HISTORY OF THE BOOK IN CANADA

VOLUME I
Beginnings to 1840

HISTORY OF THE BOOK IN CANADA

VOLUME I
Beginnings to 1840

Edited by
Patricia Lockhart Fleming,
Gilles Gallichan, and Yvan Lamonde

General Editors:
Patricia Lockhart Fleming and Yvan Lamonde

UNIVERSITY OF TORONTO PRESS
Toronto Buffalo London

© University of Toronto Press Incorporated 2004
Toronto Buffalo London
Printed in Canada

ISBN 0-8020-8943-7

Cet ouvrage est également disponible en langue française aux Presses de l'Université de Montréal
© Les Presses de l'Université de Montréal, 2004

PUM ISBN 2-7606-1768-8

Translations by/traductions par: Käthe Rothe, Wendi Petersen, Jean Chapdelaine Gagnon, and Dominique Bouchard

Printed on acid-free paper

National Library of Canada Cataloguing in Publication

History of the book in Canada / general editors: Patricia Lockhart Fleming and Yvan Lamonde.

Published also in French by Presses de l'Université de Montréal under title: Histoire du livre et de l'imprimé au Canada.
Published in cooperation with the History of the Book in Canada Project.
Includes bibliographical references and indexes.
Contents: v. 1. Beginnings to 1840 / edited by Patricia Lockhart Fleming, Gilles Gallichan, and Yvan Lamonde.
ISBN 0-8020-8943-7 (v. 1)

1. Books and reading – Canada – History. 2. Book industries and trade – Canada – History.
3. Book industries and trade – Social aspects – Canada. 4. Printing – Canada – History.
I. Fleming, Patricia   II. Lamonde, Yvan, 1944–   III. History of the Book in Canada Project.

Z206.H58 2004   002'.0971   C2004-901302-5

University of Toronto Press acknowledges the financial assistance to its publishing program of the Canada Council for the Arts and the Ontario Arts Council.

This book was made possible in part through the Canada Council for the Arts Translation Grant Programme.

 Canada Council   Conseil des Arts
for the Arts   du Canada

This book has been published with the help of a grant from the Canadian Federation for the Humanities and Social Sciences, through the Aid to Scholarly Publications Programme, using funds provided by the Social Sciences and Humanities Research Council of Canada.

University of Toronto Press acknowledges the financial support for its publishing activities of the Government of Canada through the Book Publishing Industry Development Program (BPIDP).

CONTENTS

PART SIX: PRINT AND AUTHORITY

PART SEVEN: AUTHORSHIP AND LITERARY CULTURES

ILLUSTRATIONS

Charts

Maps

Tables

GENERAL EDITORS' PREFACE

With publication of Volume 1 of *History of the Book in Canada / Histoire du livre et de l'imprimé au Canada*, Canadian book historians take their place within the network of scholars writing national histories of the book to define a field of study, to set goals for further investigation, and to provide foundations for international exchange.

Ours is a collaborative project of research and writing in French and English based at sites in Vancouver, Regina, Toronto, Montreal, Quebec, Sherbrooke, and Halifax. Volume 1: *Beginnings to 1840* will be followed by Volume 2 for 1840–1918 and Volume 3 for 1918–1980. Each volume has been developed within an expanding community of book historians, starting with an open conference where a draft table of contents was presented for discussion. Editors and other members of the volume teams then worked closely with the authors invited to write sections and case studies. A second conference for authors of each volume, held after first drafts were received and distributed, encouraged debate about the coherence of the narrative, the content and balance of individual chapters, and appropriate documentation.

The team of Volume 1 authors, drawn from a broad range of disciplines, includes pioneers who first began to investigate the history of books decades ago, as well as students who will carry the work forward. With the exception of Part Seven, which offers a regional survey of literary cultures, we challenged our colleagues to write their topics across the whole of British North America: the four Atlantic colonies, Lower and Upper Canada, and into the West. For many of us, whose research had been bounded by provincial borders, this approach led to the investigation of fresh sources and encouraged collaboration within the project team.

As a group, we have debated the meaning of the book in Canada in English and in French. While we speak of print in the lives of Canadians, we underline the role of oral transmission and manuscript publication and we trace our beginnings to Native systems of inscription and recording. In these pages, 'print' is not limited to the book in codex form; instead it encompasses newspapers, magazines, public print, forms and blanks, printed music, and illustrations in books and periodicals. As each volume of HBiC/HLIC redefines its book in Canada, the meanings shift. In the years before 1840, local imprints can be studied only within a broader framework of imported print: books and periodicals sold, read, and sometimes written here. Our firsts are transplants, soon to be replicated as settlement expanded inland. Nonetheless, patterns set in these early years were durable and define this project of Canadian book history: printing in many languages, the importance of regional presses, and a constant exchange between print and power.

In tandem with the three volumes, HBiC/HLIC has developed five databases to support the inquiries of authors and editors and to establish an infrastructure for ongoing research: Bibliography of the History of the Book in Canada / Bibliographie d'histoire du livre et de l'imprimé au Canada; Canadian Book Trade and Library Index / Index canadien des métiers du livre et des bibliothèques; Catalogues canadiens relatifs à l'imprimé / Canadian Book Catalogues; Imprimés canadiens avant 1840 / Canadian Imprints to 1840; and Manuels scolaires canadiens / Canadian Textbooks.

This volume is printed in Cartier Book, Canada's first roman typeface. Originally created by graphic designer Carl Dair, the proofs of Cartier were released on 1 January 1967 as his centennial gift to the people of Canada. To ensure that the font made a successful transition into the age of computer typesetting, designer Rod McDonald worked closely with Dair's sketches, respectfully and elegantly interpreting them into Cartier Book. In collaboration with Rod McDonald, Stan Bevington designed the HBiC/HLIC logo.

ACKNOWLEDGMENTS

The project for *History of the Book in Canada / Histoire du livre et de l'imprimé au Canada* is pleased to acknowledge the support of the Social Sciences and Humanities Research Council of Canada through the Major Collaborative Research Initiative Program for the years 2000 to 2006. This funding has enabled us to bring together editors, authors, students, and colleagues at conferences in Vancouver, Regina, Toronto, and Montreal. We have been able to recruit postdoctoral fellows for each volume and graduate research assistants at all of the sites. Their enthusiastic participation in the volumes and databases has animated every day of this project for the seven editors.

We also wish to thank the site universities for their generous support: Simon Fraser University, University of Regina, University of Toronto, McGill University, Université de Sherbrooke, and Dalhousie University, as well as the Library of the National Assembly of Quebec. At the Faculty of Information Studies, University of Toronto, which is the centre for the project and for Volume 1, we are particularly indebted to Susan Brown and Kathy Shyjak.

Among the colleagues named on the Project Advisory Board and the Project Editorial Committee, we wish to extend a particular thanks to Leslie Howsam, Germaine Warkentin, and Bruce Whiteman, who were involved in the planning of this project, and to Francess Halpenny, who has taken on a major role as adviser at the Toronto site. Joan Winearls provided expert assistance in the design of maps for Volume 1, Sandra Alston joined us at a critical stage in editing the database 'Imprimés canadiens avant 1840 / Canadian Imprints to 1840,' and Mary F. Williamson helped in the search for illustrations. The editors of Volume 1 have drawn upon the skill and judgment of text editors, Elizabeth Hulse in Toronto for English-language texts and Bettina Cenerelli (éditrice) and Yzabelle Martineau (chargée de projet) at Les Presses de l'Université de Montréal for French. The work of translation for Volume 1 has been funded by the Canada Council through the Translation Grant Programme and carried forward by Käthe Rothe and Wendi Petersen (French to English) and Dominique Bouchard and Jean Chapdelaine Gagnon (English to French).

Our publishers, University of Toronto Press and Les Presses de l'Université de Montréal, have encouraged us since we began to plan this project. We thank for their generous support Antoine Del Busso (directeur général) and René Bonenfant (éditeur) at PUM, and at UTP, Bill Harnum (senior vice-president, scholarly publishing), Siobhan McMenemy (editor), Frances Mundy (managing editor), and Ani Deyirmenjian (production manager). Ken Lewis was a meticulous copy editor and Val Cooke an inspired designer.

Throughout the project we have depended on the co-operation of libraries and archives across Canada and abroad. We owe a particular debt of gratitude to Karen Smith and John Macleod in Halifax, Suzanne Ledoux at the Bibliothèque nationale du Québec, and, at Library and Archives Canada, Jim Burant, Elaine Hoag, and Patricia Kennedy. In Toronto the staff of the Dictionary of Canadian Biography have generously made their files available to us.

Judy Donnelly, the project manager, works at the heart of this project dealing with administration and finance, as well as research and communications. For Volume 1 she supervised production of the manuscript and arranged permissions for the illustrations. The whole team has benefited from her enthusiasm and dedication.

Our greatest debt is to the authors who have agreed to write this volume and the two that will follow. They have shared their methodologies and research and broken fresh ground. Together with the editorial team, they have set Canadian book history in new directions.

HISTORY OF THE BOOK IN CANADA / HISTOIRE DU LIVRE ET DE L'IMPRIMÉ AU CANADA

HBiC/HLIC Editorial Team

Project Director: Patricia Lockhart Fleming, Faculty of Information Studies, University of Toronto.

General Editors: Patricia Lockhart Fleming; Yvan Lamonde, Département de langue et littérature françaises, McGill University.

Volume 1 Editors: Patricia Lockhart Fleming; Gilles Gallichan, Reconstitution des Débats, Bibliothèque de l'Assemblée nationale, Québec; Yvan Lamonde.

Volume 2 Editors: Yvan Lamonde; Patricia Lockhart Fleming; Fiona A. Black, School of Library and Information Studies, Dalhousie University.

Volume 3 Editors: Carole Gerson, Department of English, Simon Fraser University; Jacques Michon, Faculté des lettres et sciences humaines, Université de Sherbrooke.

Editor of Electronic Resources: Bertrum H. MacDonald, School of Library and Information Studies, Faculty of Management, Dalhousie University.

Project Manager: Judy Donnelly, Faculty of Information Studies, University of Toronto.

HBiC/HLIC Volume 1 Team

English Text Editor: Elizabeth Hulse.

French Text Editors: Bettina Cenerelli; Yzabelle Martineau.

Translators: Dominique Bouchard; Jean Chapdelaine Gagnon; Wendi Petersen; Käthe Rothe.

Cartographer: Jane Davie. Cartographic Consultant: Joan Winearls.

English proofreader: Deborah Marshall.

Indexer: Ruth Pincoe.

Post-doctoral Fellow (2000): Janet B. Friskney.

Graduate Research Assistants (Toronto): Nica Abush; Jessica Bowslaugh; Sophie Brookover; Sarah Brouillette; Pearce J. Carefoote; Amanda Collins; Maria D'Angelo; Travis DeCook; Eli MacLaren; Sophie Regalado; Patricia Richl; Andrea Rotundo; Johanna Smith; Alex Willis.

Graduate Research Assistants (Quebec): Frédéric Roussel Beaulieu; François Melançon; Mathieu Rompré.

ABBREVIATIONS

ABS	American Bible Society
ANQM	Archives nationales du Québec à Montréal
ANQQ	Archives nationales du Québec à Québec
AO	Archives of Ontario
BFBS	British and Foreign Bible Society
BRH	*Bulletin des recherches historiques*
Cat. coll.	*Catalogue collectif des impressions québécoises, 1764–1820*
CIHM	Canadian Institute for Historical Microreproductions
CO	Colonial Office (Great Britain)
DAUL	Division des archives, Université Laval
DCB	*Dictionary of Canadian Biography*
DOLQ	*Dictionnaire des œuvres littéraires du Québec*
ECP	P.L. Fleming and S. Alston, *Early Canadian Printing*
Fleming Atl.	P.L. Fleming, *Atlantic Canadian Imprints, 1801–1820*
Fleming UC	P.L. Fleming, *Upper Canadian Imprints, 1801–1841*
Hare and Wallot	J. Hare and J.-P. Wallot, *Les imprimés dans le Bas-Canada*
HBC	Hudson's Bay Company
HCQ	*Histoire du catholicisme québécois*, ed. N. Voisine
JR	*The Jesuit Relations and Allied Documents*, ed. R.G. Thwaites
LHSQ	Literary and Historical Society of Quebec
MÉM	*Mandements ... publiés dans le diocèse de Montréal*
MÉQ	*Mandements ... des évêques de Québec*
MUL, RBSCD	McGill University Library, Rare Books and Special Collections Department

MUN	Memorial University of Newfoundland
NA	National Archives of Canada (now Library and Archives Canada)
NAS	National Archives of Scotland
NBM	New Brunswick Museum
NLS	National Library of Scotland
NSARM	Nova Scotia Archives and Records Management
OCCL	*The Oxford Companion to Canadian Literature*, ed. W. Toye and E. Benson
PANB	Provincial Archives of New Brunswick
PBSC/CSBC	*Papers of the Bibliographical Society of Canada / Cahiers de la Société bibliographique du Canada*
PRO	Public Record Office (Great Britain)
RAPQ	*Rapport de l'archiviste de la province de Québec*
RHAF	*Revue d'histoire de l'Amérique française*
RSCHÉC	*Rapport de la Société canadienne d'histoire de l'Église catholique*
RTS	Religious Tract Society
SPCK	Society for Promoting Christian Knowledge
SPG	Society for the Propagation of the Gospel in Foreign Parts
TPL	Toronto Public Library, *A Bibliography of Canadiana*, and supplements
Tremaine	M. Tremaine, *A Bibliography of Canadian Imprints, 1751–1800*
TRL	Toronto Reference Library
Vlach and Buono	M. Vlach and Y. Buono, *Laurentiana parus avant 1821*

CHRONOLOGY

1751   Bartholomew Green arrives at Halifax to establish the first printing office in the northern colonies of British North America

1752   John Bushell succeeds Green after his death and begins publication of the *Halifax Gazette.* First imprints in English and French

1755   The Acadians are expelled from Nova Scotia

1759   Quebec is captured by the British

1760   Montreal surrenders to the British

1761   Anthony Henry (Anton Heinrich) takes over Bushell's printing shop in Halifax.
        James Rivington, member of a family active in the bookselling and stationery trades in London, advertises a large stock of books and stationery for sale in Halifax

1764   William Brown and Thomas Gilmore establish the first printing shop at Quebec and found the *Quebec Gazette / La Gazette de Québec*

1765   The earliest recorded almanac, 'L'almanac de cabinet,' is printed at Quebec by Brown and Gilmore
        Louis Langlois, *dit* Germain, opens the first circulating library at Quebec

1766   The first documented imprint in a Native language, a calendar in Montagnais, is printed in an edition of 1,000 copies at Quebec
        The British Stamp Act obliges printers in the North American colonies to use paper marked with a tax stamp

1774   The Quebec Act establishes French civil and British criminal law in the province of Quebec; provides freedom of religion to Roman Catholics; extends the boundaries of the province

1776   Fleury Mesplet establishes the first printing office in Montreal
First Loyalists arrive in Halifax from the American colonies
The Nova-Scotia Calendar ... for the Year ... 1777 (Halifax) includes what is probably the first illustration produced in British North America

1777   A primer with Catholic prayers is printed entirely in Mohawk by Fleury Mesplet in Montreal

1783   The end of the American Revolution brings many more Loyalists to the remaining British colonies
William Lewis and John Ryan found the first printing shop in western Nova Scotia (now New Brunswick) at Saint John and begin printing the *Royal St. John's Gazette and Nova-Scotia Intelligencer*

1784   The province of New Brunswick is created by the division of Nova Scotia

1785   Fleury Mesplet begins publishing the *Montreal Gazette / Gazette de Montréal*

1786   Alexander Morrison, bookbinder, stationer, and bookseller is active in Halifax

1787   James Robertson establishes the first printing office in St John's Island (Prince Edward Island), where he prints the *Royal American Gazette and Weekly Intelligencer*
The first German imprint, Anthony Henry's *Der Neuschottländische Calender, auf ... 1788*, is published in Halifax. The series continued until his death in 1800

1789   Periodical publishing begins with the *Nova-Scotia Magazine* (Halifax, 1789–92) and the *Quebec Magazine / Magasin de Quebec* (Quebec, 1792–4)

1790   The *Quebec Almanack / Almanach de Quebec* for 1791 (Quebec) includes a map engraved by Michel Létourneau, probably the first illustration engraved in British North America

1791   The Constitutional Act divides the old province of Quebec into Lower Canada and Upper Canada
The *Quebec Almanack / Almanach de Quebec* for 1792 (Quebec) includes an engraving of a printing press by J.G. Hochstetter, the first pictorial image engraved in British North America

1793	Louis Roy from Montreal establishes the first printing office in Upper Canada at Newark (Niagara-on-the-Lake) and founds the *Upper Canada Gazette, or American Oracle*
1797	At Quebec, Thomas Cary opens a circulating library and adds a reading room the following year
1798	Titus Geer Simons and William Waters move the government printing office from Newark (Niagara-on-the-Lake) to York (Toronto), the new capital of Upper Canada
1805	The first paper mill in British North America begins operation at St Andrews (Saint-André-Est), Lower Canada
1806	John Ryan and his son Michael establish the first printing office in Newfoundland at St John's
1807	The Ryans begin publication of the *Royal Gazette and Newfoundland Advertiser* at St John's
1808	*Colas et Colinette, ou le Bailli dupé*, by Joseph Quesnel, the first dramatic work, is published at Quebec
1813	American forces capture York, burn down the parliament building and destroy the government press
1815	George Kilman Lugrin founds the first permanent printing office in Fredericton, the capital of New Brunswick Hector Bossange, son of Parisian bookseller Martin Bossange, opens the first French bookstore, at Montreal
1818	George Dawson, a bookbinder, opens a circulating library at York (Toronto)
1819	Anthony Henry Holland, Phillip Holland, and Edward A. Moody establish the first paper mill in Nova Scotia at Hammond Plains
1820	John Carey sets up the first non-government printing shop in Upper Canada at York (Toronto)
1821	Engraver James Smillie arrives at Quebec
1824	The first lithograph known to have been produced in British North America is printed by John Adams at Quebec *St. Ursula's Convent; or, The Nun of Canada*, by Julia Beckwith Hart, the first novel by an author born in British North America, is published at Kingston, Upper Canada

1825	Completion of the Lachine Canal facilitates shipping to Lake Ontario
1826	The first paper mill in New Brunswick is in operation at Chamcook James Crooks establishes the first paper mill in Upper Canada at West Flamborough, above Dundas; a second mill begins production at York (Toronto) in 1827
1827	The first association of printers or 'typographes' is formed at Quebec
1828	The Montreal Mechanics' Institute is founded
1829	The *Christian Guardian* printing office is established at York (Toronto) by the Methodist Episcopal Church in Canada Completion of the Welland Canal facilitates shipping to Lake Erie
1830	Michel Bibaud's *Epîtres, satires, chansons, épigrammes et autres pièces de vers*, the first volume of poems by a native of Lower Canada, is published at Montreal The House of Assembly of Upper Canada specifies that its *Journal* be printed on paper made in British North America Mechanics' Institutes founded at York (Toronto), Halifax, and Quebec (1831) followed by eleven others before 1840, six in Upper Canada, two each in Nova Scotia and New Brunswick, and one in Prince Edward Island
ca. 1830	The Montreal Type Foundry is the first to manufacture type in British North America
1831	Commercial lithographic presses are in operation at Kingston (by Samuel Oliver Tazewell) and Montreal
1832	Cholera breaks out at Quebec in June, ravages Lower Canada, and spreads to Upper Canada. Total dead estimated around 13,000 York Typographical Association founded
1833	Printers' associations established at Hamilton and Montreal
1834	A second outbreak of cholera kills thousands in Nova Scotia, New Brunswick, and the Canadas
1835	Printing in Gaelic begins at Toronto, followed by Montreal in 1836 A second German printing office is established, at Berlin (Kitchener) in Upper Canada

| 1836 | Mason, Barber and Norton build a press in Toronto, the first in British North America, according to the *Royal Standard* |
| | Printers strike in Toronto |

1837	The first novel by a native of Lower Canada, *L'influence d'un livre*, by Philippe Aubert de Gaspé *fils* is published at Quebec
	Greek type is used for the first time in British North America at Montreal
	Printers form an association in Halifax

| 1837–8 | Many members of the printing trades are involved in the rebellions in Upper and Lower Canada |

| 1838 | The *Literary Garland* (1838–51), Canada's first major literary magazine, is published in Montreal |

| 1839 | Lord Durham's report recommends responsible government and the union of Upper and Lower Canada |
| | Newton Bosworth's *Hochelaga Depicta* (Montreal) features twenty illustrations of Montreal buildings by James Duncan, lithographed by P. Christie |

1840	James Evans improvises the first press in Rupert's Land (Manitoba) to print his Cree syllabary
	John Crosskill uses power printing in Halifax
	The Act of Union joining Lower and Upper Canada is passed by the British Parliament

Chronology compiled by Eli MacLaren

HISTORY OF THE BOOK IN CANADA
Beginnings to 1840

EDITORS' INTRODUCTION

This work is a collaborative history written in French and English which poses and seeks to answer a series of questions about the role of print in the lives of Canadians. The story begins with Aboriginal peoples who had lived their cultures in the northern part of North America for thousands of years. Native oral and inscribed discourse was expressed and transmitted through petroglyphs and pictographs and by means of wampum strings or belts, scrolls, totem poles, and hieroglyphic characters. When Europeans came to the shores of the Americas in search of new empires, Gutenberg's printing press was still less than a century old. Products of the same technical and intellectual revolution, the printed book and the exploration of the New World were destined to nourish each other. For Europe, North America was a revelation of which the book was to become both witness and messenger. Geography, climate, 'savage' inhabitants, fauna, and flora came to mingle with the epic of discoveries in the first accounts of explorers and the reports of missionaries, published and read throughout Europe from the sixteenth century on.

The New World offered to the Old a country to 'read,' and by means of the book, a space was opened where the imaginary, the ambitions of kings, the fervour of religion, and the taste for adventure could find expression. The diversity that marked publications about North America outlined the emergence of a new literature. Alongside the printed works controlled by political and religious authorities in France, unauthorized materials circulated without official sanction. In England the accounts of mariners in the service of the Crown who sought an imagined northwest passage to Asia were quickly published. Print also offered one of the first means of contact with Native peoples, who, rich in their own many codes of communication, did not possess a system of alphabetical writing. In order to convert these peoples, mission-

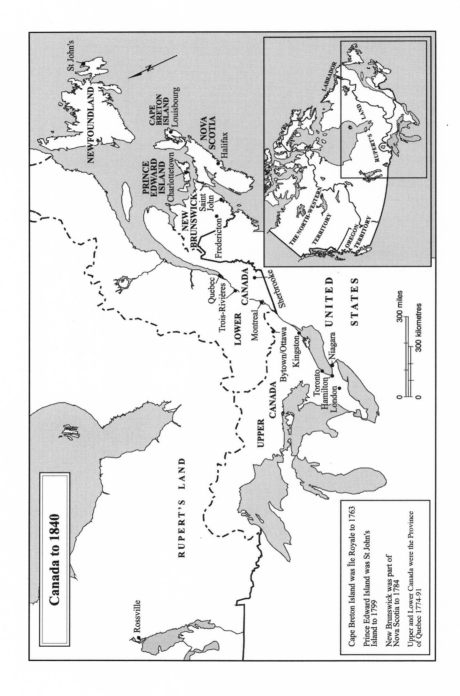

Canada to 1840

St John's

NEWFOUNDLAND

CAPE
BRETON
ISLAND
Louisbourg

NOVA
SCOTIA

Halifax

PRINCE
EDWARD
ISLAND
Charlottetown

NEW
BRUNSWICK

Saint
John

Fredericton

Quebec

Trois-Rivières

LOWER CANADA

Sherbrooke

Montreal

Bytown/Ottawa

Kingston

Niagara

Toronto
Hamilton
London

UPPER
CANADA

UNITED STATES

RUPERT'S LAND

Rossville

LABRADOR

RUPERT'S LAND

THE NORTH-WESTERN
TERRITORY

OREGON
TERRITORY

300 miles

300 kilometres

0

0

Cape Breton Island was Île Royale to 1763

Prince Edward Island was St John's
Island to 1799

New Brunswick was part of
Nova Scotia to 1784

Upper and Lower Canada were the Province
of Quebec 1774-91

Map 1.1 Canada to 1840.

aries turned to images, and adapted and invented sign systems that brought Native languages into the world of type.

While these new colonies engaged the European imagination in a literature of risk and reward, travellers and sojourners read and wrote here, their work circulated in manuscript or sent for publication abroad. It was not until 1752 that printing began in the fortified port of Halifax, founded by the British government just three years earlier to offset the return of Louisbourg to France and to encourage colonization by the British and by 'foreign Protestants,' who were intended to balance the French-speaking Acadians settled in coastal areas for more than a century. Printers who came from Boston, Philadelphia, and other cities in the Thirteen Colonies to set up the first presses in the northern colonies of British North America were already masters of their craft, with strong connections to other members of the book trades in the colonies and in Europe. For Loyalists, who were the second wave of printers in the 1780s, the ties of family and apprenticeship reinforced a shared experience of dislocation. Their personal and business connections formed a network that crossed the four Atlantic colonies well into the nineteenth century.

The commercial strategies of early printers were often broadly based in the book trades; bookselling, binding, the manufacture of blank books, and the sale of stationery and sundries were intended to balance fluctuations in the printing trade, particularly for those who did not benefit from government contracts. Until 1840 there were few printers in British North America who did not publish a newspaper. Job printing of handbills, posting notices, tickets, forms, and other daily necessities provided income with little risk. Steady sellers such as almanacs and textbooks, reports of local societies, perhaps a well-received sermon – these were the staples of the colonial press. More ambitious work could be managed with the help of an author or other sponsor or by publishing on subscription: collecting advances to cover the cost of paper and presswork.

Once newspapers and other materials were available from local presses, the circulation of print and the appetite for reading spread through the colonies in many different ways. Since the output of the colonial press was largely utilitarian well into the nineteenth century, books imported from Europe and the United States remained the choice of readers in all the provinces. Changing economic and political conditions, as well as more dependable transatlantic crossings, encouraged trade in books. However, tariffs, laws, and regulations linking books to the importation of luxury goods often limited their sale to a more prosperous clientele. Nevertheless, after 1815 the number of bookstores serving readers of both French and English expanded, and the retail trade freed itself little by little from the printer's shop to become an independent means of distribution for books and periodicals.

Churches, societies, and religious organizations were also sources for the circulation of tracts and books of devotion, in particular the Bible, considered by Protestants to be the central Christian text. More generally, benevolent societies and their libraries made possible an increasingly diversified access to printed materials. The establishment of circulating libraries, reading rooms, and other meeting places where a reader could, for a nominal sum, have access to newspapers, books, or periodicals further extended the reach of print. Their collections, as well as the holdings of certain bookstores, are known through printed catalogues, which suggest the tastes and preferences of readers in British North America. Other libraries developed to serve the needs of a more specialized clientele. The first professional libraries for lawyers and doctors appeared before 1840. Within the same period, provincial legislatures created libraries that soon ranked among the richest in the colonies.

As all these collections grew in depth and diversity in bookstores and libraries, their management, development, and classification and cataloguing required the presence of new specialists – librarians. At first they provided access only to collections and archival documents, but these keepers of books, recruited from the world of letters, journalism, and politics, gradually became sources of information and reference. Some would eventually be counted among Canada's first bibliographers.

The development of print culture depended on the spread of literacy to bring books, reading, and readers together. From its beginnings, New France was a vast, scarcely populated land, and schooling an uncertain endeavour. Even if the newcomers carried with them some small store of instruction, this legacy shrank as succeeding generations faced difficult living conditions with few institutions of learning. The British conquest did not change this social and geographic reality, which reserved education for an urban elite that would now be mainly anglophone and Protestant. Nevertheless, literacy – the ability to read and to write – increased in both the towns and the countryside. Since the role of government remained marginal in the field of education until the nineteenth century, schooling meant parish and Sunday schools conducted by clergy and members of various faiths, charity and mission schools, classes in the community, dame schools for the very young, apprenticeships for some, and private venture schools for others with the means to pay.

As learning spread through the colonies of British North America, the act of reading became both a social and a cultural practice. Reading, when conducted aloud for the benefit of an audience, joins readers and non-readers in common cause. It is also private and personal, a companion to studies and work or a participant in moments of leisure and relaxation. Whether in meditation, reflection, or the search for information or escape, reading enjoys its public and favoured spaces, atmospheres and attitudes associated with a society and a time. But above all, it requires books, and when they are costly and in short supply, they will often be much sought after and highly valued. In colonial societies where ports were closed during a long winter, readers awaited new books from Europe with an eager appetite that is hardly imaginable today.

From the early days of settlement, personal collections were formed in the homes of officials, merchants, members of the legal profession, clergymen, and politicians. Even when modest, these libraries bear witness to a special relationship between their owners and the printed page. At the beginning of the nineteenth century, some private libraries reached sizable proportions of several hundred, even several thousand, volumes, and soon book collectors and bibliophiles were to be found everywhere from the Atlantic to the banks of the Red River in the West.

Even though reading materials were often scarce in British North America, print was everywhere. In the towns it would be read aloud, officially in the square or market, solemnly in church, sociably in hotels and taverns. There were broadsides on the walls and fences and trade signs on every shop, with images to be read by the unlettered: a barrel and glass for the tavern, a watch for the jeweller, a book for the stationer. At election time, handbills and songs would be distributed at meetings and passed from neighbour to neighbour. Newspapers were delivered around the town by apprentices and posted to agents and country customers. Copies might then be routed informally through a community of readers. Imported newspapers and magazines were also shared among subscribers and would be available at reading rooms in the larger towns.

Governments were the principal publishers, responsible for almost half the printing in the eighteenth century. Ever more numerous, innkeepers were licensed by printed form every year, while traders had to post a bond for each expedition, agreeing to promote peace among the Native peoples. Lists of post offices, regulations for civic life, and calls to public meetings appeared. During cholera epidemics in the 1830s, warnings and reports were published about the spread of the disease. The development of public schooling called for more textbooks, which in turn created a new audience of young readers. Print also served readers defined by their vocations, such as lawyers, doctors, scientists, and musicians, as well as those united in worship or by common purpose in voluntary and benevolent societies.

The printing of books in Native languages, which began in 1766, included titles in Abenaki, Cree, Mohawk, Montagnais, Ojibwa, and Oneida by 1840. Publishing in French and in English started in the same year, 1752, in Halifax, where the first German work was also printed in 1788. A concentration of German settlers near Waterloo in Upper Canada subscribed for the purchase of a press in 1835; a rival to its success was established nearby in 1839. And although the community of readers was smaller, publishing in Gaelic began in 1835.

Of all the texts produced for popular reading, almanacs had no rival. Published in both cities and towns, at cheap prices in annual editions as large as 10,000 copies, they were the people's book of information and entertainment. By offering advice, organizing the world into lists, and shaping a version of history in the calendar, they created a sense of order both homely and progressive.

The links between the world of print and the power of political and religious authorities were always complex and ambiguous. Both church and state understood the potential of the printing press as a means of supporting their authority and increasing the efficiency of their administrations. But these same institutions also developed a certain mistrust of the press and the printed word.

For churches, the book was a tool to be used in preaching the gospel and for social communication. The Bible as a sacred text had been at the very origins of Christianity, and although the Gospels proclaimed, 'In the beginning was the Word,' the clergy soon saw that the spoken word was powerless without the written text. A valuable and efficient accompaniment to the former, the book sanctioned above all the orthodoxy of the messages it conveyed, particularly among Catholics, where the hierarchy was highly structured. As for government, print was a remarkable medium to ensure both administrative efficiency and the uniformity of legislative and judicial intent. It served as point of contact between the colonial administration and its subjects, it legitimized the Crown's claims to territory, and it enshrined the actions of the government in authoritative forms. From the first moment of its use, the press, which reproduced royal laws and regulations, became in the eyes of all, the true and official seal of the government.

But for both religious and political authorities, the printing press could also be adversarial, giving a voice to opposition and dispute, particularly in popular reading. Newspapers and pamphlets circulated new and sometimes disturbing ideas, in the view of established authority. Both the Catholic Church in Lower Canada and the colonial governments put in place their own strategies for controlling the press. The former tried at first to forbid or eliminate so-called vicious books, while the latter used the law to silence their opponents or even to seize the presses and imprison the publishers. Nevertheless, the effectiveness of these measures remained limited at best as the sources of print materials multiplied. In the nineteenth century, both constituted authority and apprenticeship in the practice of freedom found expression through the printed word. Religious and political reactions against the press were proof, in fact, of its strength and its capacity to both serve and contest the authorities.

The first issue of the *Halifax Gazette* (23 March 1752), which is the earliest known example of Canadian printing, reminds us of the shifting nature of literary culture and the limits of print culture. The largest of three advertisements in the newspaper was placed by Leigh and Wragg, keeping shop 'At the Sign of the Hand and Pen.' As well as teaching the basics of spelling, reading, writing, arithmetic, and bookkeeping, the partners offered night classes for 'grown Persons improving their Learning.' Leigh was also a scribe, ready to record 'Writing of all Kinds.' Other writers could in turn buy quills, pens, ink, and writing paper at the Hand and Pen. Many literary texts in the new towns of British North America were circulated only by hand and pen, copied and recopied in manuscript form, sent abroad, and read at home. Authors might find an audience or get a hearing only through recitation in drawing rooms, assemblies, and taverns. In the old province of Quebec, it was in popular songs that literary expression first found a voice.

In all the colonies, authors were readers of imported print before they were writers. Although literary standards may have been set elsewhere, the local newspaper was ready to publish a letter, an essay, or a verse. And over and over again, short-lived magazines were founded to foster native genius. Pseudonyms were common in this period, and the boundaries of literary culture elastic, encompassing religion, sermons, history, politics, and essays on philosophical and practical subjects. It was authors, printers, and readers who created literary cultures from songs sung, tales told, works written and read in early Canada.

PART ONE

PRINT AND A NEW WORLD

chapter 1

FIRST CONTACT OF NATIVE PEOPLES WITH PRINT CULTURE

Native Oral and Inscribed Discourse

CORNELIUS J. JAENEN

It is a common assumption that there is a correlation between the rise of organized knowledge and the development of some adequate form of writing, which, in turn, is assumed to require phonetic articulation. But Amerindian peoples at the time of European contact were able to communicate both information and ideas without the sorts of written and printed forms employed by Europeans or Asians. Their chief methods of communication and transmission of information were oral, representational, and what linguist Roy Harris has called 'integrational,'[1] a description that does not call into question their validity. Oral, pictorial, and print history, while recounting certain salient 'facts' of a community's past experience, adapt the recital to the socio-cultural environment and ideological climate of the present. Discourse, or human communication, is more than a mere transfer of information and opinion. All forms of transmission, written or other, indicate some point of view and context in order to communicate meaning. Print expression is as subject to interpretation and invention as its counterparts in other cultures.[2]

At first contact, Amerindians appeared to European newcomers to be devoid of 'civility' because they seemingly possessed no alphabets, written documents, or books. They were, in the words of André Thevet, 'without any law or religion whatever, living as guided by the instinct of nature.'[3] However, they were just as able as any European chronicler to recollect their past experiences. Without formal codes of law, they maintained consistent patterns of behaviour, consensus, and community standards, as well as respecting precedent and extenuating circumstances, in preserving collective harmony. In the spiritual realm, they had no creeds, scriptures, or hymnals, yet all ceremonial occasions proceeded in an orderly and traditional sequence. What Europeans elaborated and circumscribed through printed works, the Amerindians achieved largely through oral and representational transmission. Yet, there were some advantages to print culture that Amerindians did not overlook. Initially, the fact that all French readers, including those not identified as possessing supernatural powers, read a given printed text in identical fashion remained mysterious. That an initiate would pass on a message in nearly identical form was commonplace, but the word-for-word repetition of a text by various people on different occasions seemed mystical.[4]

Native 'publication' took the form of symbolic representations on rock, bark, or hides. Not unlike European printing and engraving, Native peoples had six main expressions of cultural transmission: petroglyphs, or engravings on rock; pictographs, or paintings on rock; wampum belts; bark and hide scrolls; totem poles; and hieroglyphics, the use of pictorial characters to represent a word or sound. The first recorded European awareness of Native rock art was by the Jesuit missionary Jacques Marquette near present-day Alton, Illinois, in 1673.[5] Wampum, notchings, and scrolls were designed to record past events, notable persons, and statistics. Pacific Coast chiefdoms registered genealogical and historical facts on totem poles.[6] These all replicated in a limited manner the objectives achieved by Europeans through writing and printing.[7]

The principal themes of Native pictorial recording were hunting, warfare, and supernatural intervention. Three factors determined meaning: colour, arrangement, and dimension. Red and black were the usual colours employed. Red was obtained from iron oxide (hematite), and black mostly from graphite. The medium for recording events, conveying messages, or documenting the correct recitation of a ritual varied. On the Prairies, buffalo hides were used to draw maps of trails and record the size of bison herds. The Assiniboines documented horse raids, epidemics, and the death of chiefs using symbols on hides that were carefully preserved. The Tlingits kept records on cedar slabs of the gifts given at various potlaches. The Ojibwas portrayed important events on birchbark scrolls.[8]

Rock painting and engraving were the most common and widespread vehicles for recording important issues. Naturalistic representations on rock are still to be found from Nova Scotia to British Columbia. At Milk River in Alberta, for example, a historic battle scene can be 'read.' Interpretation of this medium is much more important than for a printed document. Nevertheless, the intended message could be transmitted over a long time period. The Agawa Rock record of a raid across Lake

Superior was discovered in 1958. The same 'account' had been rendered in almost identical form on birchbark in 1852 by Ojibwa chief Shingwauk for American ethnologist Henry Rowe Schoolcraft.[9]

Wampum was the archival record of a tribe. It consisted of white cylindrical shell beads of whelks and purple beads from quahog clams that documented important rituals and treaties. An average-sized wampum was composed of eleven rows of 180 beads each, according to a Jesuit observer.[10] These records were mnemonic, designed to serve as memory aids, and they did not possess the flexibility to depict the present or the future. Agreements reached with other tribes and Europeans were duly recorded on belts or collars stored in hemp bags. When required, these were brought out by the designated keeper of the wampum, they were examined publicly, and then the agreement was 'read.' Father Joseph-François Lafitau confirmed that wampum supplied the lack of writing by making 'a local record by the words which they give these belts, each of which stands for a particular affair.' He went on to explain that 'the Iroquois, Huron and others treat matters by wampum belts ... all the Indians have annals of the sort.' Lacking an alphabet, they still had 'a way of conserving the memory of historical events and things which most merit recording.'[11] Several elders together had the responsibility of reading the wampum; thus collectively 'they forgot nothing.' Just as print gave employment to various tradespeople, so trade in discoidal beads flourished between coastal makers and inland users. Like books, wampum was both public and private property.[12]

There are many examples of the practical use of wampum. The classic example is the Thadoda-ho, the Deganawida epic of the formation of the Great Law uniting the original five Iroquois tribes. (This wampum belt was returned to the Six Nations by the Canadian Museum of Civilization in 1991.)[13] By internalizing the spatial design woven into the belt and remembering the oral tradition, it is possible to retrieve the verbal content of a wampum. This mnemonic device to 'prop up the minds' is 'read' at the condolence ritual to mourn a dead chief and install his successor.

The Iroquois associated words with gifts, so that a string of suspended presents called for an explanatory speech as each was presented. Father Barthélemy Vimont explained to French readers of the Jesuit *Relations* that 'words of importance in this country are presents'; he could have said that presents are words.[14] Similarly, Marie de l'Incarnation, mother superior of the Ursuline convent at Quebec, related that the Mohawk orator Kiotseaeton used seventeen wampum belts, or *colliers*, to relate a series of historical events through word and performance.[15]

The London *Daily Courant* reported in 1710 that four 'Indian Kings' had paid a diplomatic visit to Queen Anne. They presented her with a wampum collar recording their fidelity.[16] When in 1827 the Sulpician clergy asked the secretary of state for the colonies for confirmation of their title to the seigneury of Montreal, a Native delegate from Oka (Kanesatake) contested the claim. In evidence, he produced a wampum depicting barking dogs at each of the four corners defending Native possession.[17]

The Amerindian 'writing systems' had the advantage of sharing information and concepts without having to share the same spoken language. Too often it is still assumed that Amerindian cultures were simply earlier stages of European ones. But a better understanding of their validity results from an approach that recognizes the simultaneity of different cultural expressions. Samuel de Champlain, for example, valued Native ingenuity in communication. He used Algonquian and Huron conceptual maps, designs on bark or in the sand without mathematical grids, and strategic information to draft his own maps. He wrote that he had the Natives 'draw by hand' the map that he published in 1612 as *Carte géographique*.[18]

Although only the Mayans and some other Central American cultures developed an alphabet, a few northern groups made use of hieroglyphics. Baron de Lahontan described an Iroquoian system of recording a French expedition of 180 men, which left Montreal during the first lunar month of the Deer (July), by notches on trees. He reproduced it with a French explanation of the record. Lahontan found the system a very time-consuming method of communication; therefore he wrote: 'I have contented my self in learning only such of 'em as are most Essential; the knowledge of which I owe to Necessity more than Curiosity.'[19] This representational system appears to have enjoyed only limited diffusion. Nevertheless, it marks a significant mode of communication.

Two systems of hieroglyphics were developed by missionaries in New France. The first was by Chrestien Le Clercq, a Récollet in the Gaspésie from 1675 to 1687, who took note of a Mi'kmaq practice of pictographic writing and refined it to reproduce prayers, hymns, and sections of the liturgy.[20] The second system was elaborated in the winter of 1737–8 by Abbé Pierre Maillard on Île Royale (Cape Breton Island) from Mi'kmaq representational designs. The Natives complained that only pious works were published in hieroglyphics and that restricting them to these publications was a form of censorship. There is some evidence that Maillard had worked initially on an alphabetical system but had discarded it because it opened up access to a wide range of French publications.[21] The existence of Mi'kmaq hieroglyphic documents is of great historical importance as a factor in their retention of Catholic practices when deprived of clergy for extended periods (see illus. 1.1, p. 17).[22]

How did the Amerindians respond to European print culture? We do not know what Hochelagans thought in 1535 when Jacques Cartier, confronted with attempting to heal a paralyzed chieftain, read the opening verses of the Gospel of St John or the

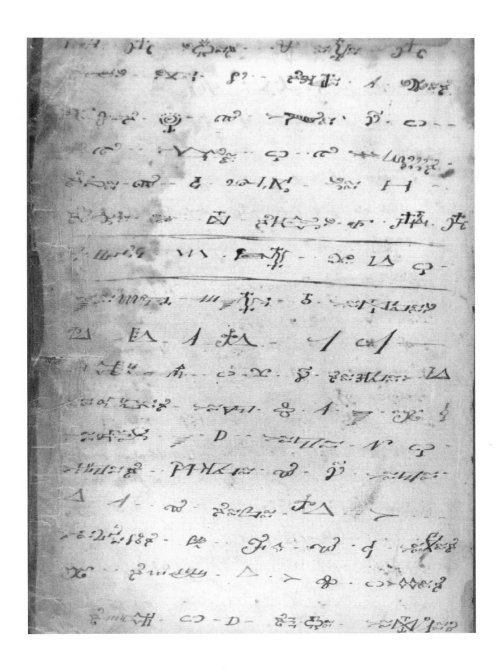

1.1 Miawpukek Mi'Kamawey prayer book (detail) in Mi'kmaq hieroglyphics (1812?–92?). Courtesy of the Miawpukek Band, Conne River, Newfoundland.

account of the Passion from his service book. Were writing and reading associated with some supernatural power? Later the Hurons, among others, were so convinced.[23]

Gabriel Sagard remarked in 1624 that the Hurons were much taken with religious illustrations, but they only counted the leaves of books.[24] Nevertheless, he had their full cooperation as he wrote a first dictionary of the language. He discovered that they had an equivalent for 'to write,' and therefore a concept of visible marks that conveyed an idea or fact but not a phonetic sound. Not all views were so positive. Marie de l'Incarnation reported that a Huron matron had harangued the elders with the accusation that the Jesuits cast evil spells on them through their prayers and 'while they read in their books.'[25] Father Pierre-Joseph-Marie Chaumonot acknowledged that 'they were convinced that we were sorcerers' casting spells, 'which were shut up in our inkstands, in our books ... consequently we dared not, without hiding ourselves, open a book or write something.'[26] Another *Relation* elaborated on the assumed influence of the printed word: 'All our power lies at the end of our tongues, in the exhibition and production of our books and Writings, the effect of which they never cease to wonder at. This is the only thing that avails us with these people, in lieu of all other ground for credibility.'[27]

It is not certain this was always the response. One wonders, for example, how impressed the missionaries were with the skilful use of memory sticks and wampum belts to recall past events; their assumption of European superiority prevented exclamations of admiration. A Native chief said recently: 'It's important that we remain different. That way, you and I will get to know the meaning of understanding. What it means to understand another man's culture.'[28] We may conclude that, although the North American Native peoples had neither paper nor print technology, they were able to achieve most of the objectives of writing and printing to the satisfaction of their own cultural imperatives. We are only now beginning to recognize the ingenuity of Native systems of signification.

Conversion through the Printed Image

FRANÇOIS-MARC GAGNON

Missionaries in New France wrote a number of commentaries about the extraordinary effect that printed images had on Native peoples. The Récollet priest Gabriel

Sagard, for instance, recounts how the young Naneogauchit (baptized Louis) asked one of the priests to open the door of his room for him, so that he could see 'if Oustachecoucou is in hell, since he died without being baptized.'[29] Sagard explains that this priest had on his wall 'a large engraving of the Judgment,' where Louis expected to find his relative depicted among the damned. Amused by the young man's naïveté, Sagard concludes, 'Some were indeed so simple that they believed these images were alive, feared them, and begged us to speak to them.'[30]

It did not take long for the missionaries to understand the use that they could make of images in converting the Native peoples. 'In truth,' Sagard commented, 'devotional images are of great benefit in this country; they look at them with admiration, consider them with attention, & understand easily what we teach them by these means.'[31] However, it was the Jesuits, more than the Récollets, who made great use of this principle. After he too became aware of the Native interest in pictures, Father Paul Le Jeune admitted, 'Oh, how fortunate it would be if all the mysteries of our faith could be well represented! These images help a great deal, and speak for themselves.'[32] A former Protestant converted to Catholicism, Le Jeune had the zeal of the neophyte and was prepared to see in the pictures 'half the instruction that one is able to give the Savages.'[33] He blamed the 'heretics', who he said were 'very much in the wrong to condemn and to destroy representations, which have so good an effect.'[34] If there was an iconophilic tradition in post-Tridentine Catholicism, it surely belongs to the Jesuit tradition, at the forefront of the Counter-Reformation. The importance that St Ignatius Loyola attributed, in his *Spiritual Exercises*, to the imagination, the faculty that produces mental images, is well known.

One would like to have a concrete representation of the illustrations that the missionaries used. Engravings on paper were employed in the field and were seldom preserved; we can therefore know them only indirectly, through descriptions written by the missionaries. On this basis, we have been able to partially reconstruct the material, to find the principal model on which it drew, and to locate what might be called its distant descendants, even though the physical origin of the sources of this material remains a mystery.[35] The missionaries provided an idea of both the content and the style of this iconography. It did not, in fact, simply illustrate a doctrine. Content and style had to represent an essential idea that would reach their audience. Very quickly, the essential concept seems to have been reduced to two elements: on the one hand, the story of salvation, from the creation of the world in six days to the Last Judgment, including the advent of Christ, his death, and his resurrection; and, on the other hand, the sins to avoid and the virtues to practise. These two themes were brought together in the last scene of the story of salvation: the portrayal of the Last Judgment, in which God punishes the wicked (or the 'infidels') and rewards the good. For this reason, eschatology seems to occupy such an important place in this iconography. Still, these depictions of the end of the world had to be understood by their intended audiences. Some representations of the Last Judgment were too confusing; according to Le Jeune, 'The devils are so mingled with the men that nothing can be identified therein.'[36] The images he had in mind corresponded more closely to the series of engravings by Pierre Landry devoted to *L'Âme bienheureuse* and *L'Âme damnée.*[37]

Father Charles Garnier gives a very clear idea of the missionaries' needs in a letter written around 1645 to his fellow Carmelite father Henri de Saint-Joseph, asking him for pictures. He begins with a list of the subjects that he would like to have portrayed: Mary, Christ, eschatology. Garnier was equally demanding with regard to the style of these images. He specifies, for example, that the people should not be portrayed 'in profile, but one should see the entire face ...; those images please them which look back at those who are looking at them,' probably those whose eyes seem to follow the viewer.[38] To be avoided were 'yellow and green, [which] scarcely please them in clothing,' he continues.[39] On the other hand, red and blue were the colours that they liked.

The idea of associating Protestants with the impious and the damned came, it seems, from the Oblate father François-Norbert Blanchet, a Canadien who worked in the missions of the Oregon Territory around 1838. To counter Protestant proselytizing, he drew a chart showing Luther and the Reformers engaged on the road of error.[40] In 1843 the Belgian-born Jesuit missionary Pierre-Jean De Smet had this image printed, which directly inspired the *Tableau synoptique de la doctrine catholique mise à la portée des sauvages*, published in an edition of five hundred copies by Desbarats in 1872 (see illus. 1.2, p. 21). Father Nicolas Point, the faithful companion of Father De Smet, depicted in one of his watercolours of his *Souvenirs des montagnes rocheuses*, painted around 1859, a tableau quite similar to the *Tableau synoptique*. The resemblance of all these documents to the *Carte du jugement* (see illus. 1.3, p. 22) is striking; this latter work, which had been made by a missionary from Brittany, Father Michel Le Nobletz (1577–1652), dated from the first half of the seventeenth century, and the missionaries in New France acknowledged that they were inspired by it. This remarkable iconographic tradition remains silent, however, about the precise details of its descent.

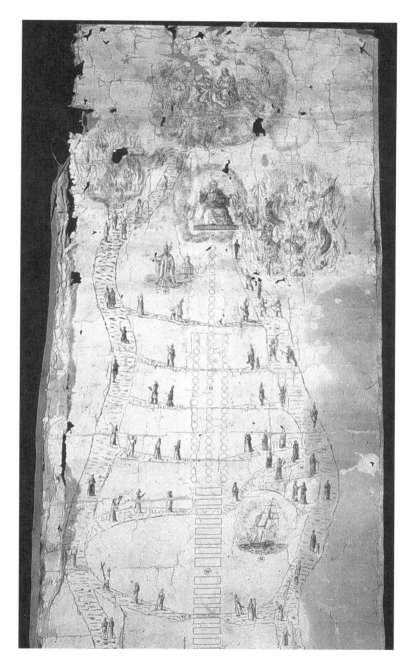

1.2 *Tableau synoptique de la doctrine catholique mise à la portée des sauvages qui n'ont encore reçu aucune instruction* (Quebec, ca. 1872); engraving on paper mounted on cloth. Courtesy of the Musée national des beaux-arts du Québec, 70.16. Photograph: Patrick Altman.

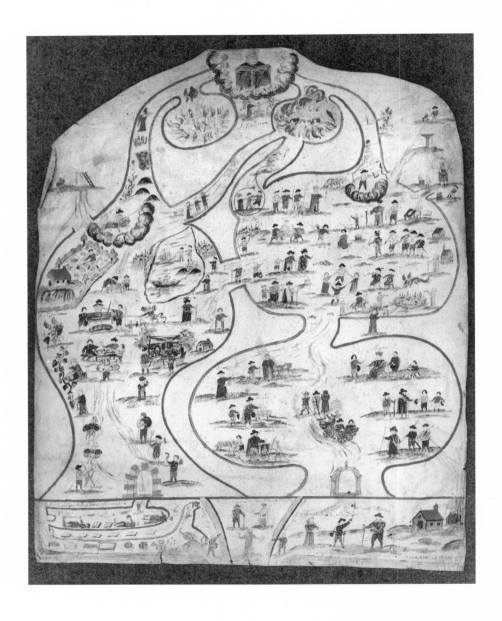

1.3   Michel Le Nobletz, *Carte du jugement, no. 1* (Brittany, early seventeenth century). Courtesy of the Evêché de Quimper, France. Photograph: le père Benoît Pruche, O.P.

chapter 2

EXPLORERS, TRAVELLERS, TRADERS, AND MISSIONARIES

French and European Writings about the New World

RÉAL OUELLET

The exploration and colonization of North America by France, between Jacques Cartier's first voyage in 1534 and the British conquest of New France in 1760, was accompanied by an abundant production of printed texts.[1] The Jesuit *Relations* alone, for example, comprised forty-one volumes published between 1632 and 1673, while Pierre-François-Xavier de Charlevoix's *Histoire et description generale de la Nouvelle France*, published in 1744, was almost two thousand pages in quarto format, not including preliminaries.[2]

For a better understanding of the nature of this production, which took place entirely in Europe, we must recall that book publishing under the *ancien régime* was marked by two main factors: the granting by government authority of privileges to print and distribute books and then, after revocation of the Edict of Nantes in 1685, competition from foreign presses, particularly the Dutch. Historians of the French book have demonstrated[3] that the privilege had three explicit objectives: 'To encourage certain booksellers in whom the government had complete trust; to battle foreign competition; to ensure publications of good quality.'[4] The privilege also allowed the control of bookstores and ensured the distribution of royal propaganda. To counter illicit trade and pirated editions, government authorities took various measures within the kingdom and at its frontiers. A first step was to deliver manuscripts to censors for evaluation in order to prevent the publication of works opposed to the monarchy, established religion, and dominant moral standards. Then the police assigned to bookstores made sure that no unlicensed books were sold, whether original works or pirated editions, French or foreign.

That the vast majority of books published on New France were printed under privilege should not come as a surprise since the colonial enterprise was encouraged or sponsored by the political and religious authorities. Thus explorer Samuel de Champlain published *Voyages et descouvertures faites en la Nouvelle France* (Paris, 1619), 'impelled,' he wrote in his dedication, 'by a due sense of the honour which I have received during the last ten years by the commissions not only, Sire, of Your Majesty, but also of the late King, Henry the Great, of happy memory, who commanded me to undertake the most exact investigations and discoveries in my power.'[5] This relationship with the governing powers was usually revealed indirectly, in the choice of publisher. One example was the Jesuit *Relations*, publication of which extended from 1632 to 1673: these volumes were published in Paris at the Cramoisy press, which was very close to the royal family. (An exception was the volume of 1638, which was published at Rouen by Le Boulenger.) The Jesuit *Relations* might, like the accounts of Jacques Cartier, Champlain, or trader and colonial promoter Nicolas Denys, become the factual record of a colonizing, missionary, exploratory, or economic activity, or, like those of Gabriel Sagard and Chrestien Le Clercq, emphasize a claim to merit and to effective action when their Récollet rivals had been thrust aside or neglected by the political authority in favour of a competing group (in this case, the Jesuits). Such a claim was made on a purely individual basis when the Récollet missionary Louis Hennepin claimed to have discovered Louisiana, and it was utterly anecdotal when Emmanuel Crespel recounted 'his shipwreck, while returning to France.'[6]

To these works by protagonists in various parts of North America were added those of official representatives, who, after having been witness to and leaders in colonization, offered broad analyses summarizing their impressions of daily life. Into this category fall the *Histoires* by lawyer Marc Lescarbot (Paris, 1609), by inspector of the Marine Claude-Charles Le Roy de La Potherie, *dit* Bacqueville de La Potherie (Paris, 1722), and by the Jesuit Charlevoix (1744), as well as the expansive treatise in comparative anthropology by another Jesuit, Joseph-François Lafitau: *Mœurs des sauvages ameriquains, comparées aux moeurs des premiers temps* (Paris, 1724). In particular, Charlevoix's *Histoire et description generale de la Nouvelle France* (Paris, 1744) is a significant work. Published in two formats (quarto and duodecimo), it was reprinted a number of times and widely read in Europe. This history also set the standards for Canadian historiography, as it remained a canonical reference for a century.

In addition to the works published with privilege were those by more unconventional figures, such as Hennepin and the military officer Baron de Lahontan.[7]

Hennepin, who changed political allegiances over the course of his life, published his *Description de la Louisiane* (1683), dedicated to Louis XIV, in Paris, but his *Nouvelle découverte* (Utrecht, 1697) and *Nouveau voyage* (Utrecht, 1698), both dedicated to William of Orange, stadtholder of Holland and king of England, Scotland, and Ireland, were published in the Netherlands. In these texts, republished and translated a number of times, he claimed to have discovered the mouth of the Mississippi River. Lahontan, who had to flee from Newfoundland to Portugal to avoid imprisonment, published the three volumes of his work in The Hague in 1702–3; he dedicated the first two volumes to Frederick IV, king of Denmark and Norway, who was part of the European coalition against France during the War of the Spanish Succession.

There are two other books to be mentioned, concerning individuals who lived in New France and who claimed to be inspired by genuine memoirs: the *Avantures* (1732) of Robert Chevalier, *dit* Beauchêne, and those of Claude Lebeau (1738).[8] Chevalier, who was probably born at Pointe-aux-Trembles (Montreal) in 1686, claimed to have accompanied Antoine Laumet, *dit* de Lamothe Cadillac, to Detroit in 1706 and to have participated in various military expeditions in New England. He may have done so, but the facts have not been verified. That he became a privateer in the West Indies, however, is unlikely. Lebeau, who presented himself as a 'lawyer in Parliament' and a 'clerk in the Beaver Office' (Bureau du Castor), was sentenced to be transferred to New France in 1729, 'no doubt for libertinism'; there he was charged the following year with the 'fraudulent circulation of counterfeit card money.'[9] As he had fled the country, he was hanged in effigy in the public square. In spite of their claim to historical accuracy, these two works are novels, based more on the readings of their authors than on events or observation in the field. Moreover, Alain-René Lesage, who had collaborated in Chevalier's work, and Lebeau had not needed to live in New France for long to be able to describe the customs of its Aboriginal and Canadien inhabitants, or to recall various events; the works of Hennepin, Lahontan, Bacqueville de La Potherie, and Lafitau provided all the information they needed.[10]

The fate of Cartier's *Relations* gives an indication of France's lack of interest in North America during the period preceding the first enterprises of colonialization in 'Canada,' as the home country was entangled in religious wars and European conflicts. An account of only the second of the three voyages Cartier made to the New World between 1534 and 1542 was published in France during the author's lifetime: *Brief récit & succincte narration* appeared in Paris in 1545. The report of his first voyage was published in Italian by Giovanni Battista Ramusio at Venice in 1565 and then in English by John Florio in London in 1580, while that of his third voyage is known to us only through a partial translation attributed to Richard Hakluyt (1600). Although various manuscripts of these accounts have been found, none can be regarded as a reflection of the intention of the presumed author. In fact, we cannot be certain that the texts credited to Cartier were written entirely by him.[11]

The first work to appear after Cartier's *Brief récit*, the *Histoire de la Nouvelle France*, published by Marc Lescarbot in 1609, is a thick octavo, to which the author added a sixty-six-page collection of his poetry, *Les muses de la Nouvelle France*. Imbued with a solid humanist culture and besotted with encyclopedic knowledge, Lescarbot accompanied Jean de Biencourt de Poutrincourt et de Saint-Just, the lieutenant-governor, and trader Pierre Du Gua de Monts to Acadia, where he lived in 1606 and 1607. His *Histoire de la Nouvelle France* is itself a composite text, both formally and thematically. In the first book, he paraphrased and combined the narratives of René de Goulaine de Laudonnière, Dominique de Gourges, and Jean de Léry to recount the French voyages to Florida, Virginia, and Brazil. In the second book, which continues the retrospective with the voyages of Cartier and Jean-François de La Rocque de Roberval and the undertakings of de Monts and Champlain, the status of the narrator changes, since the desk-bound compiler-historian becomes a witness and, up to a point, an actor in the story told. The third book describes the New World, and historical account gives way to an inventory of a territory, as the title indicates, 'in which are contained the manners and customs of life of the peoples ... and products of the lands and seas of which we have spoken in the preceding books.' Lescarbot was to publish two expanded editions of his *Histoire*, in 1611–12 and 1617–18, both in Paris.[12]

Like the Jesuit *Relations*, Champlain's monumental work was published in two major editions in the nineteenth and twentieth centuries: the first, by Charles-Honoré Laverdière, was brought out in 1870 by Desbarats, and the second, published by the Champlain Society between 1922 and 1936, was edited by Henry Percival Biggar. A *pro domo* defence of and apologia for France's colonization of North America, it relates the major steps in its author's career, interwoven with the evolution of the colony up to 1631. The first text, *Des Sauvages*, was published in Paris in 1603, a few months after Champlain returned from his voyage of exploration in the St Lawrence valley. The *Voyages* (Paris, 1613) recounts the 'discoveries along the coast of Acadia and Florida'[13] 'from the year 1604 down to 1608,'[14] and 'the voyages made to the great River St. Lawrence ... from the year 1608 until 1612';[15] the last part narrates the voyage that took place between 5 March and 26 August 1613. The *Voyages et descouvertures*, published in 1619, relates his wintering over in Huronia, near the present-day Georgian Bay, and his 1618 voyage up the St Lawrence River. After a gap of thirteen years, the *Voyages de la Nouvelle France occidentale*, published in 1632 with three different imprints,[16] was intended to give an account of the French colonial undertaking in its entirety, from its first small steps in the sixteenth century to 'the year 1631.'[17] From the outset, there is the basic problem of publication. What was retained in the 1632 edition from the texts published in 1603, 1613, and 1619, and how was this material altered? In stating that 'a Jesuit' or 'a friend' of the Jesuits had 'retouched'[18] Champlain's text to minimize the missionary work of the Récollets, Laverdière opened a broader debate. The modern editor of the *Relations*, Lucien Campeau, himself a Jesuit, has responded sharply[19] that Laverdière's position was not 'very honest'[20] and had no foundation, since 'Champlain, and no one else, not only composed the 1632 book but oversaw the printing up to completion.'[21] The debate is interesting in that it sheds light on the enormous task of rewriting that the 1632 edition involved. As he went over the versions of his *Voyages* published in 1603, 1613, and 1619, the editor cut and added considerably to construct a complete history of New France.[22] Without resolving the issue through a more detailed analysis, we can accept Campeau's hypothesis[23] that 'the printer had to work,' not on a new manuscript, but 'on the printed page'[24] of the previous editions, which would explain the many discrepancies and flawed sequences.

Another, very simple factor may explain a number of the textual transformations to the earlier *Voyages* for the 1632 edition: with the rapid development of the colony over these years, the author's perspective had changed greatly. While in 1613, for example, the title page of the *Voyages* still mentioned 'a Northern route, to travel to China,' the 1632 work is oriented entirely toward colonization of New France, with no sustained reference to the Far East. Finally, we must not minimize the importance of the criticism made by Lescarbot, who reproached Champlain for his credulity and his improbabilities.[25]

The question of the rewriting of earlier texts is another aspect that has been little studied in the tradition of French-language textual criticism. This is the case, for example, with the writings of Champlain, in which there are textual differences between the copies of a single edition, especially that of 1632. We would have to continue the work started by Laverdière and Biggar in two directions: stylistic and textological. For example, we could systematically collect all the corrections made on the available copies by examining the paper, the typefaces, the makeup of gatherings of the signatures, and so on.

The two works that were published in 1691 under the name of the Récollet missionary Chrestien Le Clercq, the *Nouvelle relation de la Gaspesie* and the *Premier etablissement de la foy dans la Nouvelle France*, which the Parisian bookseller Auroy obtained a privilege to publish on 30 December 1690, were printed at the same time, in the same shop, as the physical examination of several copies demonstrates.[26] The printer used the same paper for both books, and some signatures of *Premier etablissement de la foy* were interpolated, by error, into copies of the *Nouvelle relation de la Gaspesie*; a few cross-references from one work to the other tend to confirm this hypothesis. The physical examination of various copies also shows that the manuscript of *Premier etablissement de la foy* was probably not finalized and that it had to be revised during printing. Aside from typographic corrections, some copies bear traces of hastily made modifications.

Doubtless these blunders occurred because the Récollets, in their battle with the Jesuits for pre-eminence in the missions of New France, wanted to publish both books at the same time; the first offered the irrefutable testimony of a missionary in the field; the second, an exhaustive history, claimed to correct the exaggerations of the spiritual sons of Ignatius Loyola, who boasted of fictional conversions and minimized 'so much [the work of] the zealous, knowledgeable, and disinterested Missionaries,' as the preface states. This *pro domo* defence also brought the *Premier etablissement de la foy* into the old Jesuit-Jansenist quarrel when, in 1693, Antoine Arnaud borrowed from it freely and recopied the account published in the *Journal des sçavans* (25 June 1691) to attack the Company of Jesus.[27]

Although the importance of Lahontan's work had not yet been fully assessed at the dawn of the Enlightenment, its history is quite well known.[28] The printed work, published in three volumes in The Hague by the Frères L'Honoré, was dated 1703. The first two volumes, published together, were titled *Nouveaux voyages de Mr le baron de Lahontan, dans l'Amerique septentrionale* and *Memoires de l'Amerique septentrionale*. The third, published separately, the *Suplément aux Voyages du Baron de La Hontan*, was also found with two other title pages: *Suite du voyage de l'Amerique* and *Dialogues de Monsieur le baron de Lahontan et d'un sauvage*, dated 1704 and bearing the address 'In Amsterdam, by Boeteman's Widow, and is sold at London, by David Mortier; Bookseller in the Strand, at the Sign of Erasmus'; and a second part titled *Voyages de Portugal et de Danemarc*. A systematic study of the newspapers and correspondence of the time has revealed that the *Nouveaux voyages* and the *Memoires* had been printed and were on sale by November 1702; the *Suplément aux Voyages* followed one year later. The first two volumes were an immediate success, as witnessed by reactions in the periodicals, the publication in the summer of 1703 of a translation in English, and the appearance of two pirated editions in French, using the same fonts but different plates for the engravings and other headpieces and tailpieces. From these piracies, dated 1703 and called by bibliographers the 'à la sphère' and 'à l'ornement' editions, would be derived two branches: the isolated publication of 1707–8, which deleted the headline notes and the quotations in Greek, and the 1704–1709–1715 series. The publication of the third volume, even though the *Dialogues* provoked much comment in newspapers and correspondence, did not lead immediately to a second edition, pirated or not.[29]

This sudden success encouraged the Frères L'Honoré to republish Lahontan's work from 1705, with considerable alterations. Deleting the *Voyages de Portugal et de Danemarc*, the publisher set *Memoires* and *Dialogues* in a single volume. *Memoires* was scarcely touched, but *Nouveaux voyages* and *Dialogues* were profoundly altered by an in-house writer, Nicolas Gueudeville, who was at the time writing two periodicals for L'Honoré: *L'esprit des cours de l'Europe* and the *Journal historique*. In the preface, he stated that he had eliminated the 'low phrases,' 'cold mockeries,' and 'impediments in the narration' and had substituted a style that was 'purer, cleaner, clearer, & with a bit more finesse in the narration.'[30] In reality, Gueudeville rewrote Lahontan's text, overloading it with rhetoric and a farcical verve that diluted the geographic and, especially, the ethnographic information and turning it into an anti-France pamphlet. In the *Dialogues*, for example, he rails against the French monarch, who 'exhausts' his subjects and 'sucks [their] bones to the marrow.'[31] He suggests armed revolt to 'dethrone the Tyrant'[32] and 'lay waste to private property.'[33] In the belated response that he published to the controversial review in the *Mémoires de Trévoux*, Lahontan, who was at the time travelling in Europe in search of work, 'disavowed' this second edition, even though, he added, 'they say that it is I who augmented & corrected it with the addition of a new Preface, which they claim that I did also to disguise myself more skilfully.'[34] From this 'second' edition, disavowed by the author, stemmed the editions published in Amsterdam and probably pirated, of 1728 (*Nouveaux voyages*) and 1741 (*Nouveaux voyages, Memoires,* and *Dialogues*).

When they were published, these works drew favourable reviews in two Dutch periodicals:[35] *Histoire des ouvrages des savans* and *Nouvelles de la république des lettres.*[36] The only French journal to review them was the Jesuits' *Mémoires de Trévoux,*[37] in a highly polemical text; a bad writer and a bad Frenchman, according to the reviewer, Lahontan ought to have made of his *Voyages* 'a summary of what the Deists & the Socinians say most strongly against the submission that we owe to faith & against this captivity of reason under the empire of revelation.'[38] As this highly contentious review by the Jesuit writers demonstrates, Lahontan, whose works were revealed as hostile to Catholic France, at the outbreak of the War of the Spanish Succession, could not hope for sympathy among those in power in France. Published in Amsterdam, his books were the object of seizures, according to the 'Registre des livres arrêtés dans les visites faites par les syndic et adjoints' for 1703–42.[39]

Although we do not know the print runs of the various editions or the number of copies sold in Europe and America, we can evaluate the scope of their dissemination in intellectual circles. Advertised, critiqued, even debated in the major periodicals of the time, Lahontan's work quickly found its way into cartography (Guillaume Delisle in 1703), dictionaries and encyclopedias (John Harris, *Navigantium atque Itineratium Bibliotheca*, London, 1705; Robert Beverley, *The History and Present State of Virginia*, London, 1705; Thomas Corneille, *Dictionnaire universel, géographique et historique*, Paris, 1708), and philosophical essays (Claude Buffier, *Examen des préjugés vulgaires*, Paris, 1704). A good indication of this rapid dissemination throughout Europe is that in Germany alone, Lahontan's work influenced the thought of the theologian Jonas Conrad Schramm and the philosophers Gottfried Wilhelm Leibniz and Friedrich Wilhelm Bierling. In his inaugural philosophy lecture, given on May 1707 at the Julia Carolina Academy in Helmstedt and titled *De Philosophia Canadensium Populi*,[40] Schramm in effect used Lahontan's *Dialogues* and *Memoires* to cover the entire field of philosophy (logic, metaphysics, and the physical, moral, and political sciences). Quoting Aristotle and Plato as well, he stated that the Canadian 'Barbarians' 'are firmly knocking at the door of philosophy but do not enter because they do not have the sufficient means or because they are confined within their customs.'[41]

Three years after his lecture of 5 November 1710, alerted by a letter from Bierling, who wondered if Adario and his author were 'invented characters,' Leibniz responded five days later that Lahontan was a 'very real man, not invented, like Sadeur,' the imaginary traveller in Gabriel de Foigny's *La terre australe connue*.[42] To his correspondent, who wondered how the indigenous people of Canada could live 'in peace since they had neither laws nor public courts,' Leibniz wrote, 'It is completely true ... that the Americans in these regions live together without government but in peace; they know no struggles, nor hate, nor battles, or very few, except against men of different nations and languages. I would almost say that it is a political miracle, unknown by Aristotle and passed over by Hobbes.'[43] It easy to see how Lahontan's works largely surpassed the self-aggrandizing and documentary, even promotional, aims of traditional voyage accounts, and cut right to the heart of the ideological conflicts of his time.[44]

Although they did not cause as radical a rupture, a number of texts, such as Sagard's *Le grand voyage du pays des Hurons* (1632), Paul Lejeune's *Relations* (1633–4), and Jean de Brébeuf's *Relations* (1635), were already building a true Aboriginal anthropology, which even became comparative anthropology in 1609, with Lescarbot's *Histoire de la Nouvelle France*, and was further explored in Lafitau's *Mœurs des sauvages ameriquains* in 1724. As for Charlevoix, it suffices to place his *Histoire et description generale de la Nouvelle France* (1744) alongside the historiographical production of nineteenth-century French

Canada, in order to see the extent to which he imposed a canonical form on the subject of Canadian history.

Whether they were contesting power and colonization or acting as propaganda, the works on New France constitute the principal source of knowledge about the events that marked the history of 'French' America, as well as its human and physical geography. Furthermore, with their many maps and engraved illustrations, their narrative chapters recounting adventures in unknown lands, and their encyclopedic chapters on the habits and customs of the Native peoples and on the fauna and flora, they consolidated the image of an America as exotic as the China or Persia of that era.[45]

CASE STUDY
Marc Lescarbot's *Les muses de la Nouvelle France* (1609)
— Christian Blais

Marc Lescarbot (ca. 1570–1642), writer, translator, and lawyer, was invited to New France by Jean de Biencourt de Poutrincourt, the lieutenant-governor of Acadia.[46] From July 1606 he stayed at Port-Royal (Annapolis Royal, Nova Scotia), and in the following spring he explored the coasts of Acadia. Lescarbot is best known, however, for his historical writings; only seventeen months after his return to France in the summer of 1607, he published a three-volume *Histoire de la Nouvelle France* (Paris, 1609). Because he had been a privileged witness to the birth of a colony, some saw these volumes as the 'bestmemoirs we possess of what passed before his eyes.'[47]

Acadia inspired Lescarbot to write thirteen poems, collected under the title *Les muses de la Nouvelle France*. One of these, the *Théâtre de Neptune*, which celebrates with great pomp the return of Poutrincourt from the lands of the 'Armouchiquois' (Mi'kmaqs), is recognized as the first theatrical performance in North America (see illus. 2.1, p. 32). Although Lescarbot acknowledged at the outset that his rhymes 'were hastily made,'[48] the collection of poetry, inspired by muses who were 'unkempt and rustically garbed,'[49] would nevertheless be read throughout Europe.

The *Histoire de la Nouvelle France* and *Les muses de la Nouvelle France*, although published separately, were almost always bound together. A first edition appeared in 1609; a new edition followed in 1611, and another in 1612, all produced by Jean Millot; two more editions were published in 1617 and 1618 by

DE LA NOVVELLE FRANCE.   11

Neptune, si iamais tu as favoriſé
Ceux qui deſſus tes eaux leurs vies ont vſé;
Vray Neptune, fay nous chacun où il deſire
A bon port arriver, afin que ton Empire
Soit par-deça coneu en maintes regions,
Et bien-tot frequenté de toutes nations.

LE THEATRE
DE NEPTVNE EN LA
NOVVELLE-FRANCE

Repreſenté ſur les flots du Port Royal le quator-
zième de Novembre mille ſix cens ſix, au retour
du Sieur de Poutrincourt du païs des Armou-
chiquois.

Neptune commence revetu d'vn voile de couleur
bleuë, & de brodequins, ayant la chevelure & la barbe
longues & chenuës, tenant ſon Trident en main,
aſſis ſur ſon chariot paré de ſes couleurs : ledit chariot trainé ſur les ondes par ſix Tritons juſques à
l'abord de la chaloupe où s'eſtoit mis ledit Sieur de
Poutrincourt & ſes gens ſortant de la barque pour
venir à terre. Lors ladite chaloupe accrochée, Neptune commence ainſi.

NEPTVNE.

RRETE, Sagamos, * *arrête toy ici,*
Et écoutes vn Dieu qui a de toy ſouci.
Si tu ne me conois, Saturne fut mon pere,
Ie ſuis de Iupiter & de Pluton le frere.

*C'eſt vn mot de Sauvage, qui ſigni-fie Capi-taine.

B

2.1 Marc Lescarbot, *Le Théâtre de Neptune* in *Les muses de la Nouvelle France* (Paris, 1609). Performed in the harbour of Port-Royal (Annapolis Royal, Nova Scotia) with recitations in French, Gascon, and Mi'kmaq, this entertainment was accompanied by trumpets and cannon fire. Courtesy of the Bibliothèque nationale du Québec.

Adrian Perier; all appeared in Paris. For each, the author revised his sentences and polished his lines. Outside France, an English translation was published by George Bishop in London in 1609, and a German version by Chrysostomo Dabertzhofer in Augsburg and Hamburg in 1613. More modern editions by Tross in Paris (1866) and by the Champlain Society in Toronto (1907–14) attest to the continuing interest of researchers and collectors in *Les Muses*. Since Georges-Barthélemi Faribault in 1837, all bibliographers of New France, of Canada, and especially of Acadia have cited and described this work. Although Edme Rameau de Saint-Père and Francis Parkman simply noted its existence, other historians such as Benjamin Sulte, Lionel Groulx, and Marcel Trudel punctuate their writings with some of Lescarbot's stanzas to bring, as did the author himself, another dimension to the interpretation of the past.[50]

English Writings about the New World

I.S. MACLAREN

Whereas the first books in English about the United States resulted chiefly from colonization and settlement, most of those about what is now Canada were the product of expeditions of exploration. In book form but also in multi-volume collections, extracts in magazines, and entries in the more than two dozen English-language encyclopedias published before 1840,[51] explorers and travellers brought geography to European and American readers. The mechanism by which they did so was seldom as straightforward as the one that obtained between publishers and authors of sermons, poetry, fiction, or history. Most explorers and many travellers found themselves authors only once; thus they were seldom 'sovereign authors' and so usually acceded to the advice or pressure of publishers eager to profit from their geographical achievements by setting their accounts in narrative moulds and styles that sold best to British and, subsequently, North American readers.[52] Narratives of exploration and travel engaged the British imagination from the time of Elizabeth I, to a degree that, once the novel began, it could not resist aping them.[53] From expensively illustrated folios and quartos that pandered to armchair travellers to duodecimo guidebooks to Niagara Falls, British-based books about northern North America were chiefly commodities produced in Britain. Consequently, they reflected the vogues that occupied the British, such as early modern imperialism, naval supremacy, landscape aesthetics, political unrest and tension between the United States and the northern British colonies, the manners and customs of non-European cultures, and the culture of the French-speaking population. But these fashions meant that regions were disproportionately represented for the better part of three centuries between 1576, the date of Martin Frobisher's first Arctic voyage, and 1839, when Lord Durham published his report calling for political union between Upper and Lower Canada.

Several trends are clear: over-represented by books of exploration and travel is the Arctic, particularly the British search for a Northwest Passage; under-represented are books about treks made by refugees from the Thirteen Colonies who migrated as Loyalists to Nova Scotia and to what became New Brunswick and Upper and Lower Canada. Books by fur traders in the North and West are also disproportionately few in number. British army and naval officers clearly had greater access to the book publishing process than any other group of visitors to northern North America. Furthermore, a lack of evidence suggests that publishers did not consider there to be much purchasing power in the colonies described in their narratives of exploration and travel; while the rise of mechanics' institutes and the increase in emigration and settlement from the 1820s would change perceptions, publishers remained focused on selling to British readers. That they did so clearly bore on the ways in which books by explorers and travellers represented British North America. Any discrepancy between the realms in which explorers and travellers moved and the one in which their discoveries and experiences were brought into print, publishers themselves strove to render insignificant, thereby sustaining the illusion that the British gentleman, by making 'a tour of the world in books,' could acquire a planetary consciousness, as Daniel Defoe had phrased it.[54]

More than two dozen Britons who explored northern North America before 1840 saw individual books published in their lifetimes or had them appear shortly after their deaths.[55] Books formed the imperial means by which, from Elizabethan times onward, a Pax Britannica was announced to the world. A particular sort of book served this means initially. Although John Davis, Thomas James, and Luke Fox mark exceptions because they published books under their own names,[56] most early modern explorers found their way into print, not through discrete books, but, rather, as willing or unwitting contributors to the remarkable compendia of exploration issued by their countrymen Richard Hakluyt and Samuel Purchas. Between 1582 and 1625, these two clergymen published four compilations. As with Edward Hayes's account of Humphrey Gilbert's voyage in 1583, which appeared in *Principall Navigations* (London, 1589), and William Baffin's own accounts of his northwestern expeditions, which appeared in *Purchas His Pilgrimes* (London, 1625),[57] these works published the only extant records of some expeditions. Purchas, in his compilation, captured Abacuk Pricket's account of Henry Hudson's fateful last expedition. Not only were editions of these compilations issued throughout the centuries of Arctic exploration,[58] but the precedent they set was carried on in the form of collections of travels, such as those in the eighteenth century compiled by Awnsham and John Churchill and their successor, John Campbell, and by John Harris;[59] those in the nineteenth, such as *New Voyages and Travels* (London, 1819–23), published by Sir Richard Phillips, a furious reprinter, who lived 'parasitically upon the works of others';[60] and those in the twentieth century, such as the Coles Canadiana reprint series.

It is perhaps the case that Protestant Christianity, dedicated as it was not only to the widespread dissemination of the gospel but also to the liberation of thought and knowledge that printing had made possible, generally explains this long succession of publications by British explorers,[61] but the case of Spanish explorers on the Northwest Coast suggests that another factor was Britain's strategy to use publication as a means of securing claims on territory. This was not a practice that the Spanish chose to adopt in the eighteenth and early nineteenth centuries.

Another species of exploration and travel narrative has always been the fictitious account. Among those for northern North America is David Ingram's remarkably titled *A True Discourse*, which appeared in 1583 and was reprinted by Hakluyt in his first edition of *Principall Navigations* (1589), though he deemed it too unreliable to warrant reprinting in his second edition (1598–1600).[62] The court of Elizabeth I spurred the concept of a British Empire, often attributed to Welshman John Dee, who coined the name 'Britannia.' A passage (either northwest or northeast) to the Orient was key to this stratagem, and loath to stop at the truth, Dee championed the tale that a Welshman, Prince Madoc, had discovered the New World in the twelfth century. In the face of Spanish claims, this myth helped to legitimate Elizabeth's claim as the rightful sovereign of an Atlantic empire. Both Hakluyt, in *Principal Navigations* (London, 1598–1600) as well as the edition of 1589, and Purchas, in *Purchas His Pilgrimes*, published David Powel's story of this alleged discovery.[63]

Not all fictions were so fantastic; some enjoyed great influence without taking the form of independent books. In 1596 Juan de Fuca, a Greek pilot living in Venice, told Englishman Michael Lok that he had sailed north from California through an inlet that took him as far as an Arctic ocean. Purchas duly printed Lok's account in *Purchas His Pilgrimes*.[64] Nearly a century later, the game was still on: James Petiver, the editor of the *Monthly Miscellany*, created a Spanish explorer of the Arctic named Bartholomew de Fonte, who, along with others, sailed four ships from the North Pacific to the North Atlantic in 1640. Published in the April and June 1708 issues of his magazine, the account 'was widely credited during the eighteenth century, and several expeditions were sent to search for de Fonte's passage.'[65] As well, it provoked a public dispute in the mid-1700s between the Hudson's Bay Company (HBC) and its detractors, the latter charging that the chartered monopoly had failed to fulfill the third of its three purposes, which were to trade for furs in the Hudson Bay watershed, to settle it, and to explore for a Northwest Passage.

If exaggeration and outright invention did not furnish minor or non-existent achievements of geographical discovery or violent encounters with 'savages,' they were often responsible for descriptions of the conditions under which exploration occurred. James Cook famously lamented the neglect by published accounts to report the real circumstances of life aboard ship in the merchant marine in favour of either narratives of more modest official expeditions or altogether fabricated tales.[66] Had he lived to see its publication, the official narrative based on his own log of interactions with Nootka (now Mowachaht-Muchalaht) people at Yuquot on the west coast of Vancouver Island in March 1778 might have withered him further (see illus. 2.2, p. 37). It contains, as his log does not, the imputation to those people of 'horrid repasts' of cannibalism, an addition that his ghost writer, Bishop John Douglas, could not resist.[67]

However, fiction's sins of commission were balanced by those of omission; the reputations of explorers suffered until their writings appeared in print, often not until the twentieth century. These include fur traders Henry Kelsey, Peter Pond, David Thompson, Simon Fraser, Alexander Henry the Younger, John Rae, and Peter Warren Dease; botanist David Douglas; and Juan Francisco de la Bodega y Quadra, Alejandro Malaspina, and Dionisio Alcalá-Galiano, explorers for Spain of the Northwest Coast. Clearly, a strong correlation obtains between an explorer's reputation and the publication of a narrative under his name; subsequent scholarship alone has brought many into the regard that their journeys merited. It is almost inconceivable today to imagine the comparatively incomplete manner in which North American exploration was understood before the advent in the twentieth century of edited narratives published by the Hakluyt Society (1846–), the Champlain Society (1905–), and the Hudson's Bay Record Society (1938–83). These works spawned other less extensive series from various publishing houses, such as Macmillan of Canada and the presses of the universities of Toronto, British Columbia, and McGill and Queen's.

The chief figures in the publication of early nineteenth-century exploration narratives are John Barrow, second secretary of the Admiralty, and John Murray II, who became the official publisher for the Royal Navy during Barrow's long tenure (1804–6, 1807–45). Clearly, Barrow considered publication key to securing public and parliamentary support for an assault on the Northwest Passage in the years follow-

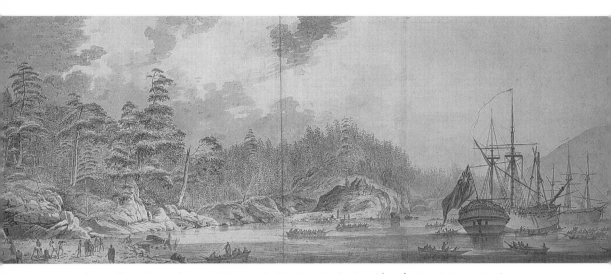

2.2 John Webber, *The Resolution and Discovery in Ship Cove, Nootka Sound* (1778). Captain James Cook and his men remained almost a month repairing the vessels and trading with the Nootkas on the Pacific shore of Vancouver Island. Courtesy of the National Maritime Museum, London, A8588.

ing the defeat of Napoleon. If Thomas Button, Henry Hudson, and others had managed to sail in salt water more than halfway across the continent two hundred years earlier, the formidable Royal Navy could surely complete the other half. Only pessimists would suggest that Hudson Bay was another cul-de-sac, like the Caribbean.

After Franklin's first overland expedition to the north coast of North America, Barrow and Murray produced his *Narrative of a Journey to the Shores of the Polar Sea* (London, 1823), the aesthetic merits of which valiantly strove to excuse the expedition's failures, including the deaths of eleven of its twenty men. Surviving correspondence indicates Barrow's keen desire to eschew the cheaper process of lithography; he urged Murray to retain the services of the brothers Finden as engravers of the sketches made by two officers on the expedition, midshipmen George Back and Robert Hood. Barrow wanted nothing less than the highest quality for any books about his cherished enterprise, and the Findens were paid twenty-three guineas on average for each of the two dozen plates that graced the narrative (others were added to the appendices). Within weeks of its appearance, even once-read copies of Franklin's *Narrative* were commanding a ten-guinea price.[68]

Barrow's involvement in many of the books from his era extended to editing them ('dishing and trimming,' he termed it in one case) to suit what he deemed popular taste and even to writing reviews for the *Quarterly Review*, published by Murray, who became and remained a close friend.[69] But with Barrow's appointment of

Franklin to the ill-fated expedition of HMS *Erebus* and *Terror* in 1845, the career of the second secretary came to an end. So too ended Murray's status as official publisher: although the frenzied search for Franklin and his crew, which lasted until 1859, produced many books about the Arctic Archipelago, they did not come from Murray and did not often receive the rich presentation that Barrow and Murray had achieved. Thus, as the heyday of exploration came to an end, so, in the case of British North America, did the era of lavish travel books. Murray, however, managed to keep jealous hold of his Arctic titles; cheaper editions are not known to have appeared until the next century.

At least by the nineteenth century, most expeditions of exploration considered a well-stocked library an essential component of their cargo. Obviously, those in ships could afford a greater tonnage; just how many men on Franklin's two land expeditions hauled books and charts over portages and across the tundra remains a nice question. Certainly, when the first expedition was reduced in the fall of 1821 to a straggling line of men marching back from Bathurst Inlet to the hoped-for refuge of Fort Enterprise, a copy of Samuel Hearne's *A Journey from the Prince of Wales's Fort, in Hudson's Bay, to the Northern Ocean*, the only book then available about the region, remained part of the load. The party of twenty men lost their way more than once. Were they consulting the chart in the inferior but lighter-weight octavo edition of Hearne's book, issued in Dublin in 1796? It would have made a more logical travelling companion than the larger quarto first edition (London, 1795). Yet the map in the octavo showed Hearne's return route across the Barrens differently from the first edition's map. The discrepancy could have confused Franklin, whose men suffered more than one delay, and contributed to the number of deaths. Certainly, the matter of a book's size bears materially on this dramatic possibility.[70]

Like books in English by explorers, those by traders and travellers remained almost exclusively a production of Britain before 1840, although American publishers routinely reissued them, seldom with permission. Travellers concerned themselves particularly with natural resources, Native peoples, scenery, possibilities for settlement and/or for growing rich, differences between the United States and British North America, and the culture of the French-speaking population. What they lacked in the exploration narrative's customary tables of measurements and observations pertaining to geography, they often made up for in data about agricultural production or vocabularies of Native groups. Infrequently before 1840 did they convey to their readers views that purported to be other than objective.[71] Interestingly, however, because a similar relationship between the officer of an institution and a publisher did not exist for other regions as, with Barrow and Murray, it did for the Arctic, and because the British government did not engage in great programs of promotion for one or another cause, as the Royal Navy did for the discovery of a Northwest Passage, the rest of British North America seems comparatively under-represented in book form before the mid-nineteenth century.

The West stands in greatest contrast to the Arctic. The HBC discouraged publication by its employees as long as it held monopolistic sway over the lands south and west of the Upper Great Lakes as far as the Pacific Ocean. Although it did not censor reading material, it gave no consent to its officers to publish their views on the fur trade or the territory that the monopoly governed. Samuel Hearne, who was an HBC man, did not live to see the publication of his *Journey* in 1795, nearly a quarter-century after the sojourns that it narrates, and after the HBC had derived whatever pecuniary benefit it could from the information his travels gathered. At last it consented to publication but apparently did not participate in the process. Hearne's work circulated in multiple manuscripts for some years, but it remains unclear how much of his book was the work of other pens. Given that at least one Grub Street hack, William Combe, would help rival trader Alexander Mackenzie into print five years later, the role of ghost writers in narratives of exploration and travel should not be discounted or underestimated.[72] Although the size of print run is unknown, there is little doubt that readers of Hearne's book were in plentiful supply, for he was paid £200 for his manuscript, more than three times what Oliver Goldsmith had netted for his popular novel *The Vicar of Wakefield* three decades earlier.[73] A few books by traders not or no longer in the employ of the HBC saw the light of day, the earliest of which by anyone with extensive experience was Joseph Robson's *Account of Six Years Residence in Hudson's Bay* (London, 1752). It contained that notorious charge, probably penned by Arthur Dobbs, that 'the Company have for eighty years slept at the edge of a frozen sea; they have shown no curiosity to penetrate farther themselves, and have exerted all their art and power to crush that spirit in others.'[74] This remarkable and accurate charge likely steeled the HBC to its policy to discourage and prohibit publication. In the event, not until the era of the upper-class sportsmen and scenery seekers (which arrived in the West in the 1840s) did its stranglehold on publication begin to loosen. Publication in 1847 of the two-volume *Narrative of a Journey round the World* (London), written for Sir George Simpson, the HBC's inland governor, would signal an easing of that control, but there are no such books for the West before 1840, and none by people travelling chiefly for pleasure.[75]

Only a few books in English concentrate on the fur trade in eastern British North America; prospects for settlement predominate. Newfoundland attracted a narrative encouraging settlement as early as 1620, when Richard Whitbourne combined his travels, both endured and imagined (including a mermaid sighting), with his advocacy that a colony be formed out of what some wished would remain exclusively a resource extraction operation.[76] In 1624 Sir William Alexander promoted the settlement of New Scotland, in what was then Acadia, without going there, as Ferdinando Gorges did for Nova Scotia in 1659.[77] After the fall of Louisbourg in 1745, another armchair traveller, William Bollan, promoted the settlement of Cape Breton.[78] Generally, however, books in English about emigration to the northern colonies were much more common after the War of 1812, especially in the 1820s and 1830s, when increased emigration from Britain was experienced by all its colonies.[79]

Interest in Quebec after the British gained control may be gauged by one publication: in the year of his death, 1761, Pierre-François-Xavier de Charlevoix published an English translation of his history of New France, first issued in French in 1744.[80] It provided the British with valuable information about the formation of their newest colony in North America.[81] Charlevoix's and other French books, such as Louis Hennepin's and the Baron de Lahontan's, supplied Jonathan Carver with much of the information in his two volumes, nearly compilations, although unacknowledged ones, of others' writings and mappings.[82]

A notable hiatus in the publication of travel books occurred during and just after the Revolutionary War. When publication resumed, it was seldom books that Loyalists wrote. Greater in number were those authored by Americans about the British colonies; before 1840 only about twenty of them appeared, about two-thirds of the number published in Britain. Also after the revolution, travel literature began to include descriptions of the attractions and deficiencies, aesthetic and economic, of Upper Canada: Surveyor General David William Smith initiated this trend with his *A Short Topographical Description of ... Upper Canada* (London, 1799). Another pattern commenced at the close of the century when Isaac Weld identified the interior of British North America as a desirable destination for scenery hunters.[83] The rage for picturesque landscape and quaint people, suspended by the Napoleonic Wars, began taking hold in Europe and the eastern United States. Enough published attention was focused on the British colonies by century's end to warrant John Pinkerton's lengthy mention of them in *Modern Geography* (London, 1802).

George Heriot's *Travels through the Canadas* (London, 1807) confirmed that books interested in landscape aesthetics and scenery could be published about British North America. Perhaps the best known of early nineteenth-century travel books in English, this quarto publication successfully presents a scenic tour in word and image from Newfoundland to Sault Ste Marie. Native North Americans and Canadiens having been subjugated by British colonial rule, these peoples figure prominently in Heriot's picturesque compositions of societies as 'honest, hospitable, religious, inof-

2.3 George Heriot, *Costume of Domiciliated Indians of North America*; aquatint by J.C. Stadler, in George Heriot, *Travels through the Canadas* (London, 1807). Courtesy of the Thomas Fisher Rare Book Library, University of Toronto.

fensive, uninformed' habitants and 'domiciliated Indians' (see illus. 2.3, above).[84] In the same vein comes John Lambert's equally well known *Travels through Lower Canada, and the United States of America* (London, 1810), three volumes quaintly illustrated by the author. Few authors and only a few publishers could regularly afford to bring out expensive illustrated editions, and these works, both published by Sir Richard Phillips, comprise two of his three entries in the field, the first having been the two-volume English translation of the Duc de La Rochefoucauld's *Travels through the United States of North America ... and Upper Canada* (London, 1799).[85] Having as keen a nose for what would sell as any nineteenth-century publisher, Phillips was not above swelling his books of travel as he saw fit, however the practice detracted from their accuracy, as the poet Robert Southey once discovered.[86]

A more typical, because more modestly produced, narrative tour of picturesque scenery is John Howison's *Sketches of Upper Canada, Domestic, Local, and Characteristic* (Edinburgh, 1821). It claimed to provide 'practical details for the information of emigrants of every class,' but its description of Niagara Falls likely accounts for three editions during the 1820s. Although no author before 1840 can accurately be considered a professional travel writer (a creation of the twentieth century), Howison, the author of remarkably popular adventure stories, was typical of many authors who would turn to travel writing, presumably because it paid well.[87] Few of these authors were resident British North Americans before 1840. The popularity – indeed, near interchangeability – of Natives, Canadiens, and Niagara as recognizably 'picturesque' matter persisted for some time; Longmans and John Maude took advantage of the craze for Niagara in the 1820s by offering his *A Visit to the Falls of Niagara in 1800* in 1826, a quarter-century after Maude saw it. Even John Murray descended from the Arctic. However, his firm's contributions were rather less predictable: George Head's *Forest Scenes and Incidents in the Wilds of North America* (1829) takes its reader to less-frequented places, and William 'Tiger' Dunlop's *Statistical Sketches of Upper Canada* (1832) is as idiosyncratic as its author. Finally, books with just enough text to hold their illustrations together were popular during the craze for the picturesque. Quebec-born Joseph Bouchette, surveyor general of Lower Canada, separated his statistical and topographical facts, published in his two-volume work, *The British Dominions in North America* (London, 1832), from his heavily illustrated, nineteen-page privately published *Views in the Canadas, New Brunswick, and Nova Scotia* [s.l., 1832?].

The strategy exemplified by Bouchette and his sons helps to show that travel books were gradually separating into well-understood sub-genres: picturesque accounts, tour guides, emigration guides, gazetteers, political assessments of the colonies, and even two compilations covering all the colonies and the Arctic, as well as tips for emigrants, by Eneas Mackenzie and Hugh Murray.[88] Sportsmen's narratives were yet to appear, but different niches in the publishing world were quickly catering to varied interests among British readers and a growing number in the United States.

In the first half of the nineteenth century, while military society dominated eastern North America, books authored by officers continued. Francis Hall, an English lieutenant, sketched the charms of Lower Canada and its people; naval lieutenant Frederick Fitzgerald De Roos hunted scenery through the United States and the Canadas; Basil Hall, a Scottish naval officer, travelled with his wife and child through the Lower Great Lakes and wrote and sketched scenery and society in the picturesque mode; James Edward Alexander travelled in military circles from Niagara to Quebec, lampooning Methodists as he went.[89] Naval officer Frederick Marryat made his presence felt in both the British colonies and the United States with the publication in London and New York of his *A Diary in America with Remarks on Its Institutions* (London, etc., 1839); he criticized conditions north of the border and excoriated egalitarian expressions of democracy in the Republic. In the same year, another officer, Walter Henry, offered up his memoirs in apparently the only book of travels by an officer published in British North America, *Trifles from My Portfolio* (Quebec, 1839).

As popular in their day as Hall, Alexander, and Marryat, other widely read nineteenth-century writers who published books in the 1830s that remarked on the British colonies include Frances Trollope, Anna Jameson, and Harriet Martineau.[90] Irish actor and author William Grattan Tyrone Power, whose work took him to the United States during 1833–5, underwent the compulsory visits to Niagara and Lower Canada and furnished a two-volume work, *Impressions of America* (London, 1836). As far as travel books are concerned, the famous brushed up against British North America but spent little time or ink on the colonies.

Two comparative absences in books of exploration and travel published before 1840 are titles by women travellers (the trio of Trollope, Jameson, and Martineau is complemented only by Frances Wright Arusmont),[91] and works that feature prominently an author's interest in flora and fauna, Pehr (Peter) Kalm's and John Bartram's in the eighteenth century marking the exceptions.[92] Otherwise, British authors and London publishers saw to it that the vogues in travel writing were regularly rehearsed for a chiefly British readership (at least in the first instance of a book's sale). It comes as no surprise that what is now Canada looks both curious and remote in these books, no less so as the period advances and the imagined gives way to the surveyed and appraised. High Arctic drama, the sublimity of Niagara, the oddity of a French-speaking British colony, and the endless wilderness and its denizens dominate the image that these works partly compose and partly reflect. Military, naval, commercial, and political institutions bring order out of the overwhelming space, which appears to offer potential, especially to the emigrant; but armchair explorers and travellers were still left with an isolated and somewhat forbidding prospect. Britain's failure to discover a Northwest Passage, which, in the end, was hardly there to be discovered, is perhaps emblematic of this general view.

CASE STUDY
Thomas James's *Strange and Dangerous Voyage* (1633)
— I.S. MacLaren

The first entire book in English about what is now Canada written by an explorer is Thomas James's, but not because his 'intended Discovery of the Northwest Passage into the South-Sea' amounted to discovery. He sailed into Hudson Bay and spent the winter of 1631–2 in James Bay, near where Henry

Hudson had wintered in 1610–11, but Luke Fox had charted those waters in the same year, as had Hudson, Robert Bylot, Thomas Button, and Jens Munk.[93]

However, James's account convinced sponsors that his expedition had succeeded because it returned home almost intact. Such casuistry was not new among explorers, but James mastered it. With his successful decision to sink his vessel in hopes that it would survive the winter (not a new idea but a little-heralded one), the book won him fame. When he published it in 1633 in London at the king's behest and perhaps involvement, North America was busy: Charles I had just awarded Lord Baltimore a charter for a new colony (Maryland), and the first *Relation* (Paris, 1632) had publicized Jesuit missions in New France. James's literary flourish rendered his book popular when another failure to find a passage would hardly have warranted notice.

His graceful prose and scientific curiosity combine in ways unmatched in exploration narratives of any age. The book fired the imaginations of poets John Milton and Samuel Taylor Coleridge, and chemist and physicist Robert Boyle quoted it extensively.[94] Scientific (especially mathematical) tabulations complement word-pictures of ice in the inland sea and of Charlton Island's boreal forest and eskers. Moreover, James included appendices by Henry Gellibrand, who discovered the variability in magnetic declination, concerning the then little understood concept of longitude, and by William Watts, chaplain to the Earl of Strafford, decrying exploration's folly and implying that the search for a Northwest Passage resulted from Spain's having duped England.[95] Invocations, intercessions, and prayers of thanksgiving punctuate the narrative. Philosophical reflections join stirring descriptions of the agony of cold, the torment of mosquitoes, and the tragedy of lives lost, as well as the drama of shipboard confrontations over navigational decisions. Yet this miscellany's most accomplished literary feature is a confession of vanity that James works into the first of two poems:

> We have with confidence relyde upon
> A rustie wyre, toucht with a little Stone,
> Incompast round with paper, and alasse
> To house it harmelesse, nothing but a glasse,
> And thought to shun a thousand dangers, by
> The blind direction of this senselesse flye.[96]

chapter 3

THE BOOK IN NEW FRANCE

FRANÇOIS MELANÇON

As a child of the Western Renaissance, the printed book followed a path that was closely linked to explorations sponsored by European states from the end of the fifteenth century. Before explorers departed, reading whetted desire and curiosity and fed their imaginations with dreams; when they returned, writing was part of a process of legitimization for territorial conquests. On the voyages themselves, books often became travelling companions.

The process of colonization left scant room for books. In the territory claimed by the French monarchy in North America, the rush for 'brown gold' (beaver pelts) relegated intellectual activities far down the list of priorities for the engagés and other colonists. The coureurs du bois could not afford to burden themselves with an object that bore no relation to their motives in joining the fur trade and served little purpose other than perhaps as a symbol of 'otherness' in the eyes of the Natives and as a cultural link to their homeland. These sentiments were shared by those cultivating the land in New France. However, the colonial experience was also born of militant Christianity and of a new political structure, the modern state. Both these social systems placed the written word at the heart of their renewal and progress, and both were able to turn to their advantage this new invention, the printing press.

It was within this context that the book was to find its place in the French territories of North America. Between the material and physical uncertainties that affected the exploitation of colonial resources and the written reports demanded by the civil and religious institutions involved, books took on different tangible forms and spread along divergent paths. In this way, they brought together the collective inheritance of New France, in part by maintaining undeniable cultural links with the home country and in part by preparing the stage for the emergence of a shared public sphere that would further strengthen the passage to British rule.

Socio-Cultural Context

There were no printing presses in New France; this is a commonplace of Canadian historical writing,[1] underlined by Pehr Kalm in 1749, among others.[2] Nevertheless, the need for a press was clear early on. A version of Diego de Ledesma's catechism in the Huron language was published at Rouen in 1630, before it was included in the history of Samuel de Champlain's voyages two years later.[3] Without doubt, the publication was intended to create an impression of the exotic rather than to be used as a practical tool for evangelization, but it confirmed at the same time the value of the printing press for missionary work.[4] In 1665 the members of the Company of Jesus at Quebec considered requesting the materials needed to publish works for their missions. The congregation of Saint-Sulpice in Montreal did likewise about twenty years later. In both cases, the efforts failed. Another attempt was made in 1748 by acting governor Roland-Michel Barrin de La Galissonière. This time a request was sent to Versailles citing the need to ease the workload of clerks in the civil administration. The royal authorities were quite favourable to the idea of establishing a king's printer in the colony, but they refused to contribute financially to the enterprise. Despite the costs of such an undertaking, the newly appointed governor, Jacques-Pierre de Taffanel de La Jonquière, pressed the case further in 1751, pointing out the political advantages of having a printing press for faster distribution of orders throughout the colony. But the proposal by the local administrators went unheeded.[5] Of the book arts, only binding was to find a modest place in the colony.[6]

The lack of a printing press in New France had three notable consequences. First, it imposed complete dependence on French presses, which followed the mercantilist economic thinking of the royal authorities. In clerical circles, however, this was not an insurmountable obstacle. Naturally, the great distances involved led to the neglect of some projects, but in spite of the hazards, many others were successfully completed. Two priests from the Séminaire des missions étrangères at Quebec had books celebrating devotion to the Holy Family published in Paris.[7] For his part, Jean-Baptiste de La Croix de Chevrières de Saint-Vallier, bishop of Quebec, entrusted the bookseller-printers Urbain Coustelier and Simon Langlois with the printing of the catechism and book of rites for his diocese, as well as a collection of earlier episcopal orders that served as a kind of ecclesiastical jurisprudence.[8] The colonial administration itself ordered the particular official forms required for the admiralty from La Rochelle or Paris, along with the change notes and bills of exchange needed to run the local economy efficiently.[9]

Further, the lack of local presses hindered the development of a colonial literature around and through which a learned collective identity distinct from that of the metropole could have taken shape. It is true, however, that the colony did not appear to offer the critical mass of educated individuals that would have made this public voice desirable. When the colonial voice did express itself, it did so through occasional literature, frequently sung.[10] In this sense, the colonial province was much the same as the other provinces of the kingdom. The centralization of the French book trade strangled the rise of the provinces in favour of Paris, which became the cultural centre of the kingdom.

Finally, recourse to European presses facilitated control by the authorities of the monarch over the production of documents relative to the colony. These documents were in fact of considerable import in the game of international politics. Baron de Lahontan, Father Louis Hennepin, and lawyer Claude Lebeau published most of their works in the Low Countries, where political intervention in the book trade was rare. Claude-Charles Le Roy de La Potherie, *dit* Bacqueville de La Potherie, who proposed the *Histoire de l'Amerique septentrionale* to the authorities in 1702, did not get permission to go to press until 1722, after the military conflicts had been resolved.[11] Many other projects never saw the light of day, such as the 'Code des procédures pour les colonies,' proposed by attorney general Mathieu-Benoît Collet, or the engineer Gaspard-Joseph Chaussegros de Léry's 'Traité des fortifications.'[12] This centrist attitude of the royal authorities concerning publishing activities was characteristic of the French book trade. Furthermore, it was supported by members of the religious establishment, who saw it as a way to preserve their orthodoxy and to prevent all doctrinal deviation among their members. It was especially obvious among the Sulpicians. The mother house in Paris insisted on reading manuscripts from every seminary in the kingdom before it granted permission to publish.[13] The revision in Paris of the texts of the Jesuit *Relations* concerning Canada came from the same attitude.

The lack of local presses left the way clear for handwritten texts,[14] but this practice was limited in New France. The various religious communities exchanged the obituaries of their members among themselves or shared extracts from one another's annals, perhaps even short devotional works written by their fellows, but little more. A few handwritten rhetorical, theological, or philosophical treatises also made the rounds in the colony, but their existence signals a pedagogical strategy centred on dictation in class and on transcription, rather than a conscious plan to counter the scarcity of printed texts. For the missionaries, copying the linguistic and pastoral works of their predecessors was founded squarely on the educational virtues of transcription; by reproducing these texts, they learned the Native languages.

Manuscript production was practised on a larger scale within the administration. The making of card money and the publication of the ordinances of the intendants, bishops' orders, and other documents circulated throughout the territory generated much written work; so much so that greater and greater pressure came to bear on the administrative clerks, as the political structures of the colony developed and the local population grew. Two hundred copies of the *Déclaration du roi, au sujet de la monnaie de cartes* were issued in the colony in 1717, and one hundred copies of each of the three proclamations concerning notarial deeds and marriage contracts in 1733.[15] Nearly twenty years later, sixty thousand printed bills of exchange were requested by intendant François Bigot to offset the increasing workload occasioned by the manuscript production of card money.[16]

Furthermore, literacy was not universal in New France, as Michel Verrette concludes in chapter 8. Far from being devalued or marginalized, the illiterate had wide rights in the *ancien régime*. The public reading aloud in a clear voice of ordinances and notarial documents, the distinctive trimming of each denomination of card money according to its value, and the recitation of the rosary in place of the reading of prayer books were all strategies designed to integrate those who could neither read nor write into a social structure that had come to be ruled by the written word.

The Spread of the Book

The lack of local presses tied colonists to European production, especially since linguistic, economic, political, and religious barriers between the French and British colonies prevented access to the book market in the Thirteen Colonies, which, in truth, were also heavily dominated by Old World production.[17] There were two commercial sources of books for New France's readers: the European retail market and the local resale market.

Books were not a first need for the majority of French subjects who had come to the colony. For some administrators, ecclesiastics, and other well-read individuals, however, there was no question of undertaking the voyage out without these companions to silent thought, especially since such men often considered a sojourn in

New France to be a transitory phase, their sights still on Versailles as the centre of their universe. A number of high administrators brought entire personal collections with them, and those who trod the colonial soil with scientific pretensions did likewise. Bishops arrived in their new diocese with their own libraries, while the Séminaire des missions étrangères, for example, made certain that its new members departing for the colony bought liturgical volumes before they left.[18]

Once established, most of these men continued to buy books on the European market. In the absence of a local book trade, colonists who wished to keep up with literary news were obliged to turn to this source of supply. Both retail merchants who provided books for the entire colony and the civil and religious institutions also drew from this source. Some claimed that it cost them much less to do so because they avoided the intermediary of the retail network and ensured their access to a market better stocked with both new and old books. The monarchy in this way provided the printed matter required by the colonial administration for matters of government and the exercise of justice, as well as that used for the celebration of mass in the chapels of its local representatives and in the fortresses. For their part, religious communities appointed an agent in the metropole to whom they delegated their purchasing.

In the local market, the choice of books was modest. Retail stalls in the colony had little to offer. Conservative businessmen, the retailers principally offered liturgical works and prayer books (especially books of hours) and spelling primers – in other words, the chief books promoted by the Catholic pastorate and in turn by educational institutions. They offered nothing new, no works of fiction, and no short-lived publications, such as the newspapers, satirical handbills, or even almanacs that were the main fare of common folk in the Old World. They could not even stock catechisms, since the parish priests themselves may have sold these to their flocks. This intervention in the local book market was not unusual. The principal colonial institutions, civil or religious, almost always short-circuited local retailers, either buying the books needed for their own use directly from France or procuring there those required for their students, to whom they resold them. At Quebec this practice was especially obvious at the Séminaire des missions étrangères and the Ursuline convent, where old account books record the existence of a small bookselling operation. The retail booksellers were left with only the meanest share of the market, which elsewhere in the kingdom constituted the working capital of the smallest booksellers.

The public sales of estates or seized property provided the only local opportunities for literate colonists to enrich their collections easily, and sometimes at very low cost, especially when the extensive collections of individuals such as businessman François-Étienne Cugnet or jurist Louis-Guillaume Verrier were offered. During the eighteenth century, more than three hundred individuals in the colonial capital attended some sixty auctions to buy books.[19]

Purchase was not the only way to acquire books. Some books circulated on loan or as gifts. Lending, through civil and religious institutions, was in fact the main way that books were circulated.Verrier, for example, frequently borrowed volumes from the legislative library of the Conseil supérieur.[20] Similarly, every religious house kept a common library where its members could, with permission of the superior of the order, borrow one or two books to enliven or vary their spiritual reading. These libraries, however, were rarely open to the public. As for books being circulated between individuals, it was often a means of sealing family, professional, or commercial ties. From the grandmother who lent a copy of the *Office de la semaine sainte* to her granddaughter and the merchant who shared leisure reading with a customer to a trader who lent the captain of a ship a book on navigation, the sharing of books formed multiple social relationships.[21]

The practice of offering books as gifts provided another dimension.[22] In bypassing the established network of retail exchanges, gift books created a strong and symbolic link between giver and receiver. Moreover, such books generally carried an implicit message, a statement about what must or should be read. The New Year's greetings offered by the Jesuits in the mid-seventeenth century were another expression of this intention, as was the devotion to the Holy Family and the Holy Angels promoted by priests of the Missions étrangères and the devotion to the Cross encouraged by the Augustinians of the Hôtel-Dieu at Quebec.[23] The efforts expended by the royal authorities to fulfill the request made jointly by missionary Jean-Louis Le Loutre, Abbé de L'Isle-Dieu, and Bishop Henri-Marie Dubreil de Pontbriand to send some two thousand devotional books to Acadia and 'Canada' convey more clearly still the prescriptive message.[24]

Books and the Colonial Territory

Books thus had a presence in New France, taking any one of a number of routes from the European production houses to their destination in North America. There too they remained within the more or less formal exchange networks that facilitated their integration into the fabric of colonial society. The territory of books mapped out by the places where they were owned, either collectively or individually, centred around certain social anchors, such as libraries. These were the centres from which written culture asserted itself and was propagated. But beyond this functional aspect, these centres also lent books an air of authority, be it divine, legal, political, intellectual, or scientific.

The religious and administrative institutions were the main seats of written culture and books in the colony. Every religious community, regular and secular, had a collection of books at the disposal of its members, usually entrusted to the care of an official or acting librarian (often the superior's assistant), who provided for their storage, care, and supervision. Access to the books was permitted, however, only through the superior, who alone authorized the reading and borrowing of books. In addition to a common library, it was not unusual to find specialized collections related to the specific goal of those organizations and distributed through their buildings according to particular needs. Such was especially the case in apothecaries and sickrooms in hospitals or in classrooms at educational establishments and boarding schools.

In addition to these collections available to priests and nuns in the communities of New France, many cells and individual rooms housed smaller collections, of which the number and subject matter varied with the interests and personal financial resources of the owner. Moreover, secular priests in parishes and missions (parochial or Native) were important promoters of culture. From Abbé Albert Davion, posted with the Tunicas, to Abbés Laboret and Claude-Jean-Baptiste Chauvreaulx, assigned to the Acadians at Grand-Pré and Pisiquid (Windsor, Nova Scotia), the brothers Nicolas-Michel and Philippe Boucher, one at Pointe-de-Lévis and the other at Île d'Orléans, and Abbé Philippe-René de Robineau de Portneuf, priest at Saint-Joachim's, each kept in his presbytery, or in whatever building stood in its stead, a quantity of books far beyond those strictly needed for the fulfilment of his duties.[25] The variety of titles and their thematic scope revealed the owner's theological and spiritual concerns and sometimes a certain intellectual curiosity or even civil involvement beyond his primary pastoral role. Similarly, most churches and chapels in the colony kept copies of the main liturgical works in the sacristy: antiphonaries, graduals, missals, and so forth.

On the administrative side, the seats of government in Montreal, Trois-Rivières, and Quebec, as well as in Acadia and Louisiana, kept a certain number of books and copies of other printed materials available for officers and senior administrators. At Quebec, in particular, as early as 1717 the royal authorities made available to members of the Conseil supérieur a collection of books in judicature that would include, nearly twenty years later, some twenty standard folio law books.

Books also found a secure place, in very different ways, at the heart of civil soci-

ety.[26] Their presence was above all an urban phenomenon. While a third of the households inventoried at Quebec for estate proceedings revealed the presence of books,
the proportion was less than one-tenth in the rural areas.[27] More often than not,
books belonged to the lettered elite, for whom they were one of the tools of daily
work, since various writing tasks fell to the head of the household. In New France
the bourgeoisies of talent and trade, along with the clergy and certain members of
the *noblesse de robe*, were the driving forces in the transmission of print culture. The
intendants and other high functionaries, the members of the Conseil supérieur, the
judges, notaries, doctors, and a great many merchants and traders dominated in this
regard. Books also played a part in the lives of urban craftsmen, although on a more
modest scale.

The Literary Heritage

While books found a foothold in the lettered and cultured circles of New France, the
works themselves created a virtual community of readers with varying skills and
expectations which recognized neither geopolitical nor social frontiers. The unify-
ing power of these books lay in the dual heritage of schooling and pastoral instruction that work habits, intellectual curiosity, and the availability of free time could
foster.

   The heart of the literary heritage of the colony was religious.[28] In those homes in
the colonial capital where books were rare, for example, there were practically no
volumes other than devotional works such as the *Heures*, the *Office de la Semaine sainte*,
and the *Vie des saints*, sometimes together with extracts from the Bible (psalms and
the Gospels). The owners of larger collections shared this same literary core, surpass-
ing it, however, in the variety of titles and the search for a deeper spiritual experience. Beyond these basic acquisitions, professional requirements pushed some
collections away from the religious into other spheres of interest: legal codes for
magistrates, bailiffs, notaries, and merchants; theological and liturgical works for
ecclesiastics; medical and pharmaceutical texts for doctors and surgeons; books on
astronomy and geometry for hydrographers and some ship captains. These interests
drove the second force of cultural transmission in the colony. The third was powered
by diverse motivations that are more difficult to determine. Financial resources, the
availability of leisure time, and intellectual curiosity, among other factors, may claim
as great a role as traditional family culture, personal ambition and activities, and self-
image. This third element developed around an eclectic curiosity about the contemporary world in full geographic and intellectual expansion (travel tales and scientific

discoveries), about its historical roots (ancient, biblical, European, and French), and about philosophical questions (moral literature). It signalled an openness to works of fiction that freely combined Greco-Latin literature (raised to canonical status in the colleges) with vernacular literature, in which dramatic and epistolary genres (close relatives of public speaking) progressively gave way to the novel (Miguel de Cervantes's *Don Quixote*, Paul Scarron's *Le roman comique*, and the works of Alain-René Lesage leading the way).

The contents of government and religious libraries were largely influenced by their social purpose. At Quebec the restoration of the catalogues of the Jesuit library and the library of the Séminaire, drawn up in 1782, confirms this tendency. The former revealed a marked prevalence of religious works, closely followed by medical books and those relative to hydrography. The seminary library, on the other hand, gave several shelves to the pedagogical works needed for the study of classical authors or the teaching of science and philosophy, in keeping with the new educational mandate it had adopted in 1764.[29] In Montreal the involvement of the religious brothers from the Hôpital général in teaching the academic rudiments also determined the composition of their collection.[30] The legislative library of the Conseil supérieur offered only law books: law codes and casebooks.

Reading

The teaching of reading was also largely coloured by religion, because instruction in this skill drew part of its legitimacy and motivation from the religious quarrels that had shaken the Christian church at the dawn of the sixteenth century. The church did not have a monopoly on promoting the access to reading, but it was by far the best equipped and the most highly structured. Thus in New France, people learned to read largely through the efforts of parochial institutions (primary schools and convents), whose curricula were set by various religious authorities.[31] The preferred learning process moved from deciphering letters, alone and in the many combinations that form syllables, to recognizing words. Traditionally, Latin was given priority. As the language of the sacred, it was the basis for both prayer and the celebration of mass. Hence the focus on learning to read aloud: learning to read was first and foremost learning to pray. Once spelling and syllabification had been mastered, the students turned to pronunciation exercises, and the formation of sentences began.

After the students had received their first communion, the church and the school initiated them into a new way of reading – the intensive reading that most devotional books validate.[32] Such reading must first be placed under the auspices of God,

acknowledged as the ultimate guardian of its admissibility. Curiosity, while tolerated, had to avoid the pitfalls of vanity and passion. The process of reading required
a linear order: 'The whole book must be read at once, without taking up another
before it is finished and without skipping any part of the book.'[33] Slowness, like the
rapture brought on by intellectual contemplation, was appropriate for a corpus of a
few chosen works, read and reread. In the end, this way of reading had a rather
pragmatic purpose: to occupy the mind in order to stave off idleness and overindul-
gence of the senses, while simultaneously reinforcing the effectiveness of the
Christian message and buttressing the shared paradigms of the community of
the faithful.

Initiation into these two ways of reading – aloud and intensive – was accompanied by an implicit ethics of reading that was reinforced by both pastoral discourse
and school books. In the eyes of the colony's ecclesiastical authorities, the choice of
books and reading material required tight control. It demanded experience and erudition beyond that of most of the faithful. Ethical choices were based on a rudimentary principle of dichotomy: on one side, the good books; on the other, the bad. The
good books included those favoured by educational institutions and the church's
various pedagogical tools (catechism, confraternity, and so forth). It was those books
which were absorbed through pragmatic reading – prayer and devotional works, as
well as the lives of the saints – that reinforced religious acts and extended ecclesiastical teachings. The second group were part of secular literature, which threatened
faith, purity, morals, and, by extension, salvation. These evil books could belong to
two classes: those that attacked religion and the church and the 'lascivious' works
about secular love, licentiousness, and ribaldry that unbridled the senses and the
imagination. Among the latter, novels and comedies topped the list.

Despite this program, many children never learned to read, especially those in
modest urban milieux and rural environments. These two groups of children generally attended school for only very short periods: one or two years, or about forty
days, just long enough to learn their catechism. As a result, the teachers' exhorta-
tions were often overtaken by the realities of daily life. Some young people left school
barely knowing how to spell, and others able to read just the Latin and French of
prayers, but others still, initiated into the techniques of writing in college or convent
or at home, easily mastered printed and handwritten texts and, little by little, transformed their reading into a silent, interior, and individual pursuit.

Not only did educational institutions not have a monopoly on the transmission
of reading skills; they also could not maintain total control over the reading choices
of the faithful. Some readers in circles familiar with written culture, such as the
colonial gentry and the bourgeois craftsmen and traders, in fact adopted a certain

3.1 Richard Short, *A View of the Jesuits College and Church / Vue de l'église et du collège des jésuites* [Quebec]; engraved by C. Grignion (London, 1761). Courtesy of the National Archives of Canada, W.H. Coverdale Collection of Canadiana, C-041504.

independence vis-à-vis the dominant discourse of the church. Baron de Lahontan, for example, spoke out against the church's moral censure of novels and comedies, railing against Abbé Étienne Guyotte of Montreal, who had physically attacked his copy of Petronius's *Satiricon*.[34] Also in Montreal, young Catherine de Villebois set the authority of her grandmother against the moral authority of a Récollet priest. Her youthful courage was a sign of how close to the surface lay the competition between rival cultural elites over reading.[35]

CASE STUDY
The Library at the Collège des jésuites
— Gilles Gallichan

After their return to New France in 1632, the Jesuits laid the foundation for a library intended to support their missionary work and the education provided at their college, which was founded three years later (see illus. 3.1, above). In France at that time, the Society of Jesus established a number of colleges endowed with well-stocked libraries. The new college at Quebec undoubtedly profited from the cultural influence and heritage of the Society of Jesus, and many gifts came to the fathers from within the order. Books were sent from France or donated by colonial administrators. As the teaching program developed and missions spread across the continent, the college library expanded as well. Works of theology, philosophy, law, medicine and pharmacology, hydrography, architecture, and the exact and natural sciences, including geometry, botany, mineralogy, and astronomy – these last useful for an understanding of the discoveries of the New World – all found a place on its shelves.

In 1716 Pierre-Michel Laure, a novice, was acting as librarian. It appears that two catalogues of the collection were drawn up, one in 1720 and the other in 1745, but neither has survived. We can assume, nevertheless, that it was the richest and most important library in New France, with a collection of several thousand works. When he visited the college in 1749, the Swedish naturalist Pehr Kalm remarked on the library and praised its orderliness.[36]

The British Conquest of New France in 1760 dealt a fatal blow to the college and its library. In 1763 the building was requisitioned by the army, and the priests sold off some of their books. When the Jesuit order was dissolved by Rome in 1773, the collection was looted and dispersed. Jean-Joseph Casot, the last member of the order in British North America and heir to its assets, bequeathed what remained of the library to the Séminaire de Québec in 1797; but he also sold some books and gave away others, particularly to the Hôpital général de Québec, the Hôtel-Dieu, the Catholic bishop, and friends and benefactors, including the printer John Neilson, who received about a hundred.

When the historian Antonio Drolet attempted to reconstruct the catalogue of the Jesuits' library, he was able to trace, by means of manuscript marks (see illus. 3.2, p. 57), about 750 titles totalling some 1,000 volumes, most preserved at the Séminaire and in the old hospitals of Quebec City.[37] An inventory has been made of a significant part of the collection at the Collège de Montréal, as well as of a few titles in the archives of the Congrégation Notre-Dame. Other fragments of the library can be found in the archives of the diocese of Quebec and the Séminaire de Nicolet.

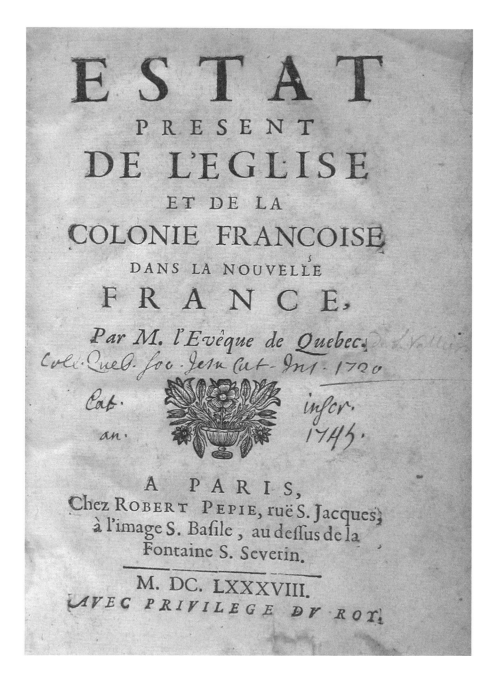

3.2 Manuscript ex libris of the Jesuit college, Quebec (1745), in a copy of Jean-Baptiste de la Croix de Chevrières de Saint-Vallier, *Estat present de l'eglise et de la colonie françoise dans la Nouvelle France* (Paris, 1688). Courtesy of the Archives de l'Archidiocèse de Québec.

PART TWO

PRINTING IN BRITISH NORTH AMERICA

chapter 4

MAPPING INNOVATION

First Printers and the Spread of the Press

PATRICIA LOCKHART FLEMING

The sloop *St. John* arrived at Halifax from Boston on 14 October 1751 with a cargo of lumber, livestock, roots, provisions, chocolate, candles, rum, and 'A printing Press & Appurtenances.'[1] Bartholomew Green, a printer 'starved out of Boston,'[2] where his family had worked in the trade for more than a century, had come to Halifax to establish a printing office, but he died before the end of October, so that it is unlikely there was time to unpack and ready the press for use.[3] John Bushell, a former partner in Boston, followed Green to Halifax and set up shop in Grafton Street in his stead, issuing the first number of the *Halifax Gazette* on 23 March 1752 (see illus. 4.1, p. 62). A skilled wood engraver as well as a printer, Bushell was proprietor of the only press in Halifax until his death in 1761, and although his imprints are not numerous, he set a pattern for the printing business in early British North America with a weekly newspaper, government orders, book work, and job printing. His earliest dated imprint, Governor Peregrine Thomas Hopson's proclamation on assuming office in August 1752, is the first example of French printing in the northern colonies,[4] and for a treaty Hopson signed with Major Jean-Baptiste Cope, 'Chief Sachem' of the Mi'kmaqs, Bushell used a two-column format for printing English and French together, heading one with rows of crowns and the other with fleurs-de-lys.[5] Among his government imprints are the first *Journal* of the House of Assembly for the province[6] and the *Acts* passed in the first assembly.[7]

Although Bushell was still named as printer in 1759, a burst of ornaments and

4.1 The *Halifax Gazette*, no. 1 (23 March 1752). Courtesy of the National Library of Canada.

typographic ingenuity marked the arrival at the press of Anthony Henry (Anton Henrich), who became a partner in 1760 and took over the business when Bushell died early in 1761. Not yet thirty, Henry settled in, welcomed a commission as king's printer in 1788, and was active until his death late in 1800. Of some 225 imprints documented or identified as his work, 65 per cent were for government. Religious titles make up another 12 per cent, crossing creeds from the New Light evangelist Henry Alline to the Anglican bishop of Nova Scotia, Charles Inglis. One devotional work was printed by subscription and intended for sale in Halifax, Boston, New York, and Philadelphia,[8] while another, printed at the expense of the missionary at Lunenburg, warned on the title page 'To be given and not to be Sold.'[9] Two series of almanacs, almost uninterrupted up to the final editions of 1801, account for 20 per cent of Henry's surviving imprints: *The Nova-Scotia Calender,* which began with the 1769 edition, and *Der Neu-Schottländische Calender,* published from 1788.[10] As Juris Dilevko explains in chapter 12, Henry was not the first to print German in British North America, but his almanac offers the most consistent use of that language until Germans had established a community in Upper Canada by the 1830s. It is not certain that Henry's newspaper 'Die Welt, und die Neuschottländische Correspondenz,' which he proposed in 1787, was ever published, although his papers in English were successful. He had continued John Bushell's *Halifax Gazette* when he took over the shop in 1761, enlarging the newspaper from a half to a full sheet in folio format. When the Stamp Act of 1765 required printers of newspapers to use paper marked with a tax stamp, Henry complied, printing on stamped paper from October 1765 to March 1766. Probably following the model of American newspapers, whose reports of local resistance to the tax they reprinted, Henry and his young assistant, Isaiah Thomas, expressed their opposition by outlining the *Gazette* text with thick mourning rules. Someone, probably Thomas, who soon left Halifax to become a leading revolutionary printer, added small devil and skull-and-crossbones cuts to mock the revenue stamp. The *Halifax Gazette* ceased publication sometime after March and was replaced in the summer by the staid *Nova-Scotia Gazette,* printed by Robert Fletcher, who superseded Henry as the government's printer. Henry countered with a popular new paper in 1769; the following year Fletcher sold his press to concentrate on bookselling, and Henry launched a third paper, the *Nova-Scotia Gazette and the Weekly Chronicle,* which he printed in Sackville Street until his death thirty years later.

In Quebec, where the Stamp Act increased the price for a ream of paper by 450 per cent, the printers William Brown and Thomas Gilmore suspended publication of the *Quebec Gazette / La Gazette de Québec* in October 1765, reminding readers that stamped paper was not required for the printing of handbills. Seven months later, publication of the newspaper resumed and, with a second interruption occasioned by the Ameri-

can invasion in 1775–6, continued for another century. Brown and Gilmore had come
to Quebec in 1764 from Philadelphia, where they had worked in the shop of William
Dunlap, a successful printer and bookseller, sometime postmaster, and protege of
Benjamin Franklin. They published the first number of the *Quebec Gazette / La Gazette
de Québec* on 21 June 1764. With new Caslon type and their signboard painted, lettered,
and mounted on a post, Brown and Gilmore, both in their mid-twenties, established
an office that was to dominate Quebec printing and bookselling for decades, from
Brown to his Scottish nephews Samuel and then John Neilson, and on to John's son
Samuel. Together they printed more than 40 per cent of all known imprints in the
northern British colonies before 1800, as well as hundreds of orders for job printing
identified only in their account books.[11] Although most of their work was in English
or French or bilingual, known then as 'double,' they printed in German, Latin, and
four Native languages – Abenaki, Mohawk (see illus. 11.1, p. 254), Montagnais (see
illus. 12.1, p. 281), and Oneida – and were the first to set music types.

The second printing office in the old province of Quebec, at Montreal, began as
a French press even though the printer, Fleury Mesplet, a native of Marseilles, had
worked in London and then Philadelphia. It was in Philadephia that he printed three
letters in 1774, 1775, and 1776 addressed by the Continental Congress to the inhabitants of Quebec encouraging them to join in rebellion. Commissioned as printer by
the Congress in 1776, Mesplet set off for Montreal, then under occupation by the
Continental Army. He arrived shortly before the troops withdrew but was detained
with his workers for almost a month. Upon their release, he set up the press and
stayed on as Montreal's only printer until his death in 1794. In a town that was not a
provincial capital, Mesplet did much less government work than Anthony Henry in
Halifax or William Brown at Quebec, just orders from the courts, the sheriff, and the
militia; but he printed other staples: almanacs in sheet and pamphlet form and periodical papers. The first, *Gazette du commerce et littéraire*, was literary and philosophical
in outlook, carrying few advertisements and little news. Suspect from the outset,
with too much Voltaire for the church and too much popular sympathy in the government's view, this small paper ceased in June 1779 when Mesplet and his editor
were arrested by executive order and held without charge for more than three years.
During his detention, Mesplet's almanac was published each year but one since the
printing office, probably directed by his wife, Marie Mirabeau, continued in a small
way with bookbinding and job printing.

Mesplet's second venture, the *Montreal Gazette / Gazette de Montréal*, published from
1785 in French and English but not always in both, succeeded as a strongly local newspaper. Including job printing, some 150 imprints are recorded from Mesplet's press,
the majority in French, though he also printed in English, Latin, and Mohawk. One of

his most ambitious projects was the publication of a translation of Richard Burn's *Justice of the Peace and Parish Officer* (London, 1755). Issued in eighteen monthly parts, *Le juge à paix* attracted 205 subscribers in Montreal, Quebec, and Trois-Rivières.[12] Mesplet also printed a few popular and current French literary works and large editions of books of devotion, some sold from his shop or sent to agents and to William Brown at Quebec, others accumulating in two inventories, the first taken when his property was sold for debt in 1785 and the second in 1794 after his death.[13] Although Mesplet's estate included binding equipment and types newly imported from Europe, there was no press, the sheriff at Montreal having owned it for almost a decade.

The political turmoil that drew Fleury Mesplet to Montreal from Philadelphia drove a second generation of printers, the Loyalists, north from the newly independent United States to Nova Scotia. John Howe, who shared Boston connections with Bartholomew Green and John Bushell, settled in Halifax in 1780 and established the *Halifax Journal* by year's end. Until he was named king's printer to succeed Anthony Henry in 1801, his output was small, fewer than forty known imprints, mostly almanacs or religious works, particularly sermons, and the monthly *Nova-Scotia Magazine* (1789–92).[14] Howe's brother-in-law and former apprentice, William Minns, had founded his own paper, the *Weekly Chronicle,* by 1786, and after Howe's two older sons, John junior, who joined his father as John Howe and Son in 1804, and David, entered the book trades, the Howe family and their partners would dominate Halifax printing well into the fourth decade. From 1801 to 1810, for example, they printed more than 75 per cent of the surviving Halifax imprints as well as their newspapers.

The other Halifax shop active in this decade was still on Sackville Street, where Anthony Henry's widow had announced, within a month of his death in 1800, that Gay and Merlin had purchased the business. Only one imprint bears Merlin's name, but Archibald Gay printed a newspaper, religious works, and four almanacs before his own death in April 1805. Elizabeth Gay, left a widow with four young children, assumed charge of the office and published under her own imprint an almanac for 1806[15] and the first number of the *Nova-Scotia and New-Brunswick Magazine* for February 1806.[16] Their newspaper, the *Nova-Scotia Gazette*, continued until that summer, but by autumn the printing office was up for sale again. John Howe Jr eventually bought the shop, still furnished with Anthony Henry's types and equipment, from James Bagnall in 1810. Henry's name was revived in the Halifax press when his godson, Anthony Henry Holland, returned from his newspaper office in Maine to establish the *Acadian Recorder* in 1813. Less conservative than the three Howe papers, Holland's *Recorder* printed John Young's 'Agricola' letters on agricultural reform from 1818 to 1821 and Thomas McCulloch's Stepsure satires, beginning in 1821. By this time Holland was also operating the first paper mill east of Quebec.

Although John Howe was the most prominent of the Loyalist printers, with a legacy secured by the entry of his youngest son, Joseph, into the trade in 1827, he was not the only one to settle in Nova Scotia after the Revolutionary War. There were also the Robertsons from Edinburgh, brothers James and Alexander, who had printed in Boston, New York, Albany, and other towns before stopping in Shelburne on the south shore in 1783. James Robertson's story is told by Warren McDougall later in this chapter. Alexander's son, James junior, joined them there and, with Thomas and James Swords of New York, published one of three newspapers serving this Loyalist settlement in the mid-1780s.[17] James Humphreys, denounced as a traitor in Philadelphia, arrived at Shelburne in 1784 and stayed the longest, returning to Philadelphia as a bookseller in 1797.[18] William Lewis, who had apprenticed with the Robertsons in Albany and been jailed there with Alexander, arrived as a captain of Loyalist militia at 'his Majesty's Loyal Settlement of St. John's River, Nova Scotia,' in 1783.[19] The company included Lewis's partner, John Ryan, who had learned printing from John Howe in Newport, Rhode Island.

When Nova Scotia was divided to create the new province of New Brunswick the following year and Saint John incorporated as a city in 1785, Lewis and Ryan were already in place printing a newspaper and proclamations for the founding governor, but the appointment as king's printer and postmaster went instead to Christopher Sower III.[20] A Loyalist regarded as another tory traitor in Philadelphia, Sower had grown up in a family of printers and typefounders in Germantown, Pennsylvania. William Lewis left Saint John soon after the rival printer set up shop, but John Ryan stayed on, eventually collaborating with Sower on a particularly fine almanac for 1792.[21] Both printers followed a familiar pattern, publishing almanacs, printing religious works, and filling orders for handbills and forms such as powers of attorney. Sower's *Royal Gazette* was official and formal, while Ryan printed more news and advertisements in the *Saint John Gazette*; his political stance had been tempered by several arrests and a trial for criminal libel early in his career with Lewis in Saint John. Although Sower was government printer, Ryan took the contract for the *Acts* and *Journals* of the assembly for several years, and when Sower resigned his offices in 1799, Ryan was named king's printer. He sold the *Saint John Gazette* to his brother-in-law, Jacob S. Mott, the son of another Loyalist printer. This network of printers, Loyalist in origin and connected by birth, marriage, and apprenticeship, persisted in New Brunswick with the success of Mott's apprentices Henry Chubb in Saint John and Chubb's brother-in-law, George Lugrin, who established the first permanent press at Fredericton, the provincial capital, in 1815.

The first presses in the capitals of Prince Edward Island and Newfoundland were also established by Loyalists, two of the original printers who moved on, James Robertson from Shelburne to Charlottetown in St John's Island (Prince Edward Island after 1799) and John Ryan from Saint John in New Brunswick to St John's, Newfoundland. James Robertson went to Charlottetown on the governor's invitation in 1787; there he published a newspaper, the *Royal American Gazette*, continuing the title he had used in New York and again at Shelburne. Though he stayed just two years, he printed the *Journals* of the House of Assembly and a substantial quarto volume of the acts passed from 1769 to 1788.[22] His journeyman William Alexander Rind, son of a Virginia printer, took over the press, but he was unable to sustain a newspaper and, from the evidence of surviving imprints, appears to have worked only for the government before he returned to Virginia in 1798, leaving the Island without a printer. Rind took along as apprentice his brother-in-law, James Bagnall, son of Loyalists who had come to Charlottetown from Shelburne. When Bagnall returned in 1804, he was appointed king's printer for Prince Edward Island. Until 1830, when he was dismissed, he struggled to keep his press in operation, with little encouragement from government and sometimes in conflict with his own interest in political reform when he sat as a member of the House of Assembly. Between 1805 and 1828 Bagnall established and discontinued six newspapers, five in Charlottetown and one in Halifax, where he printed in 1809–10. Almost all his surviving Charlottetown imprints are government work, although there is evidence that he published an almanac for 1815.[23] His successor and sometime rival was a nephew and former apprentice, James Douglas Haszard, another son of Loyalists settled in Charlottetown. A businessman as well as king's printer, Haszard, whose press would continue in the family throughout the century, succeeded in newspaper work and bookselling. In addition to official printing, he published in two genres that would be carried on by his son and grandson: almanacs and textbooks.

Newfoundland's first printer, John Ryan, was well established in Saint John, New Brunswick, when he left for the island colony in 1806, taking at least one of his printer sons with him and leaving his newspaper in the hands of a former apprentice who had become his partner. After posting a bond and agreeing to the governor's demand that he submit in advance the contents of each issue of his projected newspaper to the magistrates, Ryan and his son Michael published the first number of the *Royal Gazette and Newfoundland Advertiser* at St John's in August 1807. By 1810 Michael Ryan was printing under his own name, but his request to start a second paper was denied by the governor, who rejected a similar proposal in 1813. These restrictions on the Newfoundland press were lifted the following year when Crown lawyers in London advised that the governor did not have the power to prevent a printer from setting up shop or starting a newspaper.[24] It was another of Ryan's sons, Lewis Kelly Ryan, who founded the first reform paper in 1818, the same year that Henry David Winton arrived in St John's from London. In 1820 Winton established the town's controversial fourth paper, the *Public Ledger and Newfoundland General Advertiser*. John Ryan continued to publish the *Royal Gazette* and print for government, although the volume of work was not comparable to the other British North American colonies until after 1832, when responsible government, with an elected House of Assembly and an appointed Legislative Council, was granted to Newfoundland. Among Ryan's surviving imprints are four reports for local benevolent societies, which were his earliest job printing in St John's,[25] and seven sermons dating from 1818 to 1832, when he printed *A Warning to Ice-Hunters: A Sermon on the Profanation of the Sabbath*. Since his three sons who were printers all died young, Ryan took John Collier Withers as a partner when he withdrew from the business in 1832, some fifty years after his arrival in the British colonies as a Loyalist.

Although Quebec was divided by the Constitutional Act of 1791 into the new provinces of Upper and Lower Canada to extend British laws and customs, rather than Quebec's French civil law, to Loyalists who had settled west of Montreal and along the shores of Lake Ontario, the first press in Upper Canada was not operated by a Loyalist. The founding lieutenant-governor, John Graves Simcoe, who had commanded a Loyalist regiment in the Revolutionary War, arrived at Quebec late in 1791 and issued his first proclamation there, printed by Samuel Neilson in editions of 1,000 copies in English and 300 in French.[26] When he took the oath of office the next year in Kingston, Simcoe marked the event with another series of proclamations in French and in English, printed by Fleury Mesplet in Montreal. It was in Mesplet's office that he recruited Upper Canada's first printer, twenty-one-year-old Louis Roy, Quebec-born and trained by William Brown. Roy set up his press at Newark (Niagara-on-the-Lake), where Simcoe assembled the legislature in the autumn of 1792, and was printing by January 1793. Among his earliest imprints was Simcoe's speech at the founding legislature.[27] By April, Roy had established the *Upper Canada Gazette, or American Oracle* and was supplying administrative forms such as tavern keepers' licences and handsome location certificates framed with type ornaments. In the autumn of 1794 Roy returned to Quebec, and within a year he was publishing, with his brother, another *Montreal Gazette / Gazette de Montréal* to rival Fleury Mesplet's paper of the same name, which had been revived after his death by Edward Edwards. The Roy paper ceased by 1797, and Louis Roy moved to New York, where he died in 1799.

His successors in Upper Canada followed a similar pattern with short but productive appointments as king's printer. Gideon Tiffany, named to the post on Roy's departure, was assisted by his older brother, Silvester, a fellow printer from eastern New York State. Until the summer of 1797, when he was replaced after an indictment for blasphemy, a fine, and possibly jail, Gideon Tiffany printed laws, speeches, proclamations in English and French, and administrative forms to regulate the settlement of the new province, from survey warrants and location tickets to land grants printed on parchment. Although Tiffany proposed an almanac for 1797, it was not published, leaving only one non-official title among more than three dozen imprints from his press: *Thoughts on the Education of Youth*, by a local teacher.[28] Since the Tiffanys had always been suspected of republican sympathies, the government next appointed Titus Geer Simons, the son of a Loyalist, whose first journeymen were the Tiffanys. By 1798 Simons had as his partner William Waters, and in September that year they packed the office for shipment to York (Toronto), the new capital of Upper Canada. Waters and Simons continued to print for government, increasing the stock of administrative forms to include marriage licences and oaths of allegiance for Protestants, Quakers, and Roman Catholics. And for the election of 1800, they printed the province's first election notices.

In 1801 John Bennett, a foreman from the Neilson shop in Quebec and successor to the Roys in Montreal, was appointed king's printer, replacing Waters and Simons at York. In addition to the *Upper Canada Gazette* and work for the government in English, French, and German, he published almanacs and printed for a broader community: the Agricultural and Commercial Society, a Reformed Protestant congregation in Ernestown (Bath), and individuals engaged in political debate. Bennett left York in 1807 after a financial dispute with the government, but his successors had a monopoly in the town until 1820, when the first independent shop was established by John Carey. The only disruption occurred in 1813 after the government press was destroyed by invading American forces, who captured York. For much of the following year, government work was sent to the press in Kingston, where Stephen Miles, who had moved from Vermont to Montreal as apprentice to Nahum Mower, had been printing since 1810.

Presses were established in many more towns throughout British North America over the next three decades, reaching as far west as the Hudson's Bay Company territory in 1840. Late that year James Evans set up the Rossville Mission Press near Norway House, north of Lake Winnipeg. With type and ink of his own making and an improvised press, he printed his Cree syllabary and three hymns. Proud of his achievement as a first printer, Evans wrote, 'My types answer well.'[29]

CASE STUDY
James Robertson
— Warren McDougall

James Robertson and his brother Alexander, sons of an Edinburgh printer, had many years' experience as newspapermen in the Thirteen Colonies when they arrived at the new Loyalist settlement of Port Roseway (formerly Port Razoir, now Shelburne), Nova Scotia, in May 1783.[30] James established himself in the town, building a printing office, workers' residence, and store, and becoming a justice of the peace. The Robertsons' office was part of the commercial and social fabric of a town that soon boomed to ten thousand inhabitants. Their newspapers, the *Royal American Gazette* and the *Port-Roseway Gazetteer, and the Shelburne Advertiser*, published by Alexander's son, James junior, and Thomas and James Swords,[31] and their printing of handbills, broadsides, and pamphlets contributed to a sense of order in the new community.[32]

Printing alone could not support James, however, and he also formed a mercantile partnership with a former clerk, William Rigby. In late 1783 he went to London to try to claim £650 for losses suffered during the Revolutionary War, but received only the standard £350. He returned to Shelburne in September 1784 to face the results of unsuccessful speculation in timber, the death of Alexander, depredations made on the cash account by an apprentice, and the ongoing claim for an overpayment of £635 by Nathaniel Mills and John Hicks, with whom the Robertsons had first published the *Royal American Gazette* in New York. The sheriff seized and held his and Rigby's property, and Robertson reckoned that his losses included more than nine hundred acres of land and a house that had cost upwards of £1,000.

Nevertheless, he continued to print the *Royal American Gazette* (suspended between August 1785 and May 1786) until, in the summer of 1787, he moved his press to Charlottetown to become the first printer on St John's (Prince Edward) Island. Again he assumed positions in the community, serving as deputy postmaster, high sheriff, and marshall of the Admiralty. Though he refounded his newspaper as the *Royal American Gazette and Weekly Intelligencer* on 15 September 1787[33] and took on government printing, for which he was paid £60 a year and costs, none of these activities provided sufficient income. Despite the support of Lieutenant-Governor Edmund Fanning and the council and assembly, the imperial government would not grant him a state salary.[34]

In June 1789 Robertson left the Island for Quebec, never to return. His journeyman, William Alexander Rind, continued to print for the government under his imprint through 1790, but Robertson's salary was suspended. After unsuccessful attempts to get further compensation for his losses during the war and to be appointed king's printer in Quebec,[35] James Robertson returned to Edinburgh, where he set up shop as a printer and bookseller in 1790. He had come full circle.

The Business of Printing and Publishing

JOHN HARE AND JEAN-PIERRE WALLOT

In general, a publishing, printing, or bookselling business could not survive unless it met a certain number of conditions. It had to be able to obtain capital or credit while having available adequate equipment as well as skilled labour. It needed to ascertain beforehand a demand for printed materials, a reading public, and creative writers. Ideally, it had the patronage of the government or some public authority, churches, political parties, and other entities. Its activities had to be diversified, providing a newspaper, a printing office, paper, ink, office supplies, binding, and so on. In British North America, such businesses faced even more difficulties. Populations were sparse and scattered, often of modest means and unlettered; moreover, the people struggled with a rigorous climate. These pioneers were concerned mainly with practical issues related to their survival. Although they wanted to know about agriculture, perhaps a little about the news from Europe that affected them, and as time passed, about politics, they were not much interested in literature of the imagination. Before 1820, towns were small, trades and industry were not well developed, and the school system was inadequate. Communications were limited and difficult before the end of the War of 1812, making the circulation of printed materials even more complex. Postal costs remained high, and the problem of copyright would be addressed only after 1830. To these obstacles were added ethnic, linguistic, and religious conflicts. For the home country, the colonial 'intellectual' trade was a trade like any other; it imported raw materials from the colonies and in return exported books, magazines, and printing presses, taxed like any other finished product.

At the end of the Napoleonic Wars in 1815, some twenty presses served the territory stretching from St John's to the border at Niagara, with a scattered population of a few hundred thousand settlers. Printer-journalist-publishers often acted as agents and sellers of books and magazines from Europe and the United States; those who also ran the post office found distribution that much easier. Most of these businesses survived thanks to the demand for office supplies. They also sold official publications and government imprints; school books; sermons, hymns, and religious works, many of them ordered by churches; legal treatises; and books on practical matters. In addition, they did job printing. Much of their income depended upon the advertising in their newspapers. Local literary works were rare, most readers preferring imported and inexpensive publications.

Newspaper print runs increased over time, but remained modest. The *Quebec Gazette / La Gazette de Québec* did not have one thousand subscribers until 1812. William Lyon Mackenzie's *Colonial Advocate* (York) and the *Upper Canada Herald* (Kingston) did not reach a total of four hundred subscribers until around 1824, while subscriptions to Egerton Ryerson's *Christian Guardian* (York) climbed above a thousand (many of them Methodists) by 1830. A newspaper subscription was expensive in British North America, more than £1 per year around 1810, and the price continued to rise. On the other hand, a single copy of the paper was read by a number of people in homes, taverns, schools, and reading rooms, and these readers became more numerous after 1820.[36]

A few good libraries in Montreal, Quebec, York (Toronto), Ramsay Township, Thornhill, Pictou, and Halifax were sources of income for booksellers from the 1820s to the 1840s, as were literary and scientific societies; the most famous of these was the Literary and Historical Society of Quebec, founded in 1824. Printer-booksellers also benefited from sales to reading rooms and circulating and subscription libraries, such as Cary's, and from the newly formed mechanics' institutes, which organized courses and lectures.

General Characteristics of the Printing Business

In order to set up shop and survive, printing, publishing, and bookselling enterprises needed a certain level of literacy within or among the population. Other factors that entered into the equation were geographical distribution, degree of urbanization, average age, and level of colonial development. For the most part, the clientele of such enterprises was made up of the elites from the administration, the military, the trades, the professions, and the clergy. The business of printing and publishing was highly unstable, with many bankruptcies and closures, relocations by the printer-publisher-booksellers,[37] and the often brief lifespans of newspapers and magazines. Many of the printer-publishers were in debt, moved from one town or colony to another, emigrated from or returned to the United States, exchanged ownership of periodicals, and formed and dissolved partnerships. Nevertheless, the number of printers, binders, and engravers in Lower Canada tripled between 1820 and 1830, and continued to rise after that, proof of a profession on the road to stability.[38] Government patronage provided a measure of success, even though the state paid little and late.[39] The businesses established in one of the more populous colonies had a better chance of building a clientele. The support of one or several churches, which had hundreds or even thousands of copies of various collections printed, could also be a factor in their success.[40] In Lower Canada the need for school books, legal treatises, and Catholic catechisms and other religious works, as well as for various publications in French that were impossible to obtain from France, stimulated the production of books, assured of financing often before they were printed and of a dependable market. Nevertheless, investment was necessary, and printers used various means imported from the home country: subscriptions, newspaper advertisements, sharing of costs, or publication at the author's expense.

Aside from the patronage of the state and the churches, proprietors had a greater chance of success if they had financial support from relatives, friends, or foreign firms. For example, Charles Berger lent $4,000 to Fleury Mesplet, and Édouard-Raymond Fabre received funding from his brother-in-law Hector Bossange of Paris. William Lyon Mackenzie struggled along with the help of gifts, while John Neilson supported other printers at Quebec. Among the flourishing companies were families who had persevered in the trade for a number of generations. This was the case for the Brown-Gilmore-Neilson printing business, the Cary and Desbarats families at Quebec, the Cunnabell and Howe families in Halifax, and the Ryans in Newfoundland.[41] In some cases, the wives and daughters of printers acquired professional skills in the business and occasionally took over after the death of the proprietor; there were, in addition, a few women who specialized in printing, composition, binding, and other trades and earned a good salary.[42]

In all the colonies, the printer was often publisher, journalist, bookseller, binder, retailer of office supplies, and sometimes owner of a stationery shop as well. Between 1810 and 1840, however, many true bookstores sprang up. Books were also sold at auction, in general stores, and by peddlers hawking books and pamphlets. As well, printers acted as agents for American and European printers and publishers, selling their newspapers, books, and periodicals. These different occupations surrounding the actual business of printing were tending to disappear in Europe and the United States, but in the colonial milieu this model remained the only economically viable one, since the proprietor could hope to compensate for a deficit in one area with a profit in another. The bookselling trade, discussed by Yvan Lamonde and Andrea Rotundo in chapter 6, was the first sector in British North America to break away from the printing trades and their dependence on governments.

Political involvement was often risky. It was very much in the interest of the printer-publisher to support the government and influential people in power.[43] If he did not have a diversified enterprise, a sufficient volume of advertising in his newspaper, and generous friends or partisan support, it was difficult for him to stand up to the authorities and the various 'family compacts' that governed in the colonies.

Printers employed skilled workers, often trained on the spot or even imported. The number of employees varied over time and according to the size of the shops. For example, three people worked for Fleury Mesplet when he first arrived,[44] nine to fourteen for John Neilson between 1802 and 1814, fifteen to eighteen for Ludger Duvernay in 1837, and six to twelve for William Lyon Mackenzie.[45] Journeymen commanded high salaries, which explains why they often changed employment and why owners preferred to take on more apprentices, bound by contract for several years. In the prosperous times between 1790 and 1815, this emphasis on labour led to significantly higher rates of pay. Workers in the printing trade, always well informed, were among the first to form trade unions in North America, initially as mutual-aid societies, at Quebec (1827), York (Toronto) (1832), Hamilton (1833), Montreal (1833), and Halifax (1837).

For many years, most colonial production (not counting newspapers) consisted of publications of just a few pages, although their number and size gradually increased. Between 1764 and 1774 the number of books and pamphlets produced at Quebec averaged around four a year, 66 per cent of which were fewer than four pages in length; from 1775 to 1786 the average climbed to twelve per year, still with 61 per cent under four pages; from 1787 to 1809 the average reached twenty-one per year, of which 43 per cent had fewer than four pages; finally, from 1810 to 1820, the number of printed materials shot up to forty-eight a year, 42 per cent of which remained under four pages in length.[46] To the factors already cited explaining the scarcity of substantial publications must be added the limitations of printing offices that lacked a large enough stock of types for the rapid production of works not likely to bring in profits when the press was overflowing with regular orders. Moreover, it was not common to receive funds in advance to fulfill orders, so that the shops staggered the production of certain publications over a longer period, delaying the work until they were less busy.[47]

Four Representative Printers

It is impossible to review a representative sample of all printers and printing offices in British North America, but a few cases will be enough to illustrate how they were set up. After several moves in the United States between 1776 and 1779, Loyalist John Howe (1754–1835) settled in Halifax, where he began to publish the *Halifax Journal* on 28 December 1780. He was soon producing other printed materials: pamphlets, sermons, and almanacs. Setting himself the task of enhancing intellectual life in Nova Scotia, he started to publish the monthly *Nova-Scotia Magazine and Comprehensive Review of Literature, Politics, and News*. In 1801 he became king's printer and, in this capacity, publisher of the *Nova-Scotia Royal Gazette*, a position that brought him £140 a year until 1809 and then £175. He also made a modest sum as deputy postmaster for Nova Scotia, New Brunswick, and Prince Edward Island from 1803; this office actually brought in less than the compensation Howe paid to the previous holder of the position, hence his chronic indebtedness. His family dominated publishing in Nova Scotia; he himself controlled two newspapers, and his brother-in-law William Minns ran the *Weekly Chronicle*. Howe relinquished both appointments to his son John in 1818 and retired to devote himself to various philanthropic works. His son Joseph (1804–73), whose boundless admiration for his father lasted his entire life, took over George Renny Young's *Nova-scotian* in December 1827 and made it the most influential newspaper in the colony. The younger Howe was involved in the 'intellectual awakening' that was blowing through Nova Scotia and wrote many columns on the debates of the House of Assembly, as well as on European and North American affairs. He described the distinctive features of various regions of the colony and published his own poems in addition to the writings of several authors, including Thomas Chandler Haliburton.[48]

In Lower Canada, John Neilson (1776–1848) replaced his brother Samuel, who died prematurely in 1793, at the head of the enterprise founded by his uncle William Brown with a partner, Thomas Gilmore. Printer, publisher, and bookseller, Neilson was 'the largest consumer of paper in this country,' according to his competitor James Brown.[49] He published the *Quebec Gazette / La Gazette de Québec*, whose subscribers, half of them French-speaking, numbered more than a thousand between 1810 and 1820. Besides job printing, he produced numerous pamphlets, religious texts, and school books, as well as some more literary works, which were paid for by the author or by subscription. In 1800 Neilson secretly became the majority shareholder in the business of his main rival at Quebec, Pierre-Édouard Desbarats, and he multiplied his efforts to improve his printing equipment and the quality of his apprentices.[50] His initiatives in the publication of literary and entertaining journals, such as the *Quebec Magazine / Le Magasin de Quebec*, founded by his brother Samuel in 1792, and the *British-American Register* in 1803, failed because of the small number of subscribers and high production costs. In his bookstore, the most important in the two Canadas up to the 1810s and 1820s, Neilson sold a wide variety of office supplies, blank books, paper, and books, notably works of the Enlightenment and those of American authors. Customers could also have books bound there. He supplied the main community libraries, including that of the Assembly, and other printer-booksellers in both the Canadas with materials and books imported directly from Britain (mainly London) and the United States (Boston, New York, Schenectady, Albany, Philadelphia) or obtained through auctions. In 1818, like Joseph Howe, he entered politics and transferred his business to his son Samuel (two-thirds) and a partner, William Cowan (one-third). If we count his uncle William Brown and his brother Samuel, John Neilson belonged to one of the most durable printing and book trade dynasties of the time, since his sons Samuel and William succeeded him.[51]

The case of Ludger Duvernay (1799–1852) was different. He began his apprenticeship in 1813 at Charles-Bernard Pasteur's Montreal newspaper, *Le Spectateur*. With the

4.2 Jean-Baptiste Roy-Audy, *Portrait of Ludger Duvernay* (1832). Courtesy of the Société Saint-Jean-Baptiste, Montreal.

help of Denis-Benjamin Viger, he opened his own printing office in Trois-Rivières in 1817 and launched the first newspaper published outside Quebec or Montreal, *La Gazette des Trois-Rivières* (1817–21); it was followed by two political and literary publications: the monthly *L'Ami de la religion et du roi* (1820) and a weekly, *Le Constitutionnel* (1823–4). Although he printed a few books and pamphlets, the business never caught on because of the limit of his market. In 1826 Duvernay returned to Montreal, where he published the *Canadian Spectator* and *La Minerve* (which had about 1,300 subscribers by 1832, compared to 240 in 1827) (see illus. 4.2, above). Three years later, he acquired James Lane's printing house, located in the heart of the business district, and there he set up a new metal press, a Smith's Imperial purchased in New York; he reserved his old presses for book printing. From 1829 to 1837 Duvernay dominated publishing in Montreal, producing some thirty books and pamphlets, particularly school books, devotional works, political pamphlets, almanacs, Louis-Joseph Papineau's speeches, literary works (the poems of Michel Bibaud), the weighty three-volume *Traité sur les lois civiles du Bas-Canada* (1832–3), and, in 1836 in a pirated edition, a controversial work on both religious and political fronts, *Paroles d'un croyant*, by Félicité-Robert de La

Mennais. By 1837, he had fifteen employees. His political involvement with the Patriote party earned him lawsuits and several stays in jail. Elected to the Assembly in the summer of 1837, he took part in the rebellions and had to flee to the United States. At the request of Louis-Hippolyte La Fontaine, Duvernay returned to Montreal in 1842, resurrected *La Minerve*, and created the Association Saint-Jean-Baptiste de Montréal (the patriotic holiday dates back to 1834). His paper, the first major newspaper in the French language, survived him by almost half a century.[52]

Scotsman William Lyon Mackenzie (1795–1861) arrived in Upper Canada in 1820 and settled at York (Toronto). After various adventures, moves, and business failures, he hired a printer and launched the *Colonial Advocate* at Queenston in 1824. His weekly, renamed the *Advocate* in 1833, was a politically engaged newspaper. After he moved back to York, Mackenzie multiplied his attacks against the most prominent tories. In 1826 his adversaries ransacked his printing shop, an attack discussed by Sarah Brouillette in chapter 10. He obtained £625 in damages, enabling him to avoid bankruptcy, reimburse his most pressing creditors, and revive his business. He also clashed with the Church of England and defended the rights of American immigrants. Elected to the House of Assembly in 1828, Mackenzie quickly made his mark on various committees in the first session in 1829. A trip to the United States that same year stoked his admiration for American institutions. What happened next is common knowledge: his many battles in colonial politics, his republicanism, his repeated expulsions from the Assembly, his election as the first mayor of Toronto in 1834, his electoral defeat in 1836, and the launching of his newspaper the *Constitution* (1836–7), which advocated armed resistance to oppression by the imperial power. Following the outbreak of the rebellion in December 1837, he fled into exile in the United States, where he exhausted himself in vain conflicts. By that time, Mackenzie had produced ninety-five imprints, forty-eight under his own name and forty-seven in the name of his newspaper, the *Colonial Advocate*; he was the author of twenty-four. His greatest success as a publisher and bookseller was no doubt 'Poor Richard,' or the *Yorkshire Almanack*, followed by the 'Patrick Swift' almanacs, with print runs of 30,000 to 40,000 in 1829, 1830, and 1831.[53]

The development of printing and publishing in British North America was riddled with false starts, frequent financial difficulties, flagrant partisanship, and a few notable successes, within an impoverished and unimaginative intellectual landscape. But we must take into account the context of the time: colonization, low population levels, the slow appearance of urban centres, and the difficult and irregular communications and personal upheavals that the waves of immigrants endured as they settled one or another of the colonies. New arrivals had to leave and adjust to the heritage of the governing country. Yet in spite of its small numbers, its wide dispersal, and its colonial status, the population in British North America did not differ so fundamentally from that of the United States. In effect, the colonies, or at least their elites, took part in the development of the Western world. The start was slow, but the acceleration in the first years of the nineteenth century augured well for the future.

Subscription Publishing

MARY LU MACDONALD

Subscription publishing – inviting purchasers to pay in advance all or part of the cost of a book proposed for publication – was an established practice in Europe for books with a limited market. The system was well suited to the British North American colonies, given their small population distributed over a large territory and settler economy. Advance subscriptions protected printers and authors against financial loss. Consequently, in both French and English in all the colonies, many titles were announced first in a prospectus or advertisement seeking subscriptions. Such notices appeared as early as 1766 in the *Quebec Gazette / La Gazette de Québec* and 1770 in the *Nova Scotia Chronicle*[54] and would continue into the late nineteenth century.

Since there was no widespread distribution system, the market tended to be regional. The names on the few subscription lists that have survived are limited to residents of communities where the author or the printer could count on regional or personal interest to stimulate sales. An advertisement in the author's local newspaper, which mentioned the availability of subscription lists – usually the printing office and a shop or bookstore – was the most common means of reaching potential readers. Personal contacts could also be useful. Philippe Aubert de Gaspé *fils* relied on a Montreal friend to distribute subscription lists and collect money for *L'influence d'un livre* (Quebec, 1837), the first novel published in Lower Canada.[55]

It was customary for prospectuses to appeal to potential subscribers on the grounds of national pride or moral improvement. From the late eighteenth century on, the publication of professional and technical books was linked to the development of colonial society. Fleury Mesplet announced a translation of Richard Burn's *Justice of the Peace* in 1788 as a guide for French citizens taking their place in Quebec's legal system.[56] Later in the period, the perception of books as a means to social and material progress dominated subscription rhetoric. In both prospectuses and accompanying editorial comments, residents were enjoined to support local literary output. William A. Stephens, the author of *Hamilton; and Other Poems,* was not alone in appealing to those who 'have sufficient patriotism to patronize home productions.'[57]

Authors and printers employed many techniques to attract buyers. Often they promised to publish the names of subscribers as a sort of 'honour roll' of public-spirited citizens. We have such a list in the first novel published in Upper Canada, Julia Beckwith Hart's *St. Ursula's Convent, or The Nun of Canada* (Kingston, 1824).[58] Some prospectuses mentioned the anonymous 'respectable gentlemen' who had urged publication; others described the quality of paper, printing, or engravings in the projected work. John Richardson's name was sufficiently newsworthy that the prospectus for *The Canadian Brothers; or, The Prophecy Fulfilled* (Montreal, 1840) was printed, seemingly without charge, by newspapers from the *Quebec Gazette* to the *Western Herald* of Sandwich (Windsor), Upper Canada.[59] Accompanying editorial comments mentioned Richardson as Canadian-born, named Sir Isaac Brock and Tecumseh as characters, and as an additional incentive, identified the novel as a sequel to *Wacousta.* Financial considerations were always a factor. The prospectus for J.G. Ward's *The Spring of Life: A Didactic Poem* (Montreal, 1834) made the not-uncommon statement 'Editors who insert this Prospectus will be entitled to a copy of the work.'[60] It was also customary for the subscription price to be lower than the cost on publication.

From the available evidence, it is not possible to determine the number of subscriptions needed to make a publication economically viable. A book of prayers was printed in Halifax in 1770 with just 12 subscribers taking 46 copies.[61] Fleury Mesplet printed a medical work with the support of 33 subscribers to 126 copies,[62] while his list for Burn's *Le juge à paix,* which appeared in the *Montreal Gazette / Gazette de Montréal* through the spring of 1789, grew week by week to more than 200 names. James Dawson of Pictou, Nova Scotia, did not define 'a sufficient number' in advertisements for his tunebook, *The Harmonicon* (Pictou, 1838), although the advertisements appeared in Maritime newspapers intermittently for seven years before the work was finally published.[63] Adam Kidd claimed to have sold 1,500 subscriptions for *The Huron Chief, and Other Poems* (Montreal, 1830), and Aubert de Gaspé *fils* wrote of a necessary 256, while John Richardson complained that fewer than 200 people had subscribed for *The Canadian Brothers.* The subscription list printed in *St. Ursula's Convent* contains 147 names for 165 copies.

Not all prospectuses succeeded in attracting subscribers. There is no evidence that the edition of William Buchan's *Domestic Medicine,* projected by William Brown in 1786, was ever printed.[64] A volume of Adam Hood Burwell's poetry was proposed under his pseudonym of Erieus in 1819,[65] but it never appeared. Nor did John Howard Willis's 'The Woman Hater' (1828).[66] Also unpublished were 'The Legend of Niagara' by William Fitz Hawley, advertised in 1830, and a 'History of Canada' for which some subscriptions were collected by Hawley seven years later.[67] Many books by anonymous authors exist only as pleas for subscriptions. In addition to illustrating the workings of the trade, the prospectus, with its perception of what will persuade literate citizens to purchase a publication, tells us much about the values of their society.

Working in the Trades

CLAUDE GALARNEAU AND GILLES GALLICHAN

Pioneers of the book and printing trades arrived on the Atlantic coast and in the St Lawrence valley in the eighteenth century, armed with skills drawn from a three-century-old tradition and training acquired in the United States or Europe. Within a few decades, the first printers used the scant means at their disposal to set up a sizable production in English, in French, and in other languages, including those of Native peoples. They trained apprentices who would in turn pursue the development of the trade and build on the foundations set by a local press.

The introduction of the craft of printing and the other book trades and their subsequent expansion closely followed the demographic evolution, economic progress, and establishment of political structures in the colonies. Both craftsmen and businessmen, the printers and other book trade workers were the keepers of a highly specialized skill crucial to culture, society, and the economy. The first printers, drawn from cities in the colonies to the south, imported the typographical traditions of Scotland, England, France, Alsace, and Germany, as explained by Patricia Lockhart Fleming in this chapter. In a very short period, the Atlantic colonies and the two Canadas inherited the printing expertise of European traditions already adapted to the North American setting.

Quebec, a City of Printers

Before 1840, Quebec was a major centre for printers, as well as the economic heart of British North America. The town reached the height of its influence during the first decades of the nineteenth century, but then, as business and commerce gradually moved westward, printing activities expanded in Montreal and in Upper Canada. Before this westward migration, however, Quebec was the seat of intense activity in the field of books and printing, in French as well as in English. A major military, political, and administrative centre for the colony, the town was the meeting place for the cultural and religious life of the people. As the point of arrival for many ships from Europe, Quebec became the locus of communications and a starting point for the extensive circulation of information in printed form. The printing trade flourished there, and its rise can be traced with precision over a period of seventy-five years.

It is useful to begin with the men who practised some trade associated with printing in Quebec during this period.[68] The few directories that have come down to us[69] put the number at 145 workers, masters and craftsmen, including printers, typesetters and pressmen, bookbinders, engravers, and other workers employed in unspecified activities in the printing trades at Quebec between 1764 and 1840. Their trades developed in stages in the capital of Lower Canada. The first period of rapid expansion took place between 1790 and 1799, in the wake of the American War of Independence. The second, between 1810 and 1819, followed changes in the economic structure resulting from the European blockade and the end of war in 1815, which set off a wave of immigration that greatly enriched the population at Quebec.

Printers were more numerous than bookbinders and engravers. The directories give the names of 47 print workers without an identified trade – probably printers, journeymen, and perhaps a few writers for newspapers. Those called 'printers' were, as far as we know, the compositors and pressmen or masters. As for their linguistic heritage, 71 of the 145 were French-speaking and 74 English-speaking. In the printing trades, anglophone workers were in the majority until 1830, when francophones took the lead. Bookbinders were fewer in number. In *The Directory for the City and Suburbs of Quebec* (1790), only William Ritchie is listed. By 1822, there were four, three of whom were Canadiens: Louis Hianveux, Louis Lemieux, Charles Lefrançois, and Charles Lodge. Bookbinders often also worked as paper rulers.[70] We know of five engravers before 1800 and eight before 1840; of these, James Smillie is the best known.

Before 1800, the number of printing houses increased slowly. Until 1788, Quebec could lay claim only to Brown and Gilmore's shop. After Gilmore's death in 1773, Brown worked with a few assistants, and then his nephew, Samuel Neilson, joined him in 1789. Samuel's younger brother, John, eventually inherited the enterprise. Five other printers were active in the capital over the next decade. There were three printing offices in Quebec in 1810, six in 1822, and twelve, employing 66 workers, by 1836. The largest belonged to the Neilson family; second was the New Printing Office / Nouvelle Imprimerie, purchased in 1798 by Pierre-Édouard Desbarats, which merged in 1812 with Thomas Cary and Company and was run by Desbarats's son George-Paschal. The resurrection of the *Canadien* by Jean-Baptiste Fréchette and Étienne Parent in 1831 marked the establishment of another successful printing office, followed the year after by the establishment of the Librairie canadienne.[71]

The Role of Women and Apprentices in Printing Shops

Printers were generally men, but a few offices were headed by women. At Quebec, Marie-Josephte Voyer, wife of Pierre-Édouard Desbarats, managed her husband's printing house after his death in 1828, before her son George-Paschal took over.[72] The next year, upon the death of printer and bookseller Charles Lefrançois at Quebec, his wife, Louise Ledroit, closed his press but carried on the bookselling business.[73] There are some other examples of women directing printing offices, such as Elizabeth Gay in Halifax and, at Montreal, Marie Mirabeau, wife of Fleury Mesplet, who abandoned his newspaper, the *Gazette*, but with the permission of Governor Frederick Haldimand,[74] pursued other work in the printing house during her husband's detention at Quebec from 1779 to 1782.

Marie Mirabeau was obliged to take over her husband's business because he had not yet trained an apprentice. A few weeks before his arrest – perhaps with a foreboding of events to come – Mesplet tried to sell his two presses for 'cash money.' If the interested party did not have 'a sufficient knowledge of the art of printing,' Mesplet was prepared to offer advice 'for no monetary consideration.'[75] Such an offer from Montreal's master printer seems somewhat rash, since the apprenticeship of a novice printer required far more than a little advice. In any case, the transaction did not take place, and the printer's wife was no doubt one of the few people able to fill the orders and complete publication of *L'Almanach curieux et intéressant* for 1781 and 1782,[76] a sheet almanac, and an English-Mohawk primer.[77] The printing trades required a period of professional training governed by traditional rules for entry through apprenticeship, a practice common to all trades and professions at the time.

From the early days of their venture at Quebec, Brown and Gilmore practised this type of training in their shop, and other master printers, such as Jean-Baptiste Fréchette at the Imprimerie canadienne, who had himself apprenticed with Neilson, did likewise. Apprentices were bound to their masters, usually before a notary, between the ages of twelve and nineteen. Apprenticeship lasted between four and six years for printers and between five and seven for bookbinders. From 1790 to 1815, there were seventeen apprentice printers and six apprentice bookbinders at Quebec.[78] According to twenty-five extant contracts, the length of apprenticeship between 1830 and 1849 was from fifty-two to fifty-five months,[79] depending on the age of the apprentice at his entry into the trade: the younger the apprentice, the longer the training. Apprentices more or less became part of the master's household, much like domestic servants. In the 1780s William Brown recorded in his expense book the cost of clothing, shoes, and medical care for one of his apprentices, Sandy McDonell.[80]

The terms of the indenture (see illus. 4.3, p. 84) were similar to those of other trades, agreements observed in western Europe since the Middle Ages. Apprentices were paid between £15 and £25 a year in Neilson's shop and at Desbarats and Cary.[81] The workday, like that of other trades, was generally twelve and a half hours during the summer and eleven hours in winter. The literacy rate of apprentices was excellent. Of the fourteen young apprentices at Neilson's after 1802, eleven signed the registry every quarter, and twenty-five of the twenty-seven employed from 1830 to 1849 did likewise.[82] If a personal signature is taken as a prime indicator of literacy, apprentice printers and compositors were among the most literate, that is, the most highly educated, workers of their era.

We do not know whether apprentices were always given room and board. Since they were usually well educated, these craftsmen often became thirsty for knowledge, wanting to travel and seek out new horizons, much like their European counterparts. Some made their way to Upper Canada or New York as early as 1790, attracted no doubt by adventure and higher salaries.[83] At the same time, book trade workers must have clashed with the proprietors since occasional announcements appeared in the newspapers about the flight of an apprentice, and the publishers of the *Quebec Gazette / La Gazette de Québec* complained about the unreliability of journeymen. Apprentice printers in Europe and the United States had been notorious for their mobility since the earliest days of the press.[84]

Printers' Associations

The first printers' association, the Union typographique de Québec, was founded in 1827, and in 1836 the workers in the printing trades at Quebec came together in the Société typographique canadienne. Headed by president Adolphe Jacquies, a French immigrant printer who had arrived at Quebec about 1820, and secretary Charles Greffard, it included sixty-six members from both linguistic groups, but it existed for only eight years.[85]

In Upper Canada the York Typographical Society was formed at York (Toronto) in 1832 by twenty-four journeymen printers. By its constitution, the society tried to set minimum wages and maximum hours of work for its members, who also wanted to limit the number of apprentices in each shop. The union established a strong foun-

4.3 Indenture of Henry Chubb's apprenticeship to Jacob Mott (Saint John, 1802–9). Aged about fifteen, Henry Chubb was bound in January 1802 to Jacob S. Mott for seven years 'to learn the Art, Trade, and Mystery of a Printer.' By the terms of his indenture, he was to have 'four Quarters night Schooling' and, when he completed his term, a new suit of clothes. Jacob Mott certified on the verso of this document in September 1809 that Chubb had served his apprenticeship 'honestly and faithfully.' Courtesy of the New Brunswick Museum, Saint John, Cornwall Family Papers. Gift of Mrs Chester Brown.

dation, and in October 1836 the first labour dispute led to a strike of several weeks over the salary of printers. The workers did not win the action, but printers would continue their efforts to unionize after 1840.[86]

The Printing Office: A Social Meeting Place

The typical printer in eighteenth- and early nineteenth-century British North America was a craftsman, working with a collaborator and one or two apprentices. Sometimes his children, wife, or another family member acted as his associate, clerk, or assistant. The work was difficult and required skill and professionalism. Within such a small market, once a competitor set up shop, an inferior printer would be quickly abandoned by his clientele and obliged to move or give up the venture.

The printer's shop required relatively little space at the time, since the massive rotary presses had not yet been invented, and printing had scarcely changed since its beginnings in the fifteenth century. Ideally, the shop was well lit, with plenty of windows, because there were proofs to be read and checked, notes to be made, and orders to be written in the account books. Daylight was ideal for these tasks and saved on the cost of candles. The shop also had to be well heated and ventilated, because the printed sheets had to dry completely before being collected into gatherings. Too much humidity would also damage stocks of paper and leather, and warp the wooden parts of the press. The ideal shop had two or three rooms. The press generally occupied the centre of the main room, so that the pressman could work it easily; type cases and compositors would be placed near the windows. One room served as counter and bookstore, and the third would be for binding and the storage of paper, ink, leather, and all the other materials and accessories of the trade.

The printing office was a place for meeting and exchange, a centre of information and knowledge. People went to the printer not only to place orders but also in search of news, because this was where they would purchase newspapers, pamphlets, and, of course, books, produced locally or imported from Europe. The printer also sold stationery, almanacs, notebooks and the small bound blank books used for accounts, music paper, ink, pens, pocket knives, bone folders, inkwells, pencils, pen sets, and sealing wax. Here the clergy purchased altar cards, the ritual prayers printed in an ornamental style and mounted on cardboard to be placed against the altar during mass. The printer's shop was also the source of other imported articles, such as maps, slates, hourglasses, handwriting manuals, and even musical instruments.[87]

Printers were highly visible members of their communities, with businesses often located in the very centre of the town. In Halifax, for example, John Bushell's shop was on Grafton Street, near St Paul's Church. At Quebec, John Neilson was set up on the side of the mountain, the capital's busiest thoroughfare. In York, William Lyon Mackenzie moved several times but always stayed near King and Church Streets, at the heart of urban activity.[88]

The printing office was a gathering place for polite company, the clientele diverse and drawn from the more prosperous members of the community: men of the law, officers of justice, doctors, surveyors, clergy, military and naval officers, civil administrators, parliamentarians, merchants, craftsmen, teachers, shop assistants, clerks, students, travellers, pensioners, ladies, and members of the bourgeoisie. The printer-journalist-bookseller was a central figure in his community and in Lower Canada was often the main point of contact between French- and English-speaking citizens, between Catholics and Protestants.

In port cities, the printer's shop was especially popular when the merchant ships arrived, bringing not only new products but also the latest newspapers already four to eight weeks old from the European capitals. From these papers the printer drew materials for his own newspaper, passing on the news to the local inhabitants. The ships also brought the reams of paper so essential for the printer's work. Paper was scarce in the Canadas and the Atlantic provinces at that time, and it would be several decades before enough was produced locally to serve the colony's needs.

Historical bibliographies have established the wide variety of works produced on the presses of the earliest printers. A significant proportion of their output was job printing – handbills, 'for rent' or 'for sale' signs, and calling cards, as well as bookplates for bibliophiles and labels for apothecaries and other shopkeepers.[89]

In Halifax, Saint John, Quebec, Montreal, and York/Toronto alike, the development of the printing trades followed essentially the same model. At this period, printers usually published a newspaper from a place of business located in the town near the centres of religious and political power that would provide a goodly portion of their clientele and their revenues. Commercial notices, job printing, and bookselling were the basics of their business. The printing office was also the school for apprentices who learned the art and craft of the trade the hard way. But above all, the printer's shop was a hive of commercial activity and a focal point of cultural, linguistic, and social interaction.

CASE STUDY

Working in a Newspaper Office: The *Upper Canada Herald* in 1829–33
— Elizabeth Hulse

When John McLean was engaged as an apprentice at the *Upper Canada Herald* office in Kingston in July 1831, his annual wages were set at £12 10s. Only in his third year did he receive a raise, to £13 2s 6d for the nine months ending in April 1834. Against his wages, his employer, Hugh Christopher Thomson,[90] deducted cash advances and the cost of clothes – 'To Trowsers & vest from Oliphant' £2 2s 9d – shoes, and food. And was young McLean eager to improve himself when he acquired a copy of Mark Burnham's *Colonial Harmonist* (Port Hope, 1832)[91] for 5 shillings? His background and his subsequent career are unknown, though another John McLean was a local sheriff, and Daniel McLean became an apprentice in the same shop a year later, in October 1832. But a single surviving ledger for the *Upper Canada Herald* office for the years 1829–33 provides a glimpse into his world.[92] It also demonstrates the central role that the newspaper office played in the community.

Like McLean, the other employees were sometimes paid in kind. Against part of his wages of £2 a week between 1832 and 1834, foreman Thomas Hugh Bentley (who would later publish the paper) received eggs, potatoes, turnips, apples, butter, and cheese. Clients and suppliers also sometimes paid or were paid in kind; John McDonald of Gananoque, for whom the office printed advertising and bills, provided ten bags of bran. James Crooks of West Flamborough, to be profiled by Judy Donnelly in chapter 5, from whom the *Herald* bought printing, wrapping, and drawing paper in various sizes, was paid partly in rags. The newspaper also bought from and sold to Starr and Little, of Albany, New York, typefounders and suppliers of cases, pulleys, rollers, and ink; Smith and Brown of Belleville, papermakers; and Knowlton and Rice of Watertown, New York; as well as to other Kingston printing offices.

Since no wage book survives, we do not know how many were employed at the *Herald*, but at least a foreman or journeyman printer, one or two apprentices, and perhaps an errand boy were needed to bring out a weekly newspaper.[93] All and sundry, from the Kingston police, the commissariat, and the penitentiary to the tailor and the dressmaker, paid to advertise in the paper, and at the *Herald* office was produced a whole range of print for everyday life. For merchant Robert Cassady the shop printed 100 'Large Bills' and 200 'Blank notes'; for druggist William Binley, labels and wrappers; for the Kingston Bakery, 200 'Bread Tickets'; for the Marmora Iron Works, a prospectus. Both the Northumberland and the Midland District Agricultural Societies ordered the printing of proceedings, reports, handbills, and circulars. Daniel Ruttan was billed for a dozen subscription lists for 'Tom Thumb'; St George's Church, for 300 copies of 'Prayers'; and John Cartwright, for 1,000 copies of an election address.[94]

More ambitious was the printing of the collected *Statutes of the Province of*

Upper Canada, published by Thomson in partnership with James Macfarlane of the *Kingston Chronicle* in 1831.[95] For this volume of nearly seven hundred pages, of which at least 900 copies were produced, the office appears to have taken on several additional printers, including George Heyworth Hackstaff, who would later publish papers in Dundas and London. Employment that began with an apprenticeship or with a temporary job could eventually take a printer to his own office elsewhere in the province or beyond.

A Statistical Analysis of Early Canadian Imprints

SANDRA ALSTON AND JESSICA BOWSLAUGH

Although some statistical analysis has been carried out on imprints from particular regions and time spans in the years 1752–1840, and scholars have attempted to estimate the extent of printing and publishing activities in British North America, no comprehensive body of data has existed until now to support reliable analysis.[96] To address this lack, a database of nearly seven thousand imprints, consisting of books, pamphlets, magazines, broadsides, and job printing, has been created.[97] It should be stated at the outset that this figure does not, and cannot, encompass the entire corpus of material that may have been printed prior to 1841. Assembling the full picture would require records, with a complete accounting of all job printing, from every printer. Such records do not exist, except in a very few instances. Hugh Amory reviewed attempts by printing historians in the United States to estimate the proportion of job printing to total output, but he concluded that all have failed. We can only work from what has survived or is known from documentary evidence, and such analysis will be limited by the nature and extent of a bibliographical infrastructure.[98] Although G. Thomas Tanselle argued that this sort of data can provide merely a suggestive image,[99] it is possible to observe patterns and to draw some inferences from the data that have been accumulated.

On the basis of the records in the database,[100] we have compiled a series of charts to illustrate the analysis achieved so far. Chart 4.1 demonstrates the growth in the number of imprints by decade, from 34 in the first decade of the press in Nova Scotia to 2,667 produced in the 1830s. The intriguing dip for the years 1800–10 (from 671 to

Imprints by decade

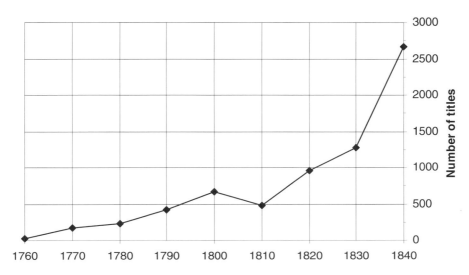

Chart 4.1 Imprints by decade.

484) needs further study. As chart 4.2 shows, the predominance of Lower Canada, where printing began in the old province of Quebec in 1764, is unquestionable. For the sake of comparison, and to understand the impact of population growth and change, the totals in charts 4.2 and 4.3 have been broken into two periods, 1752–1820 and 1821–40.[101] Just over 50 per cent of all imprints from British North America were produced in Lower Canada, a total of 3,497 titles. The output ranged from a high of 61.50 per cent (or 1,826) of all imprints printed prior to 1821 to 42.45 per cent (1,671) for 1821–40. Upper Canada was second, but only after 1820. Nova Scotia produced 19.50 per cent (579) of all imprints before 1821, compared to Upper Canada's 9.10 per cent (270) and New Brunswick's 6.24 per cent (185). For the period 1821–40, however, Nova Scotia declined in real numbers to 8.97 per cent (353), New Brunswick increased slightly to 6.63 per cent (261), and Upper Canada began the trend that would lead to its later importance as a publishing centre. Its total of 1,525 titles (38.74 per cent) comes very close to the Lower Canadian figure of 1,671 for the period 1821–40.

A certain number of imprints can be attributed only to a province, rather than to a specific town or city. However, when the place of printing can be ascertained, the geographical distribution shows striking differences among the provinces. The dominance of Charlottetown in Prince Edward Island and St John's in Newfoundland (all imprints except for one from Carbonear) is a consequence of the small population

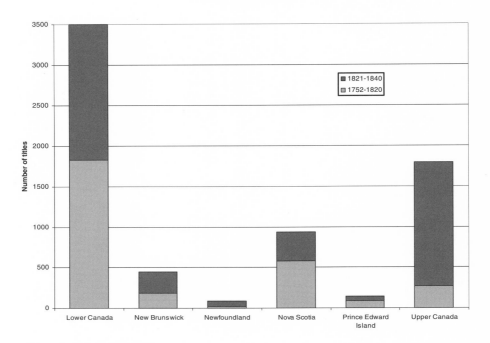

Chart 4.2 Imprints by province.

and limited number of presses in these colonies. In Nova Scotia the importance of Halifax is reflected in the total of imprints: 892 of 932 for the whole province; the rest are divided among Lunenburg, Pictou, and Shelburne. As for Lower Canada, a number of imprints (65 of 3,497) come from smaller towns with newspaper offices, such as Frelighsburgh, Saint-Charles-sur-Richelieu, Sherbrooke, Stanstead, and Trois-Rivières, but Montreal and Quebec predominate.[102] While the town of Quebec is by far the most important centre of printing in all of British North America for the years 1752–1840, with 32.50 per cent (2,245) of the titles documented, compared with Montreal's 15.48 per cent (1,069), when the figures are broken by period, the shift in the Lower Canadian press that will develop over the following decades is evident. Before 1821, Montreal's output represents only 21 per cent (385) of the imprints produced in that province; after 1820, it almost doubles to 41 per cent (685). Quebec's decline in relative importance begins: from 77 per cent (1,405) before 1821 to 50 per cent (840) in the 1821–40 period. Printing in Upper Canada before 1821 is concen-

Imprints by subject

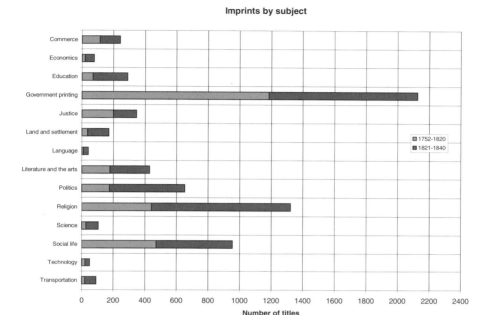

Chart 4.3 Imprints by subject.

trated in three centres: Kingston with 7 per cent (22) of the imprints, Niagara (Niagara-on-the-Lake) with 23 per cent (63), and York (Toronto) with 50 per cent (136), for all but unattributed titles. But after 1820, printing spreads to twenty-four other centres, responsible for 427 of the 1,525 imprints documented.[103] However, York/Toronto still leads, with 59 per cent of all Upper Canadian imprints; its total of 898 titles, in fact, overtakes both Quebec (840) and Montreal (685) for the period 1821–40.

To date, only limited subject analysis has been possible, but the statistics demonstrate intriguing patterns (see chart 4.3). While the importance of government printing cannot be disputed, it accounts for just under 40 per cent (1,184) of the imprints before 1821 and falls to about 24 per cent (942) in the second period. The relatively high position of the category designated 'social life' in both periods, reflects the number of almanacs printed throughout British North America. Also important is religion, which increases from 14.90 per cent in the first period to 22.35 per cent (880) of all titles in the period 1821–40.

This analysis can demonstrate in only a small way the range and extent of printing in British North America between 1752 and 1840, based on what is now known.

Would additional research into the less-documented periods, perhaps through an examination of advertisements in local newspapers and the creation of new imprint bibliographies, lead to any great change in the patterns discovered to date? One can only speculate. Until such work is completed, these 'suggestive' data can provide researchers with further questions for study in the history of the book in Canada.

chapter 5

THE MATERIAL BOOK

Adapting to Change

PATRICIA LOCKHART FLEMING

Although the word 'press' is sometimes used for a whole printing office, and even for all the materials produced there, actual printing presses are often absent from the historical record. Unlike types and paper, which are made tangible as print through the agency of a press, the machine itself remains invisible. Bibliographers, who can trace fonts and ornaments back to typefounders' specimens and match watermarks with catalogues, are seldom able to identify a printer's stock of presses without shop records or secondary evidence.

The press shipped from Boston to Halifax in 1751 would have been wooden and first imported from England (see illus. 5.1, p. 94). Although a few presses were crafted in the United States in the eighteenth century, American printers continued to favour English manufacturers until after 1800.[1] When Thomas Gilmore travelled to London in 1763 to equip a shop for Quebec, he and William Brown paid Caslon and Son £169 9s 11½ d 'for furnishing us with Types Rules &c,' which included £18 11s 6d for a 'Joiner's Bill' and £9 9s for the press.[2] After three years in the business, in June 1767, they received 'a new Printing Press with all her Appurtenances' from Kenrick Peck of London.[3] The cost, £26 8s 6d, was just 3s 6d more than the price Benjamin Franklin paid for a large English mahogany press 'made under my own Inspection with Improvements' before 1779.[4] Brown and Gilmore's new press probably joined, rather than replaced, another since the volume of printing at Quebec suggests at

5.1 J.G. Hochstetter, engraved frontispiece, *The Quebec Almanack / Almanach de Québec pour l'année 1792* (Quebec, 1791). Courtesy of the Bibliothèque nationale du Québec.

least a two-press enterprise. With less government work in Montreal, far from the capital, Fleury Mesplet's shop included 'two well-equipped presses' at the bailiff's sale in 1785.[5]

Once installed, wooden presses were durable and could be maintained by local artisans. In the Quebec office, for example, they bought a stone for the new press in 1772, paid to have a platen planed the following year, and added another press stone in 1774 and had it smoothed.[6] At York (Toronto) in 1814, a year after the government shop had been destroyed by American troops, king's printer John Cameron was having a press repaired. It lacked a number of parts, including 'inner and outer timpan' and friskets, but he expected to have these 'deficiencies' repaired locally within a week.[7]

At this time, new technologies were being introduced which would transform the printing trades over the next few decades.[8] Soon after 1800, Earl Stanhope in England invented a cast iron press strong enough to print a full sheet of paper with one pull at the bar. Rival presses were soon manufactured with levers and toggle joints to lower and raise the platen that pressed paper onto the type. In Philadelphia between 1800 and 1810 Andrew Ramage developed a more powerful wooden press with an iron platen and bed. Cheaper and more portable than the new iron presses, Ramages were used across British North America for decades. When William Lyon Mackenzie was adding a medium press to his shop for book work in 1830, George Bruce, the New York typefounder, recommended either one of the iron presses made by Robert Hoe or Samuel Rust at $230, or a Ramage, which cost $160 and was 'absolutely unrivalled except by the more costly iron presses.'[9] Three years later, when Mackenzie advertised his equipment for sale, an iron Smith's Imperial (possibly the one he bought in 1825) and a 'Handsome Foolscap Press, lately made by Ramage of Philadelphia' were two of the four presses.[10] Other printers using a Smith press in the 1830s were Joseph Howe in Halifax and Ludger Duvernay at *La Minerve* in Montreal.[11]

It is safe to assume that all the presses used in British North America up to 1840 were imported from Britain or the United States, except for one brief venture in Toronto in 1836–7. The *Royal Standard*, a new paper and the first daily in Upper Canada, announced in its second issue that 'the Press has been wholly made in this City, by Messrs. Mason, & Barber, Mechanists, and the casting done by Mr. Norton; and together is as fine a piece of work as can be executed in any part of the world – we have pleasure in thus doing justice to the Manufacturers – and pride in stating that our City is capable of producing so useful and important a piece of machinery.'[12] The press, which had cost almost one hundred pounds, fractured in early January and the *Royal Standard* office was advertised for sale in February. The next major innovations in British and American printing technology were the development of the cylinder press, which carried paper on a roller, and the application of steam power to both cylinder and large platen presses. Among the pioneers of power printing in British North America was John Crosskill of Halifax in 1840.[13]

By that year paper mills had been established in four provinces: Lower Canada (1804: St Andrews; 1815: Jacques Cartier; 1837: Portneuf), Nova Scotia (1819: Hammond Plains), New Brunswick (1826: Chamcook), and Upper Canada (1826: West Flamborough; 1827: York; 1832: Belleville).[14] Actively supported by government and the printing trades, the first two Upper Canadian mills installed papermaking machinery in the 1830s.[15] Having offered a premium to reward the founder of the industry, a contest described by Judy Donnelly in this chapter, the House of Assembly specified as early as 1830 that the whole of its *Journal* was 'to be printed on the best quality of Demi paper, of Canadian manufacture.'[16] John Eastwood, papermaker on the Don River east of Toronto, reported to the assembly in 1835 that he and his partner had 'manufactured paper last year to the value of 9000 dollars and upwards.'[17] For his part, William Lyon Mackenzie, a strong advocate of local industry, still complained when Eastwood's paper did not meet his expectations, describing it as 'detestable ... a little fairer than the ink,' in 1832 and a 'wretched rag' in 1837.[18] Other printers continued to use imported paper from Britain and the United States, marked in the finer grades with a maker's or mill name, but much of it, like the domestic paper, unmarked.

Many of the early paper mills were founded or owned by members of the book and printing trades. James Brown, a Scottish-born bookbinder and bookseller, agreed in 1804 to act as agent in Montreal for the new mill being built at St Andrews (Saint-André-Est) in the seigneury of Argenteuil. He collected rags and then sold the paper when the mill went into production in 1805. By the following year he was a shareholder, and by 1809 sole owner. Although he founded a newspaper and did other printing work, Brown continued to operate the mill until the lease with the seigneur expired in the mid-1830s.[19] Already a printer and the proprietor of a successful newspaper in Halifax, Anthony Henry Holland had the Acadian Paper Mill in operation late in 1819. In January the next year, both his *Acadian Recorder* and the *Halifax Journal* were printed on Nova Scotia–made paper. Holland later withdrew from his newspaper and operated the mill until his death in 1830.[20] At York, the papermakers John Eastwood and Colin Skinner began to publish textbooks and almanacs in the 1830s. Their first venture, *A New and Concise System of Arithmetic Calculated to Facilitate the Improvement of Youth in Upper Canada*, included among its lessons the measures of the paper trade: '24 sheets = 1 quire of paper; 20 quires =1 ream; 2 reams = 1 bundle.'[21]

Whether locally made or imported, paper was a significant cost for printers in British North America. To take one example, *The Upper Canada Christian Almanac* for 1836, printed in Toronto in an edition of 10,000 copies, cost the Upper Canada Religious Tract and Book Society £25 10s for paper, £19 for printing, and £10 4s for folding and stitching.[22] A 32-page octavo with an ornamental title on the first page, it required some 42 reams of demy paper, for which Eastwood and Skinner charged 12s per ream. Two years earlier Neilson and Cowan of Quebec were paying a similar price of 13s 6d for a ream of demy made at Portneuf.[23] On the retail side, book buyers might be offered a choice of fine or coarse paper, as was the case for the Quebec directory, which was published by subscription in 1790 at 1s for fine or 9d for coarse paper.[24] Starting with the edition for 1789, the *Almanach de Québec* was also printed on two paper stocks, with the option of blank diary leaves bound into the fine-paper copy for an extra 6d.[25] William Lyon Mackenzie went further, printing both the price and the grade of paper on the title page of his 1834 almanac: 7½d for fine paper and 5d for common.[26] Authors and others doing business with printing offices made similar choices as early as 1775, when Charles-François Bailly de Messein, himself a book collector, paid to have 100 copies of an edition of 800 playbills he was ordering for the Séminaire de Québec printed on fine paper.[27]

While paper stocks were a predictable expense in the printing office, the purchase of new type in all the necessary sizes and fonts, with small 'flowers' for borders, as well as figures, dashes, and rules, was a major investment. Brown and Gilmore's payment of £169 9s 11½d to the London typefounder William Caslon and Son to equip the shop in 1763 was followed by other orders, such as £58 2s 6d for type and ink in 1765.[28] These amounts far exceed the £30 they spent for office rent in 1766[29] and rival the £75 each that they paid themselves at the end of 1765, 'which they judge to be what a good Journeyman deserves here.'[30] The first printers at Halifax had also equipped their offices with Caslon letters and flowers, the fonts that dominated printing in England, the Thirteen Colonies, and the new republic until the late eighteenth century. Starting in the 1790s, printers in the Canadas and the Maritime colonies began to add type manufactured by Fry and Steele of London and Alexander Wilson of Glasgow to their stocks of Caslon. And with the establishment in 1796 of the first successful foundry in the United States, by Archibald Binny and James Ronaldson from Edinburgh, American types began to enter the market. The government's printing office at York, destroyed in 1813, was finally refurbished in New York in 1817 with materials costing £251 7s 6d.[31] In the following year, printers of the *Niagara Spectator* began using types from Binny and Ronaldson's Philadelphia foundry, possibly selected from their first specimen book, published in 1812. Edmund Ward framed the title page of *The Nova-Scotia Almanack* for 1819 with flowers from the same source, and in 1820 Hugh Christopher Thomson began to print with their types in Kingston. Charles Fothergill's extravagant 1824 edition of the Upper Canada *Statutes* was also printed with Binny and Ronaldson type.[32]

These and fellow proprietors who were keeping their offices and their printing up to date in the early nineteenth century with new, crisply modelled, modern-face types were also building a stock of ornamental letters for job printing and, in smaller sizes, for book work as well. There were discreet outline types at the end of the eighteenth century, then contra italics and fat faces, liberties taken with traditional black letters, durable slab serif Egyptians, playful shadowed, condensed, and perspective designs, bifurcated Tuscans, and early sans serifs. Designed first for foundries in England and Scotland, these types were copied in the United States, where the larger sizes were also cut in wood. In all their profusion, nineteenth-century ornamental types would gradually crowd out eighteenth-century ornaments, the nosegay on the title page and intricate headbands and tailpieces made up of individual printer's flowers.

John Bushell, the printer who came to Halifax in 1752, was also a skilled artisan who had designed and cut his own ornaments in wood and metal. First seen in Boston imprints from the 1730s and 1740s, three of his tailpieces and one ship cut have also been identified in early Halifax work printed by Bushell and his successor, Anthony Henry.[33] Although Fleury Mesplet, Montreal's first printer, did not make title-page vignettes, his use of French stock introduced motifs such as a liberty cap in 1784.[34] At Quebec, where bilingual work would be composed with facing title pages in French and English, the printers selected contrasting ornaments from their stock: a bouquet opposite an agricultural vignette or the Prince of Wales badge facing a sunburst (see illus. 13.1, pp. 316–17).[35]

John Bennett, who worked as John Neilson's foreman at Quebec, was named king's printer for Upper Canada in 1801. Among Neilson's papers is a list of type from Fry and Steele dated 7 August 1801 and headed with Bennett's name.[36] The order includes nine cast ornaments identified by number from the typefounder's catalogue. He took three large and one small royal arms cuts as well as a Prince of Wales badge. There was a stamp-sized ship for sailing notices in the newspaper and three artistic ornaments: a rose, a garland with musical instruments, and a tailpiece with an angel and banner printed FINIS. This modest stock, including duplicates of two of the royal arms and the ship, cost £4 3s 6d, roughly 10 per cent of his order. Bennett used the ornaments in government work and his newspaper, as well as for sermons, an almanac, and the report of a local society.

The great advantage of relief cuts, which continued to be used in popular work such as textbooks, was that they were cast in typefoundries to be set among types and printed in the same presses. Woodcuts and wood engravings, which Joan Winearls discusses in this chapter as early examples of illustrations intended for a specific text, were printed in the same way, since after the block was worked, only the image was left standing to be inked with the types. Engravings and etchings, taken in a rolling press from a design incised with tools or acid into a metal plate, were single-sheet illustrations to be inserted among the leaves of a printed book or magazine. Invented at the end of the eighteenth century, a third technique, lithography, was a process of printing from stone with greasy ink. Most often used for illustrations, maps, and music, frequently by transferring originals to the stone, lithography could also be used to print text when the printer was lacking an appropriate font of type. This was the case at York in 1833, when Samuel Oliver Tazewell printed from lithographic stone a Greek grammar for Upper Canada College.[37] The want of Greek characters was remedied in Toronto in 1840, following Montreal, where printing in Greek types dates from 1837.[38]

Working in a conservative trade at a time of accelerating industrial and technical development, the printers of British North America were both traditional and innovative. They practised old economies: saving paper by changing to a smaller font to finish the last of a text and keeping type free for other jobs by setting half-sheet gatherings in which only four leaves of an octavo, for example, would be set in type, then printed twice on a sheet of paper and split to make two gatherings of the same four leaves. Some printers made do, using worn and outdated types, while others greeted new shipments with a burst of ornaments and fancy letters in the pages of their newspapers. And even though ink could be bought by the keg, Robert Bell, a young printer discovered by Elizabeth Hulse through his marginalia, was making it 'pretty well' for the *Gore Gazette* of Ancaster in 1829.[39] Other members of the trades were ready to adopt new techniques such as printing from stereotype plates, cast from standing type, which allowed even small shops to print steady sellers without major expenses for type and composition. To speed the production of ledgers and other stationery, the *Upper Canada Gazette* office had one of the new ruling machines in operation in 1836. Less well documented is the founding sometime in the 1830s of the Montreal Type Foundry, the first to manufacture type in British North America and a leader in the continuing development of printing technology in the second half of the nineteenth century.

William Brown's Wage Book, 1775–90
— Patricia Lockhart Fleming

From 1764 to the middle of the following century, printing work at the Quebec office established by William Brown and Thomas Gilmore and carried on
by Brown's nephews Samuel and John Neilson and their successors was tabulated in a complex series of records.[40] Among twenty-six volumes of hastily
jotted daily blotters, monthly cashbooks, and formally posted journals and
ledgers for the years 1764 to 1800 is one modest book of work and wages
dating from February 1775, soon after William Brown took sole charge of the
office, to July 1790, the year following his death.[41]

     Although the entries do not account for all the work done in the shop,
it is possible to track certain printing jobs from setting of the type, through
presswork, to folding of printed sheets into gatherings for books or stitching
as pamphlets. Accounts kept by individual printers can also be charted to
show patterns of work by the week or month and to calculate rates of payment when the shop was engaged in newspaper production, job printing,
and book publication.[42]

     When Brown inaugurated the register in 1775 with his finely drawn sig-
nature facing the February accounts of Thomas Smith (see illus. 5.2, p. 101), the
shop was already engaged in a major job for the government: four treatises on
French civil law compiled by François-Joseph Cugnet, totalling 412 pages in
quarto format, to be printed in an edition of 400 copies.[43] Apart from his tasks
for the *Quebec Gazette / La Gazette de Québec* ('Three Colums' and arranging the
pages for printing), Smith worked steadily on 'Cugnets at case,' composing
types for the final four gatherings, or signatures, of *Traité de la loi des fiefs*, which
were lettered H, I, K, and L by the printers.[44] He started the shorter *Traité de la
police* by setting all eight pages of gathering A and was soon into the *Traité
abregé des anciens loix, coutumes et usages*, which they called 'Municipales.' On 18
February, Smith worked 'at Press' rather than at the type cases, printing each
sheet on the hand press (see illus. 5.1, p. 94). He was paid 7s 6d for composing
a gathering of eight pages and 3s for printing 400 copies of that same gathering, four pages on each side of the sheet.

     Although Thomas Smith took a major role in the four Cugnet volumes,
the demanding work of composition was shared among the printers. For
'Municipales,' the longest treatise at 192 pages, Smith set 127, Joseph Newsham

Work done by Thos. Smith Eor 1775

		£ s d
Febr	Three columns of L.P. for News Paper	0 .. 8 .. 3
	Seven Pages of Cugnets one letter H. to letter I.	0 .. 6 .. 6½
	Making up last Page and imposing both forms	0 .. 1 .. 0
		0 .. 15 .. 9½
6th	Four Pages of letter H. of Cugnets Case	0 .. 3 .. 9
	Seven Pages of letter I. of Cugnets Case	0 .. 6 .. 6½
	Eight Pages of letter A. Cugnets at case Police	0 .. 7 .. 6
11	Three Pages of letter B. Cugnets at case Police	0 .. 2 .. 9½
		1 .. 0 .. 7
13	Four Pages of letter D. Cugnets, police	0 .. 3 .. 9
	Letter C. at Case, Police Cugnets	0 .. 7 .. 6
	Four Pages at Case letter N. Cugnets loix Municipal	0 .. 3 .. 9
18	Letter N. Cugnets Municipales at Press	0 .. 3 .. 0
	Waited for Copy on Thursday 13th Feby	0 .. 18 .. 0
25	Five pages of letter P. at case Cugnets	0 .. 4 .. 8½
	Letter C. at case	0 .. 7 .. 6
	Letter P. at Press ..	0 .. 3 .. 0
	Four Pages of letter Q. at Case Cugnets	0 .. 3 .. 9
		0 .. 18 .. 11½
	amount	3 .. 13 .. 4½

5.2 William Brown's wage book (Quebec, 1775–90). Courtesy of the National Archives of Canada, MG 24, B 1, vol. 88, file 2.

set 42, and William Brown himself set 23 pages scattered through 10 of 25 gatherings. Only 4 gatherings are the work of a single compositor. Work at the press was also shared by Smith, Newsham, and Brown's regular press-man, Etienne Couture. Of the seven other workers whose activities in the shop between 1775 and 1790 are documented, six worked at both case and press; the seventh, Brown's slave Joe, is named only when he was at press with a waged printer, usually Thomas Chorley or Phillip Sullivan. Payments to the workers fluctuated depending on the volume of business. In early March 1775, for example, Joseph Newsham 'stood still' during much of two days 'for want of copy' and was not paid. Brown's tallies of their accounts provide figures for comparison with other trades – or to daily necessities – but they also offer a glimpse into the lives of printers such as Thomas Chorley, whose payment was often reduced by deductions for small cash advances and pur-chases from the shop, such as paper, children's books, and a prayer book in the summer of 1778.

CASE STUDY
'From patriotic motives': Upper Canada's First Paper Mill
— Judy Donnelly

Industrialist James Crooks (1778–1860), an 'omnivorous worker,'[45] added an-other feather to his cap in 1826 when he successfully claimed the £125 pre-mium offered by the House of Assembly of Upper Canada for the establish-ment of the first paper mill in the province. Although mills existed elsewhere in British North America,[46] Upper Canadian printers were still importing paper from Britain and, until 1825, duty-free from the United States.[47] The intro-duction of a 30 per-cent import duty that year made local manufacturing attractive for entrepreneurs such as the Scottish-born Crooks, whose hold-ings in West Flamborough, above Dundas, already included a gristmill, scythe factory, distillery, cooperage, inn, and general store.[48] His interest may have been piqued through his friendship with William Lyon Mackenzie, who had begun championing a mill in 1824.[49] Mackenzie and others proposed the premium, the bill for which was passed on 27 January 1826.

In March, Crooks launched his venture with a shrewdly worded appeal: 'the Subscriber hopes that persons, to whom the value of RAGS may be no object, will (from patriotic motives) lend their assistance in securing a do-mestic supply, otherwise one great object in establishing such a manufacture, namely, that of keeping the money among the colonists will be defeated.'[50] The following month he engaged 'Scotch Millwrights'[51] to construct the mill and an agent to procure qualified workers and 'apparatus' from the United States.[52] By July he had sent a 'certificate of the [mill] being in operation' to Major George Hillier,[53] civil secretary to Lieutenant-Governor Sir Peregrine Maitland, but he did not send paper samples until September,[54] when Mackenzie's *Colonial Advocate* was already using Flamborough-made paper, and the *Niagara Gleaner* advertised Crooks's wrapping paper for sale.[55] However, the Executive Council felt that the mill was only in 'partial operation,' there being no specimens of writing paper 'of the usual qualities.'[56] Undaunted, Crooks delivered six specimens on 1 December.[57] The council deemed the wove, unwatermarked paper 'satisfactory proof' of the mill's 'successful operation' and recommended that he be awarded the premium.[58]

Crooks soon reported that the mill had 'succeeded to [his] utmost expectation.'[59] The following year it was purported to be the source of paper for 'the greater portion of the inhabitants of Upper Canada, printers included,'[60] and was also shipping paper to Lower Canada.[61] Although competitors Robert Stonehouse, John Eastwood, and Colin Skinner were making paper in York (Toronto) by July 1827,[62] Crooks ran his mill until its sale in 1851 to Charles Helliwell, Eastwood's brother-in-law.[63] It was still in operation (owned at the time by Christina Bansley) when it was destroyed by fire in 1875.

Illustrations for Books and Periodicals

JOAN WINEARLS

Only a small number of illustrations were produced locally in British North America before 1840, and few craftsmen are known. The creation of illustrations for early works frequently seems random; it was probably dependent on the availability of artisans and sometimes of presses. Coincidental 'firsts' in different places are striking: woodcuts in Halifax and Montreal in 1776–7 and lithography in Montreal and Kingston in 1831. The earliest examples appear to have been stimulated by the arrival of printers and artisans from the Thirteen Colonies during and after the American Revolution. While the almost simultaneous establishment of commercial lithography in Montreal and Kingston suggests greater movement of technological information, partly through articles in local newspapers.

The methods in use were relief (woodcuts, some wood engravings, and a few typeset plans), intaglio (copper engravings or etchings), and planar (lithography). Intaglio (usually etching) was the principal technique, especially for separate prints and for some major books and magazines, from the late eighteenth century until the 1830s, when this process began to give way to the cheaper one of lithography. Any colouring in the period was added by hand. Since engravers and lithographers usually signed their work, it has been easier to identify as locally produced. Relief methods were employed throughout the period, but few local artisans have been identified before the early 1840s, in part because woodcuts were usually not signed. Wood engravings, evident in the 1830s, appear to have been imported or been part of a stereotyped edition.

City views and individual buildings were the most popular subjects of separate prints, followed by portraits, landscapes, and genre scenes.[64] Books and magazines with engravings or lithographs included a similar proportion of these subjects, together with some maps and caricatures. Woodcuts were generally used in religious works, books for children, and almanacs, and for natural history and technical illustration. Locally produced images were frequently copied from European or American originals, while small metal cuts or woodcuts were usually imported. In some cases, artists active in British North America sent their work to Britain or the United States for engraving (or lithographing) and printing, or they may have engraved it locally and had it printed abroad for better quality.

Woodcuts and Metal Cuts

Woodcuts were the earliest illustrations printed in Canada. The first known is the small view of Halifax Harbour prepared in 1776 for Anthony Henry's almanac *The Nova-Scotia Calendar ... for the Year ... 1777* (Halifax) and signed T.H.[65] It may have been by T. Hamman, who is known to have been active as a metal engraver in Halifax in the 1770s.[66] A set of eighteen fairly sophisticated woodcuts appeared in an edition of Amable Bonnefons's *Le petit livre de vie* printed by Fleury Mesplet and Charles Berger in Montreal in 1777.[67] Using circumstantial evidence, Louise Letocha has argued that these images could have been cut locally.[68] However, given the number of cuts, the absence of any known craftsman, and the short time that Mesplet had been in Montreal, it is possible that they were printed from imported blocks. Publishers in Halifax continued to favour woodcuts in the early period, influenced in part by the tradition of early North American almanacs, but perhaps also because they lacked the equipment for copper engraving. The very fine woodcut title page of Anthony Henry's *Der Neuschottländische Calender, auf ... 1788* (Halifax) may have been prepared locally (see illus. 5.3, p. 106), although not to his standards,[69] and two slightly different and more sophisticated views of Halifax were later cut for his English and German almanacs of 1793 and 1794.[70] A map for a trial report in 1791 is signed 'Engraved by T. Hamman, Halifax,' but it is in fact a relief cut of the Lunenburg coastline with typeset place names, signature, and legends.[71]

Of some forty imprints from British North America with relief illustration (excluding almanacs), an estimated two-thirds or more were produced from imported blocks or metal cuts. One or two of the other religious books published by Mesplet included small woodcuts, probably locally made, such as the rough vignette in *Pseautier de David* (Montreal, 1782).[72] The five images of the wounds of Christ engraved by the Quebec surveyor and map-maker Jean-Baptiste Duberger for the 1796 edition of *Le petit livre de vie* (see illus. 5.4, p. 106) appear in woodcut versions in editions of the same work printed at the Nouvelle imprimerie in 1800, 1809, and 1815.[73] Some religious cuts used in imprints from Lower Canada reappear in Lovell and Gibson's *Specimen of Printing Types and Ornaments* (Montreal, 1846). Stereotyped editions of religious texts produced from American plates that included illustrations were published in Upper Canada in 1834 and 1835.[74] The few illustrated books printed for children during this period use alphabet cuts and some larger genre scenes of children. Most were local reprints of English or French works; produced mainly in the 1830s, they were almost certainly from stereotype plates.

About 60 per cent of the almanacs produced in British North America before 1840 contained cuts that were used over and over again, but few other images. Much of the illustration created especially for almanacs dates from before 1800: the woodcuts produced in Halifax starting in 1776 and the early engravings from Quebec in the 1790s. A few comic and temperance almanacs in the 1830s include illustrations that resemble those in American publications. For instance, the pictures and text about the evils of alcohol in *The Nova-Scotia Temperance Almanack for ... 1835* are clearly stereotyped, possibly from the corresponding section in *The Temperance Almanac*, published in Albany, New York, in 1834.[75]

Engraving and Lithography

Samuel Neilson acquired a copper engraving press in 1779, but it appears to have been used mainly for job printing during the first decade.[76] Curiously, the earliest

5.3 Woodcut and typeset title page of *Der Neuschottländische Calender, auf ... 1788* (Halifax, 1787).
Courtesy of the National Library of Canada.

5.4 Jean-Baptiste Duberger, one of the five wounds of Christ, engraved for Amable Bonnefons,
Le petit livre de vie (Quebec, 1796). Courtesy of the Lande-Arkin Collection of Canadiana, Rare Books
and Special Collections Division, McGill University Libraries, Montreal.

known engraving was a map prepared by Michel Létourneau for Samuel Neilson's *Quebec Almanack / Almanach de Quebec, pour ... 1791*.[77] The first pictorial illustration – of a printing press – was engraved by J.G. Hochstetter for the 1792 edition of the same publication from a print in a European almanac (see illus. 5.1, p. 94).[78] Hochstetter engraved several curious allegorical images for later editions of this almanac and for the *Quebec Magazine / Le Magasin de Quebec*, as well as two portraits and a view, before 1799.[79]

More than a decade separates this activity from the engravers who appeared in Halifax and Quebec after 1810. Charles W. Torbett produced some fifteen to twenty portraits, views, and maps in Halifax magazines, newspapers, and books between 1812 and 1834, as well as trade cards and ephemera. Among his output were four views and six maps for Thomas Chandler Haliburton's *An Historical and Statistical Account of Nova-Scotia*, printed by Joseph Howe in 1829. A few artist-engravers, such as Robert Field and John Elliott Woolford, also created prints in the Maritime provinces during this period. At Quebec five or six engravers are known to have produced prints and maps in the years 1812–31, the most important of whom was James Smillie (see illus. 5.5, p. 108).

The youthful Smillie, who arrived from Scotland with his family in 1821, was the first major pictorial engraver to practise his trade at Quebec and the only one in the period for whom we have information about working conditions.[80] He engraved sixteen separate prints, twenty-two book illustrations, six maps, and a considerable amount of commercial work in the next nine years and clearly garnered much of the available trade. He was responsible for most of the views for two major publications: George Bourne's *The Picture of Quebec* (1829) and James Pattison Cockburn's *Quebec and Its Environs* (1831). For the first work, however, and despite the small size, Smillie felt it necessary to send the plates to New York for printing because of the absence of both a good copperplate press and a printer in Lower Canada. His map work was largely done for government reports. In the end, partly because of the continued use of foreign engravers and printers for major works such as those by Surveyor General Joseph Bouchette, Smillie found that he could not make a living at Quebec, and he left for New York in 1830. In the Montreal area, although five engravers are known, the best of whom was William Satchwell Leney (see illus. 10.7, p. 245) working in partnership with Adolphus Bourne, the total output was less than a third that of Quebec before 1831. No local engraving for illustration is known from Upper Canada.

The first recorded lithograph produced in British North America was the work of John Adams on the Royal Engineers press at Quebec in 1824. The Royal Engineers also had a lithographic press in Fredericton, but only a small number of prints and

5.5   Stephen Henry Gimber, frontispiece, Adam Kidd, *The Huron Chief, and Other Poems* (Montreal, 1830), engraved by James Smillie. Courtesy of the Toronto Public Library (TRL).

maps seem to have been produced (or have survived), the presses having been used mainly for government circulars. Establishment of the first commercial lithographic presses moved the centre for reproductive illustration further west. Two were in place almost simultaneously in Montreal and Kingston in 1831.[81] The first products were crude, printed on poor paper and often poorly inked, but there was a noticeable improvement in quality by 1840. Some sixty pictorial lithographs, the majority for books and magazines, were created by Adolphus Bourne, J. Greene, and others in Montreal in the period to 1840. Several major works with lithographed illustrations (although still small in size) appeared, including Newton Bosworth's *Hochelaga Depicta* (Montreal, 1839), with some twenty plates of Montreal buildings by James Duncan, lithographed by P. Christie. In Upper Canada, where lithography was introduced by Samuel Oliver Tazewell at Kingston and then at York (Toronto), seven pictorial lithographs (see illus. 10.8, p. 248) and at least twenty-four maps were produced in the first half of the 1830s. But Tazewell lacked political support for his production of government maps, and with almost no business, he eventually gave up in 1835.[82] No illustrations were produced in Upper Canada after that date until lithography became more firmly established in the 1840s and the first wood engravers arrived. To a great extent, illustrators before 1840 'found that they were working in an environment that was not yet ready for them.'[83]

Bookbinding

PATRICIA LOCKHART FLEMING

Even before printing offices were set up, the craft of bookbinding would have been practised in New France and the colonies of British North America. Service books and manuals for private prayer were embellished in the convents which excelled in embroidery, while the accounts of merchants and the maps of the military would be sewn in order or protected in folders. Simple covers could be crafted by workers in wood and leather. An inventory of seventeenth- and eighteenth-century French documents preserved in the old province of Quebec was undertaken by the Legislative Council and published in 1791. The investigation included a detailed evaluation of the condition and binding of surviving volumes stitched and sewn in homely coverings of paper, canvas, and deerskin.[84]

The first bookbinders known by name were in business by the 1760s, working for printers or, like B. Phippen in Halifax, seeking customers among the readers of early newspapers.[85] At Quebec in 1765 John Dean was paid by William Brown and Thomas Gilmore for folding, stitching, and cutting 512 copies of an alphabet book.[86] Later that year the printers sold to a merchant 2,000 copies of their first book-length work, a catechism, in sheets as it came from the press.[87] In 1767 Robert Fletcher offered the gentlemen of Nova Scotia two options for the folio *Acts* he had just printed: in sheets to be finished at their initiative or already 'neatly bound.'[88] As the book trades developed in the eighteenth century, more imprints would be advertised for sale bound in a variety of forms and finishes: stitched, interleaved with blank paper, stitched into a decorative paper covering, half bound with a leather spine and paper-covered boards, and fully bound in sheep or more costly leathers.[89] Some titles were offered in two, three, or even four bindings, each distinctly priced. The cheapest copies were stitched with a single thread drawn through all the gatherings parallel to the spine and knotted. Although this stab stitching was often regarded as a temporary finish, more than two dozen examples from the eighteenth century have survived on sermons, almanacs, and official documents from New Brunswick, Prince Edward Island, and Lower Canada. A stronger finish for stitched pamphlets and books was a wrapper of coloured or patterned paper, perhaps with a printed label. Nova Scotia binders favoured comb marbled paper in this period, while in Quebec, blue was popular as well as floral and embossed papers from Germany.[90]

Work in the bindery was often hectic, as John Neilson's records for his 1803 almanac clearly show.[91] On the sixth of January the two binders started by stitching 100 copies in blue paper; they sold another 50 almanacs in sheets to James Brown, a binder who had left Neilson's to open his own shop in Montreal. For the civil secretary's office, there was a special order for 2 copies in red morocco with 'straps to slip in pockets.' Two days later they bound 4 dozen copies, half in red sheep and half in morocco. On the twelfth they did 2 dozen in blue paper and 2 dozen in red sheep; two days later it was another 2 dozen in blue paper and 1 copy to be interleaved with writing paper and bound in calf with pockets. The following day the binders stitched another 4 dozen in blue paper and on the nineteenth put a final dozen into morocco. Over the two weeks they had bound 283 almanacs, more than two-thirds in paper. With a bindery as part of his shop and supplies stored up in the 'Garett,' Neilson offered binding for every purse and purpose (see illus. 5.6, p. 111). In 1799 one devotional work, *Instructions chrétiennes pour les jeunes gens*, could be had in sheep for 3s or 33s the dozen; in buckram 'for the schools' at 2s 9d, or 30s the dozen; and on fine paper bound in calf for 4s.[92]

5.6 Binder's ticket from the office of the *Quebec Gazette / La Gazette de Québec* (Quebec); affixed to a bound copy of the *Gazette* for 1788. Courtesy of the National Archives of Canada, RG 4, D1.

Bindings in leather, particularly calf or morocco, would often be finished with tooling in blind or gilt on the spines, and possibly around the boards. In 1766 the London stationer Kenrick Peck supplied Brown and Gilmore with binding tools and machinery, which they sold the following day, at cost and on time, to the binder Joseph Bargeas. The tools comprised a complete set of letters and figures in octavo size, a dozen 'Back Tools' for ornamenting the spines of octavos and duodecimos, and rolls for decorating the edges of the boards. Pasteboard for bindings was included, and a ream of marbled paper which cost £1, almost half the price of all the tools at £2 6s 3d.[93] Elaborate binding such as 'morocco gilt' could cost the publisher 8s 8d each, compared to basic stitching of the same work at 2½d.[94]

Since binders were trained in an apprenticeship system, styles of binding were derived from national models. At Montreal, Fleury Mesplet, whose surviving imprints are bound in every possible material,[95] looked to his own origins when he advertised copies of *L'office de la Semaine sainte* in a 'beautiful binding which imitates that of Europe.'[96] Surviving copies of this work and his *Le petit livre de vie* are consistent with French styles of the period: mottled calf, gilt on the boards and spine, with floral ornaments and fleurs-de-lys.[97] Another distinctive style underscores the traditions of the German community around Waterloo in Upper Canada in the 1830s.[98] Their books, printed in Fraktur types, were bound in calf or sheep over wooden boards with a leather strap nailed to the lower boards and fitted to a clasp on the front cover. Both the bevelling of the boards and the placement of the strap are characteristic of Pennsylvania German bindings derived from Continental models.

These and other traditional styles persisted into the nineteenth century: paper wrappers in a wider range of colours, often printed with the text of the title page enclosed in an ornamental border; durable canvas and buckram for school books; leathers and the more economical half and quarter bound styles combining leather with marbled and stencilled paper on the boards. Innovation, when it came, was seldom technical, since binding was one of the last trades to be mechanized, possibly because much of the work of folding and sewing was done by women. Instead, it was men's work that changed in the 1830s, with rollers rather than hammers to flatten the sheets and cutting machines to replace handwork.

Industrial binding traces its origin to the development of a cheap and uniform covering that simplified the binding process and filled a growing demand for affordable books in attractive covers. The earliest book cloth, a cotton dyed and sized for durability, was available in London by 1825.[99] Glazed cloth was in use by 1828, and graining of the cloth began early in the 1830s, with embossed patterns of morocco, moiré, ribbed, and florals all available within that decade. Together with their counterparts in the United States, binders in the Canadas and the Atlantic region were eager customers of the British mills, which dominated this manufacture through much of the century. Blocking of the boards and spines of cloth bindings with titles and elaborate panels in gold or blind was perfected early in the 1830s. By this time, bookbinding had emerged as a distinct trade in British North America, combining stationery work, such as paper ruling and the manufacture of blank books for record keeping, with the binding of new works.

As a link between the producers of print and their readers, binders gave material form to the printer's intentions and shaped the perception of readers, whether for a school book sturdy enough to pass down through a family of scribbling children or a gift book 'clad in silk and glittering with gold,' designed 'to grace the hand of the fair as she sits in the bosom of the family circle.'[100]

PART THREE

THE CIRCULATION OF BOOKS AND PRINT

chapter 6

COMMERCIAL NETWORKS

Importation and Book Availability

FIONA A. BLACK

In June 1795 Anna Kearny, the young wife of an officer at the Halifax Garrison 'flew to the window as soon as [her] eyes were open' to discover whether the packet signals had been raised on the flagstaffs.[1] Mrs Kearny, who revelled in recently published novels, had several reasons for such intense interest in flag signals.[2] While packet ships were forbidden by law from transporting commercial cargoes, they could carry packages and letters addressed to individuals. They were one component in the myriad legislative, commercial, and transportation infrastructures that affected book availability in British North America.[3]

Colonial trade and communication links were inevitably framed by the physical and political environments. Economies of scale, so fragile in the book trade under ideal conditions, were severely constrained, prior to the burgeoning immigration of the 1820s and the beginnings of railway building in the 1830s, by a relatively low and widely scattered population coupled with limited and slow transportation. These were some of the reasons why the early book trade in the British North American colonies was primarily concerned with importation and distribution, rather than with production, for most printed materials – with the notable exception of newspapers.

Regulations Affecting Book Importation and Distribution

For commercial cargoes of books, several British regulations affected imports. The (British) Navigation Act of 1696 reinforced an earlier act stipulating that all goods shipped to the colonies had to be transported in British (strictly speaking, English) ships. In British North America, goods carried between colonies fell under this act, although ships built in the colonies counted as 'English.' The intent was to force colonists to buy manufactured products from the home country (that is, from Britain rather than from the United States after the revolution). Colonists, however, carried on a variety of illegal trades with foreign countries, mostly European and including Ireland. Large areas of what is now Canada were not under direct imperial rule at this time, and books were conveyed, unimpeded by legislative restrictions, to the officers and men of 'The Company of Adventurers of England Trading into Hudson's Bay.' These shipments were not commercial cargoes, however; they were the result of individual or collective orders placed by officers for their personal uses or, occasionally, for libraries at fur-trade posts, and they ranged from nautical almanacs to complete sets of the *Encyclopædia Britannica*, transported by canoe to an interior trading post.[4]

Postal service evolved in tandem with developments in transportation, and the post office became an important link for information, ordering, financial dealings, and other matters related to books. Throughout the whole period to 1840, the British government administered the postal system. Early colonial and transatlantic postal services dealt with commercial as well as private mail, and the first official post office in British North America was established in 1754 in Nova Scotia. New France's first postal system was set up in 1759, during the period of military rule, and significantly, it operated between Quebec, Montreal, and Albany and ultimately on to New York. By the turn of the nineteenth century, a New York connection was relatively common for Upper and Lower Canadian suppliers of books.[5] An amendment to the Post Office Act in 1765 stipulated that postal rates in British North America were to be based on distance and number of sheets of paper.[6] By 1784 the water route from Montreal to New York took about ten days by postal courier, and service was weekly. Service between the colonies also developed, and in the late 1780s Hugh Finlay, the deputy postmaster general, launched an overland mail route between Quebec and Halifax which took fifteen weeks for a round trip. The precise numbers of post offices in any given decade have been variously estimated, but by 1820 there were more than twenty in both Lower and Upper Canada, and at least ten in the Maritime provinces.

As with all transportation methods and routes, the weather played a large role, and delivery times both across the Atlantic and north from New York were longer in the winter months. Nevertheless, postal service greatly reduced the time for the exchange of transatlantic commercial information. Individuals could use their own correspondents as book purchasers, and such orders were transported by packet ships, which often sailed alone and could set their own pace, thus reducing the overall time involved.[7] Merchant ships too could be used for transporting personal commissions, as happened when the *Adriatic* brought 'a large parcel of Magazines, Reviews and Parliamentary Registers' to Captain Kearny from his wife's uncle in England.[8]

Networks and Business Practices

No cohesive book trade existed in the British North American colonies prior to 1840. Rather, a web of separate regional networks, several of them overlapping, determined the distribution of books, and no one place had pre-eminence. In this way, the early trade in the British colonies resembled that in the United States.[9] Several elements characterized book importing and exporting, ranging from personal trade contacts to pricing practices.

Importers of books had to take into account British exporters' preference for dealing with someone known (or at least recommended by someone known) for reasons of financial security. The importance of personal and business contacts in the pre-1840 transoceanic trade should not be underestimated. Some importers, such as John Neilson of Quebec and Édouard-Raymond Fabre in Montreal, travelled to Britain and France and were thus known to an array of book wholesalers. The highly successful French-born merchant Laurent Quetton St George regularly journeyed from Upper Canada to New York to buy supplies for his merchant outlets, and these often included books.[10] Thus direct contacts between suppliers and distributors were deliberately fostered by some individuals involved in the book trade.

On the other hand, general merchants and those trading mainly in single commodities, such as tobacco, lumber, or sugar, had already established networks across the North Atlantic. Sometimes British or European booksellers would supply these merchants with stocks of books, primarily standard religious works, histories, school books, and magazines. In these cases it is possible that the impetus came from the merchant rather than from the bookseller. The merchant saw an obvious business opportunity, and the British or Irish bookseller had the advantage of dealing with a local merchant or agent. This relatively risk-free system was how at least some of the general merchants in British North American towns acquired their book stock. They bought from British suppliers, at the retail or wholesale level, in the ports of export where they had agents.

Direct connections between British North American book buyers and British and American suppliers were certainly in evidence since offers to fill direct orders were regularly, if not frequently, inserted in the colonial newspapers. For example, the retail bookselling firm of James Eastburn and Company of New York placed such an advertisement in a Montreal paper in 1819.[11] Direct orders from British North America, whether for wholesale, retail, or library use, seemed to offer some degree of financial security for the supplier. A newspaper advertisement in 1806 promoted the placing of orders directly with a publisher-bookseller in London on the grounds that 'in every part of North America, [there is] an increasing taste for English Literature, without a corresponding Increase of Facilities for obtaining the best ... Publications.'[12] For demographic, and hence economic, reasons, it was not until the second decade of the nineteenth century that British North American towns and their hinterland markets offered sufficient pull to attract scouting visits from European wholesaling booksellers.[13]

Consignments – goods shipped unsolicited – did take place to British North America, but they do not seem to have been common from British ports. There are several reasons why consignments may not have been an appealing marketing method to an overseas constituency, several of which relate to finance. Consignment shipments apparently resulted in a keen attempt by the local seller to set the prices sufficiently low to ensure that the shipment sold in its entirety. Unsold returns would not have appealed to British booksellers because of the long-distance nature of the transaction. In 1821 the Edinburgh publisher Archibald Constable wrote to John Young in Halifax, referring to books and periodicals that had been shipped to Halifax from Greenock: 'We regret to find that the Edin[burgh] Review does not suit ... and ... rather than be at the expense of receiving it back, we are willing that you dispose of it if you can, at a reduction of 25 per cent from the price charged.'[14] This comment is an indication of the relatively narrow profit margins involved in overseas shipments, and these would have constrained any speculative trade on either side of the Atlantic.

British publishers responded promptly when orders were sent to them. For example, in 1820 Archibald McQueen in Miramichi, New Brunswick, ordered books from the Edinburgh publisher Archibald Constable for a small library. Constable responded, saying, 'We shall be very glad to continue to supply the Miramichi library ... and as an earnest of our wish to encourage such undertakings we discount 15 [per cent] from the enclosed Invoice ... We shall be happy to receive your future orders.'[15] The profit margins between publisher, wholesaler, and retailer were not large enough to absorb the costs of transatlantic transportation, and charges for packing and insurance were added to the invoice.

Wholesalers

Most sellers of books in the British North American colonies, both French- and English-speaking, were general merchants. Not only did their principal line of business tend to dictate the size and quality of their book stocks; it dictated the mechanisms by which they acquired them. This was a period 'of great flux in the ... distributive capacity of the book trades' in both Britain and the colonies.[16] The evidence sug-

Table 6.1
Book exports from Scottish ports, 1783–1811, extracted from annual summary customs data
and 'normalized' (by weight) for comparative purposes

Year	Lower Canada	Nova Scotia	Newfoundland	United States
1783		1.3.8		36.2.24
1784		1.1.13		61.3.26
1789		3.2.16		9.0.10
1792	0.3.18	2.2.20		46.3.14
1801	12.3.12		6.0.0*	52.1.13
1802	2.1.21		1.1.24	169.0.12
1807	1.0.0			8.1.16
1810	0.3.21	0.1.0		2.0.12
1811	0.0.20			0.0.10
				0.2.25*

Source: Figures extracted from PRO, CUST 14/1-23, 'British and Foreign Goods and Merchandize Imported to and Exported from Scotland.' Data is included only for those years for which
British North American destinations are included. 'Lower Canada' refers to shipments to the
port of Quebec.

Note: All figures are given as hundredweight, quarters, pounds.
*Unbound books only.

gests that general merchants relied largely on wholesalers for their book stocks. The wholesale business tended to depend on regular turnover of relatively large quantities of readily accessible stock, whether of worsted stockings, hats, or books. The latest publication in philosophical rhetoric, requiring a well-educated consumer, was perhaps not as likely to be stocked by wholesalers who supplied the colonies as bundles of tried-and-true titles for the school market and light literature for readers, such as Anna Kearny, in the growing towns. New poetry, plays, and novels were more likely to sell.[17]

Investigating the largely unsung role of wholesaling stationers requires an understanding of book exporting in general. Between 1750 and 1780 a total of 596 hundredweight and 28 pounds of British-published books (i.e., a total weight of 66,752 pounds)[18] was recorded as being shipped from London to Nova Scotia.[19] Summary figures for exports from Scottish ports between 1783 and 1811 also offer a picture of book shipments to the Canadas, Nova Scotia (which included New Brunswick until 1784), and Newfoundland (see table 6.1). These figures, drawn from customs collectors' accounts, need to be treated with some caution. Newspaper advertisements in both Nova Scotia and New Brunswick clearly show that books were arriving, apparently from Port Glasgow or Greenock, in years when the customs collectors' summary statements indicate none moving to Nova Scotia or New Brunswick from any Scottish port. Circumventing high duties relating to printed books by exporting them as 'stationery' may have been common practice. Certain categories, such as Bibles, dictionaries, chapbooks, and children's books, were especially likely to have been shipped as stationery. In addition, wholesale stationers such as MacGoun's of Glasgow included books, along with paper and business ledgers, in their advertisements. Of particular relevance is the fact that MacGoun's deliberately targeted export merchants.[20]

Shipping Routes

The transportation methods to and within British North America were primarily water-borne until well into the nineteenth century, and ships, brigs, sloops, and canoes predominated in the transportation of books and other goods.[21] For climatic reasons, transatlantic book shipments were more likely to arrive in April, May, or October than in any other months.[22] Information concerning appropriate shippers, sailing schedules, and other details was of importance to both booksellers and general merchants supplying British North American readers. The major coffee houses in the principal ports on both sides of the Atlantic were the equivalent of the daily trade bulletins of the twenty-first century: dates of ship clearances and names of captains and shipping agents were regularly exchanged in the commercial and social atmosphere of such meeting places.

An example of a potentially vital publication for dealers in books is the following, from a Halifax paper in 1801:

PROSPECTUS OF A GENERAL SHIPPING AND COMMERCIAL LIST

Published at the General Post Office conformably to a plan, submitted to, and approved of by His Majesty's Post-Master General. This list exhibits a periodical account of the sailings and arrivals of merchant ships at all ports, both foreign and domestic ... Publication every Monday, Wednesday and Friday ... The list will be sent by the post ... to America at £1. 3s. per annum ... Orders will be received ... by every Postmaster in the British Settlements abroad.[23]

Such shipping and commercial lists were published in many ports including London, Glasgow, Liverpool, and New York. The names varied, but the intent of them all was to aid commerce. Local newspapers often fulfilled a similar role with the insertion of shipping information. British North American merchants could order a range of goods from British merchants, with instructions to have the goods conveyed aboard specific ships, which they knew (on good authority) to be heading for Halifax. Since this was no hit-and-miss business structure, there was time, at least in theory, to plan what books should be ordered.

All the major supplying countries (Britain, Ireland, France, and the United States) might furnish the same retailer. For example, James Brown in Montreal listed school books imported from London and Liverpool, along with a consignment of new travel books, law books, and novels from New York.[24] In general, Maritime book stocks tended to come from Britain and the United States, whereas those at Quebec were almost evenly divided, in the period 1764 to 1839, between British and French sources.[25] The St Lawrence River froze each winter, and therefore transatlantic book shipments were seasonal on that waterway to Lower and Upper Canadian towns. However, these same towns received books in any month of the year from American suppliers. For example, retailers in York (Toronto) and Brockville received books via the Great Lakes in December and January.[26] In contrast, books for the Northwest were supplied from two distinct locations: those for readers employed by the Hudson's Bay Company came exclusively through the company secretary's efforts in London; books for members of the North West Company came from Montreal. These shipments reflected the organizational structure and the headquarters of the two companies.

Local Distribution

Once imported to British North America, books could be further distributed. The development of canals, especially the Lachine Canal (completed in 1825) and the Welland Canal (completed in 1829), enhanced water-borne transportation, permitting goods to move entirely by water between Montreal and Lake Erie. Roads and the concomitant provision of stagecoaches and wagons were slow to develop, so that until at least the first decade of the nineteenth century, road transportation was uncommon or impossible between many settlements. In Nova Scotia, for example, Halifax book agents made use of coastal transport to distribute their goods around the province. A rare exception in the eighteenth century was Windsor, fifty miles away, which received newspapers and possibly books by wagon over an apparently dire road, which was the first to traverse the province. Merchants in villages such as Windsor certainly had supplies of those perennial best-sellers, Bibles, primers, and spelling books.[27] The book agents listed in the *Kingston Chronicle* in 1819 were up to two hundred miles from Kingston, considerably farther than most of the links in Nova Scotia. However, the Upper Canadian network was similar to that of Nova Scotia in that most connections were still by water, even in the second decade of the nineteenth century.

Financing

One of the major constraints on the book trade (or, indeed, on any trade) was the issue of payment for the goods. Banks, with mechanisms for the international transfer of funds in various currencies, were still evolving in this period. However, accepted practices were followed by wholesalers and retailers engaged in overseas trade. Much further research is needed to clarify the financial arrangements used by book wholesalers, but if they were dealing with larger general merchants, they were almost certainly assured prompt payment in bills drawn on reputable mercantile houses.

One method for reducing risk was to insist on a clearly defined method of payment. As the London publisher Richard Phillips emphasized in 1806,[28] 'remittances in good bills' was a requirement, and this usually meant payment from a mercantile house in London.[29] Mechanisms were rather tedious and costly for transatlantic payments for books; these could involve paper currency, bills of exchange, or promissory notes. For a variety of reasons, bills of exchange were used often in transatlantic affairs.[30] London was the centre of the credit structure, and the book trade was no different from other businesses with regard to the need for secure credit. In short, a London connection was not only important for the financial transactions of the book trades: it was often vital. The activities of the book trades of Scotland and Ireland should be interpreted within this constraining financial context, especially regarding their overseas shipments. On at least one occasion, the Scottish merchant James Dunlop in Montreal was able to speak for John Neilson at Quebec, regarding the latter's creditworthiness: 'Mr Nilson the printer of Quebec has ordered some Types from Mr Wilson. I consider him perfectly safe to credit.'[31]

The difficulty lay in the fact that commerce in books was one 'in which exceptionally long credit was expected by client retailers and customers.'[32] The supplying booksellers had to carry, in the interim, not only the production costs of the books themselves but the not inconsiderable freight and insurance costs. Overall, for at least some British wholesaling booksellers and publishers, trade to the colonies 'was hardly worth' all the effort involved.[33] Thus there was, financially, a clear advantage if books were sold (and paid for) at a local level, to merchant companies which, in turn, would send the books overseas through their own distributive network. In addition, general merchants in the colonies, who were by definition dealing in a wide array of goods, would not be so dependent financially on rapid turnover of book stock. The books handled by general merchants would form only a relatively small proportion of their entire stock. Even those in the print trades did not always expect money in payment for books and newspapers; they would accept produce such as grain, other goods, or rags in exchange, particularly in the eighteenth century.[34] In this regard, the British North American book market resembled that described by Warren McDougall for the Carolinas and Maryland.[35]

While detailed charts of the import duties for books and stationery, such as are available for the post-Confederation period,[36] have not been traced for the early period, newspapers provide evidence of such added costs. The principal sources of information are the government notices, which appeared with regularity, concerning the movement of goods north from the United States. During the French and American Revolutions, these notices clarified which essential goods could enter British North America duty free: flour, various types of timber, pitch, tar, turpentine, and so on.[37] Apparently duty on all other goods was usually the same. For example, in the summer of 1815 it was 10 per cent.[38]

Insurance costs for the trade in books to the colonies varied considerably, but they rose significantly during periods of greater risk, such as the American Revolutionary War.[39] In addition, overseas trade was burdened with relatively high freight rates. The 'for cost and charges' appearing in advertisements in British North American papers indicates clearly that retailers in the colonies could not usually absorb high insurance and shipping costs.[40] Unexpectedly, in some instances, there is evidence of the standard London price being used, even though a seller in Nova Scotia had also to cover shipping and insurance costs.[41] Furthermore, in Niagara (Niagara-on-the-Lake), a newly opened bookstore on Gate Street advertised in 1818: 'B.F. and Co. pledge themselves to sell books as low as the New York retailing prices. Library Companies, merchants, and others, who purchase by quantities, will receive a liberal discount.'[42]

A London connection was also common for books shipped to Quebec. For example, the Sulpicians purchased books in French from Dulau, a Soho bookseller, and books in English from Keating. These could have been acquired directly from the London booksellers, but the Sulpicians dealt with commissioners and 'forwarding agents' in New York, taking advantage, perhaps, of the canal route north from that city. Around 1840, other shipments arrived from Méquignon in Paris and from Mame in Tours, to help fulfill the Sulpicians' religious and educational aims.[43]

Local Costs and Pricing

In the pre-1840 period, no British or colonial legislation regulated retail book prices.[44] Evidence of the retail prices of imported books in British North America is relatively scant but nevertheless revealing. First, the expectation that, as a result of transportation over greater distances, prices would necessarily be higher in the colonies than in British provincial towns is not always supported by the evidence, although the general trend was certainly that imported books cost more than locally produced ones.[45] However, the exact effect of various factors, such as differences in paper quality or bindings, can be difficult to discern. Secondly, the apparently standard practice by booksellers in the United States of doubling the sterling price was certainly not duplicated north of the border.[46] Thirdly, prices could depend on format, and provincial booksellers in Britain could purchase books wholesale unbound, sewed, in boards, or bound,[47] whereas merchants in the colonies almost always imported books bound, to judge from customs evidence. The norm in British North America seems to have been a 25 per-cent increase over the provincial British price. For example, *Arabian Nights Entertainments* in four volumes, which sold for 12s in smaller Scottish towns,[48] was priced at 15s in Halifax; and Hugh Blair's *Sermons* was also priced at 12s and 15s respectively.[49] However, there are interesting exceptions to the 25 per-cent increase, when, for example, the price in Halifax might be lower than that in provincial British towns. On these occasions, a difference in binding or in edition may have been the critical factor. In 1789 the apparently standard price in Scotland of William Buchan's *Domestic Medicine* was 7s 6d.[50] That same year it was selling in Halifax for 5s 6d, a price that begs questions regarding the origin of the shipment and whether or not it was a pirated edition.[51]

Other price comparisons are rather more complex to make. In Quebec the local currency was in livres, which were one-twenty-fourth the value of pounds sterling, although this rate of exchange fluctuated.[52] Thus a price of 21 livres entered in a Montreal auctioneer's records for five volumes of Abbé Raynal's *Philosophical and Political History of the ... West Indies*, when converted to 17s 1d, is close to the price just four years later in Elgin, Scotland, for example (18s for six volumes of the same work).[53] Competitive prices from cheap American pirated reprints of European titles (both French and English) ensured their ready market in British North America.

The commercial availability of books in British North America was the outcome of a new and understandably fragmented business structure. London, as the centre of European credit, had vast importance, but its position was buttressed by booksellers in the colonies, upon whom the London and Parisian publishers relied for effective transatlantic distribution. Navigation acts, postal regulations, and developing transportation routes all played as critical a role in the availability of books, as did the evolving technologies of print production.

The Book Trade and Bookstores

YVAN LAMONDE AND ANDREA ROTUNDO

Bookstores were at the heart of cultural development in the colonies of British North America. However, they could exist only in a dense population that included printers, importers, general and specialized merchants, and purchasers who were literate and well-to-do – members of the civil, military, and religious elites. It was this liberal and merchant bourgeoisie that created the institutions whose development was necessarily linked to printing: parliamentary assemblies, courts, churches, schools, colleges, and various voluntary associations. Printed materials, commerce, civic life, and public opinion went hand in hand.

The bookstore as an enterprise was the culmination of a long process during which the printing trades became more autonomous and specialized: booksellers usually emerged from the printing milieu, just as publishers might be former printer-booksellers or booksellers.[54] This evolution of the bookseller's trade explains why, in the eighteenth century, an inhabitant of Halifax, Quebec, or Montreal looking for printed materials, periodicals, or books could find them in many places, and why it would not be easy to make a distinction between sellers of books and booksellers.

Precursors of the Bookseller: The Printer, the Merchant, and the Auctioneer

At first, books could be found in the office of the printer of a local newspaper, who made his primary living by job printing (broadsides, forms) and printing texts of laws, school books and religious works, and pamphlets, which he sold at his shop along with imported titles (see illus. 6.1, p. 126). He might print excerpts from imported books in his newspaper to advertise both his own publications and those of others, as did, among others, Robert Fletcher at Halifax, Henry David Winton at St John's, John Neilson at Quebec, or Fleury Mesplet at Montreal. This same model was still being used in 1812 at Kingston, in 1815 at York (Toronto), in 1825 at Niagara (Niagara-on-the-Lake), and in 1828 at Ancaster and St Catharines, where the printing office advertised in the newspaper books that it printed and published. The emergence of bookselling as an independent trade continued and intensified as the western frontier receded.

Books could also be found at the general store and in hardware stores, apothecaries, and other specialized shops, diversity being the norm. General merchants, who depended for the most part on imported goods, ordered and received a wide variety of products, including books. The Kidston family of Halifax presents the perfect example of a general merchant offering a fine range of printed materials. Printers and merchants of all sorts frequently advertised their imported stock in the newspapers, a practice that underlines anew the importance of the local press in the history of the bookstore.

Auctions often provided an opportunity for the acquisition of books. In Mont-

6.1 Advertisement for John Ruthven on the lower wrapper of John Willson, *Address to the Inhabitants of the District of Gore* (Hamilton, 1840). Courtesy of the Toronto Public Library (TRL).

real between 1778 and 1820, for example, ninety auctions held in cafés or at the auction houses of Cuvillier, Fraser, Henry, and Spragg have been documented; in Halifax, the major auction houses included Bowie and De Blois, C. and R. Hill, and John Moody and Associates. Held to liquidate the goods of other businesses, deceased individuals (see illus. 6.2, p. 128), or people leaving for or returning to Europe or the United States, auctions often put books on the block, individually or by the lot. Newspapers of the time were full of advertisements for auctions of diverse goods and books. Sometimes there were so many items for sale that the advertisement would mention the publication of a catalogue; rarely, however, have these catalogues been preserved as part of the printed heritage of Canadian materials.[55]

It seems that only four catalogues of books sold at auction before 1840 have survived from among the hundred or so titles identified:[56] the *Catalogue des bibliothèques des défunts l'honorable Adam Mabane et Alexander Gray* (1792), the *Catalogue des livres de jurisprudence* (1801), the *Catalogue of Books Composing the Library of the Late John Fleming, Esquire* (1833), and the *Catalogue of the Household Furniture, Books, and Other Effects and Property, Belonging to David Chisholme* (1836?). The last three, published in Lower Canada, are representative of the different types of auctions held at the time: in one, books of a specific genre (jurisprudence) were offered; in another (that of David Chisholme), books were among the other goods being dispersed; and in the third, a personal library (that of John Fleming) was being sold.

The *Catalogue des livres de jurisprudence, qui seront vendus par encan chez Messrs. Burns et Woolsey* listed 87 titles in French (231 volumes published between 1613 and 1801) in two main categories: canon law and civil law. The catalogue was intended to be of interest to judges and lawyers at Quebec who worked under French civil law and depended on imports from Paris to provide access to law books.[57] The auctioneers Burns and Woolsey held at least six other book auctions between 1792 and 1805, but only this catalogue has been preserved.[58] It is interesting because it reveals, in part, the state of contemporary legal knowledge, as well as certain aspects of the book business.

Many other auctions of books of a specific genre were held, for example, at Niagara, Halifax, and Quebec.[59] However, books also went under the hammer in the more general context of auctions of assorted goods. This was the case for the sale in 1837 of the belongings of the Scotsman David Chisholme (1796–1842), former coroner of Trois-Rivières, newspaper publisher, and author (see illus. 6.3, p. 129). The printed catalogue for this auction listed 563 lots that corresponded to the room divisions of the property: Dining Room, Pantry, Lobby, Drawing Room, Library, Kitchen, Stairs, Upper Lobby, Bedroom, Dressing Room, Second Dressing Room, Servant's Room, Yard,

6.2 Page from 'An Account of the Sale of the Effects of the late Major Brock sold at Auction on the 4th of January 1813' showing books sold, prices realized, and buyers' names (York [Toronto], 1813). The inventory lists thirty-eight titles (172 volumes) and one 'lot of books' among the personal effects of Isaac Brock, head of both the military command and the civil government of Upper Canada from 1811 until his death in battle at Queenston on 13 October 1812. Successful bidders included the Reverend Doctor John Strachan, George Crookshank, Major William Allan, Edward McMahon, Andrew Mercer, and John Louis de Koven. TRL, Wm Allan fonds, series VI, Miscellaneous Papers, Brock Inventory. Courtesy of Toronto Public Library (TRL).

CATALOGUE

OF THE

𝕳𝖔𝖚𝖘𝖊𝖍𝖔𝖑𝖉 𝕱𝖚𝖗𝖓𝖎𝖙𝖚𝖗𝖊,

BOOKS,

AND OTHER

EFFECTS AND PROPERTY,

BELONGING TO

DAVID CHISHOLME, ESQ.

𝕿𝖔 𝖇𝖊 𝕾𝖔𝖑𝖉 𝖜𝖎𝖙𝖍𝖔𝖚𝖙 𝕽𝖊𝖘𝖊𝖗𝖛𝖊,

BY PUBLIC AUCTION,

AT THREE RIVERS,

On THURSDAY, 5th JANUARY, 1837.

Sale to commence at TEN o'Clock.

———

The Furniture is nearly new, and of the best description ;
and the Books are principally English Editions.

The Articles and Books in the Library will be disposed of
on the Second Day of the Sale.

———

Terms Liberal :—which will be made known at the
time of Sale.

6.3 Auction catalogue for David Chisholme (1836?). Courtesy of the Bibliothèque nationale du Québec.

and Cellar. Chisholme's library contained 193 titles (646 volumes), including, among other subjects, poetry, collected works, periodicals, essays, works of history, and biographies. Most of the books had been published in London or Edinburgh, but there were also a few Canadian works. The catalogue of David Chisholme's goods reveals as much about aspects of printing history as it does about bourgeois material culture.[60]

The sale at auction of the personal library of Scottish-born John Fleming (c.1786–1832), an important businessman at Quebec and author of political and polemical works,[61] was no doubt also a cultural event that drew the local elite: collectors, wealthy individuals, and members of religious and governmental institutions. It was the largest auction of a personal library in British North America in this period, with 4,204 lots of books (10,380 volumes). The auction catalogue was published in 1833 by A. and J. Cuvillier, a firm that held at least fifteen other book auctions in Montreal between 1802 and 1815, including three that mentioned a catalogue.[62] For the Fleming sale, the catalogue was 265 pages in length and had a table of contents. It was divided into six main sections: Theology, Law and Government, National Affairs, Philosophy, Belles Lettres, and History, which were, in turn, divided into subsections. History, for example, was subdivided into Universal, Grecian, Roman, European, British, French, Asiatic, African, American, and Ecclesiastical. Each entry included the title, author's name, place and date of publication, format, and number of volumes; a few entries also included details about the binding. The titles that 'merit the particular attention of collectors for Public Institutions' were set in capital letters. The Bible subsection gives a glimpse into the wealth of this collection: 26 Bibles, dating from 1583 to 1823, originating from the major European and American printing centres. Although most of the 4,204 titles came from London, Paris, Dublin, Edinburgh, Boston, Amsterdam, Glasgow, and Lyon, the library also included titles printed in British North America (78 lots).

These three catalogues highlight the crucial role played by auctioneers in the book trade in urban areas. Collectors counted on such opportunities to build a library in which rare volumes, first acquired by others, would shine. Finally, readers could turn as well to the peddler, a seller who was second to none when it came to books for the people.

Peddlers

Country folk, usually less literate than those living in towns, could sometimes buy reading material from a peddler, who also sold his wares in town. However, competition from merchants was strong, and those in urban areas attempted to protect their businesses in law. The Nova Scotia law (1782) created 'to restrain hawkers, ped-lars, and petty chapmen, not duly licensed to trade, travelling to and fro through the country' (22 Geo. III, c. 1) was intended to protect businesses and deter sales door-to-door. The law, which ruled out the sale of farm-grown and handmade products, did not refer to printed materials and would scarcely be amended before 1815; it allowed for permits to be issued upon approval by at least three justices of the peace and for the cost of the permits to rise depending on whether the peddler was travelling with or without one or more horses.

The Lower Canadian law of 1795 (33 Geo. III, c. 8), entitled *An Act for Granting to His Majesty Duties on Licences to Hawkers, Peddlars and Petty Chapmen, and for Regulating Their Trade*, which was hardly amended before 1840, stipulated in article 13 that the law did not apply to individuals who sold 'acts of the legislature, prayer books or cat-echisms, proclamations, gazettes, almanacs, or other printed or authorized papers.' According to Egerton Ryerson, who relied on a 1799 account, the peddler's pack (or basket) most often contained calico, muslin, ribbon, strips of canvas, needles, hand-kerchiefs, shawls, cotton socks, and combs.[63] The law did not place churches on the same level as peddlers, and it described the 'authorized' printed materials that were allowed to be distributed in one way or another. But the government took precau-tions: the law on peddlers, which was passed after the French Revolution of 1789 and especially after the Terror of 1793, not only imposed the payment of a fee but obliged peddlers to take an oath of allegiance and specified that any person convicted 'of expressing seditious opinions, proffering treasonous words, maliciously spreading false news, publishing or distributing libels or seditious written or printed papers, inciting discontent in the minds of the public, and diminishing the subjects' affec-tion for His Majesty' was liable to a fine and loss of his licence.

In fact, the law on peddling only put on the record a practice that had existed since about 1770 concerning the distribution of Bibles and tracts by Protestant mis-sionaries and evangelists. With the creation and proliferation of missionary and Bi-ble societies at the turn of the nineteenth century came the dissemination of reli-gious materials by preachers such as Thaddeus Osgood in Upper Canada around 1810 or Walter Johnstone in Prince Edward Island a decade later. It was in this context that shops were opened to sell Methodist publications and that Protestant and French-speaking Swiss missionaries, well known as peddlers of 'Protestant' Bibles, were re-cruited to encourage the conversion to Protestantism of French-speaking Catholics in Lower Canada. The law passed in Upper Canada on 1 April 1818 (58 Geo. III, c. 4–5), which amended that of 1816 (56 Geo. III, c. 34), was similar in spirit, but new means of maritime transport by barque or boat were added to it.

At Cobourg or Brockville in the 1830s, books were sold alongside dry goods, groceries, dishes, and liquor. In Bytown (Ottawa), it was the clockmaker Dray who offered books for sale, according to his notice in the *Bytown Gazette* of 27 July 1839. The *Niagara Gleaner* of 16 August 1833 advertised a book sale at the Kourk Hotel. An advertisement for Joseph Wilson's 'Book-Store' in the *Hallowell Free Press* of 8 November 1831 provides a good indication of how the bookstore was born from the 'bookshop.' Only gradually in the larger towns did the bookstore emerge from the dry-goods business and the printing trade. There are many examples of the relationship between the bookstore and other businesses involved in the book trades – printers, binders, papermakers, the post office – but the dominant and lasting phenomenon was that of the bookseller-stationer.

The Emergence of the Bookstore

A systematic search of the press of the time would supply the information necessary to establish a valid geographic distribution of colonial bookstores in British North America. Even without such an inventory, we know that from the late eighteenth century, four colonial towns had bookstores. Halifax was home to the establishments of Alexander Morrison (1786) and then George Eaton (1811); Jacob S. Mott opened his bookstore (1799) in Saint John; at Quebec, Thomas Cary's bookstore (1797) was next door to his circulating library and reading room; and Montreal had Edward Edwards's bookstore (1784). Between 1800 and 1840, 'independent' bookstores, some of the better sort offering stationery and sometimes bookbinding services, as well as various imported goods, increased in the east and as far west as Berlin (Kitchener).[64] Bookstores also grew out of business relationships (Morrison-Eaton-Belcher in Halifax, Mesplet-Edwards in Montreal) and partnerships (Lesslie-Mackenzie, Horan of Quebec, Fabre), family connections (the Neilsons at Quebec, the Lesslies in Upper Canada), and among in-laws (Bossange-Fabre in Montreal). Occasionally, a printer-binder-bookseller would start a business after completing his apprenticeship with a well-established craftsman. John Bennett of York apprenticed with John Neilson at Quebec, and Henry Chubb, whose indenture is illustrated in chapter 4, trained in Saint John with Jacob S. Mott.

The birthplaces of booksellers and the supply and inventory records for their shops show that the bookstore was at origin a colonial enterprise which depended on the immigration of men and the importation of goods. Members of the book trades from Scotland (John Neilson, James Brown, George Dawson, Edward Lesslie and his sons James, John, Joseph, and William, William Lyon Mackenzie, James

Macfarlane, John Dougall, Robert Armour, Hugh Scobie) and England (William Gossip, Henry David Winton, Henry Rowsell, Thomas Cary) dominated. Jacob S. Mott was representative of those who came from the eastern United States and the Loyalist tradition. Fleury Mesplet, a native of Marseilles, came to Lower Canada via Lyon, London, and Philadelphia; Hector Bossange, a member of a leading Parisian bookselling family, received training in New York before his brother-in-law from Montreal, Édouard-Raymond Fabre, went for a period of training in Paris. A good number of these men belonged to families involved in printing or the book business in their home country or had undergone some form of apprenticeship. Such networks were fundamental, whether they linked the colony to England, Scotland, or France. Evidence of major repercussions on trade can be found at the time of the military conquest of New France and Napoleon's economic blockade which forced French imports to pass through London or the United States. It was only when the blockade ended that the arrival of Hector Bossange made the French-language bookstore a permanent reality in Montreal.

Studies of stock reveal the dependence of the colonial book trade on imports from Britain, France, and the United States and the effects of such imports on book prices. But the timing and content of bookstore advertisements in the press provide further proof of this dependence. The volume of book advertising was impressive, especially at Quebec and Halifax: between 1750 and 1820, the number of titles advertised in these cities tripled in each decade. Advertisements appeared when shipments arrived and, in towns along the St Lawrence, when the river thawed. The goods were extremely diverse, and printed materials carved out a place among the dry goods – glassware, clothing, footwear, food products, and religious objects.[65]

Bookstore Catalogues

Bookstore catalogues, another means of advertising, were more focused on books, although up to the 1830s they might sometimes contain other imported luxury items. All the major bookstores published book catalogues, printed in a newspaper or separately. William Brown, proprietor of the *Quebec Gazette / La Gazette de Québec*, published the first book catalogue (124 titles) for his bookstore in the newspaper in November 1781. Other booksellers followed suit, including John Neilson, Brown's nephew, who published catalogues in the *Gazette* in 1797 (166 titles), 1802 (244 titles), 1817 (634 titles), and 1820 (521 titles), and James Dawson, who published a 300–title catalogue in the *Novascotian* of 3 October 1832.[66] Neilson, an important bookseller, was the first to publish book catalogues separately;[67] he did so regularly between

1800 and 1819. Other booksellers published separate catalogues of which copies have survived: Clement Horton Belcher (in Halifax), Robert Armour and Hew Ramsay, Hector Bossange and Édouard-Raymond Fabre (in Montreal), Augustin-René Langlois, *dit* Germain and Thomas Cary Jr (at Quebec), and Edward Lesslie (in Toronto).[68]

In 1836 Armour and Ramsay listed 1,059 titles (1,038 of them in English) in their catalogue, which was divided into the following sections: History and Biography (87 titles), Science and Philosophy (80), Medical Works (40), Voyages, Travels, &c. (50), Novels (189), Poetical Works, &c. (98), Theology (228), Miscellaneous (163), Annuals, Illustrated Works, &c. (29), School Books (74), French Books (21), Engravings, and Paper Account Books, and Miscellaneous Articles. These titles were ordered from England (once a month), to be sent by ship in the spring, midsummer, and autumn, and from New York, Philadelphia, and Boston (once a week) for more regular delivery. A few titles published in British North America were sprinkled through the catalogue. Many of the titles in Armour and Ramsay's catalogue could also be found in the *Catalogue of Books* published by Edward Lesslie and Sons (Toronto, 1837). Their catalogue offered some fourteen hundred titles (all in English), presented in alphabetical order and then by format. That same year, Belcher's catalogue proposed 1,300 titles to potential purchasers in Halifax.

Fabre presented to his French-speaking customers 1,749 titles (at 'greatly reduced' prices) in his *Catalogue général de la Librairie canadienne* (1837), the term 'librairie' or bookstore indicating how the trade had evolved. The catalogue was divided into four parts: Literature and History (819 titles), Jurisprudence (160), Medicine (89), and Religion and Devotion (601), with a small final section for Prayer Books (54 titles) and School Books (26 titles). The price for each volume was included in the entry.

The majority of these books came from Paris, but also from London, New York, and Philadelphia. Most of the titles in the catalogue were in French, but there were titles in English (19) and in Latin (17), such as *Breviarium romanum* and *Institutiones philosophicae ad usum studiosae juventis*, by the Abbé Jérôme Demers, the first work on philosophy published in the colony. Although bookstore catalogues were quite rare before 1840, the twenty-one examples that have been located to date give a good idea of the variety of books available in the colony.

The Bookstore: A Centre of Sociability

Newspaper advertisements and catalogues enabled the bookseller to advertise merchandise, and urban and rural customers to choose their purchases, either in the store itself or by post. This clientele was made up of members of the liberal professions, the clergy, owners of small businesses, and the seigneurs of Lower Canada, to whom were added, in the English-speaking parts of the colony, government officials, merchants, officers, and artisans. Booksellers could also count on an institutional clientele as the cultural life of the colony developed: parliamentary libraries, for which booksellers might also perform binding services, schools, colleges, circulating libraries, reading and news rooms, subscription libraries and those of professionals such as lawyers and physicians, mechanics' institutes, and literary, scientific, and historical societies. While a bookseller such as Henry Rowsell of Toronto depended on purchases over the winter holiday period – 24 December being a 'ready-money day' – Stephen Miles of Kingston accepted payment in kind: 'Rags enough might be saved in every family to furnish the family with books and stationery.' It was a way to purchase books and paper while enabling more paper to be made![69]

Bookstores, like the press, made an essential contribution to the formation of a distinct local culture. While booksellers acted as agents for subscriptions to foreign periodicals or as exclusive representatives of a publisher (Belcher and Blackwood) or a collection (Macfarlane and the *Encyclopedia Americana*), they were also, more generally, socio-cultural agents. The bookstore was often a place where people got together for conversation, as at a coffee house, an inn, or a tavern. People knew that they could post a subscription list there for the publication of a novel, which was one of the very few ways to get a book produced in the colonies. Booksellers participated actively in the cultural and voluntary life of towns: James Lesslie was one of the founders of the York Mechanics' Institute in 1830, while his brother William was treasurer of a similar institute in Kingston in 1834 and Andrew MacKinlay was at the centre of development for the one in Halifax around 1835; Henry Rowsell attended all meetings of the Shakspeare Club, which became the Toronto Literary Club.

Booksellers and members of the book trades were also engaged politically with both the parties in power and those in the opposition. In Newfoundland, Henry David Winton expressed his approval of representative institutions and the emancipation of Catholics, though he later turned violently against both these causes. Among the constitutionalists were James Brown of Montreal, who led a group of loyal volunteers in 1837–8; the Armours, king's printers who opposed responsible government; and Thomas Cary of Quebec, one-time secretary to Governor Robert Prescott and founder of the anti-French *Quebec Mercury*. George Perkins Bull, an avowed government supporter, was an important figure among Orangemen in Montreal and York; James Macfarlane was very close to the executive of Upper Canada; and Henry Rowsell, a supporter of the Family Compact, went so far as to pack up the books of the lieutenant-governor, Sir John Colborne, when he left for Lower Canada. John Neilson, publisher of *La Gazette de Québec* and bookseller, supported the Patriote party in Lower Canada until it became radicalized; James and William Lesslie spent several days in prison during the Rebellions, which also disrupted the life of William Lyon Macken-zie, journalist, bookseller, and rebel leader; Édouard-Raymond Fabre's bookstore in Montreal was the meeting place for the Patriotes and a point of contact for the Comité de correspondance des députés patriotes.

The Circulating Library and the Reading Room

Among the commercial enterprises were circulating libraries and reading rooms, where one could pay for access to printed materials. Inspired by the European model, circulating libraries lent out books for a fee, and titles could thus 'circulate.' This book business, which seems to have expanded after 1810, could be either autono-mous or connected with or adjacent to a bookstore. Circulating libraries existed at Quebec (Thomas Cary Sr and Jr, Augustin-René Langlois, *dit* Germain), Montreal (William Manson, James Laughlin, John Nickless), Kingston (Stephen Miles and Miss Read), Halifax (Thomas Bennett, Mary Davis, Abdiel Kirk, D. Spence, Jacob Keefer), York/Toronto (George Dawson, Thomas Caldicott, Henry Rowsell), and St Catharines (William Mitchell). The advertisements placed in newspapers would give readers a good idea of the literary genres favoured by circulating libraries, but the *Catalogue of Cary's Circulating Library / Catalogue de la bibliothèque ambulante de Cary* (1830), the only separately printed catalogue from this period to survive,[70] shows that most of the titles offered were literary works: novels and romances, poetry, plays, and tales. The catalogue included 1,857 titles in English (4,664 volumes) and 295 in French (824 volumes), as well as the library's hours of business, the subscription fee, and condi-tions and rates for loans. Additional categories classified titles as History, Biography, Travels and Voyages, Divinity, and Miscellaneous, the last combining essays, periodi-cals (including the *Canadian Magazine*), and letters. Borrowers could also find col-lected works such as Jones's *British Essayists* in forty-five volumes, the nine-volume *Mémoires de Maximilien de Béthune, duc de Sully*, and even one of the first penny dread-fuls, *The Terrific Register; or, Record of Crimes, Judgments, Providences and Calamities* (London, 1825). Several well-known authors appeared in both French and English (Edward Bulwer-Lytton, Fanny Burney, Henry Fielding, Mme de Genlis, Mrs Opie, Bernardin de Saint-Pierre, and Sir Walter Scott). However, the vast majority of authors, who were novelists, were not as well known and appeared only once in the catalogue. Inhabitants of the town of Quebec, curious about local literature, could also borrow a few titles from Lower and Upper Canada: Julia Beckwith Hart, *St. Ursula's Convent; or,*

The Nun of Canada (Kingston, 1824); William Fitz Hawley, *Quebec; The Harp; and Other Poems* (Montreal, 1829); and Adam Kidd, *The Huron Chief, and Other Poems* (Montreal, 1830) (see illus. 5.5, p. 108).

Cary's catalogue shows clearly how the circulating library made works of literature widely available, an issue that the libraries of voluntary associations, in particular, had to come to terms with. By the late 1820s, the Edinburgh Ladies Association was funding the creation in Cape Breton, not of circulating libraries with their novels, but of travelling libraries that featured Bibles, religious tracts, catechisms, and works in Gaelic.[71]

As for reading rooms, they were set up to encourage the reading of newspapers and periodicals, and were sometimes associated with circulating libraries. These 'news rooms,' usually an initiative of printers and newspaper owners, as well as merchants, and also conducted by voluntary associations and mercantile interests, made available political, religious, and economic news, such as the prices of goods on various markets derived, for example, from European, American, and local newspapers. The advent of association libraries and mechanics' institutes, with their libraries, explains the decline and disappearance of circulating libraries and reading rooms, which from then on were integrated into the libraries of voluntary associations.[72]

In 1840, after having been available as 'dry goods' in general stores and then in 'book shops,' books were finally offered in bookstores, but they remained a luxury item. A process of national development began, working through the booksellers themselves as much as through the still tiny part of their inventory that included local imprints: descriptions of Nova Scotia or the town of Quebec and titles on law, poetry, and history.

chapter 7

SOCIAL NETWORKS AND LIBRARIES

Christian Faith in Print

Christian churches and societies active in North America prior to 1840 invested the word of God with power, authority, and meaning, believing that the 'circulation of that knowledge which flows from the sources of Divine Truth, is the most efficacious means of promoting the well-being of society, and the eternal welfare of mankind.'[1] In their collective effort to secure the New World for Christianity, these groups adopted print as an ally in disseminating that knowledge, mediating its diffusion according to their particular tenets. Simultaneously, they turned to print to produce specific denominational and organizational publications, as well as to advance and defend their spiritual, political, and social positions within the colonial milieu.

Ecclesiastics involved themselves in the circulation of religious works from the earliest days of settlement. In the 1660s Augustine sisters appealed for missals and devotional books for their patients at the hospital in Quebec.[2] Missionary work among Native groups, in turn, provoked a significant body of scriptural translations in Native languages (described by Joyce M. Banks in chapter 12), while clerical endeavour among European and Black settlers included the dissemination of religious works. During the eighteenth and early nineteenth centuries, missionaries of the Society for the Propagation of the Gospel in Foreign Parts (SPG, est. 1701), a High Church Anglican association based in England, disseminated throughout British North

America the Bibles, prayer books, and tracts they received for distribution at their own discretion.[3] They also identified cases of perceived need. In the mid-eighteenth century, London shipped French-language Bibles, prayer books, and tracts to Nova Scotia and Quebec to encourage the conversion, as well as to foster the loyalty, of French-speaking Catholic colonists. Missionaries also made requests on behalf of communities or schools where a dearth of religious publications existed. Such a situation motivated a shipment to Preston, Nova Scotia, in the 1790s to supply a newly settled group of former slaves from Jamaica.[4]

In the early nineteenth century, Protestant clerics remained instrumental in the circulation of religious publications, often through affiliations with benevolent agencies of strong religious orientation. The Reverend Thaddeus Osgood, who from 1808 to 1812 traversed the northern frontier of the United States and the Canadas on behalf of the Society for Propagating the Gospel among the Indians and Others in North America, became an agent of the Society for the Promotion of Education and Industry among the Indians and Destitute Settlers in Canada in the mid-1820s. Itinerant preaching, fundraising, and dissemination of religious publications formed the trinity of his duties for these organizations.[5] Other clerical figures joined Bible and tract societies, associations that also relied on the religious commitment of prominent government officials, military officers, local elites, and less conspicuous members of the public.[6]

Although American influence certainly existed in the field, most Bible and tract societies established in the colonies identified themselves as local affiliates of organizations based in Britain and located their activities firmly in the context of their parents' global objectives.[7] The three predominant associations were the Society for Promoting Christian Knowledge (SPCK, est. 1699), the Religious Tract Society (RTS, est. 1799), and the British and Foreign Bible Society (BFBS, est. 1804).[8] The SPCK claimed a High Church Anglican affiliation and split its mandate between education and the dissemination of religious literature; the RTS and BFBS were non-sectarian Christian organizations that embraced evangelical Anglicans. The three societies shared a common objective of facilitating access to religious works, particularly among the poor and working classes, social ranks they considered at greater risk of living in ignorance of the Christian message. Leaders of the colonial affiliates believed that the religious situation in British North America was exacerbated by the geographical isolation of many families, few of which regularly benefited from the ministrations of clergymen. 'Silent preachers,' in the form of a Bible or tract, could compensate for that circumstance; at their most efficacious, these publications offered 'encourage-

ment to the penitent, assistance to the weak, comfort to the distressed, confirmation to the strong, and triumphant views of glory for the ripe expectant of immortal-
ity.'[9] The BFBS confined its offerings to Bibles and New Testaments in a variety of
fonts and bindings. The SPCK and RTS produced extensive catalogues that included,
among other items, devotional and hymn books, scriptural studies, Christian biographies, histories, improving children's literature, and periodicals.

While publications of the three societies had circulated in British North America
in earlier years, it was after 1810 that auxiliaries and branches of the BFBS and diocesan and district committees of the SPCK began to emerge. Nova Scotia proved to be
early and fertile ground; by 1815 a diocesan committee of the SPCK had been established at Halifax, while the BFBS was represented at Halifax, Truro, and Pictou. Over
the next twenty years, affiliates of one or both of these societies appeared in settlements and townships from St John's to York Factory, in the Red River Settlement,
where the BFBS auxiliary was organized in 1821 by Hudson's Bay Company chaplain
the Reverend John West, who had been distributing religious literature since taking
up his post the previous year.[10] During the 1820s and 1830s, these organizations were
joined by auxiliaries and branches of the RTS. By 1840, colonial offshoots of the three
societies had collectively distributed several hundred thousand copies of Bibles, New
Testaments, tracts, and other religious works in a variety of languages, including
English, French, German, Gaelic, and Irish.

The two main activities of Bible and tract societies – the collection of funds and
the distribution of religious works – relied on the parent-auxiliary-branch relationship, a remarkably useful system for reaching the small and scattered settlements of
British North America. Typically, once established in a major provincial centre, an
auxiliary extended its reach outward, encouraging the formation of branches in the
smaller communities and townships in its vicinity. By this method the Upper Canada
Bible Society at Toronto claimed more than sixty branch societies or depositories in
the province by 1840 (see map 7.1, p. 141). An auxiliary and its branches acquired
annual subscriptions and donations to support the work of the parent; a portion of
the monies submitted flowed back in the form of publications, which were then
sold or distributed gratis through the auxiliaries' depositories and branches. Free
dissemination, however, was constrained by financial limitations. In 1828 the Midland District SPCK, for example, resolved that in future it would confine such distribution to tracts and small, stitched books because it had 'found that a prosecution
of the system of gratuitous distribution would too much exhaust the funds of the
institution, and thus circumscribe the sphere of its operations.'[11] Patients, prisoners,
sailors, the destitute, and Sunday school students constituted the most common

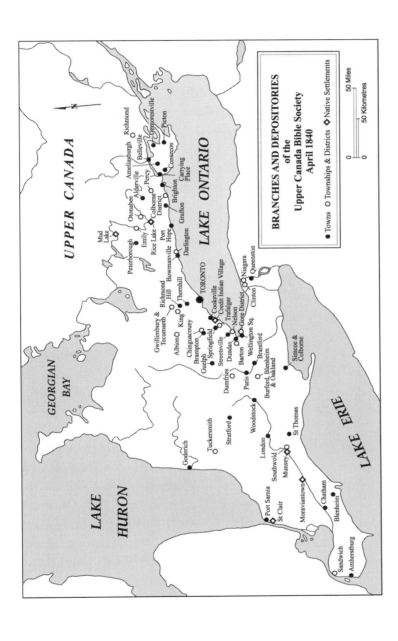

Map 7.1 Branches and depositories of the Upper Canada Bible Society, April 1840.

The Upper Canada Bible Society, one of several auxiliaries of the British and Foreign Bible Society active in Upper Canada, claimed more than sixty branches and depositories in the province in 1840. Numerous other communities in eastern Upper Canada participated in the Bible cause, but they were affiliated with auxiliaries of the British and Foreign Bible Society centred in Kingston and Montreal.

recipients of free publications, but access by these groups was often facilitated through borrowing. Sunday school students were also supported by auxiliaries of the Sunday School Union Society. Walter Johnstone, who with the blessing of a Scottish auxiliary travelled Prince Edward Island in 1820 and 1821 advocating the creation of Sunday schools, sold 'religious tracts and small books' throughout his journey.[12] During the same decade, the auxiliary in the Canadas supported libraries in Sunday schools as 'a great inducement to the regular attendance and diligent application of the children.'[13]

The system of travelling agents and colporteurs that would become common-place in Bible and tract distribution later in the nineteenth century was in its infancy prior to 1840, the Montreal Auxiliary Bible Society taking an early step in that direction in 1839.[14] Voluntary labour typified collection and dissemination between 1810 and 1840, with subscribers often exhorted to aid their societies in these activities. Military officers and Protestant clerics served the Bible cause well.[15] The BFBS and the RTS urged women in particular to undertake local visitation in a threefold effort to assess the spiritual state of their communities, identify individuals in want of reli-gious reading matter, and acquire further subscriptions and donations. A network of Ladies' Bible Associations attached to colonial branches of the BFBS took firm – and expeditious – root in the 1820s, forming 'a system of machinery unostentatious in appearance, yet powerful in reality – silent in ... progress, yet mighty in the result.'[16] Among the most committed was Guysborough's Ladies' Penny-a-Week Bible Asso-ciation, which was formed in 1823 and by 1840 had distributed over 250 Bibles and New Testaments acquired from the Halifax auxiliary.[17]

The processes of collection and distribution were not without obstacles. Winter port closures and the occasional shipwreck interfered with the arrival of publica-tions. Economic difficulties within the colonies hampered the remittance of mon-ies, leading some societies to accept payment in produce.[18] Enthusiasm waxed and waned at the local level, necessitating the periodic dispatch of a revitalizing emissary from an auxiliary. In addition, the BFBS parent engaged several individuals to pro-mote its work in the colonies. John West, who returned to British North America in 1828 at the parent's behest, was entrusted with the supplementary and delicate task of smoothing over the controversy caused by the BFBS's participation in publishing an edition of the Bible that included the Apocrypha, texts rejected by Protestants but considered integral by Roman Catholics.[19] The Reverend James Thomson, sent on a similar tour in 1838, was instrumental in the Montreal auxiliary's involvement in the French Canadian Missionary Society, a Protestant organization founded in Feb-ruary 1839 to evangelize Canadiens, who by this time were also subject to oral and literary proselytization by Swiss missionaries.[20] The Montreal auxiliary's attempts to distribute among this population directly met with substantial resistance, for the Catholic Church opposed the BFBS's fundamental principle of distributing the Bible 'without note or comment,' a tenet designed to surmount sectarian differences among Protestants but which went against Catholic belief that it was the church's responsibility to mediate the reading and interpretation of Scripture, a view shared by some Anglicans.[21]

Bible and tract societies focused most of their effort on distributing imprints sanctioned or published by their parent organizations, rather than undertaking local publication. Notable exceptions included their reports and catalogues, the former considered an invaluable tool in advertising their cause. In addition, the Toronto Auxiliary Bible Society published Ojibwa translations of portions of the Bible, the Montreal Auxiliary Bible Society sponsored two periodicals – the *Christian Register* (1823) and the *Bible Advocate* (1837–8) – and the Upper Canada Religious Tract and Book Society produced *The Upper Canada Christian Almanac* (1833–6).[22] For the most part, however, it was churches and local Christian societies that kept printers busy producing copies of their minutes, reports, constitutions, regulations, and doctrine, as well as missals, hymns, liturgies, prayers, catechisms, and school books.

Churches also used print to define, debate, advance, and defend their spiritual positions, as well as their political and social status in society, for Christianity in the colonies was fraught with sectarian differences, while accusations of disloyalty were regularly hurled against Protestant groups that had arrived in British North America from the United States. Pamphlet debates between representatives of differing religious groups were a feature of colonial life. The denominational newspapers and periodicals, which began to emerge by the 1820s and would proliferate after 1840, buttressed these irregular forays into print by providing churches with a more sustained voice on religious, political, and social matters. In the process, churches fostered a greater sense of community and furnished a forum for congregational discussion. Such publications, for which clergymen often served as subscription agents, included the Anglican *Christian Sentinel* (Montreal, 1827–9), the *Baptist Missionary Magazine* (Saint John, 1827–36), the Methodist *Wesleyan* (Halifax, 1838–52), and the Catholic *Mélanges religieux* (Montreal, 1840–52). The last of these emerged after years of debate, Bishop Jean-Jacques Lartigue having argued in 1828: 'We have urgent need of the press in order to avenge, with vigour and prudence, religion and our rights which are under attack from all sides.'[23]

The Methodist Episcopal Church in Canada, a congregation with American roots, had similarly felt the need of a press at its command.[24] In 1829 it boldly established a printing office for its newspaper, the *Christian Guardian* (York / Toronto, 1829–1925), an action the Anglicans would emulate in 1840 for the *Church* (Cobourg, Toronto, 1837–56). The Methodists' printing office in Toronto facilitated their production of denominational works and allowed the church to engage in the job printing and bookselling activities typical of colonial newspaper offices. The church's itinerant ministry, which had been selling stock from the American Methodist Book Concern (est. 1789) for some years, constituted a practised sales force. In 1833, the same year the church formed an uneasy alliance with the British Wesleyans to create the Wesleyan Methodist Church in Canada, a book depository, which became known as the Wesleyan Methodist Book Room, was established. In its entirety, this operation represented a local manifestation of a long-standing Methodist commitment to publishing and bookselling that dated back to the denomination's origins in mid-eighteenth-century England. However, it would root itself firmly in Upper Canadian soil, evolving into the largest printing, publishing, and bookselling operation in Canada by the end of the nineteenth century, one with a decidedly nationalist outlook.[25]

Church officials, missionary organizations, and Bible and tract societies shared the conviction that print was a powerful messenger. Prior to 1840, it was a messenger they embraced to serve a myriad of needs, running the gamut from Bibles and tracts through devotional works to denominational newspapers and periodicals. While individually these publications often addressed different aspects of Christian faith, practice, and politics in the northeastern part of North America, collectively they represented the intersection of the power of the word with the power of the Word, print being a chosen servant in the mission of communicating the Christian message.

Community Libraries

KAREN SMITH

The men and women who settled what is now Canada came from a wide variety of backgrounds and for differing reasons, but one underlying motivation that many immigrants shared was a desire to improve their way of life and provide a better future for their families. Educational opportunities for their children were a high priority. Among the Loyalists was a wish to recreate as quickly as possible the level of culture they had enjoyed, or aspired to, in the United States. Resourceful citizens devised a number of ways to address their need for knowledge, which drew on American, British, and European models and evolved over time as they and their communities became established. Community libraries were a way to gain access to the books they needed. The forerunners of the free public libraries that would emerge in the 1880s, these early institutions had their origins in social, philanthropic, or religious endeavours by individuals and groups.

Libraries had existed in British North America prior to 1800,[26] but the books were not generally available to the public since they were held by churches, private academies, government and fur-trading officials, or the educated elite. In some communities, churches established parochial or congregational libraries. The Presbyterian minister in Halifax in 1791, for example, urged the expansion of his library in order to make useful knowledge and religious instruction available to the congregation.[27] Though books to satisfy the colonists' spiritual needs were sometimes attainable, those that would address their commercial, educational, and cultural goals were often lacking.

The idea of individuals formally joining together and pooling their resources to select, buy, and maintain a library has been credited to the Philadelphia printer and statesman Benjamin Franklin. He came up with the concept of a subscription library, the Library Company, in 1731 as a way to mitigate for himself and his fellow tradesmen the expense of importing books they needed to improve their skills and knowledge.[28] The first subscription library in the northern colonies was established at Quebec in 1779 by Governor Sir Frederick Haldimand. His motives were partly political since he saw the establishment of a library collective as a way of 'combatting the ignorance of the populations and of encouraging good relations between the former French populations and the new British one.'[29] Haldimand had the support of both the Catholic and the Anglican bishops, and enough shares were sold to the clergy, merchants, and other members of the public to raise £500. A location was secured for the Quebec Library in the former Bishop's Palace, then a government building. The initial selection of books was carried out by the 'gentlemen chosen by the majority of subscribers to be directors,' and subscribers had some control over additions to their library. Membership was open to all, the only barrier being economic since prospective members had to be able to afford the £5 membership share and an annual fee of £2.[30]

In Montreal 'a number of public spirited gentlemen'[31] followed the Quebec model and set up a subscription library in 1796. A local directory was able to report that by 1819 the Montreal Library 'contains upward of 7000 volumes, among which are found many very scarce and expensive works.'[32] In 1800 forty-one residents of Niagara (Niagara-on-the-Lake) determined that 'nothing would be of more use to diffuse knowledge amongst us and our offspring than a library, supported by subscription.'[33] Through the efforts of Richard Cartwright, a Loyalist who wanted to improve the cultural and educational opportunities for his children, a subscription library was begun in Kingston in 1804.[34] York (Toronto) and St John's both had subscription libraries by 1810. The following year the leading citizens of Saint John met on 9 December to form the St John Society Library.[35] In 1812 Truro, Nova Scotia, had an active subscription library, where 'on every Friday, the good people assembled to exchange their books.'[36] An advertisement in the *Prince Edward Island Register* in October 1825 summoned the gentlemen of Charlottetown to establish a public library of obvious utility and benefit to them.[37] With the successful organization of the Prince Edward Island Subscription Library that year, all the British colonies had libraries in one or more major centres; indeed, ten communities in Nova Scotia had subscription libraries by then.[38]

At the same time as the first subscription libraries were being set up, a number of specialized libraries directly related to economic advancement were being established. An agricultural society was formed in Niagara in 1793 under Lieutenant-Governor John Graves Simcoe's patronage. He supported the society by providing money to buy books and by donating a set of Arthur Young's *Annals of Agriculture*.[39] When this collection was merged with the Niagara Library in 1805, it was noted that 'quite an addition was made to the library as well as to the members.'[40] In Nova Scotia a Central Board of Agriculture was founded in 1818 by the lieutenant-governor, Lord Dalhousie, and John Young, a Halifax merchant and agricultural reformer, was appointed secretary. Young, who had been educated in Scotland, was convinced that education and co-operation were vital, and he allocated funds to establish a library of agricultural works. By 1825, when the Agricultural Library of the board became the agricultural department of the Halifax Library, it contained more than 300 volumes.[41] The Montreal Agricultural Society, in the interests of promoting improved agricultural techniques, also supported education and the distribution of up-to-date information. Indeed, the twelfth of its *Rules and Regulations* in 1819 stated: 'Every member of the Society is bound to purchase a copy of such tracts as it may publish.'[42] The society also enjoyed the support of Chief Justice James Monk, who served as its president.

While the agricultural libraries were primarily utilitarian in nature, another type of specialized subscription library emerged during the same period to fulfill the demand for both knowledge and entertainment. At the major British military garrisons in Halifax, Quebec, and Montreal, when the troops were not involved in armed conflict, the large bachelor populations often found themselves with little to do.[43] In Montreal, to ease his officers' boredom, the colonel of the 26th Regiment in 1778 established a library 'where a young officer could usefully occupy himself.'[44] The British garrison at Quebec faced the same problem. At a meeting of the staff and corps on 11 May 1816, it was resolved that a 'Garrison Library would, under proper regulation, be a source of great advantage, as well as of rational entertainment, to the Officers of the Garrison of Quebec and that the plan of the Garrison Library at Gibraltar be followed.'[45] When Lord Dalhousie arrived in Halifax in 1816 to take up his position as lieutenant-governor of Nova Scotia, he found it a very dull place.[46] To amuse himself he launched an amateur theatre and gave a ball for two hundred. He also decided to use £1,000 from duties collected during the War of 1812 to set up a garrison library.[47] A large shipment of books, chosen to Dalhousie's specifications, arrived from London just before Christmas 1818.

Although primarily intended to serve their own officers, garrison libraries extended membership privileges to the local community. In Halifax, where colonial officials, members of the clergy, and other influential citizens were allowed honorary memberships,[48] the library provided a place for the military and civilians to interact socially. In St John's in 1813, a library also served as a meeting place for the military and local citizens, but in this case it was not the military who welcomed the citizens to their establishment. Instead, the St John's Library offered honorary memberships to visiting naval and army officers.[49] In all three major military centres, garrison libraries were progressive establishments, run with military precision and with a captive clientele able to afford the annual subscription fees. The libraries could thus maintain their facilities and keep their collections up to date. A traveller in 1832 remarked on the 'judiciously selected garrison library'[50] in Montreal and observed that in Halifax 'the excellent library established by the Earl of Dalhousie ... [with] a variety of standard and popular works ... must be considered a great advantage.'[51] The advantage would be extended to non-commissioned officers and privates when the British War Office decided to allow the formation of barracks libraries in 1840.[52]

The stability of the garrison libraries was in marked contrast to the situation facing some community subscription libraries by the end of the 1820s. A number of the first libraries had been the initiative of one individual or a small group. When their enthusiasm waned, it could be difficult to find others to take up the task. The Niagara Library, started with such promise in 1800, held its last meeting in March 1820 after the few active proprietors determined that their library had been too badly damaged during the War of 1812 and that they lacked enough paying proprietors to continue.[53] In Truro, the decline of the subscription library was attributed to the inability of shareholders to keep the collection current enough.[54] In a few communities the establishment of a rival subscription library with a different focus and membership eroded support for the original library. The St John Society Library at Saint John was deemed to be too undemocratic in 1821, and a rival Eclectic Society Library was founded.[55]

Regulations that had initially benefited the subscription libraries would later undermine their ability to grow. The Halifax Library limited the number of shareholders to 120, which over time pushed share prices too high for anyone from the middle classes, even when shares became available.[56] The initial share prices, while in some cases quite modest, had always been a barrier for workers and even for many in the trades. For descendants of the original settlers and ambitious immigrants who had developed into an articulate middle class by the end of the 1820s, the surviving subscription libraries, controlled by the elite, were not relevant.

A movement to address the educational needs of the working classes had been gathering momentum in Britain under the leadership of George Birkbeck, who offered public lectures at the Andersonian Institution in Glasgow in 1800. The idea was taken up and reshaped by social reformers in England, including Thomas Hodgskin, Timothy Claxton, and Lord Brougham.[57] A key element of the movement was the establishment of libraries to enable mechanics (skilled workers) to educate themselves. The movement adopted the name 'mechanics' institutes' and quickly spread to North America. The first mechanics' group to be organized in the colonies was a fraternal order, the St John's Mechanics' Society, in Newfoundland in March 1827.[58] The following year the Montreal Mechanics' Institution was established under the leadership of Presbyterian minister Henry Esson.[59] A call for donations of books was well received, and the collection had reached 500 volumes by 1835. Mechanics at Quebec had met in December 1830 and agreed to form the Quebec Mechanics' Institute, one of their chief objectives being the 'formation of a Library, the major part of which shall consist of works of a purely scientific character.'[60] In York (Toronto) newspaper publisher and politician William Lyon Mackenzie advocated the establishment of a mechanics' institute, noting that 'the establishment of institutes of this sort have, in general, been attended with the happiest consequences.'[61] The York Mechanics' Institute was formed in late 1830.[62] A 'valuable and extensive Library' was one of its first goals.[63] At about the same time, Halifax artisans under the leadership of newspaper editor Joseph Howe organized the Halifax Mechanics' Library 'for the purpose of supplying useful knowledge, at a cheap rate to all who desire it.'[64] By 1840 mechanics' institutes would also be operating in Kingston (1834), Woodstock

(1835), Brantford (1836), Cobourg (1836), and Hamilton (1839) in Upper Canada; Yarmouth (1835) and Sydney (1837) in Nova Scotia; Charlottetown (1838); and Hillsborough (1838) and Saint John (1839) in New Brunswick.[65]

The mechanics' institutes and their libraries of 'useful knowledge' were very successful in attracting members. Unlike many of the subscription libraries, which permitted access only to shareholders, the institutes welcomed members at modest rates. The presentation of courses of instruction and public lectures in conjunction with the circulation of books gave the institutes a strong profile in their communities. The important educational function they provided garnered public support and public monies. In Halifax the Mechanics' Library successfully petitioned the Nova Scotia Assembly for funds on four occasions between 1832 and 1835, while an application from the Halifax subscription library was denied.[66] The Montreal Mechanics' Institution received an annual grant of £25,[67] and the Kingston Mechanics' Institute was given $400 by the House of Assembly to purchase books and apparatus.[68] While not free, the libraries supplied an invaluable service for readers and contributed to the educational and cultural growth of their communities. The principles of equality, accessibility, and utility they embodied anticipated the development of free public libraries later in the nineteenth century.

The first major book collections in the Northwest were the private libraries of fur-trading officials who wanted to expand their reading beyond the practical works of astronomy and medicine and the morally uplifting books supplied to the posts by their companies.[69] Recognizing the benefits of a good library to both the morale and the well-being of settlers, Lord Selkirk started sending books to his Red River Colony in 1812, just a year after the first immigrants arrived. By 1822 there were 187 volumes in the library, which had been selected by Selkirk or requested by the settlers themselves.[70] That year the Red River Library was further enhanced by the 500-volume bequest of Hudson's Bay Company surveyor and explorer Peter Fidler.[71] On the West Coast the HBC surgeon at Fort McLoughlin (Bella Bella, British Columbia), William Tolmie, suggested that the books at the company's Fort Vancouver (Vancouver, Washington) trading post be circulated to the smaller posts and a subscription plan implemented, so that traders could order the books they wanted. The idea was successfully implemented in 1836.[72] It was such a success that other trading districts to the north and east adopted the idea. The concept of the subscription library, combined with HBC expertise in the transport of goods, thus allowed traders and settlers in remote areas of the Northwest access to books of their choice.

In the 1820s and 1830s a few of the literary and scientific organizations, formed to address matters of common interest, developed libraries as part of their functions.

The Literary and Historical Society of Quebec was founded in 1824, with the support of Lord Dalhousie, 'to discover and rescue from the unsparing hand of time the records which yet remain of the earliest history of Canada.'[73] Ten years later it had 360 volumes in its library. For the Natural History Society of Montreal, founded in 1827, the development of a scientific library was an important element from the society's inception; it was felt 'that the mere collection of the productions of nature would leave the design of the Society imperfect without the possession of books, that treat of such objects.'[74] By its third year the library had purchased 172 volumes and received donations of 47 more.

The content of libraries evolved over time, especially for community subscription libraries. Initially, the interest of the patrons and owners dominated. Simcoe, Selkirk, and Dalhousie had presented works on agriculture to the Niagara Library, the Red River Library, and the Ramsay Library near Perth, Upper Canada, respectively, and gifts from prominent citizens were common in the formative years. John Langhorn, an Anglican clergyman in Ernestown (Bath), Upper Canada, presented his extensive collection to the Kingston Library before he returned to England in 1813.[75] Judge James Stewart helped to launch the Halifax Library by donating a nineteen-volume set on Roman history.[76] In its first month of operation the Halifax Mechanics' Library received 238 donated volumes.[77] The books ordered, on the other hand, reflected what members wanted. The first order of 80 books in Niagara in 1801 consisted of 30 religious works; history, travel, essays, and poetry accounted for the rest. Only nine titles were fiction.[78] The first order for the Halifax Mechanics' Library in 1832 was for 35 works of fiction and 62 of basic science and reference, together with the travel accounts, memoirs, and essays popular at the time.[79]

An overview of the holdings of the Quebec, Montreal, Ramsay, and Halifax subscription libraries after each was well established reveals that current fiction constituted upwards of a third of the collections, and there was an interest in keeping up to date with developments in all aspects of human endeavour, from art to zoology. Travel literature, memoirs, and current scientific works were especially popular.[80] Both the Quebec and Montreal libraries catered to anglophone and francophone readers with separate sections of their catalogues devoted to books in English and French. But while some 40 per cent of the titles were in French at the Quebec Library in 1808, only 25 per cent of the Montreal Library's holdings in 1824 were in that language. Since the garrison libraries at Quebec and Halifax were both modelled after the Garrison Library at Gibraltar, their collections were similar. Neither library included a substantial number of French titles, and in the Quebec catalogue they were listed with German and Spanish in a short section of 'Foreign Languages, Classics, &c.' While their military and political sections were understandably large, other holdings were much like those of the community libraries. Fiction, travel, and biographies constituted over half of the collections by the time both libraries had been running for seventeen years.[81] Both civilian and military readers were interested in stocking their libraries with current literature, science, and thought.

Just as the contents of the libraries evolved, so did their memberships. The first membership shares were bought by heads of households and individuals who could afford the initial cost and annual subscriptions and who passed their shares on to their heirs. In both Halifax and Niagara, women inherited the shares of deceased fathers or husbands.[82] The rules of the Halifax Garrison Library stated that 'the ladies of families of Subscribers are allowed to subscribe and are entitled, separately, to all the privileges of subscribers.'[83] By 1835 thirty women were listed in the membership roll.

By the end of the 1830s, libraries had been established in most of the larger centres in British North America. Collectively, these institutions provided the means to advance individuals' economic, social, and cultural endeavours. While the subscription, society, and mechanics' libraries were not true public libraries freely available to everyone in the community, they did fulfill a vital role in the evolution of a stable middle class, whose members would later press their governments to provide public library services to all.

Parliamentary and Professional Libraries

GILLES GALLICHAN

Before the founding of major schools and universities, the best way for members of the professions in the colonies to expand their knowledge and follow developments in their discipline was through books. Libraries appeared very early within professional circles, a testament to the need for technical information. The practice of law, politics, and medicine first led to the creation of specialized libraries before 1840. These institutions played an important role in the society of the day; through their collections, their builders, and their users, they contributed to advances in the professions they served.

The Library of the Conseil supérieur

A law library was first created in New France within the circles of the Conseil souverain, later the Conseil supérieur de Québec. Although no lawyers were recognized in the colony, jurists and prosecutors counselled the administration in matters related to law. The Coutume de Paris was applied in New France, and the commentaries of legal advisers such as Ferrière, Domat, Pothier, or Denisart were known on the shores of the St Lawrence and often cited in the correspondence of New France's administrators.[84]

A room in the intendant's palace at Quebec was reserved for the library. It may have housed the administrator's personal collection, but after 1720 a legal collection that included classic works in French and Latin was also assembled for the needs of the Conseil and the intendant. The prosecutor Mathieu-Benoît Collet was the main proponent of the library,[85] and it is possible that the prosecutor Louis-Guillaume Verrier, who gave law courses at Quebec in the 1740s, also used it, along with notaries and military judges. However, no trace of this library was found after the Conquest; it may have been dispersed, pillaged, sold off, or repatriated to France. Nonetheless, lists surviving in the colonial archives give us a clue to at least a part of its contents.[86]

The Law Societies in Lower Canada

With the advent of British rule, the legal profession began to take shape. Governor James Murray authorized the practice of law in 1764, and lawyers soon joined together to defend their interests against the magistrates, forming the basis for the establishment of a law society.[87]

The division of the old province of Quebec into Upper and Lower Canada in 1791 created separate communities of lawyers in the new provinces. Between 1791 and 1838 the number of lawyers in Lower Canada grew from 17 to 227, but it took time for the bar to gain legal recognition. The lawyers had adversaries who feared their influence on the workings of justice. Twice, in 1823 and 1832, the parliament rejected a bill for the incorporation of a law society in Lower Canada,[88] but the jurists did not wait for official status to form their own library. Between 1801 and 1810 the need for a collection of legal texts for lawyers, judges, and students became obvious. The coexistence of French and English law required the use of various legal dictionaries and indexes, as well as classic works. Reference books had to be consulted because of changes in civil law, especially after adoption of the Napoleonic Code in 1804. Added to these problems were gaps in the collections of existing libraries, the absence of an educational institution for lawyers, and the rapid growth of publishing in law and government, not only in Lower Canada but especially in France and England.[89]

Since no specialized library existed, lawyers at Quebec could become members of the Quebec Library, which had a small law collection of 537 volumes by 1832. The parliamentary libraries were a possible source of legal information after 1802, but until 1825 they were reserved for the exclusive use of elected members, councillors, and the governor's establishment. These restrictions did not favour clerks and younger members of the profession.

The advocates' library was founded in 1811, in the midst of a political crisis that followed confrontations between the governor, Sir James Henry Craig, and the Canadien majority in the Assembly and the seizure of the newspaper *Le Canadien*. Furthermore, Pierre-Stanislas Bédard and several other members of the Assembly, also lawyers at Quebec, were among the founders of this library. Although information on the first years of the institution is scarce, we know that it was open to clerks, lawyers, and judges.[90] By 1832 the library had grown large enough and there were sufficient numbers of users to justify the hiring of a librarian. A notice was placed in newspapers,[91] and Jean-Baptiste Landry, a bailiff at various courts in the city, took the position, which he held until 1855. It was he who compiled the first catalogue of the collection in 1840.

A second law library was created in Lower Canada before 1840. At the end of the eighteenth century, lawyers in Montreal, like their Quebec colleagues, met and formed an unofficial association.[92] On 27 March 1828 the judges and lawyers of Montreal created a collective library, administered by a six-member council. Magistrates, jurists, officers of the court, and civil servants were admitted upon payment of an entry fee and an annual contribution. The initial collection of about 300 volumes, most donated by members,[93] included books on law and jurisprudence in France and England, commentaries on custom, historical works, and collections of laws and statutes.[94] Two years later, on the initiative of Chief Justice James Reid, the library became a site for legal meetings and conferences for both students and practitioners. The production of legal works was encouraged through competitions for which prizes were given. The Montreal law library thus seems to have served as the first law school.

Following the Rebellions of 1837 and 1838 and the union of Upper and Lower Canada after 1840, rumours circulated that raised fears about the future of the legal profession in Lower Canada. The city of Quebec, which had lost its status as a capital, saw the departure of many lawyers. In 1840 lawyers in Quebec and Montreal, worried about the fate of their respective libraries, applied to the Conseil spécial du Bas-Canada for incorporation.[95] The law libraries of Lower Canada were thus recognized and protected by law even before the law societies in the two cities were incorporated by an act of Parliament in 1849.

The Law Society of Upper Canada

The Law Society of Upper Canada was created by an act of Parliament in 1797 in Newark (Niagara-on-the-Lake).[96] The act was modified in 1822 to accord to the society all the rights and privileges inherent in incorporation, including that of acquiring real estate.[97] Much work by the first jurists and magistrates in Upper Canada was needed to adapt English law to a frontier colony.

In 1800 the administrators of the society considered acquiring the large personal library of Attorney General John White, who had been killed that year in a duel,[98] to use as a basis of its first collection.[99] But the acquisition was not carried through. Not until 1826 was a truly specialized library, designed initially to serve students, established, 'wherein to transact business, collect and deposit a library and to accommodate the youth studying the profession.'[100] In 1827 the solicitor general of Upper Canada, Henry John Boulton, went to London and purchased a collection of books for the sum of £291 7s 9d, overspending his budget by almost 50 per cent.[101] When the books arrived at York (Toronto) in November that year, measures were taken to set up the library in an appropriate room in the courthouse.[102] The first catalogue, printed by Robert Stanton in 1829, was distributed to members of the profession.[103] The collection included 110 titles in 264 volumes. In 1831 the library was moved to Osgoode Hall, but the Society's budget was so small that new books could not be purchased. The following year, however, the library received a donation of 50 volumes from the society's treasurer, William Warren Baldwin.[104] A year later, in 1833, the secretary, James Martin Cawdell,[105] also became librarian, and development of the library began in earnest. Donations filled the shelves, and the sum of £125 was allocated to new acquisitions. A list of the most essential works, drawn up by Robert Baldwin, included some 40 carefully chosen titles in 75 volumes.[106] Baldwin's list was sent to England, where the province's new solicitor general, Christopher Alexander Hagerman, was charged with filling the order.

In 1837 the army occupied Osgoode Hall and turned it into a barracks. The library, dislodged, was moved into a hall in the parliament buildings; as a result, an inventory and overall appraisal had to be done. These upheavals earned Cawdell an increase in his annual salary to £100. The library's worth was assessed at £800 in 1840.[107]

The Parliamentary Libraries

Parliamentary libraries made their appearance early in the nineteenth century within the sphere of elected assemblies.[108] Although printed materials had certainly circulated in the old colonial assemblies, following the example of the British Parliament, these bodies did not have libraries with a clearly defined function. The new parliamentary libraries of British North America were not based on a British model, since Westminster did not establish its library for members of Parliament until 1818, and its library for the House of Lords until 1826. It was first in France in 1796 and then in the United States in 1800 that libraries were founded to provide elected representatives with books and other printed materials.[109]

At Quebec in 1792 the members were permitted to use the services of the Quebec Library, which was housed in the Assembly building. But soon their requirements became more specific, and in 1801 a committee requested the books in French and English that were deemed necessary for legislative work. The peace that reigned at this time as a result of the Treaty of Amiens between France and Britain made it easy to acquire French books quickly. On 10 March 1802 a new committee established the library of the House of Assembly of Lower Canada, a collection of 26 titles totalling 300 volumes.[110]

In the face of this initiative, the Legislative Council decided to create its own collection. In the spring of 1802 the councillors drew up a list of 26 titles (in 180 volumes), which constituted their initial collection.[111] It expanded slowly, and the first librarian, Augustin Jordain, was engaged in 1829. This library was always more specialized and exclusive than that of the Assembly. Its catalogue was published four times between 1829 and 1834.

In 1825, when the Assembly's collection reached 5,000 volumes, the members passed a motion to make it accessible to the population of the capital between sessions. Jacques Langlois, appointed its first librarian in 1829, died during the cholera epidemic of 1832, and this calamity led to the library being closed until the following year, when the Assembly appointed as his successor the journalist Étienne Parent. Between 1810 and 1835, five editions of the library's catalogue were printed, together with supplements and acquisition lists. Over the next few years, with the support of the assistant clerk, Georges-Barthélemi Faribault, and the speaker of the Assembly, Louis-Joseph Papineau, the library developed a collection on the history of the Americas, which was intended to form the core of a national institution modelled after the Library of Congress in Washington.[112] During the political crisis of 1837–8, however, the library was closed, and it did not reopen until 1841, in Kingston.

In Upper Canada, as in the lower province, members elected to the first assemblies could use local libraries. Between 1800 and 1802 the House of Assembly of Upper Canada acquired books on law and politics and entrusted them to the clerk's care. The first books were eagerly awaited,[113] but the War of 1812 defeated these early efforts. In April 1813 the American army besieged the capital at York (Toronto) and set fire to the government building where the library was housed.[114] Three years later, with peace re-established, Parliament approved £800 of public funds to restore its library,[115] and in 1817 a parliamentary committee proposed the rules and regulations regarding the collections. The first catalogue of the new collection of 800 volumes was then published.[116]

In subsequent years, the library was moved a number of times, and there was little control over loans. In January 1827 William Lyon Mackenzie, in the *Colonial Advocate*, denounced the poor state of the parliamentary library and its management. A new legislative committee then appointed as librarian Robert Baldwin Sullivan, a young lawyer and cousin of Robert Baldwin. Efforts at development were impeded, however, when the library's budget was diverted in 1833 to purchase furniture for the Legislative Council. It was not until 1837 that yet another committee allocated a credit of £1,000 for the library. Sullivan, who had resigned in 1836, was replaced by William Winder, who published a new catalogue of the collections.

The act uniting the Canadas in 1841 forced the relocation of the capital, formerly at Quebec and Toronto, to Kingston, near the border between the two provinces. Their parliamentary libraries were also moved to the new provisional capital. The removal led to losses, thefts, and deterioration, even though the librarians, William Winder of Upper Canada and Jasper Brewer of Lower Canada, did remarkable work to limit the damage. The years of the union were a time of calamities for the parliamentary libraries. In the four Atlantic colonies, books and printed materials no doubt circulated within the legislative assemblies, but no parliamentary library was formally established before 1840.[117]

Medical Libraries

In New France, few professional libraries had existed except for those associated with educational institutions and religious congregations. However, hospitals established collections of medical and pharmaceutical works that compensated to some extent for the absence of schools and formal training. We know that at the Hôtel-Dieu de Québec a collection had already been developed in the eighteenth century and that it was destroyed when fire swept through the hospital in 1755.[118] Later, the nursing sisters received from Father Jean-Joseph Casot medical works that had belonged to the library of the Collège des jésuites. Casot also made donations to the library of the Hôpital général de Québec, which still retains a collection of books dating from the time of its foundation in 1693. Some members of the order who came from wealthy families also received from their relatives books on science and spirituality as gifts or as part of a dowry.[119] Thus the hospitals in the colony assembled specialized collections of the medical sciences and Christian meditations on charity, suffering, and death. Nuns of the Hôtel-Dieu de Montréal and the Frères Charon (Brothers Hospitallers) also had such collections before the Conquest of 1760.[120]

In time, other hospitals set up libraries of medical works, but information about these collections is sparse. The York Hospital, established in 1829 with the support of the government of Upper Canada,[121] became an important institution in the town. In 1833 Kingston had a general hospital that housed the Parliament of a united Canada, as well as its archives and library, for a time in 1841.[122] Following the great cholera epidemic of 1832, the Hôpital de la Marine was founded at Quebec, and from 1834 it treated sailors and travellers who arrived at the port suffering from various diseases. In such institutions, the doctors needed reference books and other sources of medical information to make the best possible diagnoses. Books were also essential in the local public health offices that were opened during epidemics.

The teaching of medicine, which began in Montreal and Toronto in the 1820s, also encouraged the creation of professional libraries. McGill College established its library in 1829 and published the first catalogue in 1845.[123] In Upper Canada the College of Physicians and Surgeons was incorporated in 1839, testifying to an already well organized medical profession.[124]

Conclusion

Before 1840 British North America was only opening the first chapter on specialized libraries, but the professions of law, politics, and medicine were sufficiently developed in colonial society to justify the creation of their own libraries. The numbers of practitioners, often concentrated in the cities, were sufficient to be supported by an institution. In turn, the professional libraries helped to buttress the courts in matters of law, the legislative bodies in the field of politics, and the hospitals in the practice of medicine. These professional libraries were often the first sites of training, where young practitioners came to attend lectures by their masters, to share in a common discipline, and to enhance their knowledge. In this way, libraries contributed to the advancement of professional competency and scientific learning within the colonial society.

For other professions, which were less developed at the time, we must analyze the holdings of more general libraries, since these institutions had to suffice for most demands related to trades and occupations. We must also consider whether wealthier professionals might have acquired personal libraries adapted to their needs. Such was the case for certain notaries, engineers, and surveyors. With the coming of the industrial revolution, more highly specialized publications would become available in the fields of economics, trade, and industry, and the corporate bodies of trades and professions, scientific institutions, and technical schools would go on to create a network of professional and specialized libraries.

The Library as an Institution

ERIC L. SWANICK

According to popular lore, the first library in what is now Canada was established at Port-Royal (Annapolis Royal, Nova Scotia) in 1606.[125] A modest collection of books provided by a private citizen, it had no catalogue or room set aside for its use; a single shelf sufficed. More formally, the distinction belongs to the library established by the Collège des jésuites, described by Gilles Gallichan in chapter 3. From these modest beginnings, much progress was made by 1840, and several themes emerge that would characterize libraries and the library profession in the future.

This study is based primarily on published library catalogues from the period, supplemented by histories and other sources.[126] From the fifty-six catalogues known to have been issued by 1840, approximately three dozen have been examined.[127] Those selected were representative from several perspectives. The earliest appeared in 1797, one in 1808, one in 1817, five in the 1820s, twenty-four in the 1830s, and three in 1840. Geographically, nine were from Nova Scotia, one from New Brunswick, eighteen from Lower Canada, and seven from Upper Canada. Seventeen institutions are represented, some libraries having published revisions of earlier catalogues. Many were 'social' libraries – privately owned and sponsored but 'nonetheless "public" in the distinctively eighteenth-century sense of being a space where civic, religious, and commercial values converged and overlapped.'[128] Also included were several libraries devoted to specific subjects, among them religious, military, and legal institutions, and the government libraries at Quebec and York (Toronto).

Although the catalogues vary significantly, they frequently provide, in substantial detail, information about a library's collection and practices. The prefatory material often includes the rules or bylaws of the organization, together with a list of subscribers and patrons. Some lack this information, possibly because it was posted in the library or had appeared in an earlier edition. The Montreal Library catalogue of 1797 is characteristic.[129] In the introductory material are set out the annual subscription fee, method of payment, rules for the conduct of the library association, such as the election of an executive and what constituted a quorum, membership of the various committees, responsibilities of the librarian, hours of opening, regulations governing use of the collection, and fines for damaged or lost books. This catalogue was published in English and French, as were a good number of those issued in Lower Canada during this period. Separate sections are devoted to English and French books.

The catalogues speak only in general terms, if at all, about the duties of the librarian. This individual, always male, was responsible for maintenance of the library and its collections. He was to supervise the reading room, to 'have custody and charge' of the books, and to record items borrowed and returned. The rules are often specific as to the monitoring of books for possible damage and the assessing of penalties to the borrower. The librarian's other responsibilities varied from institution to institution, but he usually handled subscriptions, fines, and other monies belonging to the society. In some instances, his salary was based in part on commissions: a portion would be determined by the fines collected. These responsibilities frequently led to his acting as the library's treasurer or secretary as well. In social libraries the librarian was responsible for posting the list of members, and in some he was instructed to print catalogues as often as 'they shall deem fit.' The regulations for the Halifax Library in 1833 state that the librarian was to act as secretary, 'shall be appointed by the Committee, and to give such security as is necessary. He shall attend in the Library Room at such hours as may be hereafter stated, have custody and charge of all the books, and receive and exchange them as required by the Shareholders, keeping an accurate account thereof.'[130] In some instances the librarian was the only person permitted to remove books from the shelves. Only for the Garrison Library at Quebec in 1821 is any assistance for the librarian recorded; the duties of a 'sub-librarian' were to include being in charge of the 'forfeits' and the list of subscribers.[131]

Most of the individuals who served as librarians in this era had other occupations. Benjamin Gerrish Gray was English master and librarian at King's College in Windsor, Nova Scotia, from 1801 to 1805. Andrew Heron, who was librarian of the Niagara Library between 1808 and 1816, was a merchant, printer, and newspaper publisher. Schoolteacher and militia officer Herbert Huntington became the first librarian of the Yarmouth Book Society in 1822. The first books acquired by the Library Society in Charlottetown in 1824 were to be 'distributed from the store of Thomas DesBrisay, the librarian.'[132] The Reverend Joseph Langley Mills, chaplain to the forces, and king's printer John Charlton Fisher served as librarian of the Garrison Library at Quebec at various times.

Only in the legislative libraries of Lower and Upper Canada was the position ever a full-time one before 1840, and then usually only when the legislature was in session. In 1834 Augustin Jourdain, librarian of the Legislative Council of Lower Canada, reported that during the session, he was required to be present every day, but that between sessions he was to open the library three days a week. Nevertheless, Jourdain affirmed that he kept the library open every day of the year except Sundays and feast days. His work consisted of keeping the collection in good order, having bindings repaired, assisting the councillors with their research, handling book loans, pursuing acquisitions, and updating the catalogue.[133] Nevertheless, the work of the legislative librarian allowed for a certain amount of free time. Étienne Parent, librarian of the assembly of Lower Canada in 1833–4, continued to publish his paper, Le Canadien, and to prepare for publication the journals of the house.

From the catalogues we can also determine the holdings of the institutions. The collections of particular types of libraries in British North America are discussed elsewhere in this volume and need not be rehearsed here (see the essays by Karen Smith and Gilles Gallichan in this chapter, and by Heather Murray in chapter 8). Making catalogues was usually the responsibility of the librarian, and he was instructed to issue them as often as necessary. In at least one instance, copies were available for purchase. Though no instructions for the cataloguing of collections have been identified for this period, it is reasonable to assume that librarians examined the catalogues of other institutions as models. The published 'catalogues' were often in fact inventories of the library's holdings as of a certain date, and provision was sometimes made for new acquisitions. Copies of the 1808 catalogue of the Quebec Library have printed additions at the end covering subsequent years. In several other catalogues, blank pages or spaces, now filled with manuscript additions in some instances, were provided to record books acquired after publication (see illus. 7.1, p. 161).

These catalogues nevertheless permit glimpses into the way that the collections were organized. Smaller collections were often shelved simply in alphabetical order,

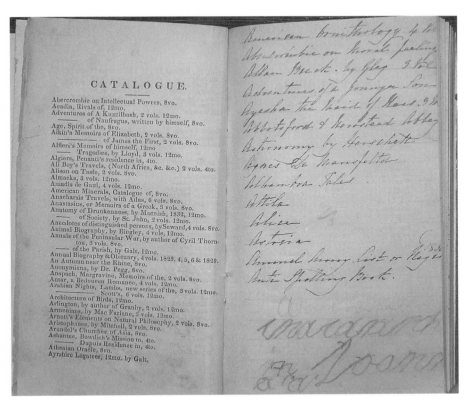

7.1 *Rules and Catalogue of the Halifax Library* (Halifax, 1833); printed page with manuscript additions. Courtesy of the Nova Scotia Legislative Library.

and arrangement by size was not uncommon. Later, broad subject divisions were used. The information provided about individual items also varies. The 1817 catalogue of the Upper Canada House of Assembly, for example, notes for each title the date of publication, the size, and the number of volumes. The size, recorded in some early catalogues, might determine the length of the loan period. Other entries indicate the relative importance placed on particular items; for example, that of the Halifax Mechanics' Institute in 1838 lists the contents of each of the forty-five volumes in the *London Encyclopedia*. Novels were frequently placed at the end of the catalogue, reflecting the relatively low status accorded this material. Often the information provided is meagre. Characteristic is a listing that identifies twenty-four volumes of the *Annual Register* but not the years held.[134] For literary works, titles are frequently given with no reference to the author. Some catalogues indicate whether more than one copy of a title was held or, in one instance, whether an item was a reference work (indicated by an 'r'), and a few provide the location. The latter was especially well recorded in the catalogues of the Lower Canada House of Assembly, which include references such as 'In the Translator's Office' or 'Clerk's Office.' Several list plans, maps, globes, and mathematical instruments held by the institution. During this period it was becoming more common to bind pamphlets together by subject. Examples appear in the Montreal Library catalogue for 1824; of several volumes of pamphlets, only two are classified as 'miscellaneous.' Each pamphlet is described in this model catalogue, which also makes use of 'see' references, such as 'Canada (Upper) Sketch of (*see Bolton*).'[135]

Little is known about the accommodation provided for most libraries in British North America before 1840. The library of the Halifax Mechanics' Institute was in 'a room not less than 15 feet square in a central location.' As no room was set aside for the New Brunswick Legislative Library in the 1820s, it was placed between the assembly and the executive council. Even in the impressive third parliament buildings erected in York in 1832, the legislative library of Upper Canada had to share space also used as a reading and committee room.[136] Not until late in the nineteenth century would libraries have buildings designated for their exclusive use.

PART FOUR

READERS AND COLLECTORS

chapter 8

THE USES OF LITERACY

The Spread of Literacy

MICHEL VERRETTE

It is not a simple matter to establish a link between the expansion of the printing of books, newspapers, and other genres and the growth of literacy, even though the cultural and social significance of print is obviously based on a potential readership. In this respect, the case of the British North American colonies before 1840 is admittedly interesting, but difficult to analyze, since local studies are often too incomplete and the written history has evolved unevenly.

A number of sources (wills, contracts, inventories, legal depositions, censuses, enlistment in the army, petitions, etc.) of unequal validity have been used to investigate literacy.[1] These sources may provide important documentation for the study of a particular social group at a specific time in history, but they are not very useful for analyzing the long-term evolution of the phenomenon of textual society as a whole. Registers of civil marriages, however, constitute an exceptional source. Existing from the sixteenth century, they cut through the population as a whole, both women and men of all social and geographic origins, and they provide direct proof of an individual's literacy: the signature.

Civil registers were well kept by the Catholic Church, and fairly complete series exist. Among Protestants, however, the division into different denominations had the effect of fragmenting information. There is also a problem of legal recognition, since the civil authorities did not automatically grant a denomination established in a village or town the right to keep marriage registers. Nevertheless, these difficulties do not diminish the documentary value of this source for the study of signature literacy, because the registers of civil status constitute the primary source of those who signed their names or declared that they did not know how to do so.

How is literacy defined? In the modern era in the Western world, to be literate meant, above all, knowing how to read. This reality is confirmed by the curriculum offered by primary schools. According to the gradation of early learning, a person who knew how to sign his or her name had normally passed through the stage of learning to read. This person was therefore literate according to the cultural criteria of the time. Statistically, the signature as an indicator no doubt overestimates the number of people who were capable of writing, underestimates the number of those who were capable of very basic reading, and offers a true picture of those who read quite fluently.[2]

New France, Quebec, and Lower Canada

Before a portrait of potential readership up to 1840 is drawn, the numerous factors that influenced the development of literacy should be identified.[3] According to data accumulated to the present, it appears that the literacy level of the French who settled in New France was higher than the average in France.[4] During the decade 1680–9, about one-quarter of the population of the new colony were literate, the men (about 30 per cent) more so than the women (about 21 per cent).[5] In the first half of the eighteenth century, the level of literacy regressed, a phenomenon observed throughout New France.[6]

A drop in literacy among the Acadian population may be explained by the perpetual state of war against the British that persisted from the early eighteenth century until the deportation of the Acadians in 1755. In addition, after the Treaty of Utrecht in 1713 the French elites, followed by some members of the religious orders who had assumed responsibility for education, left the colony, and appointments in the British administration were closed to Acadians. Nevertheless, it was not impossible for Acadians to acquire a rudimentary education.[7] A structural explanation that applied to all of New France was linked with this combination of circumstances in Acadia. The drop in the rate of literacy in the first half of the eighteenth century has to be seen in the context of settlement, colonization, and ruralization, what is called the Canadianization of the population.

It was naturally within the social elite that most readers among the Canadiens would be found at that time.[8] This elite lived mainly in towns and was composed of professionals, army officers, businessmen, and merchants. Colonial administrators and members of the clergy can also be presumed to have been literate. And others such as craftsmen, shopkeepers, government officials, and non-commissioned army officers provided an important potential readership, if not in absolute numbers, then at least in terms of their level of literacy.

As a result of their living conditions, the common people did not constitute a significant community of readers. The population was essentially rural, composed of pioneers and farmers dispersed over a vast territory, another factor limiting literacy. For colonists, whether they had just landed or had been settled for some time, the first priority was survival for themselves and their families, which ranked far above education and leisure activities such as reading. In addition, education was left to private initiatives, mainly the church. The role of the state was limited to the distribution of grants in the form of money or goods, seigneurial properties, or fiefs to assist with education. Education was in the hands of the Catholic Church, which was not interested in encouraging the mastery of reading among the general population.[9] Rather, it emphasized the training of an elite, as the haste of the Jesuits to found their college at Quebec in 1635 demonstrates.[10]

After the Conquest, the situation improved little in the St Lawrence valley. Barely one person in six or seven between 1760 and 1800 signed his or her marriage certificate. This element still constituted a limited potential readership for printers such as William Brown and Thomas Gilmore and Fleury Mesplet, who, after 1764, began to publish newspapers and other printed materials. However, people living in towns or in relatively large villages (of more than 1,000 inhabitants) were more likely to be literate.[11] The town remained by far the most favourable environment for the development of print culture.[12] As in the period before 1760, men were more likely than women to be literate,[13] and that likelihood increased somewhat if the person was anglophone and Protestant.[14] In general, those who were poor, farmers, or craftsmen were scarcely literate. In short, the typical reader in the late eighteenth century was a man, anglophone, Protestant, and usually a member of the urban elite. The literacy level in the years between 1760 and 1800 is explained by various factors. For example, among the anglophones, it should be noted that although their numbers were low, they were concentrated in towns, with a certain number in the Eastern Townships. Many had received a good education in Britain or the Thirteen Colonies. These not inconsiderable factors explain their lead over the rest of the population.

Over the last forty years of the eighteenth century, education in the colony re-

mained the prerogative of private initiatives, and the state limited itself to distributing a few subsidies to encourage people who wanted to open a school. The clergy
were still active in this area, but their human and financial resources were now very
limited. In 1789, for the first time, the colonial authorities presented a plan for a
school system that provided for a primary school in each parish, a higher-level school
in each county, and the entire system under the stewardship of a university.[15] The
bishop of Quebec, Jean-François Hubert, rejected the plan, fearing that religion would
lose importance in the future university. The church thus remained committed to
its elitist vision of education, and the majority of the population continued to be
deprived of the benefits of a parish school. Yet at the end of the eighteenth century,
the population had great need of such schools. 'In 1790, Montreal, Quebec, and Trois-Rivières, which together had a population of 33,200, had twenty schools, or one
school per 1,660 inhabitants, while in rural areas, with a total population of 128,100,
there were thirty schools, or one for every 4,270 inhabitants. The 10,000 Protestants
in the colony had seventeen schools at their disposal (one per 588 inhabitants), while
the 160,000 Catholics had forty schools (one per 4,000).'[16]

Beginning in 1800, religion became a fundamental factor in literacy and in the
development of an educated society. Over the first forty years of the nineteenth
century, the literacy rate in Lower Canada rose from one person in six and a half (15.4
per cent) in 1800–9 to one in four (25.4 per cent) in 1830–9, with still more men than
women being able at least to read. Literacy in urban areas continued to lead that in
the countryside: one person in three at Quebec, compared to one in four in Lower
Canada as a whole. From a social perspective, the upper group, with a rate reaching
up to 80 per cent, was twice as literate as the middle, at about 40 per cent; the latter
in turn had double the literacy rate of the popular segment, at 20 per cent.
Anglophones remained on the whole more literate than francophones. However,
with the arrival of immigrants of more modest origins, the social composition of the
anglophone population in Lower Canada changed, and the literacy level of the group
dropped from 65 per cent at the beginning of the period to 49 per cent in 1840.
Religious education was still a determining factor in the acquisition of basic reading
and writing. The gap between Protestants and Catholics was greater than that between anglophones and francophones.

The rise in literacy between 1800 and 1840 was not explained by economic factors, since Lower Canada did not undergo major structural changes during this period. The explanation is found more in cultural elements: the press and schooling. In
the first decades of the nineteenth century, the periodical press expanded beyond

the boundaries of the colony's urban settlements.[17] Newspapers were the least expensive printed material, the most easily accessible, and probably the least tedious to read. In addition, public education began to progress. Three laws were adopted over the period to make instruction available to a greater number of people: the first in 1801, creating royal schools; the second in 1824, called the 'Loi des écoles de fabriques'; and the third in 1829, called the 'Loi des écoles de syndics.' These laws, however, were not all equally effective. The law of 1801 succeeded in creating only a very small number of schools, the maximum for one year being 85 in 1829.[18] This law ran into administrative obstacles and the opposition of the Catholic clergy. The 1824 law on factory schools did not achieve better results, since this time the Catholic hierarchy was very much in favour but the curés did not respond to the appeals of the episcopate. As a result of avarice, it was said, or out of fear of undermining religion through education for the masses, the curés demonstrated little enthusiasm for applying the law.[19]

The success of the Loi des écoles de syndics in 1829 emerged in literacy statistics in the 1840s and 1850s. But from its beginnings it showed progress, with 465 schools and almost 15,000 students in 1829 and 1,200 schools enrolling more than 38,000 students in 1835.[20] The creation of schools, and the concomitant rise in literacy, seems thus to have flowed from a legislative will supported by government funding. The rise in literacy rates evident around 1840 was the tangible result.

Upper Canada, the Atlantic Colonies, and the West

It is more difficult to paint a clear portrait of literacy for the Atlantic colonies and Upper Canada before the mid-nineteenth century, since there are no detailed statistical studies. In the last decades of the eighteenth century, the populating of the three Maritime provinces and the region that would become Upper Canada was closely linked to the American Revolution, because the first wave of settlers consisted essentially of Loyalists from the United States. While it is reasonable to think that some Loyalists had high literacy levels, the socio-economic status of these settlers varied from one region to another.[21] Many of the first Loyalists were workers and farmers, but after 1790 a generally more literate elite from New Brunswick settled in Upper Canada, causing a shift in literacy from one province to another.

In the first half of the nineteenth century, the population of the Atlantic region and Upper Canada grew, in part because of immigration. Although some immigrants were still coming from the United States, most, numbering close to one million between the 1790s and the 1840s, were arriving from England, Scotland, Ireland, and Wales.[22] The data on these populations show very high literacy rates, but not all immigrants were prosperous.[23] Many who were of rather modest means would not be ready to contribute significantly to the development of a culture of reading and writing in a new colonial society. In addition to demographic influences, we can consider the structural factors commonly used to analyze the development of literacy. As in other new societies in the West, men were probably more literate than women, and the urban milieu probably more so than the rural. Geographic location, local wealth, and the age of the respective communities were also relevant. Religion played an important role in the growth of literacy in the English-speaking colonies. Despite the religious divisions and rivalries that marked the early history of these provinces, literacy was generally encouraged in Protestant communities.

The two cultural factors cited as agents in the rise of literacy in Lower Canada can also be measured in the Atlantic colonies and Upper Canada. The spread of the newspaper press, mapped by Travis DeCook in chapter 10, was particularly significant in Upper Canada, where a printing office had been active or was still at work in some thirty towns by 1840. Since these small shops would keep their presses busy with job work for the local community between issues of a weekly newspaper, they brought print to the very edges of settlement. And as Yvan Lamonde and Andrea Rotundo have demonstrated in chapter 6, many printing offices also stocked a modest selection of popular reading for children and families.

The progress of basic public instruction must be charted across overlapping systems of private venture schools, traditional apprenticeship, modest community and dame schools, parish and Sunday schools, and a wide range of charity schools. For most provinces, the passage of a common school act, based on the principle of local option, sanctioned and encouraged the development of local schools. In Nova Scotia, for example, the School Act of 1811 permitted communities of thirty families or households to organize schools and receive grants from the government.[24] By one estimate, some two-thirds of the children in the province were attending school for an average of twelve to eighteen months in the 1830s.[25] In New Brunswick, where the same assessment concluded that slightly more than half the children were being schooled in the 1830s,[26] monitorial schools were popular. The lieutenant-governor, George Stracey Smyth, sent his son to the first Madras school in Saint John and granted a charter in 1819, allowing the trustees to establish more schools. There were eight a year later, and by 1827 thirty Madras schools provided instruction to 1,200 pupils.[27] Smyth also paid from his own pocket the master's salary and other costs of the 'African School' to educate Black children in the province.[28] Although there were local schools on Prince Edward Island and an Acadian school at Rustico in 1815,[29] the development of a system of common schools awaited the passage of enabling legislation in 1825. Possibly one-half the island's children were being schooled by the 1830s.[30]

The Society for the Propagation of the Gospel, which was active in educational work in British North America until 1836, had established a school in Bonavista, Newfoundland, around 1727. Other SPG schools were conducted by missionaries in twenty settlements in Newfoundland at various times before 1824. Moravian missionaries opened the first school in Labrador at Nain in 1791. Charity schools and Sunday classes, often for competing faiths, remained the norm for basic instruction in Newfoundland until after the introduction of grants recognizing local educational initiatives in 1836. The most successful agency was the Newfoundland School Society, founded by Samuel Codner and supported by evangelicals within the Church of England.[31] Starting at St John's in 1824, the society had major schools in six other towns and branches in twenty-one smaller communities in 1831. It supported forty schools by 1840, but many children were still without classes.[32] Only one of eight in the population attended school in St John's, one in twenty in Trinity Bay, and one in fifty-seven in the district of Fogo.[33]

Although one of the earliest non-governmental works printed in Upper Canada was a local schoolmaster's *Thoughts on the Education of Youth*,[34] a Common School Act was not passed until 1816. Religious rivalries and the dominance of the Church of England inhibited the development of public instruction in the province, narrowing the choice of school books and limiting the recruitment of teachers. Estimates of school enrolment in the late 1830s vary, but it is unlikely that many more than half the school-aged children were enrolled in common schools in Upper Canada.[35]

To the west, in the vast territory controlled by the fur-trading companies, missionaries opened the first schools to teach the children of settlers, as well as young Natives and Métis. Both Catholics and Protestants were active at the Red River Settlement from the end of the second decade of the nineteenth century.[36] The first school for girls was opened at St Boniface in 1829 by Angélique and Marguerite Nolin, Métis women educated in Montreal.[37]

A framework for public education had been established throughout British North America by 1840, but reading and basic skills were still taught informally at home, on the job, and in the community. The number of potential readers was higher than at the beginning of the century, although the literacy rate had probably not reached 50 per cent for all the colonies. More men than women were literate, and people of means were better educated. Nevertheless, between 1800 and 1840, progress began within the working classes, and more and more people from this milieu had access to written materials. Finally, a cultural divide separated Catholics and Protestants. The latter, with a religious education based on individual reading of the Bible, received greater encouragement to learn to read.

Readers and Society

HEATHER MURRAY

Reading is a social practice, and one that has become so socially permeant that its codes and protocols may be shared by the literate and non-literate alike. Indeed – and it is the result of developments in the period examined here – one need not be a 'reader' to be part of a 'reading' culture.[38] Reading is a social act through and through, although we sometimes think of it – and certainly, it has been envisaged in this way in the past – as solitary, involuted, and ephemeral.

Reading in what is now Canada prior to 1840, we may postulate, had some ongoing characteristics:

- It occurred in a polycultural and often multilingual situation.
- It was situated in a time of deep complementarity (even interchangeability) of oral, scribal, and print forms.
- Most readers maintained cultural and linguistic affiliations with home cultures.
- An individual's level of literacy and ability to access books were determined by all of gender, ethnic origin, what we would now call class, and region of settlement.
- Reading preferences, proscriptions, and practices were often determined by religious affinity, with political allegiance assuming a similar role in the latter part of the period.
- Readers, including the most privileged, operated in a context of extremely uneven and often very restricted access to print materials.
- As a result, reading increasingly involved endeavours to increase book access and circulation and to otherwise develop a reading culture.

These presuppositions permit an equally provisional periodization of reading as considered in its social contexts: from the Native-European contact until the fall of New France (discussed in Part One of this volume), from 1760 until 1820, and from 1820 until 1840, a brief but intense era in which attitudes to reading and print were dramatically determined by the emergent political situation.

The year 1760 provides a convenient starting date for a period in which more concerted public effort bore on the question of reading. It marks, most profoundly, the consolidation of the British presence on the continent and the turning point for French-speaking residents in their own cultural development. New groups arrived, bringing with them considerable cultural capital: the Planters after the Acadian expulsion and then the Loyalists in the post-revolutionary period. Certain immigrant groups introduced additional linguistic and literary influences, and from other than European countries, among them the oratorical traditions of the Black Loyalists and, later, Black refugees who had deep connections to their African roots.[39] The first press had been established in Halifax in 1752, and another would come to Quebec in 1764. Autonomous development of the colonies was marked by the opening of the first elected assembly in Nova Scotia in 1758. The date is also useful for comparative purposes. The year 1761 saw the publication of Jean-Jacques Rousseau's *La Nouvelle Héloïse*, often considered the wellspring of a new form of modern, 'sentimental,' or empathic reading whose effects would be several, according to historian Reinhard Wittmann: a widespread 'reading mania' among the bourgeoisie, including women, a change in genre preference to belletristic and fictional materials, and a reconception of reading as doubly interiorized, occurring in both private physical space and individual psychic space.[40] For William Gilmore, in his study of reading practices and book access in rural Vermont, the year 1760 marks the consolidation of literacy skills among the urban middle classes in England, Scotland, the New England colonies, France, and Germany, with near universality in Sweden, and the beginning of the diffusion of literacy to rural areas and to non-bourgeois social groups.[41] To how great a degree these patterns would be echoed in the northern North American colonies is a question to be attempted here.

While 'private' readership may have been a conceptual development of the day, many modes of 'public' reading persisted into the period and, indeed, well into the century, necessitated in part by the scarcity of print materials. Taverns, military mess halls, printing offices, and news rooms were all characteristic locations for male reading. Handbills, posting notices, and proclamations brought print into the streets and into open spaces, while theatrical performances, political orations, and sermons remained important forms of textual transmission, especially for those with rudimen-

8.1 Anne Langton, *Interior of Blyth – John Langton, His Mother, Aunt, and Sister* (ca. 1840). Courtesy of the Fenelon Falls Public Library and the City of Kawartha Lakes, Records and Archives Facility, Schedule C4-CC1 2000809.

tary reading skills. The announcement of public proclamations and the 'lining' of hymns, when a reader would pronounce the next line to be sung by a congregation, are two examples of the augmentation that print received, while pedagogic principle and a scarcity of books and paper equally demanded that repetition and recitation, both individual and choral, were cornerstones of classroom practice.

Even within the home circle, reading was 'public' by the standards of today, dictated as much by the lack of light as by a desire for intimacy or conviviality (see illus. 8.1, above). Indeed, early accounts of 'scenes of reading' often focus on this point: the daughter of a settler recalled her mother's description of a farmhouse circle in Upper Canada, the participants reading 'turn and turn about' by 'the light of the single candle eked out by the flare from a little torch made of birchbark'; while adult-education proponent James Young remembered the men of Dumfries Township debating by the light of burning pine knots when candles were not to be found.[42] The diary of the Irish immigrant Joseph Willcocks, who lived in the York (Toronto) home of Peter Russell, for whom he clerked, gives us a picture of reading in the family circle during the winter of 1800–1. Sometimes extracts were chosen – from Swift or Ann Radcliffe's gothic *Mysteries of Udolpho*, or from the Bible or travel and historical writing, and even from New York newspapers – and sometimes longer works, either in their entirety or in extended stretches, with picaresque novels especially favoured: Fielding's *Joseph Andrews*, Smollett's *Humphry Clinker*, and Lesage's *Gil Blas*.[43] Private reading did of course exist, in bedrooms, studies, or – following the vogue of the day – gardens or picturesque natural settings (see illus. 15.2, p. 364); but one could argue that even such 'private' reading was 'public' not only in the sense that it reflected larger epistemic shifts in reading practice but because this very form of reading was encouraged and enabled through the new public institutions of reading, the libraries and literary societies.

In the later decades of the eighteenth century, libraries were primarily affiliated with organizations, whether governmental, mercantile, academic, or military. Social and subscription libraries began at the turn of the century, and these characteristically raised funds to purchase books and subscribe to British and European periodicals, whose cost in the colonies was prohibitive for most individuals.[44] The innovation quickly spread, as Karen Smith relates in chapter 7.[45] Rural dwellers in Upper Canada undertook similar initiatives: the settlers of Ennotville, a hamlet just north of present-day Guelph, began informal book exchanges as early as 1829, before moving their modest collection to the local schoolhouse.[46] Women took an active part in the establishment of social libraries, in striking contrast to their apparent exclusion from other cultural organizations in the period. The journals of Thornhill settler Mary (then Gapper) O'Brien, in the same year as the Ennotville library was founded, chronicle trips made on horseback through the bush in search of subscribers for a library and a frustrating wait of ten months for the first book parcels to arrive.[47] Commercial circulating libraries (usually attached to bookstores or stationers' or printers' shops), news rooms, and reading rooms (sometimes in the public rooms of a hotel) were other institutions for reading that developed during the time.

The period from 1820 to 1840 was marked by the spread of the 'literary society' model throughout British North America. The founders of early societies in the Canadas and the Atlantic colonies could draw on a variety of prototypes: the elite antiquarian and bibliophile societies developed in Scotland and Europe in the late eighteenth century, the reading societies of the eastern United States, such as Benjamin Franklin's famous Junto, and the public-lecture 'lyceums' that flourished in New York and New England. The French literary-political reading societies of the eighteenth century provided a further, albeit controversial, model for francophone

Lower Canada. While literary societies would develop eclectic agendas and a broader membership throughout the century, these first societies (for men only) focused on debate, discussion, and essay reading in the period prior to 1840. They often provided public cultural amenities such as lecture series and conversazioni, and sometimes they attempted to establish library collections.

While it was not the first, the Literary and Historical Society of Quebec, founded in 1824 and still extant, was undoubtedly the most successful; its dominant position was ensured by its amalgamation in 1829 with the Society for the Encouragement of the Sciences and the Arts in Canada, founded two years earlier, a society controlled by members of the francophone elite. A thriving society with a substantial museum and subscription library, it provided the standard against which other societies would set their aspirations and measure their more modest successes. The York Literary and Philosophical Society (1831) and the Halifax Athenaeum (1834) were two successor societies; both the appeal of the format and the difficulties of implementing it are illustrated by the establishment of some twenty, often short-lived, literary and debating societies in Upper Canada alone prior to 1840.[48]

In practice, societies with a more open membership and mandate stood the greatest chance of success, as demonstrated by the spread of the mechanics' institute movement in the 1820s, soon after the first was established in London, England. By mid-century, several dozen would be operating in the Canadas and Atlantic colonies. Mechanics' institutes appear to have been the first cultural organizations to invite women to attend public events such as lectures. In addition, their libraries provided the closest approximations to a true 'public' library in the period; later in the century, their collections and those of the common schools would in fact form the foundations for public libraries in their communities.

Given the scarcity of individual or familial reading records for the period, library catalogues offer, I would argue, the most accurate index of popular reading choices.[49] Subscription and mechanics' institute libraries were built through what one might call a 'plebiscite of taste' among their members: shareholders wrote suggestions in a nominations book, and final selections were made by an elected committee. Unpopular items were sometimes deaccessioned and sold to pay for fresh materials. Catalogues of these quasi-public collections lend themselves to analysis both in bulk and individually, and in several ways. The first is taxonomic – that is, through a comparative analysis of the headings used to sort materials, although not all catalogues are thus arranged.[50] The second is generic: according to the forms (periodical, monographic) and genres (history, belles lettres, for example) of different library collections. A third mode would involve an analysis of authors and titles, in order to delineate the taste of the period and to speculate on single instances of a title, interestingly rogue items, and omissions. Last, when we can match a catalogue with a constituency, we have evidence of the reading habits of particular subgroups.

The catalogues of three Halifax libraries, for example, indicate both general and specific interests and tastes.[51] In simultaneous existence in the 1830s, they nonetheless differed markedly in their memberships and inclinations. The library of the Halifax garrison was founded in approximately 1817.[52] Its privileges were extended to officers' wives and prominent local citizens.[53] The Halifax Library of 1824 numbered on its restrictive rolls the archdeacon, the chief justice, the lord bishop, and members of the powerful Uniacke family; some women held memberships in their own right. The constitution of the Halifax Mechanics' Library, founded in 1831, states that the library was intended to be 'public' and its privileges 'within the reach of any industrious person.'[54] While the collections were roughly comparable in size (approximately nine hundred items for each of the first two libraries, and some seven hundred for the Mechanics' collection), we would expect, and find, significant differences.[55]

Since only the Halifax Garrison Library subdivided its catalogue listings, a taxonomic comparison is not possible. But even a preliminary generic analysis yields some interesting results. In that library, for example, despite what we might anticipate of these seasoned campaigners, 'Novels and Romances,' at 174 volumes, is almost double any other category, with racy stories of the high life listed alongside serious fiction. Not surprisingly, 'Voyages, Travel and Geography' and 'War and Military History' occupy second and third place (at 154 and 92 volumes respectively); the category termed 'Arts, Science, Heraldry' is also sizable, in part because of its miscellaneous nature, since it includes philosophy, phrenology, and primers on playing whist. In the section 'Theology and Law,' the law predominates. On the other hand, even in the disorder of the Halifax Library catalogue, with its listings sometimes by author and sometimes by title, it is apparent that the holdings are especially strong in literature, particularly prose, with little evidence to be found of light reading. Historical subjects, memoirs and 'lives,' travel literature, and volumes of essays and letters are also numerous; law and jurisprudence seems a special interest. Although the Mechanics' library avowed that the majority of books it purchased should 'treat of useful knowledge,' the library is unexpectedly light in its holdings of practical and scientific treatises and instruction manuals; poetry, novels, travel writing, history, biography, and the fine arts are well represented, with a good dose of sermon literature.[56] Presumably this group, in common with mechanics' institutes elsewhere, refused to restrict its holdings to vocational subjects, asserting that members should be offered a liberal education.

Both patterns and puzzles emerge when we focus on the acquisition of individual writers and works.[57] Certain literary authors are encountered in all the collections: Byron, Cervantes, James Fenimore Cooper, William Cowper, Sir Walter Scott, and of course Shakespeare. One notices, as well, a strong representation of Scottish authors in all three collections, though there is no Burns in the Mechanics' collection: was it assumed each member would have a volume at home? Such overlaps indicate the commonalities, or 'canon,' of taste in the period. However, the Garrison and Mechanics' libraries have similarities not found in the Halifax Library, with shared stocks of popular favourites such as Thomas Campbell, John Gay, and Thomas Gray; the Halifax Library, on the other hand, holds a substantial amount of European literature in translation. This library, it appears, was more suited to the needs of the 'sentimental' reader; its monetary resources also allowed it to be far more current, as witnessed by a run of the Waverley novels complete to the volume released in May 1833. Both the Garrison and the Mechanics' libraries held a number of multi-volume histories of rebellions and insurrections, and the Halifax Library held a few; but one suspects these were read very differently in each location. Neither the Garrison nor the Mechanics' library extended its political sympathies as far as Thomas Paine, but the radical William Godwin's *Adventures of Caleb Williams* is found at the Halifax Library – did they read it as just another gothic?

Library catalogues are not, of course, direct evidence of the preferences and practices of their readers; they attest as much to the accidents of acquisition. Nor can too general conclusions be drawn from them. But taken as the whole, they do suggest much of the mentality of the time and of constituent groups. The very existence of all three collections, as well as their actual holdings, indicates a shared vision of reading as a form of both self- and mutual improvement. Such improvement, it was argued by cultural commentators of the day, served as a crucial agent in processes of civic and national development. In making this case, promoters of reading did not appeal only to narrowly pragmatic purposes or utilitarian motives: the term 'improvement' encompasses mental, moral, and spiritual growth, as much as 'development' could connote a cultural, political, and even religious trajectory. There is therefore no contradiction in the presence of large quantities of belletristic prose and of poetry in a library dedicated to 'useful' subjects, since such reading, if properly channelled, would cultivate both feeling and intellect and be therefore socially productive.

While such commentators were in relative agreement on the importance of 'improvement' and of reading's role in it, they were far from unanimous in their estimations of how far the colonies were achieving, or falling short of, that goal. In gauging the state of a reading culture in the early nineteenth century, we cannot always rely on contemporary accounts: emigrant agents, for example, might paint a bright picture of cultural development to lure prospective settlers, or missionaries overstate the success of a literacy campaign; on the other hand, for political or polemical purposes, writers might well exaggerate local ignorance or the paucity of resources. Anna Jameson's account in *Winter Studies and Summer Rambles in Canada* (1838) is a case in point: does she deliberately overstate the intellectual deprivation in Toronto to enhance her self-portrait as a cultural Crusoe?[58] Such divergence in the accounts is not entirely unreflective, however, since 'reading' itself differed markedly even among the literate. Susanna Moodie and John Dunbar Moodie, for example, editorializing in the decade after 1840, drew a distinction between town and country readers, the first inundated by 'vast' amounts of up-to-date information, the second acquiring 'knowledge at longer intervals' but with 'more time to make it their own.'[59] The simultaneous existence of what we might call – following Raymond Williams – residual and emergent reading methods can be illustrated by two readers at York in the 1820s, one a well-known local figure and the other soon to make his mark: Joseph Tyler and the young Robert Baldwin.[60]

When the Reverend Henry Scadding, an amateur historian, book collector, and ceaseless civic booster, staged his annual 'Log Shanty Book-Shelf' displays at the Toronto Industrial Exhibition in the late nineteenth century, he used the occasion to reflect on the culture of pre-rebellion York, his boyhood home, particularly the state of what he was to call the 'incipient literatureism' of the emerging nation.[61] In 1893 with *A Pioneer Gathering of Books of a Sententious Character*, he focused on the ability of these early readers to use their scanty supplies in thrifty and ingenious ways. Words of wisdom could be found in repeated perusals of favourites such as *Don Quixote*, *Pilgrim's Progress*, and of course the Bible; but even old almanacs and stale newspapers 'were all conned over with gratitude in the absence of other matter for consideration ... the compact set of sayings thus stored up might be compared to the old-fashioned pocket-knife which young lads aforetime were so proud to possess, containing in its handle besides several blades a great variety of little implements.'[62] For Scadding, this inventive and intensive reader was best emblematized by the eccentric Don River ferryman Joseph Tyler, a 'primitive character' noted for his extreme self-reliance.[63] Tyler had a ready stock of aphorisms and 'was ever formulating phrases and rules of conduct such as would at a later period have been not unworthy of Artemus Ward, Mr. Joshua Billings, or Abraham Lincoln himself.'[64] Under Tyler's influence, Scadding formed his own taste for 'proverbs, parables, sage summaries and saws'; he would boast that his assemblage dated from these earliest years, naming it 'A Collection Begun at York, U.C. (Toronto), 1821.'

If the example of Joseph Tyler illustrates the complementarity of orality and print in British North America, the case of Robert Baldwin shows the coexistence of scribal and print culture. In the small world of York in the second decade of the nineteenth century, Baldwin would surely have encountered Tyler, but as a reader, he was a paradigm leap away: formally educated to Tyler's autodidacticism; 'extensive' rather than 'intensive'; sentimental rather than pragmatic. The key to his early tastes is to be found in 'Poems by Robert Baldwin & Others Collected by James Samson Hunter. vol 1,' a holograph volume from 1819 intended for public, or at least coterie, circulation.[65] Baldwin attempted a number of contemporary forms, including Burnsian fragments, farewells, and impromptus to various Annas, Fannies, and Rosalines, as well as to Adeline's lock of hair; meditations on natural and sentimental subjects; and historic themes in imitation of Ossian. While the young men of his circle were mutually admiring of one another's efforts, they could also mock their susceptibility to the poetic vogue of the day.

Baldwin undertook a more public cultural project as one of the founders of the York Literary Society in 1820.[66] Ten law students and clerks convened every second Monday for 'mental improvement,' to be achieved in debate and the reading of original essays. Through discussion and the distribution of texts in oral, manuscript, and print forms, literary societies such as this one created a channel for ideas and information, a development greeted with approval, anxiety, or both. Was widespread reading a civilizing force in a new society or the forerunner of a dangerous social 'levelling'? The conservative concerns were by no means abstract; the premises of newspaper publisher and printer William Lyon Mackenzie were the de facto meeting rooms for the rebels of 1837, and according to historian Fernande Roy, the bookshop of Édouard-Raymond Fabre was the 'point de convergence' for the Montreal Patriotes.[67]

Suspicion about literacy, about the activity of reading, and about certain genres and authors was not a new phenomenon: concerns about unregulated access to sacred texts, about the enervating effects of too much reading, or about the irreality of fantasy, for example, were age-old concerns and would continue well into the century, as Carole Gerson has demonstrated.[68] But issues emerged in the 1830s that were specific to the day, and to the Canadas and the Atlantic colonies; indeed, the decade was stretched taut by conceptual contradictions. Only after the rebellion period would a firmer consensus emerge on the need for mass literacy training and for easier public access to print. The 1840s would be marked, for example, by Halifax writer George Renny Young's influential treatise *On Colonial Literature, Science and Education*, by Egerton Ryerson's innovative system of school book depositories, and by the creation in Montreal of the first branch of the Institut canadien, an influential literary-political society.

The examples discussed here demonstrate the complexity of reading and readers in British North America before 1840. For a start, they challenge the distinction between the 'public' and the 'private' reader, assumed to have developed over the course of the eighteenth century. On a theoretical level, one could argue that, paradoxically, no reader is so thoroughly 'public' as the 'private' reader, who has absorbed and adopted the protocols of reading. And the reverse is true: a resistance to literacy may involve the protection of personal or group values against imposed programs of moral or cultural assimilation. On the practical level, it is the highly trained 'private' reader – a Robert Baldwin, for example – who most strongly senses literature's social utility and takes the longest steps to promote it, to inscribe reading on the public sphere. Similarly, the differentiation between 'intensive' and 'extensive' readers may be questioned. The 'intensive' reader may have a broad access to texts through oral presentations, while the 'extensive' reader may well become the repetitive reader described by Robert Darnton as Rousseauistic, and whom we might now call Proustian. The British North American situation presents many examples of extensive readers living in an intensive world. The studious Mary Gapper O'Brien may have had the run of the Stowey Book Society's collection when she lived in Glastonbury, England, but as a settler in Upper Canada, she had quite literally to beat the bushes for books. And ferryman Joseph Tyler demonstrates a narrowing between the 'common' and the 'elite' reader. His pragmatic use of texts resembles the practice of readers trained in classical rhetoric, who mined texts for topoi to memorize.

The 'communications circuit' often deployed by book historians may also not be fully applicable to the colonial situation. Individuals could have been part of a personal or non-institutional circuit or positioned within several separate but overlapping circuits. We need schemata for 'incomplete' circuits – the highly developed 'print' culture of New France in, strictly speaking, the absence of print itself, for example – or for the personal or sub-institutional 'micro-circuits' that characterized the earliest period. Analyses are also needed for polycultural and polylinguistic systems, such as for a Métis translator, who might be positioned in two complete but overlapping circuits. As the case of Robert Baldwin demonstrates, the roles of authoring, publishing, distributing, and reading can be located not only within a single body, such as a literary society, but even within the activities of one individual. Like Henry Scadding's penknife, the reader in British North America, when opened up, may be found to contain a great variety of functions.

CASE STUDY
The Diary of Jane Ellice, Reader
— Patricia Lockhart Fleming

Safely home in Scotland for Christmas, Jane Ellice recalled in her diary 'Canada – that land of perpetual Blue Skies & glorious sunsets,' but her recent sojourn in Lower Canada was memorable in many other ways as well.[69] She had arrived in Quebec, 'music playing, colours flying,'[70] at the end of May 1838 in the party of Lord Durham, newly appointed governor-in-chief of British North America. Her husband of almost four years, Edward Ellice the younger, was private secretary to Durham. Ellice's grandfather, with his four brothers, had established the family's fur-trading and merchant connections in North America in the 1770s, and since 1795 Ellices had been seigneurs of Beauharnois on the south shore of the St Lawrence, west of Montreal.[71]

Durham's entourage remained together at Quebec until early July, when the Ellices moved on to Beauharnois. Apart from a month-long tour in the United States, with a return through Niagara and Toronto, and a visit to Quebec in October after Durham resigned his post, the Ellices lived at Beauharnois as seigneur and 'seigneuresse' (see illus. 8.2, p. 183). Jane Ellice's daily companions were her younger sister, Tina Balfour, a sketchbook, and a diary which she 'kept faithfully and fully' according to her father-in-law's wish.[72] Early on the fourth of November the seigneury was attacked and plundered during the second Patriote rising. Edward Ellice was carried off with other captives, while the women took refuge in the house of the curé and were guarded there as prisoners for almost a week. Reunited, the family left Beauharnois in an open boat, the water reflecting reprisals, 'villages burning in all directions.'[73] Two weeks later, they were on board an American ship bound for Liverpool and home.

With rumours of Patriote activities current before the rising, the young women had spoken in jest about an attack, with Tina 'certain she would act as nobly'[74] as Flora M'Ivor in *Waverley* or Cora Munro in *The Last of the Mohicans*. Reading and allusions to books enrich more than a quarter of the entries in

8.2   Katherine Jane Ellice, *The Drawing Room at the Seigneury House, Beauharnois, Lower Canada* (1838).
Courtesy of the National Archives of Canada, C-013384.

the diary that Jane Ellice kept from April to December 1838. Books were part
of her daily life: on board ship, when it was cold and foggy, she lay in bed and
read Abercrombie on moral feelings; at Beauharnois in mid-August, she finished Lockhart's life of Sir Walter Scott and began the life of Hannah More on
the following day. When she could not attend Sunday service, she read from
Scripture. As a tourist in the United States, she consulted her guidebook and
The Last of the Mohicans, which she found 'particularly interesting now we are
actually on the spot he describes so well.'[75] At Catskill Mountain she conjured
up Rip Van Winkle and in New York cited *The Water Witch*, another of James
Fenimore Cooper's novels. She read Harriet Martineau's *Society in America* in a
comfortable rocking chair in Utica, judging the style 'tiresome & prossy.'[76] An
unnamed book served on the following day as a press for two sprigs of blue-
bells 'for the sake of Bonny Scotland.'[77] The other forms of reading that served
Ellice may have included an almanac prompting her to write, 'Moon enters
first Quarter – cut your hair.'[78] She read newspapers at Quebec and Beauharnois
and later, with particular attention, when their own 'wonderful escape' was
featured in the news. At Saratoga she observed 'every one was reading the

Canada papers wth. the acct. of the affair at *Beauharnois*, occasionally stealing a glance at us to see what we looked like.'[79]

Jane Ellice's experiences as a solitary reader were framed in a series of other reading practices: intimate when she and Tina read to each other or within the family; sociable when male members of the party read aloud or recited verse and told ghost stories; and public when excerpts from newspapers were shared with a crowd. Within the Ellices' circle, books were freely borrowed and loaned or given as gifts. For Jane Ellice they were valued companions, even when Edward found her 'crying over a vol. of Sir W. Scott.'[80]

Print in the Backwoods

BERTRUM H. MACDONALD

To encourage emigration to British North America, government agencies, land companies, and individuals offered information in the form of guidebooks, which may have been among the few books that many settlers brought with them to the New World. Whether published in the home country, such as John Howison's *Sketches of Upper Canada, Domestic, Local, and Characteristic* (Edinburgh, 1821), or in the colonies, such as John Lewellin's *Emigration: Prince Edward Island; A Brief but Faithful Account* (Charlotte-Town, 1832), these compilations provided advice for those intending to emigrate.[81] In a lengthy list of items that settlers should bring with them, for example, William 'Tiger' Dunlop recommended 'books packed in barrels.'[82]

From letters that immigrants wrote to family and friends, we learn how printed materials were used and valued in the backwoods. Rural settlers had little time for reading, since the daylight hours in many months were fully occupied with agricultural activities.[83] But through reading, they sought relief from isolation and information about adapting to their new life. Publications on topics from the mundane to the scientific were studied, and books, magazines, and newspapers were borrowed from neighbours or acquired by other means. Catharine Parr Traill observed that 'every settler's library may be called a circulating one, as their books are sure to pass from friend to friend in due rotation.'[84] Although availability was a problem, and educational opportunities to develop literacy were limited, the reading interests of

8.3 Anne Langton, *Interior of John's House [Looking South]* (1837). Courtesy of the Archives of Ontario, F 1077-8-1-4-22.

backwoods residents could be as wide-ranging as their counterparts in town (see illus. 8.3, above).

Amelia Ryerse Harris, a Loyalist in Upper Canada, recorded the distress her family felt when a fire destroyed much of their first home, including 'several cases which had not been unpacked since they came from New York but had been left until a better home could be built ... the greatest loss was a Box or two of Books. Those were not to be replaced this side of New York and to a young family the loss was irreparable. A part of Pope's works, a Copy of Milton's Paradise Lost, Buchan Family Medicine, and a New Testament with commentaries was all that was saved.'[85] Intensive reading characterized Susan Burnham Greeley and her family, who lived in Haldimand Township in Upper Canada. 'We had a few very good [books] of our own that we had saved from the wreck of our fortunes in the war,' she wrote late in life, 'and these we studied over and over till I often think of what the author of WAVERLEY "says" The reason why the Scottish peasantry are so generally intelligent, is, that though they have few books, those are very good and they have to read them till they are thoroughly acquainted with the valuable information they contain, and can never forget it.'[86]

Books may have been in limited supply in many pioneer communities, but by the early decades of the nineteenth century, newspapers were becoming more common. They were often the principal reading material available to rural residents, as Anna Jameson commented.[87] Through the local papers, which reprinted news from foreign sources, settlers in remote districts were kept informed of events in Europe and the United States. They also requested papers from home. For example, William Phillips of Galt (Cambridge), Upper Canada, urged his brother in England to 'send me a newspaper as often as you can; not but we get plenty news from England, but it is all extracts, and each paper makes such extracts as suit his own politics.'[88] American newspapers such as the *Albion* of New York were also widely circulated.[89] Thomas Priestman, a settler in the Niagara District, told his brother in England in 1839: 'We have got an agraculteral paper published at Rochester in the State of N. York once a month, which I think a good deal [of]. It is both usefull and entertaining. It only costs 1/2 a dolar yearly, besides a little postage. It is prented in pamflet form and at the end of the year it makes a handsom book with a title page and index to it.'[90]

Publications on agricultural topics did not often reach rural readers in the early years, but with the formation of agricultural societies, the situation slowly changed.[91] Beginning in the late eighteenth century, province-wide and local associations were established in Nova Scotia, New Brunswick, and Lower and Upper Canada. These societies acquired, distributed, and published books and pamphlets directed to the improvement of farming.[92] The Niagara Agricultural Society, for example, acquired a 'small library on British farming,' later combined with the Niagara Library.[93] The Quebec branch of the Agricultural Society in Canada brought out *Papers and Letters on Agriculture / Papiers et lettres sur l'agriculture* in 1790, and a year later, the Society for Promoting Agriculture in the Province of Nova-Scotia published *Letters and Papers on Agriculture* (Halifax). Among the books advanced by agricultural societies was *The Letters of Agricola on the Principles of Vegetation and Tillage* (Halifax, 1822), by agricultural reformer John Young, first published in the *Acadian Recorder* between 1818 and 1821. A decade later, Joseph-François Perrault produced *Traité d'agriculture pratique ... adaptée au climat du Bas-Canada* (Quebec, 1831). William Evans's *A Treatise on the Theory and Practice of Agriculture* appeared in Montreal in 1835, and a French translation by Amury Girod the following year.[94] However, Evans's attempt to publish a journal devoted to agriculture, the *Canadian Quarterly Agricultural and Industrial Magazine*, lasted only two issues in 1838.

As early as 1770 the *Nova-Scotia Calender* was printing remedies for livestock and, in the following decade, listed fairs and markets in the province.[95] An essay, 'Sur les principes de l'agriculture,' took up almost one-sixth of the *Almanach de Québec* for 1785.[96] Almanacs directed to the farming community were first published in the early nineteenth century. *The Canadian Farmer's Almanac* for 1824,[97] printed at York (Toronto), contains several pages of hints for farmers. By the 1830s more space was being devoted to agricultural subjects. Walton and Gaylord's *Canadian Farmers' Almanac* (Sherbrooke and Stanstead) for 1838 included an eight-page essay on the improvement of swine, while Eastwood and Company's *Upper Canada Farmers' & Mechanics' Almanac* (Toronto) for 1840[98] devoted three pages to an essay entitled 'The Husbandman,' and ten to such subjects as colic and 'the gripes' in horses.

The government's continuing encouragement of the cultivation of hemp led to the publication at York in 1806 of a pamphlet in English, French, and German.[99] In 1828 Charles C. Melvin at Sandwich (Windsor), Upper Canada, compiled *Directions to Those Who Raise Tobacco in This Province* (York).[100] Also intended for settlers were early nursery catalogues. William W. Custead, of 'Dundas Street, near York,' issued his *Catalogue of Fruit & Ornamental Trees, Flowering Shrubs, Garden Seeds and Green-House Plants, Bulbous Roots & Flower Seeds* to customers in 1827.[101] His successor at the Toronto Nursery, Charles Barnhart, produced a similar catalogue in 1837.[102]

Though imported and locally published books, magazines, and newspapers were increasingly available to rural readers by 1840, reading continued to be a luxury for many, and the impact of the agricultural societies on farming practices was only gradually evident.[103]

The Uses of Literacy in the Northwest

LAURA J. MURRAY

Although the Hudson's Bay Company's main business until the twentieth century was the acquisition and sale of beaver pelts and other furs, its most substantial surviving product is paper: the company archives in Winnipeg constitute some three thousand linear metres of fur-trade documents dating back to 1671.[104] Within both the HBC and its competitor, the North West Company, literacy was the fundamental dividing line between labourers and those who had hopes of advancing to manage-

ment or ownership positions, since records, accounts, and correspondence were as
essential as furs to the success of these large trading systems, and the ability to produce or decipher writing meant access to power within the organization. The practical tie between literacy and hierarchy was reinforced by a sense among many senior
traders of the social and moral value of literacy. Beyond the demands of their employment, these men also used writing for personal reflection, ethnographic observation, and correspondence with like-minded friends, and even more fervently than
their contemporaries in Britain and New England, they considered literacy a prime
marker of civilization. In the non-business writings of fur traders intended for publication, scenes of reading and writing often seem to serve as antidotes to anxiety
about isolation and cultural contamination; in their private correspondence, arrangements for the exchange of reading material appear with frequency. The writings of
fur traders also suggest, however, that their authors inhabited a world of multiple
literacies, in which the ability of traders to interpret the behaviour of their suppliers
and neighbours, and of voyageurs and Native people to interpret the landscape and
the multilingual spoken word, was of much greater practical and cultural significance than factors and bourgeois may have recognized or admitted in writing.

The many journals, memoirs, ethnographic studies, and travel accounts produced
by fur traders cannot all be enumerated here, but a sample will suggest their range
of genre, the various circumstances behind them, and their different modes of circulation. Willard Ferdinand Wentzel's 1802 journal of the daily doings at (Great) Slave
Lake was a requirement of his position, and although it makes lively reading, it ends
sourly with a complaint: 'I hope the Company will not censure me for want of attention ... I received but 1 quire to Keep a Journal, write letters, *engagements* & give tickets
to upwards of 60 Indians last winter ... [T]herefore for the future if *exact* a Journal
from me they will[,] Please give me Paper to Keep one.'[105] In contrast, James Isham
wrote his lovingly illustrated 'Observations on Hudson's Bay' during the winter of
1743 on his own initiative, 'Being in a Disconsolate part of the world, where there is
Little conversation or Divertisment to be had,' in order to prevent 'that too common
Malady the Vapour's.'[106] Roderick Mackenzie's 'Some Account of the North West
Company,' a compendium of ethnographic information solicited from other fur traders and cross-indexed with sources as diverse as Herodotus, Lewis and Clark, Ossian,
and Johann Reinhold Forster's *History of the Voyages and Discoveries Made in the North*
(1786), was a project that he compiled after his retirement. He seems never to have
sought publication, but he was invited to join the American Antiquarian Society and
other scholarly societies on the strength of his research, and the materials he amassed

now constitute a major documentary source for the North West Company.[107] Daniel Williams Harmon sought the editorial help of a Vermont minister when he published his journal, after circulating it first among colleagues and family; it contains almost no fur-trade business but much self-reflection. John Tanner, captured in 1789 in Kentucky and raised as Anishinabe, dictated his memoir of life on the 'supply side' of the fur trade to Edwin James, a doctor at Sault Ste Marie (Michigan), and it was subsequently published in New York. Joseph Robson, Edward Umfreville, and others found patrons in England eager to publish their attacks on the Hudson's Bay Company, and Sir Joseph Banks may have sponsored Alexander Henry's colourful *Travels and Adventures in Canada and the Indian Territories* (New York, 1809). Others who desired publication were not so lucky. David Thompson, for example, was never able to afford to publish his memoirs, from which he had hoped to gain both money and renown in his old age.[108] For Alexander Mackenzie, whose exploration narrative would be widely read and earn him a knighthood, the pressure to publish became so great that he found himself on the edge of a breakdown as he edited his journals.[109]

Much of this fur-trade writing can be seen as response and contribution within a rich culture of reading among the superior officers and owners of the fur trade. Many literate traders wrote only in the line of duty, but for others, writing, be it private or public, created a virtual conversation with the world by which they measured themselves. Books, newspapers, and magazines were more available than one might expect in the Northwest, when we consider the cost and inconvenience of transporting them thousands of miles by ship and canoe.[110] Several HBC posts – Fort Vancouver (Vancouver, Washington) and Fort George (Prince George), for example – housed small lending libraries, primarily for the use of officers. Letters between traders often noted the exchange of books and periodicals, the latter being not only of interest in themselves but an important source of information about new books, which might then be ordered. Joseph Colen claimed to have a library of 1,400 volumes at York Factory in the 1790s, and the surveyor Peter Fidler donated his personal collection of 500 volumes to the Red River Library upon his death in 1822. Like the smaller collections of many of their contemporaries, these libraries included a range of material, from scientific treatises and nautical almanacs to history and fiction.[111] Traders also read literature about the Northwest. Isham, for example, had read Louis Hennepin, who himself recalled that while at 'Catarokouy' (Kingston), he 'gave [him]self much to the reading of Voyages,' which 'encreas'd [his] Ambition' for exploration.[112] Jonathan Carver draws from several previous sources, but Peter Pond, who knew the same country and people well, had little time for this second-hand information, complaining in his unpublished account that 'when [Carver] a Leudes to Hearsase he flies from facts in two Maney Instances.'[113]

Traders rarely refer to the practical use of books, though they had many technical guides and tables to hand; they emphasize instead their moral power. The Bible is sometimes mentioned as a source of guidance – stalled by wind on his first trip up the Ottawa River, Daniel Harmon 'past the Day in reading the Bible and in meditating on my present way of living, which appears to me to resemble too much that of a Savage' – but any book at all could be ascribed moral force.[114] David Thompson reported not only Samuel Hearne's declaration that Voltaire's dictionary was 'his belief, and he had no other,' but his neighbour Nor'Wester William Thorburn's low opinion of his French predecessors at Cross Lake: 'With a slight education, if any, and no books, when in their wintering houses they passed their time in card playing, gambling and dancing; which brought on disputes, quarrels and all respect was lost.' At Cumberland House in 1787, the young Thompson encountered what he took to be a warning of what he too could become in the person of a former classmate from London. 'He had been here about thirteen years, had lost all his education except reading and writing and the little of this, for the accounts of the trade appeared labor to him: he appeared in a state of apathy smoking tobacco mixed with weed, had no conversation with any person ... When we left school a Hadley's quadrant and Robertson's elements of navigation in two volumes were presented to each scholar ... I enquired if he had his, he said they had vanished long ago: here again no book, not even a bible.'[115] For Thompson, the careless loss of the navigational guide powerfully marks his classmate's downfall. Similarly, even account books had symbolic resonance for Wentzel. In 1814 he found pages of them strewn about 'in the Garret of the *Athabasca House*, mingled with the old useless *agrês* of Canoes[.] Some upon the Beams, others among the old Sails, old Kettles, Spunges, &c., &c,' and he concluded that '*one thing* Kept Pace with *another* in the decline of *once famed* Athabasca – Formerly the delight and School of the North.'[116]

The writing of fur traders presents many striking images of the act and the occasion of reading (see illus. 8.4, p. 191). William Fraser Tolmie, serving the HBC on the west coast of North America in the 1830s, used reading to transport himself home: 'Occupied till dinner time in looking over numbers of the Edr. Evg. Post, Chambers's Journal. Penny magazine & the Day – the two middle contained much useful information. Cannot justify to myself this infringing on the regular course of reading, to wit Guthrie's Geography &c but the day has not been lost as I have added a little to my stock of knowledge & while poring over these records of the past, reviews &c, old thoughts & musings come on & I almost fancy myself again in the civilized world.'

8.4 Henry James Warre, *Sir George Simpson Passing the Chats Falls, Ottawa River, in a Hudson's Bay Company Canoe* (1841). Courtesy of the Royal Ontario Museum, 995.21.92.

The cultural distance between the *Edinburgh Evening Post* and life at Fort Nisqually was as large as the physical distance, and this impression is amplified by passages in which Tolmie describes himself reading William Cowper's 'Progress of Error' as he is being paddled up the Columbia or 'sitting in the door of Bastion reading the article Duelling in the Young Mans Best Companion' while his men squared logs for the construction of a new fort.[117] Daniel Harmon's journal presents another striking example of cultural disjuncture: 'Fine weather,' he wrote in 1800 near Roche Capitaine on the Ottawa River. 'Part of the Day I have passed in reading [Fanny Burney's] Camelia or the Picture of Youth, and the remainder in shooting Pigeons and gathering Berries.'[118]

When Harmon looked up from his books, he was in fact surrounded by another form of inscription, petroglyphs, and other kinds of narration in Native and voyageur accounts, legends, and tall tales about features of the landscape, deaths and adventures, and customs of the trade. He was not literate with regard to these texts, just as he did not know how to read a rapid or a set of animal tracks. David Thompson noted that 'the removal of the smallest stone, the bent or broken twig; a slight mark on the ground, all spoke plain language to' his Native guide, a language he was eager to learn.[119] Though few fur traders shared Thompson's curiosity, their writings often inadvertently contextualize European literacy within a web of other literacies. A striking example can be found in the journals of Alexander Mackenzie. As he approached the Pacific Ocean, he reports, 'I was very much surprised by the following question from one of the Indians: "What," demanded he, "can be the reason that you are so particular and anxious in your inquiries of us respecting a knowledge of this country: do not you white men know every thing in the world?" This interrogatory was so very unexpected, that it occasioned some hesitation before I could answer it. At length, however, I replied, that we certainly were acquainted with the principal circumstances of every part of the world; that I knew where the sea is, and where I myself then was, but that I did not exactly understand what obstacles might interrupt me in getting to it; with which, he and his relations must be well acquainted, as they had so frequently surmounted them.' Mackenzie was lucky that his guides supplemented his practically useless book learning and navigational expertise by taking him on to the Pacific, where despite evidence that he was not the first European there, he 'mixed up some vermilion in melted grease, and inscribed, in large characters, on the South-East face of the rock on which we had slept last night, this brief memorial – "Alexander Mackenzie, from Canada, by land, the twenty-second of July, one thousand seven hundred and ninety-three."'[120] While this was a familiar European ritual of discovery, it is important to note that the rocks of the Pacific Coast were covered with such inscriptions. Vermilion, a major trade good, was most often used to express rather different relationships of self to land than Mackenzie's. His writing might have resembled a pictograph to those who saw it over the following years, and perhaps even been perceived as a documentation of his encounter with spirit power.

European printed texts, too, had multiple meanings in the Northwest. At Cumberland House in 1776, a Chipewyan chief showed Alexander Henry a collection of 'small prints; the identical ones, which, in England, are commonly sold in sheets to children, but each of which was here transformed into a talisman, for the cure of some evil, or obtention of some delight: – No. 1. "A sailor kissing his mistress, on his return from sea"; – this, worn about the person of a gallant, attracted, though conceled, the affections of the sex! No. 2. "A soldier in arms"; – this poured a sentiment of valour into the possessor, and gave him the strength of a giant!'[121] Henry accused HBC traders of duping the Chipewyans into attributing magical properties to the prints, but it is also possible that the Chipewyans themselves generated these explanations or considered them compatible with their beliefs. In another reinterpretation that really amounts to a reinvention of a European text, the Nlaka'pamux (Thompson) people of the interior of British Columbia include in their oral tradition a story in which God sends Coyote to fix the problems that Jesus was unable to solve. Daniel Harmon, who lived nearby not long before the arrival of the missionaries who are one distant source of this story, did not read this in *his* Bible.[122]

Obviously, then, the uses of literacy in the early Northwest cannot be simply characterized, but we can at least see that interpreting texts was a skill widely held, if variously practised, throughout the region. While writings by fur traders emphasize the value of alphabetic literacy, they also contain evidence of alternative literacies.

chapter 9

THE PLEASURES OF BOOKS

Picturing Readers

PATRICIA LOCKHART FLEMING

Conventions of portraiture familiar to early settlers in North America identified the book as an attribute of piety or culture, while shelves of books underscored learning and authority.[1] Whether formally trained or working in a vernacular tradition, artists observed these customs to characterize readers and their books throughout the colonial period. Among the earliest images are portraits, sometimes painted posthumously, of members of religious orders in New France. A well-known example of this genre is the likeness of Marie de l'Incarnation (1672), remarkable as one of the very few depictions of a woman with a shelf of books, finely bound in calf and vellum, rather than a single volume.[2] Women who sat for a likeness in the eighteenth and early nineteenth century were often captured as interrupted readers, holding an open book, put aside but carefully marked with a thumb or finger to allow the subject to engage a spectator directly before resuming her reading. Phoebe Willcocks Baldwin of York (Toronto) was painted by William Berczy in 1803 (see illus. 9.1, p. 195), about the time of her marriage to William Warren Baldwin, who was trained in both medicine and law. Described years later by her son Robert as 'the master mind of our family,' Phoebe Baldwin holds a small book, leather-bound and typical of serious private reading in this period.[3] In Montreal, Sarah Solomon (Solomons), wife of businessman and politician Thomas McCord, was painted in a similar pose by

9.1 William Berczy, *Phoebe Willcocks Baldwin* (1803–4). Courtesy of private owner.

Louis Dulongpré in 1816 (see illus. 9.2, p. 196). Little is known of her life, but among his civic offices McCord was a director of the Montreal Library.[4] It is revealing to compare the portrait of Sarah Solomon with that of Frances Brooke, author of *The History of Emily Montague*, an epistolary novel set in Quebec and published in London in 1769 (see illus. 14.2, p. 358). Brooke, painted in London by Catherine Read in 1771, holds her book close and appears to be more intimately engaged with the text, an impression enhanced by both her expression and the position of her arms and hands.

In other portraits of women, particularly in the 1830s, books shrink in size as dresses expand in volume and complexity. Two Montreal portraits from 1836 by Antoine Plamondon of Madame Thomas B. Wragg and Madame John Redpath show small books held somewhat unconvincingly amidst a sea of silk.[5] Following a similar fashion in rural New Brunswick, Thomas MacDonald, an itinerant painter, celebrated the material prosperity of settlers along the Saint John River in the 1820s and 1830s. Typical of his subjects is Eliza Jane McNally, painted at Fredericton in 1833.[6] She is dressed elaborately and seated in a stylish wooden chair holding her book firmly

9.2 Louis Dulongpré, *Portrait of Sarah Solomon* (1816). Courtesy of the McCord Museum of Canadian History, Montreal, M8355.

closed. In other MacDonald paintings the book becomes a bouquet, both book and flowers symbolizing leisure, order, and culture, hard won in a colonial economy.

A second portrait of Phoebe Baldwin with her granddaughter, Robert's eldest child, Phoebe Maria, shows her as both reader and teacher (see illus. 9.3, p. 198). It is said that she was 'probably responsible for Robert's earliest education,'[7] and after the death of his young wife and his increasing political responsibilities, she may have continued her role in reading instruction within the family circle. In this scene the unnamed artist has taken care to identify two of three books in the foreground: to the left facing the viewer is *The Ladies Magazine* in a blue paper wrapper; Maria's dog-eared pamphlet in orange paper is titled 'Infan[t] Hymns.' The large open book, printed in two columns, is undoubtedly a Bible.

Although paintings of men holding a single book are not uncommon in folk art or religious portraiture, scenes of men in their libraries constitute a more significant genre. An early example, once thought to be a self-portrait of William Berczy himself, shows a reader at ease with a well-used collection of books in various formats and finishes, shelved for convenience not for show (see illus. 9.4, p. 198). Mary Allodi has suggested that the sitter may be William Warren Baldwin, painted near the time of his marriage to Phoebe Willcocks.[8] If these portraits of the young couple are indeed a pair, they follow a pattern of conjugal readers, the woman with a single book and the man with a library. This is fully developed in the depictions of Justus Earle and Ann Earle by Thomas MacDonald (see illus. 9.5 and 9.6, p. 198). Mrs Earle, seated by a window, is an interrupted reader gazing away from a large religious book, while her husband is shown reading an elaborately bound volume, his window on the world a crowded shelf of books.

In another example of this genre, a slight disordering of the shelves forming a backdrop to Jean-Baptiste Roy-Audy's portrait *Monseigneur Rémy Gaulin* appears to be motivated by a wish to display the richly coloured edges of these fine sets of books rather than to suggest their use (see illus. 9.7, p. 199). Bishop of Kingston in Upper Canada, Gaulin is pictured with a library of religious works, substantial folios and quartos minutely lettered on the spine with title and volume number. Gaulin's likeness is similar in luxury and narrative detail to Antoine Plamondon's 1836 painting of Louis-Joseph Papineau, robed for office as speaker of the Assembly, where a careful selection of authors defines the Patriote leader: Aristotle, Cicero, Demosthenes, Charles James Fox, Thomas Jefferson, and *L'esprit des lois* of Charles de Secondat, Baron de Montesquieu.[9] More modestly armed for clerical duties in Henry Alline's New Light movement in Nova Scotia, the sombre Reverend John Payzant is shown with a Bible on his shelf and, in the foreground, a well-thumbed pamphlet from the 'Tract and Bible Society London,' dated some thirty years earlier (see illus. 9.8, p. 199). In Anthony Flower's 1824 portrait of Society for the Propagation of the Gospel missionary Robert Willis, open books speak for the clergyman (see illus. 9.9, p. 199). Printed in a compact format useful for travel in rural New Brunswick, where Flower farmed and painted, the texts are in two columns, possibly an Old Testament and the Gospels.[10] Far to the west at the Red River Settlement, a Native orator speaks for his people in Peter Rindisbacher's watercolour of a council meeting in 1823, but the shelves of books and wall maps, balanced by the British flag, suggest that power rests with the lettered minority (see illus. 9.10, p. 200).

Portraits of actual readers are less common in the early nineteenth century than later, when intimate glimpses of reading women were in vogue and painters such as Ozias Leduc and George Reid celebrated the absorption of young people in a book. One such reader pictured in this volume is Joseph Frederick Wallet DesBarres, whose achievements in mapping the east coast of North America are discussed by Bertrum H. MacDonald in chapter 12 (see illus. 12.3, p. 299). Other avid readers never captured

9.3 Anonymous portrait of Phoebe Baldwin with her granddaughter Phoebe Maria Baldwin (1833?). Courtesy of the Toronto Public Library (TRL).

9.4 William Berczy, *Man with a Bookcase* [possibly William Warren Baldwin] (1798–1804). Courtesy of the Royal Ontario Museum, 968.298.2.

9.5 Thomas MacDonald, *Mrs Ann Earle, Aged 57* (1820). Courtesy of the New Brunswick Museum, Saint John. Provenance: Brenda Dunsmore. Acc. no 2002.48.1.

9.6 Thomas MacDonald, *Mr Justus Earle, Aged 71* (1820). Courtesy of the New Brunswick Museum, Saint John. Provenance: Brenda Dunsmore, Acc. no. 2002.48.2.

9.7 Jean-Baptiste Roy-Audy, *Monseigneur Rémy Gaulin* (1838). Courtesy of the Musée national des beaux-arts du Québec, 56.469. Photograph: Jean-Guy Kérouac.

9.8 Anonymous portrait of John Payzant (1832). Courtesy of the Queen's County Museum, Liverpool, Nova Scotia.

9.9 Anthony Flower, Portrait of R. Wells [probably Robert Willis] (1824). Courtesy of the Beaverbrook Art Gallery, Fredericton, New Brunswick. Gift of Mr James H. Flower, 1987.

9.10 Peter Rindisbacher, *Captain Bulger, Governor of Assiniboia, and the Chiefs and Warriors of the Chippewa Tribe of Red Lake, in Council in the Colony House in Fort Douglas, May 22nd, 1823* (1823–4). Courtesy of the McCord Museum of Canadian History, Montreal, M965.9.

by an artist leave self-portraits by marking their books to talk to themselves, to the author, and to other readers.[11] A dramatic example of marginalia is found in James Wolfe's copy of Thomas Gray's *Elegy Written in a Country Churchyard*, which he is said to have read the night before the assault on the capital of New France, remarking, 'I would rather be the author of that piece than take Quebec.'[12] When the troops in his command defeated the French the following day, both Wolfe and the opposing commander, the Marquis de Montcalm, died. In Wolfe's copy of the elegy, a gift from his fiancée, he had marked five of the seven pages with comments and underlining, including 'The paths of glory lead but to the grave' (see illus. 9.11, p. 201).

The special relationship between author and text has already been noted in the portrait of Frances Brooke. Other examples in these pages are Ludger Duvernay holding a manuscript of his newspaper *La Minerve* (see illus. 4.2, p. 76) and Adam Kidd, whose determination to promote his own poetry is captured in a portrait where he extends to the viewer a volume bound in the patterned paper often used in Lower Canada (see illus. 14.1, p. 343). The more resilient John Galt, an established author

(7)

The boaſt of heraldry, the pomp of pow'r,
And all that beauty, all that wealth e'er gave,
Await alike th' inevitable hour.
The paths of glory lead but to the grave.

  Nor you, ye Proud, impute to Theſe the fault,
If Mem'ry o'er their Tomb no Trophies raiſe,
Where thro' the long-drawn iſle and fretted vault
The pealing anthem ſwells the note of praiſe.

  Can ſtoried urn or animated buſt
Back to its manſion call the fleeting breath?
Can Honour's voice provoke the ſilent duſt,
Or Flatt'ry ſooth the dull cold ear of Death?

  Perhaps in this neglected ſpot is laid
Some heart once pregnant with celeſtial fire;
Hands, that the rod of empire might have ſway'd,
Or wak'd to extaſy the living lyre.

  But Knowledge to their eyes her ample page
Rich with the ſpoils of Time did ne'er unroll;
Chill Penury repreſs'd their noble rage,
And froze the genial current of the ſoul.

Full

How ineffectual are often our own unaided exertions - especially in early Life? How many shining Lights owe to Patronage & Affluence what their Talents wd never procure them!

9.11 James Wolfe's copy of Thomas Gray's *Elegy Written in a Country Churchyard* (London, 1754). Courtesy of the Thomas Fisher Rare Book Library, University of Toronto.

who had written himself out of imprisonment for debt before Samuel Oliver Tazewell's lithograph appeared in the *Canadian Literary Magazine* in 1833, is recognized equally in this portrait for his role in colonizing the Huron Tract and for his biography of Byron (see illus. 10.8, p. 248).

Scenes of outdoor reading in British North America include natural landscapes, such as the harbour of Placentia in the eighteenth century described by William Barker in chapter 15 (see illus. 15.2, p. 364) and one of the legendary canoe trips of Hudson's Bay Company governor Sir George Simpson (see illus. 8.4, p. 191). Among domestic scenes of reading, William Berczy's *The Woolsey Family* (1809) shows a child reading by the window amidst the cultivated pleasures of a Quebec merchant's household.[13] A telling detail in this conversation piece is an issue of a newspaper, the *Canadian Courant and Montreal Advertiser*, partly concealed by the grandmother's sewing basket. Informal, autobiographical scenes of family reading were sketched by Jane Ellice at the seigneury of Beauharnois (see illus. 8.2, p. 183) and by Anne Langton, who pictures her family reading by lamplight (see illus. 8.1, p. 174). A more explicitly autobiographical self-portrait of a reader with his books is that of Robert-Shore-Milnes Bouchette with his caged bird, in prison in Montreal after the first Patriote rebellion and before his exile to Bermuda (see illus. 13.2, p. 329).

Child readers in the colonial period were pictured much as their parents, holding books as symbols of learning, culture, and prosperity. Informal scenes of reading instruction characterized here by the Baldwins are elaborated in classrooms such as James Peachey's etching of Mohawk children with their schoolmaster (see illus. 12.2, p. 283).

Personal Libraries and Bibliophilia

MARCEL LAJEUNESSE

A newly created country does not provide the most fertile ground for the development of a culture of the book and a taste for beautiful books. However, the first Europeans who passed through or settled in North America had come from a civilization of printing, and for them, books were tools of work, knowledge, or culture.

Large libraries were thus to be found in New France – for example, those belonging to the priests Philippe and Nicolas-Michel Boucher and to Claude-Thomas Dupuy, Louis Rouer de Villeray, and Michel Sarrazin.[14] However, simply owning books or having a library does not make the owner a bibliophile. Bibliophilia is the love of fine books: the pleasure of owning rare and valuable books, first editions, illustrated books, those with beautiful bindings.[15] In the eighteenth century, Louis-Guillaume Verrier and François-Étienne Cugnet could justly have been called bibliophiles. Verrier, attorney to the Conseil supérieur and a professor of law, put together the largest library in New France, containing more than 1,000 titles in 3,000 volumes and reflecting his scholarship in law and jurisprudence. Upon his death in 1751, Cugnet, who had arrived in New France as director of the Domaine d'Occident, left a library of 1,250 volumes on subjects such as literature, astronomy, and agriculture, an indication of his humanist and literary interests.[16] The priests Charles-Joseph Brassard Deschenaux and Jean-Baptiste Boucher, *dit* Belleville, who also had large libraries, revealed their true nature as bibliophiles through the quality of the books they collected and the eclecticism of their choices. Moreover, they generously put their libraries of more than 2,000 volumes at the disposal of the priests in their region.

A number of the libraries assembled between 1650 and 1840 (see table 9.1, pp. 204–5) stood out from the rest, notably those of Pierre-Amable De Bonne, Amable Berthelot, John Fleming, Charles Rufus Fairbanks, Robert Addison, Jonathan Sewell, and Richard John Uniacke. The composition of Judge De Bonne's library reveals a man of taste and a bibliophile imbued with the spirit of the Enlightenment.[17] Montreal businessman John Fleming holds a particular place in this company. With pronounced cultural interests, this author of poetry, polemics, and works on economics had a library of more than 10,000 volumes, including rare books and works in English, French, Spanish, and Latin. The auction of his collection is discussed by Yvan Lamonde and Andrea Rotundo in chapter 6. Lawyer Charles Rufus Fairbanks of Halifax owned a library evaluated at £500, a considerable sum at the time, which was 'one of his principal indulgences.'[18] Fur trader Peter Fidler's knowledge and uncommon love of books were evident in the 500-volume library that he built at Red River in the early decades of the nineteenth century.[19]

We know of the existence of a good number of personal libraries through the inventories and catalogues published for the book auctions that followed a death or a departure for Europe.[20] For François-Étienne Cugnet, for example, there were two catalogues, one drawn up at the time of his bankruptcy in 1741–2 and the other upon his death in 1751. A catalogue was prepared for the sale of Amable Berthelot's library in 1832, when he was leaving for a stay in Europe. Abbé Charles-

Table 9.1 Some of the most important personal libraries, 1650–1840

Name	Profession/position	Place	Size of the collection/Approximate number of books
1650–1700			
Rouer de Villeray, Louis	Notary, member of the Conseil souverain	Quebec	34 titles in 42 vols.
1700–1750			
Dupuy, Claude-Thomas	Lawyer, intendant	Quebec	575 titles in 1,045 vols.
Sarrazin, Michel	Physician, naturalist	Quebec	212 vols.
Verrier, Louis-Guillaume	Attorney of the Conseil supérieur	Quebec	997 titles in 3,000 vols.
1750–1800			
Bailly de Messein, Charles-François	Coadjutant bishop of Quebec	Quebec – Neuville	1,200 vols.
Boiret, Urbain	Superior of the Séminaire de Québec	Quebec	180 vols.
Cugnet, François-Étienne	Lawyer, seigneur, surveyor	Quebec	1,250 vols.
Dosque, Bernard-Sylvestre	Curé at Quebec	Quebec	330 vols.
Landriaux, Louis-Nicolas	Surgeon	Montreal	'outstanding' medical library *DCB*, vol. 4
Nesbitt, William	Lawyer, office holder	Halifax	'extensive library' *DCB*, vol. 4
1800–1840			
Addison, Robert	Church of England minister	Niagara	1,500 vols.
Allan, William	Businessman, office holder, judge, politician	York (Toronto)	332 vols. (bureaucrat's catalogue of 1824)
Berthelot, Amable	Lawyer, politician, author	Quebec	1,500 vols.
Boucher, Jean-Baptiste, *dit* Belleville	Priest and author	Laprairie	800 titles in 2,000 vols.
Brassard Deschenaux, Charles-Joseph	Priest and seigneur	Quebec	800 titles in 2,200 vols.
Brock, Sir Isaac	Army officer and colonial administrator	York (Toronto)	130 vols. + 'many books' (Auction, 4 Jan. 1813)

Table 9.1 Some of the most important personal libraries, 1650–1840 (*concluded*)

Name	Profession/position	Place	Size of the collection/ Approximate number of books
Cartier, Jacques	Businessman, politician	Saint-Antoine-sur-Richelieu	library on history and law *DCB*, vol. 5
Cartwright, John Solomon	Lawyer, author, politician, businessman	Kingston	'books on a vast range of subjects' *DCB*, vol. 8
Cherrier, Jacques	Priest	Saint-Denis-sur-Richelieu	400 vols.
Coffin, Thomas Aston	Office holder	Quebec	600 vols.
De Bonne, Pierre-Amable	Lawyer, judge, seigneur, politician	Quebec	251 titles in 529 vols.
Denaut, Pierre	Bishop of Quebec	Quebec	106 titles in 418 vols.
Fairbanks, Charles Rufus	Lawyer, politician, office holder, businessman	Halifax	library worth £500 *DCB*, vol. 7
Fargue, Thomas	Physician, office holder	Quebec	'one of the best private medical libraries in the colony' *DCB*, vol. 7
Fidler, Peter	Fur trader, explorer	Dauphin, Manitoba	500 vols.
Fleming, John	Businessman, author	Montreal	4,000 titles in 10,000 vols.
Foretier, Pierre	Businessman, seigneur, office holder	Montreal	389 vols.
Grant, William	Businessman, politician, office holder	Quebec	600 vols.
Hart, Ezekiel	Businessman, politician, seigneur	Trois-Rivières	remarkable library *DCB*, vol. 7
Painchaud, Charles-François	Priest	Sainte-Anne-de-la-Pocatière	566 vols.
Papineau, Joseph	Notary, politician, seigneur	Montreal	200 vols.
Perreault, Jacques-Nicolas	Merchant, seigneur, politician	Rivière-Ouelle	300 vols.
Plessis, Joseph-Octave	Bishop of Quebec	Quebec	2,166 vols.
Quesnel, Joseph	Businessman, composer, author	Montreal	725 vols.
Robinson, Joseph	Judge, politician, author	Charlottetown	'Valuable Library' *DCB*, vol. 5
Sewell, Jonathan	Office holder, lawyer, author, politician	Quebec	1,476 vols.
Sewell, Stephen	Lawyer, landowner, bureaucrat, politician	Montreal	800 vols.
Uniacke, Richard John	Lawyer, office holder, politician	Halifax	760 titles in 1,800 vols.
Whyte, James Matthew	Businessman	Hamilton	1,000 vols.

François Painchaud compiled his own catalogue around 1825,[21] while John Fleming's magnificent library merited an individual catalogue.[22] The great majority of personal libraries were dispersed at auction, their contents enriching other nascent or established libraries. A few were passed on to heirs, as was the case for the libraries of Jacques Cartier, Ezekiel Hart, Jonathan Sewell, and Richard John Uniacke; the library of Robert Addison was preserved in his parish at Niagara (Niagara-on-the-Lake).

Some collectors developed their passion for books through contact with a bibliophile. During his professional training between 1825 and 1830, François-Xavier Garneau made good use of the excellent library of notary Archibald Campbell. Similarly, in the early nineteenth century, Louis-Joseph Papineau and Augustin-Norbert Morin were apprenticed in law to Denis-Benjamin Viger, and access to his rich library awakened their love of books. Amable Berthelot and Georges-Barthélemi Faribault became bibliophiles as well, following their time as articled clerks with Jean-Antoine Panet, whose library was well known for its quality.

Ex libris in New France, Quebec, and Lower Canada

FRÉDÉRIC ROUSSEL BEAULIEU

An ex libris is the bibliophile's method of indicating his or her ownership of a book, often by means of a label or bookplate pasted inside.[23] It may take the form of a signature, a heraldic engraving, a label with a printed text, an allegorical illustration, or a mark inside the book or on the binding.[24]

Since there was no press to print labels in New France in the seventeenth century, the clergy, merchants, and the few book owners from the working classes simply used a signature as their ex libris. The Jesuits, for example, inserted a hand-written inscription: *colleg. quebec. Soc. Jes. Cat. Inscr. an. 1720* (see illus. 3.2, p. 57). Some missionaries had a modest label printed in France. On the other hand, French nobles, who formed a majority among the colonial elite, preferred the heraldic ex libris.[25] Following the example of intendant Gilles Hocquart, they had bookplates engraved and printed in France. Their coats of arms and mottoes took the place of a signa-

9.12 Detail of binding with the arms of Jean Talon, intendant of New France, 1665–8 and 1670–2, on a copy of Joanne Ludovico de la Cerda Toletano, *P. Virgillii Maronis posteriores sex libri Aeneidos argumentatis explicationibus notis illustrati* (Lugduni [Lyon], 1617). Courtesy of the Musée de l'Amérique française, Quebec.

ture,[26] since heraldic imagery represented the bearer of the arms without use of the alphabet. Others, such as the intendants Jean Talon and Jacques Duchesneau de La Doussinière et d'Ambault, had their coats of arms impressed on the bindings of their books (see illus. 9.12, above).[27]

From their first years in business at Quebec, William Brown and Thomas Gilmore printed labels to order, supplying, for example, '200 of his Names for Books'[28] to Williams Conyngham, king's procurator in 1765. In the early 1770s, Canadiens also ordered labels, the first among them being Bernard-Sylvestre Dosque, curé at Quebec from 1769 to 1774, and François Le Guerne, curé in Saint-François-de-Sales, on Île d'Orléans, from 1758 to 1789 (see illus. 9.13, p. 208). In time, bibliophiles who would

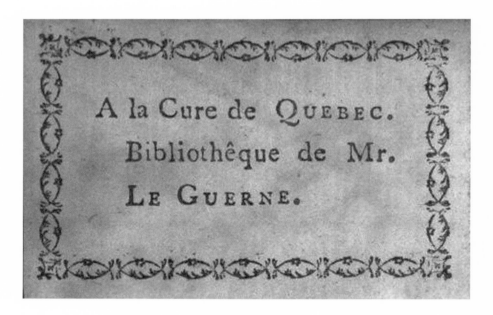

9.13 Printed ex libris of François Le Guerne, curé on Île d'Orléans, 1758–89; affixed to a copy of
Jacques Cassini, *Éléments d'astronomie par Mr Cassini, maître des comptes de l'Academie royale des sciences
et de la Société royale de Londres* (Paris, 1740). Courtesy of the Musée de l'Amérique française, Quebec.

become bishops, such as Joseph-Octave Plessis, Joseph Signay, and Pierre-Flavien
Turgeon, followed suit.

Between 1791 and 1840, signatures were the most widespread form of ex libris.
However, some community libraries, lawyers, judges, doctors, members of the clergy,
and, occasionally, women had labels printed. The manuscript ex libris of Cécile Nicot,
dit Saint-Laurent, of Quebec and the labels she had printed in 1833 illustrate this
trend well.[29] John Neilson, who succeeded his uncle William Brown at Quebec, continued to print 'Names' for book owners, filling orders of from fifty to six hundred
copies.[30] Whether ornate or simple, these printed labels did not replace the heraldic
ex libris. The bookplate of Sir James Stuart, chief justice of Lower Canada from 1838,
is one example; others can be found in the work of James Smillie, the Quebec engraver.[31] Changes in the form of the ex libris were linked both to historical development within the colony and to influences from abroad. By the mid-nineteenth century, the printed label had gained in popularity, but it remained, with few exceptions, simple in design.

The Library of Richard John Uniacke

JOHN MACLEOD

Nova Scotia attorney general Richard John Uniacke died at his 11,000-acre estate, Mount Uniacke, in 1830.[32] Born into a prominent Irish family, he had left for the New World at the age of twenty, probably because of differences with his father over his support of Irish nationalists. During the American Revolution, he was charged with treason but avoided a trial in Halifax when friends intervened. He then resumed his legal studies in Dublin, and by 1781 he had returned to Nova Scotia to practise. Great wealth followed from his appointment in 1784 as advocate general of the Vice-Admiralty Court, said to have generated over £50,000 in fees during the Napoleonic Wars and the War of 1812. His estate, with its Georgian mansion, now a museum, attests to his success.

A probate inventory of Uniacke's property after his death records a library of 260 titles in 800 volumes (see illus. 9. 14, p. 210). Another 500 law titles in 1,000 volumes were in his law office at his house in Halifax.[33] Today 280 titles remain at the Uniacke Estate Museum Park as evidence of the collecting and reading tastes of one of Nova Scotia's early leaders.[34] Many of the books reveal how he acquired them. Gifts from children and items formerly owned by mentors or ancestors are among the volumes. Sons studying abroad were given shopping lists.[35] A bibliophile who possessed his own binding tools,[36] Uniacke built complete sets using volumes from different editions, which would be rebound uniformly.[37]

His deep interest in current affairs and constitutional issues is evident in such titles as John Dickinson's *Letters from a Farmer in Pennsylvania to the Inhabitants of the British Colonies* (1774). Trade, commerce, and economic potential also drew his attention. These areas represent 44 per cent of the titles on his shelves.[38] Fiction accounts for 16.5 per cent, and religious and moral works for 11.5 per cent. An agricultural reformer, he acquired the current treatises on peat bogs, hemp, fruit trees, and livestock. He was also intrigued by the scientific advances of the day, and he owned science books and performed experiments using the apparatus he kept in the library.[39]

The overall average publication date of the titles remaining in Uniacke's library is 1781. When the books are analyzed by subject, science and technology average a very current 1794. For the nearly 45 per cent of the collection constituting history and geography, the average date is 1780, suggesting that these were lifelong interests.

9.14 Heraldic bookplate of Richard John Uniacke (1801). Courtesy of the Nova Scotia Archives and Records Management.

The religious material has an average date of 1774, while that of the literary works is 1781.[40] Irish imprints represent 16 per cent, English 68, and Scottish 10. Few of the books are American. Though no Nova Scotian imprints survive in the library, the 1830 inventory lists Uniacke's compilation of the laws of Nova Scotia, which he published in Halifax in 1805.[41] The inventory also records Thomas Chandler Haliburton's *An Historical and Statistical Account of Nova-Scotia*, published in Halifax the previous year. Despite many gaps, Richard John Uniacke's library provides a valuable insight into the intellectual interests of someone who was at the heart of Nova Scotia's political and cultural life.

Robert Addison's Library

RICHARD LANDON

When Robert Addison (1754–1829)[42] arrived at Newark (Niagara-on-the-Lake), Upper Canada, in July 1792, as a missionary of the Society for the Propagation of the Gospel, he brought with him a library of some 1,500 books dating from the sixteenth, seventeenth, and eighteenth centuries.[43] It was the largest private collection in the province.

Addison had been educated at Trinity College, Cambridge. Ordained a deacon in 1781, he served as curate at Upwell, Norfolk, for much of the following decade, when he also acquired his book collection. Several volumes are signed on the fly-leaf by William Beale, vicar of nearby Whittlesea St Mary from 1742 to 1772, and Richard Atkinson, who had preceded Addison as curate. It seems likely that he acquired their libraries in 1781 and added to them before his departure for Upper Canada.

His collection is typical for someone of his financial means at the time. It contains a large component of theology, especially the controversial commentaries and sermons of the seventeenth and eighteenth centuries. Among them are thirteen works by Offspring Blackall, bishop of Exeter; twelve by Thomas Bennet, including his 'confutations' of both popery (1701) and Quakerism (1709); and ten by the great Richard Bentley, such as his *Confutation of Atheism* (1692–3) and his Boyle sermons. Addison's oldest Bible in English seems to have been a 1599 Barker edition, and perhaps the most interesting work of theology is St Augustine's *City of God* in its first English edition of 1610 and still in its original parchment binding.

The collection, however, is by no means solely theological. Philosophy is represented by a first edition of Hobbes's *Leviathan* (1651), a 1584 Aristotle in Greek, Bacon's *Two Bookes* (1633), and Philemon Holland's translation of Plutarch (1603), and history by a 1579 English Guicciardini and a 1680 Machiavelli. The many Greek and Roman classical texts are often in the small scholarly editions published by the Elzevirs of Leyden in the seventeenth century. Poetry and fiction are not much in evidence, although Addison, Sir Thomas Browne, Defoe, Donne, Goldsmith, Johnson, Milton, Montaigne (in English), Shakespeare, Swift, and Sterne make appearances. The only work overtly about Canada that Addison brought with him is Francis Maseres's *An Account of the Proceedings of the British, and Other Protestant Inhabitants, of the Province of Quebeck, in North America, in Order to Obtain an House of Assembly in that Province* (1775).

Robert Addison died in Niagara on 6 October 1829, after nearly four decades' involvement in the public life of Upper Canada. His library survived many vicissitudes, including the invasion of the town during the War of 1812. It is, with the flourishing parish of St Mark's Anglican Church, where the books are housed, his legacy.

PART FIVE

THE USES OF PRINT

chapter 10

PRINT IN DAILY LIFE

Public Print

PATRICIA LOCKHART FLEMING

In the first issue of the *Halifax Gazette*, dated 23 March 1752, John Bushell, whose press was at last 'commodiously fixed for the Printing Business,' offered prompt and reasonable service to 'Gentlemen, Merchants, and others, as may have Occasion for any Thing in that Way.' The local merchants Nathans and Hart were among his customers that year, ordering a *Price Current*, or printed inventory, of their stock with blanks for prices to be added in manuscript.[1] A modest half-sheet passed by hand or posted on a wall, their list is one of the earliest surviving examples of free public print – notices printed to inform, amuse, persuade, or regulate.

Usually called handbills by their printers, or broadsides, to indicate a sheet or leaf of paper printed on one side only, public print links oral and written in both performance and design. Government proclamations and orders were proclaimed as well as posted in early British North America, read aloud in town by beat of the drum and on Sunday at the church door.[2] In the eighteenth century, printers could evoke ceremonious public reading by composing the text in large types and setting the royal arms to crown a proclamation. For the nineteenth-century printer, whose shop was furnished with a vocabulary of fat and ornamented letters, broadsides offered an occasion for display with contrasting types to shout out the message (see illus. 10.2, p. 221, and 12.4, p. 305). Handbills, posting notices, and proclamations – all shared public space with trade signs, painted on board or shaped in the

10.1 James Pattison Cockburn, *Neptune Inn from the Foot of Mountain Street* (1830). Courtesy of the Royal Ontario Museum, 995.21.12.

round, which encouraged even the unlettered to read the streets and countryside (see illus. 10.1, above).

For Bushell and other colonial printers, job printing, the generic term for public print as well as administrative forms and blanks, promised a steady income and quick returns since single-sheet jobs, ordered in editions of 100 or 200 copies, did not require a significant investment in paper and could be fitted into the weekly rhythm of newspaper printing and the cycle of composition and presswork for books and pamphlets. At William Brown's shop in Quebec during one week in the summer of 1778, as an example, his journeyman Thomas Chorley set the type and then worked off 100 handbills for a merchant between the composition and printing of gatherings D and E of the Douay Catechism; between E and F, he printed proclamations and one side of the *Gazette* and then composed two pages of licences for the Native trade.[3] The proclamations might have been run off from types already set for publication in the newspaper, an economy for the densely printed government notices of this period. Distribution of public print was also managed from the newspaper office, which was paid to paste up proclamations and carry notices through the town and on the road.

Although Brown's busy shop cannot be regarded as typical, it is the most extensively documented in early British North America, with twenty-six volumes of printing records surviving for the years 1763 to 1800. In the first six months after the press was set up, July to December 1764, a total of 91 printing orders were entered in the journal.[4] Thirty-eight of these imprints (totalling some 4,350 copies) are public print, texts advertising the sale of goods and land, announcing a ball, or offering a reward of £200 for information about the attackers who had cropped magistrate Thomas Walker's ear.[5] Another 38 orders for printed forms and blanks can be classed as administrative printing for public and private business, a genre discussed by Patricia Kennedy in this chapter. With warrants, summonses, bonds, and tavern keepers' licences ordered by the thousands, these jobs put another 19,000 pieces of print into circulation before the end of 1764. As the people of Quebec adjusted traditional practices to the innovations made possible by a local press, Brown and Gilmore took on more book work, printing pamphlets and books at the expense of the government, the church, and individuals.

In calculating the balance between their book work and job printing, we can document a total of almost 3,100 imprints from 1764 to 1800.[6] Some 2,400 (78 per cent) are job printing: more than 800 orders for public print and about 1,600 for administrative forms and blanks.[7] Just a fraction is known to have survived: fewer than ninety of the handbills and proclamations (11 per cent), many as single copies. Although substantial files of certain categories such as licences and land certificates remain among official papers, a mere 6 per cent of the forms and blanks have been identified and recorded. The survival of public print from early Maritime presses is even more limited. Only some three dozen public notices from eighteenth-century Nova Scotia are known, including fourteen proclamations from the very first decade of Halifax printing, when a quick succession of governors attempted to regulate public conduct: to recover wheelbarrows stolen from the King's Yard, to caution 'a fair and just Commerce with the Indians,'[8] and to observe a general thanksgiving in October 1762. The record is even thinner for early printing offices in New Brunswick and Prince Edward Island, where just a handful of imprints remains to document the circulation of proclamations, auction handbills, and reward notices before 1800.

Despite the observation of a visitor to Halifax in 1817 that 'nothing is more apt to strike an Englishman with wonder on his first arrival here, than the very marked difference, which obtains in the general management of business, and the handbills, which meet his eye every where, announcing the Public Auctions of the day,'[9] nineteenth-century handbills are almost as scarce as those printed in the eighteenth century. With few surviving printers' accounts, little systematic analysis, and uneven bibliographical records for the period from 1801 to 1840, it is impossible even to calculate what has been lost, but on the balance side, some 800 examples of public print have survived, half from presses in Upper Canada, where printing began with an official flourish in 1793.

Although record-keeping practices have probably ensured an overrepresentation of proclamations and orders among surviving single-sheet imprints, there can be no doubt that governments used print freely both to inform and to regulate the public. The War of 1812 offers just one example of an official paper trail criss-crossing the eastern part of British North America. Proclamations followed hard on the American declaration of war in June 1812. Recently appointed, the administrator of New Brunswick issued an order that he described as 'exactly similar' to a proclamation printed at Halifax the week before.[10] In Upper Canada, Major-General Isaac Brock responded in kind to the proclamation that the American brigadier-general, William Hull, had addressed to the people after he crossed the Detroit River to invade the British colonies. Brock's real answer came the following month when he captured Detroit, a victory reported at York five days later in the handbill headed *Glorious News!!!*[11] When the news reached Montreal in another five days, editors of the *Montreal Herald* relayed it to Quebec, where John Neilson published a handbill in French and English headed *More Glorious*.[12] Back across the border, Americans celebrated their victories with ballads, an early form of broadside uncommon in British North America. Only one song 'Composed by Loyal British Hero' in New Brunswick has survived to answer more than sixty American ballads written, printed, and sold during the War of 1812.[13] This tradition of verse in single-sheet format may have taken root with the Loyalists, since scattered pieces are known from Saint John as late as 1837, when *The Remembrancer* was published as a broadside to benefit widows and orphans of workers killed in the collapse of a bridge.[14]

Political handbills served a growing audience for public discourse in the nineteenth century, passed by hand or posted as the opposition took over the walls or when citizens, animated by a common cause, turned to print as a voice of persuasion. In 1811, for example, the inhabitants of St John's published their petition to the Prince Regent requesting basic services for a town grown to 10,000 but still governed as a fishery.[15] Reformers in Upper Canada and Patriotes in Lower Canada used the press to advocate constitutional reform and eventually to counsel sedition. Election time brought unparalleled freedom for debate, with a vigorous street literature represented in this chapter by two case studies: the first election in Lower Canada in 1792 and the 1836 contest in Upper Canada, the last before rebellion.

If political print divided a community, popular print reshaped it into buyers and sellers, audiences and performers. Starting with Nathans and Hart in 1752, generations of merchants, auctioneers, manufacturers, tradesmen, bankers, hotel keepers, schoolmistresses, and others ordered handbills advertising goods and services. Public entertainments were announced and organized, with thousands of posting notices, playbills, and programs. But very few records of popular pastimes survive: an 1812 circus poster from Montreal printed in black and red, an illustrated handbill for horse races at Niagara, and programs for the Toronto Regatta printed on coloured paper with a flourish of ornamental types.[16] No early playbills from British North America have been located, although William Brown printed more than 10,000 copies for the Quebec Theatre in just one season, July to December 1786. Together with 749 copies of the 750 handbills that Sergeant Mensforth ordered in 1792 to advertise the exhibition of his 'Automate ou Figure Parlante Surprenante' at the 'Caffé des Marchands' in Quebec, the theatre playbills served their purpose: read and discarded or posted and then pasted over as a palimpsest of everyday life.[17]

CASE STUDY

An Election in the Press: Lower Canada, 1792
— John Hare

The Constitutional Act of 1791 divided the old province of Quebec into two new provinces, Upper Canada and Lower Canada, each endowed with a legislative assembly. Lower Canada's assembly was composed of fifty elected members representing twenty-seven ridings. The first elections took place in June and July 1792; suffrage was based on ownership of property, but a large proportion of the adult male population had the right to vote.[18]

No other campaign until 1808 produced as many printed materials as did the elections of 1792. Samuel Neilson recorded in his account books some 70 printing jobs related to the elections, out of a total of 160 orders in his Quebec shop over the course of the year 1792. Ten were charged to the government's account and 60 ordered by candidates.[19] Most of the official documents were instructions to returning officers, but Neilson also printed 800 'Notifications in fr. & Eng: to be put up by Returning officers in all public places of resort in the respective Parishes.'[20]

Orders by individuals consisted mainly of advertisements first published in the *Quebec Gazette / La Gazette de Québec* and then reprinted as handbills. From 11 May to 13 June, Neilson published 24 such advertisements. Candidate David Lynd had 700 handbills of his advertisement headed 'To the free electors of the County of Quebec.' The *Montreal Gazette / La Gazette de Montréal* published 16 notices of this type between 21 May and 28 June, and similar advertisements appeared in William Moore's *Quebec Herald*. William Grant, a wealthy merchant and candidate in the Upper Town of Quebec, had '400 breakfast invitation Cards' printed, and John Black, a shipbuilder, ordered '150 Labels for Hats & Cocades.'[21]

Among the many pieces of separately printed electoral propaganda were songs, satires, speeches, and analyses of election issues, as well as more substantial texts such as the *Dialogue sur l'intérêt du jour*, printed by Moore in late May 1792.[22] Attributed to Jean Baillargé, this factum argued in favour of the candidacy of men of the people over that of prominent figures. Among the caricatures printed by Neilson, one entitled 'A tous les electeurs ... de la Haute Ville de Quebec' favoured the merchant candidate over the lawyer.[23] Even after the vote, Michel-Amable Berthelot Dartigny, a defeated candidate, published a ten-page pamphlet to denounce the questionable manoeuvres of his opponents.[24]

CASE STUDY
Printing an Election: Upper Canada, 1836
— Patricia Lockhart Fleming

In late May of 1836, Sir Francis Bond Head, Upper Canada's first civilian lieutenant-governor, dissolved the twelfth parliament after only two sessions. Head had arrived earlier that year well briefed about reformers in the Assembly from their recent report on grievances, a work of 570 pages printed in an edition of 2,000 copies.[25] In his opinion, it contained 'more than three times as many gross falsehoods as pages!'[26] Election to the new parliament was fought vigorously throughout the month of June in forty ridings across the province. The conservatives drew strength from the spirited leadership of the lieutenant-governor himself, and when the polls closed in early July, many reformers were swept from office.

Although printed notices had been an election ritual in Upper Canada

THE CELEBRATED HORSE
Simon Ebenezer !

WILL STAND

For Six Days only,

At the Court House, in this city,

Com'g *MONDAY,* June 20th.

The Ladies who have been obser- ved exerting themselves canvassing for Parson Draper's *son*, are parti- cularly requested to come forward to tender their votes, and SIMON will *pole*⸱ them, gratuitously.

*Pole.—A long staff ; a tall piece of timber erect ; a measure of length containing five yards and a half.—*Johnson's Dictionary.*

10.2 *The Celebrated Horse Simon Ebenezer!* (Toronto, 1836). Courtesy of the Thomas Fisher Rare Book Library, University of Toronto.

since at least 1800, participants in this contest remarked on the quantity of print in circulation. According to one observer, Head had 'flooded' the country 'with handbills and documents of various kinds written by himself and others in English, Dutch [German], and Gaelic, issued from the Tory presses, disseminating the most unfounded statements against the late members of the Assembly.'[27] From the flood of print produced by conservatives and reformers alike, almost forty handbills have survived (most in single copies), more than double the number from any other Upper Canadian election.[28] Fifteen ridings are represented and two languages, English and German. On many imprints the rhetorical flourish of a rousing speech is captured with a bold headline – *Electors Beware!!* or *Farmers Attend!!* – and expressed in contrasting types: thick egyptians, fat-face romans and italics, and shadowed or ornamented letters of recent design. Only one surviving handbill offers pictorial representation: the horse-and-groom cut at the head of a rude notice mocking the candidacy of William Henry Draper, a conservative soon elected in Toronto and then appointed to the Executive Council (see illus. 10.2, p. 221).[29]

Little is known about the distribution of election literature, but a network of readers may be inferred by repeated admonitions such as 'Let every friend to his King and Country read this document then hand it to his neighbour.'[30] The fervour of elections held over several days with open voting at the hustings is captured in printed 'state of the poll' notices. Already trailing by sixty-two votes, William Lyon Mackenzie reported on fellow reformers who would be defeated with him.[31] A second tally celebrated the conservative lead in ridings near Kingston. Headed *Victory or Death, The Rebels shall be defeated!!!* this handbill anticipates rebellion in Upper and Lower Canada the following year.[32]

Printing for Public and Private Business

PATRICIA KENNEDY

From the arrival of the first presses at Halifax and Quebec, both government officials and enterprising individuals embraced the opportunity to replicate texts efficiently and economically. Printing facilitated their efforts to collect and control information as well as to convey it, whether by circulation to a select audience or by publication to the world at large. The writing replicated in print ranged from confidential documents through texts intended to broadcast information, and included an equally diverse range of blank forms to be filled up and sent onward or returned to the office of origin (see illus. 10.3, p. 224, and 10.4, p. 225).

Hundreds of circular letters and thousands of petitions, warrants, oath certificates, and receipts survive in government archives among records of land-granting agencies before and after 1800. Records of government financial operations contain innumerable printed orders, receipts, and pay warrants, while militia records include muster rolls, certificates, and blank commissions. Records of the commission appointed in 1838 to inquire into the post office in British North America include documents printed for the commissioners, as well as circulars, instructions, and notices they collected from postmasters.

Printing saved not only the copyist's labour but also time, materials, and postage. The official besieged by a queue of applicants could quickly and accurately complete a printed form. Printing permitted much more rapid production of multiple copies when timely distribution was critical. The printed text need be proofread only once; the occasional minor error would be manually corrected by the issuing official. No mere decoration, a heraldic factotum or the royal arms served to convey an impression of state authority without the cost of ribbons and wax or the labour of impressing a seal.[33]

Blank forms were not just printed to order; notices in newspapers alerted their readers to the availability of blank forms at the printing offices. How convenient would it have been to run off a quire or two of generic receipts or bills of lading after composing and printing a specific order, or to customize from a basic format? How many purchases recorded by printers such as Brown and Gilmore were of stock forms rather than purpose-printed items to serve the needs of merchants and officials?

The layout of printed forms influenced the quantity and quality of the information gathered. The emerging science of statistics reinforced the demand for data and influenced the design of data-collecting documents. Through its rigid allocation of blank spaces, the printed form encouraged or discouraged discourse. Familiarity might breed contempt; some users confidently overwrote the printed lines to suit their needs or views or happily wrote up and down the margins or any other blank area. Others resisted, leaving the blanks blank.

The interplay between bureaucratization of government operations and the printing of forms and texts raises other questions. Did the printing of forms impose

10.3 Manuscript exemplar of a licence regulating the fur trade west from Montreal (Montreal, 1769). The men are identified in the left margin, followed by 'Quantity and Quality of Merchandize': rum, brandy, wine, guns, and ammunition. Courtesy of the National Archives of Canada, RG 4, B 28, vol. 110, part 1, p. 132.

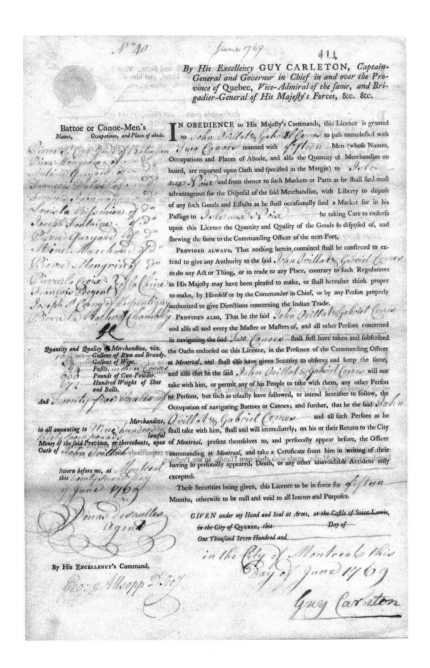

10.4 Printed fur trade licence (Quebec, 1769?). Courtesy of the National Archives of Canada, printed licence: RG 4, B 28, vol. 110, part 2, p. 411.

standardization, or did the imposition of standards demand the use of printed forms? The location tickets printed in Quebec to address the influx of Loyalist refugees faded from use after a decade as settlement patterns shifted. A second intense wave of immigration after 1815 brought a new style of printed petition for land in Upper Canada, one that addressed bureaucratic needs: places to record evidence of loyalty and of entitlement to privilege (as military veteran or child of Loyalist), file numbers or dates for survey warrants and fee receipts and other documents in the process of granting, leasing, or selling Crown lands. Consistent presentation of data made verifying the status of the claimant and the progress of the request quick and easy; the official could ignore the printed elements and find the written detail in the expected spot. Printed forms would inevitably and inexorably reinforce the bureaucratic focus on detail, regimentation, and classification.

Whether unitary or multi-part, printed forms could simultaneously serve multiple purposes. Forms could be prefaced with extracts from legislative enactments, rules and regulations, or directions and instructions to subordinate officials to guide them in recording data for local reference or in collecting it for transmission to the central agencies. Sending preprinted forms to the outlying districts for use by officials of uncertain administrative skills would instruct by example and improve the quality of responses.

Few printed forms bear an imprint, but distinguishing characteristics may allow attribution to a particular shop or printer. The types and ornamental borders on 1825 receipts for the *Canadian Courant* match those on receipts for shares in the Montreal Theatre.[34] The distinctive green paper and style of layout allow us to identify the many receipts and certificates that William Gray printed for the municipal waterworks, the venturers of a steam tow boat, the Lachine Canal Company, the Montreal Theatre, the Montreal Fire Insurance Company, and the Montreal Bank in the early nineteenth century, although he put his name to only a fraction.[35]

The increasing use of elaborate fonts, rules, and other printer's ornaments, or custom-made engraving plates, in job work for private enterprise reflects both the availability of such elements and the reshaping of print for commercial display. Elaborate engravings, whether of ships, quay-side views, or allegorical scenes, began to appear on invoices, billheads, and bills of lading, soon followed by architectural views on letterheads and insurance policies. Printing for government retained its utilitarian characteristics: dense text, few ornamental rules, ever more restrained use of the royal arms to convey authority, and larger, thicker fonts to draw attention to key words. Judicial forms, notarial contracts, and the more mundane financial forms, used as much by private enterprises as by religious bodies or social organizations, tended to exhibit a similar restraint.

For entrepreneurs and officials alike, the essential purposes for printing remained consistent: to disseminate and/or to collect and control information with efficiency and economy. Printing for public purposes not only spread the written word; it shaped how that writing was distributed and how information was recorded and gathered.

CASE STUDY
Scrip: Printing Eighteenth-Century Currency
— Patricia Kennedy

Possibly the most neglected topic in the study of job printing in British North America is the production of financial instruments to answer the chronic shortages of coin that occurred in all the colonies. The press arrived at Quebec most opportunely in 1764, since James Murray and his fellow military governors had proscribed the circulation of card money, the promissory notes inscribed on playing card stock trimmed to shapes indicative of their denominations, which the administrators of New France had issued in great quantities between 1685 and 1757.[36] Into the void soon flowed a variety of scrip printed to meet the demand for a circulating medium.

Although the absence of a printer's name on the earliest surviving examples of bills of exchange, promissory notes, and receipts prevents ready attribution to any of the colonial presses, the shop records of Brown and Gilmore and their successors at Quebec provide insight into the production of scrip and other financial documents, despite the sometimes imprecise, inconsistent, or abbreviated entries.[37] Analysis of these records reveals a difference in emphases among various professions and trades. In the first decades after the arrival of the press, army paymasters and quartermasters, the postmaster, and various other government officials ordered bills, *bons*, change notes, promissory notes, and tickets, while merchants were slow to have financial instruments printed, except for scrip – promissory notes and the chits known familiarly as *bons*[38] – which they ordered in quantities ranging from a few hundred to several thousands. The number and size of orders increased rapidly over the first decade and then dropped off sharply when coin was imported to pay British forces in the fight against the rebellious Americans.

The economic incentive to produce scrip shifted in nature and locale over the following years. Large quantities of change notes were produced for merchants at Detroit and other western posts, for Guy Johnson, superintend-

10.5 Promissory note, probably printed by Fleury Mesplet in Montreal, completed by Dobie & Badgley at Montreal, 1 May 1790. Courtesy of the National Currency Collection, Bank of Canada, 1964-0088-00473.

10.6 Beer ticket, or *bon*, for the St Roc Brewery, signed by J. Campbell at Quebec, 25 June 1814. Courtesy of the National Currency Collection, Bank of Canada, 1964-0088-00647.

ent of the Indian department, at Niagara (near Youngstown, New York), and for Patrick Sinclair, the lieutenant-governor of Michilimackinac, on the strait between Lakes Huron and Michigan. Shipping 3,400 change notes in eight denominations to Sinclair in 1779 and 8,000 notes in four denominations to John Askin at Detroit in 1781 risked only the cost of the printing and postage – £3 15s and £11 13s 4d respectively – for paper whose value as a circulating medium did not come into existence until it was countersigned by whoever promised to pay the bearer.[39]

Patterns within Quebec / Lower Canada continued to evolve as the nature of business changed and the population grew. Despite discrepancies in the shop records, we can see that as their activities increased, merchants probably began to purchase stock forms such as receipts and possibly also scrip. The promissory note for 6 livres signed by Dobie and Badgley of Montreal in 1790 might well have been a stock form printed on Fleury Mesplet's press (see illus. 10.5, p. 228). The first large-scale printing for commerce took the forms of the *bon*, or ticket promising delivery of beer (see illus. 10.6, p. 228) or other goods and services such as ferriage, and the bill, or note promising a money payment to the bearer. These forms of scrip continued into the early nineteenth century.

The Spread of Newspapers in British North America

TRAVIS DECOOK

Maps 10.1, 10.2, and 10.3 illustrate the geographical distribution and number of newspapers which began publication in three periods: pre-1801, 1801–20, and 1821–40.[40] At first glance, a westward shift is apparent: newspapers in the early period are concentrated in the Atlantic region, and the last years are characterized by an explosion of presses in Upper Canada. Before 1801, the eastern colonies predominate, with 14 newspapers started (10 of which are in Nova Scotia), double the number in Lower Canada. In the years 1801–20, the Atlantic region, at 29, continues to have the most new papers, but Lower and Upper Canada are not far behind, with 19 and 13 respectively. During this period, the spread of the newspaper press is the most balanced

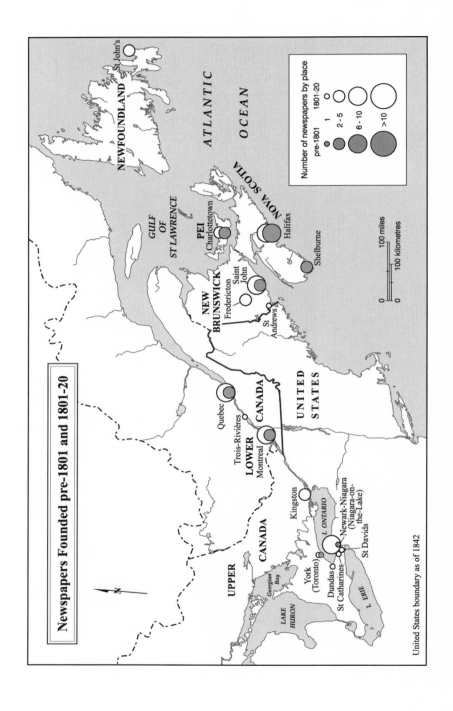

Map 10.1 Newspapers founded pre-1801 and 1801–20.

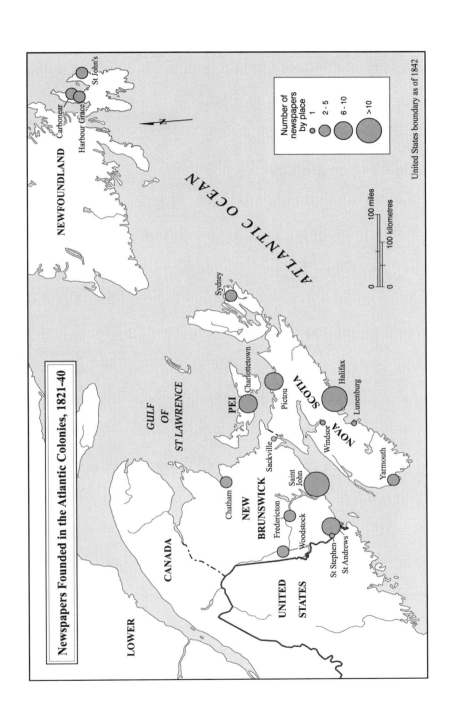

Map 10.2 Newspapers founded in the Atlantic colonies, 1821–40.

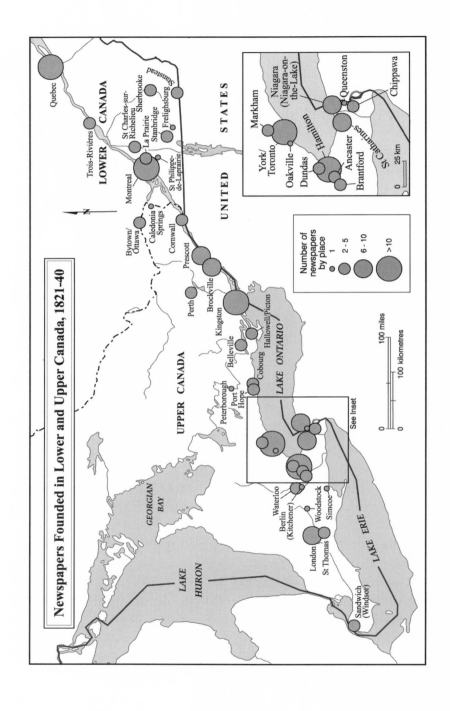

Map 10.3 Newspapers founded in Lower and Upper Canada, 1821–40.

geographically, and Upper Canada experiences the fastest growth, rising from only 2 before 1801 to 13 in 1801–20.

The 1821–40 period reveals an even greater change in Upper Canada, where the number of new newspapers increases tenfold, to 128. In these years the province has close to double the number of newspaper starts as Lower Canada. In terms of distribution within these regions, newspapers in the Atlantic region tend to be concentrated in Halifax and Saint John. In Lower Canada, Quebec is the principal location before 1801, but Montreal gains prominence after 1801, with 10 new papers to Quebec's 8, and is the publishing centre for Lower Canada after 1821, accounting for well over 50 per cent of the province's new newspapers. In Upper Canada, York (Toronto) does not become predominant until after 1820, when it eventually accounts for more than 20 per cent of the province's new presses. In this period, newspaper offices are increasingly concentrated along the western shore of Lake Ontario, from York to Niagara (Niagara-on-the-Lake).

The Newspaper Press in Quebec and Lower Canada

GÉRARD LAURENCE

Among the 120 periodical publications that appeared in Quebec and Lower Canada between 1764 and 1840, including magazines, reviews, and specialized papers of all sorts, the dominant genre – accounting for more than 70 titles, or almost 60 per cent of the total – was the newspaper. Above all, it was the prominence accorded to news that gave these publications their distinctive and permanent character, and prompted the name 'news-paper' and its synonym 'gazette,' the terms actually used in their titles. Such was the case for the first periodical published in Quebec, the *Quebec Gazette / La Gazette de Québec*, launched at Quebec in June 1764 by two young printers from Philadelphia, William Brown and Thomas Gilmore. The second title, and the first newspaper created in Montreal, the *Gazette du commerce et littéraire*, was started fourteen years later. Published in June 1778 by a French immigrant, Fleury Mesplet, it was banned after twelve months' existence. The printer, made wiser by forty months in prison, established a new publication in Montreal in 1785, more in line with the norms of the day. The *Montreal Gazette / Gazette de Montréal* was the direct ancestor of today's *Gazette*.

The Emergence of 'News-papers,' 1764–1804

In their first four decades of existence, 'news-papers,' the dominant form (seven out of the nine titles to appear), shared very stable characteristics. In a province until then completely deprived of local newspapers, the gazette filled a basic need for information. Most were published at Quebec, the capital, and came out weekly, a frequency that corresponded to the needs and means of the time. Many of the papers were written in French and in English, with line-by-line translations.[41]

In the late eighteenth century, gazettes were small four-page folios, a format prefiguring today's tabloids. They were bilingual, with each page set in two columns. Aside from the masthead, nothing differentiated the first page from those that followed.[42] There was no concern to highlight news items; rudimentary headings acted mainly as an index to the information, and there were no fixed sections for different subjects. On the whole, the text was tightly and uniformly typeset, tending to resemble the layout of a book more than that of today's newspapers. The content itself was neatly divided into two categories, editorial and advertising,[43] in proportions that varied according to the newspaper and the occasion. The editorial content was mixed; it was made up of news, excerpts and reviews of books, a variety of texts sent in by readers, and, more rarely, commentaries by the editor. In this period, foreign and international news dominated. This emphasis can no doubt be explained by the events of the times but also by the fact that the foreign press was almost the only source of news for Quebec gazettes, resulting in long delays (from a few weeks to several months) between the event and the moment when readers in Quebec found out about it.[44] Even though provincial news gained in importance after 1792, it was never dominant overall. As for local issues, news of which spread more rapidly by word of mouth, the coverage was limited. Correspondence from subscribers, urgently solicited by printers when they were short of copy, especially in winter, was an integral part of the editorial content. Finally, literature, in the broadest sense, was an indispensable element of the newspaper; it filled the roles of entertainment and instruction for the literate bourgeoisie. Advertising was generally relegated to the back of the newspaper, where notices were printed at random, without classification, and commercial advertisements jostled with government or private announcements. It was only standard cuts, the earliest form of illustration in the press, that enabled readers to sort through the contents at a glance.

During this early period, print runs of newspapers were limited to a few hundred copies. The founders of the *Quebec Gazette / La Gazette de Québec,* who set their sights on 300 subscribers, were able to persuade only 143 to take the paper, though by the mid-1780s the number had climbed slowly to between 400 and 500 copies.[45] It is estimated that Mesplet's *Gazette de Montréal / Montreal Gazette* reached almost 300 copies in 1785;[46] in 1794 the *Times / Le Cours du Tems* stated that it had 228 subscribers. Such modest circulation should not be surprising, given the sparse population and low rates of literacy, discussed by Michel Verrette in chapter 8, but also the high cost of an annual subscription, and substantial increases in postal rates.[47] Newspaper customers were therefore mainly an elite, half of them anglophones, wealthier, better educated, and more concerned with the news because of their positions and activities. The other half were francophones, a modest professional and merchant class numbering several thousand. The rest of the population had only limited access to newspapers thanks to public readings from the pulpit or the steps of the church on Sundays.

The Explosion of the Political Press, 1805–40

The situation changed radically at the turn of the nineteenth century with the appearance of the *Quebec Mercury,* created in January 1805 by Thomas Cary explicitly to defend the ideas and interests of the English merchants at Quebec. A group of members of the Assembly and other leading Canadiens launched *Le Canadien* in November 1806 to respond to the virulent attacks in the *Mercury.* This second period in the history of Quebec newspapers was marked by the rapid and massive emergence of partisan publications; from 1805 to 1840, at least 66 political papers were founded, more than half (38 of the total) in the 1830s alone. The landscape of the periodical press changed dramatically at this time. First, bilingual newspapers almost completely disappeared after 1820. Because the demarcation between the linguistic groups largely corresponded to that between the Parti canadien and the English party, the political papers of each party naturally opted for one or the other language. In spite of the fact that they were much fewer in number (20 per cent of the population), anglophones created a greater number of newspapers (33 compared to 29 established by francophones). At the same time, the geographical distribution of newspapers shifted: the town of Quebec, with some 15 new titles, was overtaken by Montreal, where some 40 papers were launched. In addition to demographic and economic factors, political realities contributed to this shift. In the opening decades of the nineteenth century, the focus of socio-economic and ethnic tensions moved to

Montreal, where extra-parliamentary conflicts were more lively and passionate, and elections more bitterly fought. It was also during this period that the first regional newspapers appeared – more than 10 in total – at Trois-Rivières and in the Eastern Townships.

Another notable change was the increasing frequency of publication. After 1820 the weeklies almost completely disappeared in favour of biweeklies, which were in turn superseded in the 1830s by triweeklies. And the daily was already emerging, at first in a hybrid form through the 'twinning' of two editions – one French, the other English (*La Gazette de Québec* and the *Quebec Gazette*, starting in 1832) – or the association between two titles (such as the *Montreal Herald* and the *Morning Courier* in 1837); some papers inched still closer to daily publication by becoming dailies during the 'business season' (generally May to October) and then returning to the triweekly format. The first true daily newspaper in British North America was the *Daily Advertiser*, which appeared in Montreal on 14 May 1833.[48]

Increased frequency allowed the news to follow events more closely, a necessity at a time when, because of the political situation in Lower Canada, more news was being generated and events were developing more rapidly. And if the daily rhythm of parliamentary debate was to be more fully reported, frequency of publication had to be considered. Finally, the expansion and changing needs of commerce called for daily publication, since the corresponding surge in advertising could not be accommodated by weeklies or biweeklies.

Given the technical means available at the time, it was difficult to increase the number of pages, but supplements of one or two pages on a separate leaf could be added when there was an abundance of news. Most newspapers remained in a folio format, but larger sheets of paper were printed, allowing the number of columns to be doubled or tripled. Between 1800 and 1810, the size of the two main gazettes at Quebec and Montreal grew from 35 by 25 centimetres to 44 by 31 centimetres. This trend accelerated when, on 9 May 1832, *Le Canadien* measured 48 by 33 centimetres, signalling that it was adopting the format 'of most other papers in this country.' An increase in size was always a response to the pressure of a growing volume of advertising, which publishers had difficulty keeping within reasonable proportions (50 per cent to 60 per cent of the total print area), especially when major political events mobilized these partisan papers.

The most important innovation was, in fact, the growing importance given to Lower Canadian affairs, less in the news – which continued to be dominated by foreign and international matters – than in the genres that served the new functions of a political press. Readers' correspondence was now filtered and directed; the newspaper was no longer seen as a marketplace where opposing ideas could be expressed, but as an assembly of partisans from which all dissenting discourse was excluded. Frequently, the editor or publisher wrote such letters, a procedure that one of them, in *La Quotidienne* of 16 December 1837, called 'building correspondence' within the newspaper office itself. From these apocryphal pieces to the editorial was only one step. The editorial article became the choicest morsel in the newspaper, since it was the strategic piece of propaganda where ideas were turned over and over, principles recalled, abuses denounced, slogans formulated, and watchwords disseminated. The main figures in journalism at the time, such as John Neilson (*Quebec Gazette / La Gazette de Québec*), Jocelyn Waller (*Canadian Spectator*), Daniel Tracey (*Vindicator and Canadian Advertiser*), David Chisholme (*Montreal Gazette*), Alexander James Christie (*Montreal Herald*), William Kemble (*Quebec Mercury*), Étienne Parent (*Le Canadien*), Adam Thom (*Montreal Herald*), and Robert Middleton (*Quebec Gazette*), made their reputations in these pages.[49] But it was not enough to tell people what they should think; they must also be allowed to judge for themselves. Hence the publication of parliamentary debates, in theory forbidden but now tolerated, through which the electors were directly informed about the conduct of their representatives and the practices of their leaders. During sessions, the parliamentary reports took up a substantial portion of the newspaper.

The resources devoted to editorial content remained, in spite of everything, modest. Even the most important journals had only a few writers. Most of the papers had a single editor, but party leaders and sympathizers willingly contributed. Since the practice of the time was not to sign articles, or to sign with only a pseudonym, it is impossible to establish the most basic statistics. Because the teams were so small, the functions were not highly differentiated; nevertheless, the position of principal editor emerged. And the journalism practised was always a 'journalism from the editor's chair,' the only roving journalist being the 'reporter' of parliamentary debates.

Clearly, such content was addressed to a traditional elite, which corresponded overall to the body of electors, still a small readership in a system of landowners' suffrage limited almost exclusively to men. Even though the prices dropped slightly,[50] a newspaper subscription, at 20s per year, was still a 'luxury product,' noted the *Écho du Pays* of 12 July 1836. A few papers in smaller format, modelled on English penny papers, began to appear, at an annual subscription of 10s per year, which could be divided into periodic payments over several months (*Montreal Transcript*). Other papers began to sell by the issue ('by peddling'). The targeted customers were artisans, whose numbers were increasing and some of whom were literate. Until 1830, only one or two newspapers printed a thousand copies, but in the following decade some may well have exceeded that number. The English-language papers, both tory and Patriote, appear to have been more popular than the French. On the eve of 1840, the *Montreal Transcript* probably had print runs of about two thousand copies. *La Minerve* declared at the same time that it had 1,300 subscribers, an unusually high number for a French-language newspaper. On 6 November 1840, the *Jean-Baptiste* set the ideal objective at two thousand copies for francophone papers: 'only then will journalism among the Canadiens have reached its peak.'

Attacks on Newspaper Printers and Their Shops

SARAH BROUILLETTE

During the first half of the nineteenth century, newspapers in British North America became primary locations for public debate and the formation of political opinion. In addition to the official controls discussed by Gilles Gallichan in chapter 13, censure was imposed extrajudicially by citizens who expressed their outrage through attacks on printers and presses.[51]

The most notorious incident was the 'types riot' in York (Toronto), when young men vandalized the printing office of William Lyon Mackenzie's *Colonial Advocate*.[52] The attack took place in the evening of 8 June 1826, publication day for the newspaper. At the time, the capital was dominated by what Mackenzie later called the 'Family Compact,' a network of office-holders closely tied to the colonial establishment. Mackenzie's *Advocate*, the second independent paper in York, was politically engaged from its founding at Queenston in 1824, commenting on parliamentary debates and attacking colonial dependence and the men who embodied it. Mackenzie and his editorial voice, 'Patrick Swift,' who revelled in defamation and scandalous caricatures, finally provoked a physical response as the angry crowd – some with family connections to Mackenzie's victims – attacked his shop. They broke down the door and set about damaging the machinery on which the *Advocate* was printed, pulling over the heavy iron press, scattering type, and throwing it into the lake.[53] The mob, according to Mackenzie, 'demolished Press, Types, Forms, Sticks, Cases, Frames,

Gallies, [and] Stands.'[54] At the time of the attack, Mackenzie was in debt and the newspaper's future precarious, but after the court awarded compensation of £625, the *Colonial Advocate* resumed publication. Samuel Peters Jarvis, the lawyer who took credit for the attack, claimed that it suited Mackenzie's own destruction of 'whatever was most valuable in public or private life.'[55] As for Mackenzie, he went on to enter politics as a Reform member of the Assembly, serve as Toronto's first mayor, and lead the Rebellion of 1837 in Upper Canada.

The second case is less well known. On 19 May 1835, Henry David Winton, printer and editor of the *Public Ledger and Newfoundland General Advertiser* in St John's, was attacked on the road by a group of people with painted faces.[56] He was struck from his horse, pummelled with a stone, and his left ear cut off. His assailants were never identified, but at the time it was thought that members of Newfoundland's Catholic community were responsible. Winton, trained as a printer and bookbinder in England, had come to Newfoundland in 1818. He founded the *Ledger* with a partner in 1820 and was owner from 1823. Initially a proponent of reform and Catholic emancipation, Winton became a vigorous critic of the political power exercised by the Catholic clergy in anticipation of the first election after representative government was granted in 1832.[57] Before the personal attack of 1835, the windows in both his printing shop and his home had been smashed by rioters bent on intimidation.[58] The assault did not moderate Winton's political voice; rather, it led him to a more entrenched position, and the *Ledger* to a more open espousal of conservative opinion. Though no individuals were charged with the crime, members of the Catholic community openly rejoiced when it happened, tearing down reward notices and singing a ballad about 'Croppy Winton.'[59]

The attacks on Winton and Mackenzie dramatize the significance of newspapers and their editors in the public life of British North America. Newspapers gave voice to political will that could lead to physical violence as well as to legislative activity.[60] Their editors contributed to the delineation of a role for print in public life and reader identity. The attack on Winton entrenched sectarian and political factionalism in Newfoundland, with readers defining their allegiances in terms of Catholic versus Protestant, reform versus conservative. However, historian Jeffrey L. McNairn has identified the attack on Mackenzie's shop as an important step in the development of public opinion, which came to hold that such matters should not be left in the hands of political or legal institutions or handled through violent intervention, but rather, should be constrained through the conscious choices of informed and politicized readers.[61]

Magazines in English

THOMAS BREWER VINCENT, SANDRA ALSTON, AND ELI MACLAREN

The first two magazines published in present-day Canada – the *Nova-Scotia Magazine* (Halifax, 1789–92) and the *Quebec Magazine / Le Magasin de Quebec* (Quebec, 1792–4) – appeared between the American Revolution and the Napoleonic Wars, a time of relative calm in North America. Following the Loyalist migration, the remaining British colonies were attempting to redefine themselves politically, economically, socially, and culturally. Production of a magazine was one of several elements of European print culture that served as tools, helping to articulate the collective character of the communities they addressed. Because both form and content of the two magazines drew heavily on established European models, they appear to have reinforced derivative cultural perspectives and social assumptions. For these societies, seeing themselves as extensions of a parent culture and not as separate entities was part of the complex of ideological issues thrown up by the Revolutionary War. However, use of the borrowed form of the magazine was marked by a struggle to adapt it to local circumstances, so that over time it came to speak as much *for* as *to* the cultural consciousness of its readership.

By the late 1780s, the basic requirement for publishing a magazine, a printing office, was in place at Halifax and Quebec, as well as in Saint John, Charlottetown, and Montreal. But such a venture presupposed other conditions. First, it assumed a critical mass of readers with a particular degree of literacy and a community of interests that the magazine could engage. Compared to the newspaper, the magazine is a more exclusive medium, making the identification of readership a crucial factor. And in Halifax and Quebec the numbers of British administrators and military officers, who formed an important part of the literate elite, fluctuated significantly. Closely linked was the problem of distribution. The realities of transportation in eighteenth-century British North America meant that the effective reach of a magazine was restricted. For both the *Nova-Scotia Magazine* and the *Quebec Magazine / Le Magasin de Quebec*, distribution was limited to a small local, if socially influential, readership.

Securing acceptable, locally authored material on a consistent basis was also essential. If the magazine hoped to be more than a conduit for texts previously published elsewhere, it had to include the work of local writers, generally amateurs for whom such contributions did not represent a priority. Otherwise, the burden of creating 'original' material would fall primarily on the editor. Finally, early magazines in British North America faced an environment that was implicitly biased against them. At best, they were perceived as provincial organs designed to transmit the culture of distant centres. The imitative form and large amount of 'borrowed' content tended to reinforce this perception. Moreover, British and American magazines, published in the acknowledged centres of cultural power and increasingly available, were potent competitors.

The *Nova-Scotia Magazine and Comprehensive Review of Literature, Politics, and News* appeared monthly between July 1789 and March 1792.[62] It was printed by John Howe in Halifax but assembled by William Cochran, who actively edited the magazine until mid-1790. Cochran, from an Irish Protestant background, had taught at Columbia College in New York for a few years before moving to Halifax in October 1788 to seek ordination in the Church of England. In Bishop Charles Inglis and his circle, he found social and cultural values compatible with his own.

Cochran looked to British magazines such as the *Gentleman's Magazine* and the *London Magazine* as his models. These consisted of digests and miscellanies of a broad range of literary and general material. As the *Nova-Scotia Magazine*'s prospectus argued, in the province 'the utility of such an undertaking is still more obvious, where few can afford to purchase the various publications whose chief merit might be united in one compilation and read at moderate expense.'[63] The magazine appears to have been designed primarily to maintain the cultural imprint of Britain on Maritime society, but Cochran also sought to encourage young local writers: 'Besides[,] a repository would be thereby provided for the literary productions of ingenious men, on subjects that particularly concern the country where we live, and which we never can expect to find discussed in English prints.'[64] What emerged was a version of 'Britishness' that had more to do with local values than with the realities of contemporary Britain. Cochran, through his selection of materials, became a cultural filter shaped significantly by the Loyalist perspective. Both what he chose to publish in the magazine and what he omitted reveal his guiding vision.

A number of recurring subjects created a sense of focus and a consistency of tone. Agriculture and education, in particular, constituted an ongoing dialogue between editor and readers. Other topics – biographies of notable figures, history, travel and exploration of 'exotic' places (including Native North American territory), science, and philosophy (mostly in essay form) – were designed to engage a more broadly based intellectual curiosity. Political issues were presented mostly as news items, and the religious sectarianism and political partisanship that characterized local debate were avoided. Also missing were such current issues as the advancement of provincial trade and commerce. Thus the vision that emerges from the pages of the *Nova-Scotia Magazine* is one of rural retirement and intellectual curiosity. It is reinforced by the pastoral and sentimental character of the poetry and fiction selected for inclusion, with their focus on the good, the beautiful, and the sweetly melancholy.

The first issue of the *Quebec Magazine, or Useful and Entertaining Repository of Science, Morals, History, Politics, &c. / Le Magasin de Quebec, ou Receuil utile et amusant de literature, histoire, politique, &c., &c.* was dated August 1792, the month the Tuileries was stormed and the French royal family imprisoned.[65] After printer Samuel Neilson's death in early 1793, the journal was continued by his brother, John Neilson, until May 1794. Though supposedly under the direction of a 'society of gentlemen in Quebec,' the magazine was in fact edited by Presbyterian clergyman Alexander Spark, who was paid £59 10s for his work over nearly two years.[66] The basic structure (digest and miscellany) was similar to that of the *Nova-Scotia Magazine* and influenced by the same models, but the journal appears to have responded to a different readership, one concerned mainly with urban, mercantile issues and much engaged in contemporary public affairs at home and abroad.

News (domestic and foreign), weather, and vital statistics were regular features and occupied significant space in each issue. Politics was a frequent subject. While some articles dealt with political theory, most were concerned with current European affairs and their implications. These were complemented by pieces on European history. The magazine also made forays into religion, literature, education, agriculture, and commerce. Selections of poetry and fiction appear to have been mainly intended to satisfy the conventions of this type of journal. How much of the contents was locally authored is difficult to judge, but the engravings, some signed by J.G. Hochstetter, were produced at Quebec (see illus. 5.1, p. 94). Consciously or unconsciously, the *Quebec Magazine / Le Magasin de Quebec*, printed in French and/or English, projected a vision of Lower Canadian society as two communities linked by certain shared concerns.

Between 1795 and the late 1810s, colonial energies were drawn into the exigencies of war, and no sustained attempt was made to publish a magazine in British North America during these years. Elsewhere magazines were changing significantly, as exemplified by such journals as the *Edinburgh Review* (established 1802) and *Blackwood's Edinburgh Magazine* (founded 1817), with their high critical standards and emphasis on original material. At the same time, the range and focus of individual magazines were narrowing, creating a more diversified and fragmented landscape. The availability, popularity, and quality of imported reviews thwarted the development of native publications. Another inhibiting factor was the broadening of newspaper journalism to include locally authored literary material. In Nova Scotia, for example, Anthony H. Holland's *Acadian Recorder* (founded 1813) would inspire such highly literate newspapers as Joseph Howe's *Novascotian* after he acquired it in 1827 and William Cunnabell's *Pearl* (1837–40).

But niches remained where locally produced magazines could address a specific readership. The post-war period saw the beginnings of sectarian journals such as John Strachan's *Christian Recorder* (1819–21), the first periodical to be attempted in Upper Canada.[67] Produced first at Kingston and then in York (Toronto), this forty-page monthly owed its existence to the energy of its editor. Strachan followed the usual practice of 'exchange' – acquiring other journals from which he could extract material in exchange for reciprocal privileges – and set up regular correspondents to obtain 'the most early religious intelligence.'[68] But from the beginning, he had difficulty finding contributors and wrote most of the 'Original Commentaries' himself. By April 1820 the magazine was composed principally of excerpts from other religious journals, and after two years' publication, it was suspended. As Strachan explained, 'the arrangements necessary for conducting a periodical publication in a colony like this, were found more difficult than had been anticipated; and although the number of Subscribers during the first year, was much greater than could have been expected, yet the expence was by no means covered.'[69]

Other Church of England periodicals encountered similar difficulties: in Lower Canada the *Christian Sentinel and Anglo-Canadian Churchman's Magazine* (Montreal) and its successor, the *Christian Sentinel,* lasted from 1827 to 1831, with a one-year hiatus, while in Nova Scotia the Lunenburg *Colonial Churchman* managed to produce six volumes between 1835 and 1841, but failed as a result of 'the inconvenience of its birth place and the want of a printer with sufficient capital and spirit.'[70] Missionary magazines in New Brunswick and Lower and Upper Canada were published with limited success, but those religious journals that could form an official relationship with their constituencies, such as the *British North American Wesleyan Methodist Magazine* (Saint John, 1840–7) and the *Canadian Christian Examiner and Presbyterian Review* (Niagara, then Toronto, 1837–40), did better. Less successful were attempts directed at other specialized markets, as Leslie McGrath demonstrates for juvenile magazines (chapter 11), Bertrum H. MacDonald for agriculture (chapter 8), and Christine Veilleux for medicine (chapter 12).

Many of the periodicals that appeared in British North America prior to 1840 were literary in focus. Jacob S. Cunnabell published two of the most important, the *Acadian Magazine, or Literary Mirror* (Halifax, 1826–8) and the *Halifax Monthly Magazine*

(1830–3). Under the editorship of Beamish Murdoch and, later, J. Scott Tremaine, the major part of the *Acadian Magazine* was written by native authors. Fiction and poetry were prominently featured, and other pieces dealt with local history and travel. There were reviews of Nova Scotian publications, and engravings of provincial scenes. Cunnabell's *Halifax Monthly Magazine* was edited by John Sparrow Thompson, who encouraged local writers but had trouble acquiring an adequate supply of material. For just six months, July to December 1836, the *Saint John Monthly Magazine* was published in New Brunswick.

Similarly, in Upper Canada the focus of most magazine publishing was literary. A prospectus appeared in 1820 for the first of several publications that James Martin Cawdell attempted, but his 'Glencawdell Portfolio' does not seem to have been printed. Cawdell renewed his efforts, and in mid-1823 part of an issue of the 'Rose Harp' was noted by the *Upper Canada Herald*.[71] In January 1835 the first number of the *Roseharp: For Beauty, Loyalty and Song* appeared; a second number was projected for May and a third for September, each to be twenty-four pages. Despite his best efforts, however, Cawdell's dream of encouraging 'a taste for literature, and the fine arts'[72] failed to materialize.

In the anglophone community of Montreal, similar attempts were equally burdened with difficulty. The *Canadian Magazine and Literary Repository,* a monthly quarto of ninety-six pages published between July 1823 and June 1825, was edited first by David Chisholme. Against the swelling of political consciousness among the francophone population, it was intended to shore up conservative British values, as the frontispiece to the inaugural volume suggests (see illus. 10.7, p. 245). The untitled engraving by William Satchwell Leney depicts two female figures; one holds an open book, and the other gestures toward a wild landscape. On the ground before them lie a book, a globe, and a protractor and square, and behind them a plow. The colonization portrayed is profound, effected by a commingling of agriculture, mathematics, geography, and literature. Surveying the precarious foothold of European civilization upon the vast North American wilderness, 'many of [whose] *native* sons and daughters remain still unblest with the light of knowledge and Christianity,' the editor purposes 'to advance ... the progress of moral improvement in all its relations to the happiness of man, and the welfare of society.'[73] The values promoted were both European, rather than Aboriginal, and British rather than French.

But a power struggle between Chisholme and the proprietors soon ripped the magazine in two.[74] In January 1824, Edward Milford, owner of the *Canadian Magazine,* and Thomas A. Turner, owner of the *Montreal Gazette,* became partners, agreeing on a financial merger of the magazine and the newspaper. But when in February,

10.7 William Satchwell Leney, engraved frontispiece for the first issue of the *Canadian Magazine and Literary Repository* (Montreal, July 1823). Courtesy of the Thomas Fisher Rare Book Library, University of Toronto.

Chisholme, who had been editor of both, discovered that his salary at the *Gazette* was to be cut as a result, he resigned, taking a number of submissions for the February issue of the magazine with him. To replace Chisholme, Turner hired his brother-in-law, Alexander James Christie, former editor of the *Montreal Herald*. Chisholme, meanwhile, attacked the proprietors of the *Canadian Magazine* in a number of local newspapers and announced his plans to launch a new journal, backed by the governor, Lord Dalhousie. The first issue of the *Canadian Review and Literary and Historical Journal*, a weighty quarto of over two hundred pages, appeared in July 1824. Its table of contents, with the articles identified in roman numerals, immediately announced its imitation of the esteemed *Edinburgh Review*. The imitation was less than successful: subsequent issues appeared in December 1824 (with an apology from the editor), March 1825, February 1826 (with the name changed to the *Canadian Review and Magazine*), and finally September 1826. The *Canadian Magazine* had ceased publication more than a year earlier.

The *Canadian Magazine* had been sold by subscription at 'Six Dollars per Annum, payable Half Yearly in advance.' A list of twenty-two agents, eleven in Lower Canada and eleven in Upper Canada, that appeared on the title page of the issue for May 1825 projected a distribution across both provinces. Its failure and that of its sibling, the *Canadian Review*, may suggest that the market for a tory magazine in the Canadas was too small to be split or that the editors and proprietors simply tired of a project marred by their own animosity.

After the single appearance of the *Rose Harp* in 1823, no periodical was published in Upper Canada until 1831. Strachan had blamed the failure of the *Christian Recorder* in part on the post-war recession, but the economy was steadily improving, as witnessed by such ambitious projects as the Rideau and the Welland Canals. The gap may have been filled by journals from Montreal, such as the *Scribbler* (1821–7), or by imports from the United States, which saw 'an extraordinary outburst of magazine activity' after 1825.[75] New attempts were made to publish a literary journal in the early 1830s, three of them in Hamilton. In 1831 A. Crosman launched the *Canadian Casket,* which was to be 'devoted to select tales, sketches from biography, natural and civil history, poetry, anecdotes, the arts, essays, and interesting miscellany.' In the fourth issue the publisher began offering a premium of three pounds to the 'writer of the best Original Tale written expressly for the *Casket* and having its scene laid in Canada.'[76] The irregular appearance of the journal was blamed on the ill health of the editor, John Gladwin, and the 'false and malicious reports of evil minded persons who endeavored to take advantage of our illness,'[77] undoubtedly a reference to Wyllys Smyth, who had launched the *Garland* just before the *Casket* ended in September

1832. Proclaiming itself 'the third attempt to sustain Canadian literature,'[78] this periodical was also to be a mixture of imported and domestic material. Despite a change in title to the *Canadian Garland* and the promise of a larger volume, doubled from eight to sixteen pages, the journal was offered for sale in November 1833, with or without its press and types. Schoolteacher Stephen Randal's *Voyageur* (1832–?), 'devoted one half to native literary productions and the remainder to good foreign selections,'[79] was also short-lived.

Rivals to these Hamilton journals were two literary monthlies published in York, the *Canadian Literary Magazine* (April–October 1833) and the *Canadian Magazine* (January–April 1833). Much more ambitious in scope than any of its predecessors in the province, the *Canadian Literary Magazine* was to appear in issues of sixty-four pages, each embellished with 'a Lithograph Engraving of some place or person distinguished in British North America' (see illus. 10.8, p. 248).[80] These attempts were followed by the equally short-lived *Mirror of Literature* (Prescott, November–December 1835) and the *Cabinet of Literature* (Toronto, 1838–9).

A new magazine had made its appearance in Montreal in December 1832.[81] Seeing the abundance of American periodicals as the chief hindrance to local writers reaching an audience, the editor sought to 'furnish … a medium through which the young aspirant to Literary honour shall become distinguished.'[82] The *Montreal Museum* was the first journal in British North America directed by a woman. The editor, Mary Graddon Gosselin, selected a range of material for inclusion, from poems and short stories to articles on popular science, education, cooking, travel, and biography. Both original work by such writers as Diana Bayley and her son, F.W.N. Bayley, and material reprinted from British and American periodicals or translated from French sources were included. Adolphus Bourne contributed illustrations of the latest fashions using his newly imported lithographic press.[83] Doubtless modelled on the successful *Ladies' Museum* (London, 1798–1832), the *Montreal Museum* distinguished itself through its editorial commentary. In the first issue, for example, the editor 'reluctantly' includes a censorious evaluation of Lady Byron's life and finds 'deficiencies' in the latest issue of an American magazine, the *Token*.

A quarto of sixty-four pages per issue, the *Montreal Museum* was printed by Ludger Duvernay. The recent addition of a new Smith's Imperial press to his shop had allowed him to print his newspaper, *La Minerve*, more quickly, thus freeing up the older presses for other work.[84] The editor of *La Minerve* at this time was Mary Graddon Gosselin's husband, Léon. Published monthly until March 1834, the magazine ran for a total of fifteen issues. It was sold by subscription at a price of 22s per year and distributed at least as far as Hamilton.

10.8 Samuel Oliver Tazewell, *John Galt*, lithograph for the *Canadian Literary Magazine* (York, May 1833). Courtesy of the Toronto Public Library (TRL). Galt is shown here as colonizer of the Huron Tract and as author of a life of Lord Byron.

Noah Webster's observation that 'the expectation of failure is connected with the very name of a Magazine'[85] is borne out by the experience in British North America. Magazines had to compete not only with imported material but also with more widely distributed local and foreign newspapers. They relied on the efforts of enthusiastic and energetic editors, but foundered on the indifference of subscribers and contributors. Most editors complained of a lack of material for their journals, and all lamented the scarcity of paying subscribers.

Subscription figures at this time are hard to determine; 'five hundred copies' is mentioned by several editors. Strachan had wanted to print five hundred of the *Christian Recorder* and 'get most of them sold,' and he accused his York publisher, George Dawson, of deception when he persuaded Strachan to print seven hundred instead, 'which greatly increased the Expence.'[86] The *Garland* (Hamilton) produced five hundred copies for a subscription list of about four hundred 'good and substantial names.' The *Canadian Magazine* in Montreal projected '400 Subscribers, [which] number is now nearly compleated, and doubtless will soon be made up.'[87] Only the publisher of *Youth's Monitor and Monthly Magazine* (Toronto, 1836) printed a list of his paid-up subscribers: twenty-three.

The difficulty of acquiring supplies and retaining employees, and even political disturbances, caused delays. Strachan was unable to publish his journal on time because of the lack of 'expected types,' while the editor of the *Canadian Christian Examiner* complained about the paper he was forced to use, announcing that he had ordered better paper from Scotland; after it arrived, 'the *Examiner* will equal any periodical in Canada as to mechanical execution.'[88] James Gedd of the *Cabinet of Literature*, in explaining the lateness of a number, alluded to 'the scarcity of hands, removing offices, and many other reasons,'[89] and in a notice inserted in the January 1838 issue of the *Christian Examiner*, the editor blamed the 'disturbed state of the frontier during the past month which required him and all the printers in the office to be on military duty.'

Given these problems, what surprises is not the delays, the many failures, and the small numbers printed but the determination of editors and publishers to prevail over previous attempts and allow a nascent cultural voice to be heard. Not until late in the period was a sustainable magazine established. The *Literary Garland* first appeared in Montreal in December 1838 and would run to December 1851. Printed by John Lovell and edited by John Gibson, it would prove to be the longest lived and most highly respected literary magazine in English in the Canadas and would most truly fulfill the role of nurturing culture in British North America.

CASE STUDY
Michel Bibaud's Encyclopedic Reviews
— Nova Doyon

Michel Bibaud (1782–1857), who launched four encyclopedic reviews between 1825 and 1842, began his journalistic career in Montreal in 1813 at Charles-Bernard Pasteur's *Le Spectateur;* in March 1817 he founded his own weekly, *L'Aurore*, with the printer Joseph-Victor Delorme.[90] He worked again with Pasteur when *Le Spectateur canadien* absorbed *L'Aurore* in September 1819. He published a collection of his own poetry, the first to appear in French in Lower Canada,[91] and a three-volume history of Canada, of which the first two volumes appeared in 1837 and 1844; a third volume was published by his son, Jean-Gaspard, in 1878.[92]

Bibaud introduced *L'Aurore* in 1817 as a 'political, literary, and anecdotal newspaper' which had more in common with a gazette than with a literary publication, because of its emphasis on current events and foreign news. His dynamic relationship with his readers demonstrated a desire to encourage reading and to stimulate the spread of knowledge. Indeed, in this newspaper, more than in his other periodicals, he published many letters from readers – signed with pseudonyms, as was the custom at the time. In his role as editor, he often entered into exchanges with them on different subjects and sometimes intervened to direct the discussion, adopting the pseudonym of a subscriber.

At the end of the eighteenth century, certain periodicals had attempted to interest the reading public with a mixture of politics, history, literature, science, and the arts.[93] When he founded his first encyclopedic review, *La Bibliothèque canadienne* (1825–30), subtitled a 'historical, scientific, and literary miscellany,' Bibaud was responding to an appeal from a correspondent in *Le Spectateur canadien*, who deplored the absence of such periodicals in Lower Canada. In this and his other reviews, which he wrote and published himself, translating, reformulating, and interpreting the texts he drew from different books and periodicals, Bibaud hoped 'to bring up to date literary monuments, historical features, or facts to the honour or advantage of the country, which have remained obscure until now ... in order to instill in our young compatriots a taste for study and instruction.'[94] He seems to have filled a real need, since his formula worked well. From a thirty-two-page monthly, *La Bibliothèque canadienne* expanded in its final year to a forty-page bimonthly. Remarkably, it survived for five years with no advertising, at a time when many periodicals lasted less than a year.[95]

When Bibaud started a weekly in 1830, he meant to continue along the lines of *La Bibliothèque canadienne* but with more resources. *L'Observateur, ci-devant La Bibliothèque canadienne* was intended to be a 'historical, literary, and political newspaper.' The change in title also marked a shift in the editorial formula. In effect, he hoped to produce a 'total periodical,' both gazette and literary anthology. Unfortunately, the public was not receptive to this concept. In the last issue, which appeared in July 1831, an anonymous reader lamented that the country could not 'support a purely literary paper'[96] and fervently hoped that the publisher would return to the format of *La Bibliothèque canadienne*. Bibaud announced therefore that, on the recommendation of his subscribers, he would once again produce a monthly.

In January 1832 he launched *Le Magasin du Bas-Canada*, a forty-page publication. In it, as a profession of editorial faith, he reprinted the prospectus for *La Bibliothèque canadienne*. The content of this review, at once literary and scientific, reflected his return to the encyclopedic formula. But Bibaud's efforts did not convince his subscribers, and without notice, *Le Magasin du Bas-Canada* ceased publication in December. It would be another ten years before he once again entered the editorial field with *L'Encyclopédie canadienne* (1842–3). Although his reviews were not all successful, it can be said that through his publishing activities, Michel Bibaud 'exerted a certain cultural influence on his milieu [and] played a unique role as a pioneer'[97] in stimulating the intellectual life of Lower Canada.

chapter 11

POPULAR BOOKS

Print for Young Readers

LESLIE MCGRATH

Reading materials for young people who lived in British North America before 1840 consisted of books brought to the colonies by settlers, publications imported by missionary societies and booksellers, and domestic imprints. Primers, catechisms, and instructional works were the most common forms of print available, but juvenile reading encompassed a far wider range of material, for 'it is a safe assumption that ... children and young people ... read what their elders were reading, namely the classics, the poets, the dramatists, the moralists and lesser moralists.'[1] We can also assume that they read newspapers, popular fiction, and other adult publications. The availability of print for children, as for adults, was limited by poverty and illiteracy, and subject to unpredictable delivery in isolated settlements, fluctuating economies, and times of war. Manuscripts, including juvenile diaries, letters, samplers, and lessons written in copybooks or on slates, were ephemeral, but their importance for children's reading in pioneer times is well documented.[2] Storytelling and songs provided the main sources of entertainment among both Aboriginal peoples and European immigrants of all ages and would later be reflected in print versions of these fireside tales.[3]

The earliest descriptions of the country written for children were brief accounts produced abroad by authors who used second-hand sources. These were followed by more lengthy narratives, such as the poetical *A Peep at the Esquimaux*, by 'A Lady'

(1825), and Diana Bayley's *Henry; or, The Juvenile Traveller* (1836). Catharine Parr Traill's *The Young Emigrants* (1826), written while the author was still in England, provided a fictionalized guide for children. With its limited plot but extensive pragmatic advice, this forerunner of Traill's more famous *Canadian Crusoes* (1852) offers an interesting contrast to what is considered the first Canadian novel for children.

Evidence of imported print for young readers appears in numerous sources. The Louisbourg records, for example, contain the inventory that creditors of bankrupt shopkeeper Jacques Rolland compiled in 1742. Among other wares, Rolland sold 'Bibliothèque bleue' publications, which included popular stories, folk tales, myths, legends, and nursery rhymes, as well as primers, or alphabets, for family use.[4] Before public education was established, the Jesuit, Récollet, Ursuline, and other orders used religious texts from France, primarily alphabets that contained prayers, to teach French-speaking and Aboriginal children. In the English-speaking colonies the Society for Promoting Christian Knowledge (SPCK) and other organizations imported tracts and instructional books in large numbers. As more schools were started, the need for textbooks with relevant local content drove a domestic book trade that in turn fostered a wider range of print. But despite legislation as early as 1801 establishing public education in Lower Canada, few communities could afford schools, and domestic textbooks were scarce. The *New-Brunswick Courier* in 1811 advocated the use of the newspaper in teaching children when other reading materials were lacking.[5]

Newspaper advertisements provide evidence of the types of books imported for more well-to-do children. The *Acadian Recorder*, for example, on 12 November 1814 advertised the contents of Abdiel Kirk's New Circulating Library, which included 'a complete musical library for Juvenile Performers,' and on 8 July 1815 it offered 'children's story books, of a superior kind, by the trunk, dozen or single books.' Consignment sales and new booksellers' stocks were also publicized; in the Halifax *Journal* of 8 June 1812, J. Hemmington's new wares included 'Janeway's Tokens; Mason's *History of Jesus*, [and] Sermons to Children,' while on 5 February 1816 the paper advertised 'Elementary Books on Arts and Sciences ... School and Children's Books, &c., a great variety and well selected,' for sale at auction by Dean and Harris.

One of the first local imprints for a child was a broadside, *A Mohawk Song and Dance*, printed 'for little Master Caldwell,' in 1780, probably at Quebec (see illus. 11.1, p. 254).[6] This early example of entertainment was an exception to the devotional literature that dominated children's reading. Although books for children were produced at presses in British North America over the following decades, some authors continued to publish their books abroad. In one study Bernard Amtmann identified 412 titles 'suitable for and available to juvenile readers, even if not always intended

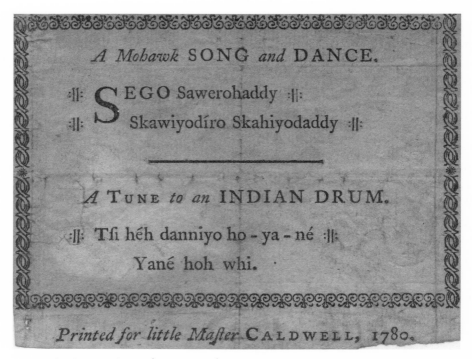

11.1 *A Mohawk Song and Dance* (Quebec, 1780). Courtesy of the Rauner Special Collections Library, Dartmouth College, 780900 broadside.

for them,' printed in the colonies or written by local residents before 1840.[7] Of these, three-quarters were printed in Lower Canada, one-tenth in Upper Canada, and one-twentieth in the Atlantic region; the remainder were published abroad. Some 215 were in French, 177 in English, and 10 in Aboriginal languages; the others were primarily Latin texts or religious works in German. If the titles are categorized by subject, religion and textbooks dominate, while fiction represents approximately one-tenth of the total. Few humorous or imaginative tales were written specifically for children, though Lindley Murray's *English Reader* contains some amusing stories. More typical of the period is the cautionary tale for young people *Charlotte Temple,* by Susanna Rowson, which was reprinted in Hallowell (Picton), Upper Canada, in 1832.[8]

Catalogues issued in British North America between 1800 and 1837 demonstrate a growing demand for children's books. The earliest known bookseller's catalogue, John Neilson's *Catalogue of English French and Latin Books, for Sale at the Printing Office* (Quebec, 1800), lists adult books and senior school texts individually by title, but just a single line about hornbooks (alphabet paddles) and children's books sums up the

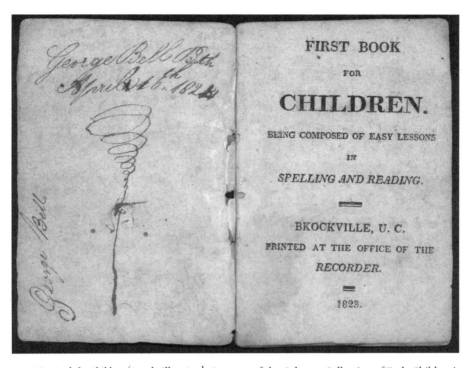

11.2 *First Book for Children* (Brockville, 1823). Courtesy of the Osborne Collection of Early Children's Books, Toronto Public Library (TRL).

juvenile stock.[9] By 1815–19 the bookstore of Hector Bossange in Montreal was offering instructional books by Arnaud Berquin, Madame Leprince de Beaumont, and Madame de Genlis and the fables of La Fontaine, together with abridged works by Plutarch, Buffon, Newton, and others.[10] In 1830 the York (Toronto) committee of the SPCK produced a catalogue of books for sale at its depository.[11] Of some 173 titles listed, 5 textbooks, 30 reward and instructional books, and 3 magazines can readily be identified as children's reading. Many of these are secular, including *The Book of Trades* and *The History of Quadrupeds*. E. Lesslie and Sons' *Catalogue of Books* (Toronto, 1837)[12] contains some fourteen hundred titles, of which nearly 100 are for children, including the 24-volume Girl's Library. The offerings range from *Aesop's Fables* and the *Arabian Nights* to *The American Juvenile Keepsake* (1825).

Given the small, uncertain markets and high cost of distribution, early printers in the colonies produced more dependable goods, such as inexpensive texts and catechisms, rather than novels and magazines (see illus. 11.2, above). Three early attempts to publish periodicals for young people were short-lived: the *Youth's Instructor* (Saint John, 1823–5), published monthly at eight pence per issue; the *Juvenile Entertainer* (Pictou, Nova Scotia, 1831–2), which appeared weekly at five shillings per annum; and *Youth's Monitor and Monthly Magazine* (Toronto, 1836),[13] at ten shillings per annum. These were instructional publications in which natural history was interspersed with moral essays and Christian religious reflections, and all were intended for literate, mature, and fairly affluent young readers.

Early books for children published locally had few illustrations, in contrast to imported books, which provided richer visual imagery. Nevertheless, in the flimsy chapbooks and early moral and instructional works produced for children in British North America to 1840, modest printers' ornaments and cuts lent interest to the text and, like the earnest stories they embellished, gave promise of works of greater imagination and delight to come.

Books of Instruction in New France, Quebec, and Lower Canada

PAUL AUBIN

For want of a clientele, the market for textbooks in New France was extremely small. Indeed, there existed only two institutions of higher learning, the Collège des jésuites for boys and the Couvent des ursulines for girls, both at Quebec; two trade schools, one in Saint-Joachim and the other run by the Frères Charon at Montreal; a few schools in household management for girls run by the nuns of the Congrégation de Notre-Dame; and the 'petites écoles,' or primary schools, of which Louis-Philippe Audet listed twenty-four outside the towns of Quebec, Montreal, and Trois-Rivières. Since there were no printing presses, the small number of textbooks in use came from France, and attempts to list them are imprecise;[14] thus we know almost nothing about the pedagogical literature in circulation, particularly in the primary schools.

Beginning in the mid-eighteenth century, however, two factors led to the development of a market for textbooks: a state structure that encouraged the creation of a school system and the public response to the government's initiatives demonstrated by school attendance, which Michel Verrette discusses in chapter 8. The first printer to arrive at Quebec in 1764 did not immediately meet the demand of schools: at the Collège de Montréal, students had to rent imported textbooks.[15] In addition, whether because of a lack of books or the following of an old custom inherited from Europe, they transcribed their coursework, thus providing a collection of unpublished manuals.[16] A list of these exists for the Collège de l'Assomption.[17] As far as possible, classical colleges used textbooks from France and gave little if any support to local pedagogical publishing, such as the *Institutiones philosophicae* (Quebec, 1835) of Abbé Jérôme Demers.

Between 1778 and 1839, forty-four printers in Quebec and Lower Canada produced 119 textbook titles, for a total of 169 publications, including reprints.[18] The output increased steadily from decade to decade, peaking in the 1830s with 70 books marketed, or 58.8 per cent of all production. The law concerning schools run by trustees, passed in 1829, resulted in a significant rise in school attendance. Montreal dominated the market, with twenty-five printing shops, followed by Quebec, with fifteen; a few more existed outside the large centres, such as George Stobbs in Trois-Rivières, Walton and Gaylord in Stanstead, and A.-C. Fortin and J.P. Boucher-Belleville in Saint-Charles-sur-Richelieu. Slightly more than half the printers (twenty-five out of forty-four) used an English name for their businesses, but the linguistic divide did not automatically restrict them to publishing in a single language. Although some anglophones, such as Armour and Ramsay, produced textbooks only in English, many other printers, notably the Neilsons (John Neilson and his son Samuel, in partnership with William Cowan, published 11 new titles, or 9.2 per cent of production in Lower Canada), printed regularly for the French-language market. A shop such as the Nouvelle Imprimerie, founded by two anglophones, changed owners several times, but francophone and anglophone used the name 'New Printing Office' when it published textbooks in English. Although 25.2 per cent (30 out of 119) of the manuals printed in Lower Canada were intended for English-language students,[19] these same books were of interest to a francophone clientele. For example, an English-language reader by Lindley Murray – the title is not specified – was used at Saint-Jean-Chrysostome de Lauzon in 1847.[20] Publishers could count on a pool of forty-eight authors who have been identified, twenty-eight of whom were francophone; more than half (twenty-seven) were teachers, and eleven, clergymen, some of whom were also teachers.

Existing at the margins of the European population, Aboriginal schools were the poor relations of pedagogical publishing. Fleury Mesplet's produced a spelling book in Mohawk in 1777 (*Iontri8aiestsk8a*) and *A Primer for the Use of the Mohawk Children* four years later, reprinted in 1827 and 1828 by the printer George Gurnett of Ancaster in Upper Canada, an edition discussed by Joyce Banks in chapter 12.[21]

Before school books began to be written locally, publishers in British North America reproduced foreign texts. Thus, for Lower Canada, with Pierre Restaut's *Abrégé des règles de versification française* (1778), France's contribution accounted for 23 titles by the end of the 1830s, or 19.3 per cent of the total production.[22] The Latin manuals of Abbé Charles-François L'Homond and Jean Palairet's readers were most often used.[23] The English-language market in Lower Canada was more dependent on foreign works than the French. Of 30 titles published in the province for anglophones, 56.6 per cent were reprints from England; a few titles came from the United States. As well, John Strachan, a Scot by birth and schoolteacher in 1809 in Cornwall, published *A Concise Introduction to Practical Arithmetic* in Montreal. A popular author in England and the United States, Lindley Murray was also a favourite among teachers in Lower Canada: between 1824 and 1865, his seven English manuals were reprinted a total of twenty-five times.[24] William Mavor, whose *The English Spelling Book* was reprinted six times between 1837 and 1874, was Murray's main competitor.[25] Another highly valued author was William Eusebius Andrews, whose *Catholic School Book* was reprinted seventeen times between 1817 and 1870 – a surprising success, since Catholics were clearly a minority among anglophones in Lower Canada.

Foreign competition for local production also occurred through the importation of books printed elsewhere. Sixty-five foreign textbooks, most of them in French, but some in English, published overseas before 1839 and circulating in Lower Canada, have been recorded in the library of the Collège de l'Assomption.[26] Of the nine textbooks whose use has been noted for one or more schools in Upper Canada before 1840, eight were printed in England or the United States and one in Montreal.[27] The American component in the importation of textbooks was notable: Mavor's *Spelling Book*, reprinted in both Lower and Upper Canada, competed with American products such as Noah Webster's readers, which were cheaper and easy to import.[28] A few years later, Jean-Baptiste Meilleur, superintendent of education for Lower Canada, and Egerton Ryerson, who occupied the same position in Upper Canada from 1844, would denounce the invasion of American textbooks into schools in their provinces.[29]

Between the textbooks printed in Europe or the United States and the publication in British North America of reprinted foreign texts, we must note those that were stereotyped. Ten or so date from before 1840, produced mainly in Upper Canada. Finally, the travels of educators from British North America in Europe and the United States – Abbé John Holmes from Lower Canada and Egerton Ryerson from Upper Canada – encouraged the use of foreign textbooks: Holmes brought many examples back from France in 1836.

The importance of the school market in the overall book trade remains to be assessed. Only a few statistics are available for Lower Canada. Between 1792 and 1812, John Neilson's bookstore, the largest in the province, sold 58,051 volumes, of which 9,477, or 16.3 per cent, were textbooks, produced locally or imported.[30] One would, however, need to know the print runs of locally produced books and the quantities of imports in order to better evaluate what share of the market textbooks occupied.

Books of Instruction in Upper Canada and the Atlantic Colonies

SARAH BROUILLETTE

Both importation and local publication of textbooks in Upper Canada and the Atlantic region were tied to the development of education and to the establishment of a publicly funded school system. No such system existed in any of the colonies before 1840.[31] Regulation through legislation was limited, much education took place in private homes and Sunday schools, and few schoolrooms possessed an adequate supply of any text. School books were believed to have a significant impact on the moral development of students, and the respective merits of various texts were debated by political and religious factions – anti-colonialist versus Loyalist, sectarian versus non-sectarian. Yet a study of what is known about the textbooks in use belies simple characterizations. Anxiety about the influence of American texts and fears about the dominance of religious works in classrooms were common, if not rational, responses. As Paul Robinson notes, the situation in the English-speaking colonies was 'a patchwork quilt – a clashing of foreign patterns held together with stitchery of uncertain origins and dubious strength.'[32]

Over half the texts known to have been used in Upper Canada before 1840 were printed in the United States,[33] and local authorship was rare. As well, American and British textbooks were frequently reprinted in the colonies, for reasons perhaps less political than financial, since stereotype plates could be imported relatively cheaply. The private market was predominant, and the purchase of textbooks was not systematically authorized even after a General Board of Education was set up in Upper Canada in 1824.[34] With Anglican bishop John Strachan at its head, it sought to displace what it perceived as a deleterious American influence in the schools. Strachan's goal was to place education under the control of the Church of England. The board allocated £150 per year for the purchase of textbooks in the province. In 1825 and 1826 it distributed the funds directly to the Society for Promoting Christian Knowledge.[35] Given that the average school book at the time cost 5d, the society could have purchased upwards of 15,000 copies with the £300.[36] The money was often used to purchase Strachan's preferred texts: the Bible and New Testament and works such as William Mavor's *English Spelling Book*, authorized by the board in 1828 and a staple throughout Upper Canada in this period (both imported and printed in Kingston in 1831, Toronto in 1836 and 1839, and Hamilton in 1839).[37] Opposition to Strachan's direct promotion of Anglican control led to the board's demise in 1833.[38]

Among other works frequently reprinted before 1840 were texts by American author Lindley Murray. His *English Reader* and its *Introduction*, which contained a broad range of eighteenth-century literature and were in no sense narrowly pedagogic, were printed regularly throughout Upper Canada and the Atlantic region between 1820 and 1840. Murray's work typified the kind of education promoted by religious leaders. His *English Reader* claimed in its title to improve both 'language and sentiments, and to inculcate some of the most important principles of piety and virtue.' The link between literacy and morality was hardly surprising during this period, since religious groups often took responsibility for teaching literacy and general knowledge, and lessons were frequently presented through religious content. As Allan Greer has observed, literacy was often considered a Christian value whose primary goal was access to the Bible. Sunday schools, where much elementary education took place, were 'evangelical to the core, ... obsessed with the written, or more precisely, with the printed word.'[39]

Despite opposition to imported texts, few locally authored works appeared. In 1829 Alexander Davidson compiled his own speller to counter the American textbooks widely used in Upper Canada. A schoolteacher in Port Hope, he created lessons with local context and included 'morning and evening prayers for every day in the week.' The book was not published until 1840, however, when it appeared as *The Canada Spelling Book*, the first book copyrighted in Upper Canada. *Kingston Chronicle* proprietor James Macfarlane expressed similar fears about American publications with contents 'not very suitable to our Constitution and Government' in an 1827 prospectus for his edition of Mavor's speller, which appeared the following year.[40]

In the Atlantic colonies, textbooks designed for local use had appeared relatively early. Making a distinction between local and imported texts, however, risks obscuring the true nature of these works. Many locally produced texts borrowed heavily from existing European or American models, and imported texts were often altered in various ways. One of the earliest books known to have been explicitly printed for students in British North America was *The Catechism of the Church of England*, which also contained 'the larger and shorter catechisms of the Church of Scotland.' Printed at the Acadian Recorder Office in Halifax in 1813, it was distributed there and through the bookstores of William Minns, George Eaton, and John Howe. Patricia Lockhart Fleming notes that Walter Bromley was collecting subscriptions for the Royal Acadian School that year and may have encouraged the publication of this catechism for the use of his students.[41] His impact on education in Nova Scotia belies claims that denominational interests controlled early instruction. The Royal Acadian School was explicitly non-denominational, arousing concern among local Anglicans and challenging the concept of education as an instrument of socio-economic control.[42] Another example of a work adapted for local use is B. Perro's *Abecedaire religieux, moral, instructif et amusant*, a French grammar printed by Edmund Ward in Halifax in 1817. In a prefatory note to the public, the author explains the difficulty of teaching French without appropriate textbooks, and thus the need to seek out a good French grammar and to have it printed locally.[43] In Prince Edward Island in 1837, James Douglas Haszard printed *Willcolkes's and Fryer's New and Much Admired System of Arithmetic and Mental Calculations*. This work was edited by local educator James Waddell and printed explicitly for his use at Charlottetown's Central Academy.[44]

Some early textbooks in the Atlantic region were more local in focus. *The Acadian Preceptor*, 'containing short and easy lessons, in prose and verse, for the use of schools,' was printed for the Royal Acadian School in Halifax in 1823. John Williams M'Coubrey printed William Charles St. John's *A Catechism of the History of Newfoundland* in St John's in 1835, and a similar book appeared later in Nova Scotia. John Henry Crosskill's *A Comprehensive Outline of the Geography and History of Nova Scotia* (Halifax, 1838) claimed to be 'arranged in a peculiar manner, which renders it applicable either as a catechism or a reading book.' Crosskill compiled the text largely from Thomas Chandler Haliburton's *An Historical and Statistical Account of Nova-Scotia* (Halifax, 1829). In the preface to the second edition (1842), he claimed that the first one thousand copies had sold out in 'several months.'[45]

After the Rebellion of 1837 in Upper Canada, American textbooks were again considered a threat to the colony, and imports from Britain more desirable. By 1838 the thirteen districts of the province boasted 651 schools and 14,776 students.[46] Not until 1841, when the Legislative Assembly of the Province of Canada passed a bill

authorizing the appointment of a superintendent of education, would public education and the selection of textbooks be centralized, but before this important reform,
as Greer notes, public opinion had already begun 'to favour the notion that all children should receive some instruction and that it was the responsibility of the state
to see that they did.'[47] In the Atlantic region the situation differed from province to
province, but there is little evidence to suggest that a systematic approach to the use
of textbooks existed before the second half of the nineteenth century.[48]

Religious Books

RAYMOND BRODEUR

In the British colonies of North America before 1840, religious books were produced to educate, enlighten, and teach the greatest possible numbers of the faithful. The socio-cultural orientation of the people who ordered these religious
works to be printed and the choices they made reveal much about the society of the
time.

The Bible

The Bible was considered the most precious of religious books because of its sacred
content. Editions were often luxurious and meticulously produced, and they had to
be approved by specialists or legitimate authorities. Before 1840 few printers in British North America undertook such an enterprise. Between July 1783 and September
1784, Peter Delaroche announced in the *Nova-Scotia Gazette* the planned publication
of a work entitled 'A Doctrinal and Practical Commentary on the New Testament,'[49]
but it was never realized. The first known Authorized Version of the Bible to be
printed in the colonies was a three-volume stereotyped edition published by John
Henry White in Halifax and then in Charlottetown in the 1820s. Joseph Wilson of
Hallowell (Picton) brought out a one-volume stereotyped edition in 1834.[50]

   While the difficulties involved in producing the whole Bible meant that few such
projects were undertaken, extracts needed for the liturgy, such as *Heures royales ...,*

contenant les épîtres et évangiles des principales fêtes de l'année ... à l'usage des Congrégations de Notre-Dame (Quebec, 1806),[51] were more common. Passages from the Bible also made their way into school books, religious narratives, and books of devotion.[52] As the basis for religious training and life, the Bible enjoyed a more widespread presence in English-speaking Protestant communities. *The Christian's Pocket Companion* (Niagara, 1819)[53] and at least three different editions of the New Testament printed in Upper Canada in the years 1830–4 should be mentioned here.[54]

Books of Devotion

Religion was not merely abstract and speculative; among the faithful, devotion was expressed through religious feeling associated with ritual observances and moral conduct. After the Conquest, few clergy were left to attend to the religious needs of Catholics. Religious communities such as the Confrérie de la Sainte-Famille[55] therefore offered them printed works useful in a life of piety and novenas dedicated to particular saints, such as the *Neuvaine à l'honneur de Saint François Xavier*.[56] Some devotional books were directed toward specific groups. For example, the Sulpician Amable Bonnefons produced an often-reprinted work entitled *Le petit livre de vie* for the faithful in the diocese of Quebec.[57] The pupils of the Ursulines, both boarders and day students, constituted another group for whom prayers were printed.[58]

While many devotional books were produced in Lower Canada, they were rare in Upper Canada. There it was more common to find collections of edifying and virtuous texts for young people, often mixed in with ordinary school readers, thereby combining moral and intellectual education. Lindley Murray's *Introduction to the English Reader* is typical of such works.[59] In Alexander Johnston Williamson's *There Is a God* (1839),[60] the author records his religious experience in verse.

Prayers, Hymns, and Psalms

Liturgical works were intended for use in religious services: rituals, ceremonials, missals, vespers, and hymnals all played a role in particular celebrations. In 1703 Bishop Jean-Baptiste de La Croix de Chevrières de Saint-Vallier had the ritual book for the diocese of Quebec printed by Simon Langlois in Paris.[61] During the eighteenth century, Fleury Mesplet in Montreal and John Neilson at Quebec printed liturgical works, including *Office de la Semaine sainte*, *Heures romaines*, and *Vêpres*. After the situation of the Catholic Church became more stable at the turn of the new century, liturgical works began to appear more regularly. Until 1820, extensive printing was carried out to restock the churches of Lower Canada with such books.

Among Protestants, publications with titles such as *A Form of Prayer to Be Used in All Churches* were common. Published under the authority of the Church of England, they were ordered by the king or his representative, typeset, and printed in the local diocese under the direction of the bishop. These texts directed the public recitation of a specific prayer decreed by the sovereign, perhaps a prayer of thanksgiving for a favour or a supplication, often accompanied by a general fast. Printers in Lower Canada received orders from the Catholic authorities to produce similar works in the form of pastorals or circulars addressed to parish priests, who were instructed to repeat them to their parishioners.

Sermons

Sermons were a type of religious work well suited to print.[62] Such publications reached a far greater public than those who attended religious services. Before 1840 more than a hundred sermons were published in the Atlantic colonies and Upper Canada. They were ordered by churches or influential groups and individuals, and printers, eager for the patronage, turned them out rapidly. The subject matter ranged from Bible passages to virtues, devotions, and sometimes funeral eulogies. Others were of a specifically political or polemical nature. As Sydney F. Wise points out, in the late eighteenth and early nineteenth centuries, these publications were a valuable conduit for the conservative, anti-revolutionary ideas being put forth by the ministers of various churches and confessional communities in British North America.[63]

Printed sermons were much more common among English-speaking Protestants: before 1800 only four sermons were published in French. The earliest of these was by David Chabrand Delisle,[64] a Church of England clergyman who, in 1787, had his funeral eulogy for merchant Benjamin Frobisher printed by Mesplet.[65] Two sermons were by Bishop Joseph-Octave Plessis,[66] and the fourth, published posthumously, by Abbé Auguste-David Hubert of Quebec.[67] Like the sermons in English, these conveyed highly conservative ideas opposed to revolution; they exhorted Canadiens to respect the legitimate authorities and submit to the Catholic clergy.

Catechisms

Catechisms are among the major legacies of the times of religious reform and the invention of the printing press.[68] In both Protestant England and Catholic France, catechisms were published from the seventeenth century.[69] For English Protestants the text remained largely unchanged from one edition to the next, but this was not the case for French Catholics, since the bishops had full prerogative over their production.

The Séminaire de Québec retains a collection of some thirty catechisms from the dioceses of France used by the missionaries of New France. The first catechism prepared for the diocese of Quebec was compiled by Bishop de Saint-Vallier and printed in Paris in 1702 by Urbain Coustelier. Part of the edition was seized by pirates and later sold in England.[70] In 1743 Bishop Henri-Marie Dubreil de Pontbriand imposed the anti-Jansenist catechism of Jean-Joseph Languet, bishop of Sens, on the diocese.[71] Ironically, the printing of Catholic catechisms in what is now Canada began with the arrival of Protestant printers at Quebec. In November 1765 the merchant Louis Langlois, *dit* Germain, ordered 2,000 catechisms from William Brown and Thomas Gilmore, at a cost of £91 16s. When the first printing sold out in less than five months, a second order was placed in 1766.[72] At that time, the Conquest had slowed the trade of books with France, but the demand for religious books was as strong as ever. So Langlois seized the opportunity to take on the role of publisher for his own benefit and that of the clergy.

In 1777 the superior of the Sulpicians in Montreal, Étienne Montgolfier, proposed to Bishop Jean-Olivier Briand that the book be split into two volumes: a small catechism to sell for 15 sols, with a revised text, and a large catechism priced at 36 sols. When the new version was offered for sale at Mesplet's, an advertisement announced, 'It is our wish that, after children have learned their alphabet, the first reader they be given should be the small catechism, which for this reason will be printed separately (from the large catechism) so it can be procured at a lower price.'[73] Thus the catechism united the two poles of cultural identity – language and religion – a formula that would often be repeated later. For in the catechism, the very act of reading drew together all priests, parents, and schoolmasters with believers of every age who were learning how to read. The undertaking was also a commercial success, reaching thousands of copies by the end of the eighteenth century.[74]

The history of the catechism in the nineteenth century largely confirms the wisdom of Montgolfier and Briand. However, between 1811 and 1815 Bishop Plessis extensively revised the small catechism of 1777, which he wished to develop in order to better prepare children for their first communion, 'whether they know how to read or not,' as he wrote in the preface. The new version of the small catechism, released in 1816, included 329 questions and answers.[75] Records show that forty-three different editions were produced by over twenty printers between 1816 and 1852 and demonstrate how successful this publication was.[76]

For English-speaking Catholics, mostly from Ireland and Scotland, William Brown printed 1,000 copies of the Douay Catechism in 1778, at a total cost of £18 10s.[77] A new edition was printed in 1800 by John Neilson.[78] However, in 1817 Bishop Plessis had his own new catechism translated into English and printed.[79] Matters progressed somewhat differently after the creation of new dioceses in the 1830s, when English-speaking bishops sought to promulgate specific catechisms, as evidenced by *The First Catechism,* approved by Bishop Alexander McDonell of Kingston in 1834.[80]

Associated with the catechisms were the numerous manuals of religious instruction created for the Native peoples, such as the *Nehiro-Iriniui* prepared by Father Jean-Baptiste de La Brosse and printed in 2,000 copies by Brown and Gilmore in 1767, at a cost of £45.[81] The Oblate missionaries in the West also produced many catechisms, some of which remained in manuscript form.[82]

After American independence, English-language Protestant catechisms were printed, but in smaller numbers than their Catholic counterparts.[83] These were not diocesan catechisms but compendia of their respective communities. In 1790 William Moore published at Quebec 'The Shorter Catechism,' 'from the true copy as now used in Scotland.'[84] Another edition of *The Shorter Catechism* appeared at Ancaster, Upper Canada, in 1828, printed 'at the Gore Gazette Office, for Robert Bell.'[85]

In 1811 the Mennonite Brethren produced *The Christian Confession of the Faith,* reprinted and sold by Joseph Willcocks at Niagara (Niagara-on-the-Lake).[86] The Methodist Episcopal Church in Canada had its *Doctrines and Discipline* printed at York (Toronto) in 1829; a year later, the Canadian Wesleyan Methodist Church published *The Doctrines and Discipline of the Canadian Wesleyan Methodists* (Hamilton, 1830).[87] In 1831 Robert Stanton published at York a work called *An Abridgement of Christian Doctrine,* which explained the catechism of the Church of England, its sacraments, feasts, and government, and the Christian's moral conduct.[88]

Not surprisingly, catechisms proclaiming a common faith were rare. Even among Catholics, when a bishop promulgated a particular catechism, it was always to the exclusion of others. Nevertheless, certain works of a prescriptive nature such as sermons sometimes took the form of catechisms. In 1822, for example, John Carey at York published *Sermon and Catechism for Children,*[89] and in 1826 Andrew Mitchell Thompson's *A Catechism for the Instruction of Communicants* appeared at Lanark, Upper Canada.[90]

The Latin term *catechesis* means 'the word that echoes,' but with the advent of the printing press, a radical change took place: the spoken word and oral tradition passed into the realm of writing. The written word that echoes becomes rather a matter of confession than of experience and, at the very least, filters experience through more controlled and immutable frameworks.

Music

NANCY F. VOGAN

During the early days of settlement, music was particularly associated with religion, leisure, and the military.[91] In many circumstances, it was transmitted orally. However, references survive of music being notated, such as an account of Marc Lescarbot transcribing the words and music of Mi'kmaq songs at Port-Royal (Annapolis Royal, Nova Scotia) in 1606–7. In New France, music instruction was provided by the Jesuits, the Ursulines, and the Sulpicians;[92] several manuscripts of compositions for Roman Catholic services have been preserved from this era. Psalm tunes used by Protestant congregations can also be found in manuscript compilations, including illustrated examples from the eighteenth century found in Nova Scotia.[93] In an early Mennonite community in the Niagara District, songbooks were copied and elaborately decorated for singing-school pupils by their teacher.[94]

Publications for use in Catholic services in New France and Lower Canada were imported from France, some of them produced especially for use in North America. Protestant congregations in the British colonies employed hymn books imported from Britain and oblong tunebooks from the United States. The tunebooks represent one of the earliest forms of music instruction produced in North America, for they usually contained theoretical introductions and some included a few secular compositions.[95] Newspaper advertisements record imported music for sale in the British colonies, but seldom identify the titles.

From 1800, when music began to be printed in British North America, through the first half of the nineteenth century, it appeared in three forms: as collections of church music, songs, or instructional material; in newspapers and magazines; and as sheet music devoted to a single composition.[96] Three printing methods were used before 1830: movable type, drawn or punched engraving, and lithography. The earliest examples in all categories were produced at Quebec or in Montreal. At Quebec in 1800, John Neilson printed *Le graduel romain à l'usage du diocèse de Québec*, a 688-page volume set with type in square chant notation on a four-line staff.[97] *The Vocal Preceptor; or, Key to Sacred Music from Celebrated Authors,* an instructional work by A. Stevenson printed in Montreal in 1811, is the earliest known example of engraved music in British North America.[98] *Nouveau recueil de cantiques, à l'usage du diocèse de Québec,* a collection prepared by Jean-Denis Daulé, chaplain to the Ursulines at Quebec, was engraved there in 1819 by Frederick Hund and printed at La Nouvelle Imprimerie.

Two years later in Montreal, William Gray printed *A Selection from the Psalms of David*, compiled by George Jenkins, with music engraved by T.G. Preston.

Music began to appear in newspapers and periodicals in the 1830s. The earliest example (and the first typeset round notation), which was published in Ludger Duvernay's *La Minerve* in 1831, is discussed by Maria Calderisi in the case study which follows. 'Favorite Waltz,' in the *Montreal Museum* of February 1833, was probably the first music lithographed in British North America. Not until John Lovell's *Literary Garland* began publication in Montreal in 1838, however, would music be included on a regular basis in a magazine; each monthly issue of this publication contains from one and a half to three pages of typeset music.[99]

In the Maritime provinces, the year 1801 marks the publication in Saint John of the earliest English-language book of music, Stephen Humbert's *Union Harmony*, but no copy of this edition is known. A second edition, published by Humbert in 1816, was printed in New Hampshire;[100] another appeared in Boston in 1831. Zebulon Estey's *New Brunswick Church Harmony* was published in 1835, and like the 1840 edition of Humbert's work, was probably produced in the United States. The first music printed from type in the Maritime provinces was the work of James Dawson of Pictou, Nova Scotia. He printed two examples from his forthcoming tune book, *The Harmonicon*, in his newspaper, the *Bee*, in 1837; the volume itself appeared a year later.[101] A second edition, also printed by Dawson, was published in 1841.

Music publications began to appear in Upper Canada in 1830. That year at York (Toronto), king's printer Robert Stanton produced *A System of Drill, for the Militia, of Upper Canada*, which included a fold-out sheet of typeset 'Bugle Sounds.'[102] Mark Burnham published his *Colonial Harmonist* in Port Hope in 1832;[103] like Humbert's, this volume was probably printed in the United States.[104] The manuscript of a proposed second edition has come to light,[105] but it seems never to have been printed. *A Selection of Psalms and Hymns* (1835), compiled for the use of Church of England congregations in the Diocese of Quebec, with music arranged by organist William Warren, was published by Stanton in Toronto, but printed in New York.[106] Alexander Davidson's *Sacred Harmony* (1838), published in Toronto by the Wesleyan Methodist Conference, was printed from stereotype plates made in New York.[107] Some later editions appeared in shape-note format.

Although sheet music may well have been printed at one of the presses in Lower Canada before 1840, two surviving examples date from that year, *The Merry Bells of England*, printed by John Lovell in Montreal, and Napoléon Aubin's *Le dépit amoureux* with music and a pictorial cover lithographed in Quebec.[108] Despite these examples, the limitations of local music publishing up to 1840 required most musicians in the

British colonies to depend on American publishers who specialized in the printing of music.

CASE STUDY
Music and *La Minerve*
— Maria Calderisi

Ludger Duvernay (1799–1852) was an experienced newspaperman by the time he acquired the Montreal biweekly *La Minerve* in January 1827, having published *La Gazette des Trois-Rivières* (1817–21) and *Le Constitutionnel* (1823–4), as well as a monthly, *L'Ami de la religion et du roi* (1820), in Trois-Rivières (see illus. 4.2, p. 76).[109] His support of the Patriote party in *La Minerve* and his involvement in the Rebellions of 1837 and 1838 and exile to the United States are well documented, but less well known is the fact that printed music appeared for the first time in a periodical in British North America on the front page of his newspaper on 19 September 1831. Four lines of music accompanying a patriotic song entitled 'La Parisienne' and a further six stanzas of text are spread across three columns at the upper left of the page. On page three, between an editorial on the use of lottery funds and another on the laying of the cornerstone for a new hospital wing, appears the following explanation:

> The famous cantata by Casimir Delavigne, la Parisienne, with music, is to be found on our first page. This costly addition to our printing equipment should prove that we spare nothing in attempting to please our readers, and it will be of great benefit in making known the melodies of new songs from Europe or others composed in this country. Music lovers wishing to make additional copies of pieces of religious or other types of music will now be able to do so at this establishment.
>
> From time to time we will publish new pieces of music which we will endeavour to find in arrangements for piano, the instrument most commonly in use.[110]

In a letter from New York to Léon Gosselin, then editor of *La Minerve*, on 23 August 1831, Duvernay wrote that he had bought a font of music from the Conner foundry, and he complained about the cost: 'over £60, nine months'

11.3 A New Year's offering in *La Minerve* (Montreal, 1832). Courtesy of the National Library of Canada.

credit.'[111] His hopes to make good use of his new luxury were not realized, however, since the only other music to appear in *La Minerve* was his New Year's offering 'L'Année 1832 (see illus. 11.3, p. 270),' and there is no evidence that his presses were engaged by other would-be music publishers.[112] Nevertheless, Duvernay's pioneering enterprise and his bow to a gentler art in the midst of a highly charged political crusade should be lauded.

Almanacs

ANNE DONDERTMAN AND JUDY DONNELLY

Almanacs were a familiar and important commodity to Europeans, with a rich history dating back to the earliest days of printing and before that to manuscript books of hours. With newspapers, they were one of the earliest products of the press in British North America, first printed in Quebec in 1765,[113] Nova Scotia in 1769,[114] New Brunswick in 1786,[115] Upper Canada in 1800,[116] Prince Edward Island in 1815,[117] and Newfoundland before 1841.[118] By that year almanacs had been produced in at least sixteen towns or cities, accounting for some ninety-six known titles or series produced by seventy-four different printers or publishers. Because almanacs were used daily and normally replaced at year-end, however, a significant number are no longer extant.

Almanacs were used as a calendar to check the day and month, holidays, feast and saints' days, and astronomical information, including sunrise and sunset, moon phases, eclipses and comets, and tides. They functioned also as ready reckoners, offering useful information such as interest and currency tables; as compendia of health and domestic advice; as agricultural and veterinary handbooks; as directories of municipal information, court sittings, military and militia lists, churches and clergy, educational institutions, societies, libraries, and other organizations; and as travel guides, providing roads and distances, sailing times, and so on. As well, they supplied entertainment in the form of verse and humorous anecdotes, historical chronologies, and, especially near the end of the period, advertisements.

Before almanacs were locally produced, they were imported in significant numbers, primarily from Great Britain, the United States, and France, and sold by stationers, general merchants, and peddlers.[119] At least one Boston almanac specifically targeted Halifax readers.[120] Imported almanacs were banned in New Brunswick in the early 1800s[121] but continued to be available elsewhere.[122] Their great disadvantage was their lack of local astronomical and community information. 'Calculated for the meridian of ... ' was an important selling point for almanac publishers; it guaranteed that content was accurate for the specific location. Charles Fothergill touted his Upper Canadian almanac of 1839 as 'not merely a *matter of fact* Text Book for all those at a distance who may desire authentic information in regard to this Province; but it constitutes an indispensable *Manuel*, from the variety and minutely detailed official intelligence which it contains, to every resident, no matter what may be his calling or avocation.'[123] Accuracy and currency were all the more critical, given that the almanac and the family Bible were often the only reference and reading materials in a household.[124]

The appearance and content of almanacs produced in British North America before 1840 show not only the influence of national models but also the printer's background. Trained in Philadelphia, Quebec's William Brown and Thomas Gilmore produced sheet almanacs (*calendriers*), a typically French and British format,[125] but with type ornaments as borders and decoration, a style characteristic of colonial American imprints. Fleury Mesplet's imprints bear the marks of a printer apprenticed in France, yet his first Montreal almanac[126] contains prognostications common to the British tradition. Over its first decade, Anthony Henry's English-language Halifax almanac[127] included the 'wit and wisdom' and domestic lore typical of American almanacs[128] and the political prognostications, chronology of world events, and weather predictions of their British counterparts.[129] His distinctive German-language almanac, printed with imported black-letter types, was based on Pennsylvania models,[130] which in turn closely resemble German exemplars, particularly *messagers boiteux*.[131] Ludger Duvernay clearly identified in his title the model for his 1830 Montreal almanac, *Guide du cultivateur ou nouvel almanac de la temperature ... d'après les almanachs allemands*.

Although innovations in style or content were introduced only gradually, almanacs in the British colonies assumed distinctive characteristics as their compilers responded to local needs and tastes; one example is the bilingual *Quebec Almanack / Almanach de Québec*.[132] In addition to English, French, and bilingual series, German-language almanacs and at least one Native-language series appeared.[133] Sheet almanacs, which served as wall calendars, were found primarily in Lower Canada at this time,[134] though they would become more widespread later in the nineteenth century. Although by 1797 the *Quebec Almanack / Almanac de Québec* had grown to 184 pages, most early almanacs were considerably more modest. Usually they were pamphlets, of 16 or more pages in octavo format, stabbed and stitched, sometimes in plain or marbled paper wrappers. Although the majority were decorated only on the title page with agriculturally themed (see illus. 11.4, p. 274) or other standard cuts, such as the royal arms, in Nova Scotia both the 'man of signs' and seasonal or 'labours of the month' cuts were used on the calendar pages. As Joan Winearls notes in chapter 5, the earliest book illustration in British North America appeared in Anthony Henry's *Nova-Scotia Calendar ... for ... 1777*.[135]

Given the importance of almanacs in daily life, the question of authorship is significant. Technical information had to be supplied by appropriately trained individuals such as surveyors, engineers, or military personnel. Maurice Simonin, an 'ancien Capitaine de Navire,' prepared the calculations for the 'Almanac de cabinet' of 1765,[136] and surveyor Samuel Holland compiled the astronomical information for at least one other Quebec almanac,[137] while fellow surveyor and mathematics teacher Bernard Kiernan did likewise in New Brunswick. But such attributions are unusual. In Nova Scotia and New Brunswick, following the British tradition, almanacs often featured pseudonymous compilers (Lilius, Theophrastus, or Scaliger) who built up a reputation and a readership. Although some content was created by almanac makers themselves, items such as recipes or domestic advice and popular verse were solicited from readers or freely copied from foreign or rival almanacs, newspapers, and other sources.

As almanacs not only tended to look similar but also frequently used identical titles, publishers began 'branding' them by adding their names to the titles – for example, *Belcher's Farmer's Almanack* or *Fothergill's Toronto Almanac*. Almanacs were also used as religious, political, or social vehicles by individuals as diverse as Montreal Patriote Ludger Duvernay, tory supporter David Dwyer in Toronto, reformer William Lyon Mackenzie (including his celebrated *Caroline Almanack ... for 1840*, printed while the rebel leader was in exile in Rochester), and temperance advocates in Nova Scotia.[138]

That almanacs were widely and intensively distributed and used is attested to by their prevalence in the marketplace and the condition of surviving examples. Print runs ranged from about 200 copies for a 1769 Quebec sheet *calendrier* to 10,000 for the 1835 *Upper Canada Christian Almanac*.[139] Mackenzie claimed to have distributed 'from 30,000 to 40,000 of the "Poor Richards"' over three years.[140] To increase sales, volume discounts were commonly offered. But although potentially lucrative, the almanac market was difficult and highly competitive. As well, almanacs were technically complex to set up, particularly the calendar and other densely packed pages. Many were published for only a few years; some for only a single issue.

For the purchaser, almanacs frequently doubled as personal diaries, and from

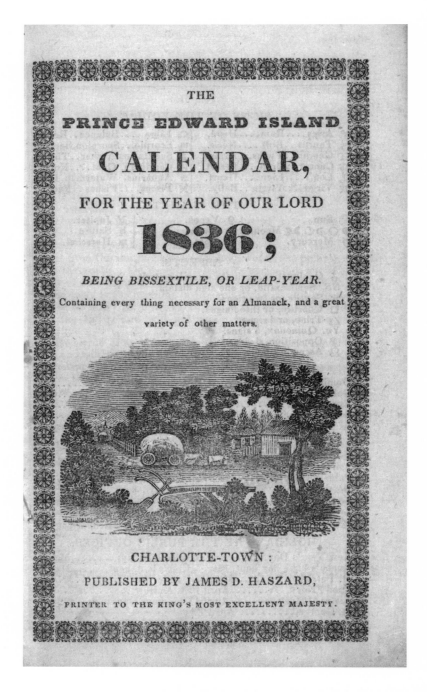

11.4 *The Prince Edward Island Calendar for the Year of Our Lord 1836; being Bissextile, or Leap-Year*
(Charlotte-town, [1835]). Courtesy of the Thomas Fisher Rare Book Library, University of Toronto.

an early period they were available interleaved with blanks. Sometimes a long series was annotated by a family or individual, such as the almanacs owned and marked by Isaac Deschamps of Halifax.[141] Owners recorded observations on the weather, ship arrivals, and details of family or working life, such as the marriages documented by a Prince Edward Island clergyman in an 1835 almanac.[142] Almanacs remain as testimony to the skills of their makers and the value placed in them by their owners.

Recipe and Household Literature

MARY F. WILLIAMSON

Recipes for food preparation and household management that were necessities in the homes of settlers appeared in manuscript collections, almanacs, periodicals and newspapers, and eventually in indigenous culinary manuals. We know from booksellers' and library catalogues and newspaper advertisements that the earliest settlers in what is now Canada were also familiar with the classic works of French, British, and American cookery.

One mission of female religious orders in New France was to nourish the poor and the sick. Today the ancient hospitals and convents of Quebec treasure well-thumbed copies of seventeenth- and eighteenth-century classic French cookbooks and confectionery manuals. These recipes, and others that evolved to take advantage of New World foods such as Indian corn, pumpkin, and maple syrup, governed the preparation of the baked goods and sweets traditionally consumed on religious feast days and often sold to the general public.[143] In the 1830s the Sisters of Providence in Montreal prepared meals for the poor from recipes that were already regarded as antique.[144]

Surviving notebooks, diaries, and manuscript collections include recipes that were collected and recorded by both men and women. In Britain and the United States – and, one assumes, in British North America – a preferred method of 'publishing' recipes was to circulate 'one's manuscript discretely to a selected group of readers.'[145] Around the turn of the nineteenth century the Claus family, originally from Germany, who came as Loyalists to Montreal and Niagara from New York, assembled instructions for currant wines, beer, mead, English 'champagne,' and shrub.[146] The editor of the *Farmers' Journal* (St Catharines, Upper Canada) presented his readers on 2 July 1828 with twenty-five recipes for cakes and puddings of mixed American and British ancestry 'from the manuscript receipt-book of a first rate house-keeper.' Before settling in Amherstburg and while leading a British regiment during the Upper Canada Rebellion of 1837, Yorkshireman Captain Henry Rudyerd filled a memorandum book and diary with recipes for fritters, 'maccaroni' pudding, and punch, together with 'Bengal currie,' 'quaffties,' and other spiced dishes that reflected his childhood in India.[147] Traditional British cakes, puddings, and desserts, vinegars, wines, and household remedies dominate the 178 recipes assembled around 1840 by Mrs W. Keppel White, an Anglican rector's wife in Harbour Breton, Newfoundland.[148]

From the late 1780s, almanacs shared recipes for curing and preserving fresh meats, fruits, vegetables, and butter for future use, the settlers' armour against starvation; for yeast, the essential component in brewing and baking; and for the ever-popular red currant and raspberry wines. Some almanacs drew special attention to recipes within their pages. Advertisements for 'The British Lady's Diary and Pocket Almanack' (Quebec, 1789) mention 'several useful recipes in cookery, pickling, preserving, &c.,' but no copies seem to have survived.[149] *Tiffany's Upper-Canada Almanac for the Year 1802* (Niagara) reproduced 'recipes for the preserving of fruits, &c' and making wines from *The Frugal Housewife* by Susannah Carter, published in London in 1742, with subsequent American editions.[150] *The Nova-Scotia Almanack for 1820* (Halifax) offered an eight-page 'Collection of Highly Approved and Valuable Receipts, for Domestic Economy.'[151] Under the heading 'For the ladies,' the 1837 *Canadian Farmers' Almanac* (Sherbrooke, Stanstead, and Montreal) reprinted nineteen recipes for puddings and pies from Lydia Child's *The American Frugal Housewife*, published between 1829 and 1836 in twenty American editions. The household hints typically provided instructions for mending china, banishing insects, and whitewashing rooms. Many almanacs included home cures for cancer, cholera, dysentery, and other bodily complaints.

The publication of cookbooks in British North America began in 1825 when Quebec bookseller Augustin- René Langlois, *dit* Germain issued Menon's *La cuisinière bourgeoise*, which had appeared in Paris in 1746. An immediate best-seller in France, this was the first cookbook directed at women. In Upper Canada, the first cookbook was *The Cook Not Mad; or Rational Cookery* (Kingston, 1831), which had been published a year earlier by Knowlton and Rice in Watertown, New York.[152] Both of these cookbooks, including their title pages, were entirely printed outside the Canadas.[153]

The year 1840 saw the almost simultaneous publication, in Montreal and Toronto, of the first original French- and English-language cookbooks. On 10 April, publisher Louis Perrault inserted an advertisement for *La cuisinière canadienne* in *L'Aurore des Canadas,* claiming, 'The Directions are all guaranteed to be foolproof, having been taken from the Journal of a former Montreal confectioner and having been tested by several families.' Eleven editions and impressions into the 1920s offered recipes for local game and fish, as well as traditional French, English, and American dishes. In August 1840, Joseph H. Lawrence at the *Christian Guardian* office in Toronto printed *The Frugal Housewife's Manual,* by 'A.B., of Grimsby,' who remains anonymous.[154] A.B.'s manual is tiny; it contains seventy-two 'useful receipts,' mostly for puddings, cakes, and desserts, with the final thirty-four pages assigned to the 'Cultivation of Vegetables.' Both sections rely heavily on American works, incorporating small variations that appear to derive from the compiler's experience.[155]

Male and female settlers brought with them to the colonies recipes for foods and beverages they had enjoyed in the old countries, quickly expanding the repertoire to include New World ingredients. While the role of cookbooks was to offer readers guidance and inspiration, what people actually cooked and consumed is more honestly reflected in manuscript recipes.

chapter 12

PRINT FOR COMMUNITIES

'And not hearers only': Books in Native Languages

JOYCE M. BANKS

Nearly all the Christian denominations active in early Canada, from first contact to 1840, published books in the languages of the peoples they hoped to convert. Roman Catholics, Anglicans, Moravians, and Methodists of every stripe carried the word of God to the Abenakis, Montagnais, Hurons, Mi'kmaqs, Six Nations, Ojibwas, Crees, and Inuit of Labrador. The apostle James called upon Christians to be 'doers of the word, and not hearers only,'[1] and some Aboriginal converts likewise proved to be 'not hearers only.' Devout Christians, they were dedicated to the conversion of their own people. Thousands of copies of the Scriptures and devotional works in Native languages were produced for use in homes, schools, and churches.[2] The majority of translations were the work of Native Christians, who almost certainly assisted in the preparation of the rest, although their work was not always acknowledged.

These publications attested to the belief that evangelism was most successful when pursued in the language of those to be converted, and they presupposed the existence of a literate society or one in which people could easily be taught to read. Despite what was done later to eradicate Aboriginal languages, the books survive, testament to the faith, dedication, and skill of both Aboriginal and European translators and their publishers. They are particularly precious as the earliest printed expressions of these languages and, given subsequent government policy, might have been among the few to survive.

The first translations available to the Native peoples were in manuscript form only. Although some materials printed for Aboriginal use consisted of broadsheets or pamphlets, most were octavo volumes, usually sturdily bound in cloth or leather. They were meant to be easily portable and inexpensive; to be sold, not given. With a few exceptions, the earliest imprints in Native languages were almanacs, primers, and catechisms. In some the words were broken down into syllables to facilitate reading. Others included an alphabet or orthography. As translation skills grew and reading ability improved, larger, more complex works were prepared, including scriptural translations, collections of psalms and hymns, and other books of devotion.

During the French regime, Catholic missionaries made the earliest translations for use among the Aboriginal peoples, preparing word lists and dictionaries with brief grammars, as well as almanacs, catechisms, and other devotional works. The few translations that were printed in France at this time demonstrated that missionaries had achieved some success in mastering the Native languages of New France; however, they were not intended for Native converts but were meant to attract support in Europe for the missions in New France. Two in the Montagnais language were printed at Rouen in 1630 for the Jesuits and reprinted as an appendix to Samuel de Champlain's *Voyages* (Paris, 1632). The earliest known musical score for a Native song also falls into this category. Gabriel Sagard, a Récollet who lived among the Hurons during 1623–4,[3] included a 'Petit eschantillon d'une chanson hurrone' in his *Histoire du Canada* (Paris, 1636). He also compiled and had published a 'Dictionaire de la langue Huronne,' issued with his *Le grand voyage du pays des Hurons* (Paris, 1632). This dictionary was meant to assist those intending to live and work among the Hurons, who could well have included traders. Early in the eighteenth century, Henry Kelsey compiled a brief vocabulary for use in the Hudson's Bay Company territories, *A Dictionary of the Hudson's Bay Indian Language*, which was published in London at company expense in 1701.[4]

Mi'kmaq

Work among the Mi'kmaqs began in 1676, when Chrestien Le Clercq, a Récollet, developed a system of hieroglyphics adapted from Native pictographic practices.[5] He referred to this writing system, the first used by missionaries among the Aboriginal peoples, in his *Nouvelle relation de la Gaspesie* (Paris, 1691). Pierre Maillard of the Missions étrangères, who was a gifted linguist and an authority on the language, expanded the system and prepared many translations when he served among the Mi'kmaqs between 1735 and 1762. Although Maillard left valuable work for the translators who followed him, no books in Mi'kmaq hieroglyphics were printed until 1866, when Christian Kauder, a Redemptorist, had *Buch das gut, enthaltend den Katechismus* published in Austria.[6] In the interval, several books in Mi'kmaq using the roman alphabet appeared, including *Alphabet mikmaque*, printed at Quebec in 1817.

Montagnais and Abenaki

To Jesuit Jean-Baptiste de La Brosse goes the honour of preparing for the press the first material in a Native language printed in what is now Canada. His 'Kalendrier perpétuel à l'usage des sauvages Montagnais, Mistassins, Papinachois, et autres,' possibly a broadside, was recorded in the accounts of Brown and Gilmore of Quebec on 25 October 1766. The edition of 1,000 copies cost the missionary £4 10s.[7] In July 1767, Brown and Gilmore printed 3,000 copies of a primer for La Brosse's use among the Montagnais.[8] Opening with the line ABEGHJIKMNOPRSTU, 'the Indian Alphabet' included a syllabarium and prayers. A second order was recorded in October of that year, suggesting another edition to be used with *Nehiro-Iriniui*, a ninety-six-page prayer book printed in an edition of 2,000 (see illus. 12.1, p. 281).[9] This work provides a catechism, prayers, and devotional exercises for the use of Catholics. With errata corrected, it was reprinted at Quebec in 1817 and 1844.[10] La Brosse also translated portions of the Bible, but with no further funds for printing, he established scriptoria at his mission schools and had his Montagnais students make manuscript copies of the translations for circulation. He 'devoted winters to the education of the Montagnais, showing them how to read and write, teaching them the catechism, liturgical rites, singing, and the rudiments of music, and training catechists to carry on his work,' and prepared a census of Montagnais Christians at his several missions, including an assessment of each person's level of literacy.[11] La Brosse had also served as a missionary among the Abenakis from 1758 to 1760, and during that period he compiled a basic dictionary of the language.[12] In 1770 he had an eight-page primer in the Abenaki language, *Akitami kakikemesudi-arenarag' auikhigan*, printed in an edition of 600 copies by Brown and Gilmore.[13]

Mohawk

The first book in the Mohawk language to be printed in the northern British colonies was a Catholic primer, *Iontri8aiestsk8a ionskaneks n'aieienterihag gaiaton sera te gari8toraragon ong8eon8e ga8ennontakon*, produced in Montreal by Fleury Mesplet in 1777.[14] This translation, by Father Jacques Bruyas, had existed in manuscript form for

NEHIRO-IRINIUi
AIAMIHE
MASSINAHIGAN,

SHATSHEGUTSH, MITINEKAPITSH,
ISKUAMISKUTSH, NETSHEKATSH,
MISHT', ASSINITSH, SHEKUTIMITSH,
EKUANATSH, ASHUABMUSHUANITSH,
PIAKÙAGAMITSH,
Gaie miſſi miſſi nehiro-iriniui Aſtſhitſh
ka tatjits, ka kueiaſku aiamihatjits ka utſhi.

UABISTIGUIATSH.

Maſſinahitſetuau, BROUN gaie GIRMOR,

1767.

12.1 *Nehiro-Iriniui Aiamihe Massinahigan* (Quebec, 1767), a Montagnais prayer book. Courtesy of the National Library of Canada.

some time, but as a later commentator has observed, 'the intricacies of the Iroquois tongue were such that [the Jesuits] could not send their work to France without personally accompanying it to see to the proof reading on the spot.'[15] He explained: 'As the letters M. and P. are wanting in ... [Mohawk] the former is replaced by an 8 which in French Iroquois does duty for a sound represented by W. in English Iroquois and the latter by K.'[16]

After the American Revolution, some two thousand Aboriginal Loyalists were granted tracts of land on the Bay of Quinte and along the Grand River in Upper Canada. Among these were Mohawks, Cayugas, Onondagas, Senecas, Tuscaroras, and Delawares, as well as Nanticokes, Tutelos, Creeks, and Cherokees.[17] Books for their use were translated into Mohawk in the belief that all could understand that language. Many of these peoples were literate Anglicans, who had brought with them the 1769 New York edition of the Book of Common Prayer, but copies were few in number. Governor Sir Frederick Haldimand was petitioned to order the printing of a new edition, and at Quebec in 1780 William Brown printed 1,000 copies of the Mohawk prayer book, paid for by royal warrant.[18] The translation was revised and corrected by Christian Daniel Claus, 'deputy agent for the Six Nations in Canada.'[19] He had an excellent knowledge of the Mohawk language, and 'so many were the improvements made that it became in his hands practically a new work.'[20] Sahonwagy, a Mohawk sachem and schoolmaster, approved the corrections for every proof sheet. More than 250 copies were delivered into the hands of the Aboriginal peoples of the region, and 600 remained unbound in Quebec two years later. According to Claus, the Catholic Natives were forbidden to use them by their priests.[21]

In 1781 a second Mohawk primer, prepared by Claus, printed at Fleury Mesplet's press, and titled *A Primer for the Use of the Mohawk Children, to Acquire the Spelling and Reading of Their Own: as Well as to Get Acquainted with the English Tongue*, was published in an edition of about 300 copies.[22] The text is in Mohawk and English on facing pages and includes an alphabet, scriptural readings, catechisms, prayers, and numerals. Claus reported to Haldimand, 'They are fond of the little Book, both old & young & I have already from the Mohawks at Niagara rec[d] Messages to send some there.'[23] Another edition was printed in London in 1786 (see illus. 12.2, p. 283),[24] and the work was twice reprinted by George Gurnett in Ancaster, Upper Canada, in 1827 and 1828, presumably for the use of the Mohawks settled along the Grand River.[25]

A new, bilingual edition of the Book of Common Prayer was published in London in 1787. To it was added a translation of the Gospel of Mark, by Joseph Brant (Thayendanegea), the pre-eminent Mohawk chief.[26] The preface states, 'Other editions were printed in the Mohawk language only; in *this*, the English is also printed

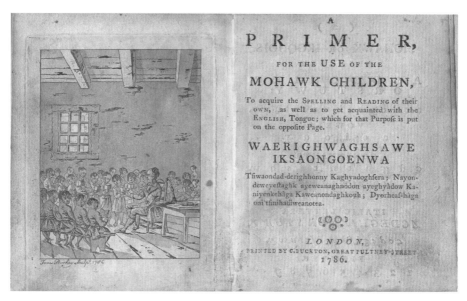

12.2 James Peachey, etched frontispiece, *A Primer, for the Use of the Mohawk Children* (London, 1786). Courtesy of the National Library of Canada.

on the opposite page. Hereby the Indians will insensibly be made acquainted with the English language; and such White People in their vicinity as chuse to learn Mohawk, will hence derive much assistance.'[27] Brant's translation of Mark was the first Gospel to be printed in Mohawk.

The British and Foreign Bible Society was established in 1804, and the first book published by this organization is said to have been *Nene karighwiyoston tsinihorighhoten ne St. John / The Gospel According to St. John in Mohawk*, printed in an edition of 2,000 copies in Mohawk and English on facing pages. An imprint date does not appear on the title page, and since the minutes for the General Committee of the BFBS for 1804–5 have not survived, there is no documentary evidence that this was indeed the society's first book, but 'folk memory' holds it to be so.[28] The translation was made by John Norton, who was of Scottish and Cherokee heritage. He was well educated and probably had some experience in printing. Joseph Brant was so favourably impressed with Norton, a soldier, teacher, and interpreter, that he adopted him, making him his deputy and successor.[29] Among the Mohawks, however, there were adverse comments about the quality of the translation.[30] Norton's text of the Gospel of John was to have been accompanied by his introductory address, but since the policy of the BFBS was to publish the Scriptures without comment, the *Address* was funded separately, although some copies of the Gospel of John are found bound with it.

Two books in Mohawk for the use of Catholics were published early in the nineteenth century. *Kaiatonsera ionterennaientag8a, sonha ong8e on8e ga8ennontag8en*, printed by Lane and Bowman in Montreal in 1816, was translated by Joseph Marcoux,[31] and *Ionteri8eienstag8a ne tsiatag ori8atogenton ogonha*, attributed to François Piquet, a Sulpician, was published in Paris in 1826.

Scriptural translations into Mohawk published in the United States began to appear in the British colonies shortly after the American Bible Society was founded in 1811. The ABS published a Mohawk edition of the Gospel of John in 1818, probably meant for use on both sides of the border. Clearly based on the BFBS edition, the reprint was 'so accurate that it copies all the typographic errors of the first edition and reproduces the page of errata at the end.'[32] When Norton was encouraged by the Society for the Propagation of the Gospel to translate the rest of the Gospels, he asked the assistance of Henry Aaron Hill (Kenwendeshon), a Mohawk catechist at St Paul's Church, Brantford. By then Norton was losing interest in the task; moreover, he believed that the Mohawks, who were becoming increasingly acculturated, would prefer to read the Bible in English.[33] The work was therefore continued by Hill alone. The establishment of a Methodist mission on the Grand River in 1822 may have encouraged his efforts, since the Methodists were happy to use his translations. The ABS published 500 copies of his bilingual Gospel of Luke in 1827,[34] of which the Methodist mission received 350.[35]

Brant's translation of the Gospel of Mark was reprinted by the New York District Bible Society in 1829, and Hill's translation of the Gospel of Matthew, corrected by John Aston Wilkes, was published at the expense of the Young Men's Bible Society of New York in 1831. The other Mohawk translations of the New Testament printed between 1831 and 1836 were also issued by this organization. Wilkes, an Englishman who had emigrated to Upper Canada in 1820, spoke Mohawk well. Hill was also assisted by William Hess, a Mohawk schoolmaster, and Elizabeth Kerr, who was a daughter of Joseph Brant. His translation of psalms and hymns went through separate printings for Anglican and Methodist use.[36] The ABS published 1,000 copies of the Book of Isaiah in 1839. This was Hill's translation, completed by Hess. Printers closer to home reprinted American translations for use among the Mohawks in the Grand River region, suggesting a clear need for such works there. In 1830 George Gurnett, then proprietor of the *Courier* newspaper in York (Toronto), reprinted a collection of hymns in English and Mohawk, originally published by the New-England Corporation.[37] This volume was subsequently reprinted at Ruthven's Book and Job Office in Hamilton in 1839.[38]

Inuktitut of Labrador

A Moravian mission was established at Nain, Labrador, in 1771 with financial assistance from the British congregation of the United Brethren. The Moravians were indefatigable translators. The first book in Inuktitut printed for use there was a hymnal, *Tuksiarutsit, attorēkset illagektunnut Labradoremetunnut*, published in London in 1809 at the expense of the Brethren's Society for the Furtherance of the Gospel. It was printed entirely in Inuktitut, except for the table of contents, which is in German, as are the names of the hymns, each with a tune number but no musical notation. The following year a harmony of the Gospels, translated by Benjamin Gottlieb Kohlmeister, was also published in London. Kohlmeister had received little formal education, but he was a good linguist who had quickly mastered the language. He lived among the Inuit for several years, first as a schoolmaster and then as supervisor of trade with the Native people. In 1818 he became general superintendent of missions, of which there were three: Nain, Okak, and Hopedale.[39]

Although the BFBS refused to publish a harmony of the Gospels because it was an adaptation of scriptural text, it did produce 1,000 copies of the Gospels of Matthew, Mark, and Luke in 1813. The Gospel of John is mentioned on the title page, but it did not appear until the following year. These books seem to have been well received. A missionary in 1814 reported that Inuit converts 'not only frequently read in the four Gospels, but evidently reflect on what they have read, propose questions to the missionaries, and ask for further information.' Those at Nain responded to printed books with 'a great desire by young and old to learn to read ..., [and] schools have been visited with great eagerness to learn, both by children and adults.'[40] The Gospels were followed by the Acts in 1816 and the Epistles in 1819; the Psalms appeared in 1830, Genesis in 1834, and Isaiah in 1837. The Gospels were revised in 1839, and the entire New Testament, revised and edited, was published by the BFBS a year later. All were produced in London.

Ojibwa

The Ojibwas[41] were one of the last of the Aboriginal peoples in the Canadas to receive books in their own language before 1840. There were two rival translators: Peter Jones, of Ojibwa and Welsh parentage, and James Evans, who was English-born. Jones was ably assisted in some of his translation work by his schoolmaster brother, John, while Evans was helped by an Ojibwa Christian, George Henry.

The first of Peter and John Jones's translations of Scripture into Ojibwa appeared in 1829 when Lieutenant-Governor Sir John Colborne 'ordered 2,000 copies of the first seven chapters of St Matthew to be printed forthwith, with the English on the opposite pages.'[42] Robert Stanton, the government printer, issued 500 copies to the Credit Mission. Two years later, the York Auxiliary Bible Society published the complete Gospel of Matthew in Ojibwa. Their plan to deliver copies to 'every Indian station in the province' was delayed only by the bad roads.[43] In the same year, Peter Jones's translation of the Gospel of John was published by the BFBS in a bilingual edition of 1,000 copies in London. Ordained as a Methodist minister in 1833, Jones continued his translation work with a *Discipline*[44] of the Wesleyan Methodist Church printed in Ojibwa and English at Toronto in 1835 and a selection of hymns published in Boston the following year.[45] This text was printed using the 'philosophical alphabet' devised by John Pickering.[46]

James Evans's first publication in Ojibwa and English appeared in 1833: *The First Nine Chapters of the First Book of Moses Called Genesis*, revised and corrected by Peter Jones,[47] was printed at the *Christian Guardian* office. Evans did not preach in Ojibwa until 1835,[48] and this book, clearly a major undertaking for him as he strove for mastery of the language, may well have required much help from Peter Jones. Evans was later to severely criticize Peter and John Jones's translation work, arguing that they 'put down the Ojibwa words as they sounded to them.'[49] Jones's translations were also attacked by Thomas Hurlburt, a non-Native Methodist missionary who spoke Ojibwa.[50] He recommended the use of a new hymn book translated by James Evans and George Henry, published in New York in 1837.[51] Evans had included a detailed orthography to assist Natives, 'the missionaries, and others ... with a little application, to read the Hymns with ease and accuracy.'[52]

Not content simply to spell out words with hyphenated syllables, linguists were now attempting to perfect the expression of Aboriginal languages in other ways. While Le Clercq and Maillard had transmitted concepts with hieroglyphics, nineteenth-century translators were seeking to express every sound in Native languages using non-Native writing systems, which would within a few years include the syllabic characters used in the Hudson's Bay Company territories as well as Isaac Pitman phonetics among the Mi'kmaqs and, later, Duployan shorthand on the West Coast. Evans had set out to develop an orthography that would more accurately represent Ojibwa words. A committee, including Peter Jones, was struck by the Canada Conference of the Wesleyan Methodist Church to pursue this work.[53] By 1836 Evans had devised an Ojibwa syllabary of eight consonants and four vowels, but it was not accepted that year by the Bible society at Toronto.[54]

The following year, he published in New York the hymn book and his *Speller and Interpreter, in Indian and English, for the Use of the Mission Schools*. It had been preceded at York in 1828 by a speller in Ojibwa, a pamphlet probably reprinted from an American title[55] and published by the Canada Conference Missionary Society. Evans's lengthy preface to his *Speller and Interpreter* includes criticism of 'others,' who could only have been Peter and John Jones. He wrote that 'almost every writer has a method of notation peculiar to himself, while none have presented us with a complete system, in which each sound is rendered invariable, by a distinct and appropriate character.' Clearly, he was moving toward the syllabic system that he was later to use. 'This want of an efficient system has presented us with a strange medley in orthography ... [S]uch representations have selected Roman characters, which, however well assured the writer might be that they did not convey exact sounds of the voice, were, in his estimation such as would answer the object in view. Others have, with greater care, selected from the English alphabet those letters which are the most analogous in sound to the modulations of the Indian voice, but without attempting to class the vowels, or even to furnish us with a synopsis of the powers of the letters; and therefore we are left to guess at the pronunciation of words.'[56]

By 1839 the Catholic missionary George-Antoine Bellecourt had served for seven years among the Saulteaux, the Ojibwa people living north of Lake Superior. He clearly recognized the need to analyze and record the grammar and syntax of the Ojibwa language, and that year he saw published at Quebec his *Principes de la langue des sauvages appelés Sauteux*. Although he had undertaken the work with great reluctance because of the difficulty of the language, he acknowledged the need for a learning aid for missionaries.[57] The work was also meant for translators and linguists. His pronunciation key was expressed in 'Remarques sur l'acception de certaines lettres de la langue sauteuse.'[58] The way in which this French speaker expressed the sounds is similar to both Evans's and Jones's orthography.

Peter Jones's last publication during this period appeared in 1840. It was a bilingual edition of *A Collection of Chippeway and English Hymns* (Toronto). Although Jones admitted that his translation had defects, he did not regard his errors to be of 'vital importance' nor did his people.[59] 'At the general council at the Credit ... [on 23] January 1840, the chiefs and principal warriors voted one hundred to five "to have the Old Ojibwa hymns reprinted, together with such others, as our Brother Peter Jones may translate, for the use of ourselves and our families."'[60] He appears to have had the volume printed at his own expense at the Conference Office in Toronto.

With it he had the last word where Evans was concerned. The 1829 edition of the hymns had long been unavailable, and some had 'complained that they were not able to read the new hymns translated by the Rev. James Evans and George Henry, ... owing to the difference in orthography.'[61] Jones included in his 'Preface' an explication of his approach to the desired orthography, but also called for the publication of an Ojibwa dictionary 'as a standard for the orthography of that language.'[62]

Cree

Evans was not on hand to rebut Jones's remarks. In 1838 he had been sent by the Canada Conference of the Wesleyan Methodist Church to the north shore of Lake Superior with a view to establishing Methodist missions there.[63] He met Crees and Ojibwas who lived the traditional nomadic life of hunters and fur trappers, that is, in circumstances where an easy reading system was needed. In 1840 the Wesleyan Methodist Missionary Society in Britain was granted permission to place missionaries in the Hudson's Bay Company territories, and Evans was appointed superintendent of missions there. He had arrived at Norway House, a major HBC trading and cargo marshalling centre, by 26 July 1840, and by 5 September he was at Rossville, a few miles away. There he established his mission and founded the Rossville Mission Press.

When and where the syllabic system he used among the Crees of that region was invented is disputed by scholars, but Evans first printed his syllabarium, or 'Cree Alphabet,' at Rossville on 15 October of the same year.[64] A simple system that the Aboriginal peoples found easy to learn, it consisted of nine symbols, each associated with a consonant and expressed in four attitudes corresponding to the vowels *e, i, o,* and *a.*

Evans is said to have used a press intended for baling furs as a printing press.[65] Types proved a much greater problem. After failing at first to make individual types, he cast a plate of lead. When it had hardened, he polished it and cut out the syllabarium, 'making a sort of stereotype plate,'[66] and printed a few sheets on 15 October. Presumably, other copies were printed later. Evans continued to experiment and appears to have been able to fashion movable type from the crude materials at hand. On 11 November he struck off 300 copies of the first three verses of the hymn *Jesus My All to Heaven Is Gone*; on 17 November he printed 250 copies of another hymn, *Behold the Saviour of Mankind*; and on 3 December an edition of *Blow Ye the Trumpet, Blow*.[67] His journal entry for that day notes, 'The Indians and children sing these hymns well, and several read with some fluency. The short time which is required to learn to read and to write arises from there being no such thing as learning to spell, every character in the alphabet being a syllable, so that when these are learned, all is learned.' Evans does not acknowledge any Aboriginal translators in preparing these hymns for the press, but it is possible that the translations were made by Henry Bird Steinhauer, an Ojibwa teacher who would join the Rossville mission in 1842. Evans goes on to state that he had 'printed about two thousand pages of hymns, &c.'[68]

James Evans's legacy went far beyond anything he might have imagined. Within thirty years, the syllabic system, further developed by others, was used throughout the HBC territories. Thousands of books were printed in syllabic characters in the several Aboriginal languages of the region, and more than a century and a half after he printed his first crude 'Cree Alphabet' at Rossville, the syllabic characters are still in use in Canada.

Conclusion

Whether the Aboriginal or European missionaries had much success as evangelizers is not at issue here, but their contribution to the culture of the Native peoples as the translators, grammarians, and lexicographers who first expressed these languages in written form has been of lasting value. Thousands of books were printed in Aboriginal languages as a result of their labours, most being the work of Native translators, a permanent testament to their abilities, to the strength of their faith, and to their determination to spread Christianity among their peoples.

Printing for New Communities in German and Gaelic

JURIS DILEVKO

English- and French-speaking communities were not the only ones of European origin served by printers in British North America. In the late 1750s, Anthony Henry (Anton Heinrich), a German-speaking printer from Alsace who had been a regimental fifer with the British forces during the Louisbourg campaign, settled in Halifax, where he became the partner of government printer John Bushell in 1760 and took over the business when Bushell died the following year.[69] Beginning in 1788, Henry published a German almanac, *Der Neuschottländische Calender*,[70] to serve the several thousand Germans who had been encouraged to settle in Nova Scotia in the 1750s to balance the French-speaking Acadians, or had arrived since the American Revolution.

The almanac, which would appear until Henry's death in 1800,[71] was intended as a direct response to the 'great number of German almanacs which are brought yearly into this province from the state of Pennsylvania and bought by the inhabitants of this country.'[72] The 1788 edition provided local historical material, such as the arrival of the first German families in Nova Scotia in 1750 and the settlement of Malagasch (Mirligueche, now Lunenburg) in 1752.

Henry also proposed to publish a weekly newspaper, to be called 'Die Welt, und die Neuschottländische Correspondenz,' beginning in January 1788. In the prospectus he wrote that it would incorporate 'all noteworthy occurrences in the four quarters of the world as they come to my ears through imported English papers generally, as also in particular, interesting matters of this province.'[73] Since he was also publishing the *Nova-Scotia Gazette and Weekly Chronicle*, he had ready access to local and international news, but no copies of 'Die Welt' have been found.

While Anthony Henry was the first to print in German letter, previewing his Fraktur types in the *Gazette* on 23 October 1787, an official notice offering a general pardon to deserters from the Hessian troops serving with the British army had appeared in English and German, set in roman and italic faces, in the *Quebec Gazette / La Gazette de Québec* in July 1783.[74] A similar notice had been printed at Quebec in an edition of fifty copies the year before.[75]

Until the 1830s, German-language publishing in the colonies was sporadic. Waves of emigration had followed the Revolutionary War, with disbanded Hessians, Palatines from New York, and Mennonites from Pennsylvania settling in eastern Upper Canada, the Niagara Peninsula, Markham north of the town of York (Toronto), and Waterloo and Woolwich Townships. These first settlers were included in a government plan to encourage the cultivation of hemp in Upper and Lower Canada. Although only the French edition of the pamphlet *Remarques sur le culture et la preparation du chanvre en Canada* has survived, it was published at York in 1806 in French, English, and German,[76] the last translated by John Paul Radelmüller of Markham, who spent eight days in York assisting the printer and correcting the work.[77]

The German population in Upper Canada expanded further after a second period of immigration began in the 1820s, this time directly from Germany as a result of poor harvests and depressed economic conditions.[78] The community in the Waterloo area, centred around Ebytown (renamed Berlin in 1833; now Kitchener), was concentrated enough by the 1830s to support a press, and it was here that Heinrich Wilhelm (later Henry William) Peterson established a printing office in 1835 to produce both a secular newspaper and Mennonite religious works.⁷⁹ German-born and schooled in Pennsylvania, he had settled in Ebytown in 1832, some six years after his first visit to the Markham community, where his father, a former printer, was the Lutheran pastor.⁸⁰ After fifty-one individuals, including the influential Mennonite bishop Benjamin Eby, agreed to buy shares at $20 each, Peterson had a printing press brought from Pennsylvania and printed the first issue of *Canada Museum, und Allgemeine Zeitung* (later *Das Canada Museum*) in August 1835.⁸¹ Each issue provided, in German with some English, materials ranging from world and local news and advertisements to poetry and serial fiction. During the Rebellion of 1837, Peterson produced two supplements reporting the events, all the while recommending restraint, non-involvement, and obedience to the authorities.⁸²

Working in conjunction with Bishop Eby, Peterson also published a variety of religious material for adults and children. A hymnal, *Die gemeinschaftliche Liedersammlung*, compiled by the bishop and containing 205 songs with a melody register, was printed on a subscription basis in 1836.⁸³ It proved so popular that an enlarged second edition was published two years later.⁸⁴ In 1839 Peterson printed a 340-page catechism, *Christliches Gemüths Gespräch vom seligmachenden Glauben*, intended for young people, with an afterword by Eby.⁸⁵ That year he also produced *Neues Buchstabir- und Lesebuch*, a Mennonite primer prepared by Eby to teach the alphabet, spelling, grammar, and punctuation through a series of religious-based exercises and simple passages from the Bible.⁸⁶ Also recorded is an almanac called the 'Neue Ober Canada Calendar' (1839–41) and a 'Meeting-Calendar' (*Ein Calendar*, 1836–), which gave the times and locations of worship services.⁸⁷

In a more secular vein, Peterson published, as a sixteen-page booklet, a German translation of the speech made by Lieutenant-Governor Sir Francis Bond Head to the Legislative Council and the House of Assembly on 20 April 1836.⁸⁸ Given his support of the government, it is an open question whether Peterson was also responsible for printing the German edition of a handbill for the Constitutional Reform Society of Upper Canada, which was harshly critical of Bond Head's actions.⁸⁹

Unlike Nova Scotia, where Anthony Henry alone represented the face of German-language publishing, the first printer did not work in isolation in Upper Canada. After Peterson turned to other pursuits, becoming a justice of the peace and registrar of the Wellington District, Heinrich Eby, the bishop's son, who had been Peterson's first apprentice, and Christian Enslin, bookbinder, bookseller, and former associate editor of *Das Canada Museum*, bought Peterson's press in 1840.⁹⁰ With Enslin as editor, they founded a newspaper, *Der Deutsche Canadier und Neuigkeitsbote* (1841–65).⁹¹ The younger Eby, who had printed a single sheet song under his own imprint as early as 1835,⁹² also expanded Peterson's involvement with birth and baptismal certificates

(*Taufscheine*), co-operating with Fraktur artists – master calligraphers who illuminated cherished family Bibles and certificates with elaborate designs – to create documents that combined printing and traditional penmanship.[93]

As revealing of the viability of the German-language press was the founding on 6 June 1839 in nearby Waterloo of a rival newspaper, *Der Canada Morgenstern* (later *Der Morgenstern*),[94] by Benjamin Burkholder, a younger printer who had come from Pennsylvania as a child. Recognizing the inevitability of change through a comment on his own conservatism, Peterson wrote in his paper that he hoped 'no one will continue to complain of a lack of adequate coverage of government affairs; we hope everyone will be satisfied now.'[95] In many ways, *Der Morgenstern* resembled *Das Canada Museum*. It too featured poetry, national and world news, and local announcements; however, it adopted a more secular, lighter tone.[96] A critical mass of German-language readers with differing tastes and values now existed to support multiple publishing enterprises.

This pattern would be replicated as other immigrant groups established themselves. Gaelic speakers from the Scottish Highlands had settled in significant concentrations in several areas of British North America by the early nineteenth century, including Cape Breton and northeastern Nova Scotia, Prince Edward Island, and the eastern part of Upper Canada. Although publishing for this community would prove to be sporadic, in 1835, the same year that Henry Peterson founded his German-language press, a catechism in Gaelic was produced in Toronto.[97] The 'spiritual songs' of the Highland schoolteacher and catechist Dugald Buchanan and Gaelic religious poetry by Peter Grant appeared in two small volumes printed in Montreal a year later.[98] And a weekly paper in English and Gaelic, titled *Tourist of the Woods, and Emigrant's Guide: Cuairtear nan coillte*, was begun at Kingston in the summer of 1840. It claimed to be the 'first Gaelic newspaper edited in America.'[99]

Translation

JEAN DELISLE

A famous saying links translation to treason, but it might better be linked to mediation. Before 1840, mediation was a factor in three major areas of translation activity – religious, administrative, and journalistic – affecting five linguistic groups: French,

English, Aboriginal languages, and, to a lesser extent, German and Gaelic, the last two already discussed by Juris Dilevko. Translation was used mainly in Quebec and Lower Canada, as a result of the British conquest of New France. Except for newspaper articles and legislative acts, many of the translations at this time appeared long after the document was written; they were, so to speak, awaiting publication. As well, a number of translations were published abroad, because the means to print them locally was lacking.[100]

Although it was not until the late 1850s that literary translation emerged, and then only timidly, relations and accounts of voyages printed in Europe in the sixteenth and seventeenth centuries, along with translations of these works, belong indisputably to the Canadian literary heritage.[101] The English-language versions of Jacques Cartier's *Voyages,* translated from the Italian by John Florio (1580); of Marc Lescarbot's *Histoire de la Nouvelle France* (1609); of accounts of discoveries by Louis Hennepin (1698) and Baron Lahontan (1703); and of Pierre-François-Xavier de Charlevoix's *Journal d'un voyage* (1761) helped to propagate across Europe the image of an immense, rugged, exotic country populated by indigenous peoples. However, translations of more conventionally literary works were rarely printed during this period; only one novel, *The History of Emily Montague* (1769), by the English writer Frances Brooke, appeared in French, in Paris in 1809.[102]

The missionaries' efforts to convert the Native peoples also encouraged translation activities, a subject studied earlier in this chapter by Joyce Banks. Chrestien Le Clercq in the late seventeenth century and Abbé Pierre Maillard in the mid-eighteenth century each worked to develop a writing system to be used in the conversion of the Mi'kmaqs of Acadia. Maillard wrote a Mi'kmaq grammar, recopied many times, which was employed to translate excerpts from the Bible, catechisms, prayers, and canticles, although these were not printed until much later, in the nineteenth century. For this work, he elaborated a hieroglyphic writing system that became part of the Mi'kmaq cultural heritage (see illus. 1.1, p. 17).[103] The manuscripts were later printed in both ideographic and alphabetic forms; a first edition appeared in Vienna in 1866. The provincial archives of Nova Scotia has preserved one of the few copies of this translation: *Buch das gut, enthaltend den Katechismus.*

Some portions of the Jesuit *Relations,* originally published in Paris, were also disseminated in the eighteenth century in Latin and Italian versions, first in Rome and then elsewhere in Italy.[104] Subsequently, booksellers and historical societies published fragments of these important ethnographic documents in English[105] before the definitive edition by Reuben Gold Thwaites appeared in Cleveland between 1896 and 1901. The translations made by Maillard and those of the *Relations* are examples of deferred publication; in both cases, a gap of several centuries separated the original text from its translation.

Among the first publications printed in Halifax, starting in 1752, were translations in English and French, including a treaty of peace and friendship.[106] Also appearing in Aboriginal languages were governors' speeches, such as one in the Oneida language by General Frederick Haldimand that was printed in 1779.[107] The British and Foreign Bible Society published a Mohawk translation of the Gospel of John in 1805, with the English text on facing pages.[108] We should also mention the publication in 1806 of the French translation of *The Poor Man's Controversy* (London, 1769), written by the English Benedictine monk John Mannock. Translated by the curé of La Prairie, Jean-Baptiste Boucher, *dit* Belleville, and published at Quebec as *Manuel abrégé de controverse: ou controvese* [sic] *des pauvres*, the work was an amalgam of catechism, devotional book, and apologetic.

Official Translation

It was with official translations that the history of translation in Canada really began. The point of departure was the surrender of Port-Royal (Annapolis Royal, Nova Scotia) in 1710. Paul Mascarene worked there as an interpreter and translator for the first governors; after him, these tasks were assumed by the provincial secretaries. Later, Isaac Deschamps translated, among other works, petitions by Acadians, a pledge of allegiance, and the deportation order of 1755.[109] During this period, three categories of administrative documents were translated: official correspondence, order books, and the council's minutes.[110]

With the Conquest of 1760 an important phase in official translation began. During the four years of the military regime, French was the de facto official language of the colony, and translation was needed for publication of official proclamations and the administration of justice. The three governors appointed at Quebec, Trois-Rivières, and Montreal were each assigned a bilingual officer as a secretary-translator. A civil regime succeeded the military administration in 1764, and from then on 'notices' were published in the *Quebec Gazette / La Gazette de Québec*. The translations in the gazette were improvised and of doubtful quality, with numerous anglicisms and barbarisms.[111] Given the need to translate laws, orders, proclamations, and other official texts into French, Governor Guy Carleton appointed jurist François-Joseph Cugnet to the position of official translator and French secretary to the governor and the council in 1768. For more than twenty years, Cugnet provided official translations in the province of Quebec. The translation of British legal vocabulary posed problems for the first translators.[112] After the Quebec Act (1774) was passed, French translation became customary in the Legislative Council, and the parliamentary status of the French language was established in January 1793. The recognition of French in both legislative chambers led to translation of the *Journals* and their appendixes, of statutes, and of all official publications.

The Constitutional Act of 1791 divided the old province of Quebec into the colonies of Upper Canada and Lower Canada. Unilingual francophone members of the Assembly in Lower Canada had to become familiar with representative institutions and British parliamentary rules. Just before the first meeting of the parliament, modelled on that of the home country, Samuel Neilson published, in English and French, *An Abstract from Precedents of Proceeding in the British House of Commons / Extraits des exemples de Procédés dans la Chambre des communes de la Grande Bretagne* (Quebec, [1792]), bringing together the regulations and orders of the British House of Commons.[113] In 1803 the Assembly asked jurist Joseph-François Perrault, who had translated Richard Burn's work on justices of the peace and parish officers in 1789, to translate a major compilation on parliamentary law, *Lex Parliamentaria*.[114] In his dedication, Perrault apologized that he had been obliged to borrow freely from English for lack of equivalent French terms.[115] Political and ideological conflicts crystallized around the translation of *Lex Parliamentaria*. In Lower Canada the treatise rapidly won the favour of francophone representatives, since it recognized the sovereignty of parliament over the monarchy. In spite of himself, Perrault had supplied ammunition to the proponents of strengthening of the legislative power over the executive.[116] Anglophone leaders viewed with disfavour this translation and the popularization of parliament, which they felt was likely to stimulate the demanding, even insubordinate, spirit of francophone representatives in the Assembly. This reaction by the British party explains why attempts to translate two other law books into French failed.[117] In these years of political agitation, the legal status of French was often thrown into question, and translation was both a political gesture and a barometer of political and linguistic tensions. Nevertheless, Perrault continued his work as a political educator, publishing a *Dictionnaire portatif et abrégé des loix et règles du parlement provincial du Bas Canada* in 1806.

The Press

The periodical press in Quebec and Lower Canada was at first largely a product of translation, and even unilingual newspapers borrowed materials from other languages. In the *Quebec Gazette / La Gazette de Québec* (bilingual until 1832), international news derived from London newspapers appeared in English and French in parallel columns.[118] It followed the North American news and official announcements, including public ordinances and regulations. In a notice on 29 May 1766, the printers asked their readers' indulgence for delays, 'as every Paragraph with us requires at least triple the Time.' Translation made the work more difficult not only for journalists but also for printers, who received orders for bilingual publications from the government or from Parliament.

Le Canadien, founded in 1806 and published until 1909 (with three interruptions), carried translated material that was significant: international news, letters, articles from the *Quebec Mercury*, and governors' speeches. In 1836 and 1839 the first translations of the Gosford and Durham reports appeared in this journal, edited at the time by Étienne Parent. *La Minerve,* founded in 1826, also contained a large number of translated articles. The editor complained of being forced, for lack of time and human and financial resources, to 'translate' the news instead of writing it: 'The publication of a French-language newspaper in Lower Canada is extremely difficult and tiresome; the Editor is reduced to laboriously translating from a foreign language almost all the pieces that fill his paper ... But we barely have the time, after all these translations, to engage in a few reflections on the affairs of the Country. And if we had to translate only foreign news ... But the authentic and official documents of our colonial policy, ... everything that can enlighten the people as to their rights, their duties, their relations with the government, comes to us in a foreign language; we must dress it in the language of the people so that they can profit from it.'[119] There does not seem to have been a 'professional' translator at *Le Canadien* or at *La Minerve* before the 1840s.[120]

Bilingualism was born with the country and is one of the fibres in its sociocultural fabric. Religious writings, official documents, and newspapers were permeated with translation. Whatever the sphere of activity in which books and printed materials were produced before 1840, translation was present. We should recall that one of the very first political publications to come off the press of Brown and Gilmore at Quebec in 1765 and advertised as 'The Grand Jury's Presentments' was soon also published in French,[121] that the printers William Vondenvelden and Pierre-Édouard Desbarats were initiated to the techniques of printing when they were translators at the *Quebec Gazette / La Gazette de Québec*,[122] or that the journals of the House of Assembly of Lower Canada were bilingual. The histories of print and of translation are inextricably entwined.

Science and Technology

BERTRUM H. MACDONALD

Explorers, colonists, and the scientific and educated communities in Europe alike were captivated by discoveries of the natural resources and plant and animal species of the New World. Thus 'inventory science,' which arose out of the Scientific Revolution and the Scottish Enlightenment of the seventeenth and eighteenth centuries, found an ideal environment in the British and French North American colonies.[123] Focused on mapping and cataloguing natural resources and phenomena, it was practised from the arrival of Europeans in the sixteenth century through the Victorian period. At Quebec in the 1760s, John Wright, 'Collector of American Seeds, for a Society of Noblemen and Gentlemen in Scotland,' published an extensive catalogue of native species, 'among which are a great many that are unknown in Europe, and not mentioned by the most famous Botanists.'[124] Although no one followed scientific pursuits full-time, both rural and urban residents were interested in the natural history of their communities. By the 1840s, with the establishment of the Magnetical and Meteorological Observatory in Toronto (1839) and the Geological Survey of Canada in Montreal (1842), scientific and engineering work would become increasingly urban-based, and careers in these disciplines begin to emerge. Access to relevant publications was necessary for scientific study of any sort. Scientific and technical books were brought to the colonies by missionaries, professionals, and lay readers, and as the colonies grew, titles on such topics would begin to appear in import notices and booksellers' announcements.

Scientific work had been pursued by a number of individuals in New France throughout the French colonial period. Mapping was especially important, and early hydrographer Jean Deshayes maintained a substantial library to support his work. As Chartrand, Duchesne, and Gingras have noted, in his library, 'One found some fifteen books on mathematics, including *Analyse des infiniments petits pour l'intelligence des lignes courbes*, a work showing its owner's interest in advanced mathematics, five books on astronomy, seven on piloting and navigation ... Deshayes also owned *Théorie des manoeuvres des vaisseaux* and eleven other volumes on meteorology and tides. He also had in his collection several copies of *La connaissance des temps*.'[125] While many practitioners were not as well equipped as Deshayes, nonetheless, some texts were essential resources for men (and a very few women)[126] who pursued scientific or technical work. At the Collège des jésuites, teachers used scientific texts published in France for instruction in physics and astronomy. Natural historians who explored the botanical and zoological features of the colonies would have needed to consult scientific titles in the course of writing their own reports. Among those producing scientific work were Pierre Boucher, governor of Trois-Rivières, whose *Histoire véritable et naturelle des moeurs et productions du pays de la Nouvelle-France* was printed in Paris in 1664. Over the next century, Michel Sarrazin, whose work appeared in the world's first scientific journal, the *Journal des sçavans*, Pierre-François-Xavier de Charlevoix, Jean-François Gaultier, and Nicolas Denys all published their natural history findings in France.

Surveyor Joseph Frederick Wallet DesBarres (see illus. 12.3, p. 299), whose *Atlantic Neptune* (London, 1774–84) has been regarded as 'one of the most remarkable products of human ingenuity, determination and industry to appear during the eighteenth century,'[127] could not have completed this massive collection of hydrographic maps and charts of the east coast of North America without recourse to the standard astronomical and hydrographic texts of the period. At his observatory in Nova Scotia, he called on three important works by French astronomers – Jacques Cassini's *Élémens d'astronomie*, Nicolas Louis de La Caille's *Éphémérides*, and Jean Picard's *Dégré du méridien*, based on the work of Maupertius and others – as well as Nevil Maskelyne's *Nautical Almanac* and Tobias Mayer's astronomical tables.[128]

Individuals who published or taught scientific subjects were not the only colonists to read about these topics. Fiona A. Black's analysis of books available in bookshops and libraries in the Atlantic colonies and Lower and Upper Canada between 1752 and 1820 shows that over 10 per cent were on scientific subjects.[129] For a comparable period, Réjean Lemoine found that upwards of 25 per cent of titles available in Lower Canada dealt with scientific topics.[130] Since only a small number of scientific and technical titles were published in the British North American colonies prior to 1840, most books and periodicals read by colonists on these topics were imported.[131]

Technical skills and knowledge were required both to reach the North American shores and to travel across the vast and varied land, some of which were acquired by experience, some from Native peoples, and some through printed materials. It is assumed that Jacques Cartier in his first voyage was guided by Martin de Hoyarsabal's work.[132] Cartier was by no means the only one to rely on published navigational resources. Maps, charts, handbooks, and other aids were widely used, as is clear from the numerous advertisements promoting their sale in eighteenth- and nineteenth-century newspapers, especially in the ports and towns along lakes and rivers. Charts for the North Atlantic and the St Lawrence River system produced by London pub-

12.3 Portrait of Joseph Frederick Wallet DesBarres, attributed to James Peachey (ca. 1785). Courtesy of the National Archives of Canada, C-135130. Gift of Mrs Doreen Desbarres Bate.

lisher David Steel could be purchased in numerous towns in the British North American colonies.[133] Stores also carried James Atkinson's *An Epitome of Navigation*, Thomas Haselden's *The Seaman's Daily Assistant*, and John Hamilton Moore's *Navigation*.[134]

   Colonial governments supported the surveying and mapping of the waters and the land. Henry Wolsey Bayfield headed extensive hydrographic survey work over four decades of the early nineteenth century. In addition to producing important charts of the Great Lakes, he also surveyed the St Lawrence River and Gulf, the coasts of Anticosti, the Magdalen Islands, Prince Edward Island, Cape Breton, Sable Island, and parts of Nova Scotia and Labrador.[135] If works by DesBarres and Bayfield were needed for navigation, accurate maps were required for settlement and utilization of the natural resources. The Bouchette family were exemplary surveyors. Joseph Bouchette Sr published a 'notable legacy' of maps, plans, and topographical descriptions.[136] Beginning with *A Topographical Description of the Province of Lower Canada* (London, 1815) in French and English, he went on to produce the two-volume *British Dominions in North America* (London, 1832) and *A Topographical Dictionary of the Province of*

Lower Canada (London, 1832). The construction of roads and canals, including the Welland and Rideau Canals in Upper Canada, in the opening decades of the nineteenth century brought engineers such as Lieutenant Colonel John By of the Royal Engineers to the colonies and introduced an increasing need for civil engineering texts.

Because scientific and technical publications were often scarce in the larger towns as well as in smaller communities, libraries became a priority of the new literary and scientific societies.[137] Soon after it was established in 1827, the Natural History Society of Montreal, for example, created a library of scientific books and periodicals.[138] This collection focused on the sciences, but other associations, such as the Literary and Historical Society of Quebec, also included scientific publications in their holdings. With the establishment of mechanics' institutes in the late 1820s and 1830s, an increasing number of libraries, though often modest in their holdings, offered scientific and technical titles.[139]

Through both imported and locally published books, manuals, periodicals, charts, and maps, colonists in the towns and on the frontier could read about an array of scientific and technical subjects. In urban settings, where these publications were more readily available, the foundations were laid for major scientific and technical work later in the nineteenth century.

Medical and Legal Print Materials

CHRISTINE VEILLEUX

In New France and in the old province of Quebec, no legislation regulated the study or the practice of law or medicine before the end of the eighteenth century, and few aspirants to either of these professions had the means to study abroad. Knowledge was transmitted by apprenticeships of unspecified duration, and no examination was required. A five-year 'clerkship,' followed by an examination, was instituted only in 1785 for lawyers and notaries and in 1788 for physicians. Practitioners who came from Europe or the American colonies generally had better training than those who had studied locally, and many brought with them specialized works, which were of great help to them in carrying out their duties. From these contacts, professionals in

British North America learned about the most popular European and American authors, which probably began to stimulate demand for the importation of their most recent works. The import trade continued to expand after 1800, as is shown by the library of Judge Richard John Uniacke, profiled by John Macleod in chapter 9.

Legal studies developed very little in the colonies between 1785 and 1840. The main areas of training remained English criminal and commercial law and the application of a colony's own regulations and practices. In the Atlantic provinces and Upper Canada, English civil law was important, while in Lower Canada, precedence was given to the Custom of Paris and Roman civil law.[140] This difference resulted from the fact that the old French law, introduced into New France with the creation of the Conseil souverain in 1663, together with the edicts, ordinances, declarations, and decrees of the Conseil d'État of the French kings, and the decrees of the Conseil souverain and orders of the intendants after 1663, were retained following the British conquest of New France, but not without opposition. The coexistence of the Custom of Paris and common law raised much dissent among both old and new subjects. The British government therefore ordered that a code summarizing the laws in force under the French regime be compiled. The responsibility for this task fell to the legal expert François-Joseph Cugnet, who in 1769 undertook the compilation of his *Extrait des édits, déclarations, règlements, ordonnances, provisions et commissions des gouverneurs généraux & intendants*. Better known as *Extrait des messieurs*, this work, edited by Attorney General Francis Maseres, was published in London in 1772–3.

The inconsistent application of laws and the inadequate training of most jurists and notaries before 1800 encouraged neither the importation of legal works[141] nor their local production. Between 1767 and 1774, the British government and the colonial administration redoubled their efforts to end the imbroglio created by the royal proclamation of 1763 and the ordinance of 1764. The grievances of the Canadiens were finally settled when the Quebec Act of 1774 sanctioned the retention of French civil law in the province of Quebec. Cugnet, disappointed at having been robbed of the exclusivity of the first codification of the country's laws, found consolation in compiling his four famous treatises on French civil law in 1775, the first to be published in British North America.[142]

From this time on, the trade in law books intensified. French-speaking jurists had access to numerous treatises on civil and Roman law, canon law, legal dictionaries, and collections of French case law, as well as several more specialized titles, such as *La nouvelle pratique civile, criminelle et beneficiale, ou, Le nouveau praticien françois*, by François Lange, and the *Lettres sur la profession d'avocat*, by Philippe-Simon Dupin. *Traité élémentaire du notariat*, by Edme Hilaire Garnier-Deschesnes, and *La Science parfaite des notaires*, by

Claude de Ferrière were among the principal works addressed specifically to notaries. English-speaking jurists were, of course, most interested in British authors, such as William Blackstone and his celebrated *Commentaries on the Laws of England;* Richard Burn, whose book *Justice of the Peace and Parish Officer* would be translated by Joseph-François Perrault as *Le juge à paix* in Montreal in 1789; and Francis Maseres, Joseph Chitty, Sir Michael Foster, Sir Edward Coke, Sir John Comyns, and Charles B. Gilbert.[143]

Nevertheless, in the years leading up to 1840, the importation of law books no longer sufficed; a system of law appropriate to the reality of British North America had to be drawn up, and it was no doubt for this reason that judicial materials were generated almost exclusively by the government. Thus one of the colony's first imprints was a form to be filled out for coroners' inquests, produced in Halifax about 1752.[144] From then on, ordinances related to the establishment of courts, to the powers of justices of the peace, and to trade, land ownership, immigration, and other subjects proliferated in the form of thousands of handbills, leaflets, and pamphlets. Adding to this production were the laws of the three Maritime provinces and after 1791, those of Upper and Lower Canada.[145] An abundance of case reports and collections of sample forms, discussed by Patricia Kennedy in chapter 10, helped jurists to keep abreast of this new reality.[146]

Records of trials, especially of those in courts of appeal, were also widely available. Collections of case law, some of them published abroad, began to appear, including works by James Stewart, Henri Desrivières-Beaubien, George Frederick Street Berton, and, in particular, Beamish Murdoch, whose collection inspired by Blackstone's *Commentaries* was of great and lasting use to lawyers in Nova Scotia.[147] Finally, the more specialized works by William Conway Keele, John George Marshall, and William Hepburn are equally noteworthy.[148]

In spite of the growing numbers of physicians after the beginning of the nineteenth century, few showed an inclination to publish texts for members of their profession. Works imported from Europe and the United States dating from the preceding century seem to have sufficed for their daily practice.[149] Among the main treatises on surgery, anatomy, and obstetrics, and other imported books and periodicals were *Domestic Medicine; or, The Family Physician* (1769), a major work by the Scottish physician William Buchan;[150] Richard Reece's *Medical Guide;* and the *American Journal of the Medical Sciences* (Philadelphia).[151] Such imports were not limited to the professional elite; the writings of populist American doctor Samuel Thomson, who rejected the advice of medical authorities and claimed that most diseases could be cured with lobelia and cayenne pepper, received an enthusiastic welcome among the reformers of Upper Canada. In 1828 a compilation of Thomson's works by Henry Lawson appeared in Kingston, and between 1831 and 1833 three editions of his *New Guide to Health* were printed in Brockville, Hamilton, and Hallowell (Picton), by William Buell Jr, Smith and Hackstaff, and Joseph Wilson respectively.[152]

James Latham, a surgeon in the British army, was probably the first to practise vaccination in British North America. In 1769 he had printed at Quebec four hundred copies of a handbill or leaflet called 'Directions for Children,' which offered a regimen for people inoculated against smallpox.[153] Although epidemics such as the Baie Saint-Paul malady in the late eighteenth century and cholera in the 1830s spurred the publication of handbills and public notices, medical texts had little to say apart from directives issued by the government or the local administration. One of the first was a pamphlet of sixteen pages entitled *Direction pour la guerison du mal de la Baie St. Paul* (Quebec, 1785), attributed to Philippe-Louis-François Badelard.[154] The major cholera epidemics of 1832 and 1834, discussed by Eli MacLaren in this chapter, mobilized the press, especially in the port cities of Halifax, Quebec, and Montreal but also in Cornwall, Kingston, Hallowell (Picton), and York (Toronto), and led to the publication of many materials intended both for the public and for health professionals. Other specialized works penned by dedicated physicians, such as Michael Underwood's *Traité sur les maladies des enfans* (Quebec, 1803) and *Remarks on Insanity and the Management of Insane Persons* (Montreal, 1840), translated from the German of J.F. Lehmann, appeared from time to time, but such initiatives were very rare. Sometimes a doctor would also spread word of his services through advertising notices. In 1792, for instance, Joseph Brown, a Montreal dentist, placed an order with Samuel Neilson at Quebec for the printing of one hundred bilingual notices called 'Directions.'[155]

In January 1826 a young doctor at Quebec, François-Xavier Tessier, published the first issue of the *Quebec Medical Journal / Le Journal de médecine de Québec* with the aim of linking all the members of the medical profession in Lower Canada. But for lack of encouragement, this bilingual bimonthly, the first of its kind in any of the provinces, ceased publication in October 1827.[156]

CASE STUDY
Facies cholerica: The Record of Cholera in Print
— Eli MacLaren

Cholera, the infection of the small intestine by the food- and water-borne bacterium *Vibrio cholerae*, invaded the city of Quebec during the immigration seasons of 1832 and 1834, spreading from there through Lower Canada to Upper Canada and, in the latter year, to Nova Scotia and New Brunswick. The horrifying and rapacious disease, characterized by diarrhea, vomiting, cramps, and epidermal discoloration, caused more than death. A dogged partner of British imperial glory, it exacerbated the political disquiet that led to the Rebellions of 1837 and 1838 in Lower Canada. Less spectacularly, it necessitated the formation of local boards of health, which, though temporary, were seminal in the development of public health management in Canada (see illus. 12.4, p. 305).[157]

The printed and manuscript record left by cholera falls into four categories: newspaper reports, government and civil documents, religious texts, and medical accounts. The newspapers first alerted individuals, including politicians, to the disease. In 1832 they caused widespread panic. By contrast, in 1834, the papers colluded in silence to play down the gravity of the disease and minimize its effect on trade.[158] The acts, circulars, proclamations, pamphlets, reports, statistical returns, and petitions published by the houses of assembly, governors, and local boards of health document the measures, numerous but too often inadequate, taken by governments against the disease. Salient among these is the act of Lower Canada that authorized municipal boards of health and established the disastrous quarantine station at Grosse-Île, which, in failing to isolate contaminated from uncontaminated ships, virtually ensured that immigrants who had escaped cholera when they sailed from Britain would contract it at their journey's end.[159] The reports of the board of health and the courts at Niagara (Niagara-on-the-Lake) also stand out: only there did violence arise, when angry citizens converged on the wharves to repulse a boat that had defied the magistrates' orders not to dock before being inspected.[160]

The religious texts consist of sermons[161] and services. The *Form of Prayer* printed by John Simpson in Fredericton early in 1832 for the Anglican churches of New Brunswick surpasses in candour the many other liturgical items specially created to address the threat of cholera. The prayer, ominous in its exhortation that people be courageous, 'lest they themselves, or others dear to them as themselves, should be smitten,'[162] sheds light on contemporary conceptions of a disease that was most readily explained as an 'awful visitation' of divine punishment.

In its issue of Monday, 11 June 1832, two days after the infected steamer *Voyageur* had reached Montreal, Ludger Duvernay's biweekly newspaper, *La*

CHOLERA BULLETIN.

Printed at the Wesleyan Office.

TO the President of the Board of Health of the Gore District:

Sir----I have this morning received a communication from Doct. GILPIN of Brantford, stating he was called to visit Three cases, which he considers exhibited characters of Spasmodic Cholera. One case, a man by the name of *Young*, proved fatal in 8 hours. The other two were convalescent when Doctor Gilpin writes.

The following is a report I submit to the Board of Health, on the above cases:

Cases of CHOLERA in the Gore District, from June 23, to June 25, inclusive----

Brantford, Cases THREE, Deaths 1, Convalescent 2.

(Signed)   SLADE ROBINSON, Pres't Medical Board.

Hamilton, June 27, 1832.

12.4 *Cholera Bulletin* (Hamilton, 1832). Courtesy of the Toronto Public Library (TRL).

Minerve, makes a passing reference to cholera in England and Ireland; the remark is tucked away among the 'Nouvelles étrangères.' Three days later the entire front page is given over to sanitary rules and regulations of the Montreal board of health; by this time, hundreds of people were dead. That this issue of Thursday, 14 June, mistakenly has the day of publication as 'lundi soir' seems a fitting typographical symbol of the confusion caused by the rapid advance of the disease. In response to such panic, these regulations constitute a veritable mobilization of print. Besides sanitary details, they order the immediate registration of all landlords, tenants, sublessees, passengers, sailors, hotel guests, butchers, and fishermen. They prescribe – in French only – that all innkeepers post the regulations and that every health officer appointed by the board be equipped with a certificate, a copy of the regulations, the names and addresses of the residents, and other documents.[163] At every house in his quartier, the officer was to identify himself, demand entry, point out all deviations from the rules, and note them in a report. The prescriptive clarity of these regulations is striking precisely because they were so ineffective in arresting the epidemic. The resentful inertia encountered by the health officers among the population was massive, and the disease itself was not reined in by posters and certificates. Yet, as they stand, the regulations are remarkable evidence of a community's yearning for the reassurance of the printed word when threatened by the unknown. They are a typographical attempt – notable for its failure – to wrest order from panic.

The full, real impact of cholera can be seen at best darkly through the glass of the printed record. 'The "facies cholerica" cannot be described in one half its horrors,' writes Joseph Workman, then a student of McGill College, in his medical dissertation of 1835; one 'never could have formed an adequate idea of it, from the most vivid description.'[164] Despite the wealth of extant documents, the print record in general falls as short as does Workman's prose in representing the wide-ranging effects of this disease, which 'in its desolating career ... spared neither age, nor sex, nor rank,'[165] nor race.

At the same time, the print culture of the day all but ignored the impact of cholera on Natives, and it is therefore difficult to determine the extent to which First Nations peoples were once again the victims of a plague brought to their shores by Europeans. That Natives too died of cholera is clear, however. In a letter dated 2 September 1834, William Jones, the Indian agent stationed at the Upper Indian Reserve on the St Clair River, writes that 'the Cholera has prevailed among the Indians of this place to a considerable extent. Yesterday we buried the 8th adult since the 18th of August. Between the 22d and 27th, inclusive, we interred one each day. The Indians have now all retired from the settlement.'[166] The light shed by this snippet of manuscript is faint, but it is enough to reveal the failure of print fully to portray the ravages of cholera in 1832 and 1834.

PART SIX

PRINT AND AUTHORITY

chapter 13

PUBLICATION AND POWER

Official Publications

GILLES GALLICHAN

A study of official publications enables us to understand the importance of links between printers and colonial governments in the eighteenth and nineteenth centuries. Publication of the acts was the duty of administrators, in accord with the judicial principle that no one should be ignorant of the law. Although this requirement greatly benefited printers, it could also put them in a position of dependence on the authorities, which might restrict their freedom of expression. And, indeed, official publications were not limited to the laws. Olga Bernice Bishop has defined them as 'any paper, map, pamphlet or book, manuscript or printed, originating in, or printed with the imprint of, or at the expense, or by the authority of any office of a legally organized government.'[1] Printed materials paid for by the government usually bore an official designation or the royal arms.

Materials Printed for the Administration

The administrators of New France would have valued a printing press in the colony, since without it the government's work was made more onerous. Documents, including paper money, often had to be copied by hand. Not only was this a slow process, but it multiplied omissions, the risk of errors, and misunderstandings because of sometimes illegible handwriting. Criers were the only way to make public – to publish in the original sense of the term – official information.[2]

In 1748 the governor, Roland-Michel Barrin de La Galissonière, requested a printer and a press for Quebec, but as François Melançon explains in chapter 3, he was not successful.[3] Consequently, the colonial administration had forms and new editions of royal decrees printed in France.[4] With the outbreak of the Seven Years War in 1756, the possibility of importing a press to New France, even in principle, was further ruled out. In the Thirteen Colonies it had been possible since the late seventeenth century to have printers produce broadsides, handbills, and legislative digests, in addition to disseminating the texts of the laws immediately by gazette or circular. Printed materials bearing the official seal of government also offered the welcome advantage to jurists and magistrates of a single, uniform text.[5] Soon after the Conquest of New France, the first press was set up in the colony. Official publications were among the earliest works produced at Halifax, at Quebec, and in each of the provinces in British North America as printing offices were established.[6] Nevertheless, it appears that governments first favoured the periodical press as the most useful means for disseminating information.

Gazettes and the Laws

Beginning in 1752, the governor of Nova Scotia, Peregrine Thomas Hopson, ordered a number of proclamations and folio laws from John Bushell.[7] He also used the columns of the *Halifax Gazette* for the same purpose. When the *Quebec Gazette / La Gazette de Québec* began publication in its turn, in 1764, the governor, James Murray, had an ordinance published in the second issue. The bilingual *Gazette* was not truly an official publication, since its interest was commerce and public information. Therefore, on 3 October 1764, Murray recognized as official publication the printing of laws and regulations of the province of Quebec in the *Gazette*, and he obliged all the priests to read these texts from the pulpit on Sundays.[8] The *Gazette* thus became a semi-official publication, its status confirmed by Governor Frederick Haldimand in 1785 when he used the newspaper to give notice of grants of public lands.

In addition to publication in the gazettes, the governors placed orders with the printers. At Quebec these would often be regulations or public notices printed as broadsides, 30 to 40 centimetres by 15 to 25 centimetres, in editions of 40 to 200 copies.[9] When the publication was not bilingual, twice as many copies would be printed in French.[10] The postal system, still in its infancy, allowed distribution of documents throughout the province. The administrators' intentions were, on the one hand, to disseminate information to the greatest number of people and, on the other, to maintain peace and public security.[11]

The King's Printer

The designation 'king's printer' appeared gradually. Over the years, official printers were appointed king's printers or printers of 'His Majesty's laws,' since they took on a legal responsibility: work to be published in the name of the executive, and thus in the name of the king, required careful printing. Anthony Henry in Halifax, William Brown and Thomas Gilmore at Quebec, and, later, William Lewis and John Ryan in Saint John, became de facto official printers, since they were the only printers in their respective towns. However, they did not immediately claim the title of king's printer. When, in 1774, William Brown published the text of the Quebec Act in a bilingual thirty-page pamphlet, he simply put after his name on the title pages 'Imprimeur de la province – Printer for the Province.' But in 1783, when he reproduced the text of the Treaty of Versailles, following the model of the London printer, he gave himself the title 'Imprimeur de sa Très Excellente Majesté – Printer to the King's Most Excellent Majesty.'[12] In New Brunswick, Christopher Sower designated himself king's printer in 1786, while in Upper Canada, Louis Roy, who was actually receiving a salary in 1793 for his printing work, did not use that title. His successors, starting with Gideon Tiffany, did so after 1795.[13] In Lower Canada, William Vondenvelden appropriated the title in 1797, and Pierre-Édouard Desbarats regularly used it on the documents that he produced in the early nineteenth century.

Before legislative assemblies were formed, the governors had sole power to award all printing contracts. In the Atlantic colonies there were few printers before 1840, and the king's printer would receive orders from the legislative assemblies and from the executive alike. Nevertheless, competition could be fierce, and some printers might agree to lower their rates and their profits in order to stay in the good graces of governors,[14] who were always able to secure the continuing loyalty of their printers.

Parliamentary Institutions and the Evolution of Official Publications

Except in Newfoundland, parliamentary assemblies were established in all the colonies in the second half of the eighteenth century. Nova Scotia began its assembly in 1758, modelled after those of the Thirteen Colonies. The administration of St John's Island, later Prince Edward Island, was formed in 1773, while the arrival of the Loyalists led to the creation of New Brunswick in 1784 and of its parliament in 1786. By the Constitutional Act of 1791, Quebec was divided into Upper and Lower Canada, and the two provinces were each given a bicameral parliament.

This new constitutional order changed the political dynamic and, as a consequence, the way that official publications were produced. The legislative branch now had the authority to have documents printed without asking for authorization from the executive. The Houses of Assembly struck printing committees charged with assisting the clerk and the speaker of the house in allocating orders to printers, following up on the work done, and reporting periodically to the house. The parliamentary printer was not necessarily the printer for the executive, as was the case in the Maritimes. The Assembly and the governor might compete for a printer's services, reflecting the constitutional rivalry between public institutions at that time. In Lower Canada the elected representatives awarded printing contracts through calls for tenders and made it a point of honour to obtain, always from the office of John Neilson, better prices than did the governor with the printers John Charlton Fisher and Thomas Cary Jr.[15]

In addition, parliaments had particular needs for new types of printed materials. The Lower Canada Assembly was the first elected body to adopt rules and regulations, which were printed by Neilson in 1793.[16] Those of Upper Canada were printed by John Bennett in 1802.[17] But the *Journals* of the parliamentary assemblies, in particular, constituted the main series of official legislative publications, since they collected the minutes of parliamentary sessions. Over the years, appendixes were added to accommodate copies of the documents from the session and the various reports submitted to the house. These printed materials dealing with roadwork, justice, land holdings, colonization, education, and public finances continue to be a fertile source for Canadian history.

The Legislative Council of the province of Quebec, created in 1774, had already inaugurated the practice of publication by ordering the printing of some twenty documents before 1792. After the establishment of an elected Assembly, however, the Legislative Council became less active in this regard. It also had its publications produced by the king's printer working within the orbit of the executive authority for official publishing. Pierre-Édouard Desbarats, king's printer for Lower Canada, published the first minutes of the upper chamber. The regular series of these journals began in 1814, and summaries of the proceedings for the sessions from 1795 to 1813 were published in 1821.[18]

In Upper Canada, Lieutenant-Governor John Graves Simcoe considered the services of a printer essential to his administration of the colony. 'The office of Printer seems to be of utmost importance,' he wrote to the secretary of state, Henry Dundas, in 1791.[19] In fact, he felt strongly enough to offer a salary to attract a printer to the new province, where living conditions were assuredly more difficult. The printer Louis Roy, who had been trained by William Brown at Quebec, took the position and began publication of the *Upper Canada Gazette* in April 1793. After 1801, his successors produced printed materials such as the *Journals* and the laws for both the executive and the legislature in Upper Canada. In April 1813, during the War of 1812, the Americans attacked York (Toronto), burning down the government buildings and destroying the official press, and from 1813 to 1815 the contract to print laws was temporarily awarded to Stephen Miles in Kingston.[20] The return of peace and the arrival of new printers in York stimulated competition. By the 1820s, they were in fierce competition for printing contracts from the legislature.[21]

In all the provinces, other legislative publications would include a few important bills, such as changes made to the legal system; electoral laws; some petitions; reports of parliamentary committees; and addresses to the governor.[22] The Assemblies of the two Canadas also approved publication of the first catalogues of their libraries. Print runs for both executive and legislative publications generally varied between 100 and 500 copies. In New Brunswick in 1786, Christopher Sower produced 100 copies of the *Journals* of the Assembly and 170 copies of the province's laws. In succeeding years, editions ranged from 200 for the *Journals* to 300 for the laws. These numbers were likely comparable in Nova Scotia, where the policy was to reserve 80 copies for the colonial administration and to sell the rest.[23] In Lower Canada the contract for the parliamentary *Journals* expanded from 100 to 400 between 1800 and 1835;[24] the edition sizes were similar in Upper Canada. Print runs for the laws and statutes were 200 copies in 1786, but probably several thousand around 1830. In 1824 the laws of Upper Canada were printed in an edition of 2,500 copies.[25] Orders of a similar size might occasionally be placed for certain documents of general interest.[26]

A certain number of legal reports were published before 1840, but the major legal series date from a later period. In Upper Canada the first judicial publications were the regulations and fee schedules of the Court of King's Bench and summaries of trials.[27] In Lower Canada the Court of King's Bench and the Court of Appeal also published their rules of conduct. Several court reports were produced, in particular, those of the political trials of the Patriotes, published in two volumes in Montreal in 1839.[28] With the publication of local jurisprudence and court-related documents, the practice of law and the training of jurists became more coherent and systematic.[29]

The first municipal documents appeared in print toward the end of the eighteenth century. Police regulations at Quebec were published in 1780 and again in 1783.[30] Regulations were printed in the town of Shelburne, Nova Scotia, in 1785; in the same year, Saint John published its charter and then in 1796, its bylaws. Shelburne also had its bylaws printed around the same time.[31] But it was generally not until the 1830s that duly constituted municipal administrations were established.

The Neilson-Fisher Affair, 1823–4

In 1823 political issues at Quebec became entangled with the privileges of the governor and the rights of printers when it came to creating an official gazette separate from the *Quebec Gazette / La Gazette de Québec*. The affair, which ended in court, pitted John Neilson's printing office against the official publisher, John Charlton Fisher. When he was elected to the Assembly for Quebec County in 1818, Neilson joined the Canadien majority in the Assembly and, at one stroke, the party opposed to the governor. Nevertheless, Neilson continued to publish the *Gazette*, the semi-official organ of the executive, and the governor's displeasure was made known to him. In order not lose the state's patronage, Neilson passed the enterprise on to his son Samuel and a partner, William Cowan. Satisfied, the governor, Lord Dalhousie, granted an official commission of king's printer to Samuel Neilson and William Cowan in 1822.

But the following year, when Neilson senior was sent with Louis-Joseph Papineau by the Assembly to London to oppose the plan for a union of the Canadas, the governor's irritation was again obvious. He withdrew the commission of king's printer from Neilson and Cowan and assigned it to Fisher, a newcomer to Quebec, who was more docile than the impetuous Neilson. What is more, the governor gave Fisher the task of producing a new *Quebec Gazette, Published by Authority / Gazette de Québec, publiée par autorité* – that is, with the exclusive right to be the first to publish the government's notices and decrees as a true official gazette. The new periodical was born in October 1823.

John Neilson rebelled against this abuse of power. The fact that a new gazette had been founded bearing the name of his newspaper meant that it was profiting unduly from the prestige and reputation, established over nearly sixty years of publication, of the *Quebec Gazette / La Gazette de Québec*. Moreover, Fisher was not a printer but a publisher, responsible for the content of the publication but not for the execution of the work. His official gazette was printed by Thomas Cary, publisher of the *Quebec Mercury*, an adversary and competitor of Neilson's paper. Neilson sued, and the affair was widely talked about in the spring of 1824, since the lawsuit challenged the governor's authority. Neilson's suit was eventually thrown out of court, and Fisher's *Gazette* enjoyed a long career, even after the Union of 1840.[32] The Neilson-Fisher affair established for the first time a distinction between the function of king's printer, who owned the press on which state documents were produced, and the official publisher, whose role was to oversee the content and legal aspects of the documents produced.

The Business of Printing

The contracts awarded to the official printer, whether by governors or by parliamentary assemblies, did not constitute a sinecure. Production costs were high, and the printer was often not paid until the document was delivered; he also would have had to assume all the costs of indexing. At Quebec the task was doubled by translations (see illus. 13.1, pp. 316–17). Around 1830, publication of the *Laws and Statutes of Lower Canada* cost about £800, a considerable sum at the time;[33] consequently, Fisher and his partner, William Kemble, had to ask the governor for an advance of funds in 1831 in order to produce the work.[34] King's printers sometimes saw their contracts cut back from one year to the next, and they had no way to protest. In practice, these orders were large and generally profitable, but they tied up the printer's stock of types, so that other orders sometimes had to be delayed or even refused. In addition, the time allotted for production was limited. In January 1813 John Neilson was summoned before a committee of the House to justify delays in the printing of parliamentary documents the previous year.[35] In Toronto, Charles Fothergill said that administrative and especially financial pressures on the king's printer were so great that one of his predecessors, John Bennett, had gone 'out of his sense.'[36]

On the other hand, official printers benefited from government favours through binding and the repair of bindings for the collections of *Journals* and laws that the government purchased from them. The printers sold subscriptions and other works produced on their presses, as well as stationery. They profited from the presence of the government and the Assembly, not only as producers of materials to be printed but also as consumers and distributors of the printed word.[37]

Assistance for Publishing

Finally, the state played a modest role in supporting publications that were not official by purchasing copies or providing funds for the printing of non-governmental works. For example, in 1814 Joseph Bouchette asked the Assembly of Lower Canada for financial assistance to publish in England a large-scale map of Lower Canada, accompanied by a complete topographical survey, under the title *Description topographique du Bas-Canada; or, A Topographical Description of the Province of Lower Canada*. The Assembly voted him £1,500 to carry through the project.[38] Fifteen years later, in 1829, when he proposed to update the work to include all the British colonies, the Assembly promised to purchase one hundred copies of his book.[39] The volumes were

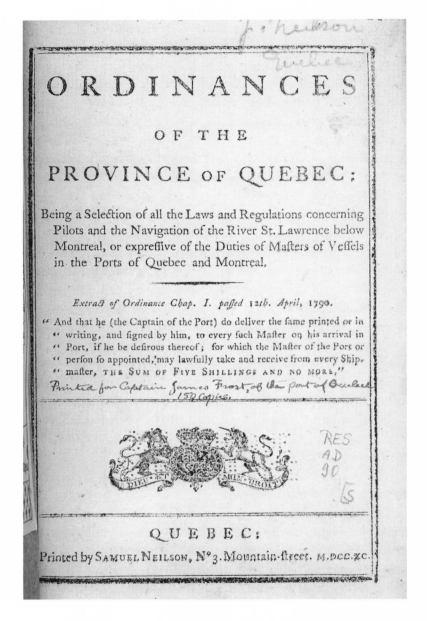

13.1 *Ordinances of the Province of Quebec* and *Ordonnances de la province de Québec* (Quebec, 1790). Printed in 'double' format with two title pages and the text in English and French on facing pages, this collection of nautical laws is ornamented with royal arms and a ship. The copy, which was signed by John Neilson and annotated 'Printed for Captain James Frost of the Port of Quebec 150 Copies,' may have been kept for Neilson's shop. Courtesy of the Bibliothèque nationale du Québec.

ORDONNANCES

DE LA

PROVINCE DE QUEBEC,

Contenant toutes les Loix et Réglemens concernant les Pilotes, et la Navigation du Fleuve St. Laurent au-deſſous de Montréal, et les devoirs des Maitres de Vaiſſeaux dans les Ports de Québec et de Montréal.

Extrait de l'Ordonnance Chap. I. paſſée le 12 Avril, 1790.

" Et que le Capitaine de Port les donne imprimés ou par écrit et ſignés
" par lui à chaque et tel Maitre à ſon arrivée dans le Port, s'il veut en
" avoir, et pour tel ſervice, le Capitaine de Port ou celui qui ſera ainſi
" nommé comme ci-deſſus, pourra recevoir de chaque et tel Maitre de
" Vaiſſeau la ſomme de cinq ſhellings et rien de plus."

A QUEBEC:

Chez SAMUEL NEILSON, N°3 Rue la Montagne. M.DCC.XC.

published in 1831 as *The British Dominions in North America*, and Bouchette asked for support from various legislatures. Nova Scotia purchased twenty-five copies.[40]

In the same spirit, Nova Scotia supported the publication in 1823 of a book by Thomas Chandler Haliburton, *A General Description of Nova Scotia*, which was superseded in 1829 by *An Historical and Statistical Account of Nova-Scotia*. The parliament of Nova Scotia also funded publication of a guide for justices of the peace in 1837.[41] These works were major undertakings that could not have been produced without financial assistance. However, although a number of similar petitions were submitted to legislatures or governors, very few authors profited from such patronage.[42] Missionary work associated with the education of Native peoples also seems to have inspired the generosity of a governor such as Sir John Colborne of Upper Canada, who financed the printing of two thousand copies of the Gospel of Matthew in Ojibwa.[43]

Official publications and semi-official gazettes were among the first products of the press in British North America. In addition to performing a practical function in administration, official publishing played an active role in the formation of colonial governments. The arrival of parliamentary institutions diminished the governors' monopoly over the award of printing contracts and drew some printers into the political debates of their times. Judicial and municipal authorities also produced their first printed materials in this period. Official publications were a dynamic force in the development of printing before 1840. They contributed to the implementation of administrative, judicial, and governmental structures that presaged the emergence of the modern state.

The Printers of Laws, Proclamations, and Official Gazettes and the King's Printers to 1840

Nova Scotia

John Bushell	1752–61
Anthony Henry	1761–6
Robert Fletcher	1766–70
Anthony Henry	1770–1800
John Howe	1801–4
John Howe and son	1804–41

Quebec / Lower Canada

William Brown and Thomas Gilmore	1764–72

William Brown	1773–89
Samuel Neilson Sr	1789–93
John Neilson	1793–4
William Vondenvelden	1795–8
Roger Lelièvre and Pierre-Édouard Desbarats	1798–9
Pierre-Édouard Desbarats	1800–22
Samuel Neilson Jr	1822–3
John Charlton Fisher	1823–5
John Charlton Fisher and William Kemble	1825–40

New Brunswick

Christopher Sower	1784–99
John Ryan	1799–1807
Jacob S. Mott	1808–14
Ann Mott and Henry Chubb	1814
George Kilman Lugrin	1814–29
John Simpson	1830–63

St John's Island / Prince Edward Island

James Robertson Sr	1787–9
William Alexander Rind	1790–8
James Bagnall	1804–8
James Douglas Haszard	1808–10
James Bagnall	1810–30
James Douglas Haszard	1830–51

Upper Canada

Louis Roy	1792–4
Gideon Tiffany	1794–7
Titus Geer Simons	1797–8
William Waters and Titus Simons	1798–1801
John Bennett	1801–7
John Cameron and John Bennett	1807–8
John Cameron	1808–13

Stephen Miles (interim at Kingston)	1813–15
Edward William McBride (interim)	1815–16
William Kemble	1816–17
Robert Charles Horne	1816–22
Charles Fothergill	1822–6
Robert Stanton	1826–41

Newfoundland

John Ryan and son	1807–14
Lewis Kelly Ryan	1814–18
John Ryan	1818–32
John Ryan and John Collier Withers	1832–47

Political Censorship

GILLES GALLICHAN

At a time when freedom of the press was still associated with licence, even with revolution, colonial governors appropriated the power to tolerate, ban, or condemn any publication over which they did not exercise full control. Under the laws in force, they could charge a printer or journalist with libel or sedition in virtue of English common law, which forbade the spread of news likely to cause disorder between the king and his subjects.[44] On this basis, lawsuits were easy, and times of war or crisis were particularly propitious for such a policy.

In New France it seems that severe control of printed materials, and of writing in general, was not necessary for the most part. With the exception of the burning of the *Anti-Coton* in 1626, there are no examples of civil authorities intervening to ban a printed work. The population was sparse and poorly educated outside the towns. Local presses did not yet exist, libraries belonged to the clergy or the elites, and even paper was a rare commodity. Under the French regime, the authorities were more suspicious of what was said or related than of what was written, printed, and read.

The arrival of the first printers at Halifax in 1751 and at the town of Quebec in

1764 was part of the evolving expansion of the printing press, which was already burgeoning in the British colonies to the south. That the printers set up shop in two colonial capitals was not a matter of chance; in the eighteenth century, printing owed its existence in large part to the patronage of governments, which placed regular and voluminous orders for various official publications. In 1765, however, an English tax law, the Stamp Act, hit the colonies, affecting local printers and shaking the foundations of the entire British empire in North America.

The Stamp Act (1765)

The Stamp Act, passed by the parliament in London, was not a censorship law per se, but its application to newspapers published in the North American colonies, including the provinces of Quebec and Nova Scotia, had the same impact as a law restricting the press. Britain wanted to raise between £60,000 and £100,000 annually in its North American colonies to replenish the kingdom's coffers. An embossed or inked mark (the stamp), indicating that a tax had been paid, had to be placed on various types of public printed materials, including court judgments, licences, insurance papers, official forms, playing cards, broadsides, pamphlets, almanacs, and newspapers. Sanctioned by George III on 22 March 1765, the law came into force on the first of November that year.

This direct tax decreed by Westminster both contravened the principle summarized in the famous slogan 'No taxation without representation' and limited access to various products affected by the measure. Merchants, jurists, and printers were the first to feel its effects. Particularly for newspaper printers, who had a small readership, the tax could sound a death knell. William Brown and Thomas Gilmore's *Quebec Gazette / La Gazette de Québec* was the first to fall. After only sixteen months in existence, the newspaper could not raise its rates without losing subscribers. Therefore it ceased regular publication on 31 October 1765, on the eve of the laws coming into force, 'by Means of the small Number of subscribers.'[45] The loss of the only newspaper in the Laurentian colony, a victim of its precarious market, suddenly deprived the colonial administration of a valuable channel of communication.

The *Halifax Gazette*, meanwhile, used stamped paper and continued publishing after 31 October. Its printers, Anthony Henry and Isaiah Thomas, could count upon a stable and loyal clientele since the newspaper had been in existence for thirteen years in Nova Scotia. However, it echoed the wave of revolt that was sweeping all of English-speaking North America; during the winter of 1765–6, the newspaper's pages were edged in black as a sign of mourning, and in addition to the reviled official stamp or in its place, some copies bore a counter-stamp in protest,[46] portraying the pirates' skull and crossbones or a little devil to represent the spirit of evil. The rebellious attitude displayed by the editor of the *Gazette* displeased the colonial authorities of Nova Scotia; they withdrew their contracts from Henry and gave them to a new printer who had arrived from London that summer.[47] The *Halifax Gazette* ceased publication on 6 March 1766, a victim of its anti-government stance. This act of censorship against Henry was one of the early clouds presaging the American Revolution.

Opposition to the Stamp Act was so great, even in Britain, that Parliament withdrew it on 18 March 1766, and on the first of May the tax was abolished. In the town of Quebec, the *Gazette* resumed publication with satisfaction on 29 May and wrote lyrically of the legislation as 'an Act more dreadful than the icy Chains of our inhospitable Winter, whose baneful Blasts spread Desolation over the Plains and stop the Source of Commerce.'[48] In Nova Scotia, however, the *Halifax Gazette* was replaced on 15 August 1766 by a new publication, the *Nova-Scotia Gazette*, printed by Robert Fletcher.

The American Revolution, 1775–86

The times were ripe for protest. The American Revolution and, later, the French Revolution stirred up a ferment of ideas and debates, which the press not only reported but participated in. The official and semi-official gazettes in the capitals, such as those in Halifax and Quebec, which published government notices, remained neutral and prudent throughout the American War of Independence. But this was not the case for the French-language gazette founded in Montreal by printer Fleury Mesplet, who arrived in the wake of the Continental army, which had occupied the town in 1775–6. His aim was to deliver the insurgents' propaganda to the Canadiens, but the need for a printer in the town became obvious, and he was able to rapidly build a clientele among merchants and the Sulpician clergy. Barely established when the troops departed, he remained in Montreal and was imprisoned for several weeks. Since the authorities had no real evidence against him, he was released to conduct his business freely. In 1778 he launched the *Gazette du commerce et littéraire* with Valentin Jautard, who edited the newspaper under the *nom de plume* 'Spectateur tranquille.'[49] In the midst of war, this liberal-minded, rebellious, and Voltairian newspaper upset the clerical and political authorities, particularly the governor, Frederick Haldimand.[50]

In 1779 Jautard opened the pages of the *Gazette* to the critical writings of the merchant and justice of the peace Pierre Du Calvet, who denounced the current legal practices as well as certain Montreal magistrates. The newspaper thus found itself in the grip of censorship by the colonial government. In its last issue on 2 June 1779, Jautard denounced the fate that had befallen him in a celebrated column titled 'Tant pis, tant mieux' (Too bad, so much the better). It contained a series of ironic maxims that ended with the expressions in the title in alternation: 'In the printing office, we put men to work at the press, and if we skin them alive, too bad. But if it makes them into better men, so much the better.'[51] Two days later, Mesplet and Jautard were taken to Quebec and imprisoned with other prominent figures suspected of sedition; they were joined by Pierre Du Calvet, who was arrested the following year. Without a trial or even formal charges, they were to remain in prison until 8 February 1783, after peace was re-established. Two years later, Mesplet began to publish a new paper, *Montreal Gazette / La Gazette de Montréal*, which pleaded in favour of constitutional parliamentary reform.[52]

After he was freed, Du Calvet went to England to protest the arbitrary nature of his imprisonment and demand more freedom in the administration of the colony. He assembled his grievances and desiderata in a pamphlet, *Appel à la justice de l'État*, which he published in London in 1784. This text was one of the founding works on constitutional reform for both Quebec and Canada. Du Calvet perished at sea in 1786, but his ideas outlived him and contributed to the introduction of parliamentary institutions in Canada.[53]

In New Brunswick the printers William Lewis and John Ryan began to publish the *Saint John Gazette* in 1783. A year later, they were accused of libel for an article on the governor's methods of distributing land to Loyalists.[54] They carried on regardless, but in 1786 they were charged once again, this time over an article criticizing the first elections in the colony, and were sentenced by the Supreme Court of New Brunswick to pay a fine.[55] After this, Ryan became compliant and less critical, and following the departure of Christopher Sower, he obtained the commission of king's printer as a reward for his good conduct.

An Era of Revolution and War, 1789–1815

The first events of the revolution of 1789 in France were greeted with sympathy in Britain and its colonies, but attitudes changed after 1792 with the fall of the monarchy and the outbreak of war between France and Britain.[56] Newspapers in Lower Canada reflected the official discourse of the parent country, and when Napoleon became a threat to Britain, simply mentioning his military genius was seen as a sign of disloyalty or even treason.[57]

The press was put to the service of war propaganda, even setting a precedent by using engravings. In 1793 John Neilson printed for the provincial secretary and registrar, George Pownall, a text entitled *Mort tragique du roi de France*, accompanied by an illustration showing the king before the guillotine. Two years later, an engraved portrait of the queen, Marie Antoinette, was also printed at Quebec, no doubt to stir up the emotions of Canadiens over the fate of their former sovereigns.[58]

Nascent parliamentary government encouraged the emergence of a politicized press. In Upper Canada, Joseph Willcocks, an elected member, attacked the House of Assembly and the courts, defending the whig point of view both in Parliament and in his newspaper, the *Upper Canada Guardian; or, Freeman's Journal* of Niagara (Niagara-on-the-Lake). The journal, founded in 1807, ceased publication in 1812. During the war that began that year, Willcocks fought on the American side and died in combat.[59]

At Quebec the *Quebec Mercury*, representing the merchant class, and *Le Canadien* confronted each other in the first years of the nineteenth century, as *Le Canadien* defended the positions of habitants, landowners, and the majority in the Assembly.[60] Published by members Pierre-Stanislas Bédard, François Blanchet, Jean-Thomas Taschereau, and Joseph Levasseur Borgia, *Le Canadien* and its opinions soon collided with those of greedy businessmen, prominent figures, and the authoritarian governor, Sir James Henry Craig. During the parliamentary crises of 1808–10, *Le Canadien* was accused of being a 'rabble-rouser' and of perpetrating 'lies and disloyalty,'[61] serious accusations at a time when Britain was at war with France.

On 17 March 1810 the governor ordered the arrest of the printer, Charles Lefrançois, and the seizure of the small press at the Imprimerie canadienne, where the newspaper was produced. Two days later, the publishers, writers, and agents of *Le Canadien* were in their turn arrested for 'treasonous practices';[62] in total, about twenty people were thrown in prison.[63] The press long remained sealed in a vault at the Quebec courthouse. Those responsible for putting out the newspaper were released after a few months, some for health reasons, but Bédard, demanding a trial that he would never receive, remained in prison until March 1811. The recall of Craig in that year and the War of 1812 brought about a political détente, but *Le Canadien* did not resume publication until 1817, with a new editorial team.

The French Revolution and the wars of the empire brought the colonial press under close scrutiny. When John Ryan left his respectable position as king's printer of New Brunswick in 1806 to open the first printing office in Newfoundland, he took with him the recommendations of the highest authorities in the colony.[64] Suspicious, the island's governor, Sir Erasmus Gower, nevertheless required Ryan to post a bond of £200 and to submit his gazette to the perusal of the magistrates before publication. Ryan was to print nothing that 'may tend to disturb the peace of His Majesty's Subjects' or raise controversy or debate, and no criticism of the British government was to appear in the paper.[65] By these means the emerging Newfoundland press was subjected to the meticulous and authoritarian control of political censorship. Up to 1815, the island's governor was able to prevent the appearance of a second newspaper. The printers Alexander Haire and Robert Lee, who wanted to start a commercial paper in St John's, had to go to London to claim their rights and force the governor to abandon this abuse of power. Ryan profited for a time from this constraint on competition, but in 1821 his son Lewis Kelly Ryan, who had established the *Newfoundland Sentinel and General Commercial Register*, had to flee the island suddenly to escape a defamation lawsuit; he died at sea.[66] Polemical writers in Newfoundland also suffered in this censorious climate. In 1812 and 1813, the St John's physician William Carson published in Scotland two reform-minded pamphlets that cost him his position as surgeon of the Loyal Volunteers.[67]

The Struggle for Freedom of the Press, 1815–36

In Upper Canada the authorities also intervened against the opposition press. The Scottish journalist Robert Fleming Gourlay was imprisoned in Niagara (Niagara-on-the-Lake) on 4 January 1819 for articles that he had published in the *Niagara Spectator*. From his cell he wrote new articles even more critical of the administration. Accused of seditious libel, he was found guilty and banned from the province on 21 August 1821. After returning to Scotland, he continued with his polemics and published notable essays on Upper Canada.[68] The publisher of the *Niagara Spectator*, Bartemas Ferguson, was also sentenced to a lengthy prison term.[69]

The journalistic career of Francis Collins, the hotheaded publisher of the *Canadian Freeman* at York (Toronto), was marked by many confrontations with the political authorities. In 1828 the governor, Sir Peregrine Maitland, and the attorney general, John Beverley Robinson, charged him with libel. His sentence of one year in prison and a stiff fine raised public sympathy for him. From his cell he continued to edit the *Freeman*, remaining just as critical of the government. The Assembly sent a petition to England on his behalf, and he received a royal pardon after forty-five weeks of detention.[70]

The figure who symbolized freedom of the press in Upper Canada at this time was William Lyon Mackenzie. In his newspaper, the *Colonial Advocate*, he criticized the tory party and the Family Compact, solidly installed in the Executive and Legislative Councils and in the House of Assembly. On 8 June 1826 Mackenzie's printing office was vandalized, an event described by Sarah Brouillette in chapter 10.[71] He took the attackers to court and obtained compensation. From then on, he was a well-known figure in the colony. Elected to the House of Assembly in 1828, Mackenzie waged his reformist battles by continuing to publish virulent articles in the *Colonial Advocate*. In 1831, following a particularly fierce attack, the House expelled him. He defended himself before his electors, on the hustings, and in the press,[72] and re-election in 1832 was a fresh triumph over the tories. He was expelled from the House several times and re-elected each time. In this climate, even the act of publishing the first Canadian edition of Thomas Paine's *Common Sense* in 1837 could be seen as a criticism of the colonial political system.[73] Mackenzie's articles and publications earned him threats and even physical assaults by some of his adversaries.

In Lower Canada a number of newspaper publishers also paid the price for expressing their opinions freely. At Quebec in 1823, John Neilson, his son Samuel, and William Cowan, who published the *Quebec Gazette / La Gazette de Québec*, challenged the authority of the governor, Lord Dalhousie, and became embroiled in a sensational trial, which they lost. In Montreal, journalists such as Jocelyn Waller of the *Canadian Spectator*, Daniel Tracey of the *Vindicator,* and Ludger Duvernay of *La Minerve* were imprisoned by the governor for press-related offences. On 16 November 1827 Waller and Duvernay were incarcerated for articles published during the hotly contested general election and also in the first weeks that the legislature was sitting. Appearing before the Court of King's Bench, they pleaded their innocence based on the right to free discussion of public affairs. They were acquitted by the jury, an outcome that led Duvernay to write in *La Minerve*, 'The country needed a newspaper like ours.'[74] In January 1832, however, Duvernay returned to prison with Daniel Tracey for articles criticizing the Legislative Council. Public meetings were organized by the Patriotes all over the province, motions of support were passed, and in Montreal several hundred people demonstrated in the streets, crying, 'Long live Duvernay and Tracey! Long live the freedom of the press! Down with the Council!' By the time Duvernay and Tracey were freed, after forty days of detention, they had become heroes to the people (see illus. 4.2, p. 76). Their return to Montreal was exultant; they were offered banquets on their way back, and a large crowd awaited their arrival. Louis-Joseph Papineau presented medals on which was engraved 'Freedom of the press is the palladium of the people.'

The notoriety pushed Tracey into politics, and in May 1832 he ran in a by-election in Montreal West, which turned into a riot. He was elected, but he died of cholera three months later. Duvernay, for his part, was imprisoned a third time in 1836 for the publication in *La Minerve* of a critique of Lower Canada's judicial and penal system. Once again, this offence increased his popularity, and people spoke of the 'triumphant imprisonment' of Duvernay. He agreed to run for office and was elected in Lachenaie in 1837, on the eve of the insurrections.

In Newfoundland in 1835, the journalist Robert John Parsons published in the St John's *Newfoundland Patriot* a sharp criticism of the despotic methods of the colony's chief justice, Henry John Boulton. The judge accused Parsons of contempt of court, summoned him to appear in his court, and sentenced him to a fine and three months in prison. A petition to reverse this unfair sentence, signed by five thousand citizens, was sent to London. Parsons finally received redress and won much recognition on the island.

Joseph Howe, self-educated, a bibliophile, a great reader, and a sharp observer, was a dominant figure in nineteenth-century Nova Scotia. From his father, a postmaster and king's printer, he had inherited the belief that newspapers were important not only for informing the people, but also for training and educating them. After 1827 he made himself well known as the publisher of the *Novascotian*, which under his direction became an important newspaper. In the 1830s, Howe published articles critical of local politicians and unscrupulous businessmen, and in January 1835 one of these earned him a charge of libel, a case discussed later in this chapter by George L. Parker. As no lawyer would agree to represent him, Howe defended himself, and before the court in March he presented a brilliant plea, regarded as a founding moment in the fight for freedom of the press.[75] His acquittal drew public acclaim, and he was soon lured into politics. The following year he entered the Assembly of Nova Scotia, where he played a prominent role for several decades.

The press in Prince Edward Island also confronted civil authorities at this time. A petition was circulated in 1823 asking London to recall Charles Douglass Smith, the lieutenant-governor. Smith, who had little tolerance for those who opposed him, was furious at the petitioners and at the printer James Douglas Haszard, who had reproduced the text of the petition in his newspaper, the *Prince Edward Island Register*. Their trial for libel stirred up debate and set a legal precedent, while Haszard received a reprimand from the court and was required to pay a fine.[76]

The Era of Insurrections, 1837–40

The years 1834 to 1837 were marked by intense publishing activity in both the Canadas. Posters, political pamphlets, constitutional tracts, and newspapers were abundant in these years of political turbulence. This energy presaged an inevitable clash between the government and the many printers, editors, and writers who supported the actions of the Patriotes and the Reformers. With the Russell Resolutions of 1837, the imperial government deprived its rebel colony of Lower Canada of parliamentary freedom. It goes without saying that the press also had to be controlled and all dissident printers silenced.

In Upper Canada, William Lyon Mackenzie, himself the leader of insurrection, had to flee Toronto and take refuge in the United States. There he fell afoul of the American authorities, who did not want to offend Britain by breaking their neutrality in this political conflict. Mackenzie finally settled in New York, where he published *Mackenzie's Gazette* and, later, other newspapers. He returned to Canada only after the amnesty in 1849 and was re-elected to the Assembly two years later.

As for Duvernay, an arrest warrant was issued against him, and he fled Montreal on 16 November 1837, entrusting his newspaper to his partners. The last issue of *La Minerve* was published a few days later, on 20 November, and it was then banned. Taking refuge in Vermont, Duvernay founded the Imprimerie du Patriote canadien in Burlington and published a newspaper of the same name there. Physically and morally ruined, he returned to Montreal in 1842 and resumed publication of *La Minerve*. He survived another ten years after these events, his career, marred by disputes and harassment, having come to a sad end.

Edmund Bailey O'Callaghan had become editor of the Montreal Irish newspaper, the *Vindicator,* in which he energetically defended the Patriote cause. On 6 November 1837 the offices of the newspaper, owned by bookseller Édouard-Raymond Fabre, were vandalized by rioters from the Doric Club, and later O'Callaghan had to go into exile in the United States, where he died in 1880.[77]

Robert-Shore-Milnes Bouchette was one of the publishers in 1837 of *Le Libéral*, the Patriote newspaper at Quebec. He was sentenced to exile in the Bermudas, but the fact that he had also been chairman of a Patriote popular assembly and had actively participated in the rebellion aggravated his case (see illus. 13.2, p. 329). He too returned to Canada after the amnesty. Charles Hunter, the other publisher of the newspaper, was arrested in March 1839 and spent several weeks in prison for having helped some Patriotes to flee and having published a newspaper that the authorities deemed 'seditious.' He died the following July.

François Lemaître was the owner and printer of *Le Libéral* at Quebec in 1837. After the newspaper was shut down in November, he launched *La Quotidienne*, a reformist and satirical newspaper in Montreal. In January 1838 his printing office on rue des Commissaires was vandalized by opponents, and he was assaulted. He was arrested and his equipment seized by the police. The owner of his press was Denis-Benjamin Viger, a businessman, member of the Legislative Council, and one of the leaders of

13.2 Robert-Shore-Milnes Bouchette, *Imprisonment of Robert-Shore-Milnes Bouchette* (1837). Courtesy of the National Archives of Canada, C-021554.

the Patriote movement, whom the *Montreal Herald* had denounced publicly as the owner of seditious newspapers. Viger himself was imprisoned from November 1838 to May 1840, and his library and papers seized by the police. He defended his rights fiercely, and the printer François Cinq-Mars, who also worked on a press owned by Viger, published a pamphlet on his imprisonment in 1840.[78]

Napoléon Aubin, who published *Le Fantasque*, another literary and satirical newspaper at Quebec, spent fifty-three days in prison in 1839 for presenting Joseph-Guillaume Barthe's poem in tribute to the exiled Patriotes. The poet himself was interned from 2 January to 3 April 1839. The imprisonment of Étienne Parent was all the more tragic, since the positions he held in *Le Canadien* had always been moderate, and his newspaper had stopped supporting the Parti Patriote in 1836. Nevertheless, he was jailed, together with the publisher of the newspaper, Jean-Baptiste Fréchette, on 26 December 1838. They were finally freed by a writ of habeas corpus on 12 April 1839. During his imprisonment, Parent continued to keep informed and even to write and publish, but the harsh conditions of his winter internment caused him to lose his hearing completely.

Exile or prison was the fate of many journalists during these years. Twenty-five Patriotes have been identified as workers in the book and printing trades in Lower Canada, not including students, teachers, and professionals.[79] Among them were printers, publishers of newspapers, and booksellers who were jailed or exiled. Even journalists, such as Parent, whose positions in the midst of turmoil were well thought out and moderate, found themselves caught up and victimized by a law that served not justice but force. Those who dared to assume the risks of press freedom often became symbolic figures, almost always swept away in the current of political engagement.

The issue of censorship of printed materials in the British North American colonies was partly the result of political crisis and the ideological confrontations that marked the 1830s, but also of the limited market and readership. Because the population of readers, purchasers, and subscribers was small, printers were forced for their business to rely on, and therefore developed a respect for, those in authority and political power. Often, the survival of the press depended on highly placed state and church officials. In the eighteenth and nineteenth centuries, printers who dared wander off the paths of orthodoxy and into the ways of criticism took great risks. Even the widespread use of pseudonyms did not reduce the dangers, since the responsibility then fell upon employees at the newspaper. The rigorous laws of the day relating to libel and slander, the lack of professional recognition for those who produced books and newspapers, and the economic influence of governments, together with the power of the police and the legal system behind them, made the realization of press freedom hazardous. However, starting with the battle against the Stamp Act, publishers and editors of newspapers sensed that this freedom presaged a new era, and some had the courage to exercise it.

CASE STUDY
Joseph Howe and Freedom of the Press
— George L. Parker

On 3 March 1835 triumphant Haligonians emerged from Province House carrying Joseph Howe, proprietor of the *Novascotian*, on their shoulders. He had just been acquitted of seditious libel by the Supreme Court of Nova Scotia.[80] For years Howe's newspaper had voiced public resentment of abuses by city and provincial administrations. On 1 January 1835 he had published a letter by his friend George Thompson, who signed himself 'The People,' accusing the non-elected Halifax 'Magistracy and Police' of wringing more than £30,000 from the people over the past thirty years.[81] At the instigation of the magistrates, Howe was prosecuted for libel. Advised that he had no case, he studied libel law, especially the imperial Libel Act of 1792, at his printing shop opposite Province House, and he conducted his own defence before the Supreme Court, presided over by Chief Justice Brenton Halliburton.[82]

During the government's stage-managed trial on 2 and 3 March, Howe did not deny the libel, but he argued the 'overwhelming public necessity'[83] for an editor to reveal official corruption and mismanagement. His speech lasted six and a quarter hours, and, as he reported to his sister, it 'startled & astonished the multitude who devoured every word like manna & what was better awed the Bench, scattered & confounded the prosecutors & what was best of all convinced the Jury.'[84] On 3 March, Attorney General Samuel George William Archibald summed up for the prosecution; Halliburton's charge to the jury followed. After ten minutes, it found Howe not guilty.

The *Novascotian* of 5 March declared that 'the PRESS OF NOVA-SCOTIA IS FREE.' All the Halifax newspapers applauded the verdict. Several magistrates resigned their posts, and nine new appointees declined to serve.[85] News of the victory spread, and in May, Nova Scotians in New York City sent him a silver pitcher.[86] The trial and his acquittal encouraged Howe to plunge into politics in the election of 1836, thus launching his public career.[87] In the provincial cabinet, he would work for responsible government for Nova Scotia, granted in principle in 1840, and for the incorporation of Halifax, which occurred a year later. Joseph Howe's oratory gave birth to a legend as powerful as John Milton's *Areopagitica* and transformed him into the voice and conscience of Nova Scotia.

Religious Censorship

PIERRE HÉBERT

The history of censorship, from the first known case in 1625 to the Act of Union of 1840, was not affected by the historic rupture of the Conquest. Instead, the practice of censorship can be divided into two periods, before and after 1800. The first saw case-by-case censorship, without predefined policy; the second, though brief, was decisive in that it made the clergy aware of the importance of more effective control, although this was instituted only after Ignace Bourget took charge as bishop of the Diocese of Montreal in 1840.

These two periods are defined by the clerical discourse found in pastoral letters and other official texts emanating from the episcopate. It is telling to observe that fourteen of these texts, proscriptive or prescriptive, are dated before 1800; only one was issued between 1800 and 1840.[88] Few pastoral letters dealt directly with books, but with the movement from the sphere of private transgression to that of public scandal and with the advent of what may be called 'imperative discourse' in the late eighteenth century, priests used them to oppose evil books.[89] One of the principal means of control consisted of 'refusing' or 'deferring' absolution to 'those who compose or sell evil books, verses, or songs.'[90] In a 'pastoral letter for special cases' – that is, when only the bishop could absolve the sinner – Jean-Baptiste de La Croix de Chevrières de Saint-Vallier, second bishop of Quebec, withheld absolution from 'those who utter in public or write something injurious against God, the Blessed Virgin, and the Saints,' as well as 'those who compose lampoons or defamatory songs.'[91]

Nevertheless, it was a long way from the words of the episcopate to the burning of books. The blight of bad books seems to have gained ground, as demonstrated by the admission made by Bishop Jean-François Hubert of Quebec in 1794: 'The reading of evil books, which are flooding the country and whose introduction we cannot block, has wreaked havoc here, even among Catholics.'[92] This statement supports the notion that censorship by the clergy was difficult, perhaps even rare. Furthermore, Hubert rejoiced that the public authorities had tried to 'proscribe the new systems' (he was probably thinking of the French Revolution), which had 'put a stop to some of the seditious and impious discourses in circulation.' There followed this surprising recognition of the clergy's weakness as censors: 'It is what those preaching the gospel could not accomplish, because they threatened only the judgments of divine vengeance.'[93]

Selective Censorship, 1625–1800

Moreover, along with this rather disorganized discourse came sporadic censorship. The first known case in New France involved the *Anti-Coton*, a pamphlet directed at Father Coton, former confessor of Henri IV.[94] As it happened, the arrival of the Jesuits in Canada in 1625 coincided with the first known book burning: 'Your R. [Reverence] must believe me,' wrote Father Charles Lalemant, first Superior of the order at Quebec, 'that we found the Anti-Coton, that it was being passed from room to room, and that in the end we burned it four months after our arrival.'[95] However, this isolated case should not be seen as the beginning of sustained censorship.

The clergy found the theatre more troubling because of incidents such as the famous 'Tartuffe Affair' in 1694 and the controversy concerning the Théâtre de société.[96] But the coming of the printing press provoked the first case of official clerical censorship against a printed work. The only 'periodical paper,' as such publications were then called, capable of stirring up eighteenth-century ideas, and all the more so because it entered into the spirit of the Enlightenment, was the *Gazette du commerce et littéraire*, which was published by Fleury Mesplet for one year between June 1778 and June 1779. The *Gazette littéraire* was disturbing not only because it provoked critical thought,[97] but also because it found fault with teachers, the government, and the judiciary. An article titled 'Tant pis, tant mieux' (Too bad, so much the better), which appeared in the issue of 2 June 1779, led to the paper's closure. The civil authorities appear to have borne primary responsibility for this censorship, but the clergy had also intervened privately. The superior of the Sulpicians, Étienne Montgolfier, had complained about the newspaper to Governor Frederick Haldimand.[98] This behind-the-scenes intervention again underlines the weakness of the clergy; had they been able to intervene publicly and vigorously, they would no doubt have done so without hesitation.

The limitations of these two types of censorship, private and case by case, became increasingly obvious. Censorship exercised in the private sphere and in the closed exchange of the confessional was quickly overtaken by the spread of printing; as for selective censorship, it was applied in reaction to a *fait accompli* and often at a time of crisis. To act in the private sphere was to ignore the idea that control of public opinion and the social means of production could result in a much broader effect; to censor case by case was to admit a failure, that of neutralizing even the appearance of multiple points of view. We should note here that, properly speaking, there was no history of censorship in Quebec before the early nineteenth century, in that a few cases do not establish practices, strategies, and coordinated actions. However, it must be said that the clergy were already defining themselves as the guardians of morals and the overseers of leisure activities, such as dance and games.

Difficult Lessons and a New Strategy (1800–40)

The nineteenth century began in a climate in which censorship was far from organized or supported by an effective authority. The spirit of independence, even insubordination, in parishes, the immense territory to be covered, and the small number of clergy, whose prestige had dwindled with the impact of the French Revolution and the Constitutional Act of 1791, all helped to prevent the development of effective censorship. The censorial apparatus that marked so profoundly the ultramontanism of the second half of the century is well known; the period from 1800 to 1840, during which freedom of the press became an issue, clearly signalled the painful passage toward this severe, even repressive, era.

The fierce attacks by the *Quebec Mercury* in 1805 on everything French more or less forced the Canadiens to respond in *Le Canadien*, from 1806 on. The decisive event was a violent song in the issue of 14 March 1810, which denounced the governor, Sir James Henry Craig, and his entourage. *Le Canadien* did, however, try to make amends:

> A song was published whose author is unknown to us, and in which the Owners of this paper have had no part; and where these verses appear: When will you dare to chase away, O People, this rabble, Whom the Governor means to pay At your expense, &c.
>
> We are sincerely distressed that such expressions should have appeared anywhere at all.[99]

The apology was in vain. Craig had *Le Canadien* seized on 17 March, and its owners were thrown into prison. The governor also asked Joseph-Octave Plessis, the bishop of Quebec, to make a gesture unprecedented in the history of the church: to read from the pulpit a proclamation emanating from the civil authority, in this case concerning the seizure of *Le Canadien*.[100] The church found itself at an impasse, since Plessis was well aware that 'it is on its [the British government's] protection that freedom of worship in the province depends.'[101] Bishop Plessis complied with the government's request. Although the church had privately pronounced itself against *Le Canadien* and against the Constitution by means of letters from Plessis, it took shelter behind Craig's proclamation to strike a final blow at *Le Canadien*.[102]

In the 1820s, Jean-Jacques Lartigue, coadjutor bishop of Montreal, aware of the weaknesses of the clergy, laid the foundation for a strategy of censorship that would be developed by his successor, Bishop Ignace Bourget. With many newspapers in existence, the local press was well established by the beginning of the decade; as well, shipments of new books were arriving from Europe more frequently, and Protestant proselytism was active, particularly through books and periodicals. Print also underlined the discord within the ranks of the Catholic clergy itself. Such was the case for the priests Augustin Chaboillez and François-Xavier Pigeon, who led a pamphlet war against Lartigue,[103] the former questioning the appointment of the bishop to head the district of Montreal, and the latter publicly contesting the dismemberment of his parish.

Given threats from outside and plots from within, Bishop Lartigue reacted. In 1828 he proposed to the archbishop of Quebec, Bernard-Claude Panet, the creation of an ecclesiastical newspaper, since, unlike other denominations, local Catholics lacked one of their own.[104] Panet responded that the time had probably not yet come for such an enterprise and that it would be difficult to find someone to take on the task. Four years later, Lartigue volunteered to manage the projected newspaper himself. Panet rejected the plan, believing that the coadjutor of Montreal, given his lack of moderation, should not assume this responsibility.[105] The project came to nothing, but Lartigue felt that he had at least made an honest attempt.[106] He saw the press simply as a tool, a means whose end seemed to be power. In 1832, when his project was about to founder, he wrote that the bishops, by not supporting his idea, were depriving themselves 'of a weapon that might have given them great power.'[107]

Bishop Lartigue was also concerned about books in general, and although he had no specific plans, he always took an interest in the dissemination of good books. He proposed to distribute through the countryside several hundred copies of *La question des fabriques,* a pamphlet by André-Rémi Hamel published in 1831,[108] and of *Exposition de la foi catholique*, by French bishop Jacques-Bénigne Bossuet.[109] On the other hand, evil books worried him, among them the pirated *Paroles d'un croyant*, by Félicité-Robert de La Mennais: 'printed in Lower Canada by means of a very discreet subscription appeal ... Ludger Duvernay and the Swiss Protestant Amury Girod had carefully worked out the publication of this anti-religious book.'[110] The bishop lamented that Catholics were taking part in the publication of *Paroles* in Montreal in 1836 and saw clearly the danger of not banning the book, which was being distributed secretly.[111]

In all his correspondence between 1828 and 1839, Lartigue hammered away at the need to control printed materials. The attacks by Chaboillez and Pigeon had shown the importance of having a religious press backed up by control of what was available to readers. If the era of innocence had ended, a certain impotence remained, since Lartigue could only draw up projects that never saw the light of day or make private gestures linked to isolated cases. On the other hand, Ignace Bourget, who had long served as Lartigue's secretary and was influenced by his bishop's opinions, laid the foundations of print censorship. The creation of the Diocese of Montreal in 1836, the recruitment of personnel around 1840, the religious revival that marked this period,[112] and the succession of the aged Lartigue by the energetic Bourget, who had learned the lessons of previous disappointments, led after 1840 to the establishment of a system of censorship based on the real power of the ecclesiastical hierarchy, freed henceforth from the power of the state.

PART SEVEN

AUTHORSHIP AND LITERARY CULTURES

chapter 14

AUTHORS AND PUBLISHING

Courting Local and International Markets

GEORGE L. PARKER

Long before printing and publishing appeared in the British North American colonies, settlers wrote about their experiences in the New World.[1] Just as their writings proclaimed their transplanted European values, so their activities revealed their notions of authorship as an elite vocation often associated with patronage from the court. During his brief sojourn at Port-Royal (Annapolis Royal, Nova Scotia) in 1606–7, Marc Lescarbot would withdraw to his room to write and to read the books he had brought from Paris. He dedicated his *Histoire de la Nouvelle France* (Paris, 1609) to the king, Henri IV, and the appended poems, *Les muses de la Nouvelle France*, to the French chancellor, Nicolas Brulart de Sillery, to whom he apologized, 'Although they are unkempt and rustically garbed consider, My Lord, the country from which they come, uncivilized, bristling with forests, and inhabited by wandering peoples.'[2]

A decade later at Bristol's Hope (Harbour Grace) in Newfoundland, Robert Hayman amused himself in the summers by translating John Owen and Rabelais and composing epigrams. When he published them in 1628 as *Quodlibets*, he modestly dedicated his 'few bad unripe Rimes' to Charles I and hoped that they would lead to further literary enterprise in Newfoundland.[3] Like later explorers and missionaries, Hayman and Lescarbot wrote for audiences back home and dedicated their books to persons of influence, in hopes of promoting colonization. This pattern would continue well into the nineteenth century as writers dedicated their works to influential patrons even as they sought to please a newer class of benefactor, their middle-class readers, in the desire to secure payment and contribute to a colonial literature.

Visitors to the colonies and local authors employed genres that were familiar to their audiences in Europe and British North America and that acted as a measure of their own skills, for education and reading fostered an awareness of literary traditions. One temporary resident between 1763 and 1767, Frances Brooke, the wife of the chaplain to the British garrison at Quebec, used the epistolary form for the first novel set in what is now Canada, *The History of Emily Montague* (London, 1769), in which she argued for the anglicization of the Canadiens. To compose his poem *Abram's Plains* (Quebec, 1789), Thomas Cary read 'harmonious' James Thomson, Alexander Pope's *Windsor-Forest*, and Oliver Goldsmith's *The Deserted Village* 'to catch their manner of writing.'[4] The statistical histories of British North America by Thomas Chandler Haliburton and William 'Tiger' Dunlop were modelled on Sir John Sinclair's multi-volume *Statistical History of Scotland* (1791–9). In his *The Charivari: or, Canadian Poetics; a Tale, after the Manner of Beppo* (Montreal, 1824), George Longmore knew his readers would recognize Lord Byron's stanzas in his anecdotes about contemporary Montreal society. Joseph Howe and his friends based their 'Club' sketches in the *Novascotian* (1830–2) on the popular 'Noctes Ambrosianae' in *Blackwood's Edinburgh Magazine*. Michel Bibaud's *Épîtres, satires, chansons, épigrammes et autres pièces de vers* (Montreal, 1830), the first volume of poems by a native of Lower Canada, received a favourable critique from *La Revue encyclopédique de Paris*, which expressed polite astonishment that a colonial could write didactic verses in the manner of Boileau, but criticized Bibaud for not adequately describing the customs of his country. Bibaud sniffed that his verses 'had not been composed with the image of France in view, but rather for that of Canada, and for readers half of whom, perhaps, had never read two lines of verse done in even the didactic manner.'[5] Literary conventions could encourage slavish imitation in mediocre writers, but they could also liberate innovative artists to develop a distinctive North American voice and vision.

These literary traditions helped writers to mediate among their overlapping physical, cultural, and psychic environments as they transmuted their wilderness experiences into realism and metaphor. If some writers idealized the frontier – usually for consumption in the home country – into a more perfect British society than the republic to the south, others bewailed their roles in a wasteland without books and the civilized amenities that they had previously enjoyed. Loyalist Jacob Bailey wrote to the Society for the Propagation of the Gospel, 'The want of books is a misfortune I sensibly feel in my present situation, for I was constrained to leave my library behind when I escaped from New England, and being so remote from the metropolis [Halifax] I can receive no assistance from others.'[6] Bailey kept in touch with intellectual currents abroad through correspondence with family and friends or through excerpts in newspapers. In such ways, authors in the colonies remained citizens of an international community with a thousand-year heritage, and this attachment illuminated lives in which melancholy and disorientation were common.

Too often this environment held challenges unknown to Europeans. Frances Brooke's character Arabella Fermor blamed the weather: 'I no longer wonder the elegant arts are unknown here; the rigour of the climate suspends the very powers of the understanding; what then must become of those of the imagination?'[7] In 1833 the recently arrived Susanna Moodie apologized to her editor that 'this chilly atmosphere, at present, is little favourable to the spirit of Poesy,'[8] but she was soon making notes about her neighbours. Her sister Catharine Parr Traill called her new home in Upper Canada 'a matter-of-fact country'[9] where no ghosts, spirits, fairies, naiads, or Druids haunted the forests and streams she now loved so much. Andrew Shiels, the blacksmith poet of Nova Scotia, complained in his preface to *The Witch of the Westcot* (Halifax, 1831) about 'the apathy for poetry that exists in Nova-Scotia,' and he observed how different were the language and customs of Nova Scotia from 'that poetical country,' the Scottish Borders, with its 'infinite associations of time, place, and circumstance.'[10] Like their colleagues in the United States, these writers found themselves in a society that esteemed the printed word only for its utilitarian value or its spiritual consolation.

This question of visibility was complicated by the fact that much writing remained in manuscript or appeared only in periodicals. For a variety of reasons, writers privately circulated their works orally and/or in manuscript for friends, correspondents, or congregations, beginning with Port-Royal's Order of Good Cheer (1606), whose members were their own composers, performers, and audience. The Old World songs, legends, and folk tales brought to the New World as part of the oral culture of French and British settlers, works usually labelled as 'anonymous,' would not be published until their North American versions were collected by antiquarians in the nineteenth and twentieth centuries. The verses of young Loyalists Jonathan Odell and Joseph Stansbury circulated in New York and Philadelphia coffee houses before their authors' flight to Nova Scotia. The poems of Joseph Quesnel and Adam Hood Burwell appeared in newspapers and magazines but were not collected in their lifetimes. Upper-class Haligonians laughed and raged as they devoured handwritten versions of Judge Alexander Croke's 'The Inquisition,' which satirized their sexual peccadilloes.[11] The young women of Deborah How Cottnam's school circulated their poems among themselves, and in academies and seminaries teenaged boys struggled over their translations of Latin poetry.

With few exceptions, authors shared the same middle- and upper-middle-class backgrounds as their British North American readers, who identified with those writers less by class ties than by language and political and religious affiliation. The list of subscribers for Julia Beckwith Hart's novel *St. Ursula's Convent* (Kingston, 1824), for example, included colonial officials and the local gentry. Many writers were gentlemen or lady dilettantes (or, like Molière's *bourgeois gentilhomme*, had aspirations to gentility), drawn from a privileged class of clergy, lawyers, public servants, teachers, and their wives, daughters, and sisters. They often published anonymously or under such pseudonyms as Portia (Deborah How Cottnam), F (Joseph Quesnel), Agricola (John Young), or Lancelot Longstaff (George Longmore). They wrote 'occasional' poetry to mark the death of a friend or a military victory, or penned the newsboy's New Year's verses for subscribers (see illus. 15.4, p. 373). Roger Viets's *Annapolis-Royal* (Halifax, 1788), like Thomas Cary's *Abram's Plains* and Cornwall Bayley's *Canada: A Descriptive Poem, Written at Quebec, 1805* (Quebec, 1806?), is a public poem that contemplates the colony's potential for agriculture and industry and concludes with apostrophes to British civilization.

Then there were the obstacles of publication and dissemination. Sometimes the quality of printing available was justification for not publishing locally. Jacob Bailey complained in 1780 to John Howe about Anthony Henry's poor printing skills, and Haliburton in 1824 criticized the high cost of printing in Nova Scotia.[12] Authors were expected to cover production costs and to market their own books, as Adam Kidd did for his *The Huron Chief, and Other Poems* (Montreal, 1830), which he hawked around Upper Canada while soliciting subscriptions for another book that was never finished (see illus. 5.5, p. 108, and illus. 14.1, p. 343).[13] What financial help there was from provincial governments was reserved for works that publicized the region or had educational value.[14] Perceiving the economic and cultural prestige of a British imprint, the English-speaking writer looked abroad for recognition (Paris was blocked for French-language writers), partly because he or she faced the same situation as the contemporary American writer, described by William Charvat as 'the struggle, in the immature economy of that time, to discover who or what his audience was.'[15] British North Americans resolved these questions in terms of the British conquest of Quebec, the American Revolution, the French Revolution, the American cultural revolution of the 1820s, and the reinvention of British North America after the 1837 rebellions. Authors in both language groups entered the nineteenth century laden with the baggage of conflicting and interpenetrating allegiances – racial, national, religious, continental – in their quest for literary flora nurtured in the rich North American soil.

This struggle was evident by 1790, when several writers addressed small, cash-

14.1 Edwin Heaton, *Adam Kidd* (1826). Courtesy of the Toronto Public Library (TRL).

starved audiences that shared their memories borne out of revolution, conquest, defeat, and exile. But they could no more live by their pens than could their contemporaries in the United States. Henry Alline published most of his works, while hardly any of Jacob Bailey's, Jonathan Odell's, or Joseph Quesnel's appeared during their lifetimes.

Henry Alline (1748–84) was an itinerant New Light minister whose family emigrated from New England before the revolution. He turned his back on the upheaval by refusing the militia service ordered by Halifax and answering God's call to preach salvation to Nova Scotians, whose neutrality he may have influenced by his own actions. During his gruelling preaching missions throughout the Maritimes, Alline often recorded, as he did on 9 May 1781, 'I ENJOYED some happy hours this day with my pen: when I found in my soul a desire that my writings might after my decease be useful; for although I preached without any notes, neither did I write many sermons, yet I wrote much on almost every essential truth of the gospel.'[16] J.M. Bumsted has called Alline 'a folk composer and troubadour, seeking to communicate his own experience in a way and in language which could be shared with his audience, most of whom were young people.'[17] In December 1780 he visited Halifax 'to commit a small piece of my writings to the press.'[18] This was the tract *Two Mites*, the first of five works printed by Anthony Henry of the *Nova-Scotia Gazette*. One was his *Hymns and Spiritual Songs* (1782?), a much enlarged version of which was the bulky manuscript that Alline was carrying at his death on his way to Boston. He handed it to the Reverend David McClure 'with direction to be particularly careful of a number of hymns, which he had prepared to be published.'[19]

Harvard-educated Jacob Bailey (1731–1808), the Loyalist Church of England missionary at Annapolis Royal, had achieved a reputation during the revolution for satiric verses on the rebels and Nonconformist ministers such as Alline. His voluminous narrative poems and several unfinished novels remained unpublished, but his sermons and shorter verses circulated in manuscript among friends. In London his fellow Loyalist, the Reverend Samuel Peters, praised the sermons and placed several of Bailey's verses in London magazines, describing them as works that 'would have done honour to Young, or Pope, or Milton.' Bailey then sent eight sermons to Thomas Brown of Halifax for forwarding to London. 'You will find them upon singular subjects, chiefly levelled against the principles of rebellion.' Although Peters wrote on 15 February 1792 that 'the cost of printing two hundred and fifty is £12, in the size of Sterne,' and that 'I intend to send you one of them printed at the next opportunity,'[20] there is no evidence they were printed.

The American Revolution redirected the career of Jonathan Odell (1737–1818), the 'most skilled and trenchant of the loyalist satirists,'[21] who was educated at the College of New Jersey (Princeton University). He contributed to the pamphlet warfare of the revolution with essays and verses in the *Gentleman's Magazine*, the *Pennsylvania Chronicle*, and *Rivington's New-York Gazette*, which warned of religious and political anarchy. Rarely has one poem caused such turmoil as his birthday song for King George III on 4 June 1776, which led to his flight from his parish in Burlington, New Jersey, with a price on his head. In New York he served the Loyalist cause as chaplain, superintendent of printing, and secretary to Sir Guy Carleton. Odell's and Joseph Stansbury's verses were set to popular British tunes and heartily sung in the messes and coffee houses of New York and Philadelphia. His satire *The American Times* was printed and sold in 1780 in London by W. Richardson, and printed in New York by James Rivington, the former Halifax bookseller. Odell prefaces his attack on the rebels with an address to his patron, George III, who had yet to pay him attention.[22] His reward came in 1784 with his appointment as provincial secretary of the new province of New Brunswick. After this promising literary career, the New Brunswick one was almost invisible, for Odell devoted his energies to administration. He wrote numerous poems for his family and friends, but his only book was *An Essay on the Elements, Accents, and Prosody of the English Language*, published in London in 1805. Yet Maritime readers during the War of 1812 must have savoured his parody of American general Stephen Van Rensselaer's defeat at Queenston Heights, 'The Agonizing Dilemma,' in the *Royal Gazette* (Saint John, 28 December 1812 – 4 January 1813).

Joseph Quesnel (1746–1809) came from a merchant family at Saint-Malo, France, and in the 1770s he frequented literary salons in Bordeaux. He would later try to establish such salons in Lower Canada. Captured by the British while on a merchant ship bound for the American colonies in 1779, he was taken to Halifax and then to Montreal, where he married and conducted business. A brief stay in revolutionary France in 1788–9 convinced him to return to Quebec. In Montreal and later, after he retired, in Boucherville, he devoted himself to writing poetry and plays. His *Colas et Colinette, ou le Bailli dupé* (Quebec, 1808) was the first dramatic work to be published in British North America. Occasionally, Quesnel complained of the lack of an appreciative audience for his writings. In 'L'épître à M. Labadie,' he echoes Boileau – 'The saddest occupation is the poet's trade' – and in 'Le dépit ridicule, ou le sonnet perdu,' he addresses his wife: 'What is the good of the trouble I take for rhyming / If no one ever has time to listen to my verse?' and considers inviting his friends to supper, locking the door, and forcing them to listen to his latest poem.[23] British traveller John Lambert seemed to confirm this dismal view when he wrote that 'the state of literature, the arts and sciences, in Canada, can scarcely be said to be at a low ebb, because they were never known to flow; and ... it is not likely that they will, in our time at least, rise much above their present level.'[24] Nevertheless, Quesnel was admired by his contemporaries, and in the twentieth century he would be judged as 'without doubt the most outstanding writer of the period, as much for the quantity and quality of his work as for his involvement in artistic and literary life.'[25]

In 1824, Julia Beckwith Hart appealed for the 'encouragement' of the 'native genius' of British North America in the preface to *St. Ursula's Convent*.[26] Her novel was part of a burst of literary and intellectual activity in the decade after Napoleon's defeat that started in newspapers from Halifax to York (Toronto), among them Anthony H. Holland's *Acadian Recorder*, Ludger Duvernay's *La Minerve*, and William Lyon Mackenzie's *Colonial Advocate*. Editors hoped that they would counter the impression, 'far too prevalent abroad, and particularly in the Mother Country, that we were comparatively ignorant and barbarous,' said Halifax lawyer Beamish Murdoch in his preface to the *Acadian Magazine* in 1826.[27] 'Very few books of any sort are printed in the colonies,' Mackenzie commented in his essay 'On Printers & Publishers' in the

Colonial Advocate on 6 April 1826. He admired the aggressive bookselling and reprint industries that were developing in the United States in the 1820s, which supplied colonial booksellers with American papers, along with pirated reprints of British authors and the major British reviews. He believed that the foreign and local circumstances needed to foster literary publishing would include literary societies and reviews to stimulate discussion.

In Halifax, Anthony H. Holland's serialization of Thomas McCulloch's 'letters' of Mephibosheth Stepsure in the *Acadian Recorder* (1821–2) led to their publication in Edinburgh in 1823. Holland himself published works aimed at the improvement of Nova Scotia, among them McCulloch's speech at the opening of the Pictou Academy, *The Nature and Uses of a Liberal Education* (1818). In Saint John, Henry Chubb initiated a rich publishing tradition in his province when in 1825 he issued Peter Fisher's *Sketches of New-Brunswick* and James Hogg's *Poems: Religious, Moral and Sentimental*. Robert Shives printed John K. Laskey's *Alethes; or, The Roman Exile* (1840), a historical romance inspired by Edward Bulwer-Lytton's popular *The Last Days of Pompeii* (1836).

Montreal bookseller and magazine publisher Joseph Nickless brought out George Longmore's poem *The Charivari* (1824), which titillated readers aware of a particularly lively local wedding several years earlier. Rival H.H. Cunningham issued reprints of Byron's *Poems on His Domestic Circumstances* (1816). When he published John Howard Willis's *Scraps and Sketches* (1831) and 'purchased the copyright from the Author,' the *Halifax Monthly Magazine* reported that 'it is the first instance of such a speculation in Lower Canada: may it succeed, "the trade" have long been the best Patrons to Old Country literature.'[28]

Among the many sermons and essays concerning civic questions that appeared in Upper Canada in the 1820s were the earliest volumes of verse: 'a rhyming defence of the jury system'[29] entitled *An Address, to the Liege Men of Every British Colony and Province in the World, by a Friend to His Species* (1822), from Hugh Christopher Thomson's *Upper Canada Herald* office at Kingston, and James Lynne Alexander's *Wonders of the West; or, A Day at the Falls of Niagara, in 1825*, printed by Charles Fothergill at York (Toronto) three years later.[30]

A literary landmark in Upper Canada in this decade was Julia Beckwith Hart's anonymously published *St. Ursula's Convent; or, The Nun of Canada* (1824), the first novel in English by a writer born in the colonies. Written in Cornwallis, Nova Scotia, and Fredericton and then completed in Kingston, where its author taught school and married stationer George Henry Hart, it was published at Thomson's *Upper Canada Herald* office. She dedicated the novel to the Countess of Dalhousie, and thanked her 147 public patrons, the subscribers. The *Canadian Magazine*'s editor, Alexander James

Christie, thought the work 'not entirely destitute of interest to a Canadian reader,' but damned it with faint praise as 'the quintessence of Novels and Romances' suitable for 'blue-stocking ladies and boarding-school misses.'[31]

Critical scorn, rather than lack of encouragement, thwarted New Brunswick native Oliver Goldsmith. He had great hopes for *The Rising Village, a Poem* (London, 1825). Since he had played Tony Lumpkin in his great-uncle and namesake's *She Stoops to Conquer*, 'the Spirit of Poetry fired my breast,'[32] and friends encouraged him to write, among them Bishop John Inglis, who wrote the preface, and his brother Henry Goldsmith, to whom the poem is dedicated. Goldsmith was clearly shaken by the negative reception of *The Rising Village*:

> My unfortunate Baubling was torn to Shreds. My first effort was criticized with
> undue severity, abused, and condemned, and why? Because I did not produce a
> poem like the great Oliver. Alas! ... I had, however, the approbation of the 'judi-
> cious few,' who thought it an interesting Production. It was very fortunate for me
> that it was the occupation of leisure Hours. My living did not depend on my
> poetical talent, lucky fellow, and in this respect I had the advantage of the
> immortal Poet [the elder Goldsmith]. After this essay I abandoned the Muses, and I
> have not had the pleasure of any further intercourse with the lovely ladies.[33]

But he did not give up. While in Saint John, he arranged for a new, revised edition of *The Rising Village*, published in 1834. When he departed the city in May 1844 for a new post in China, he was feted with addresses and testimonials from judicious admirers.

More tragic was the story of Philippe Aubert de Gaspé *fils*, a parliamentary recorder and journalist for the *Quebec Mercury* and *Le Canadien*. With the help of his father, he gathered legends, customs, and historical events into *L'influence d'un livre* (Quebec, 1837), a gothic tale of a search for the philosopher's stone. In this first novel by a native of Lower Canada, de Gaspé asks in the preface for public approbation, but he received very little from the review in *La Gazette de Québec* (10 February 1838), which called the work 'M. de Gaspé's historico-poetic mish-mash.' De Gaspé moved to Halifax to start over as a recorder but died suddenly in early 1841 and was buried in an unmarked grave.

The efforts of four writers to break into international markets signalled the emergence of professional authorship in British North America in the 1830s. Their books still carried the traditional dedication to a socially prominent patron, but the authors also had their eye on the patronage of readers. Major John Richardson, Catharine Parr Traill, Susanna Moodie, and Thomas Chandler Haliburton quickly learned that the small domestic market could not support them as popular writers. Their relations with foreign publishers are instructive: Richardson first published in London and then tried fruitlessly to succeed with domestic imprints. Moodie and Traill emigrated with established reputations and continued to publish in London, confining their publishing in the Canadas to periodicals. Haliburton's first successful Halifax publication was pirated in London, much to his pleasure.

Because imperial and international copyright laws were not geared to the protection of colonial authors, their works were frequently pirated and plagiarized in Britain, the United States, and British North America. Between the 1830s and 1923, British North America was subject to two sets of laws. As British colonies, the provinces were governed by the Literary Copyright Act of 1709, yet this protected works *first* published in Britain. As a result, Oliver Goldsmith decided not to publish the 1825 edition of *The Rising Village* in Nova Scotia 'from a conviction he might interfere with the interests of the copy right,'[34] and Richard Bentley published Haliburton's *The Clockmaker* within six months of its Halifax publication, knowing it would be difficult for Haliburton or his publisher, Joseph Howe, to take him to court. The new imperial Literary Copyright Act of 1842 took precedence in certain situations over provincial and dominion copyright until 31 December 1923. The two provincial copyright laws enacted before 1867 provided no protection outside their borders: Lower Canada's 1832 legislation, repassed by the united Province of Canada in 1841, and Nova Scotia's 1839 act, intended to support the printing industry.[35]

Although the 1709 copyright act gave the author ownership in her or his work, in practice London publishers purchased that right and used it as a monopoly to produce and distribute expensive, small first editions. They insisted on their right to supply colonial markets, even as they watched the Americans undercut them with cheap pirated reprints in British North America, where British editions were slower to arrive and exorbitantly costly. Where commerce and culture merged, Richard Bentley in London and Carey and Lea in Philadelphia would gladly negotiate with a colonial author but not with the colonial publisher; it became customary, when American publishers negotiated with British authors, to exclude other publishers and insist on retaining British North American rights.

The Canadian-born John Richardson (1796–1852), who served with his brother in the War of 1812 and then spent some twenty-five years in Britain, Europe, and the West Indies as a soldier, man about town, and writer, barely survived by his pen in spite of numerous schemes to improve his situation. When he arrived in Montreal in 1838 as a correspondent for the *Times* of London, he had already published several poems and two novels, *Écarté; or, The Salons of Paris* (London, 1829) and *Wacousta; or, The*

Prophecy (London, 1832), a historical romance set in North America during the Pontiac rebellion. The *Times* fired him for endorsing Lord Durham, and Richardson thereafter scrounged for a living in Montreal, Brockville, and Kingston, supporting himself as a newspaper editor. In his 1847 memoir, *Eight Years in Canada*, he echoed Haliburton's statement of 1838 that even the Americans did more to honour their authors. Denying any 'vanity of authorship,'[36] he contrasted the lack of encouragement he had received in the Canadas with the 'American friends'[37] who urged him to publish his sequel to *Wacousta*, *The Canadian Brothers; or, The Prophecy Fulfilled*. He sent the prospectus and letters to many papers in Montreal and Upper Canada[38] and raised about 250 subscriptions, of whom some one-third would back out.[39]

Published by Armour and Ramsay of Montreal in 1840, this edition, Richardson told William Hamilton Merritt, would be the prelude for a London one: 'I shall thereby more readily make my own terms with a London publisher.' But he realized years later he might as well have published it in Kamchatka.[40] In spite of critical acclaim and the *Literary Garland*'s prediction that it would 'establish a literary character for the country,'[41] the novel brought him no money, although its dedication to the lieutenant-governor of New Brunswick, Major General Sir John Harvey, may have helped its irascible and touchy author to enjoy a brief patronage position as manager of the Welland Canal. Subscription publishing helped to reduce what Richardson called the 'great pecuniary responsibility of the undertaking in a country so indisposed to the encouragement of literature as Canada.'[42] Adding insult to injury, he probably received no royalties from the American reprint of *Wacousta*, which was advertised for sale in Montreal in March 1841 to take advantage of the appearance of *The Canadian Brothers*. He spent his final years as a hack writer in New York, where he died, a lonely widower so poor he could not feed his Newfoundland dog.

Almost as disheartening were the circumstances of the Strickland sisters, who arrived in 1832, both recently married to half-pay officers, and ready to carve out homes in the wilderness near Lakefield, Upper Canada. In England they and their sisters had turned to writing as a source of financial support after their father's bankruptcy and death. Catharine Parr Traill (1802–99) published children's stories, and Susanna Moodie (1803–85) contributed poems and stories and produced *Enthusiasm, and Other Poems* (London, 1831) before their departure for the colonies. They were in desperate financial straits through the 1830s and quite unsuited to pioneer life, but they exploited their hardships in best-selling books about genteel upper-middle-class emigrants. Traill sent descriptive letters to her sister Agnes Strickland, who used her own reputation and influence to have Charles Knight issue these as *The Backwoods of Canada* (London, 1836) in his Library of Entertaining Knowledge. It received good reviews, went through several reprints, and was translated into German and French. Apart from the £110 that Traill received for her sale of the copyright (and an additional £15 in 1842), she 'realized that her best seller was not going to rescue her from the woods.'[43]

Moodie was determined to be a professional writer, even as she raised her children and clung to the essentials of civility. Just acquiring ink and paper and posting manuscripts were difficult. Within months of her arrival, however, she sent two poems – 'the first flight of my muse on Canadian shores' – to Dr John Sherren Bartlett, the editor of the New York *Albion*.[44] Eventually the *Palladium* (Toronto) accepted her poetry, and John Lovell and John Gibson invited contributions from her, at £5 a sheet, for their *Literary Garland* (Montreal).[45] She wrote to Sir George Arthur, the lieutenant-governor of Upper Canada, and used her reputation as a writer to persuade him to find a post for her husband. Within the year, they were out of the woods and on their way to Belleville, where John Wedderburn Dunbar Moodie had been appointed sheriff of Victoria District. For the Moodies, patronage was more than a plum; it was the difference between poverty and comfort.

Thomas Chandler Haliburton (1796–1865) won the approbation of international readers but still hoped for old-fashioned patronage to improve his standard of living. It was all part of his plan, as he explained at a dinner in Halifax in his honour in 1839, 'to resort to a more popular style' than history for the marketplace.[46] In 1824 he had considered sending the manuscript of his history of Nova Scotia to London, and he told his friend Peleg Wiswall, 'Whoever is known in this province as the author of any publication must consider that he has voluntarily brought himself to the stake to be baited by the empty barking of some and the stings & bites of others,'[47] a prescient remark from someone who would offend so many of his readers and fight with the two publishers who best served him. Within a decade, Haliburton had joined forces with Joseph Howe, the publisher of the *Novascotian*, to initiate the 'intellectual awakening of Nova Scotia,'[48] in D.C. Harvey's felicitous phrase.

In 1829, Howe published Haliburton's *An Historical and Statistical Account of Nova-Scotia*, which was critically well received but earned few profits. But *The Clockmaker; or, The Sayings and Doings of Samuel Slick, of Slickville* (1836) was immediately successful both at home and abroad, as Ruth Panofsky relates in the study that follows. Thereafter Haliburton aimed his books at an international audience. Of *The Clockmaker*, second series (1838), he wrote to his friend Robert Parker in March 1838, 'I have another volume ready for the press, which is not so local as the other, and I think better suited for English readers,' and he announced his imminent departure for London. 'While abroad [I] will lay up materials for the Clockmaker in England, which, if the work takes, I will write as soon as I return.'[49] His connection with Bentley brought Haliburton fame and money; it also influenced him to turn away from his colonial readers.

In the humorous discussion of authorship in the British colonies that concludes *The Clockmaker*, second series, Haliburton sent out feelers for a patronage plum. His Yankee peddler Sam Slick lists the authors whose literary efforts have been rewarded – the Earl of Mulgrave, appointed governor of Jamaica; Lord John Russell, made leader of the House of Commons; Sir Francis Bond Head, appointed lieutenant-general of Upper Canada; Walter Scott, made a baronet; and Edward Bulwer-Lytton, given diplomatic posts. 'The Yankee made Washington Irvin' a minister plenipo,' Slick adds. 'See if they don't send you out governor of some colony or another; and if they do, gist make me your deputy secretary, – that's a good man, – and we'll write books till we write ourselves up to the very tip-top of the ladder – we will, by gum! Ah, my friend, said [the squire], writing a book is no such great rarity in England as it is in America, I assure you; and colonies would soon be wanting, if every author were to be made a governor.'[50] In *The Letter-Bag of the Great Western* (1840), Haliburton eschews such 'mendacious effusions' and addresses his dedication to Lord Russell, 'as my Mecaenas, not on account of your quick perception of the ridiculous, or your powers of humour, but solely on account of the very extensive patronage at your disposal.' Like Robert Hayman's appeal to the king two hundred years earlier, Haliburton's dedication resulted in no choice government appointment; rather, his recompense was entry into fashionable circles, huge royalties, an honorary doctorate from Oxford, and a character, Sam Slick, who entered the popular imagination.

In London, the centre of the Anglo-American market, a new phenomenon, the seasonal best-seller, was emerging. These books were marketed through reviews, advertisements, magazine serialization, and a guaranteed purchase by the circulating libraries. Famous authors were the stuff of celebrity gossip. The intellectual support for this phenomenon came from the influential British reviews and quarterlies, such as the *Edinburgh Review*, *Blackwood's*, and the *Athenaeum*, which reached British Americans in affordable American reprint editions.

By 1840, as they embarked on the publishing waters of the Victorian era, authors in British colonies shifted their focus from a small group of elitist readers to an emerging mass audience. While conscious of being pioneers in their efforts to inaugurate a new domestic literature, they accepted their roles in the international community. The irony of their struggles for recognition is that most of them would be forgotten or ignored by twentieth-century writers, who supposed they were the first Canadian writers to face such problems.

CASE STUDY
Thomas Chandler Haliburton's *The Clockmaker*
— Ruth Panofsky

The publishing history of Thomas Chandler Haliburton's *The Clockmaker; or, The Sayings and Doings of Samuel Slick, of Slickville*, British North America's first best-selling work of fiction, showcases the vulnerable position of the colonial author and his or her publisher. Between 1837 and 1840 the first, second, and third series of *The Clockmaker* were issued in British North America, Britain, the United States, and France (in English). The sketches featured Sam Slick, a shrewd Yankee clockmaker, whose 'wise saws' and 'soft sawder,' combined with a keen grasp of 'human natur,' ensured his success with an international audience. Incredible as it may seem today, Sam Slick's popularity with nineteenth-century readers rivalled that of Charles Dickens's Sam Weller in *The Posthumous Papers of the Pickwick Club* (1836–7). Haliburton's diverse interests as a writer and thinker were reflected in an oeuvre that included history, political tracts, and fiction. The publishing history of his fiction, however, and of *The Clockmaker* series in particular – characterized by intrigue, piracy, and commercial exploitation – forms a key chapter in the early history of the book in Canada.

On 23 September 1835 the *Novascotian*, the Halifax newspaper owned and published by Joseph Howe, included the first of twenty-one sketches entitled 'Recollections of Nova Scotia.' The sketches ran until 11 February 1836 and were so admired that Howe decided to issue the complete series of thirty-three in book form. Although the title page is dated 1836, the volume in all likelihood appeared in January 1837,[51] under Howe's imprint, as the authorized, first, and only British North American edition of *The Clockmaker*, first series. The author had chosen to remain anonymous.

The Halifax edition was not protected under British or local copyright, however. The British copyright act of 1709, which required the registration of a title at Stationers' Hall prior to publication, did not ensure protection for a colonial imprint, and Nova Scotia would not pass its own copyright act until 1839. As a result, Howe was without legal recourse against Richard Bentley, whose 1837 London edition of *The Clockmaker* was issued within three months of Howe's, after a copy of the book had been brought to Bentley by an acquaintance of Haliburton's. Although Howe sought compensation from Bentley, whose edition of *The Clockmaker* he viewed as a piracy of his own, his efforts to come to an agreement with the British publisher proved futile.[52] Despite a strong desire to foster his province's cultural awareness and his successful promotion of literature and authors in the pages of the *Novascotian*, Howe faced a number of difficulties. As a book publisher, he was in a precarious financial position. He was, moreover, a poor negotiator with foreign publishers. And although well aware of the economy of the province, he overestimated Nova Scotians' interest in books of local concern.[53] The British North American edition of *The Clockmaker* was eclipsed by the British, which soon was widely available in Halifax.

Publication by Bentley held obvious advantages for Haliburton. The British publisher gave the author welcome press in his *Miscellany* and arranged reviews of his work in the *Athenaeum*, *Blackwood's Edinburgh Magazine*, and the *Times*, which encouraged international notice. When he visited London, Haliburton met other well known literary personalities through Bentley. As well, the British editions were far more attractive than those produced in Halifax and later in Philadelphia, Boston, and New York.[54] By 1838, Bentley was bringing out elegant volumes printed on quality paper and attractively and sturdily bound in purple ribbed cloth, which became the firm's signature in Britain. Not surprisingly, Haliburton soon came to regard himself as a British author who wrote primarily for a British audience.

Unfortunately for Joseph Howe, publication of *The Clockmaker* outside Nova Scotia was not restricted to Richard Bentley. In November 1837 the first, unauthorized American edition was published by Carey, Lea, and Blanchard of Philadelphia, and as early as 1838, Benjamin B. Mussey of Boston issued a separate American edition of *The Clockmaker*, first series. Howe was without legal recourse against American publishers, just as he had been with Bentley. In fact, neither Howe nor Haliburton was compensated by Carey, Lea, and Blanchard or Mussey for their unauthorized American editions. The American copyright act of 1790 provided that nothing would prohibit publication within the United States of any book written, printed, or published outside the jurisdiction of the United States by a person who was not an American citizen. Unlike his colonial publisher, however, Haliburton welcomed and later facilitated American publication of his work, as he had done with British publication.

The wholesale exploitation of a colonial work for commercial profit – at the expense primarily of Joseph Howe, who soon would regret his investment in *The Clockmaker* – escalated during the publication of the second and third series in 1838 and 1840 respectively. Although Howe's imprint appeared alongside Bentley's in the first British–British North American edition of the second series, within months he was displaced as co-publisher, his imprint removed from the title page and never to reappear in connection with *The Clockmaker*. When Haliburton would not provide Howe with a manuscript of the third series, the publisher suffered professional humiliation and further financial loss. Unable to compete with British and American publishers who could seize a colonial work as their own, Howe finally resolved to dissociate himself from *The Clockmaker* series altogether.

The appropriation by British and American publishers of *The Clockmaker*, first series, had convinced Haliburton early in his writing career of the need to protect his interest as author. Since copyright legislation was not in place to ensure this protection, he was left to his own devices, and capitalized on the international success of the first series and his reputation as the creator of Sam Slick. By offering his works to British and American publishers, he hoped to retain control over his material, thereby reducing the number of unauthorized editions and securing financial gain from his writing, which was not possible within the British North American market. Like the British and American publishers he courted, however, Haliburton acted with little regard for Joseph Howe, a man whose vision and enterprise were to exceed his grasp as a colonial publisher.

Women and Print Culture

CAROLE GERSON

The participation of women in the print history of colonial Canada can be seen as a pyramid. Its base is composed of thousands of anonymous women whose work as custodians of culture and transmitters of literacy occurred in family kitchens, schoolrooms, and religious organizations, in towns and on the remoter frontiers of settlement in French and British North America. Seldom named as individuals, few ordinary women appear in early records of the creation, contents, and consumption of Canadian print culture. Some exceptions exist: for example, women of Lower

Canada who were involved in legal claims saw their names printed in statements of case; similarly identifiable are those who placed advertisements in newspapers, joined benevolent associations that issued printed reports, or became known in death as subjects of newspaper notices, printed funeral invitations, or the rare elegy.[55] Yet even when a woman's social standing merited a separately published funeral sermon, more may be known about the clergyman who authored the text than about the woman whose demise occasioned it.[56]

In Lower Canada, where the literacy rate was lower for women than for men,[57] fortunate girls attended the convent schools run by the major teaching orders of the Ursulines at Quebec and Trois-Rivières and the Congrégation de Notre-Dame in Montreal. Here they received one or two years of intense instruction, sometimes using texts specifically prepared for local use.[58] The Catholic Church emphasized the duty of mothers to instruct their children, a responsibility that received iconographic emphasis in the recurring image of St Anne, mother of Mary, who was not only particularly popular in Lower Canada but was 'most often seen in her role as the Educatrix of the Virgin with the emphasis placed on reading.'[59] In urban English-speaking areas, educated women established reading schools for children, one of the first in the northern colonies being Elizabeth Render, whose advertisement appeared in the second issue of the *Halifax Gazette* (30 March 1752). From 1790 through 1840, as populations increased, the same pattern of domestic or private teaching soon prevailed in Upper Canada.[60]

Before 1840, women such as Diana Bayley authored some works for children, but few pedagogical texts. *Mrs. Goodman's First Step in History, Dedicated to the Young Ladies of Canada,* published by subscription in Montreal in 1827, reveals one teacher's determination to 'cultivate the mind, improve the temper, and ... excite a *taste*' for history by presenting 'extracts of as much of the History of England, as I think necessary for a young lady to commit to memory.' Her idiosyncratic curriculum adulated General James Wolfe, omitted the American Revolution, and informed students that the distinguishing events of the reign of Elizabeth I were: 'Knives first made in England. The art of making paper, introduced. Telescopes, and the art of weaving stockings, invented. Watches first brought into England from Germany.'[61]

In the daily lives of most women in the British North American colonies, religion equalled or superseded education as a principal locus of print culture, and religious works comprised much of their reading material. The funeral sermon delivered at Halifax in 1778 on the death of Mrs Margaret Green noted, 'Books of meer Amusement (Plays, Romances, Novels &c.) she seldom looked into, esteeming Time too precious to be trifled away in Vanity.'[62] In all the colonies, Protestant women joined

Bible societies, which proliferated in small and large communities from the late 1810s through the 1820s and 1830s. Their promotion of individual access to the Scriptures included local distribution of texts and fundraising for larger missionary efforts abroad, but visible female authorship of religious works relating to British North America seems to have been limited to visitors such as American evangelist Nancy Towle.[63] Unacknowledged Native and Métis women participated in the preparation of religious works in First Nations languages. In Upper Canada one or more daughters of Joseph Brant (Thayendanegea) assisted Henry Aaron Hill (Kenwendeshon) with his Mohawk translations of the Bible published during the 1830s. At Oka (Kanesatake), Charlotte de Rocheblave taught Algonquian dialects to Catholic missionary authors, while further west Métis sisters Angélique and Marguerite Nolin, based in St Boniface, opened the first school for girls in the West and enabled Father George-Antoine Bellecourt to prepare texts in Ojibwa.[64]

The association of women with imaginative literature was confirmed in 1789 by a proposal addressed to Quebec's 'Ladies and Lovers of Elegant Poetry,'[65] soliciting subscriptions for a volume of original verse. The book's failure to appear illustrates the fragility of literary culture in the colonies, although occasional local editions of popular American and European novels (whose readership the world over was largely female) attested to the faith of a few printer-publishers in a growing domestic market.[66] However, most surviving early print materials aimed at women are decidedly pragmatic in nature, including commercial notices concerning such commodities as jewellery, 'The British Lady's Diary and Pocket Almanack,' the services of 'Mrs Ward's Scouring Business,' and cookbooks.[67] Karen Smith (in chapter 7) and Heather Murray (in chapter 8) discuss women's participation in libraries, which varied from limited membership in urban institutions to Mary O'Brien's active efforts in the Upper Canadian bush.

Midway up the print culture pyramid are the women who participated in the business and commerce of books and print as members of their family enterprise, thereby replicating patterns of shared labour common in England and France. The first printer in what is now Canada, John Bushell in Halifax, relied on the assistance of his daughter Elizabeth to produce the *Halifax Gazette* from 1752 until 1761.[68] In some shops, wives worked alongside their husbands, as did Marie Mirabeau, the first spouse of pioneer Montreal printer Fleury Mesplet, and sometimes continued the business upon the death of a mate, as was briefly attempted by his second wife, Marie-Anne Tison.[69] The same path was followed by Elizabeth Gay in Halifax in 1805, Ann Mott in New Brunswick in 1814, Marie-Josephte Desbarats in Quebec in 1828, and Sophia Dalton in Toronto in 1840. These widows' ventures all proved brief: Elizabeth Gay and Ann Mott each lasted barely a year as printers, and Sophia Dalton eight as a publisher.[70]

At the apex of the print culture pyramid reside the women who were publicly visible as authors.[71] Difficult even for men in British North America before 1840, authorship for women was restricted to the few possessing sufficient time, determination, and resources to get their words into print, and was accomplished more easily in English than in French. Women in both cultures wrote copious letters and personal memoirs which sometimes circulated extensively in private family and social circles, but many such manuscripts did not appear in print until decades or even centuries after their original composition, once they acquired the status of historical documents. Examples include the 1698 memoirs of Marguerite Bourgeoys, the letters of Élisabeth Bégon and Rebecca Byles in the eighteenth century, and from the 1830s, the diaries of Lady Durham, Jane Ellice, Frances Simpson, and Mary O'Brien.

Not surprisingly, patterns of authorship for women in the British colonies reflect the different cultural histories of the two dominant language groups. Pseudonyms were more common in Lower Canada, as Bernard Andrès explains in chapter 15. Women's writing about the colonies that would become Canada was printed in French a century before anything substantial appeared in English and was usually affiliated with the Catholic Church. Marie de l'Incarnation, who published extensively in her native France, was followed by several nuns who documented the early history of their congregations. Marie Morin, the first writer born in New France, recorded the annals of the Hôtel-Dieu of Montreal, while Marie-Andrée Regnard Duplessis and Jeanne-Françoise Juchereau de La Ferté collaborated on *Les annales de l'Hôtel-Dieu de Québec, 1636–1716*. The dominance of religious paradigms affected even the work of Parisian dramatist Madame de Gomez, whose *Histoire de Jean de Calais* was republished anonymously at Quebec in 1810 with illustrations and editorial material designed to instruct young Canadiens in wisdom and virtue.

The most prominent English-speaking women authors had established careers in Britain before arriving as visitors or immigrants, and they quickly exploited the material offered by the New World. Frances Brooke was well known in London before she penned the first novel set in what is now Canada, the four-volume *History of Emily Montague* (London, 1769), after spending several years in British North America during her husband's tenure as chaplain to the British garrison at Quebec (see illus. 14.2, p. 358). Likewise, intellectual Anna Jameson's visit during her husband's posting in Upper Canada resulted in her travel account *Winter Studies and Summer Rambles* (London, 1838). The careers of Catharine Parr Traill and her sister Susanna Moodie, who were also established authors before they immigrated to Upper Canada in the

14.2 Catherine Read, *Frances Brooke* (1771). Courtesy of the National Archives of Canada, C-117373. Source: Mr Sidney Gold, England.

1830s as the wives of British half-pay officers, receive further attention from George L. Parker in this chapter and Michael Peterman in chapter 15. One young woman inspired into authorship by her father's administrative position in British North America was Henrietta Prescott, whose first book, the lively *Poems: Written in New-foundland* (London, 1839), appeared during her father's term as governor of the colony. Harrowing Atlantic voyages and shipwrecks incited two other women to publish narratives that now belong to Canada's print heritage: Lady Louisa Aylmer's *Narrative of the Passage of the Pique across the Atlantic* (London, 1837) and *Narrative of the Shipwreck and Sufferings of Miss Ann Saunders* (Providence, 1827). So appealing was colonial material that several minor English writers used second-hand sources seemingly without ever crossing the Atlantic, producing children's books such as Priscilla Wakefield's *Excursions in North America* (London, 1806) and Mary Martha Sherwood's *The Indian Chief* (London, 1830).

Before 1840, as discussed by Gwendolyn Davies and Michael Peterman in chapter 15, local publication was far more likely to occur in newspapers and journals than in book form. Books were expensive to produce and often funded by subscription, as was Margaret Blennerhassett's *The Widow of the Rock and Other Poems* (Montreal, 1824), one of the first woman-authored books of poetry to appear in the Canadas. It is likely that women, who generally possessed fewer resources than men, experienced greater difficulty in financing the printing of their work.

The elevated cultural status of both books and poetry enhanced their value as fundraisers for women in distress. In 1833 'Widow Fleck' issued a slim pamphlet of verse in Montreal, pleading to her purchasers to support a widowed mother left destitute by her husband's death from cholera. Seven years later, M. Ethelind Sawtell published *The Mourner's Tribute* (Montreal, 1840), a more robust volume with a similar appeal. In an earlier (1790) instance of this practice, the poet was the deceased husband.[72]

Apart from the print culture pyramid stands the lonely figure of Maria Monk. In view of the many women who struggled for notice as literary authors, it is ironic that the best-known female figure in the book history of pre-Confederation Canada was essentially a hoax and a victim of national, religious, and gender-based prejudices. Born in 1816 in Dorchester (Saint-Jean-sur-Richelieu), Monk first came to public attention on 14 October 1835 in a New York penny paper, the *Protestant Vindicator*, claiming to have been impregnated by a priest while attending the Hôtel-Dieu nunnery in Montreal. Several months later, the *Awful Disclosures of Maria Monk* (New York, 1836) became an instant and enduring best-seller. A sequel, *Further Disclosures*, quickly followed, and by 1860 some 300,000 copies of Monk's misadventures were in circulation in various editions. Through 1836 and 1837, refutations and affirmations of Monk's reliability churned from presses on both sides of the Atlantic, including affidavits denying the validity of her story from her mother and from the matron of the Montreal Magdalen Asylum, a refuge for wayward women where Monk had briefly resided.

Current scholarship[73] attributes principal authorship of Maria Monk's horrific tales to two unscrupulous American Protestant ministers, who exploited a vulnerable, unstable woman in order to fuel their anti-Catholic nativism. Quickly abandoned by her sponsors, Monk turned to prostitution in New York, where she is believed to have died in prison in 1849. Unlike many fraudulent texts, the narratives of Maria Monk refuse to subside into the recesses of history, and they received renewed attention when her daughter's autobiography was published in 1874. At the beginning of the twenty-first century, the new medium of electronic dissemination has stimulated a fresh phase of controversy by making Monk's texts available through Early Canadiana Online.[74]

Canada takes pride in the prominence of its women authors, noting that the first locally born author was a woman (Marie Morin), the first novel set in what is now Canada was written by a woman (Frances Brooke), and the first native-born author of a novel was likewise female (Julia Beckwith Hart). Yet other data belie the notion that the country's print culture has favoured women. In the *Montreal Museum, or Journal of Literature and the Arts* (1832–4), 'the first periodical in British North America specifically intended for female readers by a female editor,' women represent just three of the eighteen writers in English, and one of the twenty-seven writers in French.[75] Numeric tabulations quickly reveal that women cast a sliver-thin shadow on the pre-Confederation literary field, where they attained some visibility as authors and translators of fiction, poetry, memoirs, and traveller's tales, but remained absent from the weighty genres of history, sermons, science, law, and other forms of serious writing.

chapter 15

LITERARY CULTURES

Books and Reading in Newfoundland and in Labrador

WILLIAM BARKER

From the sixteenth century onwards, the wealth of the Newfoundland fishery was known to many European countries, but England and France made the most successful claims to the island and to the Labrador coastline. By the late eighteenth century, when the British had become the acknowledged colonizers of the island, a resident population (as opposed to those who summered) had become firmly established in many small communities, mainly in the southeastern part of the island. Most people were employed in the fishery, where the physical labour was great and the economic rewards minimal; others served in the military or were part of the apparatus of the merchant class, who owned the businesses upon which the communities depended. This population grew fitfully, and by the 1820s it numbered about 70,000, with some 12,000 inhabitants in St John's. A colonial government recreated many of the institutions of the home country. Schools, churches (of various competing denominations), and newspapers, with an increasing popular involvement in the rough-and-tumble of social and religious issues, and the growth of a small middle class all contributed to and were at the same time evidence of a reading culture, though not yet a literary one. Much intellectual energy was expended in political quarrels as the colony struggled toward a legislature, finally established in 1832.[1]

The development of a book culture was slow and piecemeal; it arrived, in a sense, book by book as visitors brought their reading to the island. Colonizer Robert Hayman says that he composed his book of epigrams, *Quodlibets, Lately Come Over from New Britaniola, Old Newfound-land* (London, 1628), during a fifteen-month stay in Bristol's Hope (Harbour Grace) in 1618 (see illus. 15.1, p. 363). It is unlikely such an individual would have gone on a long voyage without taking with him a small collection of books. Such reading, by the literate traveller, remained typical for many years. In the logbook of HMS *Pegasus* for the year 1786 is a watercolour by J.S. Meres that depicts the harbour of Placentia, in the foreground a boat manned by four oarsmen and in the distance two sea-going vessels (see illus. 15.2, p. 364).[2] On the hillside, overlooking the well-treed islands of this harbour, are seated two figures. One is sketching the scene, and the other reading. The book is an octavo or small quarto, and the reader holds it close to his face, clearly concentrating on the text. There must have been many other visitors who brought books (evidenced later on by auctions reported in newspapers). One certainly came with a copy of John Locke's *Second Treatise* in the edition of 1713, because a quotation from that work serves as preamble to a document establishing a community for mutual protection in St John's in 1723.[3] A group of fifty-one merchants and prominent property holders had joined together out of mutual interest to create a court of law, which sat in judgment on some fifteen cases.

Most of those who came were not, however, readers of Locke. They were poor, working-class, and probably illiterate or barely literate (the vexed term 'literate' being defined here as 'able to read books').[4] Laurence Coughlan, who preached in Carbonear and Harbour Grace from 1766 to 1773, wrote in his memoir *An Account of the Work of God* that he had 'known a Man, who could not read a Letter in a Book, go into the Wood, and cut down Timber, bring the same with the Help of a Servant, and build a Boat, rig it, and afterwards go out to Sea with the same Boat.'[5]

A culture of the book began slowly to evolve. Education and religion, not to be separated, were the prime motivators. Coughlan was just one of the ministers sent out by the Society for the Propagation of the Gospel. In his account of his few years in Newfoundland, it is clear that he encouraged readers of the Scriptures. John and Jane Noseworthy, for instance, fell under his spell, and John says, 'When I first heard you preach, I went and searched the Scriptures, to find if these Things were so; and I found, that your Preaching and the Word of God agreed.' But this testimony had to be written down by someone else, because apparently John Noseworthy did not write.[6] Coughlan's book was published in London several years after his controversial departure from Newfoundland. At the end is included a letter from a former parishioner, a woman with the initials D.O. She writes: 'Dear Sir, remember my kind Love to all my Brethren unknown; tell them, that I am poor, and beg them to send

QVODLIBETS,

LATELY COME OVER
FROM NEW 'BRITANIOLA,
OLD NEWFOVND-LAND.

Epigrams and other fmall parcels, both
Morall and Diuine.

The firft foure Bookes being the Authors owne: the
reft tranflated out of that Excellent Epigrammatift,
M^r· *Iohn Owen,* and other rare Authors:

With two Epiftles of that excellently wittie Doctor,
Francis Rablais : Tranflated out of his French at large.

All of them
Compofed and done at *Harbor-Grace* in
Britaniola, anciently called *Newfound-Land.*

By *R. H.*

Sometimes Gouernour of the Plantation there.

LONDON,
Printed by *Elizabeth All-de,* for *Roger
Michell,* dwelling in *Pauls* Church-yard,
at the figne of the Bulls-head. 1628.

15.1 Robert Hayman, *Quodlibets* (London, 1628). Courtesy of the Centre for Newfoundland Studies, Memorial University, St John's.

15.2 James S. Meres, *The Seven Islands in the Harbour of Placentia, Newfoundland*, from the logbook of HMS *Pegasus* (1786). Courtesy of the National Archives of Canada, C-002522.

me over one Book for my daily Use ... I am ashamed, that I have Nothing more to send, but please to accept of my little Fish and Berries, which I am sure you will ... Sir, I thank you for the good Books you sent us.'[7] Coughlan's memoir was to be 'Sold at Cumberland-Street Chapel,' his new parish, and the cynic wonders if this pathetic request for books had not been especially written for the London readers and Coughlan's own fundraising, rather than to reflect the needs of D.O. and others in Harbour Grace or Carbonear.

Reading, so important to the Protestant faith, was brought to the Labrador coast by the Moravians at a slightly later date. In his *Account of the Manner in Which the ... United Brethren Preach the Gospel*, August Gottlieb Spangenberg notes, 'The brethren likewise take pains to make the heathen acquainted with the holy scriptures,' following the old tradition of the church that 'an ignorant heathen be first taught to read, and afterwards instructed in all the points of Christian doctrine.'[8] They introduced the congregation to passages in the Scriptures in the oral homilies, and in that way drew them into the literate culture.[9] The Moravians also taught reading to children and even to adults, but always with one aim in mind – 'that they may learn to read the holy scriptures.'[10]

Most reading, especially in the smaller communities, was oriented to religious practice. The few schools were founded through local charity or by religious groups.[11] There were also private academies in the larger towns, but no overall state- or even church-supported system of education. It was only with the rise of St John's and the towns of Conception Bay that a reading public began to evolve.

As Patricia Lockhart Fleming has described in chapter 4, the first printing in St John's was carried out by John Ryan in 1807. By the early 1800s the city was established as the capital of the colony, and Ryan, who had been king's printer in New Brunswick, was given the position in Newfoundland.[12] The first issue of the *Royal Gazette* appeared on 27 August. Other papers followed in St John's, and by 1830 there were also newspapers in Harbour Grace and Carbonear.[13] All held strong political and religious positions in the continuous conflict between the English Protestant establishment and the Irish Catholic immigrants.

Where there are newspapers, there is also an interest in books and other printed material. The newspapers were often a source of literary reading, as those in the early nineteenth century increasingly featured excerpts from works of poetry or fiction. They also provide details about the distribution and sale of books. In issues of the *Star and Conception Bay Journal* from 1834 appear advertisements of school books for sale by D.E. Gilmour, including 'Murray's Grammar, Guy's Orthographical Exercises, Entick's Dictionary, Carpenter's Spelling.' In another advertisement are listed more advanced texts: 'History of Greece, History of Rome, Chemistry, Latin Grammar, Navigation, The Charter House Latin Grammar, School Prize Books (handsomely bound), Sturm's Reflections of the Works of God.' All these were for sale at the newspaper office. In an advertisement nearby, we read that the Carbonear Academy, run by Mr Gilmour, will soon open, and just below, 'Mrs. Gilmour begs to intimate to her friends and the public that her Seminary for YOUNG LADIES, will re-open, after the *Christmas Recess*, on Monday, January 13, 1834.' Clearly, the Gilmours were at once booksellers, stationers, and schoolteachers. The books they offered for sale do not seem to have gone beyond those school essentials.

Of great interest is a public announcement in the same newspaper dated 1 January 1834: 'The Gentlemen who have subscribed to the establishment of a PUBLIC READING ROOM, in Carbonear, are requested to attend at the House of Mr. GAMBLE, on SATURDAY Evening next, at 7 o'Clock.' The reading room was enough of a going concern by 10 March that another announcement requests the return of the first volume of the *Scottish Chiefs* to the Carbonear Book Society, 'to which Society the

BOOK belongs.' This early library is the association that naturalist Philip Henry Gosse mentions in his journal.[14] Gosse, who came from Poole, in the west of England, lived in Carbonear from 1827 to 1835 as a clerk to a fish merchant. In May 1832 he purchased at auction a copy of George Adams's *Essays on the Microscope* (London, 1787) and his reading of this work began a life-long interest in entomology.[15] But his interests and intellectual life were not solitary. There was much lending and discussion of books in leisure hours. Gosse's memoir provides a close view of the kinds of private transactions and discussions about books that were also well underway in the larger centre of St John's. The lending of private copies was basic to this culture; a poignant advertisement appeared in the *Royal Gazette* on 19 April 1810: 'It is respectfully requested that all Persons having Books belonging to the late Rev. Mr. Harries, will return them as soon as possible.'

A lively interest in a more public exchange of books and reading also obtained. As early as 1810, a reference to a St John's Subscription Library appeared in the *Royal Gazette*, but by March 1813 this library of 'Upwards of 400 volumes of well selected Books, comprising many of the works of the most celebrated British authors' was to go on sale.[16] Any former subscriber still holding books was requested to return them prior to the sale. The St John's Library Society had been founded by 1820; seven years later, a committee was able to report that 'there are actually in the Library 647 volumes, many of which are of considerable value, and are in excellent order. They however greatly regret to state, that some of the books … are in a very mutilated and defective condition.' In part, the problem was the great decline in membership; the society began with sixty-seven annual subscribers, but by 1827 the number had fallen to fifteen.[17] Occasionally we get a glimpse of what was actually being read:

> The Shareholders in the St John's Library are informed that the following BOOKS have been received, and are now ready for issuing: –
>
> Scott's Life of Buonaparte, Paul Jones, The Trial of Margaret Lindsay, Memoirs of Edmund Burke, Snodgrass's Burmese War, Campaigns in America, A Ramble in Germany, The Tor Hill, Tales of the O'Hara Family, Tales and Sketches, The Eventful Life of a Soldier, Scenes and Sketches of a Soldier's Life, Young Rifleman's Comrade, Franklin's Narrative of a Journey to the Shores of the Polar Sea, Parry's Third Voyage, Duncan's Travels, Blackwood's Magazine, Philosophical Journal, Edinburgh Review, Quarterly ditto, New Monthly Magazine.[18]

The society would later become the St John's Reading Room and Library and absorb the local Mechanics' Institute. These organizations helped to lay the basis for the largest of the reading societies, the Athenaeum, founded in 1861.[19]

Despite some promising activity, the culture centred around books was always tenuous, and they often changed hands because of the shifting circumstances of their owners. Typical are the many advertisements in the newspapers for book auctions. Generally these indicate that the owner was in the military, and the contents often suggest a conventional taste. Thus, we read of 'A quantity of BOOKS, consisting of Montefiore's Notarial Forms and Precedents, Bigland's Modern Europe, Narrative of a Voyage to the Spanish Main ... Rousseau's Letters ... Homer's Iliad and Odyssey, Beauties of Shakespeare ... Moore's Navigation, Spenser's Works, ... Pilgrim's Progress, and an assortment of Other Books ... Also, 1 Cuckoo Clock, 1 Four-Post Bedstead and Hangings (quite new) ... "all to be sold by James Clift," Auctioneer, *Who has for Sale*, Prime Corned Beef, Pork, Tea, Oranges, Pitch, Tar.'[20] Notices of such sales were a fairly frequent occurrence in Newfoundland papers. Stationers and schoolmasters and religious organizations also sold school texts, but not until the 1850s would advertisements from booksellers appear.

Book publication was very slow to get started in Newfoundland. The earliest books were produced by the newspaper printers, and most were small pamphlets. An example is the memoir of the first Congregational minister in Newfoundland, John Jones, written by a successor, Edmund Violet, in 1810, which contains a brief account of the island.[21] Though literary publishing would not really begin until George Webber's *The Last of the Aborigines: A Poem Founded in Facts* appeared in 1851, John Ryan printed sermons by Methodist George Cubit and Congregationalist James Sabine in 1818.[22] An attempt at ongoing publication was a 'Newfoundland almanack,' to be produced at the press of Henry David Winton and first advertised in 1827. It contained, 'besides the ordinary astronomical calculations, with the Fasts and Festivals ... a comprehensive Return of the Fishery and Inhabitants of the Island ... Boats and Men engaged in the Fishery,' with statistics on oil, furs, winter and summer inhabitants, births, marriages, deaths, clergy of all kinds, schools, and charitable institutions. Winton wondered if the project 'would meet with that degree of public approbation and encouragement which will warrant the present publisher in annually presenting a NEWFOUNDLAND ALMANACK, and in sparing no expense to embellish it.'[23]

From the surviving records there emerges a fairly clear picture of book culture in early colonial Newfoundland. Books were imported from abroad, and once they arrived in the island, they were circulated, often through private lending as well as through modest public collections, in what was probably a relatively small community of readers, who were also high consumers of newspapers. Given the lively debates leading up to responsible government in 1832, it is clear there were many well-informed and highly opinionated individuals in the colony, often with professional or religious training, and these would certainly have formed part of a growing community of readers.

Literary Cultures in the Maritime Provinces

GWENDOLYN DAVIES

Whether the wretched of London ever heard the 'Ballad of Nova Scotia' sung in taverns is in the realm of conjecture; but certainly, middle-class investors who read the *Gentleman's Magazine* in their coffee houses in February 1750 must have been imaginatively engaged by the clarion call: 'Let's away to *New Scotland*, where Plenty sits queen / O'er as happy a country as ever was seen.'[24] Primarily a promotional poem in the tradition of what David S. Shields has called the literature of empire,[25] the ballad nonetheless catches the intersection of Everyman's yearning for human dignity with the economy of promise. In the newly founded Halifax, the poem argues, there will be no taxes to burden, no landlords to tease, 'No lawyers to bully, nor stewards to seize.' Rather, with wood, water, forest, and stream providing plenty, 'each honest fellow's a landlord, and dares / To spend on himself the whole fruit of his cares.'

The reality for newcomers, as Alexander Grant wrote to Ezra Stiles in May 1760, was that it was the business of one-half of Halifax to sell rum and of the other half to drink it.[26] It was an image that the Board of Trade and Plantations tried to turn to its advantage in the town's early years as it gilded the pages of the *Gentleman's Magazine* with letters, articles, and illustrations encouraging colonization. Selling rum by the quart got him money 'very fast,' noted Yorkshire blacksmith G. Hick in January 1750, as he publicly invited his wife to join him for 'an easy life.'[27] Moses Harris's orderly maps of the city, embellished with benign butterflies and a conjectural porcupine, suggested that Hick and the 'Ballad of Nova Scotia' were indeed right that this was 'as happy a country as ever was seen.'[28]

It was not, however, an environment in which to foster the arts, although the founding of the *Halifax Gazette* by Bostonian John Bushell[29] on 23 March 1752 provided an outlet for regional versifiers, theatre announcements, and book advertise-

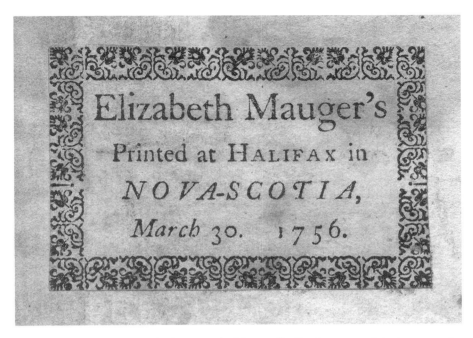

15.3 Printed bookplate of Elizabeth Mauger (Halifax, 1756); affixed to a copy of the *Spectator*, vol. 5 (London, 1739). Courtesy of the National Library of Canada.

ments. The first newspaper in what is now Canada, the *Gazette* was the forerunner of a significant series of eighteenth- and early nineteenth-century Maritime newspapers that gave literary impetus to emerging local writers. It was the *Halifax Gazette* and its successor, the *Nova-Scotia Gazette*, that enabled writers such as the anonymous author of 'On the Much Lamented Death of Mrs. Cook' (1755) to ground the conventions of funereal verse in local allusion as a way of celebrating the recently deceased 'ornament of fam'd *Chebucta's* Shore.'[30] The newspapers also alerted citizens to visiting theatrical groups such as the American Company of Comedians, who in September 1768 performed *Jane Shore*, *The Revenge*, and other dramas.[31] Most importantly for those with literary tastes, the papers in early Maritime communities excerpted passages from prominent publications, reprinted poetry from abroad, and advertised the arrival of new books. Thus readers of the *Nova-Scotia Gazette* between 1768 and 1772 could variously enjoy the dialogue of 'A Traveller' from the *Pennsylvania Chronicle*, excerpts of James Fordyce's 'Sermons to Young Women,' or Horace Walpole's poetic 'The Entail: A Fable.'[32] Advertisements for printer, stationer, and bookseller Robert Fletcher ranged from the edifying (medicinal, religious, legal, and educational) to the entertaining (Yorick's Sentimental Journey, in two volumes).[33] Fletcher's typical advertisement in 1767 announcing 'a fresh Parcel of Books lately publish'd' included Tobias Smollett's *Travels*, *The New Bath Guide* (with cuts), four plays, and six works in French.[34] With the conclusion of the Revolutionary War, Loyalist printers such as Margaret Draper, John Howe, Christopher Sower, the Motts, and the Ryans removed to the Maritimes to establish printing, bookselling, and newspaper businesses that hastened the rise of literacy and a literary culture in the region.

Life in Halifax and other Maritime outposts between 1749 and 1783 seemed largely taken up, however, with the demands of daily living. Visiting Halifax eight years after its founding, Simon Fraser of Lovat could not help but remark on the disagreeable prospect of the new settlement, noting, 'There is little more than a mile even along the shore cleard and above half a mile in breadth into the Country, the rest is impenetrable wood, the worst kind even of American, the closest, the fulest of rough underwood & swamps or morasses.'[35] But for charismatic evangelist and poet Henry Alline, moral, not physical, crudity was Halifax's most abhorrent aspect. Part of the influx of nine thousand Planter New Englanders who, after 1759, had immigrated into the areas of Nova Scotia and present-day New Brunswick left vacant by the deportation of the Acadians in 1755, he had received a rudimentary classical education in Newport, Rhode Island,[36] before moving with his family to Falmouth, outside Windsor, at the age of twelve.

Arguably Maritime Canada's first major poet, Alline turned to oral as well as printed delivery[37] in bringing his approximately five hundred spiritual 'songs' to those whom he proselytized as a revivalist New Light preacher. In so doing, he followed a pattern identified by David Hall as prevalent among semi-literate folk in seventeenth-century England and Wales, for whom 'verse had the mnemonic advantages of rhythm and rhyme.'[38] Where Alline differed from his evangelical precursors in Britain and New England was in the individualistic nature of his free-will doctrine of love and redemption, unconventionally grounded in Calvinist tradition 'but heavily influenced by the Christian Platonism of William Law and the metaphysical speculations of John Fletcher.'[39] Typical of his poems is 'Sion Comforted, or Religion Reviving,' which promises not Calvinistic terror and retribution for sinners but 'love' that 'redeem'd us from our wo!'[40] Although relatively unschooled in formal literary conventions, Alline had an unerring instinct for the power of alliterative lines, caesura, biblical resonance, and inserted vernacular. Like other hymns, 'Sion Comforted' ends with an affirmation of faith every bit as powerful as that outlined in his *Life and Journal*, a memoir begun a year after his conversion and published in Boston in 1806, twenty-two years after his death.

In many respects, Alline's journal, copied and exchanged among his followers in Nova Scotia and New England before its publication,[41] was typical of a sub-genre of 'spiritual journey' literature that circulated in Maritime Canada in the late eighteenth and early nineteenth centuries. An important influence was Jonathan Edwards's *Narrative of Surprising Conversions* (1737), which had articulated the stages through which religious revivalists would pass on their road to grace.[42] The spiritual memoirs of Alline, Jonathan Scott of Chebogue, Nova Scotia, and Mary Coy Bradley of Gagetown, New Brunswick, anticipated reader expectation by drawing upon these stock conventions, only incidentally enlivening them with Satan's titillating sexual temptations (Alline)[43] or burning 'flames of fire and brimstone' (Bradley).[44] However, beneath the conventions of Bradley's journal, readers can see into her childhood reaction to Alline's proselytizing, her economic contribution to domestic life,[45] her bitterness at gender bias against her preaching, and her resentment that marriage bound her by law 'to yield obedience to the requirements of my husband.'[46] There are tantalizing hints in her life-writing of a female resistance to conventionality not often associated with eighteenth-century Maritime women. Thus 'spiritual journey' books such as those by Bradley and Alline not only offer an important insight into eighteenth- and nineteenth-century literary taste in the Maritimes but also 'embody codes' of domestic and community patterns.[47]

However, for Anglican Loyalist refugees such as the Reverend Jacob Bailey of Annapolis Royal, who brought American and British literary tastes into late-eighteenth-century Nova Scotia, Alline and his charismatic followers were yet another manifestation of the chaos engendered by the American Revolution. In his 'Verse against the New Lights,' Bailey employed Hudibrastic poetic conventions to demean evangelical Nonconformism, conjuring up images of an incoherent Allinite pulpit-thumper who 'groans, and scolds and roars aloud / till dread and frenzy fire the crowd.'[48] Sustaining a satiric pen long after his fellow Loyalist writers had turned to more domestic genres and subject matter, Bailey nurtured his vitriol against revolutionary social disorder and evangelicalism in such major poems as 'The Character of a Trimmer' and 'The Adventures of Jack Ramble, the Methodist Preacher' (begun in 1784 and surviving in incomplete manuscript form in thirty-one books).

Bailey's literary career provides an insight into the situation of many of his fellow poets and prose writers. A paucity of publishing outlets in Nova Scotia militated against his poetry having a wide circulation. Nonetheless, his surviving correspondence demonstrates the way in which he, and Maritime writers like him, reached a readership and sustained a literary dialogue with associates. Typically, Bailey's 1779 poem 'Farewell to the Kennebec' was not only read by his friend John Hicks in New

York but was also circulated in recopied form to Mr Donnett at Fareham and Mr Lyde and the Reverend Samuel Peters in London.[49] Although Peters's letter to Bailey on 8 February 1780 recommended minor revisions in the wording and metre of the poem, he nonetheless recited Bailey's 'Farewell to the Kennebec' in a London coffee house, where the last verse 'drew sighs & Tears from many Simpathizing Persons.'[50] The surviving evidence from Bailey's correspondence thus makes it clear that, in spite of the absence of an organized infrastructure, his readers extended from Boston and London to St Andrews, New Brunswick, and Halifax. Moreover, public and private readings of literary texts increased both the reputation of the writer and the dissemination of the work. In sending a satire on fellow Loyalist poet Jonathan Odell to a friend in St Andrews in 1785, Bailey made it clear that the poem had already been read aloud in Annapolis Royal ('to amuse the Ladies') and was, by implication, to be read aloud in its new locale.

The range of Bailey's personal correspondence was augmented by the occasional appearance of his work in newspaper and pamphlet form in London, Boston, and Halifax[51] and by the circulation of his sermons in both London and Nova Scotia.[52] Although books were available in Halifax through merchants John Fletcher and Richard Kidston,[53] it is clear that Bailey, like Thomas McCulloch of Pictou forty years later, relied on the generosity of friends in Britain or the United States to fulfill his literary needs. In 1785 Samuel Peters arranged for John Predden of London to send a parcel of books directly to Bailey through a Halifax agent. The surviving correspondence and texts of Loyalist writers such as Bailey, Jonathan Odell, Deborah How Cottnam, Mather Byles, and Roger Viets provide an insight into how letters travelled; how poems, sermons, and natural histories were copied, exchanged, and read aloud; how British writers of the day such as Laurence Sterne, Frances Brooke, and Tobias Smollett were disseminated and discussed; and how committed writers such as Bailey began to lay the foundation of a literary culture in the Maritime provinces.

Although economics, geography, and personal conflicts always militated against the emergence of a Loyalist school of writing, the example of tory poets such as Bailey, Odell, and Cottnam created a regional literary and cultural consciousness that found expression in such descendants as Joseph Howe, Grizelda Tonge, and Thomas Chandler Haliburton. Moreover, Halifax's *Acadian Magazine* (1826–8) and *British North American Magazine* (1831–?) typically looked back to the Loyalist *Nova-Scotia Magazine and Comprehensive Review of Literature, Politics, and News* (1789–92) as both model and inspiration.[54] And in the values inculcated in Anglican-run schools and in universities such as King's College, Windsor, and King's College, Fredericton (University of New Brunswick), there emerged from the Loyalist experience a philosophy of evolu-

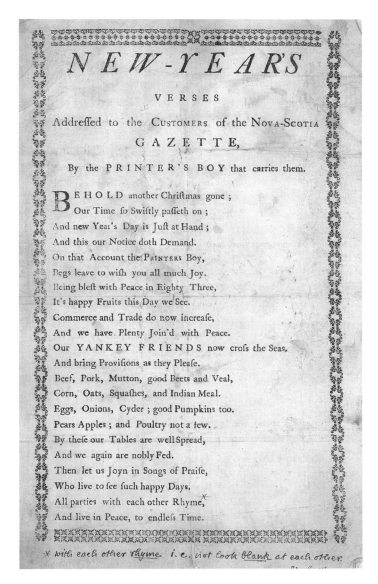

15.4 *New-Year's Verses* (Halifax, 1784). A greeting from the newspaper boy to his customers at New Year's, the carrier's address, or *étrennes*, was offered at Quebec as early as 1767, when verses were published in English and French, the latter as a song. More than seventy examples in the form of single sheets dated before 1840 have been preserved, and many others can be found printed in the newspapers of British North America. Often elaborately framed to demonstrate the printer's skill and stock of ornaments, the verses are usually topical and optimistic, frequently celebrating the role of the press in public life. Courtesy of the Nova Scotia Archives and Records Management.

tionary, rather than revolutionary, social process. Critics such as Ray Palmer Baker have argued that creativity was thwarted by the Loyalists' displacement as exiles,[55] but there nonetheless remains in the triumphant vision of social reconstruction articulated at the conclusion of Roger Viets's topographical poem *Annapolis-Royal* (Halifax, 1788) a glimpse of the resilience that led printers and booksellers, writers and readers, to turn to print culture as a way of expressing who they were in their new home in British North America. Viets's symbols of social synthesis ('gardens,' 'decent mansions,' 'spire majestic,' 'one bright centre') illustrate David Hall's observations on the importance of book history in revealing to present-day readers 'the way in which a social order' (such as that established by the Loyalists in British North America) 'can maintain itself or be subverted.'[56]

Saint John serves as a case in point. Among the early arrivals at Parrtown (as the city was initially called) were the printers William Lewis and John Ryan. At the time they began their first newspaper, the *Royal St. John's Gazette and Nova Scotia Intelligencer*, on 18 December 1783, Saint John was little more than an uphill path through the woods. The newspaper, 33 by 20.3 centimetres, was a three-column weekly which, as early as 9 September the following year, was advertising a proposal for printing by subscription one thousand copies of a book entitled 'An Accurate History of the Settlement of His Majesty's Exiled Loyalists.' Priced at 7s 6d, this history of recent events was to consist of three hundred pages in three numbers, 'on fine paper and good type,' and to include a map of Saint John and harbour; it was to be sold by a battery of Loyalist printers, including Lewis and Ryan of Saint John, John Howe of Halifax, and James Robertson of Shelburne.[57]

In spite of the competition offered by Christopher Sower's *Royal Gazette*, established in 1785, Ryan's newspaper continued to flourish as a representation of Loyalist endeavour. His advertisements began to reflect the evolution of a print culture: a book on freemasonry in July 1784; schools and school texts throughout the 1784–99 period; almanacs; bookbinder Neville Williams eager to repair old volumes; merchant E. Sand announcing a new stock of songbooks, Bibles, children's picture books, and seamen's journals; auctioneer James Hayt mounting a sale of two hundred volumes; dry-goods dealer William Campbell importing *Johnson's Dictionary* and Smollett's *Roderick Random*; or Frederictonians Ludlow, Fraser, and Robertson announcing for sale in 1798 the recently published *The New Gentle Shepherd*, local resident Lieutenant Adam Allan's reworking of Allan Ramsay's play. Interspersed with this panoply of advertisements were announcements of dramatic productions – *The Busy Body*, *The Gamester*, *The Citizen*, and *Douglass: The Noble Scotch Shepherd* – most of them performed in the Long Room of Mallard's Tavern in Saint John.

The American Revolution had escalated public dramatic performance in the United States, especially when its possibilities as propaganda were recognized. The Loyalists had brought this new-found taste for public entertainment with them in the 1780s. The 'Prologue on Opening a Little Theatre in This City, on Monday the 5th January Inst.' in 1795 is a case in point. Having asked rhetorically, 'What rais'd this City on a dreary coast, / Alternately presenting rocks and frost, / Where torpid shell-fish hardly found a bed, / Where scarce a pine durst shew a stunted head,' the presenter went on to outline the raison d'être of the new-found city: ''Twas commerce – commerce smooth'd the rugged strand, / Her streets and buildings overspread the land; / Her piers the mighty Fundy's tides control, / And navies ride secure within her mole.'[58] The prologue reiterates the place of the aesthetic, arguing: ''midst profit, still to verse repair; / Verse, which refines the pleasures of success, / Brings hope, and consolation to distress.' While this endorsement of the importance of the arts in softening the edges of commercialism says something about the eighteenth-century Loyalist vision, it also links the anonymous author's social view with his or her antecedents in New England social life.

The degree to which the Loyalists were first and foremost Americans, raised with American sensibilities and carrying American social ideas and institutions with them into British North America, is consistently and subtly illustrated through any analysis of their contributions to the evolution of a cultural infrastructure in their new home. This reality also emerges in the *Nova-Scotia Magazine*, conceived by William Cochran and printed (and later edited) by John Howe. From the beginning, it made a significant contribution to establishing a literary environment in the Maritime provinces by self-consciously urging 'young writers among the rising generation, to try their strength' in its pages.[59] To this end, Cochran published the contributions of such regional writers as 'Werter,' 'Pollio,' and 'Amicus' (Joshua Wingate Weeks), while at the same time making available to his primarily Loyalist readership the texts of such recent American literary endeavours as William Dunlap's conciliatory post-war play *The Father; or, American Shandyism*, first performed in New York in 1789. The circulation of the *Nova-Scotia Magazine* to over three hundred subscribers, ranging from farmers, barbers, and shopkeepers to churchmen, government officials, and the military, indicates that this message of social renewal undoubtedly reached a wide audience throughout the Maritime provinces, particularly given that literary works were frequently read aloud in social gatherings, thereby doubling or trebling the constituency for any piece of writing.[60]

Certainly, the twenty-two lines of a 'Poetical Letter to the Editor of the *Nova-Scotia Magazine*,' ostensibly submitted by a farmer from Cornwallis in October 1789, reinforces the sense of a general readership for the journal. Lacking the 'four crowns, two shillings and one single six-pence' necessary for a subscription to the new magazine, the farmer-poet proposes an exchange of services based on the barter system (bluenose potatoes for reading matter):

> I went home, and have been three days a contriving
> Which way I could pay for I've thoughts of subscribing:
> As cash in the country is quite out of use,
> The only way left, is to pay in produce.
> Indeed, my friend Jacob tells me, he supposes
> An honest Hibernian will deal in *bluenoses*.
> If this pay will answer, to be sure, Sir, I shall
> Become a subscriber, and pay every fall.[61]

Cochran's ironic response as 'an honest Hibernian' was that he hoped the potatoes were better than the verse, but the poem is interesting not only as a comic document of life but also as an early example in Canadian literature of the role of vernacular writing in identifying social change. It is clear from the poem that in the Cornwallis constituency, money was an increasingly visible arbiter of class and comfort, traditional religion was being challenged by secessionist faiths, and rural dwellers were feeling intellectually isolated from the urban experience.

The product of rural life himself, Cochran, during his editorship of the *Nova-Scotia Magazine*, constantly exposed readers to poetry and essays on country living. The *Acadian Recorder* essays of Agricola (John Young) of 1818–21 (thirty-eight were published in book form at Halifax in 1822 as *The Letters of Agricola on the Principles of Vegetation and Tillage*), James Irving's 'On the Southern Peasantry of Scotland' (1821),[62] Thomas McCulloch's satiric Mephibosheth Stepsure letters of 1821–3, Oliver Goldsmith's *The Rising Village* (London, 1825), Joseph Howe's 'Western Rambles' and 'Eastern Rambles' (1828–31), and Thomas Chandler Haliburton's 'Recollections of Nova Scotia' (1835) all further enhanced the themes of agricultural responsibility first articulated by the *Nova-Scotia Magazine*. These and other voices identified possibilities for financial, cultural, and educational growth that led D.C. Harvey to dub the 1820s the 'intellectual awakening of Nova Scotia.'[63] 'Agriculture, fishing, lumbering and shipbuilding forged ahead,' noted Harvey in his seminal 1936 essay, 'and the minds of the young Nova Scotians were quickened both by economic rivalry and by the literature of knowledge that was written about their province.'[64] The result was not only an increase in the economic confidence of the region but also an affirmation of cultural identity as 'poets, essayists, journalists and historians, artists, educators, controversialists and politicians strove with or against one another to lift Nova Scotians to the level of their fellow countrymen overseas.'[65]

A graduate of Glasgow who had immigrated to Halifax in 1814, John Young was not only the standard bearer for themes that McCulloch, Howe, and Haliburton were to develop in more imaginative literature; he was also one of a series of Scottish-born writers who in the early nineteenth century began to bring new influences into the literary infrastructure established by the Loyalists in the Maritimes. Some of these Scots, such as the 'Polly Bards,' who immigrated to Prince Edward Island in 1803, were Gaelic speakers who preserved in their new communities their role as a public voice for the experience of their people. The topographical poems of Calum Bàn MacMhannain (Malcolm Bàn Buchanan) and Rory Roy MacKenzie were typical in recording, after the travails of emigration, their vision of a land where 'oats grow / and wheat, in full bloom, / turnip, cabbage, and peas / Sugar from trees.'[66] Young set out in his *Acadian Recorder* essays to analyze not only the causes of a post-Napoleonic decline in Nova Scotia's economy but also the more 'enlightened mode of practice' that could 'dignify rural affairs.'[67] His elegantly written letters on topics such as composting and the Hessian fly helped to identify the role of newspapers as the most influential vehicles for public discourse and dissemination in the 1815–40 period in the Maritimes, generating not only a lively public response but also confirming for Agricola, McCulloch, and other writers the efficacy of the newspaper column as a vehicle for succinct expression, intimacy with readers, and broad, heterogeneous dissemination.

Thomas McCulloch's irascible Mephibosheth Stepsure advanced Agricola's agricultural message in a series of anonymously written letters to the *Acadian Recorder* that satirized the inhabitants of 'our town' for abandoning the plow in pursuit of fast money, upward mobility, and transitory pleasure. Serialized irregularly between 22 December 1821 and 29 March 1823 in what were ostensibly two books in the 'chronicles of our town,' the letters became a clever catalyst for reform by creating a series of archetypal misfits (Tipple, Solomon Gosling, Jack Scorem, Miss Sippit) whose moral and financial downfall was so sanctimoniously itemized by the lame, self-congratulatory Stepsure that by the end of Letter 17 he was as much object as agent of McCulloch's satire. As the controversy generated by Stepsure intensified, the sophistication of both readers and writers in the Maritimes in the 1820s was confirmed not only by the intensity of correspondents' attacks but also by the playful apocryphal sermons, nicknames, poems, and letters that emerged in the public around the series.[68] At least one memorialist has left evidence of the means by which the letters

were disseminated among rural dwellers and the effectiveness of McCulloch's anonymity in making the satires immediately pertinent to 'our town,' Nova Scotia: 'We
looked with great anxiety for the arrival of the "Recorder," and on its receipt used to
assemble in the shop of Mr. _____ to hear "Stepsure" read, and pick out the characters, and comment on their foibles, quite sure that they and the writer were among
ourselves. Great was often the anger expressed, and threats uttered against the author if they could discover him.'[69]

McCulloch's original intention even before the completion of book one on
11 May 1822 had been 'writing a novel ... I design Mephibosheth to reach at least the
twentieth letter and I have some thoughts of then adding notes and illustrations
and sending the whole home as a sample of the way in which we get on in the
western world.'[70] His experience in trying to publish the Stepsure letters in Britain
provides a case study in the frustrations facing Maritime writers aspiring to external
recognition of their talents during the 1820–40 period. McCulloch's first choice as
publisher was William Blackwood of Edinburgh, who had contributed library books
to the Pictou Academy, the influential educational institution founded by McCulloch
in 1816. But Blackwood, though confident that the humour and satire of the Stepsure
letters had 'all the pungency & originality of Swift,' nonetheless worried that the
satires had 'too much of his [Swift's] broad & coarse colouring. Taste in these things
has now a days got even more refined, and what was fit for the tea table in the days
of Queen Anne would hardly be tolerated now in the servant's hall.'[71] As a compro-
mise, he suggested that McCulloch rewrite the letters 'addressed to someone in this
country' and focus them on a 'lively and graphic picture of the state of manners,
modes of living thinking etc,' so that they could be serialized in *Blackwood's Edinburgh
Magazine* 'at the rate of ten guineas p[er] sheet.' It would be quite unnecessary, he
added, 'to make any allusion to the Letters having appeared in any of the Canadian
Papers.'[72]

Stung to the quick by Blackwood's rejection, McCulloch wrote to James Mitchell
on 3 December 1829: 'He [Blackwood] thinks me a needy hanger on upon booksellers but things are not yet so bad with me as that[.] Pray have the goodness to send for
the manuscripts without waiting for his ultimatum seal them up with my name
upon them and lay them past[.] I do not care tuppence for their publication.'[73] In
spite of his protestations, McCulloch subsequently tried to sell both the Stepsure
letters and a new novel in London, but was offered even less than Blackwood had
suggested. His failure to place either book for publication reinforces Blackwood's
argument that tastes by the mid-1820s had changed. Not surprisingly, Stepsure's references to breaking wind, uxorial discontent when a prankster slipped a hornet's

nest into Job's trousers, and the decorative effects of emptying chamber pots from gable ends during cold winter nights may have caused the publisher anxiety. But in the final analysis, as Northrop Frye has pointed out, the humour of the dour Stepsure privileged low-key irony over slapstick, and its tone, 'quiet, observant, deeply conservative in a human sense,' has not only 'been the prevailing tone of Canadian humour ever since' but also earned for McCulloch the distinction of being 'the founder of genuine Canadian humour.'[74]

His successor on the satirical landscape, Thomas Chandler Haliburton, represents a different generational approach to authorship. Whereas McCulloch had sought overseas exposure partly to make money for his children and partly to show his Scottish compatriots something of colonial life, Haliburton after the writing of his first book, *A General Description of Nova Scotia* (Halifax, 1823), self-consciously articulated to Peleg Wiswall a strategy for achieving literary success free of Nova Scotia:

> My intention was to go on progressively but steadily till I had finished the entire work, when I should send a correct Copy to my friend Francklin in London and desire him to sell it to a bookseller for the best price he could obtain if he could not sell it to give it to the printer if he would publish it at his own cost, and if he could not dispose of it to light his pipe with it ... the booksellers have administered so long to the literary appetite of the Public that they understand as it were by instinct what will be palatable and what will be removed from the table untouched. Everything however which has America for its Subject (how dull or absurd soever it may be) is read in England with avidity, and I am not altogether without hopes of being able to dispose of my labours in some way or other.[75]

Turning to book writing as much as newspaper publication, Haliburton only incidentally participated in the 1820s in the satiric-sketch tradition that so dominated the newspapers in the three Maritime provinces. Nonetheless, his involvement as both character and contributor in the politically conscious 'Club' series moderated by Joseph Howe in the *Novascotian* between 1828 and 1830 did much to hone his wit, preparing him for the double-edged satire of his Sam Slick sketches by teaching him the dramatic effectiveness of counterpointing, colloquialisms, narrative intensity, direct address, aphorisms, and caricature. It was his 'Recollections of Nova Scotia' (the first of the Sam Slick sketches) in the *Novascotian* in 1835 that escalated him to public popularity, however, for in Sam's audacious language, 'time is money' approach to life (borrowed from Benjamin Franklin), and 'go ahead' philosophy (borrowed from the popular Davy Crockett stories current in the United States), Haliburton had captured a raw antidote to the civility and hesitation that he saw as restraining colonial society. He did not forsake the agricultural themes that had energized Cochran, McCulloch, and Howe, but he appealed to a broader constituency than did farm-based Mephibosheth Stepsure by having the fast-talking Yankee clock peddler Sam Slick travel throughout Nova Scotia and, later, England, expostulating on the efficacy of initiative, energy, competitiveness, and Yankee ingenuity in achieving the economic prosperity and imperial recognition for Nova Scotia that were Haliburton's mission. Thus, although Sam reinforced rural values, he propelled readers into the nineteenth century by celebrating the advances of the industrial revolution.

In spite of Sam's Yankee irreverence, his 'gobsmackt' language and audaciousness gave him a cachet with the public that dour Mephibosheth Stepsure could never equal. Drawing upon English folk sayings and stylized New England intonation for effect, Haliburton-Slick brought unforgettable expressions such as 'raining cats and dogs,' 'quick as a wink,' and 'a stitch in time saves nine' into popular parlance among avid readers in Britain, Germany, the United States, and the British North American colonies. His pervasive influence can be measured by Jacob Norton Crowell's allusion to the sale of Sam Slick books in the goldfields of Ballarat, Australia, during 1852–5.[76]

While the newspaper sketch successfully effected social reform for McCulloch, Haliburton, and countless pseudonymous writers (such as 'A Little Bird' in the *Prince Edward Island Register*), it also exposed Nova Scotians to the literary revolution taking place in British poetry when James Irving, a former *Blackwood's* critic transplanted to Truro, Nova Scotia, began publishing his 'Letters on the Present State of English Poetry, as Exemplified in the Works of the Living Poets' in the *Acadian Recorder* in 1820. Surviving a libel suit in June 1821 against the rival *Free Press* over the issue of literary censorship and freedom of expression (including teaching unbowdlerized Shakespeare), Irving moved Maritime literature onto the stage of sophisticated literary analysis and criticism with his discussions of prosody and Romanticism in both his newspaper letters and his contributions to the *Acadian Magazine* (1827–9).

In spite of the intellectual fizz that he briefly brought to Nova Scotia literary circles in the 1820s, Irving remained on the margins of general readership by the very nature of what he wrote. In this sense, his position was not unlike that of many Maritime women associated with book culture between 1749 and 1840. Although a few conducted printing businesses in the eighteenth and early nineteenth centuries, the majority of Maritime women in the 1749–1840 period were anonymous writers and literary participants, often keeping solitary diaries as did Mercy Seccombe of Chester, Nova Scotia, in the 1760s and 1770s. Standing at the edge of ocean, night, and sky, she interpreted the secrets of the universe in the domestic terms that had informed her life, describing a shooting star as being the size of a pudding basin.[77]

Far more socialized were young urban women such as Rebecca and Eliza Byles, who could attend the private school of poet-teacher Deborah How Cottnam in Halifax, where in a few years, noted Rebecca in a 1784 letter to her Boston aunts, she expected to see women 'fill the most important offices of Church and State.'[78] At Cottnam's school, Rebecca and her sisters studied plain sewing, reading, writing, French, and dancing, but she was also sufficiently well read in standard works to be able to refer to John Locke in her letters, translate a very long sermon from French into English, read Samuel Richardson's *Pamela* and Terence's plays in French, and hear 'Pope's Homer.'[79] Though women's education underwent dramatic changes in the United States in the post-revolutionary war years,[80] there is little evidence in the curricula of schools in the Maritime provinces of tradition-breaking. Deborah Cottnam's academy, conducted first in Halifax in the 1780s and then in Saint John, positioned women in the graceful arts, teaching them the rules of prosody by having them copy poetry in penmanship classes and work verses into their samplers as an alternative form of text. Cottnam's own 'Verse for a Sampler,' disseminated under her pseudonym, 'Portia,' captured for her students the moral imperatives directing their lives as young women, and Eliza Byles's poignant post-war sampler poem, composed by her father, demonstrated the way in which a female child could be both possessed and dispossessed of voice:

> I a young Exile from my native Shore
> Start at the Flash of Arms and dread the Roar;
> My softer soul, not form'd for Scenes like these
> Flies to the Arts of Innocence and Peace;
> My Heart exults while to the attentive Eye
> The curious Needle spread the enamel'd Dye
> While varying Shades the pleasing Task beguile
> My friends approve me, and my Parents smile.[81]

The letters of Eliza and Rebecca Byles as they grew older reveal their avid interest in literature, ranging from discussions of Frances Brooke's *The History of Emily Montague*, read in Halifax only a dozen years after its publication in London, to Rebecca's topical reactions in 1821 to Sir Walter Scott and Washington Irving. Deborah How Cottnam's literary legacy manifested itself not only in the talents of her students, such as Rebecca Byles (later Almon), and her own daughter, Martha Cottnam Tonge, but also in the public literary role assumed by her great-granddaughter, Grizelda Tonge, whose handling of the Spenserian stanza form was praised by literary critic James Irving after she published 'To My Dear Grandmother, on Her 80th Birthday' in the *Acadian Recorder* on 5 March 1825. Though ostensibly dedicated to her grandmother, the poem dramatically illustrates the continuity of women's culture as Tonge acknowledges the 'power' of 'Portia's' (Deborah Cottnam's) poetic inspiration over the generations and yearns that it be effectively 'bestowed' from one generation to the next.

Grizelda Tonge's untimely death from yellow fever in 1825 while on a visit to her brother in Demerara immortalized her in the eyes of Joseph Howe, Mary Eliza Herbert, and Mary Jane Katzmann Lawson as a romantic young poet cut down in her promise. Whether she would have developed the talents identified by Irving and eschewed the marriage theme so frequently underlying female-authored works such as Anne Hecht's Saint John marriage poem of 1786 or Frederictonian Julia Beckwith Hart's *St. Ursula's Convent* (Kingston, 1824) can only be conjectured. Certainly, few Maritime female writers until Herbert in *Belinda Dalton; or, Scenes in the Life of a Halifax Belle* (Halifax, 1859) and the unpublished 'Lucy Cameron' challenged conventional roles for women. All the more interesting is the 1826 publication of the fictional 'Patty Pry' letters in the *Novascotian*, where Patty, both a flibbertigibbet preoccupied with 'dress, dancing and parties' and an intelligent reader of Shakespeare and Johnson, cynically proclaims that 'love is the article in which we deal and by which we hope to make our bread.'[82] Increasingly conscious of the need to read beneath the surface as she unravels her aunt's unhappy love story of forty years earlier, Patty clearly has already learned to exploit male paternalism and use her own charms to empower herself. Underlying her smart patter, however, the reader realizes that, although education and immigration have improved Patty's destiny over that of Aunt Tabitha in Ireland, the circumstances of female economic dependency are as immovable as ever.

One hundred years after the *Gentleman's Magazine* published the 'Ballad of Nova Scotia,' Maritime print culture had rival literary centres, Halifax and Saint John, which trumpeted their primacy in the pages of newspapers such as the Halifax *Morning Post* and the Saint John *Morning News*. Although the advantage was to shift to Saint John in the 1840s, particularly with the emergence of the literary periodical the *Amaranth*, and writers such as Douglass Huyghue ('Eugene'), Moses Perley, and Emily Beavan, there remained throughout the Maritime region at the end of the 1830s the importance of newspapers and literary periodicals as vehicles for local publication, the role of memorial literature in focusing current events, occasional book publication, and the increasing availability of international authors through the growth of libraries, serialization, and bookselling facilities. Although much was still to be achieved, 'the country,' noted Haliburton at the beginning of *The Old Judge*, had 'passed the period of youth, and may now be called an old colony.'[83]

Quebec Literature and Printed Materials: From Birth to Rebirth

BERNARD ANDRÈS

The writings that circulated in New France were those of a colony without the benefit of a printing press; they were penned for the most part by visitors from the French metropole and destined for the home country, where they would be disseminated. On the other hand, after the Conquest, the texts of the province of Quebec quickly began to be published locally from 1764. These texts were conceived, written, and published by colonists and addressed as much to their fellows in the colony as to readers in England or, more rarely, in France. New France thus passed from one empire to another, but even more from one space of reference (Europe) to another (North America). The surrender of the colony by the French to the British corresponded to a radical change of perspective for the colonists: both 'new subjects' (the Canadiens) and 'old subjects' (the English) now found themselves confronted with continental revolutions that would change forever their relationship with the land and with authority. The challenge of the American colonies to the British Crown, the challenge of French revolutionaries to the monarchy, the calling into question of the Canadiens by both – all these added up to a reconfiguration of states and states of mind.

This change in conditions of expression was decisive for the Canadiens, who could now write for other Canadiens through local channels as the press developed and as they began to have a taste for politics and intellectual exchange. It was in this new verbal context that a local literature emerged. Just as the printing press contributed to the appearance of literature in Quebec and then in Lower Canada, so the emergence of the literary left a particular mark on publishing in British North America. The complex play of correlations between the press and literature endured throughout the period from just after the Conquest to the years following the Rebellions of 1837 and 1838.

It All Began with Songs

The earliest literary manifestations appeared in a popular genre, the song. To be sure, many melodies and lyrics drawn from the traditional French repertoire were already circulating in New France, some of them adapted to local realities.[84] But with the war of the Conquest, songs took a more political turn that already reflected a sense of being Canadien, even a new patriotic spirit.[85] Although many of these songs were traced back only much later (in the nineteenth and twentieth centuries), some found a form of dissemination in their own time, as shown by accounts from the period.[86] Some transcriptions of songs can also be found in the early newspapers, among the few rhymed texts in the 'Poets Corner' of the *Quebec Gazette / La Gazette de Québec*, or in a literary column in the *Gazette du commerce et littéraire*. Later, collections were published that led to a reworking in literary form of local folklore, among them *Recueil de chansons choisies* (Montreal, 1821), collected by J. Quilliam; *Chansonnier canadien*, published by the *Montreal Herald* in 1825; and, of course, Michel Bibaud's *Épîtres, satires, chansons, épigrammes et autres pièces de vers,* printed by Ludger Duvernay in 1830. Some lyrics, naive or satirical in tone, were inspired by patriotism, the military, or love, while others addressed more daring themes (drinking songs, eating songs), or belonged to new forms of sociability or new philosophical currents (Masonic songs). When the conflict between the Canadiens and the bureaucrats was at its height, commentators in the press expressed themselves in bolder or frankly revolutionary airs, such as *Yankee Doodle* or even *La Marseillaise*, the *Marseillaise* for Canadiens going beyond the French version in calling for anarchy.[87]

The Status of Literature in the New Community

Considered a minor genre compared to poetry and belles lettres, songs nonetheless posed the question of what qualified as literary and of the uncertain paradigm that was literature at the time. Historical dictionaries note that in the eighteenth century literature was still the stuff of multidisciplinary erudition – science, arts (fine art, but also decorative arts), letters, philosophy, and so on. The republic of letters evolved from networks of scholarly correspondence and the academies into meeting places: salons, coffee houses, clubs, Masonic lodges, and reading societies. It is in this context that one must evaluate the emergence of literature in Quebec and then in Lower Canada. Here, the 'literary' may be defined as any written work going beyond the purely informative and engaging the subject matter of the text in an exchange of a controversial, argumentative, didactic, philosophical, or aesthetic nature, discourses in forms as various as articles, accounts or chronicles, memoirs, poems, songs, orations, speeches, and plays. These texts were for the most part conceived in, written for, and published in Quebec/Lower Canada.[88]

Among those who became involved in the general development of literature and printed materials in the eighteenth century were Bartholomew Green, with a press in Halifax in 1751; John Bushell and the *Halifax Gazette* the following year; William Brown and Thomas Gilmore, with the *Quebec Gazette / La Gazette de Québec* in 1764; and Fleury Mesplet, with a printing office in 1776 and the *Gazette du commerce et littéraire* two years later. In the space of some thirty years, a new 'generation of writers'[89] passed from the old image of the scholar to the new concept of the philosopher, from 'the erudite man of letters' to 'the militant man of causes.' It is the history of this essentially North American telescoping of tradition and of rupture to which one must now turn through a description of the specific context of the socio-cultural and socio-professional milieu of the time.

Neither the publishing apparatus nor the literary environment was well enough developed to allow one to speak of a 'literary institution.' In this embryonic phase,[90] a literary imagination took vague shape, supported by the arrival of the printing press; it was a state of mind still haunted by the classics. In the educational sphere, the literature taught in colleges in the colony was first and foremost that of the great Greek and Roman poets, philosophers, and orators. The preponderance of Latin is not in question; it was even the subject of a controversial article in the *Gazette littéraire* (17 June 1778). No contemporary authors or philosophers were on the curriculum of colleges at Quebec and Montreal.

Signatures and Anonymity in the Republic of Letters in Quebec and Lower Canada

This literature in formation was taken in hand by individuals who were not yet claiming the status of writer or author. For all sorts of reasons (including censorship), early writers almost never signed their texts; anonymity and pseudonymity were the norm for many years.[91] In the circles that were forming around the first gazettes, writers who were ahead of their time imagined, for the pleasure of debate, an academy or society where they could hold discussions under various pseudonyms. Camaraderie and friendship were the order of the day: 'L'ami des beaux-arts,' 'L'ami des hommes,' 'L'ami des sciences,' 'L'ami du Canadien curieux,' or 'L'ami du Président' alternated with 'Le vrai ami du vrai.' It is likely that printers and journalists accumulated a number of pseudonyms in this way,[92] perhaps also taking on female signatures such as 'Le beau sexe,' 'Angélique,' 'Henriette canadienne,' 'Philos,' 'Sophie Frankly,' 'Dorothée attristée,' and 'Félicité canadienne.'

Later, Joseph-Guillaume Barthe was to hide his 'poetic caprices' in *Le Populaire* behind the pseudonym Marie-Louise, because when it came to signatures, women at the time had more trouble than men in breaking the taboos of 'publicity.'[93] It was a matter not solely of recognition of the status of the writer in general but rather of the social roles to which the 'fair sex' was confined, including her 'natural modesty,' little suited to appearing in public places. Even in the 1830s, for every Mary Gradon Gosselin (who signed 'G' in her *Montreal Museum,* in which a small number of the texts were by women authors), how many Odile Cherriers (Anaïs) and Louise-Amélie Panets hid their identities, only to be revealed posthumously?

Networks and Generations of Writers

Between 1770 and 1790, there was much interdependence between Valentin Jautard, Pierre Du Calvet, Joseph Quesnel, Henri-Antoine Mézière, Charles-François Bailly de Messein, Joseph-Octave Plessis, and all the defenders of the 'generation of writers' called the 'generation of the Conquest.'[94] By means of the press, a new configuration appeared in the corridors of power at the time, even before a literary culture took hold. Two gazettes, including a short-lived one in Montreal (1778–9) and two no less short-lived periodicals, *Le courier de Québec: ou heraut françois* (1788) and the *Quebec Herald and Universal Miscellany* (1788–92), appeared almost as soon as the colony had two printing presses. And what is there to say about the editorial existence of the pompous Voltairian 'Académie' dreamed up by a handful of budding writers?[95]

It was not until the early decades of the nineteenth century that tighter links (but also heightened conflicts) were forged between literary men and the political and religious authorities. Also between 1805 and 1840, printing offices and centres of power proliferated, creating the conditions necessary for the formation of a true intellectual domain. Only then could one begin to talk of a sense of belonging to a socio-professional milieu, of career strategies, of a sense of the work and the author. And it was then that, among individuals such as Michel Bibaud, Joseph-Guillaume Barthe, François-Réal Angers, Odile Cherrier (Anaïs), Louise-Amélie Panet, Napoléon Aubin, and a few others, one could find forms of *habitus,* meaningful positions and oppositions, that revealed a literary ground. As the generations changed from that of the Conquest to that of the Patriotes,[96] the literary milieu came to be structured around certain publishing centres. Several examples illustrate the correlations between printed materials and a colonial literature between 1761 and 1837: first, the avatars of a manuscript published successively in the press and in pamphlet form (the La Corne case); then correspondence that became public in the form of a pamphlet (the Du Calvet case), followed by the editorial formula of *L'Almanach* and *L'Abeille*; and finally, two instances of the literary adaptation of political debates (*Les comédies du statu quo* and *Le Fantasque*).

The Adventure of a Tale of Adventure

Luc de La Corne (1711–84) is interesting both for his longevity and for the publishing history of his writings. This native-born Canadien distinguished himself militarily first during the French regime and then under the English regime. The 'général des Sauvages' was shipwrecked in November 1761, while trying to return to France with a hundred compatriots. Only seven passengers survived, including La Corne, who acted heroically. It took him three months, in the middle of winter, to return to the town of Quebec from Île Royale (now Cape Breton)! Throughout his forced march, the survivor recounted his misadventures wherever he stopped to rest, thus creating an oral tradition of this shipwreck. So circumstance made him an author, and when he returned to Montreal in March 1762, he wrote a report (in French) to the English authorities. A manuscript copy of the journal recounting this tragedy came into the hands of General Jeffery Amherst, who was then stationed at New York, and it was there that a first printed version of the account appeared in English in the *New York Mercury* on 12 April. Although it was more a report than a literary work, this brief translation was taken up and expanded in another edition, this one in French. Thus sixteen years later, La Corne (now fighting under the English flag) found himself having to defend his honour and that of all Canadiens. Implicated by General John Burgoyne for his actions at the battle of Saratoga, he denounced the accusations made against him in the London newspapers. And, the better to restore the lustre to his good name, he also published a fuller version of his account of 1762, under the title *Journal du voyage de M. Saint-Luc de La Corne, écuyer, dans le navire l'Auguste en l'an 1761*. This booklet, published in 1778 by Fleury Mesplet, was the first adventure narrative in the Quebec corpus.

A Culture Expresses Itself

In 1784 a contemporary of La Corne's, Pierre Du Calvet (1735–85), published a work with even greater repercussions for the period: *Appel à la justice de l'État*. Du Calvet, at the time a justice of the peace in Montreal, chose to have his work printed in London because he wanted to attract the attention of public opinion and the authorities in the capital. His pamphlet, or factum, was an indictment of the governor at the time, Frederick Haldimand, whom he accused of tyranny. Du Calvet made no secret of his philosophical convictions or his pro-American sentiments. For his Enlightenment ideas, he was imprisoned for almost three years, along with other intellectuals, among whom were the journalists Valentin Jautard and Mesplet.[97] When he was released, he gathered the letters and petitions that he had never stopped writing to obtain justice into a weighty 320-page collection, *Appel à la justice de l'État.* In 1784 he also published in London *The Case of Peter Du Calvet, Esq.* More than a plea in his own defence, his *Appel* was a compendium of the thought of the century and the first didactic work intended to educate Canadiens in a political sense. Of course, American propaganda, distributed widely in Quebec during the invasion of 1774–5, had already made people in the province aware of the ideas of the times.[98] However, with Du Calvet, French by origin and Canadien by adoption, one sees not only the notion of representative government take root, but also a passionate gloss on the precursors and great thinkers of the city, Pufendorf, Gratien, Grotius, Locke, and Machiavelli.

An entire literary and political culture was expressed in these writings, which were widely distributed in the province in the form of letters and collections. Proof of this dissemination may be found in the enthusiastic welcome given them by the committees at Quebec and Montreal engaged in constitutional reform, in petitions, and, later, even in the model of the constitution of 1791. At the heart of *L'Appel* was a superb 'Épître aux Canadiens,' which, for the first time, appealed to all the colonists (both francophones and anglophones) as a geographic community. It was a militant conception of literature, but also a point of convergence between manuscript and printed material, one passing the torch to the other in an ever more effective way. Both were taken in hand, this time by an author who signed his name in the name of all: 'My cause is that of the province of Quebec, just as the cause of the province of Quebec is mine.'[99] Convinced that a 'general oppression' weighed on the colony, Du Calvet in 1784 saw this as 'the natural and ordinary symptom of an approaching revolution.'[100] The same rhetoric could be found in 1791 in another pamphlet published by Fleury Mesplet. The title alone amounts to an entire plan of action: *La Bastille septentrionale, ou Les trois sujets britanniques opprimés.* Attributed to Henry-Antoine Mézière, a young Montreal 'revolutionary,'[101] this other factum denounced an arbitrary arrest in Trois-Rivières. It contained the same ideas as Du Calvet's about the correlation between the individual and the larger community.

Literature in Reviews

Mézière leads us to the next generation and to the phenomenon of literary collections, magazines, and reviews. Twenty years later, Canadiens were involved in a serious questioning of the constitution of 1791. Since the foundation of *Le Canadien* (1806), counterpart to the *Quebec Mercury* (1805) in a climate of parliamentary crisis, a new network of men of letters (in the militant sense of the term) became involved. Although most of them were active initially in politics (Étienne Parent, Ludger Duvernay, Louis-Joseph Papineau, Denis-Benjamin Viger), some, such as Michel Bibaud, Jacques Viger, Aubert de Gaspé *père* and *fils*, Louis Plamondon, and a few others, had a more traditional vision of their role. A loyalist at heart, the young Plamondon tried, with a handful of fellow lawyers, to found a literary society at Quebec. In spite of their good intentions, in 1809 they ran headlong into the distrust of the anglophone community, which saw this literary society as a political enterprise.

Three years earlier, the same Plamondon had acted on his idea of an annual publication for women. On the model of *L'Almanach des muses* (Paris), he published the *Almanach des dames, pour l'année 1807, par un jeune Canadien* (Quebec). 'To work for ladies,' 'to please and amuse,' and to encourage the production of poetry by women were the noble causes expressed only in this single issue. Although the editor used mainly French works (by Madame de Genlis, Arnaud Berquin, Fontenelle, and others), he nevertheless opened the collection with some homegrown poetry. The 'Épître consolatrice' was dedicated 'to Mr L ... who complained that his talents and his verses were not rewarded by the Government.' This long poem is interesting for more than one reason. Although Plamondon revealed neither the author nor the person to whom it was dedicated, they have since been discovered to be Joseph Quesnel and Louis Labadie.

A prolific poet, musician, and playwright, Quesnel, with several associates, had founded the Théâtre de société in 1789; the following winter, the company performed his 'comedy with ariettas,' *Colas et Colinette*. Engaged in a controversy over the theatre, he defended his art and his freedom of expression in the press. As for Labadie, an itinerant teacher and amateur poet in his spare time, he was also a travelling book salesman. For more than twenty years, he kept a voluminous diary. In 'Épître consolatrice,' Quesnel painted a sombre portrait of the reception of literature in Canada: 'In this ungrateful country, where the spirit is even colder than the climate, our talents are lost in the century in which we live.' This poem, written around 1800, deplores the lot reserved by the government for 'great minds,' while benefits showered down upon military men, 'in all ways devoid of literary talent,' and on magistrates, judges, court clerks, notaries, councillors, doctors, and even apothecaries.[102]

Fifteen years later the situation had changed, if we are to judge by Henry-Antoine Mézière's gamble with *L'Abeille canadienne* (Montreal, 1818–19). When he returned to Lower Canada in 1818, after twenty-three years, the former 'revolutionary' of *La Bastille septentrionale* was older and wiser. Conscious of having given his word to the authorities, he now talked of the 'respect due to Religion, customs, and legitimate authority.'[103] During his stay in France, he had had the opportunity to read *La Ruche d'Aquitaine* in Bordeaux. He turned this experience to his advantage by offering to Canadiens 'all that concerns the Sciences, the Arts, and Literature.' Carefully setting himself apart from the newspapers, he presented political facts only 'briefly, and separately from the conjectures that the journalists wilfully allow themselves.' *L'Abeille* introduced to Lower Canada the melancholy lyricism of French pre-Romantics such as Charles-Hubert Millevoye, Jean-François Ducis, and the celebrated Madame de Staël. De Staël was even the object of an offensive editorial in the *Gazette des Trois-Rivières*, which, taking stock of the first three issues of *L'Abeille*, called the author of *Delphine* a 'mad old woman' and taunted Mézière for some of his literary choices.[104]

Politics in Fiction(s)

If all these literary 'miscellanies' and compilations did not manage to find a loyal enough readership to guarantee their survival, it was perhaps because in the 1820s and 1830s political crisis was in the forefront of public opinion. Thus the most significant literary experiments of those decades were hybrid works inspired by current events. Two major political events marked the 1830s, the Ninety-Two Resolutions issued by the Parti patriote (1834) and the Rebellions of 1837 and 1838, and each engendered an original formula for literary activity in print in Lower Canada. While opinions were impassioned for or against the Resolutions, which had been published and discussed in the press, some writers decided to put on the stage the quirks of the 'resolutionaries' and 'anti-resolutionaries' (supporters of the status quo). Passing from the minutes of the debates in the Assembly to satirical dialogue, current events entered onto a fictional stage (some of these short plays may have been performed in private salons). 'Les comédies du statu quo' were published in *La Gazette de Québec* and *Le Canadien* and in pamphlets from April and June 1834. *La Gazette* fired the first shot on 26 April in the form of a reader's letter. Full of anecdotes satirizing the Patriotes, this dialogue brought laughing readers over to its side, causing Étienne Parent to take offence in *Le Canadien*. At first he refused to join the game, not wishing to treat lightly so serious a subject as the Resolutions. But he was soon forced to turn the formidable weapon of irony and sarcasm on his adversaries. After a second anti-resolutionary comedy appeared as a pamphlet, *Le Canadien* replied on 12 May with a third *Comédie*, this one resolutely pro-Resolutions.[105]

This humour, which came to brighten the austere *Le Canadien* at an opportune moment, was pushed to the extreme in the journalistic enterprise of Napoléon Aubin, who showed what the press owed to literature when a journalist of his calibre used a great variety of editorial formulas in order to circumvent censorship. In 1835, when the Swiss-born Aubin entered the debate, political combat was raging. The press was involved on all sides, as was the population: popular assemblies, correspondence committees of representatives, the founding of the St George's, St Patrick's, and St Andrew's societies and the Société aide-toi, le Ciel t'aidera (the Lord helps those who help themselves society). Aubin first contributed to *La Minerve* as a poet and story-teller and then as a political columnist in the debates on freedom of the press. After a pause when he worked as a parliamentary columnist at *L'Ami du peuple*, Aubin, with Aubert de Gaspé *fils*, in 1837 founded the short-lived *Le Télégraphe*, in which appeared an excerpt from *L'influence d'un livre*. This work would be considered 'the first Quebec novel.'

During the year of the first insurrection, Aubin jumped in with *Le Fantasque*. In this satirical and libertarian newspaper, he castigated the government, under cover of humour and levity, with sarcasm and wit. Although he spared no one, either in the government or among the most extreme rebels, Aubin did not stay above the fray. After an interruption of five months, because of events, he relaunched his humorous war machine against the British authorities in 1838. Lord Durham, Sir John Colborne, Thomas Ainslie Young, the chief of police at Quebec, and Symes, his assistant, were Aubin's favourite targets. But aside from these satirical jabs, the writer varied his political forms, using dystopias and imaginary travel pieces to make his point. His 'Plan de la République canadienne' combined audacity with derision, good common sense with the most far-fetched laws, and multiplied puns and pirouettes in linguistic acrobatics that mocked the censors.

On 26 December 1838 Aubin republished the poem by Joseph-Guillaume Barthe titled 'Aux exilés politiques canadiens,' and after having denounced the arrest of Étienne Parent on 31 December, he found himself also in prison for high treason. Fifty-three days in jail only sharpened the poet's wit, and he began to bring out *Le Fantasque* again in May 1839. He wrote about his arrest and feigned falling into line: 'Later I will trace in zigzag the straight line of conduct that I propose to follow in the future.' Ever the anti-authoritarian, he claimed to have enjoyed prison and continued to taunt Lord Durham. But from a literary point of view, his best contribution to the public was his parodic tale 'Mon voyage à la lune,' written with a wink and a nod to Cyrano de Bergerac, Swift, Voltaire, and his compatriots.[106] With Napoléon Aubin, the literary press in Lower Canada reached unequalled peaks that recalled the fireworks of the first *Gazette du commerce et littéraire* sixty years earlier.

Although the history of this gazette was quite brief, it had consummated the first marriage of literature and the press. At the banquet that Jautard and Mesplet offered their readers, the table was well laden. Between June 1778 and June 1779, there was a feast of articles, poetry, stories, and polemics on Voltaire, and exchanges of viewpoints about 'L'Académie de Montréal' added spice to the meal. The spirit of the Enlightenment that sparkled in these columns did not stand up to the dark hours of the American War of Independence, but it was found again in the second version of the periodical once peace returned. Other publishing links deserve mention in this panorama. The examples presented here give only a slight overview of the myriad correlations observable at the time between literature and the press. There were many manifestations of a culture of the word and persuasion, of retelling and memory, of denunciations and dreams of the future. 'I neither obey nor command anyone, I go where I want, I do what I please, I live as I can, and I will die when I must' – this motto printed in the first edition of *Le Fantasque* was as much an announcement of its fight for life as a premonition of its end. A distant descendant of the generation of the Conquest and a fellow traveller of the Patriotes, Aubin had, in his way, transposed their utopia into the literary field. Patiently, from one gazette, one magazine, one title to another, a literary culture took shape in Lower Canada. It must be said that indeed there did exist, before Durham, a people endowed with something resembling a history and a literature.

English Literary Culture in Lower Canada

CAROLE GERSON

English literary culture emerged soon after the Conquest. In 1769 the first novel set in what is now Canada was published in London: *The History of Emily Montague*, written by Frances Brooke based on her two-year sojourn at Quebec. This epistolary narrative includes many letters – some witty, some dry – voicing different characters' opinions on the politics, society, and scenery of the newly British colony, entwining features of travel writing with the conventions of romantic comedy. Several English-speaking authors who later visited or emigrated to Lower Canada wrote for a foreign audience and, like Brooke, achieved publication abroad. For example, a pair of American-born sisters, Harriet Vaughan Cheney and Eliza Lanesford Cushing,[107] who settled in Montreal in the 1830s, maintained their previous connections with Boston publishers. These instances illustrate the multiple allegiances experienced by Lower Canadian authors writing in English. Whether immigrants or locally born, and whatever their links to a specific community, province, or country, they were members of a larger world of letters dominated by the cultural power emanating from the centres of London, Boston, and New York.

In Lower Canada it took time for the English-speaking population to achieve sufficient density to support a community of letters. Despite an influx of Loyalists after the American Revolution, anglophones in 1792 numbered just 15,000, in contrast to some 140,000 francophones.[108] The vast majority of English-speaking writers, like their French-speaking compatriots, depended upon local newspapers as their principal medium of dissemination. As early as 1775–6, a 'Poets Corner,' featuring poems mainly in English, appeared in the *Quebec Gazette / La Gazette de Québec*. In both communities, the emergence of literary culture paralleled the conditions of textual production. The format of the periodical page and the taste of the times account for the dominance of briefer genres such as stories, letters, essays, lyrics, satires, and epigrams during a period when it was costly and difficult to issue lengthy works of fiction or narrative poetry in separate volumes. While Bernard Andrès, earlier in this chapter, identifies the genres of song and folklore as important roots in francophone literary culture, those who wrote in English commenced with different models, transplanted from their parent cultures abroad. One noteworthy cluster of authors, most of them born and educated in Britain, aimed especially high, producing long poems that appeared as monographs issued by local printers at the author's expense or by subscription. The list includes Thomas Cary's *Abram's Plains* (Quebec, 1789),[109] Stephen Dickson's *The Union of Taste and Science* (Quebec, 1799),[110] Cornwall Bayley's *Canada: A Descriptive Poem, Written at Quebec, 1805* (Quebec, 1806?), George Longmore's *The Charivari* (Montreal, 1824), and Adam Kidd's *The Huron Chief* (Montreal, 1830). Two modes dominate: enumerative descriptions in heroic couplets, which characterize topographical verse (Cary), and the mock-serious stanzas of Byronic parody (Longmore).

As printing offices multiplied, English readerships developed, principally in the province's major centres of Quebec and Montreal. Initially the larger town, Quebec saw the first literary activity. To inform and amuse its readers, Brown and Gilmore's bilingual *Quebec Gazette / La Gazette de Québec*, founded in 1764, printed a scattering of verse, much of it anonymous and not all of it original. Particularly intriguing are the annual New Year's verse greetings (*étrennes*) issued in both languages under the identity of the newspaper's delivery boy. Also bilingual, the monthly *Quebec Magazine / Le Magasin de Quebec* (1792–4) favoured reprinted articles, with occasional original material. Thomas Cary's *Quebec Mercury*, founded in 1805, reflected its editor's own literary proclivities in the prominence it gave to its 'poet's corner.' In Montreal, newspapers tended to follow distinct sectarian and ethnic lines: William Gray's *Montreal Herald*, founded in 1811, published verse that would appeal to Scots Presbyterians, while the Montreal *Vindicator* (founded as the *Irish Vindicator* in 1828) reproduced Irish poetry by Thomas Moore. At least half the poems in these newspapers are identified with just an initial or two or remain completely unsigned,[111] a degree of anonymity congruent with practices in British periodicals of the period. Pseudonyms tend to reflect literary conventions and classical allusions (Alpha, Caledoniensus, Flavia, A Friend, Helen, A Lady, Proteus, Quebecensis, Rusticus, A Soldier, Susan), rather than the coy and strategic veiling of identity practised by francophones, which Andrès describes.

As the political capital of Lower Canada, Quebec not only saw English-language literary activity in its early newspapers but also housed the Literary and Historical Society of Quebec, founded in 1824. Officially bilingual, the society functioned primarily in English, a situation that prevailed even after its absorption in 1829 of its French counterpart, the Société pour l'encouragement des arts et des sciences en Canada. The mandate of the LHSQ, which was instrumental in the development of Quebec's libraries, was far more comprehensive than its title suggests. In its early years, papers were read on astronomy, chemistry, engineering, agriculture, and medicine, as well as classics and the 'advantages to be derived from the cultivation of Science, Literature and Arts.' [112] This definition of the 'literary' as inclusive of all intellectual activity, although typical of its era, led one scholar to conclude, 'Indeed, it would have been more correct to name the LHSQ the "Historical and Scientific Society of Quebec."'[113]

During the early years of the nineteenth century, Montreal's growth in both population and economic significance established it as the centre of English-language literary activity in the Canadas. Of the twenty-one newspapers founded in Montreal between 1820 and 1829, seventeen were English and four were French. In contrast, during the same decade Quebec acquired six new periodicals in French and only two in English.[114] The list of English journals established in Montreal in the 1820s and 1830s reflects an impressive commitment to intellectual culture, at the same time as the brevity of their existence illustrates the precarious state of literary publishing. Discussed in 'Magazines in English' in chapter 10, the most noteworthy were the *Canadian Magazine and Literary Repository* (1823–5), the *Canadian Review and Literary and Historical Journal* (1824–6), the *Scribbler* (1821–7), the *Montreal Museum* (1832–4), and the *Literary Garland* (1838–51). Testimony to the importance of such journals in creating opportunities for authors appears in the publishing history of George Longmore's 'Tecumthe.' Initially issued in the *Canadian Review and Literary and Historical Journal* in December 1824, this verse narrative subsequently appeared in his *Tales of Chivalry and Romance*, a collection of poetry and prose published in Edinburgh in 1826. The reverse pattern was experienced by Levi Adams, another participant in the Montreal writing boom of the decade, when his mock-Byronic poem 'Jean Baptiste' appeared in the same periodical after first publication as a pamphlet. The most enduring of these periodicals, the *Literary Garland*, initiated and fostered the careers of British North America's major mid-century anglophone authors. Substantial contributors from its first two years include Eliza Lanesford Cushing, Elizabeth Mary MacLachlan (E.M.M.), Susanna Moodie, and Catharine Parr Traill. Opportunities for Montreal authors developed hand in hand with the growth of presses, whose output expanded from newspapers to periodicals and books. Of those bookseller-printer-publishers active in the 1820s and 1830s, John Lovell would outlast his predecessors and rivals Joseph Nickless, H.H. Cunningham, and Armour and Ramsay. In addition to publishing the *Literary Garland*, Lovell would become a major figure in enabling Montreal authors to publish their books at home, for local readers, and in maintaining his city's centrality for English-Canadian writers not only before Confederation but for several decades thereafter.

Literary Cultures and Popular Reading in Upper Canada

MICHAEL PETERMAN

From 1791, the year in which the old province of Quebec was divided into Lower and Upper Canada, until the 1830s, literary activity in the upper province was slow to develop. However, by 1840, despite the negative effects of depression and rebellion in the preceding decade, a strong, though still indistinctive, print culture was emerging in step with the province's growing political and economic power.

In 1791, Upper Canada had a small population and a single printing office. Three districts and their central towns vied for attention – Kingston at the eastern end of Lake Ontario, with its long-standing garrison traditions, Newark (Niagara-on-the-Lake) at the western end, in close proximity to the United States, and York (Toronto), a village with a capacious harbour, which lay between the two. That year Lieutenant-Governor John Graves Simcoe arrived in Newark, then the capital, eager to establish a political and cultural infrastructure. He acquired a government printer, for, in his words, it was crucial to 'counter the baneful effects of the News Papers of the United States, disseminated with great Industry in this Province.'[115] He also set out to found a provincial library, a system of schools, a university, and a safe and distinctive metropolitan centre. Resources, however, were few and progress was slow. The challenge from the beginning was the need to distinguish Upper Canadian political interests, social ideals, and cultural values from those south of the border, which were too near and too influential to be ignored. Moreover, since many Upper Canadians were of Loyalist origin or had family connections with the United States, it was important to emphasize the British connection.[116]

It is a truism that in the early days the demands of settlement and daily living in Upper Canada left relatively little time for cultural amenities, and the formidable distances made travel and the distribution of reading materials difficult. The literacy level was not high, especially among lower-class immigrants; in 1838 Anna Jameson reported estimates ranging from only one in twenty or thirty to one in seventy residents able to read or write.[117] Except among the better off financially, there was little disposable income or leisure time to foster literary expression or cultural development.

It fell to the growing towns, several of which vied to be the metropolis, to set standards worthy of emulation in smaller centres. In places such as Kingston and York, people of some education, usually British born and bred, began to form alliances of various sorts: agricultural associations, lending libraries, mechanics' institutes, debating societies, and literary clubs. Just as significantly, informal groups of like-minded, often wealthy people made their political influence felt. The weight of the British past largely determined what was deemed relevant, politically and culturally. The classics, philosophy, languages, science, and history all fell within the general definition of the literary, while the poem held dominion as the superior genre. Each of the British national groups promoted its favourite authors in reading rooms and local newspapers. At the same time, the American influence that Simcoe so greatly feared remained a vital force, especially through the many newspapers readily available from south of the border. Writers such as Washington Irving and Edgar Allan Poe made frequent appearances in Upper Canadian papers.

By the 1820s, newspapers had been established in several towns in the province. The triple forces that dominated journalistic content in these publications were politics, religion, and local economic interests. Experience in Upper Canada was viewed through the prism of the British connection and tinged with the *sine qua nons* of colonialism: loyalty to the Crown and the British constitution, and a commitment to religious seriousness and church membership. Political dissent was debated and criticized, and constitutional alternatives were tolerated, as were a variety of religious persuasions, but loyalty and religious values were demanded above all of, and by, the citizenry. By 1840, in the wake of the rebellions in the Canadas, these twin forces had established a virtual stranglehold over cultural life in the province.

In the late winter of 1837, before the outbreak of rebellion, Anna Jameson provided a snapshot of culture in colonial Toronto, the provincial capital. As the wife of the attorney general, she used her privileged position to gather demographic information. She was struck by the rapid growth in population, reporting that the number of Upper Canada's inhabitants had doubled in nine years to 375,000, while Toronto had doubled in five years, reaching 10,000 by 1837.[118] But for her such expansion could not mask a grim cultural inadequacy. Toronto was a mean and narrow place, 'a fourth or fifth rate provincial town, with the pretensions of a capital city.'[119] Growth in numbers there certainly was, but for Jameson, ever the cosmopolitan register, what grated was the absence of any interest not only in literature but also in science and music. Her judgment spared neither Toronto nor the province as a whole,[120] but she noted that newspapers abounded and were 'the principal medium of knowledge and communication in Upper Canada.' She counted 'about forty' papers in circulation in 1837, even as she lamented the scarcity of books and the absence of interesting magazines. Moreover, she added, it took 'about two years before any book of importance finds its way here.' With considerable archness, she concluded that 'the American reprints of the English reviews and magazines, and the Albion newspaper [published in New York], seem to supply amply our literary wants.'[121]

What Anna Jameson saw as irrevocably provincial can also be viewed in more positive terms. Her Old World standards and her privileged connections limited her opportunity to understand conditions imposed on the new province by forces beyond its borders. Contrast her responses to those of John W.D. Moodie, who arrived in Toronto early in 1838 for a month's training in the newly formed Queen's Own Regiment. Fresh from his backwoods farm north of present-day Lakefield, Captain Moodie wrote to his wife, Susanna, that he had quickly made numerous musical and literary connections in the town and several among the masters of Upper Canada College, and that he was thoroughly enjoying his leisure hours. Among these acquaintances were 'our good little friend [John] Kent,' a literary man and editor of some experience; the musical George Maynard; Walter Cavendish Crofton, who wrote under the pseudonym of 'Uncle Ben' and later edited the *Cobourg Star*; and Charles Fothergill, editor of Toronto's newest paper, the *Palladium of British America*.[122]

One's sense of the province depended in part upon one's acquaintances. In Moodie's case, we glimpse the energy and charm of a different Toronto elite from the Family Compact that Jameson encountered and resented, an elite in which musical evenings and literary expression played an important part in daily life. Toronto bookseller Henry Rowsell made journal entries during 1835–6 that provide yet another look at incipient literary energies in the city. His diary describes meetings of the Shakspeare Club (1836) and its successor, the Toronto Literary Club (1836–7), recording formal debates, papers delivered, and the stressful internal politics. Names such as the aforementioned John Kent, Dr William (Tiger) Dunlop, and Anna Jameson's husband, Robert, appear in those entries. An examination of reading tastes in Upper Canada, the literary ambitions of the province's newspapers, and the stuttering attempts to develop a market for its writers provides a more complex and promising picture of literary culture than Anna Jameson was able to grasp during her brief stay.

Education and Popular Reading

Central to the growth of reading in Upper Canada was the issue of how education was to be conducted and what it would seek to teach. It was in fact a primary battleground as the province set out to define itself in cultural and ideological terms. From the first decade of the nineteenth century, schoolteacher and clergyman John Strachan was outspoken in his celebration of the 'cause of classical learning.' Deploring Europe's political instability and the forceful platitudes of 'democratical tyranny' to the south, he sought to inculcate in his pupils a regime of sound moral principles, respect for God, patriotic love of 'that happy island' across the ocean, and the discipline of a classical education. In such principles, he argued, resided the future of the British colonies. 'In fine, the enemies of the classics are like the enemies of rank and title in society – enemies only because it is beyond their reach, or they are profoundly ignorant and the enemies of freedom.'[123] As Strachan rose in status and power, achieving by the late 1830s a well-supported stronghold within the Toronto and provincial establishment, he sedulously pursued his program of an Anglican-based elitism. Contempt for non-classical expression – be it the novel, the romance, or secular poetry; be it the rhetoric of democracy or of student-oriented educational practice – was his consistent position.

Against the weight of Strachan's educational views and those of leading spokes-men for the less hierarchical but still dogmatic denominations such as the Presbyterians and the Methodists, popular culture faced a powerful opposition in Upper Canada. Though no friend to Anglicanism, the young Methodist minister Egerton Ryerson and his public voice, the *Christian Guardian*, supported the attack upon the fictive and the unduly imaginative. Novels were mistrusted for their fanciful excesses and dangerous ideas. Indeed, prior to 1840 there was, among public commentators at least, a 'general disdain for fiction.'[124] Published lists of books for sale in Upper Canadian towns in the first two decades of the century seldom noted novels or ro-mances among their stock. The influential church newspapers spoke out against such works.[125] Nevertheless, despite many kinds of conservative resistance, the marketplace was rapidly changing even as such warnings continued. Writing in a Montreal magazine in 1824, David Chisholme would remark upon the rush of novels 'daily issuing from the press' in that city and would use the occasion to warn against their softening and weakening effects upon individuals.[126]

Thus was drawn up a battle between a firmly entrenched, elitist agenda and the growing public appetite for fiction and lighter reading. Although commentators continued to deplore 'the vicious appetites of the many,' increasing numbers of pri-vate readers found romances and novels to be both more amusing and more accessi-ble than the traditional genres. Critics might emphasize the incontestible value of poetry as literature and the trustworthiness of history and science, but readers sought out historical romances and contemporary novels because they were emotionally engaging. In the *Weekly Register*, his non-official supplement to the *Upper Canada Ga-zette*, on 26 December 1822, Charles Fothergill commented matter-of-factly on the current 'rage for novel reading' and the new journalistic fashion of publishing ex-tracts from novels. He offered a brief, well-informed history of the English, French, and Italian traditions, mentioning Richardson, Fielding, and Smollett in passing but making no judgment on their writing. Fothergill was far more open-minded about literary expression than Strachan, Ryerson, or other religious leaders. For him, Lord Byron was an icon of freedom and literary achievement. Upon Byron's death in the cause of Greek liberation, Fothergill deemed him the 'greatest Poet, and one of the most extraordinary men, of modern times.'[127] He published numerous pieces by and about him in the *Weekly Register*.

Generally, Upper Canadians looked to Britain for models of what was 'literary.' It was something practised and monitored elsewhere. One looked to the 'mother coun-try' for excellence, for models worth emulating, and for interpretations of what was valuable and worthwhile. Certain writers dominated the consciousness of Upper

Canadians during the province's first half-century; only a few were novelists. Sharing literary distinction with Shakespeare was Sir Walter Scott, whose poetry and Waverley romances pleased many of the elite not only because of his attention to Scottish heritage but also because his historical narratives were couched in worthy idealism and 'unimpeachable morality.'[128] As Carole Gerson observes, he was the single practitioner who 'made fiction respectable' in the British colonies; as such, he played a 'crucial' role 'in shaping the horizon of expectation of the Canadian literary community.'[129] Certainly, Upper Canadian magazines and newspapers lionized him, and readers eagerly sought out his books.

Sharing attention, particularly among those of Scottish descent, were Thomas Campbell and Robert Burns. The latter was the favourite poet of the Scottish people, so much so that it was not long before celebrations of Burns's birthday became yearly events in several Upper Canadian towns and cities. Campbell's *The Pleasures of Hope* (1799), which 'transplanted to North America the English village so movingly depicted in Thomas Gray's *Elegy Written in a Country Churchyard*,' influenced Dr Thomas Rolph. In his *A Brief Account* (1836), Rolph quoted a few of Campbell's lines without naming him, confident, as Heather Murray argues, that his readers would recognize Campbell's authorship without prompting.[130] Like Thomas Moore's 'Canadian Boat Song,' Campbell's *The Pleasures of Hope* offered a charming and optimistic view of the colonial experience which, regardless of its excesses, held a powerful emotional significance for many immigrants.

The Irish were not long in lionizing their famous contemporary Moore. As D.M.R. Bentley contends, 'no nineteenth-century poet with first-hand experience of Canada had a greater impact on later Canadian writers than Thomas Moore.'[131] Bentley has traced possible links between Moore's poetry and journals, particularly his 'Poems Relating to America,' and the later work of writers such as Charles Richard Weld, Charles Sangster, and Adam Kidd. Not only did Moore's 'mythopoeic aggrandizement of Canada' and his 'Edenic vision of the backwoods' make the colony attractive to prospective Irish emigrants,[132] but his poems about Ireland, including those that showcased his mastery of vernacular expression, made him a favourite of many transplanted Irish. Newspaper editors often included his poems in their 'Poetry Corner' and reported on his publications. The fact that many Irishmen became editors of papers in both Upper and Lower Canada did much to sustain Moore's popularity among local readers.

Among other popular British writers in Upper Canada were the well-established greats – William Cowper, 'the pride of moral poets,'[133] Alexander Pope, Thomas Gray, and Oliver Goldsmith, for example – and many new and appealing voices of the day, among them Joanna Baillie, Mrs Hemans, James Montgomery, Thomas Pringle, and Allan Cunningham. Much in the spotlight as the 1830s drew to a close were a number of popular new voices feeding the growing appetite for fiction in serialized and book form, such as Samuel Lover, Edward Bulwer-Lytton, and the young Charles Dickens. The popularity of Dickens's *Sketches by Boz*, *Oliver Twist*, and *Nicholas Nickleby* helped to create a new market of middle- and lower-class readers hungry for narrative excitement and social humour.

Not surprisingly, then, editors and cultural commentators in Upper Canada continued to look abroad for literary achievement and standards. Some writers sought out publishers in England. In the 1830s John Richardson found a commodious vehicle in the gothic and made an éclat with *Wacousta*, while Tiger Dunlop and Catharine Parr Traill used the premise of the emigrant handbook to present their experiences as adoptive Canadians. Nevertheless, journalism remained the province's only literary profession. Editors who proved themselves masters in the often acerbic world of Upper Canadian journalism were the best-known voices, among them William Lyon Mackenzie, Hugh Scobie, Charles Fothergill, and Hugh Christopher Thomson.

Newspapers as Literary Vehicles

From the outset, it was the local newspaper that provided literary opportunities for Upper Canadian writers. To submit a poem was to enter the arena of belles lettres and express oneself in the manner of established tradition and cultural literateness. The Old World models provided the forms and structures. At worst – which is to say, predictably – writers imitated those accepted forms; the more interesting among them sought to adapt form and convention to meet the challenge of the New World, its landscape, and its differing social conditions.

Those who wrote essays in the form of letters to the editor were typically mannered in their approach, eager to engage in controversy, to prescribe social conduct, to moralize authoritatively, or to assert a particular political agenda. Contentious local issues often drew responses in the form of animated essays or barbed, ad hominem letters. Most of these earnest, highly opinionated correspondents would never have considered writing a book for publication, though some might have asked for payment for regular submissions. The journalistic convention of the time was to adopt a pseudonym – usually an evocative, if clichéd pen name ('Nemo,' 'Truth,' or 'Atticus') – and then to enter the arena of public expression that the newspaper provided. A modicum of talent, a considerable ego, a position of local authority, or a connection to the editor helped one to garner attention.

In the *Kingston Gazette* of 1 October 1813, the editor, Stephen Miles, published a tongue-in-cheek letter of introduction from one such correspondent, identified only as T.H. It speaks with comic accuracy of the kind of writer who, driven by high self-opinion, made himself available to his local editor. On 'the tiptoe of expectancy' T.H. wrote to Miles:

> Sir – I am a man of genius, who, like many others of the same class, am sometimes in want of a little cash. It is possible, sir, you may be sometimes in need of a little of my assistance in my technical capacity; and, as I shall at all times be glad of your assistance in supplying my deficiencies, we may, if you please, establish a correspondence that may be advantageous to us both ... My genius, sir, is not confined to any particular line: it takes in the whole bounds of nature. I have already written with the highest applause, on History, Politics, Astronomy and Ethicks; but my *forte* is Poetry, and the belles-lettres. What kind of poetry do you like best? Is it the Eligiac? I give you a small specimen in that strain.

T.H. followed that effusion with examples of his prowess in the pastoral, classical, heroic, and lyric 'measures,' all modelled on 'parallel passages' from the 'greatest poets of modern times.' If Miles would only send some money, T.H. promised to supply an 'abundance of beautiful compositions.' 'What I can't write myself,' he added, 'I'll borrow.' The problem, as Stephen Miles implied, was twofold. On the one hand, editors needed to find qualified contributors whose good sense and originality merited attention. On the other, what editor, struggling to meet operating costs, could afford to pay those who were so keenly poised to submit their outpourings?

Despite such absurdities as the fictional T.H. and Toronto's self-proclaimed poet laureate 'Sir John' Smyth, it is to Upper Canadian newspapers that one must turn for the earliest evidence of literary culture in print form. The *Kingston Gazette*, for instance, provides a model from the early years of the province. Begun by Nahum Mower and Charles Kendall on 25 September 1810, the paper was one of the province's first weeklies, a four-page publication that was rich in local literary contribution. Kendall, who edited the paper before Stephen Miles took over on 17 September 1811, had a large number of Kingston and area writers to call on. Letters and articles came from 'Cato,' 'Vindex,' 'Probus,' and 'Agricola' (useful articles about agriculture were especially welcomed), and poems from 'Alcander,' 'Absalom Ready,' 'Sandy,' and 'Strephon.' Kendall published the full text of John Strachan's address at the annual examination of his Cornwall school in 1811. As well, there was a weekly feature, an article by or letter to 'The Reckoner,' published as 'Original Miscellany.' According to

Henry Scadding, 'The Reckoner' was none other than Strachan himself, the Scottish-born schoolmaster who, behind the imposing pseudonym, was articulating social advice and mapping religious values in a manner that would characterize his later rise to power.[134]

Each issue of the *Gazette* contained at least one poem, occasionally juxtaposing the work of popular British authors – Campbell and Moore, for example – with local verses written expressly for the *Gazette*. At the same time, Kendall used his paper to advertise books for sale at his office, the titles providing a kind of forum on contemporary colonial reading of the period. They ranged from 'Addison's Works' and 'Montgomery's Poems' to an extensive list of Bibles, sermons, and catechisms, and to a 'Child's Spelling-book,' a 'French Vocabulary,' and an 'American Cookery.'

Stephen Miles continued what Kendall had set in motion. New local poets appeared ('Ferdinand Friendly,' 'Flora,' 'Anti-Bacchus'), and poetic exchanges briefly flourished; 'The Reckoner' feature continued for a few more months. It was not until pressing news about the War of 1812 and General Isaac Brock's death that military matters supplanted the lively local expression that had characterized the *Gazette*'s columns. As was often the case across the province, major events, political reporting (when, for instance, the House of Assembly was in session), or a local controversy would for a time interrupt the attention to literary expression that many editors were willing to encourage.

It is not, of course, possible to identify all the local contributors who wrote under an editor's protection. He himself would have insisted upon knowing the identity of the contributor but would leave specifics to local gossip. Thus in many cases the identity of the poets, essayists, and letter writers who contributed to various papers remains a mystery. What is clear, however, is that, depending upon the inclination and politics of the editor, local newspapers often gave voice to the literary and cultural interests of citizens.

A newspaper that shared the *Kingston Gazette*'s inclinations a decade later was the *Upper Canada Gazette* under the editorship of Charles Fothergill, when wide-ranging literary expression flourished. Fothergill was appointed editor of the official government paper at York in 1822 and held the position until early 1826, when he was ousted allegedly because of his unauthorized spending as editor but more probably for his outspoken anti–Family Compact views. Fothergill used the *Upper Canada Gazette* as a forum for his own diverse interests, establishing a second section, the *Weekly Register,* to publish useful agricultural and scientific information as well as literary material and letters that addressed local and moral issues of the day. Operating with the luxury of eight pages weekly, he was often able to devote as many as five to the *Weekly Register*.

The 'literary' played a large part in Fothergill's weekly compilations. While he occasionally contributed or included pieces on 'Natural History' and agriculture, he was also attentive to the situation of the Native peoples of Upper Canada and included several essays and poems on that subject.[135] Among the local poets he published were 'Erieus' (Adam Hood Burwell) and 'Roseharp' (James Martin Cawdell), along with 'Nemo' of Belleville and 'P' of York. 'Eusebius' of Markham provided several essays (on the perniciousness of duelling and the responsibility of newspapers, for example). Fothergill was also interested in the development of theatre in York, encouraging his readers to patronize the efforts of Theatre York (1824) and the fresh enterprise of Mr and Mrs Talbot (1825).

It would be impossible in so short a compass to describe the range of newspapers in the province's first fifty years.[136] Suffice to say that they grew in number over the decades from a very few in 1810 to the 'forty' that Anna Jameson described as circulating in the province in 1837. Not all were so conspicuously supportive of a wide literary agenda as Kendall's *Kingston Gazette* and Fothergill's *Weekly Register*, but most found occasion to break with local news and the favoured political rhetoric and to make space for poetry, literate essay-writing, and, as the century developed, fiction and romantic prose pieces.

Creating a Literature

When George Parker argued, 'There was little literary publishing in Upper Canada before mid-century,' he underlined the practical truth that, 'since authorship did not pay, book publication was almost an act of faith.'[137] Literary magazines were a great risk and seldom lasted more than a few issues. Books of a literary cast were also a rarity. Printers lacked capital, and an audience willing to support the publication of volumes of poems or essays hardly existed. As a result, most such texts were self-published, typically by subscription. Nevertheless, literary expression was regarded as a sign of distinction, social accomplishment, and a confident perspective. It was the activity of a gentleman or a married gentlewoman who, because of position and ability, had something significant to contribute to the public and the ability to write forcefully, if not magisterially. For most early Upper Canadian authors, publication was seldom a means of earning an income. Rather, it was a hopeful or necessary act of self-expression in a world that regarded literature as something produced elsewhere – in Britain, Europe, or the United States.

Most prominent among the pre-1840 authors who took the chance on book publication in Upper Canada were poets who began their writing ventures in local newspapers.[138] Typically, they were males with some military or professional training. Most were British-born, and often they were at odds in terms of sensibility or politics with the prevailing social order. Most noteworthy was native-born Adam Hood Burwell (1790–1849), arguably the most important of the early poets. His long poem 'Talbot Road' first appeared in two parts in the *Niagara Spectator* in 1818, and he wrote often for newspapers and magazines under the pseudonym 'Erieus.' Consciously echoing writers such as Thomas Campbell and Oliver Goldsmith, Burwell envisioned a vibrant Upper Canadian society emerging under the heroic guidance of Thomas Talbot as wild nature was 'tamed and domesticated' along Lake Erie's shore.[139] His letters about natural history and several of his poems, including 'The Death of Brock,' appeared in Fothergill's *Weekly Register.*[140]

The most unusual among the poets were James Martin Cawdell (d. 1842) and John Smyth (d. 1852). Cawdell was a self-declared romantic who came to Upper Canada as a military officer. After leaving the army, he published poetry under the pseudonym Roseharp and several times tried to set up a magazine by the same name. His book of lyrics *The Wandering Rhymer* was published at York in 1826[141] by Fothergill, who had included some of Cawdell's poems in his newspaper two years earlier. John Smyth was the most eccentric and at the same time the most sadly pathetic. Promoting himself not only as 'Sir John' Smyth but also as 'the Genius of Canada West,' he published poems in various newspapers prior to issuing his *Select Poems* (Toronto, 1841), a book 'dedicated to Canadians.'[142]

Doctors and lawyers were noteworthy among Upper Canada's fledgling poets. Alexander Johnston Williamson (1796?–1870) was a well-travelled doctor and teacher who published several collections in Kingston and Toronto: *The Unbeliever's Prayer* (1834), *Original Poems* (1836), *There Is a God* (1839), and *Devotional Poems* (1840).[143] The Irish-born James Haskins (d. 1845), a hard-drinking doctor in the Belleville area, wrote for the *Literary Garland* and the *Church*. His collected poems appeared posthumously in 1848. Among the scribbling lawyers were John Hawkins Hagarty (1816–1900), John Breckenridge (1820–54), and Charles Durand (1811–1905). The Irish-born Hagarty practised in Toronto and used the pen name Zadig in writing for magazines and newspapers. Breckenridge, who won the Upper Canada College poetry prize for his poem 'Canada' in 1837, contributed verse to newspapers and magazines and would publish a collection, *The Crusades and Other Poems*, in 1846. Charles Durand was a contributor to numerous magazines and papers in the 1830s, often under the pseudonym Briton.

Among the emerging voices in the 1830s were Canada's first literary couple, John Wedderburn Dunbar Moodie (1797–1869), an Orcadian, and his English-born wife, Susanna (1803–85). John Moodie had already published a military memoir in Lon-

15.5 Masthead of the *Palladium of British America and Upper Canada Mercantile Advertiser* (Toronto, 1838). Courtesy of the Thomas Fisher Rare Book Library, University of Toronto.

don, and upon arriving in Cobourg in 1832, he was quick to send off poems and sketches to various American and local newspapers and magazines. Equally ambitious, Susanna Moodie sought out opportunities in the *Cobourg Star*, the New York *Albion* and its companion paper, the *Emigrant*, and various Toronto magazines. Though frustrated by the demands of their young family, their limited capital, and, after their move to the backwoods in 1834, the cost of postage, she seized what opportunities were available, notably Sumner Lincoln Fairfield's *North American Magazine*. In December 1837, in the wake of the rebellion, she sent a fervently patriotic poem to Charles Fothergill's new Toronto newspaper, the *Palladium of British America* (see illus. 15.5, above). The popular reaction to that piece, 'Canadians, Will You Join the Band. A Loyal Song,' and to several subsequent pro-British poems in that paper led directly to her recruitment as a regular contributor to a new Montreal magazine, the *Literary Garland*.[144] In Susanna Moodie's case, an adjustable patriotism and loyalty, feelings that served her as well in England as in British North America, did much for her literary aspirations in Upper Canada.

To these figures must be added other writers of wide-ranging interests. First among them is the quixotic Charles Fothergill (1782–1840), who wrote extensively, mostly about science and politics, for newspapers he edited in the 1820s and 1830s, the *Upper Canada Gazette* and the *Palladium of British America*, as well as for the *Cobourg Star*. A published naturalist before he emigrated from England in 1816, he continued to develop his passion for the study of fauna over his three decades in Upper Canada. His visionary plans for Toronto's cultural development in the 1830s included the co-founding (with Doctors William Rees and William Dunlop) of the York Literary and Philosophical Society and plans for the building of a Lyceum of Natural History and the Fine Arts, which would include a museum, art gallery, botanical garden, and zoo. In both projects, he was frustrated in part by his own failing energy and by the resilient opposition of Family Compact leaders, whom he had long delighted in criticizing.[145]

Among Fothergill's friends and acquaintances were several consequential writers. His Scarborough friend Robert Douglas Hamilton contributed essays to various magazines and newspapers, under the pseudonym Guy Pollock. William Dunlop (1792–1848) attained great prominence in Upper Canada and in Britain as a result of his popular guide for emigrants, *Statistical Sketches of Upper Canada* (London, 1832), and for 'his love of literary brawling,'[146] while Thomas Rolph (d. 1858) published an account of his travels in the West Indies, the United States, and Upper Canada in 1836[147] and also briefly edited a magazine in 1839.

Writing from the backwoods north of Peterborough, Susanna Moodie's older sister, Catharine Parr Traill (1802–99), who had also emigrated to Upper Canada in 1832, made a considerable impact with her handbook for female emigrants. *The Backwoods of Canada* was published in London in January 1836 by Charles Knight for the Society for the Diffusion of Useful Knowledge. It did not identify her as author; rather, she was simply 'the Wife of an Emigrant Officer.' The book, in the form of letters home to family and friends, offered a cheerful, detailed, and optimistic account of Traill's first two years in the backwoods. In its sympathetic treatment of emigration, settlement, and adaptation, it proved immensely popular with several waves of immigrants to British North America. Along with Anna Jameson's narrative of her year in Upper Canada, it brought both a literary and a personalized perspective upon the colony to British readers. Indeed, Jameson had read Traill's book before coming to Upper Canada and was so impressed by it that she sent a copy to her German friend Ottilie von Goethe. 'The book interested me,' she wrote, 'and pleased me very much, and it is thought to give so favourable a view of things, that they say it has made many persons emigrate.'[148]

The most prolific of pre-1840 writers was John Richardson (1796–1852). He produced several novels, blending in his fiction a love of North America's early military history with an intense, gothic, and at times erotic imagination. Richardson's on-again, off-again relationship with his native Upper Canada was evident in his journalism of the 1830s and early 1840s, as his hopes for financial success as a pioneering writer in Canada continued to elude his grasp. His *Wacousta* (London and Edinburgh,

1832) proved a dark and durable romance, one that made British North America into 'a British battleground' even as it sought to dramatize and gothicize the forest land-scape of the frontier.[149] Its success helped to open a future for writing dramatically about Upper Canada as a place. Emulating the popular American novelist James Fenimore Cooper, Richardson took as his subject the exciting and bloody history of Native-European contact along the western borders of the province that he knew well. Amidst the dark excesses of his narrative, he brought into the written record for the first time glimpses of the potential of the Upper Canadian landscape for serious fictional and dramatic treatment.

NOTES

1. First Contact of Native Peoples with Print Culture

1 G. Warkentin, 'In Search of "The Word of the Other,"'17; citing Roy Harris, *Signs of Writing* (London and New York: Routledge, 1995), part 1, chapter 2, 'Integrational Semiology.'

2 Useful insights are provided in E.H. Boone and W.D. Mignolo, eds, *Writing without Words*, and W.D. Mignolo, *Darker Side of the Renaissance*.

3 A. Thevet, *La cosmographie universelle* (Paris, 1575), 2:1013v; A. Thevet, *André Thevet's North America*, 45.

4 P. Wogan, 'Perceptions of European Literacy in Early Contact Situations.'

5 JR, 59:138–41.

6 On totem poles, see M. Barbeau, *Totem Poles.*

7 G. Mallery, *Picture-Writing of the American Indians*; A. York, R. Daly, and C. Arnett, *They Write Their Dream on the Rock Forever*; S. Dewdney, *Dating Rock Art in the Canadian Shield Region.*

8 J. Vastokas, 'History without Writing.' For locations of rock etchings and paintings, see plate 15, 'Cosmology,' in R.C. Harris, *Historical Atlas of Canada*, vol. 1.

9 S. Dewdney and K.E. Kidd, *Indian Rock Paintings of the Great Lakes*; B. Hill and R. Hill, *Indian Petroglyphs of the Pacific Northwest*; G. Tassé and S. Dewdney, *Relevés et travaux récents sur l'art rupestre amérindien.*

10 J.F. Lafitau, *Customs of the American Indians*, 1:310.

11 Ibid., 2:134; J.F. Lafitau, *Mœurs des sauvages ameriquains* (Paris, 1724), 2:211.

12 W.N. Fenton, *Great Law and the Longhouse*, 224–39.

13 F. Jennings, *History and Culture of Iroquois Diplomacy*, 14–21.

14 JR, 27:280–1.

15 Marie de l'Incarnation, *Marie de l'Incarnation ... correspondance*, 253–9, letter 92.

16 J.G. Garratt, *Four Indian Kings / Les quatre rois indiens.*

17 J. Grabowski, 'Mohawk Crisis at Kanasetake and Kahnawake.'

18 S. de Champlain, *Works*, 1:153. His 1632 map also incorporated the Native information; see R.C. Harris, *Historical Atlas of Canada*, vol. 1, plate 36.

19 Baron de Lahontan, *Voyages* (1974), 2:193–6; Lahontan, *New Voyages to North-America*, 512–15.

20 C. Le Clercq, *Premier etablissement de la foy dans la Nouvelle France* (Paris, 1691) and *Nouvelle relation de la Gaspesie* (Paris, 1691). There is no evidence that the catechism, meditations, and hymns published in these hieroglyphics by the Leopold Society of Vienna in 1866 were based on Le Clercq's work.

21 P.-A.-S. Maillard, 'Lettre de M. l'Abbé Maillard sur les missions de l'Acadie.' Maillard did not acknowledge any reliance on Le Clercq's work. The Mi'kmaq may have shown him some hieroglyphic prayers. The direct link between Mi'kmaq rock etchings and the Maillard hieroglyphics is questioned in D.L. Schmidt and M. Marshall, *Mi'kmaq Hieroglyphic Prayers*, 179.

22 B. Greenfield, 'Mi'kmaq Hieroglyphic Prayer Book.' The introduction to the NA microfilm of the Miawpukek Mi'kamawey prayer book in Mi'kmaq hieroglyphics (manuscript, 1812?–92?) says this work 'drew inspiration from the aboriginal use of totemic and other mnemonic markings,' to which users added refinements over time. (A copy of this manuscript is also held at the Centre for Newfoundland Studies.)

23 C.J. Jaenen, 'Amerindian Views of French Culture in the Seventeenth Century,' especially 113–17; P. Wogan, 'Perceptions of European Literacy in Early Contact Situations.'

24 Cited in F.-M. Gagnon, *La conversion par l'image*, 16–17.

25 Marie de l'Incarnation, *Marie de l'Incarnation ... correspondance*, 117–18, letter 50; *Marie de l'Incarnation ... correspondence*, 39.

26 *JR*, 18:40–1.

27 Ibid., 17:134–5.

28 R. Ridington, 'Cultures in Conflict,' 276.

29 G. Sagard, *Histoire du Canada* (1866), 3:628–9.

30 Ibid.

31 Ibid.

32 *JR*, 5:258–9 (1633).

33 *JR*, 11:88–9 (1637).

34 Ibid., 88–91.

35 D. Martin, 'L'estampe importée en Nouvelle-France'; F.-M. Gagnon, *La conversion par l'image*. Shenwen Li places the activity of 'conversion by imagery' in a broader context in *Stratégies missionnaires des jésuites français en Nouvelle-France et en Chine au XVIIe siècle*.

36 *JR*, 11:88–9 (1637).

37 F.-M. Gagnon, *La conversion par l'image*, figure 12.

38 *RAPQ*, 1929–30, 35–7.

39 Ibid.

40 In response to this image, the Presbyterian pastor Henry Hamon Spalding made a version showing the pope walking toward the depths of hell.

2. Explorers, Travellers, Traders, and Missionaries

1 To these, we must add a great number of texts published only in the nineteenth and twentieth centuries, such as the correspondence of Mme Bégon, Perrot's *Mémoire sur les Sauvages,* and the *Annales* of the Hôtels-Dieu at Quebec and Montreal.

2 Modern republication of the great texts of New France goes back to the nineteenth century; first were the Jesuit *Relations* (Quebec, 1858; facsimile reprint, Montreal, 1972), and Champlain's

Œuvres, edited by Laverdière (Quebec, 1870; facsimile reprint, Montreal, 1973). *The Jesuit Relations and Allied Documents ... 1610–1791*, edited by Reuben Gold Thwaites (Cleveland, 1896–1901, 73 vols; facsimile reprint, New York, 1959, 36 vols) followed. Between 1907 and 1931, under the aegis of the Champlain Society of Toronto, bilingual editions of the works by Lescarbot (1907–14), Champlain (1907–36), Denys (1908), Le Clercq (1910), and Dièreville (1931) were published. More recently, Les Presses de l'Université de Montréal, in its 'Bibliothèque du Nouveau Monde' collection, republished with a considerable critical apparatus works by the following authors: Cartier (ed. M. Bideaux, 1986), Lahontan (ed. R. Ouellet and A. Beaulieu, 1990), Charlevoix (ed. P. Berthiaume, 1994), Dièreville (ed. N. Doiron, 1997), Sagard (ed. J. Warwick, 1999), Mahieu Sagean (ed. P. Berthiaume, 1999), Le Clercq (ed. R. Ouellet, 1999), and Nicolas Perrot (ed. P. Berthiaume, 2002). Finally, the Jesuit *Relations* are now in the process of being published for the third time, with many annexed documents, by Lucien Campeau in *Monumenta Novæ Franciæ*; the nine volumes that have appeared cover the period 1602–61.

3 See especially H.-J. Martin, *Livre, pouvoirs et société à Paris au XVIIe siècle (1598–1701)*; H.-J. Martin and R. Chartier, eds, *Histoire de l'édition française*.

4 B. Barbiche, 'Le régime de l'édition,' 375.

5 S. de Champlain, *Works*, 1:207–8.

6 *Voiages du R.P. Emmanuel Crespel dans le Canada, et son naufrage en revenant en France* (Frankfurt am Main, 1742; republished there in 1752 and 1757). The printers of the 1742 and 1757 editions are not mentioned; in 1752 the work was printed by Henry-Louis Broenner.

7 Baron de Lahontan, *Œuvres complètes*.

8 *Les avantures de Monsieur Robert Chevalier, dit de Beauchêne, capitaine de flibustiers dans la Nouvelle France, redigées par M. Le Sage* (2 vols, Paris, 1732); *Avantures du s. C. Le Beau, avocat en Parlement, ou Voyage curieux et nouveau parmi les Sauvages de l'Amerique septentrionale* (Amsterdam, 1738).

9 Quoted in É. Taillemite, 'Lebeau, Claude,' *DCB*, vol. 2.

10 In the case of Lebeau, I demonstrated this fact in the introduction to Lahontan, *Œuvres complètes*, 148–50. We could also refer to É. Taillemite, who saw in Lebeau's book 'an exact tableau of the customs and character of Canadiens, even though his geographical knowledge is weak' (É. Taillemite, 'Lebeau, Claude,' *DCB*, vol. 2). Closer to the truth was the *Mémoires de Trévoux*, which called it a novel. For the chapters concerning Chevalier's adventures in the West Indies, one must add the classic account by Alexandre Olivier Exquemelin, *Histoire des aventuriers*, republished a number of times since 1686.

11 M. Bideaux, 'Introduction,' in J. Cartier, *Relations*, 36–69.

12 To these editions of *L'Histoire*, one must also add two booklets of forty-eight and forty pages in length respectively, published by Jean Millot after its first edition: *La conversion des Sauvages* in 1610, and *La relation dernière de ce qui s'est passé au voyage du sieur de Poutrincourt* in 1612, both in Paris. They were republished by R.G. Thwaites in *The Jesuit Relations*, 1:49–114 and 2:121–91; also in L. Campeau, ed., *Monumenta Novæ Franciæ*, 1:60–93 and 1:168–202.

13 S. de Champlain, *Les voyages* (1613), summary of chapters, book 1.

14 Ibid., 160.

15 Ibid., 161.

16 By Claude Collet, Pierre Le Mur, and Louis Sevestre, all in Paris. There are also copies from the 1632 edition with a title page dated 1640 and the name of Claude Collet.

17 S. de Champlain, *Les voyages* (1632), title page.

18 See ibid., 638–9, and S. de Champlain, *Œuvres*, 1272. This Jesuit may have been Jean de Brébeuf or Massé.

19 L. Campeau, 'Les Jésuites ont-ils retouché les écrits de Champlain?' 341.

20 Ibid., 343.

21 Ibid., 357.

22 Either Champlain himself or someone else. For example, as Laverdière and Biggar have noted, the marginal notes do not seem to have been revised by Champlain.

23 In 1632 interest in publishing in Europe for New France began to grow with the publication of three important works: Champlain's *Les voyages*, Sagard's *Le grand voyage*, and the first *Relation* by Lejeune.

24 L. Campeau, 'Les Jésuites ont-ils retouché les écrits de Champlain?' 355.

25 On this controversy, see F. Lestringant, 'Champlain, Lescarbot et la "conférence" des histoires.'

26 See the introduction to C. Le Clercq, *Nouvelle relation de la Gaspesie*, 107–10.

27 Cited in A. Arnaud, 'Reflexions sur un livre.' The text had first been published in 1693 in volume 7 of *La morale pratique des Jésuites*.

28 See the introduction to Baron de Lahontan, *Œuvres complètes*, 25–43, 102–6, and the bibliography, 1322–47.

29 Between 1703 and 1741, there were nine true re-editions of *Nouveaux voyages* and *Memoires* and three of *Dialogues*. To these can be added translations into English, German, and Dutch.

30 *Voyages du baron de La Hontan dans l'Amerique septentrionale*, 2 vols (Amsterdam, 1705).

31 Ibid., 2:307.

32 Ibid., 2:260.

33 Ibid., 2:280.

34 Baron de Lahontan, *Œuvres complètes*, 1014.

35 In addition, many advertisements appeared in various European periodicals.

36 *Histoire des ouvrages des savans*, August 1702, 342–50; March 1704, 122–8; *Nouvelles de la république des lettres*, January 1703, 78–97; November 1703, 545–53.

37 July 1703; text reproduced in Baron de Lahontan, *Œuvres complètes*, 1109–18.

38 Baron de Lahontan, *Œuvres complètes*, 1183.

39 The seizures concerned one copy of *Nouveaux voyages* and of *Memoires* on 4 August 1704, 18 August 1705, 26 September 1710, 28 March 1715, and 21 September 1715; and six copies on 6 February 1716 (Bibliothèque nationale de France, *ms. fr.* 21 931, f. 44, 100, 133, 141, 147, 367).

40 *De philosophia Canadensium populi in America septentrionali balbutiente dissertatio quam introductioni in philosophiam*: translated by Anne-Marie Etarian as 'La philosophie balbutiante des Canadiens,' in R. Ouellet, *Sur Lahontan*, 73–97. See also the introduction to Baron de Lahontan, *Œuvres complètes*, 121.

41 Baron de Lahontan, *Œuvres complètes*, 79.

42 R. Ouellet, *Sur Lahontan*, 98–9.

43 Ibid., 99. Leibniz returned to this theme one year later, in his *Jugement sur les œuvres de M. le comte Shaftesbury*. On the links between Baron de Lahontan and Leibniz, see the introduction to Lahontan, *Œuvres complètes*, 122–4.

44 See the introduction to Baron de Lahontan, *Œuvres complètes*, 54–68 and 82–91.

45 See the precursor book by G. Chinard, *L'Amérique et le rêve exotique dans la littérature française au XVIIe et au XVIIIe siècles*.

46 R. Beaudry, 'Lescarbot, Marc,' *DCB*, vol. 1; B. Émond, '*Les muses de la Nouvelle-France*,' *DOLQ*, 1:508–10.

47 P. de Charlevoix, *Histoire et description generale de la Nouvelle France*, 1:185; *History and General Description of New France*, 1:257–8.

48 M. Lescarbot, *Les muses de la Nouvelle France* (1609), iv.

49 Ibid., 21.

50 In *Histoire de la Nouvelle France*, Lescarbot invites his audience to read *Les muses*.

51 S.P. Walsh, *Anglo-American General Encyclopedias*, 233–4.

52 R. Chartier, *Order of Books*, 28; discussed in B. Greenfield, 'Creating the Distance of Print,' 415–17.

53 See P.G. Adams, *Travel Literature and the Evolution of the Novel*; and M. Campbell, *Witness and the Other World*.

54 D. Defoe, *Compleat English Gentleman*, 225.

55 For Arctic narratives, see A. Cooke and C. Holland, *Exploration of Northern Canada*; C. Holland, *Arctic Exploration and Development*; and E. Waterston et al., *Travellers – Canada to 1900*.

56 J. Davis, *The Worldes Hydrographical Discription* (London, 1595); T. James, *The Strange and Dangerous Voyage* (London, 1633); L. Fox, *North-West Fox* (London, 1635). James's narrative is discussed at the conclusion of this chapter.

57 This work is also known as *Hakluytus Posthumus* from the engraved title page that appears in some copies.

58 See, for example, R. Hakluyt, *Hakluyt's Collection of the Early Voyages, Travels and Discoveries of the English Nation* (London, 1809–12).

59 A. and J. Churchill, *A Collection of Voyages and Travels*, 4 vols (London, 1704); J. Harris, *Navigantium atque Itinerantium Bibliotheca*, 2 vols (London, 1705).

60 A. Boyle, 'Portraiture in Lavengro II,' 366. One of the compilers of travel accounts whom Phillips retained was John Galt. Under a pseudonym, Galt prepared *All the Voyages round the World*, issued by Phillips in 1820 and 1821. See R. Hall and N. Whistler, 'Galt, John,' *DCB*, vol. 7.

61 D.D. Hall, Introduction, in H. Amory and D.D. Hall, eds, *History of the Book in America*, 1:2.

62 D.B. Quinn and T. Dunbabin, 'Ingram, David,' *DCB*, vol. 1. No copy of *A True Discourse* is known to survive.

63 D.B. Quinn, 'Madoc,' *DCB*, vol. 1.

64 Details of the de Fuca account are discussed in G. Williams, *British Search for the Northwest Passage*, 273–6.

65 A. Cooke and C. Holland, *Exploration of Northern Canada*, 30; J. Petiver, 'A Letter from Admiral Bartholomew de Fonte,' *Monthly Miscellany* 2 (April and June 1708): 123–6, 183–6. G. Williams reprinted an abridgement of Petiver's account in *British Search for the Northwest Passage*, 277–82.

66 J. Cook, *Journals*, 1:460–1.

67 I.S. MacLaren, 'Exploration/Travel Literature.' For Cook, see [J. Cook], *A Voyage to the Pacific Ocean* (London, 1784), and *Journals*.

68 I.S. MacLaren, 'Commentary,' 304–5, 381–3nn92–3; F. Fleming, *Barrow's Boys*, 123.

69 F. Fleming, *Barrow's Boys*, 8, 199, 271, 306–10.

70 See I.S. MacLaren, 'Notes on Samuel Hearne's *Journey*.'

71 Clearly, there are exceptions, among them Anna Jameson's *Winter Studies and Summer Rambles in Canada* (London, 1838).

72 A. Mackenzie, *Voyages from Montreal ... through the Continent of North America* (London, 1801). See

F. Montgomery, 'Alexander Mackenzie's Literary Assistant'; I.S. MacLaren, 'Alexander Mackenzie and the Landscapes of Commerce.'

73 Richard Glover, 'Editor's Introduction,' in S. Hearne, *Journey from the Prince of Wales's Fort*, xliii.

74 J. Robson, *An Account of Six Years Residence*, 6. For the attribution of the book's attacks on the HBC, see G. Williams, 'Arthur Dobbs and Joseph Robson,' and *Voyages of Delusion*, 215.

75 For other early books about the West, see E. Waterston et al., *Travellers – Canada to 1900*; B.B. Peel, *Peel's Bibliography of the Canadian Prairies to 1953*.

76 R. Whitbourne, *A Discourse and Discovery of New-Foundland* (London, 1620).

77 W. Alexander, Earl of Stirling, *An Encouragement to Colonies* (London, 1624); F. Gorges, *America Painted to the Life*, 4 pts (London, 1659).

78 W.D. Bollan, *The Importance and Advantage of Cape Breton* (London, 1746).

79 Nearly fifty books written by travellers interested in emigration were published before 1840. Many are listed in E. Waterston et al., *Travellers – Canada to 1900*.

80 P.-F.-X. de Charlevoix, *Journal of a Voyage to North America*, 2 vols (London, 1761).

81 On translation, see Jean Delisle's article in chapter 12. Later in the eighteenth century, books in French, such as La Rochefoucauld-Liancourt's *Voyage*, were translated into English almost immediately.

82 J. Carver, *Travels through the Interior Parts of North-America* (London, 1778), and *The New Universal Traveller* (London, 1779).

83 I. Weld, *Travels through the States of North America, and the Provinces of Upper and Lower Canada* (London, 1799).

84 G. Heriot, *Travels through the Canadas*, 254–5, 244.

85 Phillips did, however, publish three modest books from the search for the Northwest Passage – Thomas M'Keevor's *A Voyage to Hudson's Bay* (1819), Alexander Fisher's *Journal of a Voyage of Discovery, to the Arctic Regions* (1819), and the anonymous *Letters Written during the Late Voyage of Discovery in the Western Arctic Sea* (1821) – all part of his ambitious New Voyages and Travels series (1819–23). None of these met the standard either of his earlier books by Heriot and Lambert or of the Arctic books that Murray published with Barrow.

86 A. Boyle, 'Portraiture in Lavengro II,' 364.

87 R. Morrison, 'John Howison of *Blackwood's Magazine*,' 192.

88 E. Mackenzie, *An Historical, Topographical, and Descriptive Account of the United States of America, and of Upper and Lower Canada* (Newcastle upon Tyne, 1819); H. Murray, *Historical Account of Discoveries and Travels in North America*, 2 vols (London and Edinburgh, 1829).

89 F. Hall, *Travels in Canada and the United States* (London, 1818); F.F. De Roos, *Personal Narrative of Travels in the United States and Canada* (London, 1826); B. Hall, *Travels in North America* (Edinburgh, London, and Philadelphia, 1829); J.E. Alexander, *Transatlantic Sketches* (London and Philadelphia, 1833).

90 F. Trollope, *Domestic Manners of the Americans* (London and New York, 1832); A. Jameson, *Winter Studies and Summer Rambles in Canada* (London, 1838); H. Martineau, *Travels in America* (London, 1838).

91 F. Wright, *Views of Society and Manners in America* (London and New York, 1821). Two well-known women writers' works are not travel books: Frances Brooke's epistolary novel *The History of Emily Montague* (London, 1769) and Catharine Parr Traill's settler narrative *The Backwoods of Canada* (London, 1836). In 1806 Priscilla Wakefield published an account of travels

to Quebec, Montreal, and Kingston in 1793 as the letters of two men, entitled *Excursions in North America* (London), but she may never have travelled to North America.

92 P. Kalm, *Travels into North America*, 3 vols (Warrington and London, 1770); J. Bartram, *Observations on the Inhabitants, Climate ... and Other Matters ... from Pensilvania to ... the Lake Ontario in Canada* (London, 1751).

93 Munk's book preceded James's by nine years but, of course, was published in Danish.

94 For Milton, see I.S. MacLaren, 'Arctic Exploration and Milton's "frozen Continent"'; for Coleridge, see J.L. Lowes, *Road to Xanadu*, 121–3, 129–30, 155; for Boyle, see A. Cooke, 'James, Thomas,' *DCB*, vol. 1.

95 T. James, *Strange and Dangerous Voyage*, [135]. Indeed, almost a century would pass after James's voyage and book before England resumed its search for a Northwest Passage.

96 Ibid., 39.

3. The Book in New France

1 The suggestion that Bishop Henri-Marie Dubreil de Pontbriand had a portable press has now been completely discredited. See J. Hare and J.-P. Wallot, 'Les imprimés au Québec (1760–1820).'

2 P. Kalm, *Voyage*, f. 758; Marie de l'Incarnation to the Mother of Saint-Joseph, 12 September 1670, cited in Marie de l'Incarnation, *Correspondance*, 883; J. Navières to Mademoiselle Navières de Deschamps, October 1737, cited in J. Navières, *Lettres inédites*, 13.

3 D. de Ledesma, *Doctrine chrestienne* (Paris, 1632); see J. Sabin, *Bibliotheca Americana*, 10:163; reprinted in Samuel de Champlain, *Les voyages de la Nouvelle France occidentale* (Paris, 1632). Following Father Jean de Brébeuf's translation is Father Énemond Massé's translation into Montagnais of the Dominican oratory texts.

4 Already confirmed by missions in Asia and South America; see G.A. Bailey, *Art on the Jesuit Missions in Asia and Latin America*.

5 C.-H. Laverdière and H.-R. Casgrain, eds, *Journal des jésuites*, 335; L. Tronson to F. Vachon de Belmont, [1683], cited in A. Fauteux, *L'introduction de l'imprimerie au Canada*, 4; NA, MG 1, Series B, vol. 89, President of the Conseil de la Marine to the Marquis de La Jonquière, 4 May 1749, fol. 68v; NA, MG 1, Series C11A, vol. 97, Extracts of letter from de La Jonquière and Bigot, 1751, fol. 260v. For a more in-depth look at these projects, see F. Melançon, 'La circulation du livre au Canada sous la domination française.'

6 Archives de la paroisse Sainte-Anne-de-Varennes, Livre de comptes, 1725 à 1899, in M. Filion, *Paroisse Sainte-Anne-de-Varennes, 1692–1992*, 40; Archives de la paroisse Notre-Dame de Montréal, 'Compte rendu du marguillier Pierre Guy,' 1741, and 'Compte rendu du marguillier Jacques Charly,' 1742, cited in É.-Z. Massicotte, 'Libraires-papetiers-relieurs à Montréal au XVIIIe siècle,' 298; Archives des ursulines de Québec, Journal de recette & dépense de 1715 à 1746.

7 [L. Ango des Maizerets], *La solide dévotion à la Très-Sainte Famille*; C. Glandelet, *Office de la Sainte Famille*. There are no known extant copies of the latter.

8 J.-B. de Saint-Vallier, *Catéchisme du diocèse de Québec* (Paris, 1702); *Rituel du diocèse de Québec* (Paris, 1703); J.-B. de Saint-Vallier, *Statuts, ordonnances, et lettres pastorales* (Paris, 1703).

9 NA, MG 1, Series C11A, vol. 92, Letter from Bigot to the minister, Quebec, 25 October 1748, fol. 117–19; ibid., vol. 93, 25 October 1749, fol. 301–302v.

10 A. Fauteux, 'Bataille de vers autour d'une tombe.'

11 Baron de Lahontan, *Nouveaux voyages de Mr le baron de Lahontan, dans l'Amerique septentrionale* (La Haye, 1703); L. Hennepin, *Nouvelle decouverte d'un tres grand pays situé dans l'Amerique* (Utrecht, 1697); C. Lebeau, *Avantures du Sr. C. Le Beau* (Amsterdam, 1738); C.-C. Bacqueville de La Potherie, *Histoire de l'Amérique septentrionale* (Paris, 1722).

12 NA, MG 1, Series C11A, vol. 37, Declaration of the Conseil de la Marine, [Versailles], 18 June 1717, fol. 247–247v; ibid., vol. 50, Letter from Beauharnois to the minister, Quebec, 1 October 1728, fol. 91–2.

13 See letters 3, 49, and 57, in L. Tronson, *Correspondance*, vol. 1.

14 F. Moureau, ed., *De bonne main*; H. Love, *Culture and Commerce of Texts*.

15 NA, MG 1, Series C11A, vol. 38, Letter from Vaudreuil and Bégon to the Conseil de la Marine, 6 November 1717, fol. 57; ibid., vol. 59, Letter from Beauharnois and Hocquart to the minister, 3 October 1733, fol. 103.

16 Ibid., vol. 96, Letter from Bigot to the minister, 10 October 1750, fol. 32.

17 When it managed to shake off these restrictions, American print was often in the form of diplomatic or military newspapers inquiring into the affairs of the neighbours up and down the continent's east coast. For more on the situation in the British colonies in North America, see J. Raven, 'Importation of Books during the Eighteenth Century.'

18 See, for example, J.-C. Dubé, *Les intendants de la Nouvelle-France*, 199–220; J.-E. Roy, 'Notes sur Mgr de Lauberivière,' 8–9.

19 This is a considerable number of purchasers (281), given the number of book owners (314) revealed in the city's post-mortem inventories for the same period; see G. Proulx, *Les Québécois et le livre, 1690–1760*, 45.

20 ANQQ, greffe J.-B. Decharnay, Inventory of goods belonging to Louis-Guillaume Verrier, 10 January 1759.

21 ANQQ, greffe J.-A. Saillant, Inventory of goods belonging to Jean Lemoine, 8 March 1751; greffe L. Chambalon, Inventory of the community of goods of the late Pierre Pellerin de Saint-Amand and Louise des Mousseaux, 5 March 1704; ibid., Inventory of the community of goods belonging to Claude Pauperet, 7 April 1707.

22 N.Z. Davis, 'Beyond the Market.'

23 See H.-M. Boudon, *Œuvres complètes*, vol. 3, col. 128ff; F.-X. Duplessis, *Lettres*, 196, 205, 216–17, 237, 242–3, 250–1.

24 N.-M. Dawson, *Le catéchisme de Sens en France et au Québec*, 33–41.

25 A. Maheux, 'La bibliothèque du missionnaire Davion au dix-huitième siècle'; Laboret, '[Liste d]es livres que jaz apporté de Paris à la grand pré dans l'acadie,' in Centre d'études acadiennes, Saint Charles-aux-Mines, Registre des baptêmes, mariages et sépultures de l'église, 5 juillet 1739 – 10 novembre 1748; R. Brun, *Pionnier de la nouvelle Acadie*, 32; R. Olivier, *Philippe Boucher, curé en Nouvelle-France*; P.-G. Roy, 'Bibliothèque de l'abbé Nicolas Boucher, curé de St-Jean de l'Ile d'Orléans,' 157–9; P.-G. Roy, 'La bibliothèque du curé Portneuf'; B. Haché and M. McClaughlin, 'Le livre en Acadie avant 1840.'

26 See the first surveys: A. Roy, *Les lettres, les sciences et les arts au Canada*; A. Drolet, *Les bibliothèques canadiennes*. For more in-depth studies, see G. Proulx, *Les Québécois et le livre 1690–1760*; G. Proulx, *Les bibliothèques de Louisbourg*; L. Dechêne, *Habitants et marchands de Montréal au XVIIe siècle*, 386, 391, 468, and 476; M. Robert, 'Le livre et la lecture dans la noblesse canadienne,

1670–1764'; L. Lavoie, 'La vie intellectuelle et les activités culturelles à la forteresse de Louisbourg, 1713–1758.'

27 G. Proulx, *Loisirs québécois*, 44.

28 Ibid., 82ff.; F. Melançon, 'La migration d'un objet culturel.'

29 M. Laurent, 'Le catalogue de la bibliothèque du Séminaire de Québec.'

30 F. LeFebvre, 'La bibliothèque des frères Charon.'

31 Schooling was not uniformly available throughout the colony. In sparsely populated areas, there were few schools, convents, or private tutors; even where these existed in greater numbers, not everyone attended. Populations in the towns enjoyed many educational opportunities, and some people took greater advantage of these privileges than others; see R. Magnuson, *Education in New France*.

32 For the debates surrounding intensive reading and other reading styles, see G. Cavallo and R. Chartier, *Histoire de la lecture dans le monde occidental*.

33 Musée de la civilisation, Québec, Fonds Séminaire de Québec, Séminaire 95, no. 23, 'Reglement particulier,' [après 1692], 16.

34 Baron de Lahontan, *Nouveaux voyages dans l'Amérique septentrionale*, in *Œuvres complètes*, 1:314.

35 É. Bégon, *La correspondance*, 195.

36 P. Kalm, *Voyage de Pehr Kalm au Canada en 1749* (f. 718), p. 239.

37 A. Drolet, 'La bibliothèque du Collège des jésuites.'

4. Mapping Innovation

1 PRO, CO 221, vol. 28, f. 136.

2 H. Amory, 'New England Book Trade,' 315.

3 Biographies of many of the individuals discussed here appear in the *DCB*. Imprints are described in Tremaine, *ECP*, and the other standard bibliographies. For eighteenth-century newspapers, see Tremaine, pp. 594–653.

4 Nova Scotia, Governor, 1752–6 (Hopson), *Une proclamation* (Halifax, 1753): *ECP* 5A.

5 Nova Scotia, Treaties, *Treaty/Traite* (Halifax, 1753): Tremaine/*ECP* 9.

6 Nova Scotia, House of Assembly, *Journal* (Halifax, 1758): Tremaine/*ECP* 17.

7 Nova Scotia, Laws, statutes, etc., *Acts* (Halifax, 1759): Tremaine/*ECP* 19.

8 W. Doyle, *The Universal Prayer* (Halifax, 1770): Tremaine/*ECP* 146.

9 P. Delaroche, *The Gospel of Christ Preached to the Poor* (Halifax, 1773): Tremaine 177.

10 Tremaine 119; Tremaine/*ECP* 503.

11 Transcribed in *ECP*, pp. 416–511.

12 R. Burn, *Le juge à paix* (Montreal, 1789): Tremaine/*ECP* 583.

13 R.W. McLachlan, 'Fleury Mesplet,' 268–70, 280–302.

14 Tremaine, pp. 653–6.

15 *An Almanack, for the Year of Our Lord, 1806* (Halifax, 1805): Fleming Atl. NS34.

16 Fleming Atl. NS41.

17 Tremaine, pp. 612–17; see also *ECP* 426A.

18 J.N. Green, 'English Books and Printing,' 294.

19 Tremaine, p. 597.

20 Also spelled Sauer or Saur.

21 *The British American Almanack* (Saint John, 1791): Tremaine/ECP 688.

22 St John, Island of, Laws, statutes, etc., *Acts* (Charlotte-Town, 1789): Tremaine 619.

23 'Prince Edward Island Calendar' (Fleming Atl., p. 160).

24 P. O'Flaherty, 'Ryan, John,' *DCB*, vol. 7.

25 Benevolent Irish Society (St John's), *Report* (1807), *Rules and Constitution* (1807), *Appendix* (1808); Society for Improving the Condition of the Poor (St John's), *An Account* (1808): Fleming Atl. Nfld1–4.

26 Upper Canada, Lieutenant-Governor, 1791–9 (Simcoe), *A Proclamation* (Quebec, 1792): Tremaine/ECP 815.

27 Upper Canada, Lieutenant-Governor, 1791–9 (Simcoe), *Speech* (Newark, 1793): Tremaine 863.

28 R. Cockrel, *Thoughts on the Education of Youth* (Newark, 1795): Tremaine 929.

29 B. Peel, *Rossville Mission Press*, 9.

30 For information on the Robertsons, see especially NSARM, MG 100, vol. 214, no. 23; NAS, CS96/4286, Sequestration of James Robertson, 1808; M. Robertson, 'The Loyalist Printers: James and Alexander Robertson'; D.C. McMurtrie, *Royalist Printers at Shelburne, Nova Scotia*; F.L. Pigot, 'Robertson, James,' *DCB*, vol. 5; C.S. Humphrey, 'Robertson, James,' *American National Biography*, 18:624–5. On the Robertsons' Loyalist claims, see PRO, AO 13/116 and AO 13/19, March to July 1784, and AO 13/137, no. 522–5, March 1790.

31 Tremaine, pp. 614–17.

32 For Robertson's imprints in Shelburne and Charlottetown, see Tremaine and *ECP*.

33 Tremaine, pp. 646–7.

34 PRO, CO 226/12, 377–79, Gov. Fanning to Lord Sydney, 6 December 1788; 420, Lord Grenville to Fanning, 20 October 1789.

35 G. Palmer, *Bibliography of Loyalist Source Material in the United States, Canada and Great Britain*, 819.

36 Louis-Généreux Labadie used the *Quebec Gazette / La Gazette de Québec* in class in the late eighteenth century; see NA, MG 24, B 1, vol. 1, 1791. The *New-Brunswick Courier* of 2 May 1811 invited its readers to use the newspaper to learn to read among the family; see G.L. Parker, *Beginnings of the Book Trade in Canada*, 23. For the *Christian Guardian*, see J. Stabile, 'The Economics of an Early Nineteenth-Century Toronto Newspaper Shop,' 59.

37 Experienced pressmen and typographers were much in demand, received high wages, worked all year round, and moved often. The correspondence of the Neilson printing office contains innumerable references to their instability; see J. Hare and J.-P. Wallot, 'Les imprimés au Québec (1760–1820),' 92 and 100.

38 C. Galarneau, 'Les métiers du livre à Québec (1764–1859),' 145–6.

39 In 1775 William Brown published four legal works by François-Joseph Cugnet for the government. In spite of a promise of payment by May, he had to wait until November (Tremaine 197). Brown waited six months before receiving the £106 10s 8d owed him by the government (Warrant, 10 October 1784, private collection).

40 Samuel Neilson printed 9,000 catechisms in 1792; see J.-P. Wallot, 'Frontière ou fragment du système atlantique ,' 11. In Halifax in 1816, 7,253 books were distributed by missionaries; see G.L. Parker, *Beginnings of the Book Trade in Canada*, 20.

41 See C. Galarneau, 'Les métiers du livre à Québec (1764–1859),' 149–50.

42 See ANQQ, P 193/19, 'Salaires des employés.'

43 The Neilson family lost the exclusive rights to government contracts in 1823 when John

became politically active; see G. Gallichan, *Livre et politique au Bas-Canada, 1791–1849*, 115–22; see also G. Gallichan's discussion of political censorship in chapter 13.

44 'Requête de Mesplet au Congrès des États-Unis en date du 1er août 1783,' cited in R.W. McLachlan, 'Fleury Mesplet,' 251.

45 For Mesplet, see R.W. McLachlan, 'Fleury Mesplet'; for Neilson, see his payroll book in ANQQ, P 193/19, and C. Galarneau, 'Les métiers du livre à Québec (1764–1859),' 157; on Mackenzie, see P. Fleming, 'William Lyon Mackenzie as Printer,' 13–17.

46 J. Hare and J.-P. Wallot, 'Les imprimés au Québec (1760–1820),' 80–1. Impressive quantities of handbills and forms, most of them lost, were also produced; see the studies in chapter 10 by Patricia Lockhart Fleming and Patricia Kennedy. Surviving examples of single-sheet imprints recorded in the HBiC/HLIC database, discussed in this chapter by Sandra Alston and Jessica Bowslaugh, more than double the totals of books and pamphlets discussed here.

47 Thus, Neilson printed the *Journal de la Chambre d'Assemblée* between 31 January and 7 August 1801; see J. Hare and J.-P. Wallot, *Les imprimés dans le Bas-Canada, 1801–1810*, 99–100.

48 M.M. Beck, 'Howe, John,' *DCB*, vol. 6, and 'Howe, Joseph,' *DCB*, vol. 10.

49 S. Chassé, R. Girard-Wallot, and J.-P. Wallot, 'Neilson, John,' *DCB*, vol. 7.

50 Ibid. In 1848 the stock in the Neilson printing shop and bookstore alone was worth £2,717 7s 7d.

51 The inventory of the Neilsons' community of property, made almost twenty years after John's death, still listed £30,143 6s 8d of debts owing and £692 in personal estate, against only £25 in liabilities (ibid.).

52 J.-M. Lebel, 'Duvernay, Ludger,' *DCB*, vol. 8.

53 F.H. Armstrong and R.J. Stagg, 'Mackenzie, William Lyon,' *DCB*, vol. 9; Fleming UC 479, 531, and 715.

54 Tremaine 77, 146.

55 L. Lacourcière, 'Aubert de Gaspé, fils [1814–1841].'

56 Tremaine 549, 583.

57 Prospectus for *Hamilton; and Other Poems* (Toronto, 1840) in *Hamilton Gazette*, 13 January 1840; Fleming UC 1330.

58 Fleming UC 219.

59 *Quebec Gazette*, 11 September 1839; *Western Herald*, 18 September 1839.

60 *Cobourg Star*, 5 February 1834.

61 W. Doyle, *Universal Prayer* (Halifax, 1770): Tremaine 146.

62 R. Jones, *Remarques sur la maladie contagieuse de la Baie Saint Paul* (Montreal, 1787): Tremaine 517.

63 *Bee* (Pictou), 12 August 1834.

64 Tremaine 476; 'The Canadian Surveyor' had been proposed the year before: Tremaine 470.

65 *Gleaner, and Niagara Newspaper*, 5 August 1819.

66 *Gazette* (Montreal), 6 October 1828.

67 'The Legend' is mentioned in the *Canadian Courant* (Montreal), 10 February 1830. The 'History of Canada' is known only because of published complaints by those who had paid five shillings in advance; see the *Morning Courier* (Montreal), 12 March 1838, and the *Quebec Gazette*, 5 February 1840. A prospectus for Hawley's *Quebec, the Harp, and Other Poems* (Montreal, 1829) appeared in the Montreal *Gazette*, 2 July 1829.

68 C. Galarneau, 'Les métiers du livre à Québec (1764–1859),' 145.

69 The only extant directories for the town of Quebec are for the years 1790, 1791, 1792, 1822, and 1826 (DAUL, P 282).

70 C. Galarneau, 'Les métiers du livre à Québec (1764–1859),' 144–8; M. Allodi and R. Tovell, *An Engraver's Pilgrimage.*

71 C. Galarneau, 'Les métiers du livre à Québec (1764–1859),' 148–9. The research archives on printing and the book trades assembled by Claude Galarneau can be consulted at DAUL, P 282.

72 C. Galarneau, 'Les Desbarats: Une dynastie d'imprimeurs-éditeurs (1794–1893),' 130.

73 J.-M. Lebel, 'Lefrançois, Charles,' *DCB*, vol. 6.

74 J.-P. de Lagrave, *L'époque de Voltaire au Canada*, 199.

75 'À vendre,' *Gazette du commerce et littéraire*, 28 April 1779.

76 In 1781 Marie Mirabeau worked with Edward William Gray, who was also from Philadelphia; see *ECP*, p. 518.

77 J.-P. de Lagrave, *L'époque de Voltaire au Canada*, 199. Marie Mirabeau also did bookbinding; see Tremaine 331, 351, 354, 355.

78 J.-P. Hardy and D.-T. Ruddel, *Les apprentis artisans à Québec 1660–1815*, 99–113.

79 J.-F. Caron, 'Les apprentis à Québec de 1830 à 1849,' 71, 77, 102–8.

80 *ECP*, p. 420. William Brown also occasionally hired printers by the day, and he owned a black slave named Joe, who worked as a pressman in his shop; see T.P. Lemay, 'Joe,' *DCB*, vol. 4.

81 In York (Toronto) in 1826, William Lyon Mackenzie also paid his apprentices £15; see P. Fleming, 'Canadian Printer's Apprentice in 1826,' 14.

82 ANQQ, P 193/19, 'Salaire des employés'; J.-F. Caron, 'Les apprentis à Québec de 1830 à 1849,' 71.

83 C. Galarneau, 'Les métiers du livre à Québec (1764–1859),' 153–4.

84 Ibid., 154.

85 Ibid.

86 P. Fleming, 'Printing Trade in Toronto: 1798–1841,' 63.

87 For example, see *Quebec Gazette / La Gazette de Québec*, 15 April 1802, supplement, and *Le Canadien*, 31 January 1834.

88 E. Hulse, *Dictionary of Toronto Printers, Publishers, Booksellers*, 162.

89 M. Brisebois, *The Printing of Handbills in Quebec City 1764–1800*, xxv–xxviii.

90 For an account of Thomson's career, see H.P. Gundy, 'Thomson, Hugh Christopher,' *DCB*, vol. 6.

91 Fleming UC 598.

92 AO, F 4269. The *Herald* was published from 1819 to 1851. This ledger is marked 'C.'

93 NA, RG 5, A 1, vol. 75, pp. 39882–90, John Macaulay to George Hillier, 1825.

94 Most of these items have not been located; for imprints from the *Herald* office that are known, see the index in Fleming UC.

95 Fleming UC 572.

96 The period to 1800 for British North America as a whole has been documented by Marie Tremaine's *A Bibliography of Canadian Imprints, 1751–1800*, supplemented by Patricia Lockhart Fleming and Sandra Alston's *Early Canadian Printing*. For subsequent years, Fleming has covered Upper Canada in her *Upper Canadian Imprints, 1801–1841* and the Atlantic provinces in *Atlantic Canadian Imprints, 1801–1820*. Milada Vlach and Yolande Buono's *Catalogue collectif des impressions québécoises, 1764–1820* records the holdings of twelve Quebec libraries.

97 The 'Canadian Imprints to 1840 / Imprimés canadiens avant 1840' database is a research project of the History of the Book in Canada / Histoire du livre et de l'imprimé au Canada which has attempted to compile a record of all Canadian imprints, except for newspapers, for the years 1752–1840. Entries drawn from the bibliographies and catalogues cited in note 96 have been supplemented by catalogue records from a number of libraries, including the Bibliothèque nationale du Québec and the University of Toronto (two databases that allowed Z35.50 searching in imprint data), records from the Canadian Institute for Historical Microreproductions, and a data file from the National Library of Canada. The HBiC/HLIC project is indebted to Elaine Hoag (National Library of Canada) and Suzanne Ledoux (Bibliothèque nationale du Québec) for identifying imprints and providing records from their institutions' catalogues. The 'Canadian Imprints to 1840 / Imprimés canadiens avant 1840' database is available at the HBiC/HLIC website.

98 H. Amory, Appendix 1, 'A Note on Statistics,' in H. Amory and D.D. Hall, eds, *A History of the Book in America*, 1:504–18.

99 G.T. Tanselle, 'Some Statistics on American Printing, 1764–1783.'

100 Records in the database contain author and title information; as full an imprint as could be ascertained from the sources available; attribution of the place of publication, if only at the provincial level; date of printing; and one of twelve generic subjects.

101 The same chronological division has been applied to the analysis of newspapers in chapter 10.

102 One hundred of the 3,497 Lower Canadian imprints are attributed only to that province, with no town or city identified.

103 Three other towns had newspapers but no known imprints.

5. The Material Book

1 J. Bidwell, 'Printers' Supplies and Capitalization.'

2 NA, MG 24, B 1, vols 49, 50, 7 June 1764.

3 NA, MG 24, B 1, vol. 49, 20 June 1767.

4 J. Bidwell, 'Printers' Supplies and Capitalization,' 168.

5 R.W. McLachlan, 'Fleury Mesplet,' 269.

6 NA, MG 24, B 1, vol. 49, end of April 1772; vol. 100, 10 May 1773; vol. 102, 1 and 25 August 1774.

7 NA, RG 5, A 1, vol. 19, pp. 8350–2; quoted in Fleming UC 88.

8 B. Dewalt, *Technology and Canadian Printing*, 24–9.

9 AO, F 37, Bruce to Mackenzie, 24 April 1830.

10 *Colonial Advocate*, 28 November 1833.

11 B. Dewalt, *Technology and Canadian Printing*, 27; M. Lemire, ed., *La vie littéraire au Québec*, 2:188.

12 *Royal Standard*, 11 November 1836.

13 D.C. Harvey, 'Newspapers of Nova Scotia,' 289.

14 G. Carruthers, *Paper in the Making*; for the Belleville mill, see AO, F 4269, 335.

15 P.L. Fleming, 'Paper Evidence,' 34–5.

16 Upper Canada, House of Assembly, *Journal: Appendix* (1831), 177: Fleming UC 579.

17 Upper Canada, House of Assembly, *Journal: Appendix* (1835),[11] 22: Fleming UC 887.

18 *Colonial Advocate*, 11 October 1832; *Constitution*, 13 September 1837.

19 L. Chéné, 'Brown, James,' *DCB*, vol. 7.

20 G. Tratt, 'Holland, Anthony Henry,' *DCB*, vol. 6; Fleming Atl. NS183.

21 W. Phillips, *A New and Concise System of Arithmetic* (York, 1833), 28: Fleming UC 723.

22 Fleming UC 898.

23 NA, MG 24, B 1, vol. 172, 4907.

24 *The Directory for the City and Suburbs of Quebec* (Quebec, 1790): Tremaine 650.

25 Tremaine 544.

26 *A New Almanack for the Canadian True Blues* (York, 1834): Fleming UC 715.

27 Séminaire de Québec, *Le monde démasqué*: Tremaine 214.

28 NA, MG 24, B 1, vol. 49, 24 June 1765.

29 Ibid., 29 November 1766.

30 Ibid., 31 December 1765.

31 Thomas Fisher Rare Book Library, University of Toronto, MS coll. 131, box 22, Francis Gore, 27 February 1817.

32 Fleming UC 242.

33 *ECP* 17, 19, 63; for the ship cut, see the *Halifax Gazette*, 31 October to 7 November 1766.

34 *L'écu de six francs*: Tremaine 416.

35 Agricultural Society in Canada, Quebec Branch, *Papers and Letters on Agriculture / Papiers et lettres sur l'agriculture* (Quebec, 1790): Tremaine 623; *Quebec Almanack / Almanac de Québec* (Quebec, 1794): Tremaine 869.

36 NA, MG 24, B 1, vol. 177, 6490.

37 *An Introduction to Greek Declension*: Fleming UC 708.

38 John Larkin, *Eklekta Mythistorias*.

39 E. Hulse, 'Printer Writes Home,' 6.

40 NA, MG 24, B 1; ANQM, P 1000-3-360; ANQQ, P 192, 193.

41 The volumes are described and listed in *ECP*, pp. 417–21. Brown's wage book is NA, MG 24, B 1, vol. 88, file 2.

42 Examples are found in *ECP* 200, 268, 280, 281, 332, 335, 337, 495, 623, 661.

43 Tremaine/*ECP* 197–200; the fourth volume is *Extraits des edits, declarations, ordonnances et reglemens*. All were published at Quebec 'Chez Guillaume Brown' in 1775.

44 Since the unit of work for a printer was the sheet of paper to be put on the press, each sheet was lettered in alphabetical order, a marking that would then be used by the binder to assemble the folded sheets, or gatherings, in correct sequence. For Cugnet in quarto format, each sheet of paper was printed with eight pages of text, four per side, and then folded twice to make a gathering of four leaves or eight pages.

45 'Cuesta Profile,' 33.

46 See G. Carruthers, *Paper in the Making*, for other mills.

47 P.L. Fleming, 'Paper Evidence,' 25.

48 T.M. Bailey, 'Crooks, James T.,' *Dictionary of Hamilton Biography*, 1:55. See also D. Ouellette, 'Crooks, James,' *DCB*, vol. 7.

49 'United States paper comes to this Province duty free. If the government had offered liberal encouragement to a paper maker, he would have saved us £3000, Halifax, a year' (*Colonial Advocate*, 3 June 1824).

50 *Colonial Advocate*, 23 March 1826, and *Niagara Gleaner*, 30 March 1826.

51 AO, F 37, James Crooks to W.L. Mackenzie, 10 April 1826. J.A. Blyth, however, states that the mill was erected by Irish immigrant Joseph Barber ('The Development of the Paper Industry,' 126–8).

52 Crooks had to 'go all the way to Jersey' to obtain the equipment. See AO, F 37, James Crooks to W.L. Mackenzie, 16 May 1826.

53 NA, RG 5, A 1, vol. 78, p. 42216, Crooks to Hillier, 18 July 1826. Crooks inquires why his earlier submission of the certificate has not been acknowledged. No reply from Hillier has been located.

54 NA, RG 1, E 3, vol. 14, p. 27, 19 September 1826.

55 *Colonial Advocate*, 2 September 1826; *Niagara Gleaner*, 23 September 1826.

56 NA, RG 1, E 3, vol. 14, p. 28, 5 October 1826.

57 The samples survive in ibid., pp. 30–5. The cream-coloured, trimmed paper is two sizes, likely foolscap and half-sheets of small royal or imperial.

58 Ibid., p. 30, 26 December 1826.

59 James Crooks to William Hands, 7 February 1827, quoted in N.L. Edwards, 'Establishment of Papermaking,' 72.

60 Quoted in N.L. Edwards, 'Establishment of Papermaking,' 72.

61 Mackenzie states: 'We are glad to learn that Mr. Crooks is getting customers for printing paper in Montreal' (quoted in P.L. Fleming, 'Paper Evidence,' 30).

62 *Colonial Advocate*, 26 July 1827.

63 J.A. Blyth, 'Development of the Paper Industry,' 128.

64 M. Allodi, *Printmaking in Canada*. I have relied heavily on this indispensable source for information on separate prints and on engraving and lithography in the period.

65 Tremaine/*ECP* 224.

66 H. Piers and D.C. Mackay, *Master Goldsmiths and Silversmiths of Nova Scotia and Their Marks*, 157–8.

67 Tremaine/*ECP* 251.

68 L. Letocha, 'Le premier livre illustré imprimé au Québec,' 5–7; and L. Dusseault-Letocha, 'Les origines de l'art de l'estampe au Québec,' 51ff.

69 Tremaine 503. Henry implies in the introduction that he would have imported the woodcuts with his German types if he had realized that 'such things could not be properly made [locally].'

70 Tremaine/*ECP* 751, 824.

71 *The Trials of George Frederick Boutelier and John Boutelier, for the Murder of Frederick Eminaud* (1791): Tremaine/*ECP* 697.

72 L. Dusseault-Letocha, 'Les origines de l'art de l'estampe au Québec,' 89–95; Tremaine/*ECP* 374. See also Tremaine/*ECP* 394.

73 Tremaine/*ECP* 980, 1162.

74 *The Holy Bible* (Hallowell [Picton], 1834): Fleming UC 760; Amos Blanchard, *Book of Martyrs* (Kingston, 1835): Fleming UC 823.

75 R. Sagendorph, *America and Her Almanacs*, 240–1.

76 *ECP*, p. 419.

77 Tremaine 630.

78 Tremaine 695.

79 M. Allodi, *Printmaking in Canada*, 13–23, and personal communication.

80 M. Allodi and R.L. Tovell, *Engraver's Pilgrimage*.

81 M. Allodi, *Printmaking in Canada*, 80–1.

82 J. Winearls, 'Printing and Publishing of Maps in Ontario before Confederation,' 59–61; M. Allodi, *Printmaking in Canada*, 91–2.

83 A.E. Davis, *Art and Work*, 36.

84 Quebec, Province, Legislative Council, *Ancient French Archives / Anciennes archives françaises*: Tremaine 734.

85 *Nova Scotia Chronicle and Weekly Advertiser*, 17–24 January 1769.

86 [Primer] (Quebec, 1765): Tremaine 65.

87 Catholic Church, *Catechisme du diocèse de Sens* (Quebec, 1765): Tremaine 59.

88 Nova Scotia, Laws, *The Temporary Acts* (Halifax, 1767): Tremaine 114.

89 Eighteenth- and nineteenth-century bindings are described in *ECP*, Fleming UC, and Fleming Atl.; some of this material was also compiled in an unpublished paper on book-binding in Canada prepared for the National Museum of Science and Technology by Patricia Lockhart Fleming (1995).

90 R.J. Wolfe, *Marbled Paper*, plate 25 for comb patterns and plate 10 for German papers.

91 NA, MG 24, B 1, vol. 94, no. 2.

92 P.H. Humbert, *Instructions chrétiennes* (Quebec, 1799): Tremaine 1126.

93 NA, MG 24, B 1, vol. 49, 9 and 10 June 1766.

94 Agricultural Society in Canada, Quebec Branch, *Papers and Letters on Agriculture / Papiers et lettres sur l'agriculture* (Quebec, 1790): Tremaine 623.

95 Tremaine/ECP 231.

96 *Gazette du commerce et littéraire*, 24 February 1779.

97 ECP 251, 282.

98 Fleming UC 949, 1323, 1551, 1554.

99 D. Ball, *Victorian Publishers' Bindings*.

100 J. Simpson, *The Canadian Forget Me Not* (Niagara, 1837): Fleming UC 1136.

6. Commercial Networks

1 NSARM, MG 1, no. 526A, entry for 6 June 1795.

2 Ibid., entry for 3 October 1795: 'Read the Banish'd Man till Bed time.'

3 F.A. Black, 'Book Availability in Canada, 1752–1820.'

4 F.A. Black, 'Beyond Boundaries.'

5 For the French connection, see Y. Lamonde, 'La librairie Hector Bossange,' 80.

6 5 Geo. III [1765], c. 25.

7 J.E. Harrison, *Until Next Year*.

8 NSARM, MG 1, no. 526A, entry for 1 July 1795.

9 J.N. Green, 'From Printer to Publisher,' 29.

10 Quetton St George advertised at least two such shipments to York in 1804; see *Upper Canada Gazette*, 15 September and 15 December 1804.

11 *Montreal Herald*, 22 May 1819.

12 *Nova Scotia Royal Gazette*, 17 April 1806.

13 For example, see T. Fairbairn's advertisement in the Halifax *Free Press*, 20 July 1819.

14 NLS, MS 791, Archibald Constable, Letter-book, 1820–2, Constable to John Young, Halifax, 26 March 1821.

15 Ibid., Constable to Archibald McQueen, Miramichi, 19 August 1820.

16 J. Raven, *Judging New Wealth*, 13.

17 Ibid., 21.

18 This weight, using McDougall's method of calculation, represents approximately 89,000 volumes; see W. McDougall, 'Copyright Litigation in the Court of Session,' 15. It is possible that some of the thousands of volumes sent to Nova Scotia were being transshipped to ports in the Thirteen Colonies or the West Indies.

19 The customs data are held, in varying formats, at PRO, CUST 14/1-23; and NAS, E504. The annual summary accounts from which they are drawn did not detail which port the books were being sent to, simply which colony.

20 Glasgow University, Special Collections, Eph N/139, advertising broadside for MacGoun's Stationery Warehouse. Through the Scottish Book Trade Index, this firm has been linked to Archibald MacGoun Jr, who was at the stated address from 1797 to 1800.

21 C.A. Andreae, *Lines of Country*, 3.

22 Evidence drawn from pre-1820 British North American newspaper announcements of ship arrivals.

23 *Nova Scotia Royal Gazette*, 20 August 1801.

24 *Montreal Gazette / Gazette de Montréal*, 10 December 1810.

25 R. Lemoine, 'Le marché du livre à Québec,' 165.

26 *Upper Canada Gazette*, 15 December 1804, p. 4, advertised by Quetton St George; and *Kingston Gazette*, 16 January 1813, p. 3, advertised by H. Spafford & Co.

27 NSARM, MG 3, vol. 236, Horton's Landing, King's County, Account Book, 1793–4; Colchester Historical Society Archives, D13, 89.37, James Patterson, Account and Day-book, 1802–3; NSARM, mf. 13512, Windsor Account Book, 1778–[82?].

28 *Nova Scotia Royal Gazette*, 17 April 1806.

29 J. Raven, 'Establishing and Maintaining Credit Lines Overseas,' 144–62 passim.

30 Ibid.

31 NAS, GD 1/151, James Dunlop to Alexander Dunlop, 16 December 1798.

32 J. Raven, 'Establishing and Maintaining Credit Lines Overseas,' 144.

33 Ibid., 154.

34 An example concerning the acceptability of payment in produce is an advertisement by the printer John Bennett in the *Upper Canada Gazette*, 28 April 1804. Rags were requested in the *Kingston Gazette*, 30 October 1810. Grain was requested by Mower and Kendall, printers of the *Kingston Gazette*, for their agent in York, Quetton St George; see *Kingston Gazette*, 19 February 1811.

35 W. McDougall, 'Scottish Books for America,' 25–7.

36 Cf. Canada, Customs Department, *Trade and Navigation, Unrevised Monthly Statements*.

37 For example, *Acadian Recorder*, 3 June 1815.

38 Ibid.

39 J. Raven, 'Establishing and Maintaining Credit Lines Overseas,' 150–1.

40 See, for example, the merchants Brymer and Belcher's advertisement, *Royal Gazette and Nova Scotia Advertiser*, 9 March 1790.

41 *Nova Scotia Gazette and Weekly Chronicle*, 7 May 1771.

42 J.R. Johnson, 'Availability of Reading Material for the Pioneer in Upper Canada,' 132.

43 M. Lajeunesse, 'Le livre dans les échanges sulpiciens Paris-Montréal.'

44 J. Feather, 'The English Book Trade and the Law,' 57.

45 R. Lemoine, 'Le marché du livre à Québec,' 164.

46 Rick Sher, e-mail to author, 13 March 1996; information supplied by James Green.

47 *The London Catalogue of Books ... 1811* states that the books were sewed or in boards (with the exception of school books) and offers a separate price list for binding.

48 *Catalogue of the Public Library at Hawick* (1792): NLS, mf. 52 [18(1)].

49 *Royal Gazette and Nova Scotia Advertiser*, 23 June 1789; and I. Forsyth, *A Catalogue of the Elgin Circulating Library* (1789).

50 I. Forsyth, *A Catalogue of the Elgin Circulating Library*; *Catalogue of the Public Library at Hawick* (1792): NLS, mf. 52 [18(1)].

51 *Royal Gazette and Nova Scotia Advertiser*, 21 July 1789.

52 Fortunately, the auctioneer's clerk in Montreal entered his calculations of exchange as well as the livre value of the sale; see NA, MG 19, A 2, series III, vol. 144, Sales at Vendue.

53 This example taken from ibid., Sale of William Harkness's Goods, 20 June 1785, Sold to B. Hart. The Elgin price is from I. Forsyth, *A Catalogue of the Elgin Circulating Library*.

54 Y. Lamonde, *La librairie et l'édition à Montréal*. Biographies of most of the printers, journalists, and booksellers mentioned here are included in the *DCB*. We thank Patricia Lockhart Fleming for making available to us her documentation on Upper Canada.

55 Y. Lamonde and D. Olivier, *Les bibliothèques personnelles au Québec*.

56 Y. Lamonde, B. MacDonald, and A. Rotundo, 'Canadian Book Catalogues / Catalogues canadiens relatifs à l'imprimé,' available on the HBiC/HLIC website; the catalogues used here are described in this database.

57 R. Lemoine, 'Le marché du livre à Québec,' 132.

58 Y. Lamonde, B. MacDonald, and A. Rotundo, 'Canadian Book Catalogues / Catalogues canadiens relatifs à l'imprimé.'

59 'Will be Sold by Public Auction, On Tuesday the 13th day of July, a Large Collection of Medical, Surgical, and Historical Works, [the property of the late Dr. Kerr] [...] at 7 o'clock [...] J. Thorner, Auctioneer, Niagara. June 23d, 1824' (*Niagara Gleaner*, 26 June 1824); '[Auction Sale by Wm. Allan] of a Valuable library of books and about 100 volumes on fortifications and gunnery [...] [Halifax] 1830' (*Novascotian* [Halifax], 4 February 1830, cited in S. Greaves, 'Book Culture in Halifax in the 1830s,' 8); 'Une grande collection de livres de droit, de littérature, de religion, de médecine [...] en français, et en anglais, dont il sera préparé des catalogues avant le jour de la vente' (*Le Canadien* [Quebec], 23 October 1835, cited in Y. Lamonde and D. Olivier, *Les bibliothèques personnelles au Québec*, 91).

60 Y. Lamonde and D. Olivier, *Les bibliothèques personnelles au Québec*, 91.

61 P. Deslauriers, 'Fleming, John,' *DCB*, vol. 6.

62 Y. Buono, 'Imprimerie et diffusion de l'imprimé à Montréal de 1776 à 1820,' 203–5.

63 Ryerson quoted in B.S. Osborne, 'Trading on a Frontier,' 61–2; see also S. Jaumain, 'Le colporteur dans le Québec du XIXe siècle,' 13–18; G.L. Parker, *Beginnings of the Book Trade in Canada*, 19–20.

64 Clement Horton Belcher, Andrew and William MacKinlay, and William Gossip in Halifax;

James Dawson in Pictou; Henry Stamper in Charlottetown; Henry David Winton in St John's; Stephen Humbert and George Blatch in Saint John; John, Samuel, and William Neilson and Joseph Crémazie at Quebec; James Brown, Henry H. Cunningham, Merrifield and Co., Hector Bossange, John Nickless, Édouard-Raymond Fabre, Thomas A. Starke, George Perkins Bull (left for York [Toronto] in 1833), Robert and Andrew Armour, and Charles-Philippe Leprohon in Montreal; William Buell in Brockville; J.B. Cheesman, Thomas Tomkins, and James Macfarlane in Kingston; the Lesslie family in York, Kingston, and Dundas, with whom William Lyon Mackenzie had a short-term partnership in Dundas before moving to York, and where George Dawson, the Methodist Book Room, James and Thomas A. Starke, Thomas Ford Caldicott, Henry Rowsell (also established in Kingston), and Hugh Scobie were in business. James Ruthven in Hamilton and Emanuel Christian Enslin in Berlin were also booksellers. In addition to these well-established bookstores, there was Rufus Colton's 'Book-Store,' located 'in the village of Saint-Thomas,' as the *St. Thomas Liberal* of 15 May 1833 announced.

65 F.A. Black, 'Book Availability in Canada, 1752–1820,' 65 and 120; '"Advent'rous Merchants and Atlantic Waves,"' 171; 'Searching for the "Vanguard of an Army of Scots" in Early Canadian Book Trade'; Y. Lamonde, 'La librairie Hector Bossange de Montréal (1815–1819) et le commerce international du livre,' 190–1; C. Galarneau, 'Le commerce du livre à Québec (1766–1820)'; E. Hulse, *Dictionary of Toronto Printers, Publishers, Booksellers*.

66 R. Lemoine, 'Le marché du livre à Québec,' 25 and 91; S. Greaves, 'Book Culture in Halifax in the 1830s,' 9.

67 S. Alston, 'Canada's First Bookseller's Catalogue.'

68 A complete description can be found in Y. Lamonde, B. MacDonald, and A. Rotundo, 'Canadian Book Catalogues / Catalogues canadiens relatifs à l'imprimé.'

69 H. Rowsell, journal, entry of 24 December 1835, quoted in F.N. Walker, *Sketches of Old Toronto*, 133; H.P. Gundy, 'Publishing and Bookselling in Kingston since 1810,' 22–3.

70 A catalogue for George Dawson's York Circulating Library was published in the *Upper Canada Gazette* (York), 26 February 1818; cited in F. Black, 'Searching for the "Vanguard of an Army of Scots,"' 91.

71 K. Donovan, '"May Learning Flourish,"' 108.

72 J.L. McNairn, *Capacity to Judge*, 144–8.

7. Social Networks and Libraries

1 Quebec Diocesan SPCK, *Report*, 16th (1835), 5.

2 JR, 49:209, 211 (1664–5); 50:163 (1665–6); 51:115 (1666–7); 52:109 (1667–8).

3 SPG, *Classified Digest of the Records*, 88–177, 798.

4 Ibid., 110–11, 136, 116–17.

5 T. Osgood, *Canadian Visitor*.

6 J. Fingard, '"Grapes in the Wilderness,"' 7–10.

7 The American Bible Society, for example, granted 816 Bibles and New Testaments to the British colonies between 1816 and 1830 (C. Lacy, *Word-Carrying Giant*, 68). For a history of the American Bible Society, see P.J. Wosh, *Spreading the Word*. Unless otherwise indicated, general statements about Bible and tract society activity in British North America are based on the

reports of local societies available on CIHM. In addition to those cited elsewhere, reports of the following societies were consulted: Bible Society of Upper Canada, Halifax Diocesan Committee SPCK, Kingston Auxiliary Bible Society, Kingston RTS, Lunenburg District SPCK, New Brunswick Auxiliary Bible Society, Newcastle District SPCK, Niagara District Committee SPCK, Richmond Hill Branch Bible Society, Society for Converting and Civilizing the Indians in Upper Canada, York (later Toronto, then Upper Canada) Auxiliary Bible Society, York Committee SPCK. On activity in Upper Canada, see J.A. Wiseman, 'Bible and Tract.'

8 For histories of these societies, see W.O.B. Allen and E. McClure, *Two Hundred Years*; S.G. Green, *Story of the Religious Tract Society*; and G. Browne, *History of the British and Foreign Bible Society*.

9 Niagara RTS, *Report*, 1st (1834), 8; and Upper Canada Religious Tract and Book Society, *Report*, 1st (York, 1833), 10.

10 J. West, *Substance of a Journal*, 66, 28, 34.

11 Midland District SPCK, *Report*, 2nd (Kingston, 1828), 5.

12 W. Johnstone, *Travels in Prince Edward Island*, 20.

13 Sunday School Union Society of Canada, *Report*, 2nd (Montreal, 1824), 22–3.

14 Montreal Auxiliary Bible Society, *Report*, 19th (1839), 8–29.

15 J. Fingard, '"Grapes in the Wilderness."'

16 Charlotte County Auxiliary Bible Society, *Report*, 1st (St Andrews, 1824–6), 10–11.

17 Guysborough reports in Nova-Scotia Auxiliary Bible Society, *Reports*, 10th–12th (Halifax, 1825–32), 14th (1835–6), 16th–18th (1836–41).

18 Nova-Scotia Auxiliary Bible Society, *Report*, 8th (1822–3); and Montreal Auxiliary Bible Society, *Report*, 12th (1832), 5.

19 E.C. Woodley, *Bible in Canada*, 28–40; G. Browne, *History of the British and Foreign Bible Society*, 2:323–7; and L. Howsam, *Cheap Bibles*, 13–15.

20 R. Hardy, *Contrôle social et mutation de la culture religieuse au Québec*, 23–45. See also R.M. Black, 'Different Visions.'

21 J. Fingard, '"Grapes in the Wilderness,"' 16.

22 Fleming UC 677, 750, 812, 898.

23 Cited in T.-M. Charland, 'Projet de journal ecclésiastique de Mgr Lartigue,' 41.

24 A. Green, *Life and Times*, 134.

25 J.B. Friskney, 'Towards a Canadian "Cultural Mecca."'

26 A. Drolet, in *Les bibliothèques canadiennes, 1604–1960*, describes the many private and religious libraries in all parts of British North America. See also Y. Lamonde, 'Social Origins of the Public Library in Montreal.'

27 E. Townsend et al., *Sentinel on the Street*, 29.

28 J.N. Green, 'English Books and Printing,' 262.

29 Frederick Haldimand to Richard Cumberland, 2 March 1779, quoted in F.C. Würtele, 'Our Library,' 31.

30 Ibid., 37.

31 *An Alphabetical List of the Merchants, Traders, and Housekeepers Residing in Montreal*, 24.

32 Ibid.

33 J. Carnochan, 'Niagara Library, 1800–1820,' 338.

34 J.A. Roy, *Kingston*, 31 and 120.

35 PANB, MS. M 1986. 13, J.R. Harper, 'Social History of New Brunswick,' 112.

36 Editorial by Jotham Blanchard in the *Colonial Patriot* (Pictou) of 1832, quoted in C.B. Fergusson, *Mechanics' Institutes in Nova Scotia*, 19.

37 *Prince Edward Island Register*, 27 October 1825.

38 V.L. Coughlin, *Larger Units of Public Library Service in Canada*, 35.

39 J.J. Talman, 'Agricultural Societies of Upper Canada,' 545–6.

40 J. Carnochan, 'Niagara Library, 1800–1820,' 341.

41 J.S. Martell, *The Achievements of Agricola and the Agricultural Societies, 1818–25*, 9 and 15.

42 C.F. Grece, *Facts and Observations Respecting Canada*, 159.

43 E.K. Senior, *British Regulars in Montreal*, 9.

44 A. Drolet, *Les bibliothèques canadiennes, 1604–1960*, 110.

45 *Regulations and Catalogue of the Quebec Garrison Library* (1824), 2.

46 Earl of Dalhousie, *The Dalhousie Journals*, 1:22.

47 Ibid., 1:75.

48 S.B. Elliott, 'Library for the Garrison and Town,' 5.

49 E. Chappell, *Voyage of His Majesty's Ship Rosamond to Newfoundland*, 244.

50 J. Macgregor, *British America*, 2:512.

51 Ibid., 84–5.

52 C. Whitfield, *Tommy Atkins*, 102.

53 J. Carnochan, 'Niagara Library, 1800–1820,' 344.

54 C.B. Fergusson, *Mechanics' Institutes in Nova Scotia*, 19.

55 PANB, MS. M 1986. 13, J.R. Harper, 'Social History of New Brunswick,' 114.

56 G.A. Campbell, 'Social Life and Institutions of Nova Scotia in the 1830's,' 149.

57 J. Blanchard, 'Anatomy of Failure,' 393.

58 R.H. Cuff, 'Mechanics' Society,' 489. Although this society offered 'educational opportunities,' it was the St John's Mechanics' Institute (1849) that provided a reference library.

59 N. Robins, 'Montreal Mechanics' Institute: 1828–1870,' 374.

60 *Catalogue and Rules of the Library & Reading Room of the Quebec Mechanics' Institute* (1841), i.

61 W.L. Mackenzie, *Catechism of Education*, 28.

62 See TRL, Toronto Mechanics' Institute fonds, 1831–83, for the records of this institute and correspondence with others in Upper Canada.

63 *York Commercial Directory, ... 1833–4*, 133.

64 'Editorial,' *Acadian Recorder*, 22 October 1831, quoted in G.A. Campbell, 'Social Life and Institutions of Nova Scotia in the 1830's,' 114.

65 V.L. Coughlin, *Larger Units of Public Library Service in Canada*, 38.

66 NSARM, MG 100, vol. 175, no. 34b, Assembly Petitions – 1832.

67 N. Robins, 'Montreal Mechanics' Institute: 1828–1870,' 375.

68 E.C. Bow, 'Public Library Movement in Nineteenth-Century Ontario,' 3.

69 M. Payne and G. Thomas, 'Literacy, Literature and Libraries in the Fur Trade,' 44.

70 D.E. Ryder, 'The Red River Public Library, June 1822,' 36–7.

71 M. Payne, *The Most Respectable Place in the Territory*, 76.

72 Ibid., 76–7.

73 F.C. Würtele, 'Our Library,' 29.

74 Natural History Society of Montreal, *First Annual Report* (Montreal, 1828), 4.

75 W. Canniff, *History of the Settlement of Upper Canada*, 348.

76 D.C. Harvey, 'Early Public Libraries in Nova Scotia,' 437.

77 'Monthly Record,' *Halifax Monthly Magazine*, December 1831, pp. 335–6.

78 J. Carnochan, 'Niagara Library, 1800–1820,' 339, 351–2.

79 *Catalogue of Books in the Halifax Mechanics' Library* (1832), 3–17.

80 The library catalogues analyzed were *Catalogue of English and French Books in the Quebec Library at the Bishop's Palace* (1808), *Catalogue of the Books in the Montreal Library* (1824), *Rules and Catalogue of the Halifax Library* (1833), and *Articles and Catalogue of the Ramsay Library* (Kingston, 1836: Fleming UC 986). The Quebec Library had been established for twenty-nine years, the Montreal Library for twenty-eight years, the Halifax Library for nine years, and the Ramsay Library for seven years.

81 *Catalogue of Books in the Garrison Library of Quebec* (1833) and *Rules and Catalogue of the Halifax Garrison Library* (1835) were consulted for this overview.

82 'List of the Shareholders of the Halifax Library, November 1833,' in *Rules and Catalogue of the Halifax Library* (1833), 14–15; J. Carnochan, 'Niagara Library, 1800–1820,' 342.

83 *Rules and Catalogue of the Halifax Garrison Library* (1836), 9.

84 J.-E. Roy, 'L'ancien Barreau au Canada,' 254–5.

85 A. Morel, 'Collet, Benoît-Mathieu,' *DCB*, vol. 2.

86 G. Gallichan, 'L'État québécois et ses bibliothèques,' 80–1.

87 C. Veilleux, *Aux origines du Barreau québécois*.

88 Ibid., 37–60.

89 M. Nantel, *La bibliothèque du Barreau et les archives judiciaires de Montréal*, 56.

90 G. Gallichan, *La bibliothèque du Barreau de Québec*, 9–11.

91 *Gazette de Québec*, 26 October 1832.

92 P. Beullac and E. Fabre Surveyer, *Le centenaire du Barreau de Montréal*, 12.

93 Ibid., 13.

94 M. Nantel, *La bibliothèque du Barreau et les archives judiciaires de Montréal*, 3–4.

95 'Ordonnance pour incorporer la Bibliothèque des avocats de Québec,' *Ordonnances faites et passées par … le Conseil spécial … du Bas-Canada*, 5:575, 4 Vic., c. 49. The parliamentary constitution of Lower Canada was suspended in March 1838.

96 Upper Canada, *Statutes*, 37 Geo. III, c. 13; see also C. Moore, *Law Society of Upper Canada*.

97 On the incorporating acts of the Law Society of Upper Canada, see C. Moore, *Law Society of Upper Canada*, 15–16, 61–4.

98 E.G. Firth, 'White, John,' *DCB*, vol. 4.

99 W.R. Riddell, *The Legal Profession in Upper Canada*, 83.

100 Memorandum from the Law Society of Upper Canada to Lieutenant-Governor Peregrine Maitland, 29 April 1826, cited in W.R. Riddell, *Legal Profession*, 84.

101 Ibid.

102 The courthouse and the prison were, at the time, on the north side of King Street, between Toronto and Church Streets.

103 C. Moore, *Law Society of Upper Canada*, 68–9.

104 Dr W.W. Baldwin was the father of Robert Baldwin.

105 R.L. Fraser, 'Cawdell, James Martin,' *DCB*, vol. 7.

106 W.R. Riddell, *Legal Profession in Upper Canada*, 101.

107 Ibid., 92.

108 G. Gallichan, 'Les Parlements et leurs bibliothèques,' 145–8.

109 J. Marchand, *La Bibliothèque de l'Assemblée nationale*, 34–48; J. Conaway, *America's Library*, 5–25.
110 G. Gallichan, *Livre et politique au Bas-Canada*, 224–5.
111 Ibid., 229–31.
112 Ibid., 237–301.
113 F.M. Watson, 'A Credit to This Province,' 4–5.
114 In reprisal, the following year the British army set fire to the Capitol in Washington and destroyed the Library of Congress. See J. Conaway, *America's Library*, 22–3.
115 Upper Canada, *Statutes*, 56 Geo. III, c. 25.
116 Fleming UC 118.
117 G. Gallichan, *Livre et politique au Bas-Canada*, 305; *Development of the New Brunswick Legislative Library*.
118 A. Drolet, *Les bibliothèques canadiennes*, 26.
119 Marie de l'Assomption, *Bibliographie d'ouvrages anciens de médecine gardés à l'Hôpital général (1669–1874)*.
120 Y. Lamonde, *Les bibliothèques de collectivités*, 35.
121 Fleming UC 472.
122 The building, designed by Montreal architects Wells and Thompson, was erected between 1833 and 1835. See G. Deschênes and L. Noppen, eds, *L'hôtel du Parlement*, 35.
123 Y. Lamonde, *Les bibliothèques de collectivités*, 47.
124 Fleming UC 1339.
125 L.S. Garry and C. Garry, eds, *Canadian Libraries in Their Changing Environment*, 4.
126 For historical background, see G. Gallichan, 'Bibliothèque et culture au Canada après la conquête, 1760–1800'; L.S. Garry and C. Garry, eds, *Canadian Libraries in Their Changing Environment*; Y. Lamonde, *Les bibliothèques de collectivités à Montréal*. The legislative libraries of Lower and Upper Canada are described in J.-C. Bonenfant, 'La Bibliothèque de l'Assemblée nationale et ses bibliothécaires,' and F.M. Watson, 'A Credit to This Province.'
127 The catalogues are listed in the Canadian Book Catalogues / Catalogues canadiens relatifs à l'imprimé' database, available on the HBiC/HLIC website.
128 R.W. Beales and J.N. Green, 'Libraries and Their Users,' 400.
129 *Catalogue of English and French Books in the Montreal Library / Catalogue des livres francois et anglais dans la Bibliotheque de Montreal (1797)*.
130 *Rules and Catalogue of the Halifax Library* (1833), 7.
131 *Regulations and Catalogue of the Quebec Garrison Library* (1821), [24].
132 V.L. Coughlin, *Larger Units of Public Library Service in Canada*, 91.
133 G. Gallichan, *Livre et politique au Bas-Canada*, 284–8.
134 *Constitution, Rules and Bye Laws of the Halifax Mechanics' Library* (1838).
135 *Catalogue of Books in the Montreal Library* (1824).
136 F.M. Watson, 'A Credit to This Province,' 13.

8. The Uses of Literacy

1 On the sources and definition of literacy, see M. Verrette, 'L'alphabétisation de la population de la ville de Québec de 1750 à 1849'; and M. Verrette, *L'alphabétisation au Québec, 1660–1900*. These studies offer a synthesis of historians' writings on this issue.
2 R. Chartier, 'Les pratiques de l'écrit.'

3 L. Stone, 'Literacy and Education in England: 1640–1900.'

4 L.-J. Dugas, 'L'alphabétisation des Acadiens, 1700–1850'; F. Ouellet, 'Fréquentation scolaire, alphabétisation et société au Québec et en Ontario jusqu'en 1911,' 267ff.

5 M. Verrette, *L'alphabétisation au Québec, 1660–1900*, 92.

6 Ibid.; L.-J. Dugas, 'L'alphabétisation des Acadiens, 1700–1850.'

7 M. Basque, *De Marc Lescarbot à l'AEFNB*, 33–4.

8 M. Verrette, *L'alphabétisation au Québec, 1660–1900.*

9 Ibid.

10 C. Galarneau, *La France devant l'opinion canadienne*, 35.

11 Y. Lamonde, *Histoire sociale des idées au Québec*, 1:71.

12 C. Lessard, 'L'alphabétisation à Trois-Rivières de 1634 à 1939,' 92; M. Verrette, *L'alphabétisation au Québec, 1660–1900*, 124ff.

13 M. Verrette, *L'alphabétisation au Québec, 1660–1900*, 112.

14 Ibid., 127–8.

15 L.-P. Audet, *Histoire de l'enseignement au Québec*, 1:331.

16 Y. Lamonde, *Histoire sociale des idées*, 1:78.

17 C. Galarneau, 'La presse périodique au Québec de 1764 à 1859,' 144.

18 L.-P. Audet, *Histoire de l'enseignement au Québec*, 1:344.

19 A. Dufour, *Tous à l'école: État, communautés rurales et scolarisation au Québec*, 37.

20 Ibid., 42.

21 R.D. Francis et al., *Origins: Canadian History to Confederation*, 197.

22 P. Axelrod, *Promise of Schooling*, 8.

23 M. Verrette, *L'alphabétisation au Québec, 1660–1900*, 142.

24 Nova Scotia School Act (1811), 51 Geo. III, c. 8.

25 C.E. Phillips, *Development of Education in Canada*, 134.

26 Ibid.

27 Madras School, *Annual Report of the State of the Madras School in New-Brunswick for the Year 1820* (Saint John, 1820): Fleming Atl NB88.

28 D.M. Young, 'Smyth, George Stracey,' *DCB*, vol. 6.

29 W.B. Hamilton, 'Society and Schools in New Brunswick and Prince Edward Island,' 119.

30 C.E. Phillips, *Development of Education in Canada*, 133–4.

31 W.G. Handcock, 'Codner, Samuel,' *DCB*, vol. 8.

32 W.B. Hamilton, 'Society and Schools in Newfoundland.'

33 C.E. Phillips, *Development of Education in Canada*, 133.

34 R. Cockrel, *Thoughts on the Education of Youth* (Newark, 1795): Tremaine 929.

35 C.E. Phillips, *Development of Education in Canada*, 134; J.D. Wilson, 'Education in Upper Canada,' 209.

36 M.R. Lupul, 'Education in Western Canada before 1873.'

37 D. Chaput, 'Nolin, Jean-Baptiste,' *DCB*, vol. 6.

38 I am referring not only to the fact that illiterates may function well in a reading culture through publicly mediated access to texts or through proxy but also to the paradoxical situation of the illiterate in a literate society: no one is more firmly defined by a reading culture than those putatively excluded from it.

39 On the orature (oral literature) of the Africadians, see G.E. Clarke, 'Introduction.'

40 R. Wittmann, 'Was There a Reading Revolution at the End of the Eighteenth Century?' 295–301.

41 W.J. Gilmore, *Reading Becomes a Necessity of Life*, 20.

42 *Mail and Empire* (Toronto), 18 January 1927, transcribed in Ennotville Women's Institute, Tweedsmuir History compilation, Ennotville Historical Library; J. Young, *Reminiscences of the Early History of Galt*, 72.

43 NA, MG 24, C 1, Letterbook and Diary. The diary was published as J. Willcocks, 'Diary.'

44 The term 'social library' is sometimes used to refer to the library or book-lending practices of an already-existent circle or association; subscription libraries recruited members and supported the collection through fees. In practice, the two appear to be virtually synonymous in this period.

45 See also S. Greaves, 'Book Culture in Halifax in the 1830s,' 3.

46 Still in existence, this is the last remaining social library in Ontario.

47 AO, F 592, Diary entry, 5 February 1829.

48 A further discussion of literary societies prior to 1840 is found in H. Murray, *Come, Bright Improvement!* 23–52.

49 Private library lists may or may not indicate current tastes (materials may be inherited, for example), while wills may omit the most treasured items, since these are assumed to remain in the family circle. In addition, it is notoriously difficult to generalize from individual tastes. Booksellers' lists also pose interpretive difficulties: no matter how canny a judge of the market a bookseller may be, inventories do not usually tell us who bought the book and never tell us why.

50 Taxonomy is addressed in Y. Lamonde, *Les bibliothèques de collectivités à Montréal* and 'Universal Classification'; for an application of the proposed classification to the Institute canadien de Montréal's catalogues, see Y. Lamonde, *Territoires de la culture québécoise*.

51 *Constitution, Rules & Bye Laws of the Halifax Mechanics' Library* (1834); *Rules and Catalogue of the Halifax Garrison Library: with a List of Subscribers* (1835); *Rules and Catalogue of the Halifax Library* (1833).

52 The library is sometimes dated to 1816 and sometimes to 1817. While the Quebec garrison had a much earlier library, the one at Halifax was probably the first to be supported by the garrison by rates. It is now the Cambridge Military Library at Royal Military Park (see S.B. Elliott, 'A Library for the Garrison and Town,' 4).

53 S.B. Elliott, 'Library for the Garrison and Town,' 4.

54 *Constitution, Rules & Bye Laws of the Halifax Mechanics' Library*, [1], 2.

55 There is some ambiguity about the size of the Mechanics' Library holdings: while a manual count reveals approximately 720 items, the accession numbers run to 1,200, possibly because they record volumes rather than titles.

56 *Constitution, Rules & Bye Laws of the Halifax Mechanics' Library*, [1].

57 Analysis of author holdings is complicated by the fact that subscription libraries typically held many volumes of 'elegant extracts,' 'beauties,' 'curiosities,' and other forms of anthologies; an author absent in monograph form may be well represented in this way.

58 Jameson seems to deliberately undercount the number of bookstores, library collections, and literary societies extant during the time of her visit and does not mention the plans to develop both a lyceum and a provincial university. See, for example, her cultural 'audit' in *Winter Studies and Summer Rambles in Canada*, 1:270–5.

59 J. D. Moodie and S. Moodie, 'To the Public.'

60 R. Williams, *Marxism and Literature*, 121–7.

61 H. Scadding, *Horace Canadianizing*, 18.

62 H. Scadding, *Pioneer Gathering of Books*, [1].

63 H. Scadding, *Toronto of Old*, 163.

64 H. Scadding, *Pioneer Gathering of Books*, 4.

65 TRL, Robert Baldwin papers. Despite the title, there is both poetry and prose in the volume, the poems appear to have been authored by Robert Baldwin primarily, and the editor was Baldwin's friend James Hunter Samson (not Samson Hunter). In all probability, no further volumes were produced.

66 AO, F 43, Literary Society of York, Resolutions and Regulations.

67 F. Roy, *Histoire de la librairie au Québec*, 39; see pp. 35–63 for a more general discussion of the political and cultural role of the booksellers.

68 C. Gerson, *Purer Taste*.

69 K.J. Ellice, *Diary*, 170. In a study of Ellice's diary, Carol Shields concluded, 'Her preference for the broomsticks-and-potatoes variety of reportage suggest [sic] that she is a reliable witness and that her journal is weighted more in favour of fact than of fiction' ('Three Canadian Women,' 53). My thanks to Suzy Aston for her useful observations on Ellice's diary in my book history course in 2001.

70 K.J. Ellice, *Diary*, 32.

71 J.M. Colthart, 'Ellice, Edward,' *DCB*, vol. 9.

72 K.J. Ellice, *Diary*, 7.

73 Ibid., 144.

74 Ibid., 131.

75 Ibid., 81.

76 Ibid., 98.

77 Ibid., 99.

78 Ibid., 157.

79 Ibid., 154–5.

80 Ibid., 71.

81 For other examples of settlers' guides, see E. Waterston et al., *Travellers – Canada to 1900.*

82 W. Dunlop, *Statistical Sketches of Upper Canada, for the Use of Emigrants*, 9–10.

83 C. Haight, *Life in Canada Fifty Years Ago*, 180.

84 C.P. Traill, *The Backwoods of Canada* (1836), 290.

85 J.J. Talman, ed., *Loyalist Narratives from Upper Canada*, 135.

86 Ibid., 78–9.

87 A. Jameson, *Winter Studies and Summer Rambles in Canada*, 1:271.

88 W. Phillips to T. Phillips Jr, 14 July 1839, quoted in W. Cameron, S. Haines, and M. McDougall Maude, eds, *English Immigrant Voices*, 295.

89 J.J. Talman, 'Life in the Pioneer Districts of Upper Canada, 1815–1840,' 166; also A. Jameson, *Winter Studies and Summer Rambles in Canada*, 2:140.

90 A.J.L. Winchester, '"Scratching Along amongst the Stumps,"' 55.

91 J.J. Talman, 'Agricultural Societies of Upper Canada,' 545.

92 Ibid.

93 R.L. Jones, History of Agriculture in Ontario, 1613–1880, 159–60.

94 *Traité théorique et pratique de l'agriculture* (Montreal, 1836–7).

95 Tremaine 127, *ECP* 350.

96 Tremaine/*ECP* 412.

97 Fleming UC 191.

98 Fleming UC 1384.

99 Fleming UC 39. Only the French edition has been located. See also Tremaine 687, 721.

100 Fleming UC 383.

101 Fleming UC 317.

102 Fleming UC 1087.

103 J.S. Martell, *Achievements of Agricola*; J. McCallum, *Unequal Beginnings*.

104 The Hudson's Bay Company Archives are now part of the Provincial Archives of Manitoba.

105 MUL, RBSCD, MS 472, MASS 2356a, W.F. Wentzel, 'Journal Kept at Slave Lake, 1802,' 13; emphasis in original. One quire is twenty-four sheets of paper.

106 J. Isham, *Observations*, 4.

107 NA, MG 19, C 1, R. Mackenzie, 'Some Account of the North West Company Containing Analogy of Nations Ancient & Modern.'

108 D. Thompson, *Narrative*, lxvi.

109 See Mackenzie's letter of 1794 in L.R. Masson, ed., *Les bourgeois*, 1:44.

110 See F.A. Black, 'Beyond Boundaries'; J.H. Beattie, '"My Best Friend"'; M. Payne and G. Thomas, 'Literacy, Literature and Libraries'; J.M. Cole, 'Keeping the Mind Alive.'

111 F.A. Black, 'Beyond Boundaries'; L.D. Castling, 'Red River Library'; D. Lindsay, 'Peter Fidler's Library.'

112 J. Isham, *Observations*, 93; L. Hennepin, *Nouvelle découverte*, 24–5.

113 P. Pond, 'Narrative,' 39.

114 D.W. Harmon, *Sixteen Years*, 32.

115 D. Thompson, *Narrative*, 8, 41, 43.

116 MUL, RBSCD, MS 472, MASS 2356, W.F. Wentzel to Roderick Mackenzie, 28 February 1814, 48–9; emphasis in original. (I have changed the word 'Spunges' from the McGill transcription.)

117 W.F. Tolmie, *Journals*, 248, 169, 272.

118 D.W. Harmon, *Sixteen Years*, 27.

119 D. Thompson, *Narrative*, 90.

120 A. Mackenzie, *Journals*, 323, 378. It is interesting to note that when, some years later, Tolmie tried to get Native people to show him Mackenzie's inscription, they directed him to 'some Indian hieroglyphics marked with red earth' instead. On the same day that Tolmie notes the 'stupidity' of his guide in misconstruing the plates in Franklin's journal, he does not call himself stupid for not understanding the 'hieroglyphics' (W.F. Tolmie, *Journals*, 297–8).

121 A. Henry, *Travels*, 335. (A. Dobbs, in his *Account*, noted that the Native people were 'very fond of all kind of Pictures or Prints, giving a Beaver for the least Print' [42].)

122 J. Ramsey, 'Bible in Western Indian Mythology.'

9. The Pleasures of Books

1 L.J. Docherty, 'Women as Readers'; Y. Lamonde, 'La représentation de l'imprimé dans la peinture et la gravure québécoises (1760–1960).'

2 A. Vachon, Rêves d'empire, 316.

3 M.S. Cross and R.L. Fraser, 'Baldwin, Robert,' *DCB*, vol. 8.

4 E.K. Senior, 'McCord, Thomas,' *DCB*, vol. 6.

5 M. Béland, ed., *Peinture au Québec*, 426–7.

6 J.R. Harper, *A People's Art*, 87.

7 M.S. Cross and R.L. Fraser, 'Baldwin, Robert,' *DCB*, vol. 8.

8 M. Allodi, *Berczy*, 183.

9 M. Béland, ed., *Peinture au Québec*, 420–3.

10 Thanks to John Macleod, who brought this painting to our notice, and to Ann Lowe and Laurie Glen, of the Beaverbrook Art Gallery, and Peter Laroque, of the New Brunswick Museum, for sharing the results of their research on Anthony Flower.

11 H.J. Jackson, *Marginalia*.

12 E.M. Lloyd, 'Wolfe, James,' *Dictionary of National Biography*, 21:767–75.

13 M. Allodi, *Berczy*, 218–20.

14 A. Roy, 'Ce qu'ils lisaient,' 200, 206–7; J.-C. Dubé, 'Les intendants de la Nouvelle-France et la République des lettres,' and *Claude-Thomas Dupuy, intendant de la Nouvelle-France*. As well as Dupuy, known for his encyclopedic 1,045-volume library, other intendants had large libraries: Jacques de Meulles, François de Beauharnois de La Chaussaye, Raudot father and son, Michel Bégon de La Picardière, and Gilles Hocquart. Most of the individuals discussed here are the subjects of biographies in the *DCB*.

15 Y. Devaux, *L'univers de la bibliophilie*.

16 C. Nish, *François-Étienne Cugnet, 1719–1751*.

17 [P.-G. Roy], 'La bibliothèque du juge de Bonne.'

18 D.A. Sutherland, 'Fairbanks, Charles Rufus,' *DCB*, vol. 7.

19 J.G. MacGregor, *Peter Fidler*; D. Lindsay, 'Peter Fidler's Library.'

20 See, for example, the after-death inventories of the priests Nicolas and Philippe Boucher, Louis Rouer de Villeray, Urbain Boiret, Bernard-Sylvestre Dosque, Jean-Baptiste Boucher, *dit* Belleville, and Charles-Joseph Brassard Deschanaux; of the bishops Charles-François Bailly de Messein, Pierre Denaut, and Joseph-Octave Plessis; and of Louis-Guillaume Verrier, Pierre Foretier, Pierre-Amable De Bonne, Richard John Uniacke, Ezekiel Hart, and Jonathan Sewell. See also Y. Lamonde and D. Olivier, *Les bibliothèques personnelles au Québec*.

21 Y. Lamonde and D. Olivier, *Les bibliothèques personnelles au Québec*, 117.

22 A. Cuvillier and J. Cuvillier, *Catalogue of Books Composing the Library of the Late John Fleming, Esquire* (Montreal, 1833).

23 G. Meyer-Noirel, *L'ex libris: Histoire, art, techniques*, 12.

24 E. Castle, *English Book-Plates*, 3.

25 R.H. Stacey, *Canadian Bookplates*, 3.

26 DAUL, P 245/29, no. 5758. The University of British Columbia, McGill University (Masson Collection), and the Bibliothèque nationale du Québec (Collection Gagnon) also hold collections of Canadian ex libris.

27 The Fonds ancien de la Bibliothèque du Séminaire de Québec contains several books bearing the coats of arms of Jean Talon and of Jacques Duchesneau.

28 NA, MG 24, B 1, vol. 50, p. 37.

29 DAUL, P 245/2, no. 267-28.

30 See NA, MG 24, B 1, vols 50, 55, 58, 69, 80, 81, 84, and 86, and *ECP*, pp. 424–512 for additional orders.

31 S. Harrod and M.J. Ayearst, *List of Canadian Bookplates*, 139. For examples of heraldic bookplates etched or engraved by James Smillie, see M. Allodi and R.L. Tovell, *Engraver's Pilgrimage*, nos 11, 14, 41, and 42.

32 For an account of his life, see B.C. Cuthbertson, 'Uniacke, Richard John,' *DCB*, vol. 6, and *The Old Attorney General*.

33 Uniacke's will provided for his law books to remain for the use of his sons, six of whom had studied law, as long as any wished to practise. Afterwards they were to be sold. An auction poster dated only 'Monday' is extant (NSARM, MG 1, vol. 1769, no. 42b).

34 After Uniacke's death, the estate was occupied for more than a century by the family, who added books to the library and may have kept or lost items. In 2000 the remaining books were examined, and 280 titles were identified as Uniacke's, of which 155 appear in the 1830 inventory. At least 94 books with his bookplate are not found in the 1830 inventory.

35 J.M. Beck, in 'Uniacke, James Boyle,' *DCB*, vol. 8, mentions that Uniacke kept his son James busy with requests for 'livestock, spinning-wheels, engravings, books.' Only three books have booksellers' tickets (all British).

36 The tools are listed in Nova Scotia Museum of Cultural History, Uniacke MS 3, 'Inventory of house furnishings,' 1830. This is a room-by-room inventory made by sons Richard and Andrew.

37 For evidence of this practice, see volumes of the 1797 edition of Edward Gibbon's *The History of the Decline and Fall of the Roman Empire* bound to match volumes from an 1802 edition.

38 This analysis is based on subject headings assigned by the Nova Scotia Museum library to the 280 remaining titles identified as Uniacke's.

39 Nova Scotia Museum of Cultural History, Uniacke MS 3, 'Inventory of house furnishings,' 1830.

40 This analysis is based on the call numbers assigned by the Nova Scotia Museum library when the collection was entered into its catalogue.

41 See Fleming Atl. NS37. The laws were found in a 1956 inventory but have since disappeared.

42 H.E. Turner, in 'Addison, Robert,' *DCB*, vol. 6, details his career in Upper Canada, including his land speculation and his political activities. See also F. Habermehl and D.L. Combe, *St. Mark's*, chapters 1–3.

43 For a list of books in Addison's library, see W.J. Cameron and G. McKnight, *Robert Addison's Library*. This catalogue does not include any books published after 1792, and Addison certainly acquired more after that date.

10. Print in Daily Life

1 Bushell set a full imprint as the final line: 'HALIFAX: Printed by John Bushell, 1752' (Tremaine 3).

2 In Nova Scotia the public reading of a law 'on the Parade of Halifax, after Notice by beat of Drum' was 'deemed a sufficient Publication' (1758: 32 Geo. c. 22); when the *Quebec Gazette / La Gazette de Québec* was suspended in 1765, publication by beat of drum, reading by the curates, and posting in the three major towns was deemed 'a sufficient Publication' for 'Ordinances, Proclamations, &c.' (*ECP* 72).

3 NA, MG 24, B 1, vol. 88, file 2: Chorley; the catechism is Tremaine 280.

4 NA, MG 24, B 1. Printing records for 1764 to 1800 are transcribed in *ECP*, pp. 416–511.

5 Quebec (Province), Governor, 1764–8 (Murray), [Reward notice] (Quebec, 1764): Tremaine/ *ECP* 43.

6 The total includes printing work entered in the accounts as well as surviving imprints not recorded there but located and described in Tremaine and *ECP*.

7 It is difficult to provide comparable statistics since many bibliographies exclude job printing. Noting that his figures reflect only a portion of 'the real bread-and-butter of the colonial printer,' Peter Parker tabulated an average of 35 per cent job printing in Philadelphia for selected years from 1758 to 1800. With the federal government located there after 1790, the proportion of job printing rose above 50 per cent (P. Parker, 'Philadelphia Printer,' 37–8).

8 Nova Scotia, Lieutenant Governor, 1761–3 (Belcher), [A Proclamation] (Halifax, 1762): *ECP* 30A.

9 *Free Press* (Halifax), 2 September 1817.

10 New Brunswick, Administrator, 1812–13 (Smyth), [A Proclamation] (Saint John, 1812): Fleming Atl. NB39.

11 Upper Canada, President, 1811–12 (Brock), *Proclamation* (1812): Fleming UC 75; *Glorious News!!!* (York, 1812): Fleming UC 65.

12 *More Glorious* (Quebec, 1812): M. Brisebois, *Impressions,* 166.

13 *A New Song, on Peace, and Conquered Bonaparte* (Saint John, 1814): Fleming Atl. NB50; G. Bumgardner, 'Vignettes,' 44–6.

14 George Bond, *The Remembrancer* (Saint John, 1837).

15 [Petition of Inhabitants] (St John's, 1811): Fleming Atl. Nfld10.

16 *Mrs. Redon's Benefit* (Montreal, 1812): M. Brisebois, *Impressions,* 178; *Niagara Race Meeting* (1840): Fleming UC 1440; *Toronto Regatta* (Toronto, 1839): Fleming UC 1335; *Toronto Regatta* (Toronto, 1840): Fleming UC 1469.

17 Mensforth, *Aux curieux et spéculatifs* (Quebec, 1792): Tremaine 788.

18 P. Tousignant, 'La première campagne électorale'; J. Hare, *Aux origines du parlementarisme québécois,* 47–61, 149–206.

19 Tremaine 761–81; *ECP* 770A–781; Vlach and Buono 0223.

20 *ECP,* p. 490.

21 *ECP,* pp. 491–2.

22 Tremaine 767; Vlach and Buono 0438.

23 M. Allodi, *Printmaking in Canada / Les débuts de l'estampe imprimée au Canada,* 10–11; *ECP* 775A.

24 M.A. Berthelot Dartigny, *Conversation au sujet de l'élection de Charlesbourg* (Quebec, s.d.): Tremaine 761.

25 Upper Canada, Parliament, House of Assembly, Select Committee on Grievances, *Seventh Report* (Toronto, 1835): Fleming UC 892.

26 F.B. Head, *Narrative,* 7.

27 *The Elections – or, A Plain Dialogue* (1836): Fleming UC 938.

28 Twenty-seven handbills (twenty-six unique) were preserved in a scrapbook known only in microform (CaOTUTF mfm 2 in Fleming UC) until it was acquired by the Thomas Fisher Rare Book Library at the University of Toronto in 1999 as 'Scrapbook formerly belonging to James Lesslie.'

29 *The Celebrated Horse Simon Ebenezer! Will Stand for Six Days Only* (1836). 'Simon Ebenezer' would be Simon Ebenezer Washburn, who held appointment with Draper as a reporter in the Court of King's Bench.

30 Constitutional Reform Society, *The Supplies* (1836): Fleming UC 931; *Thirteen Reasons* (1836): Fleming UC 1001. Only one notice records the number printed: 2,500 in support of the

reformers Thomas Parke and Elias Moore, who were re-elected in Middlesex. See *The British Constitution For-Ever* (1836): Fleming UC 912.

31 W.L. Mackenzie, *Streetsville Hustings* (1836): Fleming UC 967.

32 Fleming UC 1074.

33 For commentary on the use of the royal arms and heraldic factotums in printed documents, see P. Kennedy, 'Impressions of State Authority.'

34 NA, MG 19, A 2, series 3, vols 40–1, pp. 4442, 4446, 4454, and 4637.

35 Examples appear scattered through NA, MG 19, A 2, series 3, vols 28–47 and 58–9.

36 Two examples of card money from the 1740s are illustrated in A.B. McCullough, *Money and Exchange in Canada to 1900*, 28.

37 For the Brown/Neilson shop records, see *ECP*, pp. 417–511.

38 An example of a *bon* from 1788 is illustrated in A.B. McCullough, *Money and Exchange in Canada to 1900*, 27.

39 *ECP*, pp. 454, 460.

40 This study was based on the following sources: for the period to 1800, Tremaine, pp. 595–653; for 1801 to 1840, S. Ellison, *Historical Directory of Newfoundland and Labrador Newspapers, 1807–1987; Nova Scotia Newspapers: A Directory and Union List, 1752–1988; New Brunswick Newspaper Directory, 1783–1996 / Répertoire des journaux du Nouveau-Brunswick, 1783–1996;* H. Boylan, *Checklist and Historical Directory of Prince Edward Island Newspapers, 1787–1986;* A. Beaulieu and J. Hamelin, *La presse québécoise des origines à nos jours*, vol. 1; Fleming UC n1–145.

Totals should be treated with caution since some titles are known only from a brief contemporary reference or a prospectus and may be magazines rather than newspapers. And while newspaper starts capture the vitality of an expanding press, they do not reflect the stability of papers that continued for decades, even to the present day.

41 On this question, see G. Laurence, 'La distribution linguistique de la presse au Québec,' 123–5, which deals specifically with the period 1764–1840.

42 It is thus completely anachronistic to speak of the front page of a newspaper during this period.

43 The advertisements, a mixture of public notices, classified advertisements, and actual commercial advertising, were still far from being exploited as the main source of funding for the newspaper.

44 Before 1810, delays in the transmission of news from Europe to British North America were in the order of two to three months. Around 1840, with the appearance of the transatlantic steamship, these delays were cut by more than half.

45 J.-P. Wallot, 'Frontière ou fragment du système atlantique,' 9–10.

46 The few figures available are those that the newspapers themselves supplied; they must therefore be treated with caution.

47 In the eighteenth century, subscriptions were generally annual or semi-annual, and one had therefore to agree to lay out a substantial sum all at once. Newspapers were usually sent by mail.

48 True dailies – those published daily 'year-round' – did not appear in Canada East until the beginning of the 1850s.

49 For accounts of the careers of all these individuals, see the *DCB*.

50 For example, and taking account of the changes in formats and increased publication

frequency: 1805, *Quebec Gazette / La Gazette de Québec* (35 by 25 centimetres, weekly): 20s per year; 1811, the *Montreal Herald* (52 by 33 centimetres, weekly): 15s per year; 1826, *La Minerve* (37 by 26 centimetres, biweekly): 20s per year; 1832, the *Quebec Mercury* (42 by 28 centimetres, triweekly): 20s per year; 1833, the *Daily Advertiser* (daily/triweekly): 30s per year; 1840, the *Montreal Herald* (daily/triweekly): $6 per year.

51   See J.M. Bumsted, 'Liberty of the Press,' 524.

52   The best information on this incident comes from the accounts of those involved. See W.L. Mackenzie's *The History of the Destruction of the Colonial Advocate Press* (York, 1827), and S.P. Jarvis's *Statement of Facts, Relating to the Trespass, on the Printing Press* (York, 1828). See also C. Raible, *Muddy York Mud*, 8–10; G.M. Craig, *Upper Canada*, 111–14; F.H. Armstrong and R.J. Stagg, 'Mackenzie, William Lyon,' *DCB*, vol. 9.

53   W.L. Mackenzie, *The History of the Destruction of the Colonial Advocate Press*, 1.

54   Ibid.

55   S.P. Jarvis, *Statement of Facts*, 18.

56   P. O'Flaherty, 'Winton, Henry David,' *DCB*, vol. 8; also P. O'Flaherty, *Old Newfoundland*, 138.

57   P. O'Flaherty, 'Winton, Henry David.'

58   P. O'Flaherty, *Old Newfoundland*, 151–5.

59   Ibid., 163.

60   For comparable attacks in the United States, see R.G. Silver, 'Violent Assaults on American Printing Shops, 1788–1860.'

61   J.L. McNairn, *Capacity to Judge*, 143.

62   Tremaine, pp. 653–6.

63   *Royal Gazette* (Saint John), 27 October 1789.

64   Ibid.

65   Tremaine, pp. 656–8. The subscription book for the *Quebec Magazine / Le Magasin de Quebec* is in NA, MG 24, B 1, vol. 46, file 8.

66   Tremaine, p. 656.

67   For detailed information about journals published in Upper Canada to 1840, see Fleming UC j1–11.

68   *Christian Recorder*, February 1820, p. 446.

69   Ibid.

70   Quoted in G.E.N. Tratt, *Survey and Listing of Nova Scotia Newspapers*, 83.

71   *Upper Canada Herald*, 22 July 1823. No copies have been located.

72   *Roseharp*, 1 January 1835, [p. 1].

73   *Canadian Magazine and Literary Repository*, July 1823, p. 6; italics in original.

74   M.L. MacDonald, 'Some Notes on the Montreal Literary Scene.'

75   F.L. Mott, *History of American Magazines*, 340.

76   *Canadian Casket*, 3 December 1831, p. 29.

77   Ibid., 18 September 1832, p. 143.

78   *Garland*, 15 September 1832, p. 7.

79   K. Greenfield, 'Randal, Stephen,' *DCB*, vol. 7. Randal was also responsible for *Randal's Magazine* (Picton, 1837).

80   Fleming UC j4.

81   A. Beaulieu and J. Hamelin, in *La presse québécoise*, 1:74, state that a single issue in French, titled

Musée de Montréal, had appeared in October 1832, but no copies have been located; and M.L. MacDonald, in 'The *Montreal Museum*, 1832–1834,' concludes that the reference the authors saw was to the French prospectus.

82 *Montreal Museum*, December 1832, p. 2.
83 M. Allodi, 'Bourne, Adolphus,' *DCB*, vol. 11, and *Printmaking in Canada / Les débuts de l'estampe imprimée au Canada*, no. 40.
84 M. Lemire et al., *La vie littéraire au Québec*, 2:188.
85 *American Magazine*, February 1788, p. 130.
86 Quoted in Fleming UC, p. 447.
87 Thomas A. Turner to A.J. Christie, 22 February 1824; quoted in M.L. MacDonald, 'Some Notes on the Montreal Literary Scene,' 35.
88 *Examiner*, March 1837, wrapper.
89 *Cabinet of Literature*, March 1838, wrapper.
90 On Bibaud's career, see C. Cyr, 'Bibaud, Michel,' *DCB*, vol. 5. See also F. Roy, '1837 dans l'oeuvre historique de trois contemporains,' 63–9; and P. Savard, '*Histoire du Canada* de Michel Bibaud,' in *DOLQ*, 1:345–7.
91 *Épîtres, satires, chansons, épigrammes et autres pièces de vers* (Montreal, 1830).
92 *Histoire du Canada sous la domination française* (Montreal, 1837); *Histoire du Canada et des Canadiens, sous la domination anglaise* (Montreal, 1844). Bibaud, a sometime schoolteacher, also published *L'arithmétique en quatre parties* (Montreal, 1816) and *L'arithmétique à l'usage des écoles élémentaires du Bas-Canada* (Montreal, 1832).
93 See K. Landry, '"Les avantages que la presse procure au public."'
94 *La Bibliothèque canadienne* 1.1 (June 1825): [1].
95 See A. Beaulieu and J. Hamelin, *La presse québécoise des origines à nos jours,* 1:1–110.
96 *L'Observateur* 2.26 (2 July 1831).
97 J. d'A. Lortie, ed., *Les textes poétiques du Canada français*, 2:682.

11. Popular Books

1 B. Amtmann, *Early Canadian Children's Books*, v.
2 See, for example, Susanna Moodie's *Roughing It in the Bush* (London, 1852), 2:108, for reading lessons using trays of sand during this period.
3 F. Lepage, *Histoire de la littérature pour la jeunesse*, 25.
4 C. Moore, *Louisbourg Portraits*, 96, 288.
5 Cited in G.L. Parker, *Beginnings of the Book Trade in Canada*, 23.
6 Tremaine/ECP 334.
7 B. Amtmann, *Early Canadian Children's Books*, v.
8 Fleming UC 645.
9 See S. Alston, 'Canada's First Bookseller's Catalogue,' 23.
10 Y. Lamonde, 'La librairie Hector Bossange de Montréal,' 73–4.
11 Fleming UC 491.
12 Fleming UC 1111b.
13 Fleming UC j9.
14 A.E. Gosselin, *L'instruction au Canada*, 229–30; L.-P. Audet, *Histoire de l'enseignement au Québec*, 1:152.

15 O. Maurault, *Le Collège de Montréal*, 51.

16 C. Galarneau, 'Demers, Jérôme,' *DCB*, vol. 8.

17 R. Olivier and F. Boulet, *Catalogue descriptif de quelques manuels scolaires manuscrits*.

18 M. Tremaine recorded textbooks of which no copies remain. She lists an alphabet printed by Brown and Gilmore in 1765 and republished several times in thousands of copies (Tremaine 65), as well as other readers from between 1766 and 1788 that have not survived. See also the catalogue on the 'Manuels scolaires québécois' website. The main collection is housed at the Université Laval; most of the religious teaching communities have also preserved textbooks. For religious books, catechisms, and similar works, see Raymond Brodeur's contribution in this chapter.

19 Because we lack statistics, we do not know the school attendance of anglophones in Lower Canada. Yvan Lamonde has compiled an index for the island of Montreal: the number of anglophone students taught free of charge rose from 712 in 1825 to 1,100 in 1835; see Y. Lamonde and C. Beauchamp, *Données statistiques*, 45. As well, J.A. Dickinson notes the boom in English immigration to Lower Canada between 1812 and 1840 (from 30,000 to 180,000 immigrants); see J.A. Dickinson, 'L'anglicisation,' 84–5. It should be noted that no textbooks intended for anglophones were printed in Quebec in the eighteenth century, while printers produced 18 titles for this readership during the 1830s alone. In addition, we would need to be able to compare francophone and anglophone student populations. C. Galarneau gives a ratio of one school per 4,000 francophones, compared to one school per 600 anglophones in 1790; see C. Galarneau, 'L'école, gardienne de la langue,' 100.

20 P. Aubin and M. Simard, *Les manuels scolaires*, 38, 52.

21 Tremaine 265 and 355; Fleming UC 332 and 391.

22 Taken into account are only the reprintings of foreign works in their entirety; thus we have not included French textbooks that were altered, such as the *Nouveau traité d'arithmétique* by the Frères des écoles chrétiennes, published in Montreal in 1838, which reproduced a French textbook after the measurement system was changed; see P. Aubin, 'La pénétration des manuels scolaires de France au Québec,' 8.

23 Textbooks in Lower Canada were influenced by French pedagogy. N. Voisine thus attributes to the Frères des écoles chrétiennes the substitution of Latin for French in reading lessons; see N. Voisine, 'L'église, gardienne de la langue,' 97. This was the case in France, but in Lower Canada, before the arrival of the first brothers in Montreal in 1837, the market comprised 14 readers republished from France or written in the province, starting with the *Grand alphabet*, published at Quebec in 1800. This spelling book was in Latin, but the 13 others were in French. Of course, the newspapers of Lower Canada advertised textbooks from France, including a certain number written in Latin that may have been used. The use of French to teach reading was nevertheless common in Lower Canada before the priests arrived.

24 C. Monaghan, *Murrays of Murray Hill*.

25 For editions of Murray and Mavor printed in Upper Canada before 1840, see Fleming UC.

26 R. Olivier, *Bibliographie d'anciens manuels scolaires étrangers*.

27 J.D. Wilson, 'Common School Texts in Use in Upper Canada prior to 1845,' 45–6. We can suppose that the number of foreign textbooks used in Upper Canada was very high; see F.A. Black, '"Horrid Republican Notions,"' 11.

28 G.L. Parker, *Beginnings of the Book Trade in Canada*, 24.

29 In this regard, the study of advertisements in newspapers announcing imported textbooks is promising; see F.A. Black, '"Horrid Republican Notions."'

30 Y. Lamonde and C. Beauchamp, *Données statistiques*, 96–7. Religious books were accounted for separately. For the year 1782 alone, 9,000 titles, 'almost all of them catechisms,' were purchased, no doubt mainly by schools. The proportion of sales that textbooks represented in Neilson's bookstore was certainly increased in this way.

31 For the history of education in Upper Canada and the Atlantic region, see S.E. Houston and A. Prentice, *Schooling and Scholars*; K.F.C. MacNaughton, *Development of the Theory and Practice of Education*; P. Robinson, *Where Our Survival Lies*; and F.W. Rowe, *Education and Culture in Newfoundland*.

32 P. Robinson, *Where Our Survival Lies*, 7.

33 J.D. Wilson, 'Common School Texts in Use in Upper Canada,' 42. Wilson provides a detailed list of the texts in use in various parts of the province.

34 V.E. Parvin, *Authorization of Textbooks*, 7–9.

35 B. Curtis, 'Schoolbooks and the Myth of Curricular Republicanism,' 311.

36 Ibid., 312.

37 For textbooks printed in Upper Canada during this period, see Fleming UC.

38 J.D. Wilson, 'Common School Texts in Use in Upper Canada,' 39.

39 A. Greer, 'Sunday Schools of Upper Canada,' 179.

40 Fleming UC 323. The Board of Education also paid Macfarlane to print 2,000 copies of Mavor's speller on large cardboard sheets for classroom use (B. Curtis, 'Schoolbooks and the Myth of Curricular Republicanism,' 312).

41 Fleming Atl. NS93.

42 J. Fingard, 'Bromley, Walter,' *DCB*, vol. 7.

43 Fleming Atl. NS138.

44 M. Brisebois, *Impressions*, 30.

45 G.L. Parker, 'Crosskill, John Henry,' *DCB*, vol. 8.

46 V.E. Parvin, *Authorization of Textbooks*, 13.

47 A. Greer, 'Sunday Schools of Upper Canada,' 180.

48 See F.W. Rowe, *Education and Culture in Newfoundland*, and K.F.C. MacNaughton, *Development of the Theory and Practice of Education*.

49 Tremaine 396.

50 Fleming UC 760.

51 Vlach and Buono 261.

52 See, for example, *Histoire abrégée de l'Ancien Testament* (Montreal, 1815): Vlach and Buono 393.

53 Fleming UC 137a.

54 Fleming UC 464 (York, 1830), 692 (Kingston, 1833), 761 (Kingston, 1834).

55 Vlach and Buono 178, 179. Another example is *La dévotion aux SS. Anges Gardiens*, produced by Fleury Mesplet in 1783: Vlach and Buono 206.

56 Vlach and Buono 556–61; another edition was produced in 1825 in Saint-Philippe. There were also other publications that spoke of devotional activities, such as Alexis Du Monceau's *Exercice très dévot envers S. Antoine de Padoue*: Vlach and Buono 223–5.

57 Tremaine 251, 980, 1083, 1162; Vlach and Buono 106–7.

58 Vlach and Buono 733–6.

59 Fleming UC 164 (Niagara, 1821), 483 (Kingston, 1830), 629 (Hallowell [Picton], 1832), 1314 (Toronto, 1839).

60 Fleming UC 1388.

61 O. Hubert, *Sur la terre comme au ciel*.

62 The sermons published in small format were circulated as pamphlets. Bishop Charles Inglis's sermon, dating from 1787 (Tremaine 516), was thirty-two pages long, but most were between sixteen and twenty pages. Sermons are identified in Tremaine, Vlach and Buono, *Cat. coll.*, Fleming Atl., and Fleming UC.

63 S.F. Wise, 'Sermon Literature and Canadian Intellectual History.'

64 J. Lambert, 'Chabrand Delisle, David,' *DCB*, vol. 4.

65 Tremaine 512.

66 Tremaine 1140; *Cat. coll.* 0860–1.

67 Tremaine 987; *Cat. coll.* 0660.

68 The first 'printed' catechism is attributed to Luther in 1527.

69 É. Germain, *Langages de la foi à travers l'histoire*.

70 F. Porter, *L'institution catéchistique au Canada*, 107–8.

71 N.-M. Dawson, 'Le paradoxal destin d'un catéchisme.'

72 Tremaine 59, 76.

73 *Cat. coll.* 0493.

74 Tremaine 699, 700, and 701.

75 The 1815 edition included 332 questions and answers.

76 R. Brodeur, ed., *Les catéchismes au Québec, 1702–1963*, 25–36.

77 Tremaine 280.

78 The Douay Catechism was later reprinted in a volume entitled *The Sincere Catholick's Companion* (Quebec, 1800, 1802): Tremaine 1168.

79 *Cat. coll.* 0491.

80 Fleming UC 766.

81 Tremaine 105; L.-P. Hébert, 'Le *Nehiro-Iriniu* du Père de La Brosse.'

82 G. Carrière, *Dictionnaire biographique des oblats de Marie-Immaculée au Canada*.

83 No studies have yet been carried out on the print materials used in Sunday schools.

84 *Quebec Herald*, 16 August 1790; Tremaine 636.

85 Fleming UC 432.

86 Fleming UC 61.

87 Fleming UC 441, 466.

88 Fleming UC 521.

89 Fleming UC 176.

90 Fleming UC 300.

91 H. Kallmann, *History of Music in Canada*, 27.

92 E. Gallat-Morin and J.-P. Pinson, eds, *La vie musicale en Nouvelle-France*, 33–60, 82–8, 109–22.

93 See N.F. Vogan, 'The Robert Moor Tunebook and Musical Culture in Eighteenth-Century Nova Scotia.'

94 M.S. Bird, *Ontario Fraktur*, 20–1, 50–4.

95 For information on early tunebooks, see J. Beckwith, ed., *Sing Out the Glad News*.

96 H. Kallmann, 'Publishing and Printing,' 1090.

97 Tremaine/*ECP* 1167.

98 M. Calderisi, *Music Publishing in the Canadas*, 11.

99 Ibid., 19–22.

100 Fleming Atl. NB59.

101 B.H. MacDonald and N.F. Vogan, 'James Dawson of Pictou and *The Harmonicon.*'

102 Fleming UC 497.

103 Fleming UC 598.

104 M. Calderisi, *Music Publishing in the Canadas*, 12.

105 J. Beckwith, *Psalmody in British North America*, 19.

106 Fleming UC 826. An edition without music had appeared the year before; see Fleming UC 770.

107 Fleming UC 1197a.

108 M. Calderisi, *Music Publishing in the Canadas*, 40–7.

109 On Duvernay's career, see J.-M. Lebel, 'Ludger Duvernay et la Minerve'; and J.-M. Lebel, 'Duvernay, Ludger,' *DCB*, vol. 8. On his newspapers, see also A. Beaulieu and J. Hamelin, *La presse québécoise*, vol. 1.

110 Author's translation.

111 ANQQ, Fonds L. Duvernay, no. 95, Duvernay to Gosselin, New York, 23 August 1831.

112 M. Calderisi, *Music Publishing in the Canadas.*

113 Brown and Gilmore's sheet almanac, 'Almanac de cabinet' (Quebec): Tremaine 57. This may have been modelled on the 'almanachs de cabinet' popularized in seventeenth-century Paris. See R. Chartier and D. Roche, 'Les pratiques urbaines,' 427.

114 Anthony Henry's 'Nova-Scotia Calender' (Halifax): Tremaine 119.

115 Christopher Sower's *Astronomical Diary* (Saint John): Tremaine 446.

116 Sylvester Tiffany's 'Upper Canada Almanack': Tremaine 1113. An almanac proposed by Gideon Tiffany at Newark (Niagara-on-the-Lake) in 1796 was not published; see Tremaine 979.

117 'The Prince Edward Island Calendar for ... 1815' (Charlottetown): Fleming, Atl., p. 160. In early 1792, Charlottetown printer William A. Rind published a calendar issue by issue in the *Royal Gazette*, lamenting the lack of 'Encouragement from the Community' to produce a proper almanac (Tremaine, p. 648).

118 Although Henry Winton had proposed a 'Newfoundland almanack' in 1827 (see William Barker's essay in chapter 15), there is no evidence of publication. The earliest example known is *The Newfoundland Almanac* for 1841 (St John's), but since Joseph Templeman's preface discusses 'the success which attended his first publication' and states that he has 'introduced much additional matter,' there was likely a previous edition.

119 *Nova Scotia Chronicle and Weekly Advertiser*, 20 June 1769.

120 *Mein and Flemings Register ... for 1768.*

121 See Henry Chubb's warnings that purchasers of illegally imported almanacs were 'liable to a prosecution' (*New-Brunswick Courier*, 6 December 1818).

122 'Dutch [i.e., German] and English Almanacks' were offered for sale at Jones and Thomas's store in Niagara (*Gleaner*, 13 December 1823).

123 Advertisement for *The Toronto Almanac and Royal Calendar of Upper Canada for 1839* (*Kingston Chronicle*, 11 May 1839).

124 In 1845 Frances Beavan recalled the reading materials she had seen years earlier in a native New Brunswicker's house: 'On a small shelf is laid the library, which consists but of the

bible, a new almanac, and Humbert's Union Harmony' (*Sketches and Tales Illustrative of Life in the Backwoods of New Brunswick*, 31).

125 See R. Chartier and D. Roche, 'Les pratiques urbaines,' and M. Perkins, *Visions of the Future*.

126 *Almanach encyclopédique, ou chronologie ... 1777*: Tremaine 225.

127 A. Dondertman, 'Anthony Henry, "Lilius," and the *Nova Scotia Calendar*.'

128 M.B. Stowell, *Early American Almanacs*.

129 On early English almanacs, see B. Capp, *Astrology and the Popular Press*.

130 Preface to *Der Neuschottländische Calender ... 1788* (Halifax): Tremaine 503.

131 The authors are grateful to Hans-Jürgen Lüsebrink for bringing this similarity to their attention.

132 Published at Quebec from 1791 to 1841 by members of the Neilson family. Later issues contain little French text.

133 Brown and Gilmore's 'Indian Kalendar,' 1768–73, 1793 (Tremaine 122, 822, and 1078) and 'Indian Almanack,' 1779–86, 1798 (Tremaine/ECP 273, Tremaine 1078). No copies have been located.

134 Examples include the 'Almanac de cabinet' (Tremaine 57) and the *Calendriers ... pour Montreal* published by Ludger Duvernay in the 1820s (*La Minerve*, 29 December 1828). There are no extant copies of the only known Upper Canadian sheet almanacs, all from Niagara; see Fleming UC, p. 458.

135 Tremaine/ECP 224.

136 See Tremaine 57.

137 See Tremaine 157.

138 *Nova Scotia Temperance Almanack* (Halifax, 1834–6).

139 'Calendrier de cabinet pour ... MDCCLXX': Tremaine 128; *The Upper Canada Christian Almanac, for ... 1835*: Fleming UC 812.

140 W.L. Mackenzie, *Sketches of Canada and the United States* (London, 1833); quoted in Fleming UC 479.

141 The almanacs are in Special Collections, Killam Library, Dalhousie University.

142 *Prince Edward Island Calendar ... 1835* (Charlottetown, [1834]), Halifax Public Library copy. Thomas Ridout recorded his experiences during the War of 1812 in an interleaved copy of the 1813 *Quebec Almanac*; see T. Ridout, *Ten Years of Upper Canada*, 180n.

143 Marius Barbeau scoured archives in Quebec for references to food and recipes. See 'Boulangerie, patisseries et friandises' in his *Saintes artisanes II*, 83–148.

144 M.A. Martin, *L'Institut de la Providence*, 1:281–3.

145 J. Theophano, *Eat My Words*, 191–2.

146 NA, MG 19, F 1, vol. 13, pt 2, Notebook, 461–74.

147 TRL, Boulton papers, Diary of Capt Henry Rudyerd, 20 July 1837 – January 1841.

148 Centre for Newfoundland Studies Archives, MF-216 ARCH.

149 Tremaine 579.

150 Fleming UC 7.

151 Fleming Atl. NS164.

152 Fleming UC 523.

153 For a full publication history of this and later Canadian cookbooks, see Elizabeth Driver's *Culinary Landmarks*.

154 In an advertisement in the *Christian Guardian*, 19 August 1840, *The Frugal Housewife's Manual* is said to be 'by a Canadian Lady.' Only two copies have been located (Fleming UC 1389).

155 The first twenty recipes in the *Manual* are also found in Colin Mackenzie's *Five Thousand Receipts* (4th American ed., 1839). Most of the instructions for vegetable cultivation were borrowed from Charles Crossman's *The Gardener's Manual* (Albany, New York, 1835), which accompanied packets of seeds grown by the Shakers of Mount Lebanon, New York, and sold throughout Upper Canada.

12. Print for Communities

1 James 1:22.

2 For bibliographical details and background information about books in Native languages discussed in this article, see J.C. Pilling, *Bibliography of the Algonquian Languages, Bibliography of the Eskimo Language*, and *Bibliography of the Iroquoian Languages*. For editions of biblical texts, see also T.H. Darlow and H.F. Moule, *Historical Catalogue of Printed Editions of Holy Scripture*.

3 J. Rioux, 'Sagard, Gabriel,' *DCB*, vol. 1.

4 K.G. Davies, 'Kelsey, Henry,' *DCB*, vol. 2.

5 G.-M. Dumas, 'Le Clercq, Chrestien,' *DCB*, vol. 1.

6 This work was reprinted in Restigouche in 1921.

7 Tremaine 75.

8 Tremaine 106.

9 Tremaine 105.

10 Ibid.

11 L.-P. Hébert, 'La Brosse, Jean-Baptiste de,' *DCB*, vol. 4.

12 Ibid.

13 Tremaine 147.

14 Tremaine 265.

15 R.W. McLachlan, *First Mohawk Primer*, 5. See also C. Jaenen, 'Bruyas, Jacques,' *DCB*, vol. 2.

16 R.W. McLachlan, *First Mohawk Primer*, 6.

17 B. Graymont, 'Thayendanegea,' *DCB*, vol. 5.

18 *Order for Morning and Evening Prayer / Ne Yakawea*: Tremaine 335.

19 D. Leighton, 'Claus, Christian Daniel,' *DCB*, vol. 4.

20 R.W. McLachlan, *First Mohawk Primer*, 8.

21 Tremaine 335.

22 Tremaine 355.

23 Ibid.

24 Ibid.

25 Fleming UC 332 and 391.

26 See Tremaine 335.

27 'Preface,' in The Book of Common Prayer, ii.

28 Thanks are owed to Rosemary Mathew, Bible Society's Library, Cambridge University Library, who carried out detailed research in response to several questions about early publications of the BFBS in Native languages.

29 C.F. Klinck, 'Norton, John,' *DCB*, vol. 6.

30 R.E. Ruggle, 'Kenwendeshon,' *DCB*, vol. 6.

31 B. Whiteman, *Lasting Impressions*, 35.

32 J.C. Pilling, *Bibliography of the Iroquoian Languages*, 130.

33 R.E. Ruggle, 'Kenwendeshon,' *DCB*, vol. 6.

34 Ibid. Ruggle dates this work to 1828.

35 Ibid.

36 Ibid.

37 Fleming UC 484.

38 Fleming UC 1276.

39 J.K. Hiller, 'Kohlmeister, Benjamin Gottlieb,' *DCB*, vol. 7.

40 BFBS, *Tenth Report* (1814), 55–6.

41 'Chippewa' and 'Ojibwa' (or Ojibway) were once used interchangeably, but 'Ojibwa' is now preferred in Canada, though 'Chippewa' is sometimes used for Ojibwa living to the east, south, and southwest of the Great Lakes. 'Saulteau' (or Sauteau or Salteaux), the name used by the French for peoples living north of Lake Superior, is an Ojibwa dialect.

42 *Part of the New Testament of Our Lord and Saviour Jesus Christ, Translated into the Chippewa Tongue, from the Gospel by St. Matthew / Pungkeh ewh ooshke mahzenahekun tepahjemindt owh ketookemahwenon kahnahnauntahweenungk. Jesus Christ*: Fleming UC 435.

43 *Mesah oowh menwahjemoowin, kahenahjemood owh St. Matthew. Kahkewagwonnaby kiya tyentennagen. Kahahnekahnootahmoobeungig keahnoonegoowod enewh*: Fleming UC 516.

44 *Part of the Discipline of the Wesleyan Methodist Church in Canada*: Fleming UC 903.

45 *Nvgvmouinvn genvnugvmouat igiu anishinabeg anvmiajig.*

46 J. Pickering, *Essay on a Uniform Orthography*. The need for a standard orthography was clearly recognized elsewhere as well. The continuing efforts of contemporary linguists were described by Max Müller in *Proposals for a Missionary Alphabet*, which he submitted to the Alphabetical Conference in 1854. The conference subscribed to the use of a standard missionary alphabet, 'where there was no important national literature clinging to a national alphabet' (49). Ostensibly, simplicity was the goal, since members of the conference believed that 'to increase the number of letters is tantamount to diminishing the usefulness of the alphabet' (44), but their efforts resulted in an alphabet of eighty-three characters, including diphthongs, based on the roman alphabet.

47 Fleming UC 693.

48 D.B. Smith, *Sacred Feathers*, 153.

49 Ibid.

50 Ibid., 185.

51 *Nu-gu-mo-nun O-je-boa an-oad ge-ë-se-üu-ne-gu-noo-du-be-üng uoô Muun-gou-duuz gu-ea Moo-ge-gee-seg ge-ge-noo-ŭ-muu-ga-oe-ne-ne-oug.*

52 'Preface,' in ibid., 6.

53 G.M. Hutchinson, 'Evans, James,' *DCB*, vol. 7.

54 Ibid.

55 *Spellings for the Schools in the Chipeway Language / Ah-ne-she-nah-pa, Oo-te-ke-too-we-nun*: Fleming UC 401.

56 'Preface,' in J. Evans, *Speller and Interpreter*, 4–5.

57 G.-A. Bellecourt, *Principes de la langue des sauvages appelés Sauteux*, iv.

58 Ibid., v.

59 D.B. Smith, *Sacred Feathers*, 185.

60 Ibid.

61 'Preface,' in P. Jones, *Collection of Chippeway and English Hymns*, iii.

62 Ibid., iv.

63 G.M. Hutchinson, 'Evans, James,' *DCB*, vol. 7.

64 B.B. Peel, *Rossville Mission Press*, 9.

65 M.V. Ray, 'Introduction,' in J. Evans, *Cree Syllabic Hymn Book*, 7. Ray also suggests how the mistaken idea that the earliest Rossville books were printed on birchbark may have originated.

66 From Evans's journal, 13 October 1840, cited in B.B. Peel, *Rossville Mission Press*, 9.

67 Ibid., 11.

68 Ibid.

69 H.K. Kalbfleisch, *History of the Pioneer German Language Press of Ontario*, 13–17; D.G. Lochhead, 'Henry, Anthony,' *DCB*, vol. 4.

70 Tremaine/*ECP* 503. On the title page of this edition, Henry used *Der Hochdeutsche Neu-Schottländische Calender*.

71 The last edition was for the year 1801; see Fleming Atl. NS 3.

72 Tremaine 503.

73 Tremaine, pp. 234–5, 619–20.

74 *Quebec Gazette / La Gazette de Québec*, 10, 17, 24 July 1783.

75 2 February 1782: *ECP*, p. 461.

76 Fleming UC 39. John Neilson published a French edition in Quebec (Hare and Wallot 123).

77 Radelmüller was paid £4 6s (NA, RG 1, E 15 B, vol. 16, account 26).

78 H. Lehmann, *German Canadians*, 66–79.

79 Several years earlier William Lyon Mackenzie, explaining that 'application having been made to me by a number of respectable settlers to establish a German Newspaper in this town,' had offered to enlarge his *Colonial Advocate* and print it in English and German using 'the black-letter type commonly used in Dutch papers printed in Pennsylvania.' He was prepared to 'carry this project into effect' whenever the settlers subscribed £200 to outfit the shop (*Colonial Advocate*, 1 January 1829).

80 H.K. Kalbfleisch, 'Peterson, Heinrich Wilhelm,' *DCB*, vol. 8.

81 Fleming UC n57.

82 Kalbfleisch, *History of the Pioneer German Language Press of Ontario*, 23.

83 Fleming UC 949.

84 Fleming UC 1200.

85 Fleming UC 1323.

86 Fleming UC 1290.

87 Fleming UC, pp. 456–7.

88 Rede Seiner Excellenz, Sir Francis Bond Head, Lieutenant Gouverneurs der Provinz Ober Canada (copy in Thomas Fisher Rare Book Library, University of Toronto). For an English edition, see Fleming UC 1048.

89 Fleming UC 934.

90 T. Eadie, 'Enslin, Christian,' *DCB*, vol. 8.

91 Fleming UC n58.

92 H.K. Kalbfleisch, *History of the Pioneer German Language Press of Ontario*, 21.

93 M.S. Bird, *Ontario Fraktur*; E.R. Good, *Waterloo County Itinerant Fraktur Artists*.

94 Fleming UC n142.

95 H.K. Kalbfleisch, *History of the Pioneer German Language Press of Ontario*, 24.

96 Ibid., 29.

97 *Leabhar aithghearr a' cheasnachaidh*: Fleming UC 905.

98 *Laoidhean spioradail*: TPL 7400; *Dain spioradail*: TPL 7407.

99 Fleming UC n54.

100 For more information, see J. Delisle, *La traduction au Canada / Translation in Canada, 1534–1984*; J. Delisle and G. Lafond, eds, *Histoire de la traduction / History of Translation*.

101 P. Stratford, *Bibliographie de livres canadiens traduits / Bibliography of Canadian Books in Translation*, xi.

102 The literary work of Frances Brooke was widely distributed in Europe and translated into several languages. See L. McMullen, 'Moore, Frances (Brooke),' *DCB*, vol. 4.

103 C. Gallant, 'L'influence des religions catholique et protestante sur la traduction des textes sacrés à l'intention des Micmacs dans les provinces Maritimes,' 101. A new edition of this work was published in Restigouche in 1921 by the *Micmac Messenger*.

104 R.G. Thwaites, 'Introduction,' *JR*, 1:41.

105 Ibid.

106 Tremaine/*ECP* 9.

107 Tremaine 325.

108 TPL 771.

109 G. Tratt, 'Deschamps, Isaac,' *DCB*, vol. 5.

110 C. Gallant, 'L'Acadie, berceau de la traduction officielle au Canada,' 73.

111 P.-A. Horguelin, 'Les premiers traducteurs (1760 à 1791),' 20.

112 For the general quality of translations during this period, see P. Daviault, 'Traducteurs et traductions au Canada.'

113 Tremaine, 812; for the period 1751–1800, information and references on the work in various languages of the early printers can be found in the appendixes and indexes of *ECP*, 417–523, 575–600.

114 Tremaine 583; *Cat. coll.* 0265 and 0855; G. Gallichan, *Livre et politique au Bas-Canada, 1791–1849*, 127–43.

115 See also J. Hare, 'La formation de la terminologie parlementaire et électorale au Québec: 1792–1810.'

116 G. Gallichan, *Livre et politique au Bas-Canada, 1791–1849*, 133.

117 *Precedents of Proceedings in the House of Commons*, by John Hatsell, and William Blackstone's treatise on criminal law.

118 F.-J. Audet, 'William Brown (1737–1789),' 106.

119 *La Minerve*, 17 November 1828.

120 G. Demers, 'La traduction journalistique au Québec (1764–1855),' 139.

121 F.-J. Audet, 'William Brown (1737–1789),' 99; Tremaine 66 and 67.

122 G. Gallichan, *Livre et politique*, 112.

123 S.E. Zeller, *Inventing Canada*, 4.

124 *ECP* 118.

125 L. Chartrand, R. Duchesne, and Y. Gingras, *Histoire des sciences au Québec*, 27.

126 C.M. Chu and B.H. MacDonald, 'Public Record.'

127 D.W. Thomson, *Men and Meridians*, 1:107.

128 R.L. Bishop, 'J.F.W. DesBarres: An Eighteenth-Century Nova Scotia Observatory.'

129 F.A. Black, 'Book Availability in Canada, 1752–1820,' chapter 3.

130 R. Lemoine, 'Le marché du livre à Québec.'

131 See, for example, the lengthy list of 'Books for Sale at the Store of James Dawson,' published in the *Bee* (Pictou, Nova Scotia) from 1 November 1837 through 7 February 1838.

132 L. Chartrand, R. Duchesne, and Y. Gingras, *Histoire des sciences au Québec*, 15.

133 F.A. Black, 'Book Availability in Canada, 1752–1820,' 72.

134 Ibid., 99.

135 D.W. Thomson, *Men and Meridians*, 1:191.

136 Ibid., 1:268.

137 See, for example, A.C. Dunlop, 'Pictou Literary and Scientific Society.'

138 B.H. MacDonald, 'In Support of an "Information System."'

139 C.B. Fergusson, *Mechanics' Institutes in Nova Scotia*.

140 F.-J. Audet, 'Les débuts du barreau de la province de Québec,' 227.

141 R. Lemoine, 'Le marché du livre à Québec,' 135–6.

142 Tremaine/*ECP* 197–200.

143 R. Lemoine, 'Le marché du livre à Québec,' 176–84; É. Langlois, 'Livres et lectures à Québec, 1760–1799,' 95–6; G. Labonté, 'Les bibliothèques privées à Québec (1820–1829),' 191–5; C. Veilleux, 'Les gens de justice à Québec, 1760–1867,' 466–9; *Le juge à paix*: Tremaine 583.

144 *Halifax ss: An Inquisition Indented, Taken at Halifax, within the Said County of Halifax ... before Samuel Shipton, Gent. Coroner* (Halifax, 1752–60): Tremaine 2.

145 For a bibliography of works on law published in British North America before 1840, see C. Rollins and J. Lynn-George, *Law to 1900 / Droit d'avant 1900*.

146 S. Normand, 'L'imprimé juridique au Québec du XVIIIe siècle à 1840.'

147 J. Stewart, *Reports of Cases Argued and Determined in the Court of Vice-Admiralty at Halifax in Nova-Scotia* (London, 1814); H. Desrivières-Beaubien, *Traité sur les lois civiles du Bas-Canada* (3 vols, Montreal, 1832–3); G.F.S. Berton, *Reports of Cases Adjudged in the Supreme Court of the Province of New Brunswick* (Fredericton, 1835); B. Murdoch, *Epitome of the Laws of Nova-Scotia* (4 vols, Halifax, 1832–3). See also K.G. Pryke, 'Murdoch, Beamish,' *DCB*, vol. 10.

148 W.C. Keele, *A Brief View of the Township Laws up to the Present Time* (Toronto, 1835) and *The Provincial Justice, or Magistrate's Manual* (Toronto, 1835): Fleming UC 838, 839; J.G. Marshall, *The Justice of the Peace, and County and Township Officer in the Province of Nova Scotia* (Halifax, 1837); W. Hepburn, *The Solicitor's Manual* (Toronto, 1837): Fleming UC 1104.

149 C. Galarneau, 'L'enseignement médical à Québec (1800–1848),' 58–62.

150 This title was reprinted many times. One version proposed at Quebec around 1786, however, seems never to have been published. See Tremaine/*ECP* 476.

151 R. Lemoine, 'Le marché du livre à Québec,' 197, 214; Y. Morin, 'Les niveaux de culture à Québec, 1800–1819,' 103–4.

152 J.J. Connor and J.T.H. Connor, 'Thomsonian Medical Literature and Reformist Discourse in Upper Canada'; Fleming UC 545, 654, 733.

153 Tremaine/*ECP* 136.
154 J. Bernier, 'Badelard (Badelart), Philippe-Louis-François,' *DCB*, vol. 5; Tremaine/*ECP* 454–5. The question of authorship is reviewed in *ECP* 454–5.
155 Tremaine 754; see also *ECP* 698A.
156 G. Janson, 'Tessier, François-Xavier,' *DCB*, vol. 6.
157 This case study is greatly indebted to G. Bilson, *Darkened House*, and R. Lemoine, 'Les brochures publiées.' Bilson's study discusses policies of public health as a reaction to cholera; see particularly 114–15. For a discussion of cholera as a scourge of the British Empire, see R. Lemoine, 'Les brochures publiées,' 35.
158 G. Bilson, *Darkened House*, 70–1.
159 Bas-Canada, *Acte pour l'établissement de bureaux sanitaires* (Quebec, 1832).
160 Niagara District, General Board of Health, 26 June 1832: Fleming UC 631; Niagara District, General Quarter Sessions, 25 June 1832: Fleming UC 632.
161 Two examples are J. Bethune, *A Sermon Preached on Wednesday, February 6, 1833* (Montreal, 1833), and George Jehoshaphat Mountain, *A Retrospect of the Summer and Autumn of 1832* (Quebec, 1833).
162 Church of England, *A Form of Prayer*, 11.
163 'Règles et règlemens, ordres et directions, faits et établis par le Bureau de santé, dans et pour les cité, port et havre de Montréal,' *La Minerve*, 14 June 1832.
164 Joseph Workman, *Medical Inaugural Dissertation on Asiatic Cholera* (Montreal, 1835), 30.
165 Ibid., 5.
166 AO, F 454, William Jones to Col. James Givens, 2 September 1834.

13. Publication and Power

1 O.B. Bishop, *Publications of the Governments*, v.
2 Some early newspapers used the word 'Herald' or 'Héraut' in their titles, evoking the officer who loudly proclaimed to the public the laws, regulations, and such news as wars, the death of the king, or the birth of the dauphin.
3 F. Melançon, 'La circulation du livre au Canada sous la domination française,' 41; A. Fauteux, *L'introduction de l'imprimerie au Canada*, 5.
4 It should be noted that England did the same for its colonies where printing had not yet been established.
5 D.D. Hall, 'Chesapeake in the Seventeenth Century,' 61–2.
6 The colony of Cape Breton had a separate government from 1764 to 1820, but no printer was established on the island during this time.
7 Tremaine 4–8; *ECP* 5A–7B.
8 G. Gallichan, *Livre et politique*, 108.
9 Tremaine 43–55; *ECP* 43–55B.
10 Tremaine 89.
11 P.L. Fleming, 'Des publications pour la paix, l'ordre et le bon gouvernement,' 13–14.
12 Tremaine 188, 398.
13 W. Colgate, 'Louis Roy: First Printer in Upper Canada,' 123.
14 Tremaine 520, 560, 644.

15 G. Gallichan, *Livre et politique*, 113–14.

16 Tremaine 836.

17 Fleming UC 17.

18 G. Gallichan, *Livre et politique*, 113–14.

19 J.G. Simcoe to H. Dundas, London, 12 August 1791, quoted in W. Colgate, 'Louis Roy: First Printer in Upper Canada,' 123.

20 From 1793 to 1798, official publications in Upper Canada had been produced at Newark, later called Niagara (now Niagara-on-the-Lake); Fleming UC 80.

21 Fleming UC 307, 351.

22 See, for example, Fleming UC 87, 454–5.

23 Fleming Atl. NS37, NS123; Tremaine 713, 790.

24 See the motions for print runs in the *Journaux de la Chambre d'assemblée*. Editions were published in French and English. See also G. Gallichan, 'La session de 1836,' 241–2.

25 Fleming UC 242.

26 Fleming UC 1058.

27 Fleming UC, pp. 536–7.

28 N.-E. Dionne, *Inventaire chronologique*, 3:288, 290, 364.

29 S. Normand, 'L'imprimé juridique au Québec du XVIIIe siècle à 1840.'

30 Tremaine 341; *ECP* 403A, 403B.

31 Tremaine 467, 468, 469, 1020. Saint John also published regulations in 1817 and 1820, and Halifax printed a draft charter in 1814; see Fleming Atl. NB67, NB94, NS105.

32 G. Gallichan, 'La Gazette officielle.'

33 The speaker of the Assembly was paid a salary of £1,000 per year. At the beginning of the century, Nova Scotia allocated £550 to publish the consolidation of its laws (1758–1804), plus £100 to bind the volumes.

34 NA, RG 1, E 15 A, vol. 210, 4 May 1831.

35 *Journaux de la Chambre d'assemblée du Bas-Canada*, 12–15 January 1813; NA, MG 24, B 1, vol. 2, 264.

36 Excerpt from the *York Observer*, quoted in *Quebec Gazette / La Gazette de Québec*, 21 July 1825, p. 3.

37 B.H. MacDonald, 'La publication des livres.'

38 Bouchette received only £500.

39 C. Boudreau and P. Lépine, 'Bouchette, Joseph,' *DCB*, vol. 7.

40 W.H. Laurence, '"Never Been a Very Promising Speculation,"' 51.

41 Ibid., 54–60.

42 Ibid., 76–8.

43 Fleming UC 435.

44 D. Houde, 'La liberté de la presse en droit anglais, américain et canadien,' 125; F.M. Greenwood and B. Wright, 'Introduction: State Trials, the Rule of Law, and Executive Powers in Early Canada.'

45 *Quebec Gazette / La Gazette de Québec*, 31 October 1765.

46 B. Murdoch, *History of Nova-Scotia, or Acadie*, 2:446–58.

47 Tremaine, pp. 599–601.

48 *La Gazette de Québec / Quebec Gazette*, 29 May 1766.

49 J.-P. de Lagrave and J.G. Ruelland, *Premier journaliste ..., Valentin Jautard*, 4–28.

50 J.- P. de Lagrave, *L'époque de Voltaire au Canada*, 161–95.

51 *Gazette du commerce et littéraire*, 2 June 1779.

52 Tremaine, pp. 623–4; J.-P. de Lagrave, *L'époque de Voltaire au Canada*, 257–90; J.-M. Fecteau and D. Hay, 'Government by Will and Pleasure instead of Law,' 150–4.

53 J.-P. Boyer, *'Appel à la justice de l'État' de Pierre du Calvet*, 64–85.

54 Tremaine, p. 665.

55 P. O'Flaherty, 'Ryan, John,' *DCB*, vol. 7; D.G. Bell, 'Sedition among the Loyalists.'

56 C. Galarneau, *La France devant l'opinion canadienne, 1760–1815*, 225 ff.

57 Ibid., 287.

58 M. Allodi, *Printmaking in Canada / Les débuts de l'estampe imprimée au Canada*; Tremaine 842, 949.

59 F.M. Greenwood and B. Wright, 'Parliamentary Privilege,' 418–23.

60 Hare and Wallot, pp. 315–27.

61 'Aux souscripteurs,' *Le Canadien*, 19 November 1808.

62 F. Ouellet, 'Bédard, Pierre,' *DCB*, vol. 6.

63 Hare and Wallot, pp. 215–20; J.-M. Fecteau et al., 'Sir James Craig's "Reign of Terror."'

64 He had previously had some trouble with the law, which, in spite of his loyal services, might have raised the governor's mistrust.

65 P. O'Flaherty, 'Ryan, John,' *DCB*, vol. 7.

66 Ibid.

67 P. O'Flaherty, 'Carson, William,' *DCB*, vol. 7; Fleming Atl. Nfld8, Nfld10.

68 S.F. Wise, 'Gourlay, Robert Fleming,' *DCB*, vol. 9; B. Wright, 'Gourlay Affair.'

69 R.L. Fraser, 'Ferguson, Bartemas,' *DCB*, vol. 6.

70 H.P. Gundy, 'Collins, Francis,' *DCB*, vol. 6.

71 Mackenzie recounted the details of this attack in a publication in 1827. See Fleming UC 324; P.L. Fleming, 'William Lyon Mackenzie as Printer.' The circumstances of the lawsuit created turmoil in the legal class, since some of the attackers were lawyers or law students. See C. Moore, *Law Society of Upper Canada*, 73–4.

72 Fleming UC 621.

73 Fleming UC 1126.

74 D. Monière, *Ludger Duvernay*, 72; J.-M. Lebel, 'Duvernay, Ludger,' *DCB*, vol. 8.

75 The court sat in the hall now occupied by the Nova Scotia Legislative Library; see J. Howe, *Speeches and Public Letters*, 1:82.

76 I.R. Robertson, 'Haszard, James Douglas,' *DCB*, vol. 10; J.M. Bumsted, 'Liberty of the Press in Early Prince Edward Island, 1823–9,' 522–39.

77 J. Monet, 'O'Callaghan, Edmund Bailey,' *DCB*, vol. 8.

78 G. Parizeau, *La vie studieuse et obstinée*, 70–9; F. Ouellet and A. Lefort, 'Viger, Denis-Benjamin,' *DCB*, vol. 9; *Mémoires relatifs à l'emprisonnement de l'honorable D.-B. Viger*.

79 J.-P. Bernard, *Les Rébellions de 1837–1838*, 290–315.

80 B. Cahill, 'R. v. Howe (1835) for Seditious Libel.'

81 Howe published two letters by George Thompson ('The People') on the subject. See the *Novascotian*, 20 November 1834 and 1 January 1835.

82 J. Howe, *Speeches and Public Letters*, 1:23. Chapter 2 contains Howe's speech, Archibald's reply, and Halliburton's charge to the jury. Howe's speech is also recorded in the *Novascotian*, 12 March 1835.

83 J. Howe, *Speeches and Public Letters*, 1:59.

84 B. Cahill, 'R. v. Howe (1835) for Seditious Libel,' 731.

85 J.M. Beck, 'Fool for a Client,' 39–40. Even eighty-two-year-old John Howe, a former magistrate with an unsullied reputation, was dragged into the recriminations that spring.

86 J. Howe, *Speeches and Public Letters*, 1:83.

87 J. Howe, *My Dear Susan Ann*, 175, Howe to Susan Ann Howe, 3 July 1835.

88 A complete examination of pastoral letters is found in P. Hébert and P. Nicol, *Censure et littérature au Québec*, 182–221.

89 This involved mainly 'Mandement du jubilé pour la ville de Québec'; see *MÉQ*, 5 March 1771, 2:224, 230–1.

90 Mgr de Saint-Vallier, 'Avis donnés aux curés et missionnaires dans une assemblée ecclésiastique tenue à Québec,' *MÉQ*, 5 February 1694, 1:311.

91 Mgr de Saint-Vallier, 'Mandement pour les cas réservés,' *MÉQ*, 10 March 1694, 1:329.

92 Mgr Hubert, 'Mémoire sur le diocèse de Québec, 1794,' *MÉQ*, 1794, 2:487.

93 Ibid.

94 The exact title is *Anti-Coton, ou Réfutation de la lettre déclaratoire de la doctrine des Pères Jésuites conforme aux décrets du concile de Trente, par le Père Coton* (Paris, 12 December 1610).

95 'Relation de ce qui s'est passé en la Nouvelle-France ou Lettre du P. Charles Lalemant, supérieur de la Mission de Canada, de la Compagnie de Jésus, au père Hiérosme Lalemant son frère,' in *Mercure françois*, 13.1. In 'Le monde de l'imprimé,' Danielle Rainville states that *Anti-Coton* 'was burned by the Catholic Gravé' (13). We were not able to verify this statement.

96 On this subject, see J. Laflamme and R. Tourangeau, *L'Église et le théâtre au Québec*.

97 We have, however, tried to demonstrate that, contrary to accepted opinion on the subject, this newspaper was produced essentially by Mesplet and Valentin Jautard themselves, under cover of some thirty different pseudonyms. See J. Cotnam and P. Hébert, 'La *Gazette littéraire* (1778–1779).'

98 E. Montgolfier to F. Haldimand, 2 January 1779, quoted in J.-P. de Lagrave, *Fleury Mesplet*, 165.

99 *Le Canadien*, 14 March 1810.

100 It should be noted that Craig, who had just dissolved the Parliament of Lower Canada and who was worried about the presence of a number of seditious Canadiens, was not at all satisfied with the clergy's role in the *Le Canadien* affair. Priests subscribed to this newspaper and seem to have supported the ideas that it presented; see Mgr Plessis to J.-H. Roux, 22 March 1810, *RAPQ*, 1927–8, 272. In the same letter, Plessis says that Craig summoned him to demand a firm position from the clergy on this issue.

101 Mgr Plessis to M. François Noiseux, 22 March 1810, *RAPQ*, 1927–8, 273.

102 On the role of the clergy, see L. Lemieux, *L'établissement de la première province ecclésiastique*, 67–71; G. Chaussé, *Jean-Jacques Lartigue*, 63–5.

103 On the affair of the priests Chaboillez and Pigeon, see P. Hébert and P. Nicol, *Censure et littérature au Québec*, 48–56.

104 Mgr Lartigue to Mgr Panet, 28 July 1828, *RAPQ*, 1942–3, 25; 30 November 1828, ibid., 37.

105 Mgr Lartigue to Mgr Panet, 11 February 1832, *RAPQ*, 1942–3, 134; Mgr Panet to Mgr Lartigue, 16 February 1832, *RAPQ*, 1935–6, 229; T.-M. Charland, 'Un projet de journal.'

106 Mgr Lartigue to Jacques Paquin, curé in Saint-Eustache, 17 March 1832, *RAPQ*, 1942–3, 138.

107 Mgr Lartigue to Mgr Panet, 24 January 1832, *RAPQ*, 1942–3, 132; he expressed this idea again a month later: Mgr Lartigue to Mgr Panet, 20 February 1832, *RAPQ*, 1942–3, 135.

108 Mgr Lartigue to P.-F. Turgeon, 3 January 1832, *RAPQ*, 1942–3, 129.

109 Mgr Lartigue to Mgr Signay, 10 January 1832, *RAPQ*, 1942–3, 130.

110 *HCQ*, 2:1, 382. Regarding the condemnation of *Paroles d'un croyant,* see Y. Lamonde, *La philosophie et son enseignement au Québec (1665–1920)*, 96–114; on the pirated edition of *Paroles d'un croyant*, see D. Monière, *Ludger Duvernay et la révolution intellectuelle au Bas-Canada*, 88.

111 Mgr Lartigue to Mgr Signay, 1 May 1836, *RAPQ*, 1944–5, 188.

112 On the question of whether this was a religious renewal or religious awakening, see René Hardy's analysis in 'À propos du réveil religieux dans le Québec du XIXe siècle.' Hardy gives considerable importance to the 1820s with regard to the origin of a religious awakening; we see the same period as also important in the movement toward religious censorship.

14. Authors and Publishing

1 For background information on the writers discussed here, see R.P. Baker, *History of English-Canadian Literature to the Confederation*; F. Dumont and J.-C. Falardeau, eds, *Littérature et société canadiennes-françaises*; C.F. Klinck et al., eds, *Literary History of Canada*; M. Lemire, ed., *Dictionnaire des oeuvres littéraires du Québec (DOLQ)*, vol. 1, *Des origines à 1900*; M. Lemire, ed., *La vie littéraire au Québec*, vol. 1, 1764–1805; D. Mativat, *Le métier d'écrivain au Québec (1840–1900)*, chapters 8 and 9; G.L. Parker, *Beginnings of the Book Trade in Canada*; W. Toye and E. Benson, eds, *Oxford Companion to Canadian Literature (OCCL)*.

2 M. Lescarbot, *History of New France*, 3:461–513, contains the original French version of *Les muses de la Nouvelle France.*

3 [Robert Hayman], *Quodlibets, Lately Come Over from New Britaniola, Old Newfound-land* (London, 1628), A2.

4 Thomas Cary, *Abram's Plains: A Poem* (Quebec, 1789), preface: Tremaine 585.

5 Isidore Lebrun's review in the *Revue encyclopédique de Paris* was reprinted in *La Minerve,* 20 October 1831, p. 1. Bibaud signed his reply in *Le Magasin du Bas-Canada* 1 (January 1832): 23.

6 J. Bailey, *Frontier Missionary*, 177.

7 F. Brooke, *The History of Emily Montague* (1985), 103.

8 S. Moodie, *Letters of a Lifetime*, 90, Moodie to the editor of the *Albion*, New York, 14 February 1833.

9 C.P. Traill, *Backwoods of Canada* (London, 1836), 153–4.

10 A. Shiels, *The Witch of the Westcot* (Halifax, 1831), preface, unpaged.

11 Thomas B. Vincent explains in the introduction to his edition of Croke's 'The Inquisition' that 'at least five manuscript copies of the original version are extant,' one at the NSARM, two at the NBM, Saint John, one at Harvard University, and one at Queen's University, Kingston. Croke made significant revisions to the poem for his English readers when it was published in his 1841 collection *The Progress of Idolatry*. See T.B. Vincent, *Narrative Verse Satire in Maritime Canada*, 144–5.

12 NSARM, MG 1, 94, GA 10, Jacob Bailey to John Howe, 31 December 1780; and T.C. Haliburton, *Letters*, Haliburton to Peleg Wiswall, 7 January 1824.

13 M.L. MacDonald, 'Kidd, Adam,' in *OCCL*.

14 See W.H. Laurence, '"Never Been a Very Promising Speculation."'

15 W. Charvat, *Literary Publishing in America, 1790–1850*, 9.

16 H. Alline, *Life and Journal* (Boston, 1806), 124.

17 H. Alline, *Hymns and Spiritual Songs* (Sackville, NB, 1987), ix.

18 H. Alline, *Life and Journal* (1806), 98, 117.

19 Ibid., 177. McClure's two letters to Alline's parents conclude this volume. At least four editions of his *Hymns and Spiritual Songs*, as well as his *Life and Journal*, were issued in New England.

20 J. Bailey, *Frontier Missionary*, 178–9.

21 T. Vincent, 'Odell, Jonathan,' in *OCCL*.

22 C.D. Edelberg, *Jonathan Odell*, 117–18.

23 For these poems and their translations, I am indebted to J.E. Hare, 'Quesnel, Joseph,' *DCB*, vol. 5.

24 J. Lambert, *Travels through Canada*, 1:318.

25 M. Lemire, *La vie littéraire au Québec*, 1:139.

26 D.G. Lochhead, 'Editor's Introduction,' in J.C.B. Hart, *St. Ursula's Convent* (1991), xxv.

27 'Preface,' *Acadian Magazine* 1 (July 1826): i–ii.

28 'Literary Notice,' *Halifax Monthly Magazine* 1 (February 1831): 366. This writer may not have known about Howe's purchase of Haliburton's *An Historical and Statistical Account of Nova-Scotia* (Halifax, 1829).

29 H.P. Gundy, 'Literary Publishing,' 176.

30 Fleming *UC* 178, 246.

31 'New Publications,' *Canadian Magazine, and Literary Repository* 2 (May 1824): 464.

32 O. Goldsmith, *Autobiography*, 11.

33 Ibid., 12.

34 O. Goldsmith, 'Prospectus,' *Novascotian*, 26 March 1834.

35 The basic British copyright act before 1840 was the 1709 Literary Copyright Act (8 Anne, c. 19). The 1842 act was the Literary Copyright Act (5 & 6 Vic., c. 45). The pre-Confederation acts were Lower Canada, *An Act for the Protection of Copy Rights* (2 Wm IV, c. 53) [1832], which was confirmed in 1841 by the Province of Canada as *An Act for the Protection of Copy Rights in this Province* (4 & 5 Vic., c. 61); and Nova Scotia, *An Act for Securing Copy Rights* (2 Vic., c. 36) [1839].

36 J. Richardson, *Eight Years in Canada* (Montreal, 1847), 93.

37 Ibid.

38 J. Richardson, *The Canadian Brothers* (1992), xli–xlv.

39 J. Richardson, *Eight Years in Canada* (1847), 104, 108.

40 W.F.E. Morley, *Bibliographical Study of Major John Richardson*, 5. Richardson made his comment in the 1851 New York edition of *Wacousta*.

41 Note in the *Literary Garland* 1 (September 1839): 487.

42 J. Richardson, *Eight Years in Canada*, 104.

43 C. Gray, *Sisters in the Wilderness*, 125.

44 S. Moodie, *Letters of a Lifetime*, 90–1, Moodie to the editor of the *Albion*, New York, 14 February 1833.

45 S. Moodie, *Roughing It in the Bush* (London, 1852), 2:194–5.

46 'Dinner to Thomas C. Haliburton, esq. the Historian of Nova Scotia, and Author of The Clockmaker,' *Novascotian*, 12 June 1839.

47 T.C. Haliburton, *Letters*, 15, Haliburton to Peleg Wiswall, 7 January 1824.

48 D.C. Harvey, 'The Intellectual Awakening of Nova Scotia.'

49 T.C. Haliburton, *Letters*, 94, Haliburton to Robert Parker, 24 March 1838.

50 T. C. Haliburton, *The Clockmaker* (1995), 434, 435–6.

51 B. Nesbitt, 'The First *Clockmakers*,' 95. See also G.L. Parker, 'Editor's Introduction,' in T.C. Haliburton, *The Clockmaker* (1995), xxix.

52 A detailed account of the relationships among Haliburton, Howe, and Bentley is provided in G.L. Parker, 'Editor's Introduction,' in T.C. Haliburton, *The Clockmaker* (1995). Letters from Haliburton to Bentley are reprinted in T.C. Haliburton, *Letters.*

53 G.L. Parker, 'Another Look at Haliburton and His Publishers,' 87.

54 Ibid., 89–90.

55 'Poem on Miss Willcocks' (Quebec, 1784): Tremaine 444.

56 T. Wood, *A Sermon Occasioned by the Death of ... Mrs. Abigail Belcher* (Halifax, 1771): Tremaine 162; B. Phelps, *Death ... in a Sermon, Occasioned by the Death of Mrs. Jane Chipman* (Halifax, 1775): Tremaine 212.

57 M. Verrette, *L'alphabétisation au Québec, 1660–1900*, 92.

58 *Formulaire de prières* (Montreal, 1777): Tremaine/ECP 258.

59 K.R. Murray, 'Sainte Anne,' 73.

60 E.J. Errington, *Wives and Mothers*, 210.

61 *Mrs. Goodman's First Step in History*, iii, iv, 22.

62 J. Seccombe, *A Sermon Occasioned by the Death of Mrs. Margaret Green*: Tremaine, 301.

63 N. Towle, *Some of the Writings and Last Sentences of Adolphus Dewey* (Montreal, 1833).

64 Joyce M. Banks, in chapter 12, describes the role of Elizabeth Kerr, Brant's daughter, in assisting Henry Aaron Hill. Christiana Brant was the Mohawk 'princess' who was working on biblical translations in 1824; see *Faith of Our Fathers*. See also D. Chaput, 'Charlotte de Rocheblave' and 'The "Misses Nolin."'

65 'A Collection of Original Poems': Tremaine 589.

66 Susanna Rowson's 1791 novel, *Charlotte Temple*, appeared in Upper Canada in 1832: Fleming UC 645.

67 'Catalogue of Books and Jewellery' (Quebec, 1784): Tremaine 443; 'The British Lady's Diary and Pocket Almanack' (Quebec, 1789): Tremaine 579; 'Handbill ... ' (Quebec, 1789): Tremaine 622.

68 L.M. Hudak, *Early American Women Printers and Publishers*, 210–19.

69 C. Galarneau, 'Mesplet, Fleury,' *DCB*, vol. 4; H.P. Gundy, *Early Printers and Printing*, 17; A. Fauteux, *Introduction of Printing into Canada*, chapter 4:16.

70 Fleming Atl., pp. 25, 75; I.R. Dalton, 'Simms, Sophia (Dalton),' *DCB*, vol. 8.

71 The following discussion is drawn from M. Brunet, 'Les femmes dans la production de la littérature francophone du début du XIXe siècle québécois,' and C. Gerson, *Canada's Early Women Writers.*

72 William McMurray, 'Two Poems' (Quebec, 1790): Tremaine 643.

73 P. Sylvain, 'Monk, Maria,' *DCB*, vol. 7.

74 N. Lester, *Le livre noir du Canada anglais*, 125–9.

75 M.L. MacDonald, 'The *Montreal Museum*,' 139, 146.

15. Literary Cultures

1 P. O'Flaherty, *Old Newfoundland*, 148.

2 NA, R5434-0-0-E (C-2522); reproduced in P. Neary and P. O'Flaherty, *Part of the Main*, 48.

3 J.A. Webb, 'Leaving the State of Nature,' 164. Webb reprints the text of the document, which is in PRO, CO 194/7, pp. 246–52.

4 David G. Alexander, in 'Literacy and Economic Development in Nineteenth-Century Newfoundland,' estimates literacy rates on the island from 1836, the date of the first census; see also G. Corbett, 'Literacy,' 316–17.

5 L. Coughlan, *Account of the Word of God in Newfoundland*, 19.

6 Ibid., 87, 94.

7 Ibid., 168.

8 A.G. Spangenberg, *Account of the Manner in Which the ... United Brethren Preach the Gospel*, 74.

9 This condition of literacy via orality, which is very old in Europe, is well described for sixteenth-century France in N.Z. Davis, 'Printing and the People.'

10 A.G. Spangenberg, *Account of the Manner in Which the ... United Brethren Preach the Gospel*, 81.

11 These schools are described in A. Hamilton, *Account of the State of the Schools in ... Newfoundland*.

12 See also E.J. Devereux, 'Early Printing in Newfoundland.'

13 S. Ellison, *Historical Directory of Newfoundland and Labrador Newspapers*, provides an excellent survey of extant papers.

14 P.H. Gosse, 'Philip Henry Gosse's Account of His Years in Newfoundland, 1827–1835.'

15 D. Wertheimer, 'Gosse, Philip Henry,' *DCB*, vol. 11.

16 *Royal Gazette*, 15 November 1810, 25 February 1813. For the beginnings of libraries in Newfoundland, see also R. Konrad, 'Libraries,' 289.

17 *Public Ledger and Newfoundland General Advertiser*, 13 February 1827.

18 Ibid., 2 November 1827.

19 L. Whiteway, 'The Athenaeum Movement.'

20 *Public Ledger and Newfoundland General Advertiser*, 27 March 1827.

21 E. Violet, *Remarks upon the Life and Manners of the Rev. John Jones* (St John's, 1810): Fleming Atl. Nfld6.

22 G. Cubit, *Jesus Christ the Supreme Governor and Only Foundation of the Christian Church* and *Observations on the Nature, Evidences, and Authority of the Christian Religion*; and J. Sabine, *A Sermon in Commemoration of the Benevolence of the Citizens of Boston*: Fleming Atl. Nfld13–15.

23 *Public Ledger and Newfoundland General Advertiser*, 20 April 1827.

24 Anonymous, 'Ballad of Nova Scotia,' *Gentleman's Magazine*, February 1750, xxx; reprinted in C. Gerson and G. Davies, eds, *Canadian Poetry from the Beginnings through the First World War*, 29.

25 D.S. Shields, *Oracles of Empire*, 3–17.

26 Quoted in J.M. Bumsted, *Henry Alline, 1748–1784*, 15.

27 G. Hick to 'My dear and loving wife,' 30 November 1749, *Gentleman's Magazine*, January 1750.

28 M. Harris, 'A Plan of the Harbour of Chebucto and Town of Halifax' and 'A Plan of the Town of Halifax in Nova Scotia,' *Gentleman's Magazine*, February 1750.

29 For biographies of Bushell and many of the other individuals discussed in this article, see the *DCB*.

30 *Halifax Gazette*, 1 March 1755.

31 See, for example, the advertisements in *Nova-Scotia Gazette*, 1, 3, and 15 September 1768.

32 *Nova-Scotia Gazette*, 24 March 1768, 14 April 1768, and 14 July 1772.

33 *Nova-Scotia Gazette*, 28 July 1768.

34 *Nova-Scotia Gazette*, 26 November 1767.

35 Lt Col. Simon Fraser to Bailie James Fraser, 28 June 1757, in A. Macdonald, *The Old Lords of Lovat*

and Beaufort, 136. I wish to thank Mary Bogaard of Sackville, New Brunswick, for drawing this letter to my attention.

36 J.M. Bumsted, *Henry Alline, 1748–1784*, 5.

37 *Hymns and Spiritual Songs* was published in Boston in 1786 and went through further editions in Dover, New Hampshire (1795, 1797), and Storington-Port, Connecticut (1802).

38 D.D. Hall, *Cultures of Print*, 52.

39 S.A. Marini, *Radical Sects of Revolutionary New England*, 42.

40 C. Gerson and G. Davies, eds, *Canadian Poetry from the Beginnings through the First World War*, 37.

41 J. Beverley and B. Moody, 'Introduction,' *The Life and Journal of the Rev. Mr. Henry Alline* (1982), 23–4.

42 C.C. Goen, *Revivalism and Separatism in New England, 1740–1800*, 13–14.

43 J. Beverley and B. Moody, 'Introduction,' *The Life and Journal of the Rev. Mr. Henry Alline* (1982), 47–50. Jonathan Scott's spiritual journal has been published as *The Journal of the Reverend Jonathan Scott*, ed. H.E. Scott Jr.

44 M. Bradley, *A Narrative of the Life and Christian Experience of Mrs. Mary Bradley, of Saint John, New Brunswick, Written by Herself* (Boston, 1849), 28. For the original narrative, see New England Historic Genealogical Society, Boston, S61, series B, BIOG 2B4, 'Mary Bradley.'

45 M. Bradley, *A Narrative of the Life*, 50.

46 Ibid., 106. See also M. Conrad, 'Mary Bradley's Reminiscences,' 92, and G. Davies, *Studies in Maritime Literary History, 1760–1930*, 26–8.

47 D.D. Hall, *Cultures of Print*, 35.

48 NSARM, MG 1, vol. 100, reel 14, 904, 428–31. This poem is reprinted in C. Gerson and G. Davies, eds, *Canadian Poetry from the Beginnings through the First World War*, 38–40, as '[Verse against the New Lights].'

49 NSARM, MG 1, vol. 92a, no. 139, John Hicks to Jacob Bailey, 26 October 1779; no. 146, G. Lyde to Jacob Bailey, 15 February 1781; vol. 93, no. 34, Samuel Peters to Jacob Bailey, 8 February 1780.

50 Ibid., Samuel Peters to Jacob Bailey, 8 February 1780.

51 In a letter, William Clarke indicates that he published Bailey's letter on the state of the Loyalist refugees in the London *Publick Advertiser* circa 21 March 1783; see NSARM, MG 1, vol. 93, no. 80, William Clarke to Jacob Bailey.

52 NSARM, MG 1, vol. 93, no. 54, William Clarke to Jacob Bailey, 1782. Clarke says that he has not seen Bailey's sermons yet but will get them from Samuel Peters. This comment suggests either publication or circulation.

53 For the book importation and selling practices of John Fletcher and Richard and James Kidston, see F.A. Black, 'Book Availability in Canada, 1752–1820, and the Scottish Contribution,' especially 73–5 and 193–6.

54 'Address,' *Acadian Magazine* 1 (January 1827): 278–9, and 'To The Public,' *British North American Magazine* 1 (February 1831): 2.

55 R.P. Baker, *History of English-Canadian Literature to the Confederation*, 51.

56 D.D. Hall, *Cultures of Print*, 53.

57 *Royal St. John's Gazette*, 9 September 1784; Tremaine 421.

58 NSARM, MG 1, vol. 1610, no. 86, 'Prologue on Opening a Little Theatre at St. Johns, New Brunswick.'

59 'To the Public,' *Nova-Scotia Magazine* 1 (June 1790): n.p. For a discussion of the *Nova-Scotia*

Magazine, see also G. Davies, 'Literary Study of Selected Periodicals from Maritime Canada: 1789–1872,' 15–97, and G. Davies, '"Good Taste and Sound Sense."'

60 D.C. Harvey, 'Intellectual Awakening of Nova Scotia,' 108. Harvey says that 'very few plain, blunt men' subscribed to the *Nova-Scotia Magazine*. However, a cross-referencing of the Halifax names on the subscription list with those in NSARM, Vertical Mss. File, 'Assessment Rolls of Halifax, 1792–93,' ed. Terrence Punch, reveals that a number of barbers, labourers, artisans, servants, and shopkeepers subscribed to the journal.

61 *Nova-Scotia Magazine* 1 (November 1789): 389.

62 *Acadian Recorder*, 14 July 1821.

63 D.C. Harvey, 'Intellectual Awakening of Nova Scotia,' 116, 119.

64 Ibid., 116.

65 Ibid., 119.

66 Malcolm Bàn Buchanan, 'Emigration of the Islanders,' in M. MacDonell, 'Bards on the "Polly,"' 37. Rory Roy MacKenzie's 'The Emigration' appears on page 38 of the same issue. Both poems are presented in Gaelic and in English translation.

67 J. Young, *The Letters of Agricola on the Principles of Vegetation and Tillage* (Halifax, 1822), ix and 22. See also J.S. Martell, *Achievements of Agricola and the Agricultural Societies, 1818–25.*

68 For readers' response to the Stepsure letters and their later publishing history, see G. Davies, 'Editor's Introduction,' in T. McCulloch, *The Mephibosheth Stepsure Letters* (1990), xvii–lxxi.

69 W. McCulloch, *Life of Thomas McCulloch, D.D., Pictou*, 73.

70 NSARM, MG 1, vol. 793, no. 69, Thomas McCulloch to Simon Bradstreet Robie, 9 February 1822.

71 NLS, Acc. 5643/B8, Letter-books, 480–3, William Blackwood to John Mitchell, 31 December 1829.

72 Ibid., 133–7, William Blackwood to John Mitchell, 15 December 1828.

73 NSARM, MG 1, vol. 553, no. 46, Thomas McCulloch to James Mitchell, 3 December 1829.

74 H.N. Frye, 'Introduction,' to Thomas McCulloch, *The Stepsure Letters* (1960), iii–ix.

75 NSARM, MG 1, vol. 79, folder 1, Tho. C. Haliburton to 'Dear Sir' (Peleg Wiswall), 7 January 1824.

76 NSARM, MG 1, vol. 1419, file 1, item A, 128, Jacob Norton Crowell, 'Pencillings on Sea and on Shore, or a Voyage to Australia.' On the publishing history of Haliburton's *Clockmaker* series, see Ruth Panofsky's case study in chapter 14.

77 For a discussion of Mercy Seccombe's diary, see G. Davies, 'Poet to Pulpit'; see also G. Davies, '"Old Maidism Itself."'

78 NA, MG 23, D 6, Rebecca Byles to her aunt, 24 March 1784.

79 Ibid.

80 L.K. Kerber, *Women of the Republic*, 185–285, and M.B. Norton, *Liberty's Daughters*, 256–94.

81 NA, MG 23, D 6, 111, p. 5, Eliza Byles to her aunts.

82 *Novascotian*, 29 June 1826.

83 T.C. Haliburton, *The Old Judge* (London, [1849]), 1:6.

84 J. d'A. Lortie, ed., *Les textes poétiques du Canada français: 1606–1867.*

85 B. Andrès, 'D'une mère patrie à la patrie canadienne.'

86 P. Monette, ed., *Le rendez-vous manqué avec la Révolution américaine.*

87 'Sur le triomphe de Tracey et de Duvernay,' in *Chansons politiques du Québec*, 1:299–301.

88 B. Andrès, *Les lettres de la Conquête (1759–1799)*.

89 B. Andrès, 'La génération de la Conquête.'

90 B. Andrès, 'Les lettres d'avant la lettre.'

91 M. Brunet, 'Anonymat et pseudonymat au XIXe siècle.'

92 J. Cotnam and P. Hébert, 'La *Gazette littéraire* (1778–1779).'

93 J. Roy, 'Stratégies épistolaires et écritures féminines,' 521.

94 B. Andrès, 'La génération de la Conquête.' For all of these writers and a synthesis of works about them, see B. Andrès and M.A. Bernier, eds, *Portrait des arts, des lettres et de l'éloquence au Québec (1760–1840)*.

95 B. Andrès, 'Le fantasme du champ littéraire dans la *Gazette de Montréal* (1778–1779),' and N. Doyon, 'L'Académie de Montréal (1778): Fiction littéraire ou projet utopique?'

96 B. Andrès and M.A. Bernier, 'De la génération de la Conquête à celle des Patriotes.'

97 B. Andrès, 'Y a-t-il un intellectuel dans le Siècle?'

98 P. Monette, ed., *Le rendez-vous manqué avec la Révolution américaine*; Vlach and Buono 282.

99 P. Du Calvet, *Appel à la justice de l'État* (London, 1784), 66.

100 Ibid., 151.

101 I. Beaulé, 'Henri-Antoine Mézière.'

102 Quoted in J. d'A. Lortie, ed., *Les textes poétiques du Canada français*, 1:445, 447.

103 H.-A. Mézière, 'Prospectus,' *L'Abeille canadienne*, 1 August 1818.

104 *Gazette des Trois-Rivières*, 15 September 1818.

105 N. Desjardins, 'La théâtralisation du politique.'

106 L. Villeneuve, '*Le Fantasque* de Napoléon Aubin.'

107 Biographies of many of the authors discussed here appear in the *DCB*.

108 M. Lemire, ed., *La vie littéraire au Québec*, 1:348.

109 Tremaine 585.

110 Tremaine/*ECP* 1124.

111 D.M.R. Bentley, 'Poems in Early Canadian Newspapers.'

112 F.C. Würtele, *Index of the Lectures, Papers and Historical Documents*, xlii.

113 G. Bernatchez. 'La Société littéraire et historique du Québec,' 188.

114 M. Lemire, ed., *La vie littéraire au Québec*, 2:108.

115 J.G. Simcoe, *Correspondence*, 3:298.

116 G.L. Parker, *Beginnings of the Book Trade in Canada*, 24.

117 A. Jameson, *Winter Studies and Summer Rambles in Canada* (1838), 1:34.

118 Ibid., 36–7.

119 Ibid., 30.

120 As Clara Thomas has argued, Jameson's intense dislike of her husband and his colonial friends coloured her view of the city during her year-long stay. She had come to Upper Canada with the purpose of seeking a divorce.

121 A. Jameson, *Winter Studies and Summer Rambles* (1838), 1:271. The Reverend George Mortimer had provided a more optimistic picture of the available reading matter four years earlier. Describing York in 1833, he reported, 'We have two monthly magazines published in York, and three or four newspapers, and from New York we have two weekly newspapers, designed expressly for English readers – the *Albion* and the *Emigrant*, full of English news and English literature; so that in a month or six weeks, we have all the cream of the London and country news, as well as the best of the lighter articles from the British periodicals.' He

also mentions cheap reprints of some British periodicals and a variety of American magazines and series, which allowed him 'to furnish [his] family with an extent of literature far beyond [his] capabilities in England' (G. Mortimer, *Life and Letters*, 197).

122 S. and J. Moodie, *Letters of Love and Duty*, 72–3. Both Kent and Maynard were ordained ministers and Upper Canada College teachers; all were English emigrants.

123 J. Strachan, 'An Address ... at the Last Annual Examination of His School, in *Kingston Gazette*, 3 September 1811.

124 C. Gerson, *Purer Taste*, 19.

125 The Methodist *Christian Guardian*, which began publication in 1829, had one of the largest circulations in the province by 1832. Using the newspaper's records, Julie Stabile has found 1,250 subscribers on the rolls in 1830 and 1,100 in 1834 (J. Stabile, 'Economics of an Early Nineteenth-Century Toronto Newspaper Shop,' 59). George L. Parker calls it 'obligatory reading for all classes and factions' (*Beginnings of the Book Trade in Canada*, 57).

126 David Chisholme, 'St. Ursula's Convent, or the Nun of Canada,' *Canadian Review and Literary and Historical Journal* 1 (July 1824): 49–53.

127 *Weekly Register*, 8 July 1824.

128 C. Gerson, *Purer Taste*, 68.

129 Ibid., 69.

130 H. Murray, *Come, Bright Improvement!* x.

131 D.M.R. Bentley, *Mimic Fires*, 80.

132 Ibid., 86, 83.

133 *Kingston Gazette*, 14 January 1811.

134 See J. Strachan, *John Strachan: Documents and Opinions*, 25–31.

135 Fothergill owned land on the north shore of Rice Lake and had become a friend to and spokesman for the Mississaugas still resident in that area.

136 For newspapers published in the province, see Fleming UC n1–145.

137 G.L. Parker, *Beginnings of the Book Trade in Canada*, 74, 67.

138 I include here only those who published a book or a number of poems in Upper Canada prior to 1840, though a few exceptions to this one-book requirement have been made. Writers such as Adam Kidd, whose *The Huron Chief* was published in Montreal in 1830, are excluded.

139 D.M.R. Bentley, *Mimic Fires*, 106.

140 Burwell's 'The Death of Brock' appeared in the *Weekly Register* on 1 January 1824. Several essays were published in the paper in 1823.

141 Fleming UC 279.

142 Mary Lu MacDonald's *Literature and Society in the Canadas* has much valuable bibliographical and biographical information about Upper Canadian writers. See also the *DCB* for biographies of many of the writers discussed here.

143 Fleming UC 820, 1083, 1388, 1510.

144 M. Peterman, 'Reconstructing the *Palladium of British America*.'

145 H. Murray, 'Frozen Pen, Fiery Print, and Fothergill's Folly.' See also her *Come, Bright Improvement!* 13, 41–3.

146 G. Draper and R. Hall, 'Dunlop, William,' *DCB*, vol. 6.

147 T. Rolph, *A Brief Account* (Dundas): Fleming UC 992.

148 See J. Johnston, *Anna Jameson*, 111. As Johnston points out, Jameson does not identify Traill by

name or the book by title. However, her description perfectly fits Traill's book, especially in its cheerful attention to the interests of female emigrants. In fact, Jameson adds in the same letter, 'I wish much that I were going to live such a life, instead of residing in a small, vulgar, factious city [Toronto], where I shall be afraid to speak, almost to think, lest I should inadvertently hurt Mr. Jameson's interests.' The letter is dated 1 October 1836, seven months after Traill's book was first published.

149 M.L. MacDonald, *Literature and Society in the Canadas*, 143.

SOURCES CITED

Archival Sources

Archives des ursulines de Québec
Journal de recette et dépense de 1715 à 1746

Archives nationales du Québec à Montréal
P 680, Fonds Ludger Duvernay, 1805–52
P 1000-3-360, Neilson collection

Archives nationales du Québec à Québec
Greffes: J.-B. Decharnay
        J.-A. Saillant
        L. Chambalon
P 192, Fonds Famille Neilson, 1693–1953
P 193, Fonds Imprimerie Neilson, 1790–1895

Archives of Ontario / Archives publiques de l'Ontario
F 37, Mackenzie-Lindsey family fonds, 1687–1973
F 43, Thomas Ridout family fonds, 1786–1894
F 454, William Jones fonds, 1831–9 (AO microfilm reel MS 296)
F 592, Mary Sophia O'Brien fonds, 1828–[31?] (AO microfilm reel MS 199)
F 4269, *Upper Canada Herald* ledger, 1829–33

Bibliothèque nationale, Paris
Ms. fr. 21931, Registre des livres arrêtés dans les visites faites par les syndic et adjoints, 1703–42

Centre des études acadiennes
Registre des baptêmes, mariages et sépultures de l'église Saint-Charles-aux-Mines, 5 juillet 1739 – 10 novembre 1748

Centre for Newfoundland Studies Archives, Memorial University
MF-216 ARCH, Gladys E. Soulsby Collection
Miawpukek Mi'kamawey prayer book, [1812?–92?] (photographic facsimile; original held by the Miawpukek Band of the Mi'kmaq Tribe, Conne River; microfilm copy, NA, mf. M-8638)

Colchester Historical Society Archives
D13, 89.37, James Patterson fonds, Account and Day-book, 1802–3 (NSARM, mf. 10953)

Division des archives, Université Laval
P 245, Fonds Fournier
P 282, Fonds Claude Galarneau

McGill University Libraries, Rare Books and Special Collections Division
MS 472, Masson Papers; available on-line at http://digital.library.mcgill.ca/nwc/

Musée de la civilisation, Québec
Fonds Séminaire de Québec

National Archives of Canada / Archives nationales du Canada (now Library and Archives Canada)
MG 1:   Fonds des Colonies, 1540–1898
            Série B, Lettres envoyées, 1663–1789
            Série C11A, Correspondance générale; Canada, 1540–1784
MG 19: Fur trade and Indians
            A 2 [R7712-0-7-E], Ermatinger estate fonds, 1758–1966
                Jacobs-Ermatinger estate, 1758–1862
            C 1 [R2155-0-7-E], Masson collection, 1784–1857
                Archives collection, 1785–1857
            F 1 [R5236-0-7-E], Claus family fonds, 1755–1886
MG 23: Late eighteenth-century papers
            D 6 [R6131-0-1-E], Mather Byles Jr and family fonds, 1757–1837
            J 7 [R5434-0-0-E], Logbook of HMS *Pegasus*, 1786 (microfilm reel C-4848)
MG 24: Nineteenth-century pre-Confederation papers
            B 1 [R7325-0-0-E], Neilson Collection, 1666–1912
            C 1 [R2809-0-9-E], Joseph Willcocks fonds, 1799–1822
RG 1:   Executive Council: Quebec, Lower Canada, Upper Canada, Canada, 1764–1867
            E 3, Upper Canada: Executive Council, Submissions on state matters
            E 15, Board of Audit of the provincial public accounts
            E 15 A, Quebec and Lower Canada, 1759–1841
            E 15 B, Upper Canada, 1792–1841
RG 5:   Provincial and civil secretaries' offices: Upper Canada, Canada West
            A 1, Upper Canada sundries, 1766–1841

National Archives of Scotland
CS 96, Court of Session Productions, ca. 1760–1840

E 504, Customs records, 1742–1830
GD 1/151, James Dunlop Letters, 1773–1815

National Library of Scotland
Acc. 5643/B8, Letter-books
MS 791, Archibald Constable & Co., Letter-book, 1820–2

New England Historic Genealogical Society
S61, series B, BIOG, 2B4, Mary Bradley

Nova Scotia Archives and Records Management
MG 1:   Papers of families and individuals
         10-17A, Almon family fonds
         18-83, Mather Byles Almon business papers
         91-104, Jacob Bailey fonds
         167-75, Thomas Cantley documents
         181-218, Chipman family fonds
         526A, Anna Kearny fonds
         550-8, Thomas McCulloch papers
         793, Simon B. Robie documents
         1419, Evelyn Richardson papers
         1595-613, Bliss family papers
         1769, Crofton James Uniacke papers
MG 3:   Business papers
         236, Horton's Landing, King's County, Account Book, 1793–4
MS 100: Documents, newspapers items, miscellaneous items
         214, Berry papers
Mf. 13512, Windsor Account Book, 1778–[82?]

Nova Scotia Museum of Cultural History
Uniacke MS 3, Inventory of house furnishings, 1830

Provincial Archives of New Brunswick / Archives provinciales du Nouveau-Brunswick
MS. M 1986.13, J.R. Harper, 'Social History of New Brunswick'

Public Record Office, London (now National Archives)
AO 12, American Loyalists Claims, series I, 1776–1831
AO 13, American Loyalists Claims, series II, 1780–1835
CO 194, Colonial Office and predecessors: Newfoundland, Correspondence, 1696–1922
CO 221, Colonial Office and predecessors: Nova Scotia and Cape Breton Miscellanea, 1730–1861
CO 226, Colonial Office and predecessors: Prince Edward Island Original Correspondence, 1769–1873
CUST 14, Ledgers of imports and exports, Scotland, 1755–1827

Thomas Fisher Rare Book Library, University of Toronto
MS coll. 131, Canadian Documents Collection

Toronto Reference Library
Henry John Boulton papers
Robert Baldwin papers

Published Sources

Adams, Percy G. *Travel Literature and the Evolution of the Novel.* Lexington: University Press of Kentucky, 1983.

Alexander, David G. 'Literacy and Economic Development in Nineteenth-Century Newfoundland.' In *Atlantic Canada and Confederation: Essays in Canadian Political Economy*, ed. Eric W. Sager, Lewis R. Fischer, and Stuart O. Pierson, 110–43. Toronto: University of Toronto Press in association with Memorial University of Newfoundland, 1983.

Allen, William Osborne Bird, and Edmund McClure. *Two Hundred Years: The History of the Society for Promoting Christian Knowledge, 1698–1898.* 1898. Reprint, New York: Burt Franklin, 1970.

Alline, Henry. *Hymns and Spiritual Songs.* With an Introduction by John M. Bumsted. Sackville: Ralph Pickard Bell Library, Mount Allison University, 1987.

– *The Life and Journal of the Rev. Mr. Henry Alline.* Ed. James Beverley and Barry Moody. Hantsport: Lancelot Press, 1982.

Allodi, Mary. *Berczy.* Ottawa: National Gallery of Canada, 1991.

– *Printmaking in Canada: The Earliest Views and Portraits / Les débuts de l'estampe imprimée au Canada: Vues et portraits.* Toronto: Royal Ontario Museum, 1980.

Allodi, Mary, and Rosemarie L. Tovell. *An Engraver's Pilgrimage: James Smillie in Quebec, 1821–1830.* Toronto: Royal Ontario Museum, 1989.

An Alphabetical List of the Merchants, Traders, and Housekeepers Residing in Montreal: To Which Is Prefixed a Descriptive Sketch of the Town by Thomas Doige. Montreal: James Lane, 1818.

Alston, Sandra. 'Canada's First Bookseller's Catalogue.' *PBSC/CSBC* 30.1 (Spring 1992): 7–26.

American National Biography. Ed. John A. Garraty and Mark C. Carnes. Vol. 18. New York: Oxford University Press, 1999.

Amory, Hugh. 'The New England Book Trade, 1713–1790.' In *A History of the Book in America*, vol. 1, *The Colonial Book in the Atlantic World*, ed. Hugh Amory and David Hall, 314–46. Cambridge and New York: Cambridge University Press, 2000.

Amory, Hugh, and David D. Hall, eds. *A History of the Book in America*, vol. 1, *The Colonial Book in the Atlantic World.* Cambridge and New York: Cambridge University Press, 2000.

Amtmann, Bernard. *Early Canadian Children's Books, 1763–1840: A Bibliographic Investigation into the Nature and Extent of Early Canadian Children's Books and Books for Young People / Livres de l'enfance & livres de la jeunesse au Canada, 1763–1840: Étude bibliographique.* Montreal: B. Amtmann, 1976.

Andreae, C.A. *Lines of Country: An Atlas of Railway and Waterway History in Canada.* Erin: Boston Mills Press, 1997.

Andrès, Bernard. 'D'une mère patrie à la patrie canadienne: Archéologie du patriote au XVIIIe siècle.' *Voix et images* 78 (Spring 2001): 474–97.

– *Écrire le Québec: De la contrainte à la contrariété; essai sur la constitution des lettres.* Études et documents. Montreal: Éditions XYZ, 2001.

– 'Le fantasme du champ littéraire dans la *Gazette de Montréal* (1778–1779).' *Études françaises* 36 (2000): 9–26.

– 'La génération de la Conquête: Un questionnement de l'archive.' *Voix & images* 59 (Winter 1995): 274–93.

– 'Les lettres d'avant la lettre: Double naissance et fondation.' *Littérature* 113 (March 1999): 22–35.

– *Les lettres de la Conquête (1759–1799)*. Cahiers du CELAT. Sainte-Foy: Université Laval, forthcoming.

– 'Y a-t-il un intellectuel dans le Siècle? ou Penser au Québec à la fin du XVIIIe siècle.' In *L'inscription sociale de l'intellectuel,* ed. Manon Brunet and Pierre Lanthier, 43–60. Quebec/Paris: Presses de l'Université Laval / L'Harmattan, 2000.

Andrès, Bernard, and Marc André Bernier. 'De la génération de la Conquête à celle des Patriotes.' In *Portrait des arts, des lettres et de l'éloquence au Québec (1760–1840)*, ed. Bernard Andrès and Marc André Bernier, 15–46. Sainte-Foy: Presses de l'Université Laval, 2002.

– eds. *Portrait des arts, des lettres et de l'éloquence au Québec (1760–1840)*. Sainte-Foy / Paris: Presses de l'Université Laval / L'Harmattan, 2002.

Andrès, Bernard, and Nancy Desjardins, eds. *Utopies en Canada (1545–1845)*. Figura, textes et imaginaires, no. 3. Montreal: Département d'études littéraires, Université de Québec à Montréal, 2001.

Ango des Maizerets, Louis. *La solide devotion à la Très-Sainte Famille de Jésus, Marie, et Joseph. Avec un catéchisme qui enseigne à pratiquer leurs vertus.* Paris: Florentin Lambert, 1675.

[Arnaud, Antoine]. 'Reflexions sur un livre [...] intitulé.' In *Premier établissement de la foy dans la Nouvelle France: Œuvres de Messire Antoine Arnaud,* 699–720. Paris and Lausanne: S. d'Arnay, 1780.

Aubin, Paul. *Le manuel scolaire dans l'historiographie québécoise.* Sherbrooke: GRÉLQ, Université de Sherbrooke, 1997.

– 'Les manuels scolaires québécois.' Available on-line at: http://www.bibl.ulaval.ca/ress/manscol/.

– 'La pénétration des manuels scolaires de France au Québec – un cas-type: Les frères des Écoles chrétiennes, XIXe–XXe siècles.' *Histoire de l'éducation* 85 (Jan. 2000): 3–24.

Aubin, Paul, and Michel Simard. *Les manuels scolaires dans la correspondance du Département de l'instruction publique, 1842–1899: Inventaire.* Sherbrooke: GRÉLQ, Université de Sherbrooke, 1997.

Audet, Francis-J. 'Les débuts du barreau de la province de Québec.' *Cahiers des Dix* 2 (1937): 207–35.

– 'William Brown (1737–1789): Premier imprameur, journaliste et libraire du Quèbec; sa vie et ses oeuvres.' *Transactions of the Royal Society of Canada*, 3rd ser., 26 (1932): 97–112.

Audet, Louis-Philippe. *Histoire de l'enseignement au Québec, 1608–1840.* 2 vols. Montreal: Holt Rinehart and Winston, 1971.

Axelrod, Paul. *The Promise of Schooling: Education in Canada, 1800–1914.* Themes in Canadian Social History. Toronto: University of Toronto Press, 1997.

Bailey, Gauvin Alexander. *Art on the Jesuit Missions in Asia and Latin America, 1542–1773.* Toronto: University of Toronto Press, 1999.

Bailey, Jacob. *The Frontier Missionary: A Memoir of the Life of the Rev. Jacob Bailey.* Ed. W.S. Bartlet. Boston: Ide and Dutton, 1853.

Baker, Ray Palmer. *A History of English-Canadian Literature to the Confederation: Its Relation to the Literature of Great Britain and the United States.* Cambridge: Harvard University Press, 1920.

Ball, Douglas. *Victorian Publishers' Bindings.* Williamsburg, VA: Book Press, 1985.

Barbeau, Marius. *Saintes artisanes II: Mille petites adresses.* Montreal: Fides, 1946.

– *Totem Poles.* 2 vols. Ottawa: Roger Duhamel, 1964.

Barbiche, Bernard. 'Le régime de l'édition.' In *Histoire de l'édition française*, vol. 1, *Le livre conquérant, du Moyen Âge au milieu du XVIIe siècle*, ed. Roger Chartier and Henri-Jean Martin in collaboration with Jean-Pierre Vivet, 367–77. Paris: Promodis, 1982.

Basnage de Beauval, Henri. *Histoire des ouvrages de Savans.* Rotterdam, 1687–1709. Vol. 1, 1701–4. Reprint, Geneva: Slatkine Reprints, 1969.

Basque, Maurice. *De Marc Lescarbot à l'AEFNB: Histoire de la profession enseignante au Nouveau-Brunswick.* Edmundston: Les Éditions Marévie, 1994.

Beales, Ross W., and James N. Green. 'Libraries and Their Users.' In *A History of the Book in America,* vol. 1, *The Colonial Book in the Atlantic World,* ed. Hugh Amory and David Hall, 399–404. Cambridge and New York: Cambridge University Press, 2000.

Beattie, Judith Hudson. '"My Best Friend": Evidence of the Fur Trade Libraries Located in the Hudson's Bay Company Archives.' *Épilogue* 8.1 (1993): 1–32.

Beaulé, Isabelle. 'Henri-Antoine Mézière: D'épistolier à pamphlétaire.' Master's thesis, Université de Québec à Montréal, 1996.

Beaulieu, André. *La première bibliothèque canadienne: La bibliothèque des jésuites de la Nouvelle-France, 1632–1800 / The First Canadian Library: The Library of the Jesuit College of New France.* Ottawa: BNC/NLC, 1972.

Beaulieu, André, and Jean Hamelin. *La presse québécoise des origines à nos jours.* Vol. 1 (1764–1859). Sainte Foy: Presses de l'Université Laval, 1973.

Beavan, Frances. *Sketches and Tales Illustrative of Life in the Backwoods of New Brunswick, North America: Gleaned from Actual Observation and Experience during a Residence of Seven Years in That Interesting Colony ...* London: Routledge, 1845.

Beck, J.M. 'A Fool for a Client: The Trial of Joseph Howe.' *Acadiensis* 3.2 (Spring 1974): 27–44.

Beckwith, John. *Psalmody in British North America: Humbert, Daulé, Jenkins, Burnham.* Toronto: Institute for Canadian Music, Faculty of Music, University of Toronto, 2002.

– ed. *Sing Out the Glad News: Hymn Tunes in Canada; Proceedings of the Conference Held in Toronto, February 7 and 8, 1986, Organized by the Institute for Canadian Music, Faculty of Music, University of Toronto.* Toronto: Institute for Canadian Music, 1987.

Bégon, Élisabeth. *La correspondance de Madame Bégon, 1748–1753.* Ed. Claude de Bonnault. Quebec: Imprimerie de roi, [1935].

Béland, Mario, ed. *La peinture au Québec, 1820–1850: Nouveaux regards, nouvelles perspectives.* Quebec: Musée du Québec, Publications du Québec, 1991.

Bell, D.G. 'Sedition among the Loyalists: The Case of Saint John, 1784–6.' In *Canadian State Trials,* vol. 1, *Law, Politics, and Security Measures, 1608–1837,* ed. F. Murray Greenwood and Barry Wright, 223–40. Toronto: University of Toronto Press, 1996.

Benoît, R. Albert. 'L'influence de la traduction sur notre parler.' *Le Canada français* 8 (May 1922): 251–71.

Benson, Eugene, and William Toye, eds. *The Oxford Companion to Canadian Literature.* 2nd ed. Toronto: Oxford University Press, 1997.

Bent, William, comp. *The London Catalogue of Books, with Their Sizes and Prices. Corrected to August MDCCCXI.* London: W. Bent, 1811.

Bentley, D.M.R. *Mimic Fires: Accounts of Early Long Poems of Canada.* Montreal and Kingston: McGill-Queen's University Press, 1994.

– 'Poems in Early Canadian Newspapers.' Available on-line at: http://www.uwo.ca/english/canadianpoetry/canpoetry/.

Bernard, Jean-Paul, comp. *Les Rébellions de 1837–1838: Les Patriotes du Bas-Canada dans la mémoire collective et chez les historiens.* Montreal: Boréal Express, 1983.

Bernatchez, Ginette. 'La Société littéraire et historique du Québec (The Literary and Historical Society of Quebec) 1824–1890.' *RHAF* 35.2 (Sept. 1981): 179–92.

Beullac, Pierre, and E. Fabre Surveyer. *Le centenaire du Barreau de Montréal, 1849–1949.* Montreal: Ducharmes, 1940.

Bibaud, Michel. *Épîtres, satires, chansons, épigrammes et autres pièces de vers.* Montreal: La Minerve, 1830.

– *Histoire du Canada et des Canadiens sous la domination anglaise.* Montreal: Lovell et Gibson, 1844.

– *Histoire du Canada sous la domination française.* Montreal: John Jones, 1837.

'La bibliothèque de Mgr de Lauberivière.' *Bulletin des recherches historiques* 1 (1895): 10.

'La bibliothèque du curé Portneuf.' *Bulletin des recherches historiques* 54 (1948): 227–30.

Bidwell, John. 'Printers' Supplies and Capitalization.' In *A History of the Book in America*, vol. 1, *The Colonial Book in the Atlantic World*, ed. Hugh Amory and David D. Hall, 163–83. Cambridge and New York: Cambridge University Press, 2000.

Bilson, Geoffrey. *A Darkened House: Cholera in Nineteenth-Century Canada.* Social History of Canada. Toronto: University of Toronto Press, 1980.

Bird, Michael S. *Ontario Fraktur: A Pennsylvania-German Folk Tradition in Early Canada.* Toronto: M.F. Feheley Publishers, 1977.

Bishop, Olga Bernice. 'The First Printing Press in Canada, 1751–1800.' In *Books in America's Past: Essays Honoring Rudolph H. Gjelsness*, ed. David Kaser, 129–48. Charlottesville: University Press of Virginia, 1966.

– *Publications of the Governments of Nova Scotia, Prince Edward Island, New Brunswick, 1758–1952.* Ottawa: National Library of Canada, 1957.

Bishop, Roy L. 'J.F.W. DesBarres: An Eighteenth-Century Nova Scotia Observatory.' In *Profiles of Science and Society in the Maritimes prior to 1914*, ed. Paul A. Bogaard, 65–81. Fredericton and Sackville: Acadiensis Press and the Centre for Canadian Studies, Mount Allison University, 1990.

Black, Fiona A. '"Advent'rous Merchants and Atlantic Waves": A Preliminary Study of the Scottish Contribution to Book Availability in Halifax, 1752–1810.' In *Myth, Migration and the Making of Memory, Scotia and Nova Scotia, c. 1700–1990*, ed. Marjory Harper and Michael E. Vance, 157–88. Halifax/Edinburgh: Fernwood Publishing / John Donald Publishers Limited, 1999.

– 'Beyond Boundaries: Books in the Canadian Northwest.' In *Across Boundaries: The Book in Culture & Commerce*, ed. Bill Bell, Philip Bennet, and Jonquil Bevan, 91–115. Winchester and New Castle, DE: St. Paul's Bibliographies and Oak Knoll Press, 2000.

– 'Book Availability in Canada, 1752–1820, and the Scottish Contribution.' Ph.D. diss., Loughborough University, 1999.

– '"Horrid Republican Notions" and Other Matters: School Book Availability in Georgian Canada.' *Paradigm – Journal of the Textbook Colloquium* 2 (July 2001): 7–18.

– 'Searching for the "Vanguard of an Army of Scots" in the Early Canadian Book Trade.' *PBSC/ CSBC* 38 (Autumn 2000): 65–99.

Black, Robert Merrill. 'Different Visions: The Multiplication of Protestant Missions to French-Canadian Roman Catholics, 1834–1855.' In *Canadian Protestant and Catholic Missions, 1820s–1960s: Historical Essays in Honour of John Webster Grant*, ed. John S. Moir and C.T. McIntire, Toronto Studies in Religion, no. 3, 49–73. New York: Peter Lang, 1988.

Blanchard, Jim. 'Anatomy of Failure: Ontario Mechanics' Institutes, 1835–1895.' *Canadian Library Journal* 38 (1981): 393–8.

Blyth, J.A. 'The Development of the Paper Industry in Old Ontario, 1824–1867.' *Ontario History* 62 (June 1970): 119–33.

Bollème, Geneviève. *Les almanachs populaires aux XVIIe et XVIIIe siècles: Essai d'histoire sociale.* Livre et sociétés: Études et mémoires pour servir à l'histoire de la civilisation du livre, no. 3. Paris: Mouton and Co., 1969.

Bonenfant, Jean-Charles. 'La Bibliothèque de l'Assemblée nationale et ses bibliothécaires.' In *Livre, bibliothèque et culture québécoise: Mélanges offerts à Edmond Desrochers, s.j.*, ed. Georges-A. Chartrand, vol. 2, 641–9. Montreal: ASTED, 1977.

Boone, Elizabeth Hill, and Walter D. Mignolo, eds. *Writing without Words: Alternative Literacies in Mesoamerica and the Andes*. Durham: Duke University Press, 1994.

Bouchot, Henri. *Les ex-libris et les marques de possession du livre*. Paris: Rouveyre, 1891.

Boudon, Henri-Marie. *Œuvres complètes de Boudon, grand archidiacre d'Évreux, réunis pour la première fois dans un ordre logique et analogique: Renfermant ses divers opuscules ascétiques et un très-grand nombre de lettres et d'exhertations jusqu'ici inédites*. 3 vols. Ed. Jacques-Paul Migne. Paris: Éditeur aux Ateliers catholiques, 1856.

Bow, Eric C. 'The Public Library Movement in Nineteenth-Century Ontario.' *Ontario Library Review* 66.1 (March 1982): 1–16.

Boyer, Jean-Pierre. *'Appel à la justice de l'État' de Pierre du Calvet, champion des droits démocratiques au Québec*. Quebec: Septentrion, 2002.

Boylan, Heather, comp. *Checklist and Historical Directory of Prince Edward Island Newspapers, 1787–1986*. Charlottetown: Public Archives of Prince Edward Island, 1987.

Boyle, A. 'Portraiture in Lavengro II: The Publisher – Sir Richard Phillips.' *Notes and Queries* 196 (1951): 361–6.

Brisebois, Michel. *Impressions: 250 Years of Printing in the Lives of Canadians / Impressions: 250 ans d'imprimerie dans la vie des Canadien(ne)s*. [Ottawa]: Fitzhenry & Whiteside and the National Library of Canada, 1999.

– *The Printing of Handbills in Quebec City, 1764–1800: A Listing with Critical Introduction*. Montreal: Graduate School of Library and Information Studies, McGill University, 1995.

Brodeur, Raymond, ed. *Les catéchismes au Québec, 1702–1963*. Sainte-Foy/Paris: Presses de l'Université Laval / Éditions du CNRS, 1990.

Brooke, Frances. *The History of Emily Montague*. Ed. Mary Jane Edwards. Centre for Editing Early Canadian Texts, no. 1. Ottawa: Carleton University Press, 1985.

Browne, George. *The History of the British and Foreign Bible Society: From Its Institution in 1804, to the Close of Its Jubilee in 1854*. 2 vols. London: Bagster and sons, 1859.

Brun, Régis. *Pionnier de la nouvelle Acadie, Joseph Gueguen, 1741–1825*. Moncton: Éditions d'Acadie, 1984.

Brunet, Manon. 'Anonymat et pseudonymat au XIXe siècle: L'envers et l'endroit de pratiques institutionnelles.' *Voix et images; L'édition littéraire au Québec* 14.2 (Winter 1989): 168–82.

— 'Les femmes dans la production de la littérature francophone du début du XIXe siècle québécoise.' In *Livre et lecture au Québec (1800–1850)*, ed. Claude Galarneau and Maurice Lemire, 167–80. Quebec: Institut québécois de recherché sur la culture, 1988.

Bumgardner, Georgia B. 'Vignettes of the Past: American Historical Broadsides through the War of 1812.' *Printing History* 7/8 (1982): 37–48.

Bumsted, J.M. *Henry Alline, 1748–1784*. Toronto: University of Toronto Press, 1971.

– 'Liberty of the Press in Early Prince Edward Island, 1823–9.' In *Canadian State Trials*, vol. 1, *Law, Politics, and Security Measures, 1608–1837*, ed. F. Murray Greenwood and Barry Wright, 522–46. Toronto: University of Toronto Press, 1996.

Buono, Yolande. 'Imprimerie et diffusion de l'imprimé à Montréal de 1776 à 1820.' Master's thesis, Université de Montréal, 1980.

Cahill, Barry. '*R. v. Howe* (1835) for Seditious Libel: A Tale of Twelve Magistrates.' In *Canadian State*

Trials, vol. 1, *Law, Politics, and Security Measures, 1608–1837*, ed. F. Murray Greenwood and Barry Wright, 547–75, 731–2. Toronto: University of Toronto Press, 1996.

Calderisi, Maria. *Music Publishing in the Canadas, 1800–1867.* Ottawa: National Library of Canada, 1981.

Cameron, Wendy, Sheila Haines, and Mary McDougall Maude, eds. *English Immigrant Voices: Labourers' Letters from Upper Canada in the 1830's.* Montreal and Kingston: McGill-Queen's University Press, 2000.

Cameron, William J., and George McKnight. *Robert Addison's Library.* Hamilton, ON: Printed at McMaster University for the Synod of the Diocese of Niagara, 1967.

Campbell, George A. 'Social Life and Institutions of Nova Scotia in the 1830's.' Master's thesis, Dalhousie University, 1949.

Campbell, Mary. *The Witness and the Other World: Exotic European Travel Writing, 400–1600.* Ithaca: Cornell University Press, 1988.

Campeau, Lucien. 'Les Jésuites ont-ils retouché les écrits de Champlain?' *RHAF* 5.3 (Dec. 1951): 340–61.

– ed. *Monumenta Novæ Franciæ.* 9 vols. Rome: Monumenta hist. Soc. Jesu, 1967–.

'Le Canada à l'époque de la "Révolution atlantique" (fin XVIIIe siècle–début XIXe siècle).' *Annales historiques de la Révolution française*, année 45 (1973): 321–435.

'Canadian Imprints Database / Imprimés canadiens.' Available on-line at: http://acsweb2.ucis.dal.ca/ hbicdb/english/imprints.html and http://acsweb2.ucis.dal.ca/hbicdb/francais/imprimes.html.

Canniff, William. *History of the Settlement of Upper Canada (Ontario) with Special Reference to the Bay of Quinté.* Toronto: Dudley and Barnes, 1869.

Capp, Bernard. *Astrology and the Popular Press: English Almanacs, 1500–1800.* London and Boston: Faber & Faber, 1979.

Carile, Paolo. *Le regard entravé: Littérature et anthropologie dans les premiers textes sur la Nouvelle-France.* Sillery: Éditions du Septentrion, 2000.

Carnochan, Janet. 'The Niagara Library, 1800–1820.' *Transactions of the Canadian Institute* 4 (1892–3): 336–56.

Caron, Jean-François. 'Les apprentis à Québec de 1830 à 1849.' Master's thesis, Université Laval, 1985.

Carrière, Gaston. *Dictionnaire biographique des oblats de Marie-Immaculée au Canada.* 3 vols. Ottawa: Éditions de l'Université d'Ottawa, 1976.

Carroll, E.G. 'History of Printing.' *Canadian Antiques Collector* 8.1 (1973): 43–5.

Carruthers, George. *Paper in the Making.* Toronto: Garden City Press Cooperative, 1947.

Cartier, Jacques. *Relations.* Ed. Michel Bideaux. Montreal: Presses de l'Université de Montréal, 1986.

Carver, Jonathan. *Travels through the Interior Parts of North America.* London: Printed for the author and sold by J. Walter, 1778.

Castle, Egerton. *English Book-Plates: An Illustrated Handbook for Students of Ex-libris.* London: George Bell and Sons, 1892.

Castling, Leslie D. 'The Red River Library: A Search after Knowledge and Refinement.' In *Readings in Canadian Library History*, ed. Peter F. McNally, 153–66. Ottawa: Canadian Library Association, 1986.

Catalogue collectif des impressions québécoises, 1764–1820. Milada Vlach and Yolande Buono. Quebec: Bibliothèque nationale du Québec, 1984.

Catlin, George. *Letters and Notes on the Manners, Customs, and Conditions of the North American Indians.* London: D. Bogue, 1844. Reprint, New York: Dover Publications, 1977.

Cavallo, Guglielmo, and Roger Chartier. *Histoire de la lecture dans le monde occidental.* Paris: Éd. du Seuil, 1997.

Champlain, Samuel de. *Œuvres de Champlain.* Ed. Charles-Honoré Laverdière. 3 vols. Quebec: Geo.-E. Desbarats, 1870.

– *Les voyages du Sieur de Champlain Xaintongeois, capitaine ordinaire pour le roy, en la marine […].* Paris: J. Berjon, 1613.

– *Works of Samuel de Champlain.* 6 vols and portfolio of maps. Ed. H.P. Biggar et al. Toronto: Champlain Society, 1922–36.

Chansons politiques du Québec. Vol. 1, *1765–1833.* Ed. Maurice Carrier and Monique Vachon. Montreal: Leméac, 1977.

Chappell, Edward. *Voyage of His Majesty's Ship Rosamond to Newfoundland and the Southern Coast of Laborador.* London: J. Mawman, 1818.

Chaput, Donald. 'Charlotte de Rocheblave: Métisse Teacher of the Teachers.' *Beaver* 308.2 (Autumn 1977): 55–8.

– 'The "Misses Nolin" of Red River.' *Beaver* 306.3 (Winter 1975): 14–17.

Charland, Thomas-Marie. 'Un projet de journal ecclésiastique de Mgr Lartigue.' *Rapport de la Société canadienne d'histoire de l'Église catholique* 24 (1956–7): 39–54.

Charlevoix, Pierre-François-Xavier de. *Histoire et description generale de la Nouvelle France, avec le journal historique d'un voyage fait par ordre du roi dans l'Amérique septentrionale.* 4 vols. Paris: Rollins fils, 1744.

– *History and General Description of New France.* Trans. from the original edition and ed., with notes, by John Gilmary Shea. 6 vols. New York: F.P. Harper, 1900.

Chartier, Roger. *The Order of Books: Readers, Authors, and Libraries in Europe between the Fourteenth and Eighteenth Centuries.* Trans. Lydia G. Cochrane. Stanford: Stanford University Press, 1994.

– 'Les pratiques de l'écrit.' In *Histoire de la vie privée*, vol. 3, *De la Renaissance aux Lumières*, ed. Philippe Ariès and Georges Duby, 113–61. Paris: Éditions du Seuil, 1999.

Chartier, Roger, and Daniel Roche. 'Les pratiques urbaines de l'imprimé.' In *Histoire de l'édition française*, vol. 2, *Le livre triomphant, 1660–1830*, ed. Roger Chartier and Henri-Jean Martin in collaboration with Jean-Pierre Vivet, 402–29. Paris: Promodis, 1984.

Chartrand, Luc, Raymond Duchesne, and Yves Gingras. *Histoire des sciences au Québec.* Montreal: Boréal, 1987.

Charvat, William. *Literary Publishing in America, 1790–1850.* Philadelphia: University of Pennsylvania Press, 1959.

Chaussé, Gilles. *Jean-Jacques Lartigue, premier évêque de Montréal.* Montreal: Fides, 1980.

Chinard, Gilbert. *L'Amérique et le rêve exotique dans la littérature française au XVIIe et au XVIIIe siècles.* Paris: Droz, 1934. Reprint, Geneva: Slatkine, 1970.

Chu, Clara M., and Bertrum H. MacDonald. 'The Public Record: An Analysis of Women's Contributions to Canadian Science and Technology before the First World War.' In *Despite the Odds: Essays on Canadian Women and Science*, ed. Marianne Gosztonyi Ainley, 63–73. Montreal: Véhicule Press, 1990.

Clarke, George Elliott. 'Introduction: Fire on the Water; A First Portrait of Africadian Literature.' In *Fire on the Water: An Anthology of Black Nova Scotian Writing*, vol. 1, *Early and Modern Writers 1785–1935*, ed. George Elliott Clarke, 11–29. Porter's Lake, NS: Pottersfield Press, 1991.

Clément, Diane, and Martine Malenfant. *Les Sciences médicales du XVIIe au XIXe siècle: La Bibliothèque du Séminaire de Québec.* Ed. Danielle Aubin. Quebec: Musée de la Civilisation, 1998.

Cole, Jean Murray. 'Keeping the Mind Alive: Literary Leanings in the Fur Trade.' *Journal of Canadian Studies* 16.2 (Summer 1981): 87–93.

Colgate, William. 'Louis Roy: First Printer in Upper Canada.' *Ontario History* 43 (1951): 123–42.

Conaway, James. *America's Library: The Story of the Library of Congress, 1800–2000.* New Haven: Yale University Press, 1999.

Connor, Jennifer J., and J.T.H. Connor. 'Thomsonian Medical Literature and Reformist Discourse in Upper Canada.' *Canadian Literature / Littérature canadienne* 131 (Winter 1991): 140–55.

Conrad, Margaret. 'Mary Bradley's Reminiscences: A Domestic Life in Colonial New Brunswick.' *Atlantis* 7.1 (Fall 1981): 92–101.

Cook, James. *The Journals of Captain James Cook on His Voyages of Discovery.* 4 vols. Ed. J.C. Beaglehole. Cambridge: The Hakluyt Society at the University Press, 1955–68.

Cooke, Alan, and Clive Holland. *The Exploration of Northern Canada, 500–1920: A Chronology.* Toronto: The Arctic History Press, 1978.

Corbett, George. 'Literacy.' In *Encyclopaedia of Newfoundland and Labrador*, ed. Joseph R. Smallwood et al., vol. 3, 316–19. St John's: Harry Cuff Publications, 1991.

Cotnam, Jacques, and Pierre Hébert. 'La *Gazette littéraire* (1778–1779): Notre première œuvre de fiction?' *Voix et images* 20 (Winter 1995): 294–312.

Coughlan, Laurence. *An Account of the Word of God, in Newfoundland, North-America, in a Series of Letters, to Which Are Prefixed a Few Choice Experiences; Some of Which Were Taken from the Lips of Persons, Who Died Triumphantly in the Faith.* London: W. Gilbert, 1776.

Coughlin, Violet L. *Larger Units of Public Library Service in Canada.* Metuchen, NJ: Scarecrow Press, 1968.

Craig, Gerald M. *Upper Canada: The Formative Years, 1784–1841.* Toronto: McClelland & Stewart, 1963.

'Cuesta Profile: Escarpment "Wonder Man" Built 19th Century Empire.' *Cuesta: A Niagara Escarpment Commission Publication*, Spring 1981, 33–5.

Cuff, Robert H. 'Mechanics' Society.' In *Encyclopedia of Newfoundland and Labrador*, ed. Joseph R. Smallwood et al., vol. 3, 489–90. St John's: Harry Cuff Publications, 1991.

Curtis, Bruce. 'Schoolbooks and the Myth of Curricular Republicanism: The State and the Curriculum in Canada West, 1820–1850.' *Histoire sociale / Social History* 32 (Nov. 1983): 305–29.

Cuthbertson, Brian. *The Old Attorney General: A Biography of Richard John Uniacke.* Halifax: Nimbus, 1980.

Dalhousie, George Ramsay, Earl of. *The Dalhousie Journals.* Ed. Marjory Whitelaw. Vol. 1. Ottawa: Oberon Press, 1978.

Darlow, T.H., and H.F. Moule. *Historical Catalogue of Printed Editions of Holy Scripture in the Library of the British and Foreign Bible Society.* New York: Kraus Reprint Corp., 1963.

Daviault, Pierre. 'Traductuers et traduction au Canada.' *Transactions of the Royal Society of Canada*, 3rd ser., 38 (1944): 67–87.

Davies, Gwendolyn. '"Good Taste and Sound Sense": The Nova-Scotia Magazine (1789–92).' In *The Atlantic Anthology*, vol. 3, *Critical Essays*, ed. Terry Whalen, 5–22. Toronto and Charlottetown: ECW Press and Ragweed, 1985.

– 'A Literary Study of Selected Periodicals from Maritime Canada: 1789–1872.' Ph.D. diss., York University, 1979.

– '"Old Maidism Itself": Spinsterhood in Eighteenth- and Nineteenth-Century Literary and Life-Writing Texts from Maritime Canada.' In *Mapping the Margins: The Family and Social Discipline in Canada, 1700–1975,* ed. Nancy Christie and Michael Gauvreau, 235–46. Montreal and Kingston: McGill-Queen's University Press, 2004.

– 'Poet to Pulpit to Planter: The Peregrinations of the Reverend John Seccombe.' In *Making Adjustments: Change and Continuity in Planter Nova Scotia, 1759–1800,* ed. Margaret Conrad, 189–97. Fredericton: Acadiensis Press, 1991.

– *Studies in Maritime Literary History, 1760–1930.* Fredericton: Acadiensis Press, 1991.

Davis, Angela E. *Art and Work: A Social History of Labour in the Canadian Graphic Arts Industry to the 1940's.* Montreal and Kingston: McGill-Queen's University Press, 1995.

Davis, Natalie Zemon. 'Beyond the Market: Books as Gifts in Sixteenth-Century France.' *Transactions of the Royal Historical Society,* 5th ser., 33 (1983): 69–88.

– 'Printing and the People.' In *Society and Culture in Early Modern France: Eight Essays,* 189–226. Stanford: Stanford University Press, 1975.

Dawson, Nelson-Martin. *Le catéchisme de Sens en France et au Québec.* Quebec: Éditions Nota bene, 2000.

– 'Le paradoxal destin d'un catéchisme à double nationalité: L'histoire du manuel de Mgr Languet à Sens et à Québec.' Ph.D. diss., Université Laval, 1989.

Dechêne, Louise. *Habitants et marchands de Montréal au XVIIe siècle.* Paris: Plon, 1974.

Defoe, Daniel. *The Compleat English Gentleman.* 1729. Ed. Karl Büllbring. 1890 facsimile reprint, Folcroft: Folcroft Library, 1982.

Delisle, Jean. *La traduction au Canada, 1534–1984 / Translation in Canada, 1534–1984.* Ottawa: Presses de l'Université d'Ottawa, 1987.

Delisle, Jean, and Gilbert Lafond, eds. *Histoire de la traduction / History of Translation.* Ottawa: Université d'Ottawa, 2002.

Demers, Ginette. 'La traduction journalistique au Québec (1764–1855).' *Traduction terminologie et rédaction* 6.1 (1993): 131–47.

Deschênes, Gaston, and Luc Noppen, eds. *L'hôtel du Parlement, témoin de notre histoire.* Quebec: Assemblée nationale, 1986.

Desjardins, Nancy. 'La théâtralisation du politique au temps des patriotes: Les Comédies du statu quo (1834).' Master's thesis, Université de Québec à Montréal, 2003.

Devaux, Yves. *L'univers de la bibliophilie.* Paris: Pygmalion and Gérard Watelet, 1988.

The Development of the New Brunswick Legislative Library, 1841–1991. Fredericton: Legislative Library, 1991.

Devereux, E.J. 'Early Printing in Newfoundland.' *Dalhousie Review* 43 (Spring 1963): 57–66.

Dewalt, Bryan. *Technology and Canadian Printing: A History from Lead Type to Lasers.* Ottawa: National Museum of Science and Technology, 1995.

Dewdney, Selwyn. *Dating Rock Art in the Canadian Shield Region.* Art and Archaeology Occasional Paper 24. Toronto: Royal Ontario Museum, 1970.

Dewdney, Selwyn, and Kenneth E. Kidd. *Indian Rock Paintings of the Great Lakes.* 2nd ed. Quetico Foundation Series. Toronto: University of Toronto Press, 1967.

Dickinson, John A. 'L'anglicisation.' In *Le français au Québec: 400 ans d'histoire et de vie,* ed. Michel Plourde, 80–91. Saint-Laurent: Fides and Publications du Québec, 2000.

Dictionary of Canadian Biography. Vols 1–8. Toronto: University of Toronto Press, 1966–85.

Dictionary of Hamilton Biography. Vol. 1. Ed. T. Melville Bailey. Hamilton, 1981.

Dictionary of National Biography. Ed. Sir Leslie Stephen and Sir Sidney Lee. Vol. 21. 1900. Reprint, London: Oxford University Press, 1965.

Dictionnaire des oeuvres littéraires du Québec. 2 vols. Ed. Maurice Lemire. 2nd ed. Montreal: Fides, 1980.

Dionne, Narcisse-Eutrope. *Inventaire chronologique des livres, brochures, journaux et revues publiés en diverses langues dans et hors la province de Québec*. 4 vols. Montreal: Bibliothèque nationale du Québec, 1905–12.

Dobbs, Arthur. *An Account of the Countries Adjoining to Hudson's Bay ...* London: Printed by J. Robinson, 1744.

Docherty, Linda J. 'Women as Readers: Visual Interpretations.' *Proceedings of the American Antiquarian Society* 107.2 (1997): 335–88.

Dondertman, Anne. 'Anthony Henry, "Lilius," and the *Nova Scotia Calendar*.' *PBSC/CSBC* 29 (Fall 1991): 32–50.

Donovan, Kenneth. '"May Learning Flourish": The Beginnings of a Cultural Awakening in Cape Breton during the 1840's.' In *The Island: New Perspectives on Cape Breton's History (1713–1990)*, ed. Kenneth Donovan, 89–112. Fredericton/Sydney: Acadiensis Press / University College of Cape Breton Press, 1990.

Doyon, Nova. 'L'Académie de Montréal (1778): Fiction littéraire ou projet utopique?' *Mens* 1 (Spring 2001): 115–40.

Driver, Elizabeth. *Culinary Landmarks: A Bibliography of Canadian Cookbooks, 1825–1950*. Toronto: University of Toronto Press, forthcoming.

Drolet, Antonio. 'La bibliothèque du Collège des jésuites (essai de reconstitution).' *RHAF* 14.4 (March 1961): 487–544.

– *Les bibliothèques canadiennes, 1604–1960*. Ottawa: Cercle du Livre de France, 1965.

Dubé, Jean-Claude. *Claude-Thomas Dupuy, intendant de la Nouvelle-France, 1678–1738*. Montreal: Fides, 1969.

– *Les intendants de la Nouvelle-France*. Montreal: Fides, 1984.

– 'Les intendants de la Nouvelle-France et la République des Lettres.' *RHAF* 29 (June 1975): 31–48.

Dufour, Andrée. *Tous à l'école: État, communautés rurales et scolarisation au Québec de 1826 à 1859*. Montreal: Hurtubise HMH, 1996.

Dugas, Louis J. 'L'alphabétisation des Acadiens, 1700–1850.' M.A. thesis, Université d'Ottawa, 1992.

Dulong, Gaston. 'L'anglicisme au Canada français: Étude historique.' In *Études de linguistique franco-canadienne: Communications présentées au XXXIVe Congrès de l'Association canadienne-française pour l'avancement des sciences, Québec, novembre 1966*, ed. Jean-Denis Gendron et George Straka, 9–14. Quebec: Presses de l'Université Laval, 1967.

Dumont, Fernand, and Jean-Charles Falardeau, eds. *Littérature et société canadiennes-françaises*. Quebec: Presses de l'Université Laval, 1964.

Dunlop, Alan C. 'The Pictou Literary and Scientific Society.' *Nova Scotia Historical Quarterly* 3 (June 1973): 99–116.

Dunlop, William. *Statistical Sketches of Upper Canada, for the Use of Emigrants*. London: J. Murray, 1832.

Duplessis, François-Xavier. *Lettres du P.F.-X. Duplessis de la Compagnie de Jésus*. Ed. Joseph-Edmond Roy. Lévis: Mercier et Cie, 1892.

Dusseault-Letocha, Louise. 'Les origines de l'art de l'estampe au Québec.' Master's thesis, Université de Montréal, 1975.

Edelberg, Cynthia Dubin. *Jonathan Odell: Loyalist Poet of the American Revolution*. Durham: Duke University Press, 1987.

Edwards, Nina L. 'The Establishment of Papermaking in Upper Canada.' *Ontario History* 39 (1947): 63–74.

Ellice, Katherine Jane (Balfour). *The Diary of Jane Ellice*. Ed. Patricia Godsell. Ottawa: Oberon Press, 1975.

Elliott, Shirley B. 'A Library for the Garrison and Town: A History of the Cambridge Military Library, Royal Military Park, Halifax, Nova Scotia.' *Epilogue/Épilogue* 8 (Fall/automne 1989): 1–11.

Ellison, Suzanne. *Historical Directory of Newfoundland and Labrador Newspapers, 1807–1987*. St John's: Memorial University of Newfoundland Library, 1988.

Errington, Elizabeth Jane. *Wives and Mothers, Schoolmistresses and Scullery Maids: Working Women in Upper Canada, 1790–1840*. Montreal and Kingston: McGill-Queen's University Press, 1995.

Evans, James. *Cree Syllabic Hymn Book*. Toronto: Bibliographical Society of Canada, 1954.

Faith of Our Fathers: A Century of Victory 1824–1924; The 100th Annual Report of the Methodist Missionary Society. Toronto: Methodist Missionary Society, 1924.

Fauteux, Aegidius. 'Bataille de vers autour d'une tombe.' *Mémoires de la Société royale du Canada*, 3rd ser., 25 (1931): section 1, 47–60.

– *L'introduction de l'imprimerie au Canada: Une brève histoire*. Montreal: Compagnie de papier Rolland, 1957.

– *The Introduction of Printing into Canada: A Brief History*. Montreal: Rolland Paper Co., 1957.

Feather, John. 'The English Book Trade and the Law 1695–1799.' *Publishing History* 12 (1982): 51–75.

Fecteau, Jean-Marie, and Douglas Hay. 'Government by Will and Pleasure instead of Law: Military Justice and the Legal System in Quebec, 1775–83.' In *Canadian State Trials*, vol. 1, *Law, Politics, and Security Measures, 1608–1837*, ed. F. Murray Greenwood and Barry Wright, 129–71. Toronto: University of Toronto Press, 1996.

Fecteau, Jean-Marie, F. Murray Greenwood, and Jean-Pierre Wallot. 'Sir James Craig's "Reign of Terror" and Its Impact on Emergency Powers in Lower Canada, 1810–1813.' In *Canadian State Trials*, vol. 1, *Law, Politics, and Security Measures, 1608–1837*, ed. F. Murray Greenwood and Barry Wright, 323–78. Toronto: University of Toronto Press, 1996.

Fenton, William N. *The Great Law and the Longhouse: A Political History of the Iroquois Confederacy*. Norman: University of Oklahoma Press, 1998.

Fergusson, C. Bruce. *Mechanics' Institutes in Nova Scotia*. Halifax: Public Archives of Nova Scotia, 1960.

Fetherling, Douglas. *The Rise of the Canadian Newspaper*. Toronto: Oxford University Press, 1990.

Filion, Mario. *Paroisse Sainte-Anne-de-Varennes, 1692–1992*. [s.l., s.n.], 1991.

Filion, Paul-Emile. 'La première bibliothèque canadienne: Le Collège des Jésuites à Québec; historique et contribution à l'inventaire du fonds.' In *Livre, bibliothèque et culture québécoise: Mélanges offerts à Edmond Desrochers, s.j.*, ed. Georges-A. Chartrand, 273–98. Montreal: ASTED, 1977.

Fingard, Judith. '"Grapes in the Wilderness": The Bible Society in British North America in the Early Nineteenth Century.' *Histoire sociale / Social History* 5.9 (avril/April 1972): 5–31.

Fleming, Fergus. *Barrow's Boys*. New York: Atlantic Monthly Press, 1998.

Fleming, Patricia Lockhart. *Atlantic Canadian Imprints, 1801–1820: A Bibliography*. Toronto: University of Toronto Press, 1991.

– 'A Canadian Printer's Apprentice in 1826.' *Devil's Artisan* 9 (1982): 13–17.

– 'Des publications pour la paix, l'ordre et le bon gouvernement.' *Fac-similé / Facsimile*, Special issue (September 1997): 13–14.
– 'Paper Evidence in Toronto Imprints, 1798 to 1841.' *PBSC/CSBC* 29 (1980): 22–37.
– 'The Printing Trade in Toronto: 1798–1841.' In *Sticks and Stones*, ed. John Gibson and Laurie Lewis, 47–68. Toronto: Toronto Typographic Association, 1980.
– 'A Study of Pre-Confederation Ontario Bookbinding.' *PBSC/CSBC* 11 (1972): 53–70.
– *Upper Canadian Imprints, 1801–1841: A Bibliography.* Toronto: University of Toronto Press in co-operation with the National Library of Canada, 1988.
– 'William Lyon Mackenzie as Printer, 1824–1837.' *Devil's Artisan* 5 (1981): 3–12; 6 (1981): 3–19.
Fleming, Patricia Lockhart, and Sandra Alston. *Early Canadian Printing: A Supplement to Marie Tremaine's 'A Bibliography of Canadian Imprints, 1751–1800.'* Toronto: University of Toronto Press, 1999.
Forsyth, Isaac. *A Catalogue of the Elgin Circulating Library, Containing a Select and Valuable Collection of Books, by the Latest and Best Authors; on History, Divinity ... and Miscellaneous Literature. Which are lent to read ...* Elgin, Scotland: Isaac Forsyth, 1789.
Fournier, Jacques. 'La Bibliothèque des Augustines de l'Hôtel-Dieu de Québec: Étude d'un fonds ancien.' Master's thesis, Université de Montréal, 1983.
Fournier, Paul-André. 'L'ex-libris et les formes changeantes de l'expression identitaire dans les arts graphiques du XVe siècle à nos jours.' Ph.D. diss., Université Laval, 1996. 2 vols.
Francis, R. Douglas, Richard Jones, and Donald B. Smith. *Origins: Canadian History to Confederation.* Toronto: Holt, Rinehart and Winston, 1988.
Friskney, Janet B. 'Towards a Canadian "Cultural Mecca": The Methodist Book and Publishing House's Pursuit of Book Publishing and Commitment to Canadian Writing, 1829–1926.' Master's thesis, Trent University, 1994.
Gagnon, François-Marc. *La conversion par l'image: Un aspect de la mission des jésuites auprès des Indiens du Canada au XVIIe siècle.* Montreal: Bellarmin, 1975.
– 'Vue de face ou de profil: Essai sur l'iconographie indienne de George Catlin.' In *L'"Indien," instance discursive: Actes du colloque de Montréal, 1991,* ed. Antonio Gómez-Moriana and Danièle Trottier, 223–48. Candiac: Éditions Balzac, 1993.
Gagnon, Philéas. *Essai de bibliographie canadienne: Inventaire d'une bibliothèque comprenant imprimés, manuscrits, estampes, etc. relatifs à l'histoire du Canada et des pays adjacents, avec des notes bibliographiques.* 2 vols. Quebec and Montreal: P. Gagnon, etc., 1895–1913.
Galarneau, Claude. 'Le commerce du livre à Québec (1766–1820).' Seminar papers by Jacqueline Roy-Cloutier, Jacques-Antoine Auguste, Gilles Gallichan, Céline Cyr-Lemire, and Michel Verrette. Université Laval, 1977.
– 'Les Desbarats: Une dynastie d'imprimeurs-éditeurs (1794–1893).' *Cahiers des Dix* 46 (1991): 125–49.
– 'L'école, gardienne de la langue.' In *Le français au Québec: 400 ans d'histoire et de vie,* ed. Michel Plourde, 99–102. Saint-Laurent: Fides and Publications du Québec, 2000.
– 'L'enseignement médical à Québec (1800–1848).' *Cahiers des Dix* 53 (1999): 37–64.
– *La France devant l'opinion canadienne, 1760–1815.* Quebec: Presses de l'Université Laval, 1970.
– 'Les métiers du livre à Québec (1764–1859).' *Cahiers des Dix* 43 (1983): 143–65.
– 'La presse périodique au Québec de 1764 à 1859.' *Transactions of the Royal Society of Canada* 22 (1984): 143–66.
Gallant, Christel. 'L'Acadie, berceau de la traduction officielle au Canada.' *Cultures du Canada français* 2 (Autumn 1985): 71–8.
– 'L'influence des religions catholique et protestante sur la traduction des textes sacrés à

l'intention des Micmacs dans les provinces Maritimes: Du livre de prières de l'abbé Maillard (1710–1762) à la traduction des Évangiles par Silas Tertius Rand (1810–1889).' *Traduction terminologie et rédaction* 3 (1990): 97–109.

Gallat-Morin, Élisabeth, et Jean-Pierre Pinson, eds. *La vie musicale en Nouvelle-France.* Cahiers des Amériques, no. 1. Quebec: Septentrion, 2003.

Gallichan, Gilles. *La Bibliothèque du Barreau de Québec, l'émergence d'une institution.* Montreal: Wilson et Lafleur, 1994.

– 'Bibliothèque et culture au Canada après la conquête, 1760–1800.' In *Livre, bibliothèque et culture québécoise: Mélanges offerts à Edmond Desrochers, s.j.,* ed. Georges-A. Chartrand, vol. 1, 299–310. Montreal: ASTED, 1977.

– 'L'État québécois et ses bibliothèques.' In *Les bibliothèques québécoises d'hier à aujourd'hui,* ed. Gilles Gallichan, 79–100. Montreal: Les Éditions ASTED, 1998.

– 'La Gazette officielle: Une longue et difficile naissance.' In *La Gazette officielle du Québec: 125 ans d'édition gouvernementale,* 23–33. Quebec: Les Publications du Québec, 1994.

– 'Le *Lex Parliamentaria* ou le Bas-Canada à l'école parlementaire.' *PBSC/CSBC* 25 (1986): 38–62.

– *Livre et politique au Bas-Canada, 1791–1849.* Sillery: Septentrion, 1991.

– 'Les Parlements et leurs bibliothèques, ou les chemins documentaires de la démocratie.' *Documentation et bibliothèques* 47.4 (Oct.–Dec. 2001): 145–8.

– 'La session de 1836.' *Cahiers des Dix* 55 (2001): 191–284.

Garratt, John G. *Four Indian Kings / Les quatres rois indiens.* Ottawa: Public Archives of Canada, 1985.

Garry, Loraine Spencer, and Carl Garry, eds. *Canadian Libraries in Their Changing Environment.* Downsview, ON: Centre for Continuing Education, York University, 1977.

Gauvreau, Danielle. *Québec, une ville et sa population au temps de la Nouvelle-France.* Sillery: Presses de l'Université du Québec, 1991.

Germain, Élisabeth. *Langages de la foi à travers l'histoire: Approche pour une étude des mentalités.* Paris: Fayard-Mame, 1972.

Gerson, Carole. *Canada's Early Women Writers: Texts in English to 1859.* The CRIAW Papers. Ottawa: CRIAW/ICREF, 1994.

– *A Purer Taste: The Writing and Reading of Fiction in English in Nineteenth-Century Canada.* Toronto: University of Toronto Press, 1989.

Gerson, Carole, and Gwendolyn Davies, eds. *Canadian Poetry from the Beginnings through the First World War.* Toronto: McClelland & Stewart, 1994.

Gidney, R.D. 'Elementary Education in Upper Canada: A Reassessment.' In *Education and Social Change: Themes from Ontario's Past,* ed. Michael B. Katz and Paul H. Mattingly, 3–27. New York: New York University Press, 1975.

Gilmore, William J. *Reading Becomes a Necessity of Life: Material and Cultural Life in Rural New England, 1780–1835.* Knoxville: University of Tennessee Press, 1989.

Glandelet, Charles. *Office de la sainte Famille.* [s.l., s.n.], 1702.

Godechot, Jacques. *Histoire de l'Atlantique.* Paris: Bordas, 1947.

Goen, C.C. *Revivalism and Separatism in New England, 1740–1800: Strict Congregationalists and Separate Baptists in the Great Awakening.* Middletown: Wesleyan University Press, 1987.

Goldsmith, Oliver. *The Autobiography of Oliver Goldsmith.* Toronto: Ryerson Press, 1943.

Good, Edgar Reginald. *Waterloo County Itinerant Fraktur Artists.* Kitchener: Pochauna Publications, 1977.

Gosse, Philip Henry. 'Philip Henry Gosse's Account of His Years in Newfoundland, 1827–35.' *Newfoundland Studies* 6 (Fall 1990): 210–66.

Gosselin, Amédée-Edmond. *L'instruction au Canada sous le régime français (1635–1760)*. Quebec: Lafamme & Prouix, 1911.

Grabowski, Jan. 'Mohawk Crisis at Kanasetake and Kahnawake.' *European Review of Native American Studies* 5.1 (1991): 11–14.

Grant, Campbell. *The Rock Art of the North American Indians*. Cambridge: Cambridge University Press, 1983.

Gray, Charlotte. *Sisters in the Wilderness: The Lives of Susanna Moodie and Catharine Parr Traill*. Toronto: Penguin Books of Canada, 2000.

Greaves, Susan. 'Book Culture in Halifax in the 1830s: The Entrenchment of the Book Trade.' *Epilogue* 11 (Spring 1991): 1–19.

Grece, Charles F. *Facts and Observations Respecting Canada, and the United States of America*. London: J. Harding, 1819.

Green, Anson. *The Life and Times of the Rev. Anson Green, D.D.* Toronto: Methodist Book Room, 1877.

Green, James N. 'English Books and Printing in the Age of Franklin.' In *A History of the Book in America*, vol. 1, *The Colonial Book in the Atlantic World*, ed. Hugh Amory and David Hall, 248–98. Cambridge and New York: Cambridge University Press, 2000.

– 'From Printer to Publisher: Mathew Carey and the Origins of Nineteenth-Century Book Publishing.' In *Getting the Books Out: Papers of the Chicago Conference on the Book in 19th-Century America*, ed. Michael Hackenberg, 26–44. Washington, DC: Center for the Book, Library of Congress, 1987.

Green, Samuel G. *The Story of the Religious Tract Society for One Hundred Years*. London: Religious Tract Society, 1899.

Greenfield, Bruce. 'Creating the Distance of Print: The Memoir of Peter Pond, Fur Trader.' *Early American Literature* 37 (2002): 415–38.

– 'The Mi'kmaq Hieroglyphic Prayer Book: Writing and Christianity in Maritime Canada, 1675–1921.' In *The Language Encounter in the Americas, 1492–1800: A Collection of Essays*, ed. Edward G. Gray and Norman Fiering, 189–229. New York and Oxford: Berghahn Books, 2000.

Greenwood, F. Murray, and Barry Wright. 'Introduction: State Trials, the Rule of Law, and Executive Powers in Early Canada.' In *Canadian State Trials*, vol. 1, *Law, Politics, and Security Measures, 1608–1837*, ed. F. Murray Greenwood and Barry Wright, 3–51. Toronto: University of Toronto Press, 1996.

– 'Parliamentary Privilege and the Repression of Dissent in the Canadas.' In *Canadian State Trials*, vol. 1, *Law, Politics, and Security Measures, 1608–1837*, ed. F. Murray Greenwood and Barry Wright, 409–49. Toronto: University of Toronto Press, 1996.

– eds. *Canadian State Trials*. Vol. 1, *Law, Politics, and Security Measures, 1608–1837*. Toronto: University of Toronto Press, 1996.

Greer, Allan. 'L'alphabétisation et son histoire au Québec: État de la question.' In *L'imprimé au Québec: Aspects historiques (XVIIIe–XXe siècles)*, ed. Yvan Lamonde, 25–51. Quebec: Institut québécois de recherche sur la culture, 1983.

– 'The Pattern of Literacy in Quebec, 1745–1899.' *Histoire sociale / Social History* 11.22 (Nov. 1978): 295–335.

– 'The Sunday Schools of Upper Canada.' *Ontario History* 67 (1975): 169–84.

Gundy, H. Pearson. *Early Printers and Printing in the Canadas*. Toronto: Bibliographical Society of Canada, 1957.

– 'Literary Publishing.' In *Literary History of Canada: Canadian Literature in English*, ed. Carl F. Klinck et al., 174–88. Toronto: University of Toronto Press, 1965.

– 'Publishing and Bookselling in Kingston since 1810.' *Historic Kingston* 10 (1962): 22–36.

- 'Samuel Olivier Tazewell, First Lithographer of Upper Canada.' *Humanities Association Review / Revue de l'Association des humanités* 27 (1976): 466–83.

Habermehl, Fred, and Donald L. Combe. *St. Mark's: Persons of Hopeful Piety.* Niagara-on-the-Lake, ON: Archives Committee of St Mark's, 2000.

Haché, Bernard, and Mireille McClaughlin. 'Le livre en Acadie avant 1840.' In 'Rapport de recherche réalisée dans le cadre du projet Histoire du livre et de l'imprimé au Canada / History of the Book in Canada.' Moncton, 2001.

Haight, Canniff. *Life in Canada Fifty Years Ago: Personal Recollections and Reminiscences of a Sexagenarian.* Toronto: Hunter Rose, 1890.

Haliburton, Thomas Chandler. *The Clockmaker, Series One, Two, and Three.* Ed. George L. Parker. Centre for Editing Early Canadian Texts, no. 10. Ottawa: Carleton University Press, 1995.

- *The Letters of Thomas Chandler Haliburton.* Ed. Richard A. Davies. Toronto: University of Toronto Press, 1988.

Hall, David D. 'The Chesapeake in the Seventeenth Century.' In *A History of the Book in America*, vol. 1, *The Colonial Book in the Atlantic World*, ed. Hugh Amory and David D. Hall, 55–82. Cambridge and New York: Cambridge University Press, 2000.

- *Cultures of Print: Essays in the History of the Book.* Amherst: University of Massachusetts Press, 1996.

Hamilton, Anthony. *An Account of the State of the Schools in the Island of Newfoundland: Established or Assisted by the Society for the Propagation of the Gospel in Foreign Parts.* London: C. and J. Rivington, 1827.

Hamilton, Walter. *French Book-Plates.* London: George Bell and Sons, 1896.

Hamilton, William B. 'Society and Schools in New Brunswick and Prince Edward Island.' In *Canadian Education: A History*, ed. J. Donald Wilson, Robert M. Stamp, and Louis-Philippe Audet, 106–25. Scarborough, ON: Prentice-Hall of Canada, 1970.

- 'Society and Schools in Newfoundland.' In *Canadian Education: A History*, ed. J. Donald Wilson, Robert M. Stamp, and Louis-Philippe Audet, 126–44. Scarborough, ON: Prentice-Hall of Canada, 1970.

- 'Society and Schools in Nova Scotia.' In *Canadian Education: A History*, ed. J. Donald Wilson, Robert M. Stamp, and Louis-Philippe Audet, 86–105. Scarborough, ON: Prentice-Hall of Canada, 1970.

Hardy, Jean-Pierre, and David-Thiery Ruddel. *Les apprentis artisans à Québec, 1660–1815.* Montreal: PUQ, 1977.

Hardy, René. 'À propos du réveil religieux dans le Québec du XIXe siècle: Le recours aux tribunaux dans les rapports entre le clergé et les fidèles.' *RHAF* 48 (Autumn 1994): 187–212.

- *Contrôle social et mutation de la culture religieuse au Québec, 1830–1930.* [Montreal]: Boréal, 1999.

Hare, John. *Aux origines du parlementarisme québécois, 1791–1793: Étude et documents.* Sillery, Quebec: Septentrion, 1993.

- 'La formation de la terminologie parlementaire et électorale au Québec: 1792–1810.' *Revue de l'Université d'Ottawa* 46 (Oct.–Dec. 1976): 460–75.

Hare, John, and Jean-Pierre Wallot. 'Les imprimés au Québec (1760–1820).' In *L'imprimé au Québec: Aspects historiques (XVIIIe–XXe siècles)*, ed. Yvan Lamonde, 77–125. Quebec: Institut québécois de recherche sur la culture, 1983.

- *Les imprimés dans le Bas-Canada, 1801–1840: Bibliographe analytique*, vol. 1, *1801–10.* Montreal: Presses de l'Université de Montréal, 1967.

Harmon, Daniel Williams. *Sixteen Years in the Indian Country: The Journal of Daniel Williams Harmon.*

Ed. W. Kaye Lamb. Toronto: Macmillan, 1957. Originally published as *A Journal of Voyages and Travels.* Andover, 1820.

Harper, J. Russell. *A People's Art: Primitive, Naïve, Provincial, and Folk Painting in Canada.* Toronto: University of Toronto Press, 1974.

Harris, R. Cole, ed. *Historical Atlas of Canada.* Vol. 1. Toronto: University of Toronto Press, 1987.

Harrison, Jane E. *Until Next Year: Letter Writing and the Mails in the Canadas, 1640–1830.* Waterloo, ON: Wilfrid Laurier University Press for the Canadian Postal Museum–Canadian Museum of Civilization, 1997.

Harrod, Stanley, and Morely J. Ayearst, comp. *A List of Canadian Bookplates: With a Review of the History of Ex-libris in the Dominion.* Ed. Winward Prescott. Boston: Society of Bookplate Bibliophiles, 1919.

Hart, Julia Catherine Beckwith. *St. Ursula's Convent; or, The Nun of Canada, Containing Scenes from Real Life.* Ed. Douglas G. Lochhead. Centre for Editing Early Canadian Texts, no. 8. Ottawa: Carleton University Press, 1991.

Harvey, D.C. 'Early Public Libraries in Nova Scotia.' *Dalhousie Review* 14 (1934–5): 429–43.

– 'The Intellectual Awakening of Nova Scotia.' In *Historical Essays on the Atlantic Provinces*, ed. G.A. Rawlyk, 99–121. Toronto: McClelland & Stewart, 1967.

– 'Newspapers of Nova Scotia.' *Canadian Historical Review* 26 (1945): 279–301.

Head, Francis Bond. *A Narrative.* 2nd ed. London: J. Murray, 1839.

Hearne, Samuel. *A Journey from the Prince of Wales's Fort in Hudson's Bay to the Northern Ocean, 1769, 1770, 1771, 1772.* Ed. Richard Glover. Toronto: Macmillan, 1958.

Hébert, Léo-Paul. 'Le *Nehiro-Iriniu* du Père de La Brosse ou "L'influence d'un livre."' In *Une inconnue de l'histoire de la culture: La production des catéchismes en Amérique française*, ed. Raymond Brodeur et Jean-Paul Rouleau, 57–83. Sainte-Foy: Éditions Anne Sigier, 1986.

Hébert, Pierre, and Patrick Nicol. *Censure et littérature au Québec: Le livre crucifié (1625–1919).* Saint-Laurent: Fides, 1997.

Hennepin, Louis. *A New Discovery of a Vast Country in America.* Reprinted from the second London issue of 1698, with facsimiles of original title-pages, maps, and illustrations. 2 vols. Introduction, notes, and index by Reuben Gold Thwaites. Chicago: A.C. McClurg & Co., 1903. Reprint, Toronto: Coles Pub. Co., 1974.

– *Nouvelle decouverte d'un tres grand pays situé dans l'Amerique, entre le Nouveau Mexique et la mer glaciale, avec les cartes, & les figures necessaires, & de plus l'histoire naturelle & morale, & les avantages, qu'on en peut tirer par l'établissement des colonies.* Utrecht: Chez Guillaume Broedelet, 1697.

Henry, Alexander, the elder. *Travels and Adventures in Canada and the Indian Territories.* Ed. James Bain. Boston, 1901. Originally published New York, 1809. Reprint, New York: Burt Franklin, 1969.

Hill, Beth, and Ray Hill. *Indian Petroglyphs of the Pacific Northwest.* Saanichton: Hancock House Publishers, 1974.

Holland, Clive. *Arctic Exploration and Development c. 500 B.C. to 1915: An Encyclopedia.* New York: Garland, 1994.

Horguelin, Paul-A. 'Les premiers traducteurs (1760 à 1791).' *Meta* 22 (March 1977): 15–25.

Houde, Danièle. 'La liberté de la presse en droit anglais, américain et canadien.' *Cahiers de droit* 13 (1972): 121–93.

Hounsom, Eric Wilfrid. *Toronto in 1810.* Toronto: Ryerson Press, 1970.

Houston, Susan E., and Alison Prentice. *Schooling and Scholars in Nineteenth-Century Ontario.* Toronto: University of Toronto Press, 1988.

Howe, Joseph. *My Dear Susan Ann: Letters of Joseph Howe to His Wife, 1829–1836.* Ed. M.G. Parks. St John's: Jesperson, 1985.

- *The Speeches and Public Letters of Joseph Howe.* 2 vols. Ed. Joseph Chisholm. Halifax: The Chronicle Publishing Company Ltd, 1909.

Howsam, Leslie. *Cheap Bibles: Nineteenth-Century Publishing and the British and Foreign Bible Society.* Cambridge: Cambridge University Press, 1991.

Hubert, Ollivier. *Sur la terre comme au ciel: La gestion des rites par l'Église catholique du Québec (fin XVIIe– mi XIXe siècle).* Sainte-Foy: Presses de l'Université Laval, 2000.

Hudak, Leona M. *Early American Women Printers and Publishers, 1639–1820.* Metuchen, NJ, and London: Scarecrow Press, 1978.

Hulse, Elizabeth. *A Dictionary of Toronto Printers, Publishers, Booksellers, and the Allied Trades, 1798–1900.* Toronto: Anson-Cartwright Editions, 1982.

- 'A Printer Writes Home.' *Devil's Artisan* 12 (1983): 3–8.

Isham, James. *Observations on Hudson's Bay, 1743–1749.* Ed. E.E. Rich. Publications of the Champlain Society. Hudson's Bay Company Series, 12. London: Champlain Society for the Hudson's Bay Record Society, 1949.

Jackson, Heather J. *Marginalia: Readers Writing in Books.* New Haven and London: Yale University Press, 2001.

Jaenen, Cornelius J. 'Amerindian Views of French Culture in the Seventeenth Century.' In *Out of the Background: Readings on Canadian Native History,* ed. Robin Fisher and Kenneth Coates, 102–33. Toronto: Copp Clark Pitman Ltd, 1988.

Jameson, Anna. *Winter Studies and Summer Rambles in Canada.* 2 vols. London: Saunders and Otley, 1838.

- *Winter Studies and Summer Rambles in Canada.* Ed. James J. Talman and Elsie McLeod Murray. Toronto: Nelson, 1943.

Jaumain, Serge. 'Le colporteur dans le Québec du XIXe siècle: Contribution à l'histoire comparée.' Master's thesis, Université d'Ottawa, 1985.

Jennings, Francis. *History and Culture of Iroquois Diplomacy: An Interdisciplinary Guide to the Treaties of the Six Nations and Their League.* Syracuse: Syracuse University Press, 1985.
The Jesuit Relations and Allied Documents: Travels and Explorations of the Jesuit Missionaries in New France, 1610– 1791: The Original French, Latin and Italian Texts with English Translations and Notes. 73 vols. Ed. Reuben Gold Thwaites. Cleveland: Burrows Bros, 1896–1901. Reprint, New York: Pageant Book Company, 1959.

Johnson, J.R. 'The Availability of Reading Material for the Pioneer in Upper Canada: Niagara District, 1792–1841.' Master's thesis, University of Western Ontario, 1982.

Johnston, A.J.B. *La religion dans la vie à Louisbourg (1713–1758).* Ottawa: Direction des lieux et des parcs historiques nationaux, Service canadien des parcs, Environnement Canada, 1988.

Johnston, Judith. *Anna Jameson: Victorian, Feminist, Woman of Letters.* Aldershot, England, and Brookfield, VT: Scholar Press, 1997.

Johnstone, Walter. *Travels in Prince Edward Island, Gulf of St. Lawrence, North-America in the Years 1820– 21.* Edinburgh: D. Brown, 1823.

Jones, Robert Leslie. *History of Agriculture in Ontario, 1613–1880.* Toronto: University of Toronto Press, 1946. Reprint, 1977.

Kalbfleisch, Herbert Karl. *The History of the Pioneer German Language Press of Ontario, 1835–1918.* Toronto: University of Toronto Press, 1968.

Kallmann, Helmut. *A History of Music in Canada, 1534–1914.* Toronto: University of Toronto Press, 1960.

- 'Publishing and Printing.' In *Encyclopedia of Music in Canada*, ed. Helmut Kallmann, Gilles Potvin, et al., 1090–1. 2nd ed. Toronto: University of Toronto Press, 1992.

Kallmann, Helmut, Gilles Potvin, Kenneth Winters, Robin Elliott, and Mark Miller, eds. *Encyclopedia of Music in Canada*. 2nd ed. Toronto: University of Toronto Press, 1992.

Kalm, Pehr. *Voyage de Pehr Kalm au Canada en 1749*. Ed. Jacques Rousseau and Guy Béthune. Montreal: Pierre Tisseyre, 1977.

Kennedy, P. 'Impressions of State Authority.' In *Genealogica & Heraldica: Proceedings of the 22nd International Congress of Genealogical and Heraldic Sciences in Ottawa, August 18–23, 1996*, ed. Auguste Vachon, Claire Boudreau, and Daniel Cogné, 373–84. Ottawa: University of Ottawa Press, 1998.

Kerber, Linda K. *Women of the Republic: Intellect and Ideology in Revolutionary America*. Chapel Hill: The Institute of Early American History and Culture, University of North Carolina Press, 1980.

Kesterton, Wilfred H. *A History of Journalism in Canada*. Toronto: McClelland & Stewart, 1967.

Klinck, Carl F., et al., eds. *Literary History of Canada: Canadian Literature in English*. 2nd ed. Toronto: University of Toronto Press, 1976–90.

Koeppel, Adolph. *The Stamps That Caused the American Revolution: The Stamps of the 1765 British Stamps Act for America*. Mahasset, NY: Town of North Hamstead American Revolution Bicentennial Commission, 1976.

Konrad, Ruth. 'Libraries.' In *Encyclopaedia of Newfoundland and Labrador*, ed. Joseph R. Smallwood et al., vol. 3, 289–94. St John's: Harry Cuff Publications, 1991.

Labonté, Gilles. 'Les bibliothèques privées à Québec (1820–1829).' Master's thesis, Université Laval, 1986.

Lacourcière, Luc. 'Aubert de Gaspé, fils [1814–1841].' *Cahiers des Dix* 40 (1975): 275–302.

Lacy, Creighton. *The Word-Carrying Giant: The Growth of the America Bible Society (1816–1966)*. South Pasadena: William Carey Library, 1977.

Lafitau, Joseph-François. *Customs of the American Indians Compared with the Customs of Primitive Times*. 2 vols. Ed. and trans. William N. Fenton and Elizabeth L. Moore. Toronto: Champlain Society, 1974–7.

- *Mœurs des sauvages ameriquains, comparées aux moeurs des premiers temps*. 2 vols. Paris: Saugrain l'aîné, Charles Estienne Hochereau, 1724.

Laflamme, Jean, and Rémi Tourangeau. *L'Église et le théâtre au Québec*. Montreal: Fides, 1979.

Lagrave, Jean-Paul de. *L'époque de Voltaire au Canada: Biographie politique de Fleury Mesplet (1734–1794)*. Montreal: L'Étincelle, 1993.

- *Fleury Mesplet (1734–1794), imprimeur, éditeur, libraire, journaliste*. Montreal: Patenaude éditeur, 1985.

Lagrave, Jean-Paul de, and Jacques G. Ruelland. *Premier journaliste de langue française au Canada: Valentin Jautard, 1736–1787*. Sainte-Foy: Les éditions Le Griffon d'argile, 1988.

Lahontan, Louis Armand de Lom d'Arce, baron de. *New Voyages to North-America*. Reprinted from the English ed. of 1703, with an introduction, notes, and index by Reuben Gold Thwaites. Chicago: A.C. McClurg, 1905.

- *Œuvres complètes*. Ed. Réal Ouellet in collaboration with Alain Beaulieu. 2 vols. Bibliothèque du Nouveau Monde. Montreal: Presses de l'Université de Montréal, 1990.

- *Voyages du baron de Lahontan dans l'Amérique septentrionale*. 2 vols. Montreal: Éditions Élysée, 1974.

Lajeunesse, Marcel. 'Le livre dans les échanges sulpiciens Paris-Montréal au cours de la première moitié du 19e siècle.' In *Livre et lecture au Québec (1800–1850)*, ed. Claude Galarneau and Maurice Lemire, 133–47. Quebec: Institut québécois de recherche sur la culture, 1988.

Lambert, John. *Travels through Canada, and the United States of North America, in the Years 1806, 1807,*

1808; to Which Are Added, Bibliographical Notices and Anecdotes of Some of the Leading Characters in the United States. 3rd ed. 2 vols. London: Baldwin, Cradock and Joy, 1816.

Lamonde, Yvan. *Les bibliothèques de collectivités à Montréal (17e–19e siécle): Sources et problèmes.* Montreal: Bibliothèque nationale du Québec, 1979.

– *Histoire sociale des idées au Québec: Vol. 1, 1760–1896.* Montreal: Fides, 2000.

– *La librairie et l'édition à Montréal (1776–1920).* Montreal: BNQ, 1991.

– 'La librairie Hector Bossange de Montréal (1815–1819) et le commerce international du livre.' In *Livre et lecture au Québec (1800–1850)*, ed. Claude Galarneau and Maurice Lemire, 59–92. Quebec: Institut québécois de recherche sur la culture, 1988.

– 'La librarie Hector Bossange de Montréal (1815–1819) et le commerce internationale du livre.' In *Histoire de la littérature pour la jeunesse: Québec et francophonies du Canada,* ed. Françoise Lepage, 181–218. Orléans: Éditions David, 2000.

– *La philosophie et son enseignement au Québec (1665–1920).* Montreal: Hurtubise HMH, 1980.

– 'La représentation de l'imprimé dans la peinture et la gravure québécoises (1760–1960).' In *Portrait des arts, des lettres et de l'éloquence au Québec (1760–1840)*, ed. Bernard Andrès and Marc André Bernier, 73–98. République des lettres. Sainte-Foy: Presses de l'Université Laval, 2002.

– 'Social Origins of the Public Library in Montreal.' *Canadian Library Journal* 38 (1981): 363–70.

– *Territoires de la culture québécoise.* Sainte-Foy: Presses de l'Université Laval, 1991.

– 'A Universal Classification for the Study of Nineteenth-Century Libraries and Booksellers.' *Libraries & Culture* 24 (Spring 1989): 158–97.

Lamonde, Yvan, Bertrum H. MacDonald, and Andrea Rotundo. 'Canadian Book Trade Catalogues / Catalogues canadiens relatifs à l'imprimé.' Available on-line at: http://acsweb2.ucis.dal.ca/hbicdb/english/catalogues.html and http://acsweb2.ucis.dal.ca/hbicdb/francais/catalogues.html.

Lamonde, Yvan, and Claude Beauchamp. *Données statistiques sur l'histoire culturelle du Québec, 1760–1900.* Chicoutimi: Institut interuniversitaire de recherches sur les populations, 1996.

Lamonde, Yvan, and Daniel Olivier. *Les bibliothèques personnelles au Québec: Inventaire analytique et préliminaire des sources.* Montreal: Bibliothèque nationale du Québec, 1983.

Landry, Kenneth. '"Les avantages que la presse procure au public": Le discours stratégique de quelques prospectus de journaux et de périodiques canadiens avant 1840.' In *Portrait des arts, des lettres et de l'éloquence au Québec (1760–1840)*, ed. Bernard Andrès and Marc André Bernier, 295–311. Sainte-Foy: Presses de l'Université Laval, 2002.

Langlois, Égide. 'Livres et lectures à Québec, 1764–1799.' Master's thesis, Université Laval, 1984.

Laurence, Gérard. 'La distribution linguistique de la presse au Québec.' In *Le français au Québec: 400 ans d'histoire et de vie,* ed. Michel Plourde, 123–6. Saint-Laurent: Fides and Publications du Québec, 2000.

Laurence, W.H. '"Never Been a Very Promising Speculation": Requests for Financial Assistance from Authors of Non-Fiction Books to Nova Scotia House of Assembly, 1800–1850.' *PBSC/CSBC* 39.2 (Autumn 2001): 45–78.

Laurent, Monique. 'Le catalogue de la bibliothèque du Séminaire de Québec, 1782.' Ph.D. diss., Université Laval, 1973.

Laverdière, Charles-Honoré, and Henri-Raymond Casgrain, eds. *Journal des jésuites.* Montreal: Éditions François-Xavier, 1973.

Lavoie, Laurent. 'La vie intellectuelle et les activités culturelles à la forteresse de Louisbourg, 1713–1758.' *Man and Nature / L'homme et la nature* 4 (1985): 129–38.

Lebel, Jean-Marie. 'Ludger Duvernay et la Minerve: Étude d'une enterprise de presse montréalaise de la première moitié du XIXe siècle.' Master's thesis, Université Laval, 1982.

Le Clercq, Chrestien. *Nouvelle relation de la Gaspesie.* Ed. Réal Ouellet. Montreal: Bibliothèque du Nouveau Monde, 1999.

Lee, Brian North. *Early Printed Book Labels: A Catalogue of Dated Personal Labels and Gift Labels Printed in Britain to the Year 1760.* Pinner, England: Private Libraries Association and the Bookplate Society, 1976.

LeFebvre, Fernand. 'La bibliothèque des frères Charon.' *Bulletin des recherches historiques* 64.3 (July–Sept. 1958): 67–77.

Lehmann, Heinz. *The German Canadians, 1750–1937: Immigration, Settlement & Culture.* Ed. and trans. Gerhard P. Bassler. St John's: Jesperson Press, 1986.

Lemieux, Lucien. *L'établissement de la première province ecclésiastique au Canada, 1783–1844.* Montreal: Fides, 1968.

Lemire, Maurice, ed. *La vie littéraire au Québec.* 2 vols. Sainte-Foy: Presses de l'Université Laval, 1991.

Lemoine, Réjean. 'Les brochures publiées au XIXe siècle afin de lutter contre le choléra: Essai bibliographique.' *Cahiers du livre ancien du Canada français* 1 (Summer 1984): 35–41.

– 'Le marché du livre à Québec, 1764–1839.' Master's thesis, Université Laval, 1981.

Lepage, Françoise, ed. *Histoire de la littérature pour la jeunesse: Québec et francophonies du Canada.* Orléans: Éditions David, 2000.

Lescarbot, Marc. *The History of New France.* 3 vols. Ed. W.L. Grant. Toronto: Champlain Society, 1907–14.

Lessard, Claude. 'L'alphabétisation à Trois-Rivières de 1634 à 1939.' *Cahiers nicolétains* 12 (Sept. 1990): 83–117.

Lester, Normand. *Le livre noir du Canada anglais.* Montreal: Intouchables, 2001.

Lestringant, Frank. 'Champlain, Lescarbot la "conférence" des histoires.' *Quaderni del Seicento Francese* 6 (1984): 69–88.

Letocha, Louise. 'Le premier livre illustré imprimé au Québec.' *Bulletin de la Bibliothèque nationale de Québec* 10.3 (Sept. 1976): 5–7.

Li, Shenwen. *Stratégies missionnaires des jésuites français en Nouvelle-France et en Chine au XVIIe siècle.* Paris and Quebec: L'Harmattan / Presses de l'Université Laval, 2001.

Lindsay, Debra. 'Peter Fidler's Library: Philosophy and Science in Rupert's Land.' In *Readings in Canadian Library History,* ed. Peter F. McNally, 209–29. Ottawa: Canadian Library Association, 1986.

Lortie, Jeanne d'Arc, ed. *Les textes poétiques du Canada français: 1606–1867.* 12 vols. Montreal: Fides, 1987–.

Love, Harold. *The Culture and Commerce of Texts: Scribal Publication in Seventeenth-Century England.* Amherst: University of Massachusetts Press, 1998.

Lowes, John Livingstone. *The Road to Xanadu: A Study in the Way of the Imagination.* Boston: Houghton Mifflin, 1955.

Lupul, Manoly R. 'Education in Western Canada before 1873.' In *Canadian Education: A History,* ed. J. Donald Wilson, Robert M. Stamp, and Louis-Philippe Audet, 241–64. Scarborough, ON: Prentice-Hall of Canada, 1970.

Macdonald, Archibald. *The Old Lords of Lovat and Beaufort.* Inverness: Northern Countries Newspaper and Printing and Publishing Company, 1934.

MacDonald, Bertrum H. 'In Support of an "Information System": The Case of the Library of the

Natural History Society of Montreal.' In *Readings in Canadian Library History 2*, ed. Peter F. McNally, 217–40. Ottawa: Canadian Library Association, 1996.

– 'La publication des livres: Le rôle clé des gouvernements et des organismes gouvernementaux / Getting the Book Published: The Instrumental Role of Governments and Their Agencies.' *Fac-similé / Facsimile* 19 (May 1998): 13–18.

MacDonald, Bertrum H., and Nancy F. Vogan. 'James Dawson of Pictou and *The Harmonicon*: Sacred Music for Victorian Maritimers.' *PBSC/CSBC* 38.2 (Fall 2000): 33–64.

MacDonald, Mary Lu. *Literature and Society in the Canadas, 1817–1850*. Lewiston: E. Mellen Press, 1992.

– 'The *Montreal Museum*, 1832–1834: The Presence and Absence of Literary Women.' In *Women's Writing and the Literary Institution / L'écriture au féminin et l'institution littéraire*, ed. C. Potvin et al., 139–50. Edmonton: Research Institute for Comparative Literature, University of Alberta, 1992.

– 'Some Notes on the Montreal Literary Scene in the Mid-1820's.' *Canadian Poetry* 5 (Fall/Winter 1979): 29–40.

MacDonell, Margaret. 'Bards on the "Polly."' *Island Magazine*, no. 5 (Fall–Winter 1978): 34–9.

MacGregor, James Grierson. *Peter Fidler: Canada's Forgotten Surveyor, 1769–1822*. Toronto: McClelland & Stewart, 1966.

Macgregor, John. *British America*. Vol. 2. Edinburgh: W. Blackwood, 1832.

Mackenzie, Alexander. *The Journals and Letters of Sir Alexander Mackenzie*. Ed. W. Kaye Lamb. Toronto: Macmillan of Canada / Hakluyt Society, 1970.

Mackenzie, William Lyon. *Catechism of Education*. York: Colonial Advocate Press, 1830.

MacLaren, I.S. 'Alexander Mackenzie and the Landscapes of Commerce.' *Studies in Canadian Literature* 7 (1982): 141–50.

– 'Arctic Exploration and Milton's "frozen Continent."' *Notes and Queries* 229 (1984): 325–6.

– 'Commentary: The Aesthetics of Back's Writing and Painting from the First Overland Expedition.' In *Arctic Artist: The Journal and Paintings of George Back, Midshipman with Franklin, 1819–1822*, ed. C. Stuart Houston, 275–310. Montreal and Kingston: McGill-Queen's University Press, 1994.

– 'Exploration/Travel Literature and the Evolution of the Author.' *International Journal of Canadian Studies / Revue internationale d'études canadiennes* 5 (Spring/printemps 1992): 39–68.

– 'Notes on Samuel Hearne's *Journey* from a Bibliographical Perspective.' *PBSC/CSBC* 31.2 (Fall 1993): 21–45.

MacNaughton, Katherine F.C. *The Development of the Theory and Practice of Education in New Brunswick 1784–1900*. Fredericton: University of New Brunswick, 1946.

Magnuson, Roger. *Education in New France*. Montreal and Kingston: McGill-Queen's University Press, 1992.

Maheux, Arthur. 'La bibliothèque du missionnaire Davion au dix-huitième siècle.' *Canada français* 27 (March 1940): 650–61.

Maillard, Pierre-Antoine-Simon. 'Lettre de M. l'Abbé Maillard sur les missions de l'Acadie et particulièrement sur les missions Micmaques.' *Soirées canadiennes* 3 (1863): 290–426.

Malchelosse, Gérard. 'La bibliothèque acadienne.' *Cahiers des Dix* 19 (1954): 263–86.

Mallery, Garrick. *Picture-Writing of the American Indians*. 2 vols. New York: Dover Publications, 1972.

Mandements, lettres pastorales, circulaires et autres documents publiés dans le diocèse de Montréal depuis son érection. 15 vols. Montreal: J. Chapleau & Fils, 1869–1952.

Mandements: Lettres pastorales et circulaires des évêques de Québec. 6 vols. Quebec: Imprimerie générale A. Coté, 1887–90.

Marchand, Jean. *La Bibliothèque de l'Assemblée nationale: Histoire de ses origines, de sa constitution officielle et de ses développements, sous l'administration de Camus et de Druon jusqu'à la construction de la bibliothèque actuelle.* Bordeaux: Société des Bibliophiles de Guyenne, 1979.

Marie de l'Assomption, sœur. *Bibliographie d'ouvrages anciens de médecine gardés à l'Hôpital général (1669–1874).* Montreal: Bibiothèque des Archives de l'Hôpital général de Québec, 1978.

Marie de l'Incarnation. *Marie de l'Incarnation, ursuline (1599–1672): Correspondance.* Ed. Guy Oury. Solesmes: Abbaye Saint-Pierre, 1971.

– *Marie of the Incarnation (1599–1672): Correspondence.* Ed. Guy Oury. Trans. Dominic Kelly. Cartron, Sligo: Irish Ursuline Union, 2000.

Marini, Stephen A. *Radical Sects of Revolutionary New England.* Cambridge: Harvard University Press, 1982.

Martell, James Stuart. *The Achievements of Agricola and the Agricultural Societies, 1818–25.* Halifax: Public Archives of Nova Scotia, 1940.

Martin, Denis. 'L'estampe importée en Nouvelle-France.' Ph.D. diss., Université Laval, 1990.

Martin, Henri-Jean. *Livre, pouvoirs et société à Paris au XVIIe siècle (1598–1701).* 2 vols. Geneva: Droz, 1969.

Martin, Henri-Jean, and Roger Chartier, eds. *Histoire de l'édition française.* Vol. 1, *Le livre conquérant, du Moyen Âge au milieu du XVIIe siècle.* Vol. 2, *Le livre triomphant, 1660–1830.* Paris: Promodis, 1982, 1984.

Martin, Marie Antoinette. *L'Institut de la Providence: Histoire des Filles de la charité servantes des pauvres dites Soeurs de la Providence.* 6 vols. Montreal: Providence (Maison Mère), 1925.

Massicotte, Édouard-Zotique. 'Libraires-papetiers-relieurs à Montréal au XVIIIe siècle.' *Bulletin des recherches historiques* 36.5 (May 1930): 298–9.

Masson, L.R., ed. *Les bourgeois de la compagnie du Nord-Ouest: Récits de voyages, lettres et rapports inédits relatifs au nord-ouest canadien.* 2 vols. Quebec, 1890.

Mativat, Daniel. *Le métier d'écrivain au Québec (1840–1900): Pionniers, nègres ou épiciers des lettres?* Montreal: Triptyque, 1996.

Maurault, Olivier. *Le Collège de Montréal, 1767–1967.* 2d ed. Ed. Antonio Dansereau. Montreal, 1967.

McCallum, John. *Unequal Beginnings: Agriculture and Economic Development in Quebec and Ontario to 1870.* Toronto: University of Toronto Press, 1980.

McCoy, James C. *Jesuit Relations of Canada 1632–1673: A Bibliography.* Paris: Arthur Rau, 1937.

McCulloch, Thomas. *The Mephibosheth Stepsure Letters.* Ed. Gwendolyn Davies. Centre for Editing Early Canadian Texts, no. 7. Ottawa: Carleton University Press, 1990.

– *The Stepsure Letters.* Introd. H. Northrop Frye. Toronto: McClelland & Stewart, 1960.

McCulloch, William. *Life of Thomas McCulloch, D.D., Pictou.* Truro, 1920.

McCullough, A.B. *Money and Exchange in Canada to 1900.* Toronto: Dundurn Press in co-operation with Parks Canada and the Canadian Government Publishing Centre, 1984.

McDougall, Warren. 'Copyright Litigation in the Court of Session, 1738–1749, and the Rise of the Scottish Book Trade.' *Edinburgh Bibliographical Society Transactions* 5, part 5 (1988): 2–31.

– 'Scottish Books for America in the Mid-18th Century.' In *Spreading the Word: The Distribution Networks of Print, 1550–1850,* ed. Robin Myers and Michael Harris, 21–46. Winchester and Detroit: St Paul's Bibliographies and Omnigraphics, 1990.

McLachlan, R.W. *The First Mohawk Primer.* Montreal: [s.n.], 1908.

– 'Fleury Mesplet, the First Printer at Montreal.' *Proceedings and Transactions of the Royal Society of Canada,* 2nd ser., 12 (1906): section 2, 197–309.

McMurtrie, Douglas C. *The Royalist Printers at Shelburne, Nova Scotia.* Chicago: privately printed, 1933.

McNairn, Jeffrey L. *The Capacity to Judge: Public Opinion and Deliberative Democracy in Upper Canada, 1791–1854.* Toronto: University of Toronto Press, 2000.

Melançon, François. 'La circulation du livre au Canada sous la domination française.' *PBSC/CSBC* 37.2 (Autumn 1999): 35–58.

– 'Émergence d'une tradition catholique de lecture au Canada.' *Cahiers de la recherche en éducation* 3.3 (1996): 343–62.

– 'Façonner et surveiller l'intime: Lire en Nouvelle-France.' In *Discours et pratiques de l'intime*, ed. Manon Brunet and Serge Gagnon, 17–45. Quebec: Institut québécois de recherche sur la culture, 1993.

– 'La migration d'un objet culturel: Le livre en Nouvelle-France.' In *Mémoires de Nouvelle-France*, ed. Phillipe Joutard and Thomas Wien. Quebec: Septentrion, forthcoming.

Meyer-Noirel, Germaine. *L'ex-libris: Histoire, art, techniques.* Paris: Picard, 1989.

Mignolo, Walter D. *The Darker Side of the Renaissance: Literacy, Territoriality, and Colonization.* Ann Arbor: University of Michigan Press, 1995.

Monaghan, Charles. *The Murrays of Murray Hill.* New York: Urban History Press, 1998.

Monette, Pierre, ed. *Le rendez-vous manqué avec la Révolution américaine.* Montreal: Chez Triptyque, forthcoming.

Monière, Denis. *Ludger Duvernay et la révolution intellectuelle au Bas-Canada.* Montreal: Québec-Amérique, 1987.

Montgomery, Franz. 'Alexander Mackenzie's Literary Assistant.' *Canadian Historical Review* 18 (June 1937): 301–4.

Moodie, Susanna. *Letters of a Lifetime.* Ed. Carl Ballstadt, Elizabeth Hopkins, and Michael Peterman. Toronto: University of Toronto Press, 1985.

– *Roughing It in the Bush.* First Published 1832. Toronto: Bell & Cockburn, 1913. Reprint, Toronto: Prospero, 2000.

– *Roughing It in the Bush; or, Life in Canada.* 2 vols. London: R. Bentley, 1852.

Moodie, Susanna, and John Moodie. *Letters of Love and Duty: The Correspondence of Susanna and John Moodie.* Ed. Elizabeth Hopkins, Michael Peterman, and Carl Ballstadt. Toronto: University of Toronto Press, 1993.

– 'To the Public.' *Victoria Magazine* 1 (Sept. 1847): 1–2.

Moore, Christopher. *The Law Society of Upper Canada and Ontario's Lawyers, 1797–1997.* Toronto: University of Toronto Press, 1997.

– *Louisbourg Portraits: Life in an Eighteenth-Century Garrison Town.* Toronto: Macmillan of Canada, 1982.

Morin, Yvan. 'Les niveaux de culture à Québec 1800–1819: Étude des bibliothèques privées dans les inventaires après décès.' Master's thesis, Université Laval, 1979.

Morley, William F.E. *A Bibliographical Study of Major John Richardson.* Toronto: Bibliographical Society of Canada, 1973.

Morrison, Robert. 'John Howison of *Blackwood's Magazine*.' *Notes and Queries* 240 (1995): 191–3.

Mortimer, George. *The Life and Letters of the Rev. George Mortimer, M.A., Rector of Thornhill, in the Diocese of Toronto, Canada West.* Compiled by Rev. John Armstrong. London: Aylott and Jones, 1847.

Mott, Frank Luther. *A History of American Magazines.* Cambridge: Harvard University Press, 1970.

Moureau, François, ed. *De bonne main: La communication manuscrite au XVIIIe siècle.* Paris and Oxford: Universitas and Voltaire Foundation, 1993.

Muller, F. Max. *Proposals for a Missionary Alphabet: Submitted to the Alphabetical Conferences Held at the Residence of Chevalier Bunsen in 1854.* London: A. & G.A. Spottiswoode, 1854.

Murdoch, Beamish. *A History of Nova-Scotia, or Acadie.* 3 vols. Halifax: James Barnes, 1865–7.

– 'Preface.' *The Acadian Magazine* 1 (July 1826–June 1827): i–ii.

Murray, Heather. *Come, bright Improvement! The Literary Societies of Nineteenth-Century Ontario.* Toronto: University of Toronto Press, 2002.

– 'Frozen Pen, Fiery Print, and Fothergill's Folly: Cultural Organization in Toronto, Winter 1836–37.' *Essays on Canadian Writing* 61 (Spring 1997): 41–70.

Murray, Kathleen R. 'Sainte Anne as Symbol of Literacy in Quebec Culture.' *Quebec Studies* 30 (Fall 2000/Winter 2001): 70–8.

Nantel, Maréchal. *La Bibliothèque du Barreau et les archives judiciaires de Montréal.* Montreal: *La Revue du Barreau* 6.2 (Feb. 1946): 56–64.

Navières, Joseph. *Lettres inédites du missionnaire J. Navières sur le Canada (1735–1737).* Ed. Ludovic Drapeyron. Paris: Institut géographique de Paris, Charles Delagrave, 1895.

Neary, Peter, and Patrick O'Flaherty. *Part of the Main: An Illustrated History of Newfoundland and Labrador.* St John's: Breakwater Books, 1983.

Nesbitt, Bruce. 'The First *Clockmakers.*' In *The Thomas Chandler Haliburton Symposium*, ed. Frank M. Tierney, 93–102. Reappraisals: Canadian Writers 11. Ottawa: University of Ottawa Press, 1985.

New Brunswick Newspaper Directory, 1783–1996 / Répertoire des journaux du Nouveau-Brunswick, 1783–1996. 2nd ed. Revised and updated by Muriel Daniel. Fredericton: Council of Head Librarians of New Brunswick, 1996.

Nish, Cameron. *François-Étienne Cugnet, 1719–1751: Entrepreneur et enterprises en Nouvelle-France.* Histoire économique et sociale du Canada français. Montreal: Fides, 1975.

Normand, Sylvio. 'L'imprimé juridique au Québec du XVIIIe siècle à 1840.' Paper presented at the History of the Book in Canada, Volume I, Open Conference, Toronto, November 2000. Available on-line at: http://www.hbic.library.utoronto.ca/vol1normand_en.htm.

Norton, Mary Beth. *Liberty's Daughters: The Revolutionary Experience of American Women, 1750–1800.* Boston: Little, Brown, 1980.

Nova Scotia Newspapers: A Directory and Union List, 1752–1988. Inventory compiler, Lynn Murphy; cataloguer, Brenda Hicks; with assistance from Anjali Vohra. Halifax: School of Library and Information Studies, Dalhousie University, 1990.

L'Observateur, ci-devant La Bibliothèque canadienne. Montreal, 1830–1.

O'Dea, Agnes C. *Bibliography of Newfoundland.* 2 vols. Ed. Anne Alexander. Toronto: University of Toronto Press in association with Memorial University of Newfoundland, 1986.

O'Flaherty, Patrick. *Old Newfoundland: A History to 1843.* St John's: Long Beach Press, 1999.

Olivier, Réjean. *Bibliographie d'anciens manuels scolaires étrangers employés au Collège de L'Assomption depuis 1832 jusqu'au début de 1900.* L'Assomption: Collège de L'Assomption Bibliothèque, 1979.

– *Philippe Boucher, curé en Nouvelle-France: Catalogue descriptif et explicatif de quelques-uns de ses livres.* Based on *Le curé Philippe Boucher, 1665–1721*, by J. Edmond Roy. L'Assomption: Collège de l'Assomption Bibliothèque, 1983.

Olivier, Réjean, and Fernand Boulet. *Catalogue descriptif de quelques manuels scolaires manuscrits datant de 1811, au début du XXe siècle en possession des Archives, exposés à la Bibliothèque à l'occasion de la Semaine nationale de l'éducation du 30 mars au 30 avril 1981.* L'Assomption: Collège de L'Assomption Archives et bibliothèque, 1981.

Osborne, Brian S. 'Trading on a Frontier: The Function of Peddlers, Markets, and Fairs in Nineteenth-Century Ontario.' *Canadian Papers in Rural History* 2.2 (1980): 59–81.

Osgood, Thaddeus. *The Canadian Visitor: Communicating Important Facts and Interesting Anecdotes Respecting the Indians and Destitute Settlers in Canada and the United States of America.* London: Hamilton and Adams, [1829?].

Ouellet, Fernand. 'Fréquentation scolaire, alphabétisation et société au Québec et en Ontario jusqu'en 1911: Les francophones et les autres.' *Cahiers Charlevoix: Études franco-ontariennes* 2 (1997): 263–349.

Ouellet, Réal. *Sur Lahontan: Comptes rendus et critiques (1702–1711).* Quebec: L'Hétrière, 1983.

Oury, Guy. *Marie de l'Incarnation, 1599–1672.* 2 vols. Quebec: Presses de l'Université Laval, 1973.

Palmer, G. *Bibliography of Loyalist Source Material in the United States, Canada and Great Britain.* Westport: Meckler Pub., 1982.

Palmer, Robert Roswell. *The Age of the Democratic Revolution: A Political History of Europe and America, 1760–1800.* 2 vols. Princeton: Princeton University Press, 1959.

Pariseau, Claude. *La Bibliothèque du Collège de Québec.* Occasional Paper. Montreal: McGill University, Graduate School of Library Science, 1972.

Parizeau, Gérard. *La vie studieuse et obstinée de Denis-Benjamin Viger.* Montreal: Fides, 1980.

Parker, George L. 'Another Look at Haliburton and His Publishers Joseph Howe and Richard Bentley: The Colonial Author and His Milieu.' In *The Thomas Chandler Haliburton Symposium*, ed. Frank M. Tierney, 83–92. Reappraisals: Canadian Writers 11. Ottawa: University of Ottawa Press, 1985.

– *The Beginnings of the Book Trade in Canada.* Toronto: University of Toronto Press, 1985.

Parker, Peter J. 'The Philadelphia Printer: A Study of an Eighteenth-Century Businessman.' *Business History Review* 40 (Spring 1966): 24–46.

Parvin, Viola Elizabeth. *Authorization of Textbooks for the Schools of Ontario, 1846–1950.* Toronto: University of Toronto Press, 1965.

Payne, Michael. *The Most Respectable Place in the Territory: Everyday Life in Hudson's Bay Company Service, York Factory, 1788–1870.* Ottawa: National Historic Parks and Sites, Environment Canada, 1989.

Payne, Michael, and Gregory Thomas. 'Literacy, Literature and Libraries in the Fur Trade.' *Beaver* 313.4 (Spring 1983): 44–53.

Pearson, David. *Provenance Research in Book History: A Handbook.* London and New Castle: British Library and Oak Knoll Press, 1998.

Peel, Bruce B. *Peel's Bibliography of the Canadian Prairies to 1953: Based on the Work of Bruce Braden Peel.* Ed. Ernie B. Ingles and N. Merrill Distad. Toronto: University of Toronto Press, 2003.

– *Rossville Mission Press: The Invention of the Cree Syllabic Characters and the First Printing in Rupert's Land.* Montreal: Osiris, 1974.

Perkins, Maureen. *Visions of the Future: Almanacs, Time, and Cultural Change, 1775–1870.* Oxford: Clarendon, 1996.

Peterman, Michael. 'Reconstructing the *Palladium of British America*: How the Rebellion of 1837 and Charles Fothergill Helped to Establish Susanna Moodie as a Writer in Canada.' *PBSC/CSBC* 40 (Spring 2002): 7–36.

Phillips, Charles Edward. *The Development of Education in Canada.* Illus. Fay Edwards and Priscilla Hutchings. Toronto: Gage, 1957.

Pickering, John. *An Essay on a Uniform Orthography for the Indian Languages of North America: As published in the Memoirs of the American Academy of Arts and Sciences.* Cambridge: University Press, Hillard & Metcalf, 1820.

Piers, Harry, and Donald C. Mackay. *Master Goldsmiths and Silversmiths of Nova Scotia and Their Marks.* Halifax: Antiquarian Club, 1948.

Pilling, James C. *Bibliography of the Algonquian Languages.* Washington, DC: Government Printing Office, 1891.

– *Bibliography of the Eskimo Language.* Washington, DC: Government Printing Office, 1887.

– *Bibliography of the Iroquoian Languages.* Washington, DC: Government Printing Office, 1888.

Pond, Peter. 'The Narrative of Peter Pond.' In *Five Fur Traders of the Northwest,* ed. Charles M. Gates, 9–59. Minneapolis: Minnesota Society of the Colonial Dames of America, University of Minnesota Press, 1933.

Porter, Fernand. *L'institution catéchistique au Canada: Deux siècles de formation religieuse, 1633–1833.* Montreal: Éditions Franciscaines, 1949.

Proulx, Gilles. *Les bibliothèques de Louisbourg, Fortress de Louisbourg.* Ottawa: Parcs Canada, 1974.

– *Loisirs québécois: Des livres et des cabarets, 1690–1760.* [Quebec]: Service canadien des parcs, région du Québec, 1987.

– *Les Québécois et le livre, 1690–1760.* Ottawa: Parcs Canada, 1985.

Raible, Chris. *Muddy York Mud: Scandal & Scurrility in Upper Canada.* Creemore: Curiosity House, 1992.

Rainville, Danielle. 'Le monde de l'imprimé et l'Église au Québec, 1880–1960.' M.A. thesis, École de bibliothéconomie, Université de Montréal, 1983.

Ramsey, Jarold. 'The Bible in Western Indian Mythology.' In *Reading the Fire: Essays in the Traditional Indian Literatures of the Far West,* 166–80. Lincoln and London: University of Nebraska Press, 1983.

Rapport de l'archiviste de la province de Québec. Quebec: Ministère des affaires culturelles, 1920/21–1959.

Raven, James. 'Establishing and Maintaining Credit Lines Overseas: The Case of the Export Book Trade from London in the Eighteenth Century, Mechanisms and Personnel.' In *Des personnes aux institutions: Réseaux et culture du crédit du XVIe au XXe siècle en Europe,* ed. Laurence Fontaine et al., 144–62. Louvain-la-Neuve: Bruylant-Academia, 1997.

– 'The Export of Books to Colonial North America.' *Publishing History* 42 (1997): 21–49.

– 'The Importation of Books during the Eighteenth Century.' In *A History of the Book in America,* vol. 1, *The Colonial Book in the Atlantic World,* ed. Hugh Amory and David D. Hall, 183–97. Cambridge and New York: Cambridge University Press, 2000.

– *Judging New Wealth: Popular Publishing and Responses to Commerce in England, 1750–1800.* Oxford: Clarendon Press, 1992.

Rawlyk, George A. *The Canadian Fire: Radical Evangelism in North America, 1775–1812.* Montreal and Kingston: McGill-Queen's University Press, 1994.

Richardson, John. *The Canadian Brothers; or, The Prophecy Fulfilled; A Tale of the Late American War.* Ed. Donald Stephens. Centre for Editing Early Canadian Texts, no. 9. Ottawa: Carleton University Press, 1992.

– *Eight Years in Canada: Embracing a Review of the Administration of Lords Durham and Sydenham, Sir Chas. Bagot, and Lord Metcalf, and Including Numerous Interesting Letters from Lord Durham, Mr. Chas. Buller and Other Well Known Public Characters.* Montreal: Cunningham, 1847.

Riddell, William Renwick. *The Legal Profession in Upper Canada in Its Early Periods.* Toronto: Law Society of Upper Canada, 1916.

Ridington, Robin. 'Cultures in Conflict: The Problem of Discourse.' In *Native Writers and Canadian Writing,* ed. W.H. New, 273–89. Vancouver: UBC Press, 1990.

Ridout, Thomas. *Ten Years of Upper Canada in Peace and War, 1805–1815: Being the Ridout Letters.* Toronto: William Briggs, 1890.

Robert, Mario. 'Le livre et la lecture dans la noblesse canadienne, 1670–1764.' Master's thesis, Université du Québec à Montréal, 2000.

– 'Le livre et la lecture dans la noblesse canadienne, 1670–1764.' *RHAF* 56 (Summer 2002): 3–27.

Robertson, Marion. 'The Loyalist Printers: James and Alexander Robertson.' *Nova Scotia Historical Review* 3.1 (1983): 83–93.

Robins, Nora. 'The Montreal Mechanics' Institute: 1828–1870.' *Canadian Library Journal* 38 (Dec. 1981): 373–9.

Robinson, Paul. *Where Our Survival Lies: Students and Textbooks in Atlantic Canada*. Halifax: Atlantic Institute of Education, Dalhousie School of Library Service, 1979.

Robson, Joseph. *An Account of Six Years Residence in Hudson's Bay*. London: J. Payne and J. Bouquet, 1752.

Rollins, Caron, and Jann Lynn-George, comp. *Law to 1900: A Bibliography Selected from the Catalogue of the Canadian Institute for Historical Microreproductions* (CIHM) / *Droit d'avant 1900: Une bibliographie tirée du catalogue de l'Institut canadien de microreproductions historiques* (ICMH). Ottawa: Canadian Institute for Historical Microreproductions / Institut canadien de microreproductions historiques, 1997.

Rowe, Frederick W. *Education and Culture in Newfoundland*. Toronto: McGraw-Hill Ryerson, 1976.

Roy, Antoine. 'Ce qu'ils lisaient.' *Cahiers des Dix* 20 (1955): 199–215.

– *Les lettres, les sciences et les arts au Canada sous le régime français*. Paris: Jouve et Cie, 1930.

Roy, Fernande. '1837 dans l'œuvre historique de trois contemporains des événements: Bibaud, Christie et Garneau.' In *Les Rébellions de 1837–1838: Les Patriotes du Bas-Canada dans la mémoire collective et chez les historiens*, ed. Jean-Paul Bernard, 63–89. Montreal: Boréal Express, 1983.

– *Histoire de la librairie au Québec*. Montreal: Leméac, 2000.

Roy, James A. *Kingston: The King's Town*. Toronto: McClelland & Stewart, 1952.

Roy, Joseph-Edmond. 'L'ancien Barreau au Canada.' Conférence donnée devant le Barreau de Québec dans la Salle de le Cour d'assises par J.-Edmond Roy, notaire à Lévis, au mois de février 1897. Montreal: Théoret, 1897. Also published in *La Revue légale* 3 (1897): 231–302.

– 'Notes sur Mgr de Lauberivière.' *Bulletin des recherches historiques* 1.1 (Jan. 1895): 4–11.

Roy, Julie. 'Stratégies épistolaires et écritures féminines: Les Canadiennes à la conquête des lettres (1639–1839).' Ph.D. diss., Université de Québec, 2003.

Roy, Pierre-Georges. 'Bibliothèque de l'abbé Nicolas Boucher, curé de St-Jean de l'Ile d'Orléans.' *Bulletin des recherches historiques* 30.5 (May 1924): 152–9.

– 'La bibliothèque du curé Portneuf.' *Bulletin des recherches historiques* 54.8 (Aug. 1948): 227–30.

– 'La bibliothèque du juge de Bonne.' *Bulletin des recherches historiques* 42.3 (March 1936): 136–43.

Roy, Raymond, Yves Landry, and Hubert Charbonneau. 'Quelques comportements de Canadiens au XVIIIe siècle d'après les registres paroissiaux.' *RHAF* 31.1 (June 1977): 49–73.

Rutherford, Paul. *The Making of the Canadian Media*. McGraw-Hill Ryerson Series in Canadian Sociology. Toronto and New York: McGraw-Hill Ryerson, 1978.

Ryder, Dorothy E. 'The Red River Public Library, June 1822.' *PBSC/CSBC* 22 (1983): 36–55.

Sabin, Joseph. *Bibliotheca Americana: A Dictionary of Books Relating to America, from Its Discovery to the Present Time*. Continued by Wilberforce Eames and completed by R.W.G. Vail. 29 vols in 15. New York: [s.n.], 1868–1937.

Sagard, Gabriel. *Histoire du Canada, et voyages que les frères mineurs recollects y ont faicts pour la conversion des infidels depuis l'an 1615*. 4 vols. Paris: C. Sonnius, 1636. Reprint, Paris: Tross, 1866.

Sagendorph, R. *America and Her Almanacs: Wit, Wisdom & Weather, 1639–1970*. Dublin, NH: Yankee, 1970.

Scadding, Henry. *Horace Canadianizing: Early Pioneer Life in Canada Recalled by Sayings of the Latin Poet Horace; Being the Log Shanty Book-Shelf Pamphlet for 1894*. Toronto: Copp Clark, 1894.

– *A Pioneer Gathering of Books of a Sententious Character, Comprising Proverbs, Parables, Sage Summaries* and Saws, Being the Contents of the Log Shanty Book-Shelf for the Year 1893, in the Pioneer's Lodge, Exhibition Park, Toronto. Toronto: Copp Clark, 1893.

– Toronto of Old. Abridged and ed. F.H. Armstrong. Toronto: Oxford University Press, 1966.

Schmidt, David L., and Murdena Marshall. Mi'kmaq Hieroglyphic Prayers: Readings in North America's First Indigenous Script. Halifax: Nimbus Publishing, 1995.

Schramm, Jonas Conrad. 'La philosophie balbutiante des Canadiens.' Trans. Anne-Marie Etarian. In Sur Lahontan: Comptes rendus et critiques (1702–1711), ed. Réal Ouellet, 73–97. Quebec: L'Hêtrière, 1983.

Scott, Jonathan. The Journal of the Reverend Jonathan Scott: Genealogical Notes on the Scott, Marbury, Thwing, Ring, and Bass Families. Ed. Henry E. Scott Jr. Boston: New England Historic Genealogical Society, 1980.

Senior, Elinor Kyte. British Regulars in Montreal: An Imperial Garrison, 1832–1854. Montreal and Kingston: McGill-Queen's University Press, 1981.

Shields, Carol. 'Three Canadian Women: Fiction or Autobiography.' Atlantis 4.1 (Autumn 1978): 49–54.

Shields, David S. Oracles of Empire: Poetry, Politics, and Commerce in British America, 1690–1750. Chicago: University of Chicago Press, 1990.

Shiels, Andrew. The Witch of the Westcot: A Tale of Nova Scotia in Three Cantos; and Other Waste Leaves of Literature. Halifax: Joseph Howe, 1831.

Silver, Rollo G. 'Violent Assaults on American Printing Shops, 1788–1860.' Printing History 1.2 (1979): 10–18.

Simcoe, John Graves. The Correspondence, with Allied Documents Relating to His Administration of the Government of Upper Canada. 5 vols. Collected and edited by E.A. Cruikshank. Toronto: Ontario Historical Society, 1923.

Smallwood, Joseph R., et al., eds. Encyclopaedia of Newfoundland and Labrador. 5 vols. St John's: Newfoundland Book Publishers [and others], 1981–94.

Smith, D.B. Sacred Feathers: The Reverend Peter Jones (Kahkewaquonaby) and the Mississauga Indians. Lincoln: University of Nebraska Press, 1987.

Society for the Propagation of the Gospel in Foreign Parts. Classified Digest of the Records of the Society for the Propagation of the Gospel in Foreign Parts, 1701–1892: (with Much Supplementary Information). London: Published at the Society's Office, 1893.

Spangenberg, Rev. August Gottlieb. An Account of the Manner in Which the Protestant Church of the Unitas Fratrum or United Brethren Preach the Gospel and Carry On Their Missions among the Heathen. [Trans from the German.] London: H. Trapp, for the Brethren's Society for the Furtherance of the Gospel, 1788.

Stabile, Julie. 'The Economics of an Early Nineteenth-Century Toronto Newspaper Shop.' PBSC/CSBC 41.1 (Spring 2003): 43–75.

Stacey, Robert H. Canadian Bookplates. Toronto: Subway Books, 1997.

Stone, Lawrence. 'Literacy and Education in England: 1640–1900.' Past and Present 42 (Feb. 1969): 69–139.

Stowell, Marion Barber. Early American Almanacs: The Colonial Weekday Bible. New York: Burt Franklin, 1977.

Strachan, John. John Strachan: Documents and Opinions, a Selection. Ed. J.L.H. Henderson. Toronto: McClelland & Stewart, 1969.

Stratford, Philip. Bibliographie de livres canadiens traduits de l'anglais au français et du français à l'anglais / Bibliography of Canadian Books in Translation: French to English and English to French. Ottawa: Conseil canadien de recherche sur les humanités / The Committee on Translation of the Humanities Research Council of Canada, 1977.

Talman, James John. 'Agriculture Societies of Upper Canada.' *Ontario Historical Society Papers and Records* 27 (1931): 545–52.

– 'Life in the Pioneer Districts of Upper Canada, 1815–1840.' Ph.D. diss., University of Toronto, 1930.

– ed. *Loyalist Narratives from Upper Canada.* Toronto: Champlain Society, 1946.

Tanner, John. *A Narrative of the Captivity and Adventures of John Tanner.* Ed. Edwin James. New York: Carville, 1830. Reprint, Minneapolis: Ross and Haines, 1956.

Tanselle, G. Thomas. 'Some Statistics on American Printing, 1764–1783.' In *The Press and the American Revolution*, ed. Bernard Bailyn and John B. Hench, 315–63. Worcester: American Antiquarian Society, 1980.

Tassé, Gilles, and Selwyn Dewdney. *Relevés et travaux récents sur l'art rupestre amérindien.* Montreal: Laboratoire d'archéologie de l'Université du Québec à Montréal, 1977.

Theophano, Janet. *Eat My Words: Reading Women's Lives through the Cookbooks They Wrote.* New York: Palgrave, 2002.

Thevet, André. *André Thevet's North America: A Sixteenth-Century View.* Ed. Roger Schlesinger and Arthur P. Stabler. Kingston and Montreal: McGill-Queen's University Press, 1986.

Thompson, David. *David Thompson's Narrative, 1784–1812.* Ed. Richard Gilchrist Glover. Toronto: Champlain Society, 1962.

Thomson, Donald W. *Men and Meridians: The History of Surveying and Mapping in Canada.* 3 vols. Ottawa: Queen's Printer, 1966–9.

Tobin, Brian, and Elizabeth Hulse. *The Upper Canada Gazette and Its Printers, 1793–1849.* Toronto: Ontario Legislative Library, 1993.

Tolmie, William Fraser. *The Journals of William Fraser Tolmie, Physician and Fur Trader.* Ed. Howard T. Mitchell. Vancouver: Mitchell Press, 1963.

Toronto Public Library. *A Bibliography of Canadiana, Being Items in the Public Library of Toronto, Canada, Relating to the Early History and Development of Canada.* Ed. Frances M. Staton and Marie Tremaine. Toronto: Public Library, 1934.

– *A Bibliography of Canadiana: First Supplement.* Ed. Gertrude M. Boyle with the assistance of Marjorie Colbeck. Toronto: Public Library, 1959.

– *A Bibliography of Canadiana: Second Supplement.* 4 vols. Ed. Sandra Alston with the assistance of Karen Evans. Toronto: Metropolitan Toronto Library Board, 1985–9.

Tousignant, Pierre. 'La première campagne électorale des Canadiens en 1792.' *Histoire sociale* 15 (1975): 120–48.

Townsend, Elizabeth, et al. *A Sentinel on the Street: St. Matthew's United Church, Halifax, 1799–1999.* Halifax: Nimbus, 1999.

Toye, William, and Eugene Benson, eds. *The Oxford Companion to Canadian Literature.* 2nd ed. Toronto: Oxford University Press, 1997.

Traill, Catharine Parr. *The Backwoods of Canada: Being Letters from the Wife of an Emigrant Officer, Illustrative of the Domestic Economy of British America.* London: C. Knight, 1836.

Tratt, Gertrude E.N. *A Survey and Listing of Nova Scotia Newspapers, 1752–1957, with Particular Reference to the Period before 1867.* Halifax: Dalhousie University, 1979.

Tremaine, Marie. *A Bibliography of Canadian Imprints, 1751–1800.* Toronto: University of Toronto Press, 1952.

Tronson, Louis. *Correspondance de M. Louis Tronson.* Ed. Louis Bertrand. Paris: Librairie Victor Lecoffre, 1904.

Umfreville, Edward. *The Present State of Hudson's Bay, 1743.* London: Stalker, 1790.

Vachon, André. *Rêves d'empire: Le Canada avant 1700.* Ottawa: Public Archives of Canada, 1982.

Vastokas, Joan M. 'History without Writing: Pictorial Narratives in Native North American.' In *Gin Das Winan: Documenting Aboriginal History in Ontario,* ed. Dale Standen and David McNab, 48–64. Toronto: Champlain Society, 1996.

Veilleux, Christine. *Aux origines du Barreau québécois, 1779–1849.* Sillery: Septentrion, 1997.

– 'Les gens de justice à Québec, 1760–1867.' Ph.D. diss., Université Laval, 1990.

Verrette, Michel. *L'alphabétisation au Québec, 1660–1900: En marche vers la modernité culturelle.* Sillery: Septentrion, 2000.

– 'L'alphabétisation de la population de la ville de Québec de 1750 à 1849.' *RHAF* 39.1 (Summer 1985): 51–76.

Villeneuve, Lucie. '*Le Fantasque* de Napoléon Aubin: Mutation du genre utopique et jeux de mascarades.' In *Utopies en Canada (1545–1845),* ed. Bernard Andrès and Nancy Desjardins, 145–71. Figura, textes et imaginaires, no. 3. Montreal: Département d'études littéraires, Université de Québec à Montreal, 2001.

Vincent, Thomas B., ed. *Narrative Verse Satire in Maritime Canada, 1799–1814.* Ottawa: Tecumseh Press, 1978.

Vlach, Milada, and Yolande Buono. *Laurentiana parus avant 1821.* Montreal: Bibliothèque nationale du Québec, 1977.

Vogan, Nancy F. 'The Robert Moor Tunebook and Musical Culture in Eighteenth-Century Nova Scotia.' In *Planter Links: Community and Culture in Colonial Nova Scotia,* ed. Margaret Conrad and Barry Moody, Planters Series, no. 4, 154–64. Fredericton: Acadiensis Press, 2001.

Voisine, Nive. 'L'église, gardienne de la langue.' In *Le français au Québec: 400 ans d'histoire et de vie,* ed. Michel Plourde, 93–7. Saint-Laurent: Fides and Publications du Québec, 2000.

– ed. *Histoire du catholicisme québécois.* 4 vols. Montreal: Boréal, 1984–91.

Walker, Frank Norman. *Sketches of Old Toronto.* Don Mills, ON: Longmans Canada, 1965.

Wallot, Jean-Pierre. 'Frontière ou fragment du système atlantique: Des idées étrangères dans l'identité bas-canadienne au début du XIXe siècle.' *Historical Papers / Communications historiques,* 1983, 1–29.

– 'La Révolution française au Canada, 1789–1838.' In *L'image de la Révolution française au Québec, 1789–1989,* ed. Michel Grenon, 61–104. Montreal: Hurtubise HMH, 1989.

Walsh, S. Padraig. *Anglo-American General Encyclopedias: A Historical Bibliography, 1703–1967.* New York: R.R. Bowker, 1968.

Warkentin, Germaine. 'In Search of "The Word of the Other": Aboriginal Sign Systems and the History of the Book in Canada.' *Book History* 2 (1999): 1–27.

Waterston, Elizabeth, et al. *The Travellers – Canada to 1900: An Annotated Bibliography of Works Published in English from 1577.* Guelph, ON: University of Guelph, 1989.

Watson, Fiona M. '*A Credit to This Province': A History of the Ontario Legislative Library and Its Predecessors, 1792–1992.* Toronto: Ontario Legislative Library, 1993.

Webb, Jeff A. 'Leaving the State of Nature: A Locke-Inspired Political Community of St. John's, Newfoundland, 1723.' *Acadiensis* 21.1 (Autumn 1991): 156–65.

West, John. *The Substance of a Journal during a Residence at the Red River Colony, British North America; and Frequent Excursions among the North-West American Indians, in the Years 1820, 1821, 1822, 1823.* London: L.B. Seeley and Son, 1824.

Whiteman, Bruce. *Lasting Impressions: A Short History of English Publishing in Quebec.* Montreal: Véhicule Press, 1994.

Whiteway, Louise. 'The Athenaeum Movement: St. John's Athenaeum (1861–1898).' *Dalhousie Review* 50 (1970–1): 534–49.

Whitfield, Carol. *Tommy Atkins: The British Soldier in Canada, 1759–1870.* Ottawa: Parks Canada, 1981.

Willcocks, Joseph. 'The Diary of Joseph Willcocks from Dec. 1, 1799, to Feb. 1, 1803.' In *The Province of Ontario – a History, 1615–1927*, ed. Jesse Edgar Middleton and Fred Landon, vol. 2, 1250–322. Toronto: Toronto Dominion Publishing Co., 1927.

Williams, Glyndwr. 'Arthur Dobbs and Joseph Robson: New Light on the Relationship between Two Early Critics of the Hudson's Bay Company.' *Canadian Historical Review* 40 (1950): 132–6.

– *The British Search for the Northwest Passage in the Eighteenth Century.* London: Longmans, for the Royal Commonwealth Society, 1962.

– *Voyages of Delusion: The Quest for the Northwest Passage.* New Haven: Yale University Press, 2002.

Williams, Raymond. *Marxism and Literature.* Oxford: Oxford University Press, 1977.

Wilson, J. Donald. 'Common School Texts in Use in Upper Canada prior to 1845.' *PBSC/CSBC* 9 (1970): 36–53.

– 'Education in Upper Canada: Sixty Years of Change.' In *Canadian Education: A History*, ed. J. Donald Wilson, Robert M. Stamp, and Louis-Philippe Audet, 190–213. Scarborough, ON: Prentice-Hall, 1970.

Wilson, J. Donald, Robert M. Stamp, and Louis-Philippe Audet, eds. *Canadian Education: A History.* Scarborough, ON: Prentice-Hall, 1970.

Winchester, Angus J.L. '"Scratching Along amongst the Stumps": Letters from Thomas Priestman, a Settler in the Niagara Peninsula, 1811–1839.' *Ontario History* 81 (1989): 41–58.

Winearls, Joan. 'The Printing and Publishing of Maps in Ontario before Confederation.' *PBSC/CSBC* 31 (Spring 1993): 59–61.

Wise, Sidney F. 'Sermon Literature and Canadian Intellectual History.' In *Canadian History before Confederation*, ed. J.M. Bumsted, 253–69. Georgetown: Irwin-Dorsey, 1979.

Wiseman, John A. 'Bible and Tract: Disseminating Missionary Literature in Nineteenth-Century Ontario.' *Publishing History* 18 (1985): 69–83.

Wittmann, Reinhard. 'Was There a Reading Revolution at the End of the Eighteenth Century?' In *A History of Reading in the West*, ed. Guglielmo Cavallo and Roger Chartier, trans. Lydia G. Cochrane, 284–312. Cambridge: Polity Press, 1999.

Wogan, Peter. 'Perceptions of European Literacy in Early Contact Situations.' *Ethnohistory* 41 (1994): 407–29.

Wolfe, Richard J. *Marbled Paper: Its History, Techniques, and Patterns.* Philadelphia, 1990.

Woodley, Edward C. *The Bible in Canada.* Toronto: J.M. Dent, 1953.

Wosh, Peter J. *Spreading the Word: The Bible Business in Nineteenth-Century America.* Ithaca: Cornell University Press, 1994.

Wright, Barry. 'The Gourlay Affair: Seditious Libel and the Sedition Act in Upper Canada, 1818–19.' In *Canadian State Trials*, vol. 1, *Law, Politics, and Security Measures, 1608–1837*, ed. F. Murray Greenwood and Barry Wright, 478–504. Toronto: University of Toronto Press, 1996.

Würtele, Frederick C., comp. *Index of the Lectures, Papers and Historical Documents Published by the Literary and Historical Society of Quebec ... 1829 to 1891.* Quebec: Morning Chronicle, 1891.

– 'Our Library.' *Transactions of the Literary and Historical Society of Quebec* n.s. 19 (1889): 29–73.

York, Annie, Richard Daly, and Chris Arnett. *They Write Their Dream on the Rock Forever: Rock Writings of the Stein River Valley of British Columbia.* Vancouver: Talonbooks, 1993.

York Commercial Directory, Street Guide and Register, 1833–4. Compiled by George Walton. York: G. Walton, 1834.

Young, James. *Reminiscences of the Early History of Galt and the Settlement of Dumfries, in the Province of Ontario.* Toronto: Hunter, Rose, 1880.

Zeller, Suzanne E. *Inventing Canada: Early Victorian Science and the Idea of a Transcontinental Nation.* Toronto: University of Toronto Press, 1987.

CONTRIBUTORS

Sandra Alston is the Canadiana specialist at the University of Toronto Library. Author of the *Second Supplement* to the Toronto Public Library's *A Bibliography of Canadiana* (1985–9), she has recently published, with Patricia Lockhart Fleming, *Toronto in Print* (1998) and *Early Canadian Printing: A Supplement to Marie Tremaine's 'A Bibliography of Canadian Imprints, 1751–1800'* (1999).

Bernard Andrès, a professor of literature at the Université du Québec à Montréal, is a member of the Royal Society of Canada and of the Société des Dix. His publications include *Écrire le Québec* (2001), *L'énigme de Sales Laterrière* (2000), and with Marc André Bernier, *Portrait des arts, des lettres et de l'éloquence au Québec, 1760–1840* (2002).

Paul Aubin, after working for organizations, including the Ministère des affaires culturelles du Québec and the Institut québécois de recherche sur la culture, is now an independent researcher affiliated with the Centre interuniversitaire d'études québécoises at Université Laval and Université du Québec à Trois-Rivières. For the last ten years, he has concentrated his research on the history of textbooks, first those of Quebec and now Canada.

Joyce M. Banks holds a PhD from the University of London. She is retired from the National Library of Canada, where she was curator of the Rare Book Collection.

William Barker is president of the University of King's College in Halifax and also teaches in the English Department of Dalhousie University. His research is in aspects of literature, education, and printing, mainly during the English Renaissance. His most recent publication is an edition in English of the *Adages* of Erasmus (2002).

Fiona A. Black, of Dalhousie University's School of Library and Information Studies, researches and publishes in two principal book history areas: Scottish contributions to Canadian book availability, and applications of geographic information systems for print culture research. She is an editor of Volume 2 of HBiC/HLIC.

Christian Blais, who holds a bachelor's degree in history from Université Laval (1998) and a master's in history from the Université de Montréal (2001), specializes in the history of the Gaspésie, Acadie, and Quebec politics. He is the co-editor of a history of the lieutenant-governors of Quebec and currently works on the reconstitution of the Quebec parliamentary debates at the Bibliothèque de l'Assémblée nationale.

Jessica Bowslaugh holds honours bachelor of arts and master of information studies degrees from the University of Toronto. She is currently interested in the intellectual history of Ontario, as represented in nineteenth-century community libraries and newspapers.

Raymond Brodeur, professor in the Faculté de théologie et de sciences religieuses, Université Laval, is director of the Groupe de recherche sur l'enseignement religieux au Québec et sur la catéchèse actuelle, and of the Centre d'études Marie de l'Incarnation. His publications include *Catéchisme et identité culturelle dans le Québec de 1815* (1998) and *Les catéchismes au Québec* (1990).

Sarah Brouillette is a doctoral candidate in English and the Collaborative Program in Book History and Print Culture at the University of Toronto. Her research concerns globalization and literary publishing.

Maria Calderisi was music librarian at the National Library of Canada, responsible for reference services and for the development and maintenance of the print component of the Music Division. She is the author of *Music Publishing in the Canadas / L'édition musicale du Canada: 1800–1867* (1981), based on her MMA thesis (McGill University, 1975).

Gwendolyn Davies is dean of graduate studies and associate vice-president, research, at the University of New Brunswick. A member of the English Department, she has authored or edited five books on Canadian literature and has published journal articles and biographies for the *DCB* on writers of the Atlantic provinces. She has served as president of the Bibliographical Society of Canada.

Travis DeCook is a doctoral candidate in English and the Collaborative Program in Book History and Print Culture at the University of Toronto. His research interests include Renaissance literature, theory, and cultural history.

Jean Delisle is director of the École de traduction et d'interprétation at the Université d'Ottawa. A specialist in the history of translation, he is the author of a dozen works, including *Au cœur du trialogue canadien* (1984), *La traduction au Canada* (1987), *Les alchimistes des langues* (1990), *Les traducteurs dans l'histoire* (1995), *Portraits de traducteurs* (1999), and *Portraits de traductrices* (2002).

Juris Dilevko is an assistant professor in the Faculty of Information Studies, University of Toronto. His research interests focus on various aspects of librarianship, and his work has appeared in such journals as *American Studies*, *Library Quarterly*, and *Library and Information Science Research*.

Anne Dondertman is assistant director, Thomas Fisher Rare Book Library, University of Toronto. Her professional background is in rare book cataloguing and the digitization of special collections; her personal research interests lie in nineteenth-century imprints and twentieth-century Canadian literary alternative press publications.

Judy Donnelly is the HBiC/HLIC project manager and holds an MLS from the University of Toronto. She is co-compiler, with Carl Spadoni, of *A Bibliography of McClelland and Stewart Imprints, 1909–1985: A Publisher's Legacy* (1994), has published several articles on Canadian almanacs, and is a contributing editor to *DA: A Journal of the Printing Arts*.

Nova Doyon of the Département d'études littéraires, Université du Québec à Montréal, is completing a doctoral thesis in which she compares the role of the press in the development of the literary cultures of Quebec and Brazil during the first decades of the nineteenth century. She is collaborating in the preparation of an anthology, *La conquête des lettres au Québec (1759–1799)*.

Patricia Lockhart Fleming teaches in the Faculty of Information Studies and the Collaborative Program in Book History and Print Culture at the University of Toronto. Her research interests include the material form of Canadian imprints and the intersection of analytical bibliography and book history. She is the project director of HBiC/HLIC, a general editor, and an editor of Volumes 1 and 2.

Janet B. Friskney is a post-doctoral fellow with HBiC/HLIC. Her work to date includes publications on the Methodist Book and Publishing House (William Briggs / Ryerson Press) and McClelland and Stewart's New Canadian Library series.

François-Marc Gagnon is a member of the Order of Canada, professor emeritus of the Université de Montréal, and director of the Gail and Stephen A. Jarislowsky Institute of Studies in Canadian Art, Concordia University. He has published extensively on Paul-Émile Borduas and the Automatiste movement and retains an interest in early manifestations of art in Canada.

Claude Galarneau studied at Quebec and Lyons, and obtained his doctorate from the Université de Paris. Between 1953 and 1990 he taught in the History Department at Université Laval, where he is professor emeritus. The author of numerous books and articles on books and printing, he received the Marie Tremaine Medal of the Bibliographical Society of Canada in 1990.

Gilles Gallichan studied library science at the Université de Montréal and obtained his doctorate in history from Université Laval in 1990. He is interested in the history of the book, bibliography, and libraries. He currently works on the reconstitution of the Quebec parliamentary debates before 1963, at the Bibliothèque de l'Assemblée nationale du Québec. He is an editor of Volume 1 of HBiC/HLIC.

Carole Gerson is a professor in the English Department at Simon Fraser University, where she teaches and researches Canadian literary and publishing history. She has published many books and articles on early Canadian fiction and poetry and Canadian women writers, including a study of Emily Pauline Johnson (Tekahionwake). She is an editor of Volume 3 of HBiC/HLIC.

John Hare, a historian of Quebec literature and social life and professor emeritus at the Université d'Ottawa, has published numerous articles, as well as bibliographies and editions of texts, notably *Les Canadiens français aux quatre coins du monde: Bibliographie commentée des récits de voyages avant 1900* (1964). With Jean-Pierre Wallot, he published *Les imprimés dans le Bas-Canada 1801–1810* (1967) and other studies of early Quebec printing.

Pierre Hébert, professor in the Département des lettres et communications at Université de Sherbrooke, is a specialist in Quebec literature and the field of censorship. He has published, among other works, studies of Lionel Groulx and Jacques Poulin, several articles on censorship, and the first volume of a history, *Censure et littérature au Québec: Le livre crucifié (1625–1919)* (1997).

Elizabeth Hulse is the author of *A Dictionary of Toronto Printers, Publishers, Booksellers, and the Allied Trades, 1798–1900* (1982) and of numerous articles related to the book trades in Toronto. A former rare books librarian and archivist, she is the English-language text editor for HBiC/HLIC.

Cornelius J. Jaenen, professor emeritus in history, University of Ottawa, specializes in New France, Amerindians, ethnicity, multiculturalism, and early Christianity. Among his publications are *Friend and Foe* (1976), *The Role of the Church in New France* (1985), *Emerging Identities* (1986), *The French Regime in the Upper Country of Canada during the Seventeenth Century* (1996), and *The Apostle's Doctrine and Fellowship* (2003).

Patricia Kennedy joined the Manuscript Division of the Public (later National) Archives of Canada in 1968, where her responsibility for records of the British regime engendered an abiding interest in the interplay between bureaucratic processes and record-keeping practices. She has contributed articles on strategies for archival research to volumes 1 and 2 of *Canadian State Trials*.

Marcel Lajeunesse, who holds a PhD, has served as professor and director at the École de bibliothéconomie et des sciences de l'information at the Université de Montréal since 1970. From 1994 to 2002, he was vice-dean in the Faculté des arts et des sciences. His research interests include Quebec publishing and the history of the book, libraries, and information studies.

Yvan Lamonde teaches Quebec history and literature at McGill University. He has published books and articles on the history of printing, libraries, and bookselling in Quebec, as well as *Histoire sociale des idées au Québec*, volumes 1 (1760–1896) and 2 (1896–1929). He is a general editor of HBiC/HLIC and an editor of Volumes 1 and 2.

Richard Landon is director of the Thomas Fisher Rare Book Library and a professor of English at the University of Toronto. His areas of research include book history and bibliography, and he has recently published *Literary Forgeries and Mystifications* (2003).

Gérard Laurence, a professor in the Département d'information et de communication at Université Laval, specializes in the history of media in Quebec and Canada. After conducting research on the history of television and radio in Quebec, he has been studying the evolution of the press in Quebec to 1884, a project which will constitute the first synthesis on the subject.

Bertrum H. MacDonald is associate dean (research), Faculty of Management, Dalhousie University, and editor of electronic resources for HBiC/HLIC. His primary research interest focuses on the diffusion of scientific information, particularly among Canadian scientists, from the nineteenth century to the present.

Mary Lu MacDonald holds a doctorate in history from Carleton University and is an independent researcher resident in Halifax. She is the author of *Literature and Society in the Canadas, 1817–1850* (1992) and of 'Reading between the Lines: An Analysis of Canadian Literary Prefaces and Prospectuses,' in *Prefaces and Manifestoes* (1990).

Eli MacLaren is a PhD candidate in the Department of English and the Collaborative Program in Book History and Print Culture at the University of Toronto. He is currently researching the strictures placed on literary authorship by the publishing environment of nineteenth-century Canada.

I.S. MacLaren teaches history and literature at the University of Alberta. Exploration and travel writing and painting, history of the book, environmental history, and the Canadian painter Paul Kane are his research interests. Current projects include a biography of the mapper of the Canadian Rockies, phototopographer M.P. Bridgland; the voyage of Thomas James, 1631–2; and an interactive website about Kane.

John Macleod is an archivist who works at the Nova Scotia Archives and Records Management in Halifax. He compiles the Nova Scotia section of the bibliography of publications concerning the history of the Atlantic region that appears in the semi-annual journal *Acadiensis*.

Warren McDougall is an honorary fellow of the Centre for the History of the Book at the University of Edinburgh, and secretary of the Edinburgh Bibliographical Society. He writes on the eighteenth-century Edinburgh bookseller Charles Elliot and on the international Scottish book trade, and is co-editor of the projected *History of the Book in Scotland*, vol. 2 (1707–1800).

Leslie McGrath is curator of the Osborne Collection of Early Children's Books, Toronto Public Library. She holds a BA and MLS from the University of Toronto, where she is currently enrolled in the doctoral program at the Faculty of Information Studies, in the Collaborative Program in Book History and Print Culture.

François Melançon studies the social history of cultural practices in early Quebec. He specializes in the history of the book, reading, education, and literacy under the French regime. His publications include 'Le livre en milieu colonial d'Ancien Régime: L'exemple de la Nouvelle-France,' in *Les mutations du livre et de l'édition dans le monde, du XVIIIe siècle à l'an 2000* (2001).

Heather Murray teaches in the English Department at the University of Toronto. She is the author of *Working in English: History, Institution, Resources* (1996) and *Come, bright Improvement! The Literary Societies of Nineteenth-Century Ontario* (2002). Her research interests include the history of reading, the development of English literature and literary studies in Canada, and the rhetoric of social reform movements.

Laura J. Murray is associate professor of English at Queen's University, where she teaches and pursues research in the areas of American and Aboriginal studies, literary theory, and copyright.

Recent articles have appeared in *Ethnohistory*, *American Quarterly*, *New England Quarterly*, and *American Literary History*.

Réal Ouellet, a member of Centre interuniversitaire d'études sur les lettres, les arts et les traditions (CELAT), was professor at Université Laval. Author of studies on the novel, the theatre, and the travel narrative, he has also edited major texts of New France: Lahontan (1990), Sagard (1990 and 1999), Champlain (1993 and 2002), and Le Clercq (1993).

Ruth Panofsky, of the Department of English, Ryerson University, specializes in Canadian literature, publishing history, and textual studies. She has published numerous articles on Thomas Chandler Haliburton.

George L. Parker taught at the Royal Military College of Canada, Kingston, for many years and now resides in Halifax. He is the author of *The Beginnings of the Book Trade in Canada* (1985) and numerous articles on publishing history and copyright, and he edited Thomas Chandler Haliburton's *The Clockmaker, Series One, Two, and Three* (1995) for the Centre for Editing Early Canadian Texts project.

Michael Peterman teaches English and Canadian studies at Trent University, where he is principal of Catharine Parr Traill College. His research interests are Canadian and American writing, particularly nineteenth-century English-Canadian literary culture; he has written extensively on Robertson Davies, Susanna Moodie, and Catharine Parr Traill, and is currently at work on Irish-Canadian writers James McCarroll and Isabella Valancy Crawford.

Andrea Rotundo is a PhD student at the Faculty of Information Studies, University of Toronto, in the Collaborative Program in Book History and Print Culture. Her research focuses on the catalogues of booksellers, publishers, auctioneers, and public and private libraries.

Frédéric Roussel Beaulieu has completed a master's thesis at Université Laval. He specializes in political history and in the history of the book and printing. A former trainee in parliamentary history at the Bibliothèque de l'Assemblée nationale du Québec, he is the author of 'Les débats parlementaires au service de l'histoire politique,' *Bulletin d'histoire politique* (2003).

Karen Smith is the special collections librarian at the Killam Library, Dalhousie University. She is interested in all aspects of early Nova Scotia print culture.

Eric L. Swanick is head of special collections, Simon Fraser University. He has published articles recently in *Acadiensis*, *Amphora*, *Parenthesis*, and the *DCB*.

Christine Veilleux holds a doctorate in history from Université Laval. She has worked for the Canadian Institute for Historical Microreproductions since 1981 and the Société littéraire et historique de Québec since 1997. Among her publications are *Aux origines du Barreau québécois, 1779–1849* (1997) and numerous articles in the *DCB* and in specialized journals.

Michel Verrette, who holds a doctorate from Université Laval, is an associate professor at the Collège universitaire de Saint-Boniface, where he has taught since 1989. He specializes in

European history, particularly cultural history, and literacy. His most recent publication is *L'alphabétisation au Québec, 1660–1900: En marche vers la modernité culturelle* (2002).

Thomas Brewer Vincent of the Department of English, Royal Military College of Canada, Kingston, has published widely on the early literature of Maritime Canada and has pioneered the development of electronic bibliographical research tools to aid the study of early Canadian cultural development.

Nancy F. Vogan, who is professor of music at Mount Allison University, is the author of numerous articles on the history of music and music instruction and co-author, with J. Paul Green, of *Music Education in Canada: A Historical Account* (1991).

Jean-Pierre Wallot is director of the Centre de recherche en civilisation canadienne-française, Université d'Ottawa, and visiting professor in the Département d'histoire. Alone or with others, he has published a dozen books and more than 130 articles. A member of the Order of Canada, and the Royal Society of Canada, he has received numerous awards. He was national archivist of Canada from 1985 to 1997.

Mary F. Williamson, senior scholar, fine arts bibliographer (retired), and adjunct faculty in the Graduate Department of Art History, York University, is interested in Canadian culinary history and the illustration of books and periodicals in Canada up to the Second World War. She has made contributions on culinary history to many periodicals and newsletters.

Joan Winearls is the former map librarian of the University of Toronto Library and the author of, among other publications, *Mapping Upper Canada, 1780–1867: An Annotated Bibliography of Manuscript and Printed Maps* (1991) and *Art on the Wing: British, American and Canadian Illustrated Bird Books from the Eighteenth to the Twentieth Century* (1999).

INDEX

Page references in italics indicate the presence of an illustration. An italic *c* following a page reference indicates a chart; an italic *m* indicates a map; an italic *t* indicates a table. Magazines and newspapers published in British North America are listed under the headings 'magazines by title' and 'newspapers by title.'

Fairfield, Sumner Lincoln (1803–44), 406

Fargue, Thomas, 205*t*

Faribault, Georges-Barthélemi (1789–1866), 33, 155, 206

Ferguson, Bartemas (ca. 1792–1832), 325

fiction. *See* novels and fiction

fictitious accounts, 25, 35–6, 359, 382

Fidler, Peter (1769–1822), 149, 189, 203, 205*t*

Field, Robert (ca. 1769–1819), 107

Finden brothers (engravers), 37

Finlay, Hugh (ca. 1730–1801), 116

First Book for Children (Brockville, 1823), 255

First Catechism, The, 266

Fisher, Alexander (d. 1838), 414n85

Fisher, John Charlton (1794–1849), 160, 312, 314, 315, 319

Fisher, Peter (1782–1848), 346

Fleck, Widow (fl. 1833), 359

Fleming, John (ca. 1786–1832), 127, 130, 203, 205*t*, 206

Fletcher, Robert (fl. 1766–85), 63, 110, 125, 318, 322, 369–70

Flower, Anthony (painter), 197, *199*

Foigny, Gabriel de (ca. 1630–92), 30

Fonte, Bartholomew de (fl. 1640), 35–6

Fordyce, James (1720–96), 369

Foretier, Pierre (1738–1815), 205*t*

format: of almanacs, 272–3; of bilingual publications, 61, 98, 234, 282, 283, 286, 287, *316–17*; of exploration texts, 33, 38; of newspapers, 234, 236, 237, 439n50; and pricing, 123–4

forms, blank, 68, 69, 215, 216, 217, 223–9, 302; design and layout, 223, 226; examples of, *84, 225, 228*; and statistical data, 223, 226

Forster, Johann Reinhold (1729–98), 188

Fort George (Prince George, BC), 189

Fort Nisqually, 191

Fort Vancouver (Vancouver, Wash.), 149, 189

Fothergill, Charles (1782–1840), 98, 272, 315, 320, 346, 398, 399, 401, 403–4, 406–7

Fothergill's Toronto Almanac, 273

Fox, Luke (1586–1635), 34, 44

France: books about New France in, *23,* 23–33,

57; books imported from, 48–53, 123, 253, 267, 298; New France's dependence on presses in, 46–7; privileges to print, 23, 24; publishing in, 23–4, *32,* 47

Franklin, Benjamin (1706–90), 64, 93, 145, 175, 379

Franklin, Sir John (1786–1847), 37–8, 435n120

Fraser, Simon (1776–1862), 36

Fraser, Simon, Master of Lovat (1726–82), 370

Fréchette, Jean-Baptiste (ca. 1791–1857), 82, 329

Fredericton, 374; booksellers in, 374; King's College, 372; newspapers in, 230*m,* 231*m* (*see also specific titles under* newspapers by title); printing in, 66, 304

freedom of the press, 327, 330–1

Frelighsburgh, Lower Canada, 90, 232*m*

French Revolution, 123, 322, 323–4, 334, 383

Frères Charon, 157, 256

Frobisher, Martin (1539?–94), 34

Frugal Housewife's Manual, The, 277

Fuca, Juan de (1536–1602), 35

fur trade, 34, 36; licences for, *224–5*

fur traders, 34, 36, *191;* books and libraries of, 116, 149, 189; literacy and reading of, 187–93; writing by, 34, 36, 39, 188–9, 190

Gaelic (language), 137, 140, 222, 292, 377

Galt, John (1779–1839), 200, 202, *248,* 413n60

Garneau, François-Xavier (1809–66), 206

Garnier, Charles (1605 or 1606–49), 20

gatherings (of pages for binding), 100–1, 110, 422n44

Gaulin, Rémi (1787–1857), 197, *199*

Gaultier, Jean-François (1708–56), 298

Gay, Archibald (printer), 65

Gay, Elizabeth, 65, 82, 356–7

Gedd, James, 249

Gellibrand, Henry (1597–1636), 44

gemeinschaftliche Liedersammlung, Die, 291

Geological Survey of Canada, 297

Germain, Augustin. *See* Langlois, *dit* Germain, Augustin-René

German (language), 63, 64, 140, 222, 289–92;

libraries, circulating, 136–7, 175, 253, 365–7

libraries, community, 144–51, 176–7

libraries, garrison, 147, 150–1, 177–8

libraries, law, 53, 127, 152–4, 203

libraries, medical, 156–7

libraries, parliamentary, 135, 155–6, 162

libraries, personal or household, 130, 184, 202–6, 204–5*t*, 209–12; of clergy and missionaries, 48–9, 51, 145, 199, 211–12; illustrations of, *174, 185, 198, 199*; legal collections, 154; in New France, 49, 52, 436n14; in the Northwest, 149, 189; preservation of, 206; subject scope of, 52, 209–10, 211, 433n49

libraries, professional or specialized, 146, 151–8

libraries, science and technology, 297–300

libraries, social, 175, 433n44

libraries, subscription, 135, 145–6, 147–8, 175, 176, 366, 433n44

libraries, travelling, 137

libraries in religious institutions, 50, 51, 53, 55–7, 145

literacy, 165–72, 180; and advancement in the fur trade, 187–8; definitions of, 165, 166, 362; factors influencing, 166; link with morality, 188, 260; multiple and alternative literacies, 172–4, 188, 191–3, 216, 362; of Native peoples, 278–89, 364; in New France, 48, 53, 166–7; of printing apprentices, 83, 84; and Protestantism, 167, 168, 172, 364; of settlers, 169–70; sources for, 165–6; in Upper Canada, 396; in urban centres, 167–9. *See also* education; reading

Literary and Historical Society of Quebec, 72, 150, 176, 300, 394

literary and scientific societies, 72, 149–50, 175–6, 389, 394. *See also* individual societies

Literary Copyright Act (1709), 348

literary magazines, 243–9

literary translation. *See* translation(s)

literature and literary works: definitions and traditions of, 340–1, 368, 371, 384–5, 394, 399–400; in library catalogues, 161, 177–8; literary cultures, 52–3, 361–408; in

magazines, 243–51, 350, 372, 375–6, 389–90, 395; manuscript circulation of, 341, 344, 357, 371, 456n11; in newspapers, 358; in newspapers – Lower Canada, 234, 384, 385, 386, 390–1, 392, 393, 394; in newspapers – Newfoundland, 365; in newspapers – Nova Scotia, 243, 345, 346, 350, 368–70, *373, 376–7,* 379, 382, 385; in newspapers – Prince Edward Island, 380; in newspapers – Upper Canada, 291, 345, 346, 350, 401–4, 406

lithography, 37, 99, 103, 107, 109, 247, *248*; for music, 268; for text, 99

Locke, John (1632–1704), 362, 381

Lodge, Charles (bookbinder), 81

London, Upper Canada, 232*m*

Longmore, George (b. ca. 1793–1867), 342; *The Charivari,* 340, 346, 393; *Tales of Chivalry and Romance,* 395; 'Tecumthe,' 395

Louis XVI, king of France (1754–93), 324

Louisbourg, 253

Lovell, John (1810–93), 249, 268, 350, 395

Lower Canada: censorship in, 322–4, 326–30, 332–6; copyright legislation, 348, 457n35; education and schools in, 167–9, 256–9, 442n19; election of 1792, 219–20; government printing in, 310, 311, 312, 314, 315, *316–17, 318–19*; importation of books, 119*t*; imprints from, 89–91, 90*c*; legal code, 301; literary culture of, 383–95; music publication in, 267–8, 269–71, *270*; newspapers in, 230*m*, 232*m*, 233–8, 326–7; paper mills in, 96, 97; parliamentary library in, 155; peddling law in, 131; predominance in publishing, 89, 90*c*; translation in, 295–6; travel books on, 40–3. *See also* Quebec (old province)

Loyalists: cultural background of, 144–5, 185, 371, 372, 374–5, 393; literacy rates of, 169–70; Native peoples as, 282; in printing trades, 65–9, 370; travel books by, 34

Lugrin, George Kilman (ca. 1792–1835), 66, 319

Lunenburg, NS, 90, 231*m*, 290

Lushington, Henrietta. *See* Prescott, Henrietta

Lynd, David (ca. 1745–1802), 220

paper: for binding, 110, 111, 200; cost of, 63, 97; grades of, 79, 97; imported, 86, 96, 102; measures of, 97; pasteboard, 111; rags for making, 102, 135, 425n34; scarcity of, 86; and the Stamp Act (1765), 63, 321–2

paper mills, 65, 87, 96–7, 102–3; machinery for, 96

paper ruling, 81, 99

Papers and Letters on Agriculture / Papiers et lettres sur l'agriculture (Quebec), 186

Papineau, Joseph (1752–1841), 205*t*

Papineau, Louis-Joseph (1786–1871), 76, 155, 197, 206, 314, 326, 389

Parent, Étienne (1802–74), 82, 155, 160, 237, 329–30, 389, 390–1

Parsons, Robert John (ca. 1802–35), 327

Pasteur, Charles-Bernard (newspaper publisher), 75, 250

Patriotes and Patriote party, 77, 136, 180, 182, 269, 313, 326–7, 328–30; and literary culture, 386, 390–2; Ninety-Two Resolutions (1834), 390

patronage: government, 72, 73, 315, 318, 321, 342; private (for authors), 339, 344, 350–1

Payzant, John (1749–1834), 197, *199*

Peachy, James (d. 1797), 202, *283*, *299*

peddlers, 130–1, 389

Peep at the Esquimaux, A, 252

periodicals. *See* magazines

Perley, Moses Henry (1804–62), 382

Perrault, Jacques-Nicolas, 205*t*

Perrault, Joseph-François (1753–1844), 186, 295, 302; *Dictionnaire portatif et abrégé des loix et règles du parlement provincial du Bas Canada,* 295; *Traité d'agriculture pratique ... adaptée au climat du Bas-Canada,* 186

Perrault, Louis (1807–66), 276

Perro, B., 261

Perth, Upper Canada, 232*m*

Peterborough, Upper Canada, 232*m*

Peters, Samuel (fl. 1779–96), 344, 372

Peterson, Heinrich Wilhelm (later Henry William) (1793–1859), 290–1

Petiver, James (1663 or 1664–1718), 35

petroglyphs, 14–15, 191

Phillips, Sir Richard (1767–1840), 35, 41, 414n85

philosophy publications, 134, 257

Phippen, B. (bookbinder), 110

Picard, Jean (1620–82), 298

pictographs, 14–15, 192, 435n120

Picton, Upper Canada. *See* Hallowell

Pictou, NS, 79, 90, 140, 231*m*, 268, 427n64

Pictou Academy, 346, 378

Pigeon, François-Xavier (1778–1838), 335

Pinkerton, John (1758–1826), 40

Piquet, François (Sulpician), 284

pirated editions, 28, 76, 124, 335, 346, 348, 352–4

Plamondon, Antoine (1804–95), 195, 197

Plamondon, Louis (1785–1828), 389

Plessis, Joseph-Octave (1763–1825), 205*t*, 208, 264, 265, 266, 334, 386, 455n100

Poe, Edgar Allan (1809–49), 396

poetry: ballads and songs, 218, 253, 254, 368, 384; in exploration narratives, 44; funereal, 369; in Gaelic, 292, 377; manuscript circulation of, 180, 341, 371, 372, 456n11; in newspapers and magazines, 394, 404, 405–6; New Year's verses, 342, *373,* 394; occasional, 342; publication of, 250, 340, 344, 346; public reading of, 371–2; sampler verses, 381; by women, 341, 356, 359, 381, 382

Point, Nicolas (1799–1868), 20

political handbills, 218, 219–20, 222

Pond, Peter (1739/40–1807), 36, 189

'Poor Richard,' or the Yorkshire Almanack, 77, 273

Port Hope, Upper Canada, 232*m*, 260

Portneuf, Lower Canada: paper mill in, 96, 97

Port-Royal (Annapolis Royal, NS), 31, 32, 158, 294, 339, 341. *See also* Annapolis Royal, NS

postal system, 116, 310

postmasters, 71, 74

Post Office Act (1765), 116

Powel, David (1522?–96), 35

Power, William Grattan Tyrone (1797–1841), 43

Prescott, Henrietta (later Lady Lushington) (d. 1875), 358

Prescott, Upper Canada, 232*m*

Preston, NS, 139

Preston, T.G. (fl. 1821), 268

prices: of books, 79, 110, 123–4; of magazines, 246, 247, 256, 376; of newspapers, 72, 237; of paper, 63, 97; of presses, 93, 95; of type and ornaments, 97–8, 269, 271

Pricket, Abacuk (fl. 1610), 35

Prince Edward Island (St John's Island), 67, 70, 131, 142, 146, 311, 319; education in, 171, 261; Gaelic speakers in, 292, 377; imprints from, 89, 90, 90*c*; newspapers in, 67, 230*m*, 231*m*, 327

Prince Edward Island Calendar, 274

printers, 61–78, 80–8, 93–102; apprentice-ships, 74, 82–3, *84*; associations or trade unions, 74, 83, 85; as booksellers, 71–2, 73, 75, 86, 125, *126*, 133; compositors, 81, 100–2; of government publications, 318–20; mobility of, 74, 83, 88, 418n37; New Year's verses, *373*; numbers of in Quebec, 81; political activities of, 63–8, 73, 75, 76, 77, 321–31; pressmen, 81, 85, *94*, 100–2; slaves as, 102, 420n80

printing offices, 71–8, 80–8; attacks on, 77, 238–9, 328; of churches and religious organizations, 143–4, 335; early spread of, 61–9, 230*m*; economics of, 71–4; employees of, 73–4; family connections, 65, 66, 67, 68, 73, 74–5; paper mills owned by, 96–7; records of, 87, 100, *101*, 102, 217; social role of, 85–6; workday in, 83, 102

printing press(es), 93–6, *94*; cylinder press, 96; engraving press, 99, 105; importation of, 93, 95; iron, 95; lack of in New France, 46–7; lithographic press, 107, 109, 247; made in Toronto, 95–6; numbers of, 71, 93, 95; Ramage press, 95; Smith's Imperial, 76, 95, 247; steam-powered, 96; wooden, 93, *94*, 95

print runs. *See* edition sizes or print runs

privileges to print, 23, 24

probate inventories, 52, 165, 209, 436n20

proclamations: oral publication of, 437n2; printing of, 215–18; scribal publication of, 48

promissory notes, 227, 228, 229

Protestant missionaries, 284–9, 334; book collections of, 211–12; books distributed by, 131, 138–44; French-speaking, 131, 142

Protestants and Protestantism: catechisms for, 266; and literacy rates, 167, 168, 171, 172, 364; role of print for, 138–44. *See also* specific denominations (Church of England, Methodists, etc.)

Pseautier de David, 105

pseudonyms, 385–6; in almanacs, 273; for cookbooks, 277; in newspapers and magazines, 237, 250, 322, 375, 380–2, 385–6, 394, 395, 401–5, 407, 455n97; of women, 342, 357, 381–2, 386, 394, 395, 407

public prayers, 264, 304

Purchas, Samuel (1575?–1626), 34–5, 35

Quebec (old province): American invasion of (1774–5), 63–4, 388; literary culture of, 383–8, 392; translation in, 294–5. *See also* Lower Canada

Quebec (town): bookbinders in, 81, 110, 254–5; booksellers in, 117, 125, 132, 133, 134, 135, 254–5, 427n64; books imported to, 123; engravers in, 105, 107; Garrison Library at, 147, 150–1, 159, 160; Hôtel-Dieu, 56, 156–7, 357; illustrations of, *55*, *216*; imprints from, 90, 91; job printing in, 216–17; libraries in, 136, 145, 150, 153, 155, 394; lithography in, 107; magazines in, 75, 242; Mechanics' Institute, 148; music publishing in, 267, 268; newspapers in, 63–4, 230*m*, 232*m*, 233–7, 314, 321, 324, 328, 329, 394 (*see also specific titles under* newspapers by title); printers' associations in, 74, 83; printers in, 63–4, 80–2, 86, 216–17; as a printing centre, 80–1, 90, 91; printing statistics for, 74, 90, 91

Quebec Act (1774), 295, 301, 311

Quebec Almanack / Almanach de Québec, 94, 97, 107, 187, 272

Quebec Theatre, 219

Queenston, Upper Canada, 77, 232*m*

Quesnel, Joseph (1746–1809), 205*t*, 342, 345, 386, 389; *Colas et Colinette*, 345, 389; 'L'épître

Rossville Mission Press, 69, 288, 289
Rouer de Villeray, Louis (1629–1700), 203, 204*t*
Rousseau, Jean-Jacques (1712–78), 173
Rowsell, Henry (1807–90), 133, 135, 136, 398
Rowson, Susanna (Haswell) (1762–1824), 254
Roy, Louis (1771–99), 68, 311, 312, 319
Royal Acadian School, 261
Royal Engineers, 107, 300
Roy-Audy, Jean-Baptiste (1778–1848), 76, 197, *199*
Rudyerd, Henry (captain), 276
rural settlements, 175, 184–7
Russell Resolutions (1837), 328
Rust, Samuel (press maker), 95
Rustico, PEI, 171
Ruthven, John (bookseller), *126*, 285
Ryan, John (1761–1847): in Newfoundland, 67, 68, 73, 320, 324–5, 365; in Saint John, 66, 311, 319, 323, 374
Ryan, Lewis Kelly, 67, 320, 325
Ryan, Michael (1784–1829), 67
Ryerson, Egerton (1803–82), 131, 181, 258, 399

Sabine, James (1774–1845), 367
Sackville, NB, 231*m*
Sagard, Gabriel (fl. 1614–36), 18–19; 'Dictionaire de la langue Huronne,' 279; *Le grand voyage du pays des Hurons*, 30, 279
Sahonwagy (d. after 1787), 282
St Andrews, NB, 230*m*, 231*m*
St Andrews (Saint-André-Est), Lower Canada: paper mill in, 96
St Boniface, 171
St Catharines, Upper Canada, 136, 230*m*, 232*m*
Saint-Charles-sur-Richelieu, Lower Canada, 90, 232*m*
St Davids, Upper Canada, 230*m*
St John, William Charles, 261
Saint John (formerly Parrtown), 132, 218, 313, 374–5, 382; booksellers in, 132, 374, 427n64; libraries in, 146, 148; Mechanics' Institute, 149; newspapers in, 66, 230*m*, 231*m*, 233, 374 (*see also specific titles under newspapers by title*); printers in, 66, 84, 374

St John's, 362, 365; booksellers in, 125, 135, 365, 427n64; imprints from, 89, 218, 367; libraries in, 146, 147, 148, 366; Mechanics' Institute, 367; newspapers in, 67–8, 230*m*, 231*m*, 239, 365 (*see also specific titles under newspapers by title*); printers in, 67–8
St John's Island. *See* Prince Edward Island
St John's Library Society, 366
St John's Mechanics' Society, 148
St John Society Library (Saint John), 146, 148
St John's Reading Room and Library, 366
St John's Subscription Library, 366
St Philippe-de-Laprairie, Lower Canada, 232*m*
St Stephen, NB, 231*m*
St Thomas, Upper Canada, 232*m*, 427n64
Saint-Vallier, Jean-Baptiste de La Croix de Chevrières de (1653–1727), 46, 57, 263, 265, 332
Sand, E. (Saint John merchant), 374
Sandwich (Windsor), Upper Canada, 187, 232*m*
Sarrazin, Michel (1659–1734), 203, 204*t*, 298
Saulteux, 287, 448n41
Sawtell, M. Ethelind (author), 359
Scadding, Henry (1813–1901), 179–80, 182, 403
schools. *See* education and schools
Schramm, Jonas Conrad, 30
science and technology publications, 297–300
Scobie, Hugh (1811–53), 133, 401
Scott, Jonathan (1744–1819), 371
Scott, Sir Walter (1771–1832), 136, 178, 182, 183, 184, 351, 400
scribal publication, 47–8, 224, 309. *See also* manuscript circulation
scrip, printing of, 227, 229
scrolls (bark and hide), 14
Seccombe, Mercy, 380–1
Selkirk, Thomas Douglas, 5th Earl of (1771–1820), 149, 150
Séminaire des missions étrangères (Quebec), 46, 49
serial publishing, 291, 346, 352–3, 377, 401
Sermon and Catechism for Children, 266
sermons, published, 68, 264, 304, 355, 367, 372, 444n62
Seven Years War (1756–63), 200, 310